WITHDRAWN
UTSA LIBRARIES

KING LEOPOLD'S RULE
IN AFRICA

Motherhood.
Bangala Woman and Child.
From the Bronze by Herbert Ward.

KING LEOPOLD'S RULE
IN AFRICA

BY

EDMUND D. MOREL

(E. D. M.)

AUTHOR OF

"AFFAIRS OF WEST AFRICA," "THE BRITISH CASE IN FRENCH CONGO"
"THE CONGO SLAVE STATE," "THE EMPIRE'S COTTON SUPPLY"
"THE SIERRA LEONE HUT-TAX INSURRECTION"
"TRADING MONOPOLIES IN WEST AFRICA," ETC. ETC.

WITH ILLUSTRATIONS AND MAPS

NEGRO UNIVERSITIES PRESS
WESTPORT, CONNECTICUT

Originally published in 1904
by William Heinemann, London

Reprinted in 1970 by
Negro Universities Press
A Division of Greenwood Press, Inc.
Westport, Connecticut

Library of Congress Catalogue Card Number 70-132078

SBN 8371-4647-X

Printed in the United States of America

TO THE MEMORY OF

MY MOTHER

THIS BOOK IS DEDICATED

PREFACE

THE struggle in England against the misrule of the Congo State really dates from September, 1896, when the Aborigines Protection Society, tired of making representations to the authorities in Brussels, appealed to the British Government. Its appeal fell on deaf ears. In the spring of the following year, Sir Charles Dilke brought the question, together with other matters connected with Africa, before the House of Commons, and suggested that the British Government should approach the Powers with a proposal for an international conference, "with a view to the adoption and enforcement of further measures for securing equitable treatment of the natives of Africa." He was generally supported by Mr. Sydney Buxton, Mr. McKenna, Mr. Thomas Bayley, Mr. John Burns, and Sir George Baden-Powell. The Congo State found an apologist in Captain Bethell, and the suggestion was declined by the Government.

The debate was followed by a public meeting, held under the auspices of the Aborigines Protection Society, at which Mr. John Morley, Sir Charles Dilke, and Mr. Courtney spoke. From that time onwards, Mr. H. R. Fox-Bourne, the Society's secretary, stimulated by the published diary of Glave, by the disclosures of the Swedish missionary, Sjoblöm, and the Irish missionary, Murphy, and by reports from other sources, has waged a gallant fight against Congo State methods, culminating in the publication of his book, "Civilisation in Congoland," early in 1903.

Some five years ago the author of the present volume, whom circumstances some years previously had led to take an interest in West African questions generally, became convinced that the system of government carried on by the authorities of the Congo State was a bad and wicked system, inflicting terrible wrongs upon the native races, and that the conception of tropical African development upon which it rested was one that ought to be struggled against without pause or abatement of energy in the interests of humanity, of European honour, and European statesmanship in the Dark Continent. To that conviction the author has ministered to the extent of his capacity and opportunities ever since, as an independent free lance in the columns of the *Nineteenth Century, Contemporary Review, Speaker, Morning Post, Daily News, Daily Chronicle, Pall Mall Gazette, West African Mail*, and many other publications; in one or two foreign journals; in several pamphlets,* and in two volumes, "Affairs of West Africa" † and "The British Case in French Congo." In the course of this work the author, who was not acquainted, previous to 1901, with either Sir Charles Dilke or Mr. Fox-Bourne, who between them had borne up to that time the whole brunt of the fight, came into touch with these gentlemen, with whom he has been privileged on many occasions to co-operate.

The movement for reform thus inaugurated by the Aborigines Protection Society in 1896, made slow but appreciable progress in the education of public opinion. Towards the close of 1901 it received an impetus through the representations sent to the Foreign Office by fifteen British Chambers of Commerce, protesting against the treatment of British merchants in the French Congo. It became apparent to the Chambers more closely interested in the subject, that the hardships undergone by certain British firms in the French Congo were wholly attributable to the theoretical adoption by France of the system of State appropriation, or State-delegated appropriation of the land and the raw material yielded by the land, which is the bedrock of Congo State methods, and which France had applied to the French Congo in an evil moment. The action of the Chambers, at first confined to French Congo, not only widened, therefore, but became concentrated, as logically was bound to be the case,

* Published in 1901, 1902, 1903, and 1904.
† Since translated into French by M. Duchêne, Chief of the African Division of the French Colonial Office.

PREFACE

upon the Congo State, and at the annual meeti[ng of the] Associated Chambers of Commerce in 1903 a reso[lution was] carried to the effect that the "principles and practice [introduced] into the administration of the Congo Free State [in the] areas of the Conventional Basin of the Congo" we[re contrary] to the Act of Berlin, and that the Government should be invited, in conjunction with the other Signatory Powers, to bring about reform.

The intervention of the Chambers of Commerce strengthened the movement in many respects. The Congo Government, however, saw therein the opportunity to represent the whole agitation as got up by "Liverpool merchants," jealous of Antwerp's growing importance as a rubber market; and its various henchmen, in Belgium and outside of it, have with somewhat monotonous persistency reiterated that amusing fiction on every possible occasion, and probably in every known European language. In point of fact, the only appreciable British material interest in the Congo State is exercised very strongly in favour of the present *régime*.

The author of this volume, who has no commercial interest of any kind whatsoever in Africa, was in 1902 invited, through his work as a writer on West African questions, to become a member of the Committee of the West African Section of the Liverpool Chamber of Commerce.* This circumstance the Congo crowd have positively revelled in, and the author has been made the butt of extravagant personal abuse. A pamphlet was even brought out in English and distributed broadcast, written by a person of the name of Demetrius C. Boulger,† in which it was stated, *inter alia*, that "Mr. Morel and his patrons want the control of the rubber trade, which, as a motive, is contemptible." ‡ Insinuations of this character have been useful in the sense that they have enabled one to insist in season and out of season upon the fundamental issue at stake.

---

* Which position he resigned this year.
† "The Congo State is not a Slave State," by Demetrius C. Boulger. London : Sampson Low, Marston & Company. Price 6*d*.
‡ See also the issues of that strangely misnamed publication, "La Vérité sur le Congo," issued fortnightly from Brussels in the interests of the Congo Government.

PREFACE

To put the Congo State in the pillory and pelt it is comparatively easy, for elements of conviction increase every day. To make people understand that the ill treatment of the Natives does not belong—even in the superlative degree it has attained on the Congo—to that class of regretable incidents from which the history of no Colonial Power is altogether free, has been, and is, a task of greater difficulty. To become an efficient power for good of a lasting kind, humanitarian feeling must be constructive. It is not enough to denounce a wrong; it is necessary to show how that wrong originates, and to put forward a practical remedy. In this respect the process of instructing Public Opinion still lacks in completeness, and the recently formed Congo Reform Association has a great and useful task to perform.

The wrong done to the Congo peoples originates from the substitution of commerce, which is based upon the recognition by Europe of native ownership in land and in the produce of the land (which the native alone can gather), with the consequent onus upon the European to PURCHASE that produce which modern industrialism requires; by a system based upon the right of a European State to expropriate the Native of tropical Africa from his land and from the produce of the land (which produce constitutes in tropical Africa the element of commerce), with the consequent elimination of the onus upon the European to PURCHASE produce which has ceased to belong to the gatherer of it. The only remedy lies in the reversal by civilisation of the latter system set up in the Congo territories, a system as immoral in conception as it is barbarous in execution, and disastrous to European prestige in its ultimate effects. It was worth while, and it continues to be worth while, to incur misrepresentation in the effort to make clear beyond possibility of doubt that the destruction of commercial relationship between the European and the African in tropical Africa means the enslavement of the African, and is the fundamental cause of all the abominations of Congo State control.

The alliance between humanitarian sentiment and practical knowledge of tropical African conditions was cemented at the Mansion House meeting, held under the auspices of the Aborigines Protection Society in May, 1902, with Mr. Alfred

PREFACE xiii

E. Pease, M.P., in the Chair, supported by Sir Charles Dilke, Sir Alfred Lyall, and others, and, either by delegate or by letter, by the London, Liverpool, and Manchester Chambers, by the African Society, and by the Colonial Society of Germany. The resolutions passed expressed the opinion that the provisions of the Berlin Conference "as regards the protection of Native populations" had been violated "by proceedings ruinous to those Native populations," and called upon His Majesty's Government to confer with the Signatory Powers to the Act to take steps "with a view to fulfilment of their joint obligations." In December of that year "Affairs of West Africa" appeared, in which a few chapters were devoted to Congo State misrule. The publication of this volume was followed almost immediately by Mr. Fox-Bourne's far completer indictment, "Civilisation in Congoland." About this time the movement for reform received the powerful support of Mr. Alfred Emmott, M.P. for Oldham, and not long afterwards that of Mr. W. T. Stead, Dr. Clifford, and Dr. Grattan-Guinness, head of the Congo-Balolo Mission.* Resolutions of censure upon Congo State methods were passed in succession by the Associated Chambers of Commerce, by the Free Church Council, and by the London Branch of the International Union.† On March 2, 1903, Viscount Cranbourne replied negatively in the House of Commons to a question put by Sir Charles Dilke, asking "whether the Government had taken or proposed to take steps towards procuring the co-operation of the principal Signatories to the Berlin Act in efforts to restrain the abuses which had grown up under the rule of the Congo Free State in violation of the provisions of that Act." On March 12 an answer of a similar kind was made by Viscount Cranbourne to questions by Mr. Channing and Mr. Lansfield. Viscount Cranbourne admitted, however, that Consular reports had been received by the Government pointing to the existence of

---

* It should also be mentioned that the Aborigines Protection Society appealed directly to the Belgian Parliament.

† The warm thanks of all who are interested in this question is due to the *Morning Post* for the conspicuously able and persistent manner in which it has urged inquiry into Congo State methods. It would be difficult to over-estimate the value of the work performed by the *Morning Post*.

"acts of cruelty and oppression" in the Congo territories. On May 5, the Rev. W. M. Morrison, a missionary just home from the Congo, delivered an account of his experiences before a meeting convened by the Aborigines Protection Society, presided over by Dr. Clifford, and supported by Sir Charles Dilke, by several members of Parliament, including Messrs. Bayley, Emmott, and Samuel, and a number of other people. Sir Charles Dilke moved, and the author seconded, a resolution once more appealing to the Government to take concerted action.

These persistent efforts were destined to meet with their reward at last. Soon after the above meeting it became known that a day had been secured for a debate in the House on a motion put down by Mr. Herbert Samuel. The debate took place on May 20. After speeches by Mr. Samuel, Sir Charles Dilke, Mr. Alfred Emmott, Sir John Gorst, Viscount Cranbourne, Lord Edmund Fitzmaurice, and the Prime Minister, who admitted the existence of an "overwhelming case," the House adopted without a single dissentient voice a resolution pledging the Government to "confer with the other Powers, Signatories of the Berlin General Act, by virtue of which the Congo Free State exists, in order that measures may be adopted to abate the evils prevalent in that State." The British Note was presented to the Powers in August last.

Meanwhile Mr. Roger Casement, permanent British Consul in the Congo State, an official " of wide African experience," * had been conducting a personal investigation in the Upper Congo. The appalling account of his experiences is now before the world, and has been followed by a further debate in Parliament, in the course of which absolute unanimity prevailed as to the essentiality of putting an end to the present horrors. So far as British action alone is concerned, a constructive policy was on that occasion placed before His Majesty's Government, which was supported by all the speakers in the debate, and which Lord Percy admitted to be "practical."

The fact that Mr. Roger Casement was investigating on the spot became known towards the end of 1903, and the

* British Note.

nature of his report was shrewdly surmised. Indeed, the verdict of any competent, and therefore impartial, British official could only have been identical with the verdict of instructed Public Opinion at home. It remains to be said that Mr. Casement, whose reputation already stood high, performed the difficult and unpleasant task entrusted to him with extraordinary ability, and that his report might have been written by a machine—a painfully eloquent machine—so judicious, and free from bias or prejudice is its tone.

The publication of the official report, prefaced by an exceedingly scathing and contemptuous appreciation by Lord Cromer touching his own experiences in the Lado enclave, infused fresh fire into the movement for Congo reform, in the shape of new helpers in the cause and a great accretion of public strength. Dr. Guinness started a series of public lectures early in the year in Scotland, drawing large audiences. Although head of a missionary organisation, Dr. Guinness dropped all sectarianism in his lectures, which were purely humanitarian in character. Early in the year, also, the first steps were privately taken to concentrate individual effor into one organisation whose sole aim and object would be the enlightenment of Public Opinion on this particular question. The work of founding that organisation devolved largely upon the author of this volume, who, with the cordial co-operation and assistance of Mr. Alfred Emmott, M.P., Mr. John Holt, and others, was placed in the position of being able, within two months of the idea taking root, to announce the creation of the Congo Reform Association at the Philharmonic Hall, Liverpool, on March 23, at a demonstration presided over by Mr. Emmott.

The aims of the Association are the restoration to the Natives of the Congo of the rights guaranteed to them by the Berlin and Brussels Acts. Otherwise stated, it has come into being to help on the work of Congo reform, in perhaps a completer and more systematised form by appealing on a simple issue to a much wider public than had been approached hitherto. The Presidency of the Association has been accepted by Earl Beauchamp, and its supporters already include ten Peers and some forty Members of Parliament, amongst others such men as Mr. John Morley, the Earls of Aberdeen, Darnley, Listowel, and Norbury; Lords Brassey, Tweedmouth, Ffrench, Kinnaird, Denman, and Overtoun; the Bishops of Liverpool, Durham, Rochester, and St. Asaph; virtually all the prominent leaders of Nonconformity; members of Parliament of both sides, including Sir Charles Dilke, Sir John Kennaway, Sir Gilbert Parker, John Burns, Austin Taylor, Richard Bell; well known personalities like Mr. St. Loe Strachey, Professor Bosworth Smith, Rev. Stephen Gladstone, Mr. W. A. Cadbury, Dr. E. Wilmot Blyden, and many others, together with prominent foreigners, either with personal knowledge of Africa and her peoples, or with special qualifications, such as Prince Boris Czetwertynski, Count Hans Coudenhove, Herr Ludwig Deuss, Professor Poulteney Bigelow, etc.*

Such in brief is the record of British effort against an evil which is both gigantic and unique.

The clear and absolute duty of the Powers is to rid the Congo territories of the misrule which is decimating the population. They can do so, if they will, without the slightest difficulty. The condition of affairs on the Congo is an affront to humanity. Britain in taking the lead in protesting against that condition of affairs, is animated by no selfish motives. The entire movement is primarily due to the dogged determination of a few individuals who knew the facts, and were determined to do what in them lay to make the truth known to the world. It is emphatically not a movement for which official initiative openly or secretly engineered is responsible. That the support of other civilised peoples whose Governments also have their portion of moral responsibility will eventually be forthcoming is not to be doubted. But to obtain that support, unflagging effort, undeterred by disappointment, is essential.† If we organise

---

* It is significant of the unanimity of feeling prevailing in Great Britain that men, who in matters political and religious are strongly, even violently opposed, have found themselves able to co-operate in this cause, and it is a tribute to the belief in the unselfishness of the Association's aims, that foreigners should have allied themselves to a British organisation.

† In August last, the Executive Committee of the Congo Reform Association expressed the wish that the author of this volume should present, on their behalf, a memorial to President Roosevelt, and should participate in the Boston Peace Congress, where the Congo Question was

our forces, and pursue resolutely the course which duty and honour alike order us to follow, the issue is certain. It is a struggle well worth the waging. Our forefathers smashed the over-sea slave-trade, and we shall root out the modern inland slave-trade on the Congo. The difference between the two evils is that the latter is more destructive of human life and human happiness, and more demoralising in its cumulative effects than the former was, even at the height of its power.

E. D. MOREL.

HAWARDEN,
1904.

to be discussed, as the representative alike of the Congo Reform Association, and of other Associations and Societies with which the former is on terms of cordial and sympathetic co-operation.

INTRODUCTION

THE object of this book is to place before all men who claim the epithet of civilised, the condition of the Congo territories after nearly twenty years of King Leopold's rule.

It has seemed to me that at the present stage in the struggle against an evil which has attained enormous proportions, something more was required than a recapitulation of pre-existing records. I have thought that an effort should be made to explain with some fulness the inward causes leading to those outward effects of which the Congo territories are, and have been, for a considerable period, the scene. This I have endeavoured to do by defining the radical distinction between the development of tropical Africa by trade, which involves the recognition of Native rights in land and forest produce; and the exploitation of Tropical Africa through the methods introduced, legalised, and upheld by King Leopold, *the sole arbiter of and legislator for the destinies of the Congo Natives.*

I have tried to show that a humane, common-sense and just treatment of the Native races of tropical Africa by the European Powers reposes upon certain fundamental principles, which, if set aside, must inevitably lead to the adoption of an alternate policy profoundly immoral in itself, maintainable by force alone, and bound in the long run to prove economically and politically disastrous.

CONTENTS

PART I.—HISTORICAL

CHAP.		PAGE
I.	THE BERLIN ACT	3
II.	THE ANTECEDENTS OF THE BERLIN ACT	8
III.	THE SEQUEL TO THE BERLIN ACT AND THE CONSTITUTION OF THE CONGO STATE	17

PART II.—THE NEW AFRICAN SLAVE-TRADE

IV.	COMMERCIAL DEVELOPMENT *VERSUS* COERCION	31
V.	HOW THE STATE DESTROYED LEGITIMATE TRADE IN THE UPPER CONGO	39
VI.	THE ECONOMIC TEST OF CONGO STATE RULE	44
VII.	THE FINANCIAL TEST OF CONGO STATE RULE—THE BENEFICIARIES BY GOVERNMENT SLAVERY	59
VIII.	THE "PROPERTY" PLEA—THE CONGO STATE'S MAIN LINE OF DEFENCE	75
IX.	NATIVE LAND-TENURE, TRADE, AND LABOUR	89
X.	THE THIRD TEST OF CONGO STATE RULE—MILITARISM, MURDER, MUTILATION, AND THE TRAFFIC IN ARMS	102

PART III.—THE NEW SLAVE-TRADE IN BEING

(*The Working of the System as it affects the Natives*)

XI.	CONGO STATE CONTROL IN THE CENTRAL DISTRICT (THE MONGALLA)	127
XII.	CONGO STATE CONTROL IN THE CENTRAL DISTRICT (THE MONGALLA—THE CAUDRON CASE)	135
XIII.	CONGO STATE CONTROL IN THE CENTRAL DISTRICT (LOPORI AND MARINGA)	154
XIV.	CONGO STATE CONTROL IN THE NORTHERN DISTRICT	171

CONTENTS

CHAP.		PAGE
XV.	CONGO STATE CONTROL IN THE DOMAINE DE LA COURONNE	179
XVI.	CONGO STATE CONTROL IN THE WESTERN DISTRICT (KASAI)	189
XVII.	CONGO STATE CONTROL IN THE EASTERN DISTRICT	201
XVIII.	CONGO STATE CONTROL IN THE SOUTH-EASTERN DISTRICT (KATANGA)	209
XIX.	CONGO STATE CONTROL ON THE RIVER BANKS	220
XX.	CONGO STATE CONTROL IN THE LOWER CONGO	229
XXI.	THE GENERAL CONDITION OF NATIVE LIFE UNDER CONGO STATE RULE	235

PART IV.—THE WORKING OF THE SYSTEM AS IT AFFECTS INTERNATIONAL COMMERCIAL INTERESTS

XXII.	RABINEK'S PERSONALITY AND HISTORY	259
XXIII.	THE KATANGA COMPANY AND THE CONGO STATE: RABINEK'S RELATIONS WITH BOTH	267
XXIV.	THE PLOT AND THE ARREST	275
XXV.	THE TRIAL, THE SENTENCE, AND THE END	285

PART V.—THE CONGO DEBATE IN THE BELGIAN HOUSE OF REPRESENTATIVES

XXVI.	FIRST DAY'S PROCEEDINGS	299
XXVII.	SECOND DAY'S PROCEEDINGS	312
XXVIII.	THIRD DAY'S PROCEEDINGS	327
XXIX.	THE LESSONS OF THE DEBATE	339

PART VI

XXX.	THE ATTEMPT TO DISCREDIT CONSUL CASEMENT'S REPORT	355

APPENDIX 373–466

LIST OF ILLUSTRATIONS

Motherhood . . . . *Photogravure Frontispiece*	
	Facing page
Portrait of the Author	8
The Cause of the Modern African Slave Trade . . .	24
Indiarubber Sheds at Baringa	24
Portrait of the Right Hon. Sir Charles W. Dilke, Bart., M.P.	32
Natives of the Nsongo District (Abir Concesssion, etc.) . .	48
Portrait of Alfred Emmott, Esq., M.P.	64
Portrait of Mr. Roger Casement	80
Portrait of Mr. H. R. Fox-Bourne	96
Children mutilated by Congo Soldiery	112
Natives shot and mutilated by Congo Soldiery	128
Nsala of Wala in the Nsongo District (Abir Concession) . .	144
In the Mission Village of Lulanga	160
Two Wretched Mongo Women (Abir Concession) . . .	168
Manyanga Natives, Cataracts Region (Lower Congo) . .	176
Native Prisoners at Boma taking the Air	192
Native Method of Mending a Broken Leg	208
The Native at Home (French Congo)	208
"Hostages" sharpening Sticks in Palm Avenue, Baringa . .	224
Indiarubber "Hostages" chained by the Neck, etc. . . .	224
Typical Barrack House under Civilized Administration . .	240
Police Barracks at Matadi	240
Portrait of Gustav Maria Rabinek, aged 18	272

LIST OF ILLUSTRATIONS

	Facing page
Portrait of Gustav Maria Rabinek aged 22	272
Scene in the Cataracts Region (Lower Congo)	288
The Agents of the Modern African Slave Trade	304
Portrait of M. Emile Vandervelde	320

MAPS

Copy of the Map of Rabinek's Concession	256
Map of the Congo Territories	466

PART I

HISTORICAL

THE BERLIN ACT
THE ANTECEDENTS OF THE BERLIN ACT
THE SEQUEL TO THE BERLIN ACT, AND THE
  CONSTITUTION OF THE CONGO STATE

CHAPTER I

THE BERLIN ACT

How it was brought about—Its aims—The principles it laid down—
Its trustee

"In the Name of Almighty God."*

EVENTS of public policy are seldom dictated by causes other than the material interests which the Government that may be concerned considers necessary to uphold, on behalf of the nation with whose mandate it is for the time being entrusted. The contention holds good in the case both of Democracies and Autocracies. Those interests in themselves may be perfectly respectable and legitimate, or they may be the reverse ; the fact remains, that, as a rule, the aim of every Government is to promote the interests of its own people, to the exclusion and, if necessary, to the detriment of the interests of other peoples. The sentiment is natural, and until the millennium is reached, frontiers abolished, and universal brotherhood established as a working basis, its selfishness is as justifiable in ethics as it is inevitable in practice. Yet there have been occasions when the Government of a country has been moved by a sentiment divorced from selfishness—a sentiment of broad humanity, in its true sense. Sometimes, where the form of government is democratic, its action has been due to public opinion unmistakably expressed ; sometimes to the intense convictions of a great statesman supreme at its council-board. Sometimes it has been due to the lofty ideals of a ruler wielding autocratic power to an unlimited extent. These noble exceptions have not been numerous, but they have occurred, and no student of history is ignorant of them.

Now, although international jealousies contributed very largely to the Berlin Conference of 1885, it is unquestionable that the spirit displayed at that Conference and the policy it laid down were alike inspired by humanitarian motives—*practical* humanitarian motives. The existence of international

* Opening to the Berlin Act.

s in Equatorial Africa was admitted, and the desire
y them expressly stipulated, as one of the principal
s for the Conference. But apart from that, there
..__ . sible throughout the deliberations which took place in
the course of the framing of the clauses of the Act, a desire
to protect the natives of Africa from injustice and expropriation; to guarantee them in the peaceful possession of their
land and property; to check, as far as possible, inter-tribal
warfare and the slave-raiding operations of Arab half-castes;
and to maintain and develop trade. Particular stress was
laid upon the latter point, it being universally recognised that
commercial intercourse is, above all things, the surest medium
for the advancement of communities from a state of primitive
barbarism to a greater knowledge of arts and crafts, and,
generally speaking, to a higher conception of life.

The motives which guided the members of the Conference
can best be understood by the following extracts from the
discussions.

Prince Bismarck, in his opening speech, said:

" In convoking the Conference, the Imperial Government was guided
by the conviction that all the Governments invited share the wish to bring
the natives of Africa within the pale of civilisation by opening up the
interior of that continent to commerce. . . ."

" The fundamental idea of this programme is to facilitate the access of
all commercial nations to the interior of Africa. . . ."

" The natural development of commerce in Africa gives birth to the
very legitimate desire to open up to civilisation the territories which are
at present unexplored and unoccupied. . . ."

Sir Edward Malet, representing Great Britain, said:

" I cannot forget that the natives are not represented amongst us, and
that the decisions of the Conference will, nevertheless, have an extreme
importance for them. The principle which will command the sympathy
and support of Her Majesty's Government will be that of the advancement of legitimate commerce, with securities for the equality of treatment of all nations, and for the well-being of the native races. . . ." *

" But I think this Conference, on careful examination of the question,
will recognise the necessity of providing more in detail for the absolute
equality of treatment of the subjects of all Powers as regards duties and
direct and indirect taxes, residence, liberty to trade and travel, use of
roads and railroads, coasting trade, and religious freedom. . . ." †

" I make it a point of placing it on record that the *régime* of freedom
of commerce in the Conventional Basin of the Congo . . . is without
limit as to duration. . . ." ‡

---

* Protocol No. 1. Protocols and General Act of the West African
Conference, presented to both Houses of Parliament by Command of Her
Majesty, March, 1885.
† Protocol No. 1, *op. cit.*
‡ Protocol No. 8, *op. cit.*

THE BERLIN ACT

Mr. Kasson, representing the United States, said:

"It was the earnest desire of the Government of the United States that these discoveries should be utilised for the civilisation of the native races, and for the abolition of the slave-trade; and that early action should be taken to avoid international conflicts likely to arise from national rivalry in the acquisition of special privileges in the vast region so suddenly exposed to commercial enterprise. If that country could be neutralised against aggression with equal privileges for all, such an arrangement ought, in the opinion of my Government, to secure general satisfaction. . . ."*

The Marquis of Penafiel, representing Portugal, said that his Government

"shares entirely the far-reaching ideal, so nobly expressed . . . that commercial relations which will become extended in the African Continent will serve the cause of peace and humanity." †

Baron Lambermont, representing Belgium, and Baron de Courcel, representing France, affixed their signatures to the report of the "Commission charged with examining the project of declaration relating to freedom of commerce in the Basin of the Congo, and its affluents," which report contains the following passages :—

"In immense countries, where communications are rare or imperfect, where the traffic is carried on by primitive or special means, where, in fact, the administrative machinery is in a great part wanting, reason in harmony with experience advises leaving to commerce a great liberty of action. . . ."

"No doubt whatever exists as to the strict and literal sense which should be applied to the term 'in commercial matters.' It refers exclusively to traffic, to the unlimited power of every one to sell and to buy, to import and export products and manufactured articles. No privileged position can be conferred under this head; the way remains open without any restrictions to free competition in the domain of commerce."

"To develop commerce it is not sufficient to open ports or to remove custom-house barriers. Without merchants there is no commerce. If one wishes to attract merchants towards distant countries still imperfectly known, it is necessary to surround with guarantees that which is of essential interest to them, their persons, their goods, the acquisition of property, the right of inheritance, and the exercise of professions. Such is the object of the stipulation which terminates Article 5. It protects not only merchants, but comprises all foreigners and the pioneers of civilisation as well as those of commerce. . . ." ‡

Baron de Courcel made the additional declaration:

"But beyond the special stipulation of Article 4, we have recognised and sanctioned a certain number of principles which assure the application of freedom of commerce in the Basin of the Congo against all

---

* Protocol No. 3, *op. cit.* † Protocol No. 2, *op. cit.*
‡ Annex 1 to Protocol 4, *op. cit.*

infraction in the future. The prohibition of differential duties, of monopolies or privileges, and of all inequality of treatment to the prejudice of persons belonging to a foreign nationality is affected by no limitation of time. The good which results therefrom should be considered as a definite acquisition." *

At the final sitting of the Conference, Prince Bismarck made use of these words :

" The resolutions which we are about to sanction formally secure to the trade of all nations free access to the interior of the African Continent. The guarantees which will be provided for freedom of trade in the Basin of the Congo . . . are such as to afford the most favourable conditions for the development and security of the trade and industry of all nations. In another series of regulations you have shown much careful solicitude for the moral and physical welfare of the native races, and we may cherish the hope that the principle adopted in a spirit of wise moderation will bear fruit and will help to introduce these populations to the advantages of civilisation." †

His sentiments were echoed by Count de Launay, representing Italy, who remarked :

" Whatever may be the future reserved for our work, which is subject to the vicissitudes of all things human, we can, for the present at least, testify that we have neglected nothing in the bounds of possibility for opening as far as the centre of the African continent a wide route to the moral and material progress of the native tribes, and the development of the general interests of commerce. We have at the same time aided the cause of religion, of peace, and of humanity, and enlarged the field of international law." ‡

These aspirations expressed by the plenipotentiaries are to be found embodied, in brief, in the following clauses of the Berlin Act :—

" Article 1. The trade of all nations shall enjoy complete freedom.

" Article 5. No Power which exercises, or shall exercise, sovereign rights in the above-mentioned regions shall be allowed to grant therein a monopoly or favour of any kind in matters of trade.

" Article 7. All the Powers exercising sovereign rights or influence in the aforesaid territories bind themselves to watch over the preservation of the native tribes, and to care for the improvement of the conditions of their moral well-being, and to help in suppressing slavery, and especially the slave-trade."

Thus, as it might have been supposed for many years, if not for all time, a vast portion of Equatorial Africa had been deliberately excluded from international rivalry ; a vast field had been thrown open to the legitimate trade of all nations ; a policy had been devised which would serve as an example and moral in the relations of all European States with the

---

* Protocol No. 8, *op. cit.* † Protocol No. 10, *op. cit.*
‡ Protocol No. 10, *op. cit.*

natives of Africa, a policy at once broad, practical, and humane, a policy truly civilising, upright, and sound.

The "Congo Free State" was solemnly recognised as a friendly State, and became a distinct entity under the sympathetic sponsorship of the Powers. To King Leopold II. of Belgium, constitutional monarch of a neutral country, was assigned the trusteeship of this great territory so brimful of possibilities, was entrusted this great experiment which seemed to inaugurate an era of lofty effort and high moral purpose. How came it that King Leopold should have been selected to that proud position, and how has King Leopold fulfilled his trust?

CHAPTER II

THE ANTECEDENTS OF THE BERLIN ACT

The Conference of 1876—Foundation of the International Association—The germination of a "State"—The professed objects of King Leopold—His specific pledges.

" Is it necessary for me to say that in inviting you to Brussels, I have not been guided by egotism? No, gentlemen, if Belgium is small, Belgium is happy and content with her lot . . . but I should be pleased to think that this civilising movement had been inaugurated from Brussels."—KING LEOPOLD, September 12, 1876, at the International Conference held in Brussels, from which was born the "International Association for the Exploration and Civilisation of Central Africa."

"The spirit of this proposed government is free trade, free commerce, unrestricted enterprise, self-supported arbitration on all subjects likely to provoke misunderstandings between man and man, impartial adjudication on all points between subjects irrespective of colour, creed, or nationality; paternal care of each of its subjects' rights, whether black or white, irrespective of rank or social status; encouragement of all enterprise likely to promote the well-being of the State; abstention from interference in domestic and private matters where the public welfare is unconcerned; in short, a government paternal, just, discreet, calculated to promote happiness and contentment." — STANLEY, at the Manchester Town Hall, October 21, 1884, urging the recognition by Great Britain of the International Association.

" With regard to the question, how it is proposed to govern the Congo State, the legislation of the Congo territory, subject to the supervision and control of the Association, shall be based upon the principles of law recognised by civilised nations, and upon the philanthropic principles set forth in the well-known plan of the Association, whose aim is to civilise Africa by encouragement given to legitimate trade. . . ."—Manifesto of the International Association, which subsequently became the "Independent State of the Congo."

AFRICA, the *terra incognita* of the Western world, the land of darkness and of mystery, of monstrous fables and eccentric legends, passed by swift transition in the sixties and seventies of last century to be the cynosure of all eyes, the loadstar of popular imagination, and in a lesser degree the preoccupation of European Governments. This revolution in modern thought concerning Africa had been brought about by the

Photograph by THE AUTHOR *Elliott & Fry*

THE ANTECEDENTS OF THE BERLIN ACT

sensational discoveries of Burton, Speke and Grant, Baker and Schweinfurth, and Livingstone. In 1876, King Leopold II., constitutional monarch of Belgium, which owed its political independence to the London Congress of 1830, and the preservation of its threatened neutrality to the action of the British Government in 1870, invited an international Conference to Brussels, to consider the best means which could be devised to open up the centre of the Dark Continent to European civilisation. Dreams of colonial expansion had before that date been nursed by the Belgian monarch, who was careful, however, to assure the assembled explorers and scientists at Brussels of the absolute disinterestedness of his intentions. The upshot of the Conference was the creation of an "International Association for the Exploration and Civilisation of Central Africa," and of which King Leopold naturally assumed the presidency.

After some tentative efforts on the part of the Association from the East Coast, which did not lead to anything practical, Stanley suddenly emerged at the mouth of the Congo, from his celebrated voyage across the continent, revealing to the world the existence and course of that mighty river.

King Leopold, realising the immense importance of the discovery, and its possible effect upon the vaguely ambitious projects he was harbouring, hastened to get in touch with the great explorer, whose services he succeeded in enlisting. The energies of the Association, and of the *Comité d'Etudes du Haut Congo**—a sort of dual organisation, responding to one sole directing will, the King's—were henceforth concentrated upon the Congo. Stanley went out on behalf of the Association in 1879, and again in 1882, making treaties with chiefs, founding posts, and establishing a plausible basis in Africa for pending developments on the European chess-board.

Step by step the real motives inspiring the King's initial action in 1876 were coming to the fore. In the earliest stages His Majesty invited, in effect, the world to regard him as a second Henry the Navigator. As a philanthropist he has ever posed, but by 1880 the idea of an African State of which he should be the European sovereign had already defined itself very clearly in His Majesty's mind, and given to his philanthropy that severely practical side for which it has been ever remarkable.

With the rivalry between Stanley and de Brazza on the banks of the Congo, and the dispute between France and the Association in respect to the Niadi-Kwilu, it is unnecessary

* Which had been created in 1880.

to deal here. These historical incidents have been frequently narrated, with slight variations as to dates and motives, by Mr. Fox-Bourne,* by M. Cattier,† M. Jean Darcy,‡ and others; and apart from the fact that I could not hope to improve upon what has been written hitherto on that subject, my object is to steer clear of all matters not absolutely germane to the question at issue. The event that precipitated the rapidly maturing plans pursued by King Leopold with a pertinacity which, had the outcome of his intervention been anything but what it is, could be described as magnificent, was the Anglo-Portuguese Treaty of February 26, 1884, which Sir Charles Dilke and, subsequently, Lord Edmund Fitzmaurice (Lord Lansdowne's brother), were prominently concerned in drafting. By this Treaty Portugal's claim to the coast-line between the 8° and 5° 12″ of latitude south was recognised by Great Britain, together with a strip of territory on both sides of the river Congo as far as Noki, Portugal thus obtaining the mouth of the river. In exchange for the recognition of this claim, which, as Sir Charles Dilke puts it, "historically considered, was, in my opinion good," § Portugal pledged herself, amongst other things, to a moderate tariff, and to a strict equality of commercial treatment for all nations. The objects of this Treaty were several, but to King Leopold it conveyed a plain intimation that the true aims of the Association had been perceived by the British Government, and that the African sceptre fondly caressed in his imagination was slipping from his grasp. But King Leopold rose to the occasion, and succeeded in bringing off a signal diplomatic victory.

General Henry Sandford ‖ (King Leopold's political bagman for America, as Stanley had become his mouthpiece for England) reported glibly about territory having been ceded to the Association "for the use and benefit of free states established and being established"—what a grisly satire it seems in these days!—and begged for American recognition of the Association as an "independent State." The United States Government acceded to this request. This action, undertaken, as has long since been apparent, on assurances for which there was no basis in fact, confers a peculiar

* "Civilisation in Congoland." H. R. Fox-Bourne (P. S. King & Son).
† "Droit et Administration de l'Etat Indépendant du Congo." F. Cattier.
‡ "Cent années de rivalité coloniale." Jean Darcy.
§ "Civilisation in Africa." *Cosmopolis.*
‖ Subsequently one of the two American representatives at the Berlin Conference.

responsibility upon the American people in connection with the state of affairs prevailing in the Congo territories to-day.*

Simultaneously with the successful efforts to win over America, Stanley went to London and Manchester to stir up the West African mercantile community against the Treaty, which was not popular in Europe, and not favoured by the merchant firms established on the Congo (who were then doing a very considerable trade), for the identical reasons which Stanley skilfully played upon in addressing his English audiences. The London and Manchester Chambers of Commerce believed what Stanley told them as to the aims of King Leopold, and, backed by the Press, started what Sir Harry Johnston has called "a nonsensical agitation" against the Treaty. The difficulties of the British Government, already considerable, were intensified by the home opposition, and finally the Treaty was abandoned.

Meanwhile the international position in Africa was singularly complicated. The interests of France, Portugal, England, and the Association—that is to say, King Leopold —were all more or less involved. An inextricable jumble was the result, and when Bismarck suggested a conference, the various parties concerned acquiesced. Whatever may have been uppermost in the famous Chancellor's thoughts at the time, there can be no doubt that the Conference embodied a great idea and a grand ideal.

The Conference met, took expert advice, discussed and elaborated with extreme care a series of principles which should regulate European policy in Tropical Africa. The result of the Conference, so far as the Association was concerned, was a foregone conclusion before it had completed its labours. Indeed, before the Conference closed, the lead given by the United States had been followed by the Powers of Europe. But the recognition desired, and obtained by King Leopold, was a recognition founded upon certain pledges specifically made by his representatives. In the

* The American Government did not ratify the Berlin Act, but its representatives took a prominent part in the Conference, as also in the Brussels Conference, and concluded, moreover, in 1891 a separate treaty with the Congo State, which secured to American citizens "the treatment of the most favoured nation in all that relates to rights, privileges, exemptions," etc. It should be borne in mind that in his message to Congress (December, 1883) explaining the reasons for the initiative taken by the United States in recognising the Association, President Arthur said, "The objects of this Society are philanthropic; it does not aim at permanent political control." The gravity of the special obligation resting upon the American Government is fully recognised in the American Memorial addressed to Congress and presented by Senator Morgan on April 19, 1904.

"Exchange of Declarations" between the British Government and the Association, done at Berlin on December 16, 1884, the Association is described as having been "founded by His Majesty the King of the Belgians, for the *purpose of promoting the civilisation and commerce of Africa, and for other humane and benevolent purposes.*" It is further stated in that document (the "Free States" myth being studiously kept to the fore):

"That the Association and the said Free States will do all in *their* power to prevent the slave-trade, and to suppress slavery." On the faith of these assurances the British Government declared "their sympathy with, and approval of, the humane and benevolent purposes of the Association." Those pledges given by the Association were amplified and set forth clearly and succinctly in the General Act of the Conference of Berlin, signed by the Powers collectively, which Act became the charter of the new State's existence, as is expressly admitted in the Belgian code of laws known as the *Pandectes Belges*, and as was no less explicitly avowed at the close of the Conference by Count van der Straeten-Ponthoz, delegate for Belgium, in the following terms :

"The Acts of the Conference give practically effect to the bold and generous ideas conceived by His Majesty. The Belgian Government and nation will, therefore, gratefully adhere to the work elaborated by the High Assembly, *thanks to which the existence of the New State is henceforth assured, whilst rules have been laid down by which the general interests of humanity will profit.*"

The Powers believed in the pledges of King Leopold; pledges categorically defined in the "Exchange of Declarations" with Great Britain and the United States; pledges recapitulated by the President of the International Association, Colonel Strauch, in the following terms :

"The Conference to which it is my duty to render homage would, I venture to hope, consider the accession of a Power *whose exclusive mission is to introduce civilisation and trade into the centre of Africa* as a further pledge of the fruits which its important labour must produce;"

pledges given in reiterated and glowing periods, and doubtless quite sincerely at the time, by Stanley before the London and Manchester Chambers of Commerce. King Leopold had devoted his revenues to the work of the Association; he had given expression to such earnest and philanthropic sentiments, he appeared to be animated by feelings so eminently worthy of respect and admiration, that Mr. Busch, the representative of Germany, presiding over the last sitting of the

THE ANTECEDENTS OF THE BERLIN ACT 13

Conference, was only saying what was the generally accepted opinion at the time when he declared:

"We all do justice to the high aim of the undertaking to which His Majesty the King of the Belgians has affixed his name."

Such were the circumstances under which King Leopold, constitutional monarch of Belgium, became trustee for one million square miles of African territory, and guardian of, perhaps, some twenty million Africans.

It is, I think, especially important to-day, that no shadow of doubt should be entertained by a single person in regard to the nature of the pledges given by King Leopold to the world, through his representatives, at the time the Congo State was in process of birth, and prior, therefore, to its baptism. The statements already quoted cannot, of course, allow of hesitation on the point; nevertheless, we shall find much valuable and additional proof in the speeches delivered by Stanley on behalf of the Association in London * and Manchester in 1884.† Here are some extracts from the London speech on "Civilisation and Commerce":

"We wish" (*i.e.* the Association) "to secure equal rights to all, and the utmost freedom of commerce...."

"While we travelled through and through the Congo lands, making roads, stations, negotiating for privileges, surveying the vast area, teaching and preparing the natives for the near advent of a bright and happy future for them, winning them by gentleness, appeasing their passions, inculcating commercial principles, showing to them the nature of the produce that would be marketable ‡ when the white man should come; and everywhere accepted as their friends and benefactors...."

"Commerce cannot expand in a new-born region like the Congo Basin, if it is not relieved of all fear of that dread Portuguese tariff."

"At the Conference" (the Conference of 1876, at which King Leopold disclaimed all "egotism") "it was recommended to establish hospitable and scientific stations under a flag, which was to be blue with a gold star in the centre, figurative, I suppose, of the morning star, forerunner of the light that was to shine over the Dark Continent. One of the objects of the Association was to influence as much as possible the suppression of the slave-trade in the interior."

"The purpose of the Association is to compel commerce and industry to follow it eagerly by the very inviting prospects held before commercial and industrial enterprise."

At Manchester, on October 21, 1884, those magnificent

---

* Supplement to the *Chamber of Commerce Journal*, Sept. 19, 1884.

† Manchester Chamber of Commerce. Special meeting held on Tuesday, October 21, 1884, in the large room of the Town Hall, Albert Square, Manchester.

‡ Will the reader please note the word "marketable," and refer to Chapter VI. ?

promises and sentiments were renewed. Stanley, who had been staying the day previous with Mr. J. F. Hutton, President of the Manchester Chamber of Commerce, the father of my friend Mr. J. Arthur Hutton, the present Chairman of the West African Section of that Chamber, had so impressed his host that the latter, upon introducing Stanley to the meeting at the Town Hall, exclaimed—

"He is here to tell us that these millions on the banks of the Congo are eager for our trade ; he is here also to show us how the freedom of those Africans may be maintained, and how the complete freedom of commerce of all countries may be established, and how all the customs houses and all vexatious restrictions and impediments to trade may be utterly abolished and swept away from the banks of the Congo."

Freedom of commerce, synonymous with the freedom of the native—that was, and is, the truth—the truth we are preaching now ; the truth embodied in the Berlin Act ; the truth enunciated by Stanley ; the truth King Leopold and his agents bound themselves on their personal honour and by public pledges to adhere to. Let us remember these solemn and reiterated pledges as we follow the developments of a surprising evolution.

On a par with assurances of freedom to the native, encouragement of commerce, suppression of evils, holy horror of the hateful tariff, were the protestations of philanthropic motive. Listen to them !

"Whatever you do contrary to the Association, or adverse to its aspirations, you cannot impoverish the Association. The £500,000 sterling which it has given away to the Congo it gave freely, the thousands of pounds which it may give annually it gives without any hope of return further than a sentimental satisfaction, therefore you cannot injure it pecuniarily." (Manchester.)

"Scheme we have none, further than to civilise the Congo Basin, discountenance the slave-trade, keep the road thither open and untaxed for commerce to enter, improve communications in every possible way to the extent of its means, keep the peace between man and man, and administer what wise laws may be framed for our guidance, and such as are necessary in Christian communities." (Manchester.)

"This society has as little to do with Belgium, as a State, as any society in Manchester. It is simply a private society, with a rich prince at the head, whose home is in Belgium, and, therefore, it has its headquarters in Brussels. A sentiment animates it—viz. good will to all men, white or black, a spirit of free trade, and unrestricted intercourse." (Manchester.)

"Though they understand the satisfaction of a sentiment when applied to England, they are slow to understand that it may be a sentiment that induced King Leopold II. to father this International Association. He is a dreamer, like his *confrères* in the work, because the sentiment is applied to the neglected millions of the Dark Continent. They cannot appreciate rightly, because there are no dividends attached to it, this restless, ardent,

THE ANTECEDENTS OF THE BERLIN ACT 15

vivifying and expansive sentiment, which seeks to extend civilising influences among the dark races, and to brighten up with the glow of civilisation the dark places of sad-browed Africa. . . . Who knows but that in some distant future the memories of the founders of the International Association will be also revered as the principal factor in the civilisation of regenerated Africa?" (London.)

"Regenerated Africa." I wonder whether Sir Henry M. Stanley, cited to-day (unjustly, I believe, for Sir Henry is an invalid living in the glorious pioneering days of the past, with no knowledge of the sordid ends to which his great work has been applied) * in conjunction with Sir Hugh Gilzean Reid, Sir Alfred Jones (Consul for the Congo State in Liverpool), and Mr. Demetrius Boulger, as defenders of the Congo State, ever reads his old speeches.

Is it surprising that such eloquence won over his hearers? Is it surprising that the Manchester Chamber of Commerce expressed by resolution " its warm sympathy with the earnest efforts of His Majesty the King of the Belgians to establish civilisation and free trade † in the Upper Congo," and recommended that " the Independent State or States proposed to be founded there may be recognised by all nations, and that the beneficent work there inaugurated may be ultimately extended throughout the whole of that river from its source to its mouth." No wonder the Anglo-Portuguese Treaty was unpopular in England! No wonder that a score of splendid men gathered at first round the blue banner with the golden star! No wonder the Aborigines Protection Society enrolled King Leopold as one of its members! No wonder that all Europe, bowing in respectful admiration at the philanthropy of a royal "Peabody," at the re-incarnation with added virtues born of advancement in culture and civilisation, of a Henry the Navigator, feeling the utmost confidence in the integrity, the sense of honour and enlightened statesmanship of the Belgian monarch, placed the fate of

---

* Since these words were written the great explorer has passed away. Taking the man's work as a whole, there is nothing grander in the history of exploration and geographical discovery. And there is nothing more pitiful than the results which have followed that work. In a recently published article by Sir Harry Johnston, the latter says of Stanley, "The last year of his life was certainly embittered by the gradual growing conviction that he had been the indirect means of placing in the Congo Basin a Power more unscrupulous and more disastrous in its results than might have grown up under the flag of Islam." What a picture of infinite pathos!

† *Trade* already existed in the Upper Congo, as Stanley specially emphasised (see Chapter VII.), but the desire was to keep it "free"—free from interference by vexatious enactments. Do not let us forget this. That *trade* itself could be threatened never entered the head of any one.

millions of African natives, and the destiny of an immense portion of the Dark Continent, with all its promises of future good for Africa and for Europe, in the hands of the "rich prince," who, scorning dividends, imbued with views the highest and loftiest which could enrich the human mind and stir the human heart, had prepared the way for a "Regenerated Africa!"

CHAPTER III

THE SEQUEL TO THE BERLIN ACT, AND THE CONSTITUTION OF THE CONGO STATE

There is an impression, very widely existing among the people in the Congo State, that when this money is voted by the Brussels Conference, there will be war and raids instead of any beneficial result, and that great evils will grow far greater than the slave-trade, as existing at present. (Hear, hear.) We contend that it ought to be suppressed by judicious efforts, by the extension of legitimate commerce, by fair consideration for the natives, by being just to the Arabs and enlisting their sympathy, and not by exterminating the natives or the Arabs in a series of wars."—Mr. F. W. Fox.*

FIVE years had passed since the foundation of the "Congo Free State"—a short five years, which had brought many lessons, unpalatable disclosures, bitter disillusion. The veil of philanthropic motive concealing the face of the Congo sphinx had been brushed aside somewhat, and the features which it concealed were not nearly so benign as the world had had reason to expect from the many honeyed words previously uttered. Strange tales were filtering through from Africa anent the treatment of natives by the Belgian agents of the new State. Somehow or other they hardly tallied with the antecedent professions of humanitarian purpose. One heard of numerous combats; of cannibal Bangalas in the employ of the State who feasted upon the bodies of natives slain in these encounters; of Congo State officers receiving tribute of slaves and ivory—for all the world like the half-caste Arabs whose evil deeds they were denouncing up hill and down dale. With the chief of these same Arabs,† the Congo State, through Stanley, had contracted a singular alliance, installing him as Governor of Stanley Falls, furnishing him with a specimen of that flag which was to have been the "forerunner of the light that was to shine over the Dark Continent;" buying that ivory from him of which " every

* Speaking at the Conference of African merchants, held at the rooms of the London Chamber of Commerce, November 4, 1890.
† Hamed-ben-Mohamed, otherwise Tippu-Tib.

pound weight," according to Stanley, had "cost the life of a man, woman, or child," and selling it in Europe, while severely taxing its export where merchants were concerned. All this might be susceptible of explanation, but it was rather surprising. It did not accord, somehow, with that glowing report to the "Sovereign-King," of which the first paragraph read as follows : " La repression de la traite des esclaves a été l'un des objets principaux poursuivis par votre Majesté dès l'origine des entreprises belges au Congo." That was all very well, and there had been some skirmishes with Arab bands ; on the other hand, there was that hoary-headed old sinner, master at Stanley Falls, furnishing the State with ivory "for gold payable at Zanzibar." A singular military complexion, too, for a philanthropic undertaking, was being given to the State. Between 1885 and 1888 the military forces of the State had doubled. In 1889 they reached a total of 23 officers, 29 non-commissioned officers, and 2200 "regulars;" but the most cheerful expectations were officially held out as to forthcoming increases. "We can count," ran an official report, "in the Bangala country alone upon 5000 militia, and in the neighbourhood of the Aruwimi and Stanley Falls upon at least 3000 men." Here was a prospect of unlimited military expenditure which the "rich prince" was, apparently, caressing. A "series of military operations" undertaken to "rally" the populations of Upoto, N'Dobo, Yambinga, etc., had seemingly necessitated the import in 1888 of "three maxims and sixteen bronze cannons." Men rubbed their foreheads and wondered whether they were dreaming. The merchants in the Congo, instead of finding an ally in the new State, had discovered a formidable competitor. Trade, instead of being encouraged, was being heavily handicapped. Advantage had been taken of the silence of the Berlin Act in the matter of export duties, to impose export duties aggregating £50,000 on a year's export trade of £175,000 ! The most fantastic licences had been clapped upon every object used by traders. A man had to pay £2 for every rowing-boat, £4 for every sailing-boat, £14 for every steam-lighter, £40 for every steamer over 50 tons burthen ; 5*d*. per square yard for lodgings for black workmen, 8*s*. 4*d*. per head for every black workman. Rubber was taxed £20 per ton ; ivory, £80 per ton. The merchants hardly saw the force of being made to pay for the military adventures in operation above the Cataracts. It was not part of the bargain. They began to sigh for that defunct Anglo-Portuguese Treaty. More curious still, the State, which had passed a decree proclaiming all "vacant land" to be its property, was beginning to display a singular method of interpreting the word "vacant." The grotesque absurdity of a regulation forbidding the hunting of the elephant "throughout the whole extent of the State's territory without special permission," when three-quarters of the Congo territories were even unexplored, was seen to have a peculiar side to it in view of the State's own transactions in that article. Another regulation prohibiting the trade in rubber and gumcopal in the Aruwimi district under penalty of a fine of 50 to 2000 francs, was hardly less singular. In short, the character of the new dispensation was already as unlike its published programme as chalk from cheese.

Meanwhile Cardinal Lavigerie was preaching a holy crusade against the African internal slave-trade. He found a zealous convert, needless to remark, in the philanthropic Sovereign of the Congo State, to whom it is said Lavigerie suggested the assassination of the worthy Governor of Stanley Falls, the eminently respectable Tippu-Tib.* King Leopold preferred to summon a Conference at Brussels, of which the Brussels General Act was the outcome. This Conference, to which the signatory Powers of the Berlin Act adhered, as well as the United States, which had not ratified the former, laid down a series of the most excellent rules. Its virtual, although not intended, effect was to give King Leopold a plausible justification for raising an enormous army of cannibal mercenaries wherewith to destroy the power of the Arab slave-traders (who held enormous stocks of ivory), and to levy import duties to help to pay for the military conquests and promenades he was planning.

It is of little avail to cry over spilled milk, but one cannot but feel amazed at the fatuity of the Powers—Holland excepted—in allowing themselves to be so entirely hoodwinked. However, hoodwinked they were, and all the pledges of the International Association and its agents with regard to the preservation of "free trade"—that is to say, of trade unhampered by those unpleasant customs dues, the fear of which had destroyed the Anglo-Portuguese Treaty—went by the board. The merchants protested in no uncertain voice. The Dutch Government gave them its support, and at a meeting held at the London Chamber of Commerce on November 4, 1900, under the chairmanship of Sir Albert Rollit, M.P., British, French, Dutch, and Portuguese merchants vigorously denounced the hypocrisy of Africa's regenerator, whose Government—in the words of M. Beraud —"has done nothing whatever in the interests of traders that

* Pierre Mille, "Au Congo Belge."

they found there." They were accused, for their pains, of wishing to encourage the slave-trade! The half-dozen pamphlets which were bandied about at that time by upholders and critics of the Leopoldian *régime* did not leave much shred of respectability to the "Independent State of the Congo," whose champions failed to meet the damaging exposure of its methods, as already apparent beneath the mask of philanthropic intent. But the Powers had committed themselves. Holland could not hold out alone indefinitely. The merchants had prepared their bed, and they had to lie on it. In brief, King Leopold had his way, and with prestige enormously increased, fortified by loans contracted with Belgium, which but for the Brussels Act he would probably not have obtained, provided with an additional source of revenue which might under certain circumstances have become considerable, the Sovereign of the Congo State started upon his African career in grim earnest.

At this stage it is necessary to touch upon the personal part played by, and the individual responsibility of King Leopold in framing the policy pursued by the Congo State since 1890.

It has been the custom, it is even now the custom, of people who prefer to indulge in vague and nebulous statements rather than *face the facts as they are*, to lay the blame for the evil policy which has been put into operation, and for the evil deeds which have necessarily accompanied it, upon the King's advisers in Brussels, and the King's agents in Africa. The contention is wholly and absolutely at variance with the constitution of the State in the first place, and with demonstrable facts in the second place. It is also contrary to common sense. We need not go beyond Belgian authorities to prove this, superfluous as any argument on the subject must be to all who are acquainted with the Congo problem.

The most able and learned treatise on the constitution of the "Independent State of the Congo" is the work of Professor F. Cattier, of the Brussels University. In Part III., under the title of "Droit public et droit administratif" he defines in its judicial aspect the distinction between the "essential principles of the Belgian Constitution (Droit Public)" and the "essential principles of the Congo Constitution (droit Public Congolais)."

"In Belgium," says Professor Cattier, "the King is but one of the trustees of the national sovereignty. Belgium is a constitutional monarchy. Quite different is the situation in the Independent State of the Congo. Sovereignty does not reside in the Congolese nation, it is vested in the person of the Sovereign. Leopold II. is not the trustee, but the titulary of sovereignty. All the rights and all the duties of Government *are summarised and incorporated in his person.** In Belgium the nation has in its Constitution arranged for the delegation of the attributes of sovereignty. It has created and organised its powers, regulated its forms and means of action, guaranteed specific rights to citizens. In the Congo the Sovereign, being the titulary of the sovereignty absolute (*toute entière*) is the direct fountain-head of the legislative, executive, and judicial power. He can, if he chooses, exercise these powers directly and personally. He can, if he prefers it, delegate the execution of the same to certain officials or bodies of officials. That delegation has no other fountain-head but his will. He settles as he pleases the nature and the limits of the delegation to which he consents. He can, at any moment, cancel or modify them. His will cannot meet with any judicial obstacle. Leopold II. would say, from this point of view, and with greater accuracy than did Louis XIV., 'The State, it is I.' . . . Leopold II., titulary of Congolese Sovereignty, exercises it without being checked by any constitutional link. He is the absolute master of the whole of the internal and external activity of the Independent State. He can frame such laws as may appear good to him to settle questions of public and private law, *except respect due to treaties.*† The organisation of justice, the army, the financial systems, the industrial and commercial *régimes*, are established freely by himself according to the idea, be it accurate or faulty, which he has of their utility or efficacy. He regulates with the same independence all the external relations of the State : the despatch and reception of diplomatic and consular agents, the treaties, the negotiations, the alliances and the general policy of a State *dependent upon him alone.*‡ In a word, Leopold II. *possesses personally and exercises personally,*§ save where he thinks it advisable to delegate them to others, all the prerogatives that popular custom (*droit des gens*) recognises to *Sovereign States.*‖ No constitutional rule confines the exercise of these prerogatives. *On the other hand, his will is subordinate to the respect of international treaties which the Congo State (l'Etat du Congo) has concluded.*" ¶

That is plain enough. Trustee to the Powers for the performances of certain pledges, King Leopold, apart from this, is the lord and master absolute over one million square miles of African territory, and over the lives of many millions of human beings, not even the judicial establishment being independent. How could it be, under such a *régime* of absolute and unlimited despotism? The judicial establishment** of the Congo State cannot, indeed, be treated seriously. That there are some well-intentioned men connected with it need not be doubted, but they cannot go beyond a certain point. At a given stage their capacity for usefulness disappears.

* Italics mine.
† Italics Professor Cattier's.
‡ Italics mine.
§ Italics Professor Cattier's.
‖ Italics Professor Cattier's.
¶ Italics Professor Cattier's.
** For fuller particulars of the Judicial establishment of the State, the reader is referred to F. Cattier, *op. cit.*, Speyer, " Comment nous governons le Congo," and Lycops, " Codes congolais et lois usuelles."

They cannot expose the system of the Government whose servants they are, much less condemn it. The judge who presides over the Court of First Instance at Boma is an official named by the King, and revocable at his pleasure: the Boma Appeal Court is composed of a president and two judges, revocable *ad nutum*. The minutes of the trials and judgments passed by these Courts upon individuals guilty of perpetrating atrocities upon the natives are invariably suppressed by the Government. Then there is the famous *Conseil Supérieur* in Brussels, constituted in 1889, and composed of individuals named without exception by the King. Another peculiarity of the judicial establishment is that a Belgian condemned in the Congo for atrocities upon the natives cannot be prosecuted in Belgium should he succeed in escaping thereto, or should the local authorities deem it better policy to allow him to slip quietly away; equally curious is the circumstance that such an official, deeming himself unjustly dealt with by the Congo Courts, cannot compel the Congo "Government" to prosecute him in his own country, try he ever so hard.* Truly Congo "justice" is a fearful and wonderful thing, and when an unhappy individual unconnected with the Administration or the Trusts gets into its clutches, woe betide him. The Stokes and Rabinek affairs are cases in point. But this is by the way.

To return to the constitution of the Congo State. If the reader be not satisfied with the judicial exposition of Professor Cattier, let him turn to M. Wauters, the historian of the Congo State.

"The Congo State being an absolute monarchy, it is evident that one does not find therein, properly speaking, separate and independent legislative, judicial, and administrative powers. . . . All the power emanates from the Sovereign, who exercises them himself (*par lui même*) or by his delegates. He consults, if he thinks well, the *Conseil Supérieur* at Brussels. . . . The Sovereign manifests his will in the form of decrees, countersigned by the Secretary of State."

And, if further reference be necessary, we may consult M. Alfred Poskine, a "commercial and consular" authority, author of an interesting study on the Congo.†

"Let us repeat, after so many others, what has become a platitude: the success of the African work (*l'œuvre africaine*) is the result of an autocratic Government, that is to say, of the work of a single man, guided by a single thought—'homo unius libri,' said the Romans of a remarkable man; it is the work of a sole directing will, without being hampered by the hesitation of timorous politicians, carried out under his sole

---

* See the Tilkens Case, Part V.   † "Bilans Congolais," 1900.

responsibility, intelligent, thoughtful, conscious of the perils and the advantages, discounting with an admirable prescience the great results of a near future."

Finally, the words of M. Van Eetvelde, Congo State Secretary, may be given:

"To-day, it is to your Majesty that the State belongs, and upon whom devolves the care of providing for its destinies, in the triple interest of the native peoples, the mother country, and civilisation." *

Thus do the leading Belgian authorities tell us in no uncertain voice—that which is claimed by King Leopold himself, and by his admirers—that he, and he alone, *is* the Congo State; that he, and he alone, initiates and directs, and has ever initiated and directed, its policy; that its financial, administrative, and judicial system responds to the workings of his will; that the agents he appoints in Europe and in Africa are merely the instruments of his conceptions; and that their careers depend wholly and absolutely upon strict obedience to instructions.

After this disgression we may once more take up the thread of the narrative.

The opposition of Holland which delayed the final ratification of the Brussels Act until January, 1892, did not trouble King Leopold, who forthwith commenced to put his plans into execution. The expenditure estimates for 1891, legalised by the Decree of November 29, 1890, were eloquent of the nature of the policy about to be inaugurated, for out of a total estimated expenditure of 4,544,931.87 francs, military expenses (*Force Publique*) figured to the amount of 2,271,628 francs, or 50 per cent.

The year following the Brussels Conference saw the inauguration of the New Policy in its three distinct, yet closely related branches.

1. A war of extermination against the Arabs.
2. A career of conquest in the Nile Valley beyond the frontiers of the State.
3. The rubber and ivory tax—the necessary corollary of the other two.

The first serious collision with the Arabs occurred in October 27, 1891; the second on May 6, 1892. Battle then succeeded battle; Nyangwe, the Arab stronghold, was captured in January, 1893, and with the surrender of Rumaliza in January, 1894, the campaign came to an end. If the extermination of the Arabs had been followed by a decent

* *Bulletin Officiel*, January, 1897.

native policy, it would perhaps have been justified, notwithstanding the fearful havoc and disgusting incidents with which the process was accompanied,* but never were words more prophetic than those uttered by Mr. F. W. Fox in November, 1890, and which are placed at the head of this chapter.

"There is an impression very widely existing among the people in the Congo State that when the money is voted by the Brussels Conference, there will be war and raids, instead of any beneficial result, and that great evils will grow—far greater than the slave-trade existing at present."

When we see to-day what has replaced Arab rule; when we remember that at the very time this slaughter was going on—slaughter between natives armed by Arabs and natives armed by King Leopold's agents—the Congo State was putting into operation a system of so-called "taxation" on human beings, in rubber and in ivory, more selfish than the system of the Arab, who lived on the land and was interested in it to that extent; and infinitely more cruel and more degrading in its cumulative effect upon the natives. When we bear in mind that the State has merely substituted itself for the Arab, as the ivory monopolist of the Upper Congo territories; when we think of these things, when the records of the last decade are before us, the word "hypocritical" is inadequate to express the conduct of an institution which has claimed ever since to have been animated with sentiments of the purest philanthropy, in ridding the Upper Congo of inconvenient competitors for the acquisition of the rich ivory stores of the country.

Concurrently with the Arab war, the Sovereign of the Congo State was flinging column after column into the Nile Basin. Expedition followed expedition into the Bahr-el-Ghazal, and the territory beyond the 4th parallel of lat. north. In June, 1893, the "blue banner with the golden star" was run up at Dufile and Kiri; and a Belgian expedition pushed as far north as the confines of Darfur. At first both British and French protested against these "filibustering promenades;" but in 1894 King Leopold, who had been negotiating with France for the joint occupation of the Bahr-el-Ghazal, finding the French Government dilatory in coming to an arrangement, induced the British Government to conclude a most unfortunate Convention (August 14, 1894) which did much to strain Anglo-French relations, has brought

* The cannibal Batetla, allies of the State, feasted upon the dead and wounded upon the battle-field. These appalling scenes are fully described by Dr. Hinde in " The Fall of the Congo Arabs."

THE CAUSE OF THE MODERN AFRICAN SLAVE TRADE—INDIA-RUBBER SHED
(The rubber is cut up into small pieces, and is then allowed to dry on the large platform)
(Photo by Mr. Herbert Frost)

INDIA-RUBBER SHEDS AT BARINGA
(Photo by Mr. Herbert Frost)

us nothing but embarrassment, and which materially assisted in precipitating the two nations to the brink of war.

All these adventures necessitated the expenditure of vast sums of money which had somehow to be acquired, and the unhappy native of the Congo territories was made to bear the burden.

We may now pause to examine the contention which has been advanced by the Congo State and its supporters. In its official defence, in its reply to the British Note, and in subsequent official publications, the Congo State seeks to justify the native policy it definitely inaugurated in 1891 and 1892, and which it has since pursued, by the necessity of raising funds somehow and anyhow to meet its expenses. The argument appears to have found some support even among critics of the State's methods. To my mind it is quite unsustainable. King Leopold was given the trusteeship of the Congo territories on certain specifically enunciated lines. To quote a writer whose persistent whitewashing of the State's actions has contributed somewhat to confuse the public mind:

> "Europe did not say to the King or his representatives, 'You have done so well in Central Africa, you have established so clear a title to its possession, that we assign you the Congo region as your fair share in the partition of Africa, and leave you to govern it as you see fit;' the Powers, I say, did nothing of the kind. They acquiesced in what had been done, and they sanctioned the creation of the State, but they laid down the strictest regulations for its conduct, and they defined the work it was to accomplish."

These sentences, needless to remark, were framed before King Leopold had begun to argue—a recent phase of his Majesty's diplomatic methods—that the Powers had nothing to do with the creation of the State! The sentences are strictly true. Assuming that the declaration of the Brussels Conference may be interpreted as justifying the State's war of extermination against the Arabs, that Conference also broke with one of the chief stipulations of the Berlin Act, in order to sanction the imposition of import duties wherewith to provide the necessary funds for the purpose. Had a system calculated to foster trade been adopted by the Congo State in the six years which elapsed between its creation and the commencement of the Arab war, the moneys derivable from that source would have been considerable. Stanley, whom we may presume was in a position to be acquainted with the facts, declared in 1884 that the volume of trade which had been built up along 68 miles of Congo coast-line, and 110 miles on the banks of the Lower River, amounted in those days to £2,800,000. Now, a very large proportion of that trade, as will be shown more clearly in Chapter VII., was due to the labour of the natives of the Upper Congo above Stanley Pool, and became, when the European merchants pushed further up the Lower Congo, concentrated to an appreciable extent in the Lower Congo, the entire course of which was incorporated by the Berlin Act in the Congo State. A 10 per cent. duty on that trade would have produced a large sum. It has always appeared to me that the Powers showed a most strange lack of perception in crediting for one moment the assurances of King Leopold and his agents in respect to that monarch's alleged financial philanthropy. Seeing that they were desirous of sanctioning the creation of an "Independent State" in Tropical Africa, they should have recognised that import duties for revenue purposes were essential. It is, however, no less true that the "Independent State" would never have been created but for the explicit assurances of its founder that no import duties would be levied on trade, and that the whole affair was really the sort of hobby of a "rich prince" who wished for no return on his capital, and who incarnated the chivalrous generosity of a bygone age *plus* the attribution of a pronounced humanitarian sentiment, product of more recent times. Be that as it may, the point which I wish to accentuate is this, that a great trade existed in the Lower Congo when the Congo State was born; that, presuming King Leopold's promised effort to develop trade had been carried out, the existing trade would by 1890 probably have increased, or at least not decreased; so that when authorised to raise funds on trade wherewith to tackle the Arabs, a great revenue would have been ready at hand. The policy of the State—between 1885 and 1890—had been, however, to hamper trade in every conceivable way, and its volume had already become perceptibly reduced. But in addition to such funds as were procurable in 1890 from the levying of import duties on the reduced trade existing in the Lower Congo, it must not be forgotten that the immediate result of the Arab war was (1) to place in the hands of the State the vast stock of ivory (and other valuables) that had been accumulated by the Arabs in their strongholds (at Kasongo alone ivory to the value of not far short of £25,000 was captured),* (2) and, further, to substitute for the Arabs,

---

* "We also took about twenty-five tons of ivory, ten or eleven tons of powder, millions of caps, cartridges, for every kind of rifle, gun, and revolver perhaps ever made." "The granaries throughout the town were stocked with enormous quantities of rice, coffee, maize, and other food, etc."—Dr. Hinde, *op. cit.*

the agents of the State as monopolists of the ivory contained in the country, which they proceeded to collect by measures differing but little, and in the matter of expenditure, differing probably not at all, from those of their predecessors. Then, again, it must not be forgotten that if the purchase of rifles, ammunition, and accoutrements in Europe for the regular levies of the State cost money, on the other hand, the expenses connected with the commissariat of the State's cannibal regulars and irregulars were infinitesimal, the bodies of the slain on the Arab side being sufficient for all purposes, seeing that each individual cannibal had "at least one body to eat,"* and, indeed, more than he could comfortably manage, because cases of death through surfeit or indigestion were not unknown.† On the whole, it may be estimated that the expenditure involved in exterminating the Arabs was very largely recouped. The filibustering expeditions Nilewards must, certainly, have been a source of great expense to the State; but in this case the Sovereign of the Congo State could not invoke the slightest mandate from the Powers. To his own unsatiable ambitions alone were these expeditions, with all the loss of life and international complications to which they gave rise, attributable. When, therefore, the Congo State and its apologists plead justification for the native policy pursued since 1891, the contention may be unhesitatingly refuted, on material as well as humanitarian grounds.

The State's economic policy—which is its native policy—is explained fully, and discussed from every aspect, in Parts II. and III. It has been attended, and is being attended, with persistent and well-nigh incredible—were the facts not built upon an unshakable foundation of truth—barbarity; a barbarity necessary and inevitable to the maintenance of the system. It is accompanied by the up-keep of an enormous and constantly increasing army armed with Albinis, and a cloud of irregulars armed for the most part with cap-guns.‡ It is characterised by perpetual warfare, slaughter, and depopulation all over the country. The flag which was to symbolise freedom, justice, and progress has become synonymous with grinding oppression, outrage, rapine, and massacre. Trade has been destroyed, and a system of Government slavery more atrocious than the periodical raids of Arab halfcastes instituted in lieu thereof.

It is with mingled loathing and impatience that one

---
* Dr. Hinde. † Dr. Hinde.
‡ They are, however, armed in many cases with the Albini.

contemplates the events of the last eighteen years—loathing for the cruel avariciousness, the callous indifference to human life, the odious hypocrisy which have characterised the methods of the Congo State, methods unrelieved by a single redeeming feature;* impatience at the pusillanimity and indifference of the Powers; the lack of courage, and the absence of plain speaking on the part of those who have known the truth for years, and held their peace; the gross misrepresentations of a few individuals.

But if "the mills of God grind slowly, they grind exceeding small." It cannot be that this abomination shall endure much longer; and those of us who in the face of calumny and threats have fought the fight—and in so doing, claim to have performed no more than an obvious duty which the statesmen of Europe should themselves have taken in hand long ago—think we see at last, "high in the heavens the flash of an uplifted sword, and the gleam of the arm of the avenging angel."

* The enterprise and dogged determination of Colonel Thys and his partners in building the Congo railway, together with the commercial activity displayed by the companies he formed, belong to a different category of events. Due credit is given to them in various parts of this volume. The position of the Thys group, or what remains of it, towards the Congo State, *i.e.* the King, is at best one of armed neutrality.

PART II

THE NEW AFRICAN SLAVE-TRADE

COMMERCIAL DEVELOPMENT *VERSUS* COERCION

HOW THE STATE DESTROYED LEGITIMATE TRADE IN THE UPPER CONGO

THE ECONOMIC TEST OF CONGO STATE RULE

THE FINANCIAL TEST OF CONGO STATE RULE — THE BENEFICIARIES BY GOVERNMENT SLAVERY

THE "PROPERTY" PLEA—THE CONGO STATE'S MAIN LINE OF DEFENCE

NATIVE LAND-TENURE, TRADE, AND LABOUR

THE THIRD TEST OF CONGO STATE RULE—MILITARISM, MURDER, MUTILATION, AND THE TRAFFIC IN ARMS

CHAPTER IV

COMMERCIAL DEVELOPMENT *VERSUS* COERCION

"To deny to the natives the right to sell ivory and rubber produced by the forests and plains belonging to their tribes, which forests and plains form part of their hereditary natal soil, and with which ivory and rubber they have traded freely from time immemorial, is a veritable violation of natural rights." — Protest of Messrs. URBAN, BRUGMANN, THYS, and WEINER in 1892.

"I cannot forget that the natives are not represented amongst us, and that the decisions of the Conference will nevertheless have an extreme importance for them. The principle which will command the sympathy and support of Her Majesty's Government will be that of the advancement of legitimate commerce, with security for the equality of treatment of all nations, and for the well-being of the native races."—Sir E. MALET at the Berlin Conference, Protocol, November, 1884.

I HAVE been fortunate in coming into the possession of a number of extracts from letters written by Belgians and Frenchmen connected with the Belgian trading companies of the *Rue Bréderode*,* and carrying on, about the time the new policy was inaugurated, their ordinary business in the Upper Congo. These letters, which throw a flood of light upon the proceedings of the Congo State's representatives thus early in the day, are descriptive of events which have characterised to an increasing degree of intensity the policy of the Congo State from that time onwards. The difference between then and now lies in the fact that all independent merchants †—all merchants at all, in fact—have long since disappeared, and we can only rely nowadays upon the courage of some English or American missionary, in the relation of chance travellers, or in the not always disinterested account of

---

* The Thys group.

† Under present circumstances, the operations of the Thys group can hardly be termed "commercial," for they are based upon the common assumption of prior ownership by the white man of the elements of trade—that is, of the forest produce. Nevertheless, there is reason to hope and believe that the procedure adopted by the *Société Anonyme Belge*—the principal "Thys" Company unabsorbed by the Government —compares favourably with that adopted by the Government and the Great Trusts.

ex-officials or ex-servants of the Trusts to acquaint us with what is going on. The extracts I am about to give are also extremely valuable, inasmuch as they are explanatory of the transition stage between the extinction of trade and the substitution in lieu of it, of Government slavery. They are the connecting link, as it were, between the two epochs. At the time these letters were written home, the New Policy was in process of inauguration. Hitherto the native had been looked upon by the merchants established in the country as the owner of the products of the soil which the merchants wished to acquire by legitimate purchase, as everywhere else in Western Africa. Commercial relationship had been established in the ordinary way, and long before the Congo State had come into existence. The native, attracted by the merchandise offered for sale by the white man, gathered the produce of the forests and brought it to the factories for sale. Thus has trade been built up between the white man and the black wherever the former has penetrated into the interior of the western half of the continent. The letters show us the characteristic and necessary accompaniments *in Africa* of introducing as a working policy a conception of African development, whereby the native is relegated from the position of owner of the forest products, which he has been accustomed *to sell*, to that of a lawless and ownerless serf on the estate of " Bula Matadi." *

There is always a danger which those of us who have long ago mastered the essentials of the Congo problem are in fear lest we should overlook, in our endeavours to make others see what is so clear to us with equal clearness. One doubts sometimes whether it be possible for the ordinary reader who does not habitually interest himself in African questions, to grasp the absolute revolution which so fundamental a change in the relationship between the white man and the black must occasion in the daily life, in the general conditions, in the "moral and material" outlook of the native population. To realise the full significance of such a revolution, the reader must unconsciously allow some play to his

---

* Native name for the Congo State—Stanley's old name. The origin of this name is not generally known. Stanley was so christened in the year 1883 by the inhabitants of the village of M'Fufu near Vivi. One day a man came rushing into the village with the news that a strange white man was breaking stones. It was Stanley blasting the rocks to make a horizontal road for the transport, in sections, of his boat the *L'en Avant*. In the Ba-Congo language, Ntadi means stone ; the plural being formed by prefixes, Ntadi is Matadi in the plural. Thus Bula Matadi, the man who broke the stones ; and the place where his blasting operations first took place, has preserved the name Matadi.

Photograph by   *H. Walter Barnett*

THE RIGHT HON. SIR CHARLES W. DILKE, BART., M.P.
(The first to raise the Congo question in the House of Commons)

imagination in order that he may construct a mental picture which shall crystallise into tangible substance the meaning of the written words conveyed to his brain. If his imagination be divorced from all acquaintance with African conditions, the effect of his unconscious efforts may fall far short of accuracy. That is what one dreads—that the bald description of the revolution wrought in *the life* of the African native, through the application of a policy of appropriation of land and products, devised in Brussels, may not be fully understood by merely stating, as though one were dealing with a mathematical problem, the main lines of difference between that policy and the practice of legitimate commerce.

I detest sensationalism, and this appalling Congo business is replete with so many elements of horror that the reader may well be spared anything beyond the enumeration of facts, which in themselves are sufficiently repulsive without any attempt at "piling on the agony." But the policy of appropriation of the native's land and the products thereof *is the key to the whole Congo problem;* and I almost feel that the reader will forgive me if I endeavour to give a brief sketch representing the legitimate and illegitimate development of Equatorial Africa, and their respective effects upon the African.

Imagine a broad river, with brown, discoloured waters. From either bank stretches a vast sea of dark, impenetrable bush, broken here and there by clearings where native villages are situate, containing anything from 500 to 5000 inhabitants. Round them are plantations of bananas and various crops, large or small, according to the needs of the population—well or ill kept, according to the relative degree of prosperity of the people and to individual characteristics. Here and there the bush yawns back from the riverside, and a village will be found within a few hundred yards of the bank, for where there is a river there is fish, and large numbers will be caught for local consumption, or for bartering with inland villages against other food. In the cooler hours of the day, the men-folk will hunt or fish, weave mats, make knives, work brass wire, or smoke and laze and discuss local affairs, while the women attend to household matters, work in the plantations, gather firewood, and spend many an hour over the intricacies of their *coiffure;* and the children will play about, the elders helping in the fishing operations, or keeping off the grey parrots from committing havoc with the young crops. At night the fires will be lit, and the glow of the embers will flicker on dark forms squatting round, smoking, and listening perhaps to the professional story-teller spinning "fairy tales" by the yard; or, if the moon be shining brightly, and the sky free from clouds, a wild dance will take place in the street of the village—a dance continued for many hours, and only brought to an end by the physical exhaustion of the performers. They are happy, these people, in their primitive way. Life goes on with much the same monotony as at home. An occasional affray between villages will come as an exciting diversion, accompanied by a good deal more sound and fury than bloodshed; a herd of elephants may wreck the plantations, a storm swamp some canoes, fish may be scarce, but on the whole existence is distinctly passable. There are no telephones, no rates and taxes, not even a fiscal policy. In those native communities there are good men and bad, just as at home—good according to their lights, bad according to their individual characters, just as at home. Their lights are not our lights, but who shall say which bring the greatest happiness? They have no workhouses in the forest, no unemployed, no paupers.

On a sudden a whisper is carried on the wings of the wind; it gathers in volume. The news flies from village to village, the drums are sounded summoning the people to the palaver. A steamer is coming up the river with white men on board. Do they come in peace or war? It will soon be known, for the steamer has anchored, and its occupants are parleying with the shore. Then comes the intelligence that all is well. The white men have come in peace, and with many marvellous articles to sell. Within an enormous radius the news is conveyed by drum, and within a day or two every village knows what are the white man's wants. It is ivory that he wants—ivory live or dead, ivory cut from the freshly killed elephant, or ivory stacked in the compounds of the chiefs. Ivory; but also the sap from the great vines which grow so luxuriously in the forest, thick sometimes as a man's thigh. The white man's servants have told the villagers on whose land they are even now erecting a dwelling and a store, how to collect that sap; that he will buy as much as the people will bring him; and that he will give gaudy handkerchiefs, and cloth, brass wire, beads, iron pots, and copper rods for it, and many more wonderful things that he has— armlets and leglets, looking-glasses, hair-pins with wonderful heads, bright-coloured glass, such marvels as will drive every native lady in the country wild with anticipation, and into an eager and enthusiastic factor in promoting a taste for rubber-collecting on the part of her lord.

To these primitive folk it is a mine of desirable objects

suddenly brought before their delighted vision, a toy-shop, whose contents a moderate degree of labour will bring within arm's reach; for the man will sit down and make bracelets and anklets out of the brass rods, the brass wire will do to ornament spear-shafts, knives, and axes, and what man will not covet one of those gaily striped cloths which will make him a finer peacock than his fellows? As for the women, well, if the iron hoes represent a decided improvement on the primitive agricultural implements with which they have, hitherto, been fain to rest content, what can be thought of the articles of personal adornment? * If Lofinda has set her heart upon that string of bright blue beads, Yamina must have that kerchief with the gorgeous checks; and shall not Bikela, the comely one, see her beauty reflected in that curious shiny thing, brighter even than the spear of Molobo her lover?

Thus is trade born in Western Africa, the trade between the white man and the African: the only incentive to the widening in the horizon of the African, the only incentive to acquire new ideas, to develop arts and crafts; the awakening of desires before undreamt of—a page in the evolution of the human race. And as more white men

* There are still people to be found who think that the African native is a brute beast impervious to human sentiment, and that a writer who endeavours to paint a different picture is sentimentalising in order to improve his case. To such people I commend the following extracts from the book of Mr. Herbert Ward (*op. cit.*). He deals only with the Congo natives, who have many traits, repulsive in our eyes, born of environment and the natural craving of the human machine for meat, which is seldom procurable in many parts of the Congo territories.

"A native of the Upper River will embrace his wife ere he sets out on a fighting expedition, or will fondle his child, and even condescend to give the infant its morning bath in the river if the mother be unable to perform the task. . . . On one occasion I happened to be journeying from Stanley Pool to Boma . . . along with a party of eighty or one hundred Bangala men. . . . Probably twenty women accompanied the party, wives of the head men. . . . After five days' weary marching our path led us to the fords of the Luasa River, through whose swollen waters, running now breast high, we had to wade. . . . The party crossed without much difficulty, beyond a wetting of the bare skin, but the force of the current was such that the fatigued women found trouble in keeping their feet and battling their way across. One very young and frail-looking girl feared to enter the stream, and stood hesitating on the nearer bank, when her husband, a strapping young fellow of twenty-five or so, seeing her anxiety, turned back from the point he had reached in the water, and, tenderly gathering her up in his arms, placed her upon his shoulder. Thus burdened he stepped again into the river and bore her safely to the other side, the girl clinging to his head and neck the while with every mark of confidence and affection."

Such quotations could be multiplied a hundred-fold.

come, so the African learns. He is a very shrewd man, the African ; the capacity for barter, the keenness to bargain, are marked characteristics. He will go to the store of white man No. 1 and look at it, and the store of white man No. 2 and look at that, and gradually out of the earlier relationship will develop ruling market prices, and commerce will have taken a place in the black man's mind and the black man's life, which is for his good ; for the good of the European merchant, who risks his health and his capital on the commercial instincts of the Negro—for no one but the Negro can gather the produce of the soil the European desires ; for the good of the European Administrator, who levies customs dues on his countryman's goods in order that he may bring improvements into the black man's country and give facilities to the European merchant; for the good of the Europeans in the far-off Western world, who handle the product of the black man's labour. Thus, and thus alone, can tropical Africa be legitimately developed by the white man.

But what is that vague and meaningless rumour coming from afar? Why are the faces of the white merchants troubled? Who are these other white men who come in big steamers, with many black men in uniforms and carrying rifles? As yet they know it not, our forest-dwellers, who since the advent of the first white men have extended their villages and plantations and prospered amazingly. As yet they know it not, but these other white men, these soldiers with guns, are the heralds of the dawn, the dawn of "moral and material regeneration"—"Bula Matadi." And soon the process begins. In each village soldiers come summoning the chiefs to attend the great palaver of "Bula Matadi." They enter the villages, do those soldiers, full of insolent swagger, and ere they leave, after delivering their message, have interfered with women, stolen fowls, and perchance robbed the plantations of a bunch or two of bananas. From all the villages around the chiefs and head men attend the great palaver in fear, knowing not what it may portend. They are not kept long in suspense. Each chief is asked the number of able-bodied males in his village ; the figure is put down by the representative of "Bula Matadi" in a book. Each chief is then told that his village must furnish so many baskets of rubber every moon, so many goats and fowls, so much cassava ; all ivory must be brought to "Bula Matadi," no ivory and no rubber must be taken to the white men at the factories ; such is the order of "Bula Matadi." The chiefs depart, bewildered, angry, sullen, and afraid.

COMMERCIAL DEVELOPMENT V. COERCION

That night, and the next and the next, councils are held in every village. Runners to the white men in the factories report that the latter are powerless; they will still buy rubber and ivory, but only by stealth, for "Bula Matadi" will not let them buy openly. The people are filled with consternation; there is a babel of many tongues; divers opinions are expressed. Is not the country theirs, and the trees, and the vines in the forest? Are they the slaves of "Bula Matadi"? Shall they be treated not as men but as monkeys? How shall they live if their goats, their fowls, their cassava, and their bananas must be taken to the big palaver camp every moon? What is "Bula Matadi" that they should no longer gather rubber for the sellers of cloths and beads? Let "Bula Matadi" beware lest the spears of the young men pierce the soldiers that steal! Have they become women? They will collect rubber as before for the white sellers of cloth.

The next day a party from the village, laden with rubber, starts for the nearest factory. One man creeps back at nightfall broken, bleeding, and trembling. He reports the party was stopped by soldiers who fell upon them not far from the factory, and stole the rubber. They resisted; Bogasu was killed, the others, beaten and buffeted, were dragged before the representative of "Bula Matadi," who ordered them to be flung upon their faces, when they were cruelly beaten with whips, so cruelly that blood flowed. Then they were "tied up," and the survivor was told to go back to his village, and inform the chief that he had disobeyed the orders of "Bula Matadi" by sending rubber to the factory. If the offence were repeated, "Bula Matadi" would send soldiers to the village to punish him. The other men would be kept as hostages for the hundred basketfuls of rubber due from the village at the full moon. Terror mingled with fury now reigns supreme in the village. Let the soldiers come.

The moon is almost at its full when a messenger arrives from the camp of "Bula Matadi." It is a reminder that the time for payment of the rubber is nearly at hand. If it is not forthcoming, the anger of "Bula Matadi" will vent itself upon those who have dared to disregard instructions. The messenger is heard in sombre silence. The quantity of rubber required could not be gathered if the population of the village were twice what it is.

The soldiers of "Bula Matadi" have come and gone, and all is over: a short, fierce resistance, a crackling fusillade, cries of agony, and a dull glare lighting up the sombre recesses of the forest. The sun sets on blackened ruins, smouldering ashes, and ruined crops; while here and there outstretched figures lie prone. The survivors—men, women, and children—are crouching, bereft of shelter, in the forest. And so they crouch for days, subsisting on roots and herbs. Then one by one they slink back furtively to the site of their former homes. Little by little a measure of confidence returns, huts are rebuilt, seed is sown. Diminished in numbers, shaken but not quite broken in spirit, the community settles down once more. And then—then another visit from the soldiers of "Bula Matadi," another summons to the camp, renewed demands coupled with a pointing of the moral. They have not forgotten it, poor souls. No longer can resistance be entertained. A couple of soldiers are stationed permanently in the village, where they rape and steal to their heart's content. As for the villagers themselves, they are no longer men, but weary slaves. All day long, and for days together in the forest getting rubber, striving to satisfy insatiable demands, unmercifully flogged if the amount gathered falls short of the amount required, wandering ever further afield, away from their homes, unable to attend to their plantations, demoralised, degraded, all the manhood driven out of them. If such be the lot of the men, what of the women? The village, formerly clean and well kept, becomes dirty and neglected. Indifference and despair eat into the hearts of the people; mortality increases, many seek refuge in the forest and perish miserably, while others may finally be successful in finding shelter in some other village further removed from "Bula Matadi's" immediate sphere of operations. The village empties and decays; it is played out, and the representative of "Bula Matadi" shifts his quarters to the nearest "untapped district." In a few years, or perhaps only in a few months, since the advent of "Bula Matadi" and his soldiers, the swiftly encroaching bush has covered up all traces of what was once, before the blasting breath of a "moral and material regeneration" passed over the land, a little community in the African forest with its joys and its sorrows, its elements of badness and its elements of good, primitive, savage, but as happy perchance, as important assuredly to itself, as any cluster of thatched roofed cottages in sunny Devon.

Overdrawn? No, the description, minus all its repulsive details, of an event a thousand times repeated on the Congo; an illustration of the New African Slave Trade, which prevails wherever "Bula Matadi" has obtained a foothold from Banana to the Great Lakes.

And now for the letters.

CHAPTER V

HOW THE STATE DESTROYED LEGITIMATE TRADE IN THE UPPER CONGO

"It is permissible for the native to find by work the remuneration which contributes to augment his well-being. Such is, in fact, one of the ends of the general policy of the State to promote the regeneration of the race by instilling into him a higher idea of the necessity of labour." *

"Yambuya, February 6, 1891.

"My relations † with the State have hitherto been of the best. I have never opposed any of the laws of the Congo State, and if my relations with Messrs. W—— and V—— ‡ are strained, it is because I have objected to their sending their people armed with loaded guns to the very neighbourhood of my factory, threatening natives who had come to trade with me. . . . It is impossible any longer to buy anything. The country is ruined. The passengers in the steamship *Roi des Belges*, Messrs. F——, G——, T——, M——, von H——, and Captain K——, have been able to see for themselves that from Boutya, half a day's journey below our factory of Upoto, to Boumba inclusive, there is not an inhabited village left; that is to say, four days' steaming through a country formerly so rich, to-day entirely ruined.

"O. S."

"Equateur, April 24, 1891.

"There is much rubber here, but the natives will not bring it in. . . . M. R—— declares that we are forbidden to ask the natives to fetch rubber. They are supposed to be entitled to bring it without being told, but they cannot be asked to fetch any ! ! ! M. B——, *Commissaire* at Bangala, despatched latterly a large quantity of rubber ; I am told that it has not been bought, but is the product of tribute levied upon the chiefs !

"A. P."

"Gongo, Dona, October 20, 1891.

"I find it necessary to report the proceedings of the State. . . . The other day I bought 100 kilos of ivory. The next day, Etiaka, the former village chief where our factory is established, who fled five months ago after the cruelties inflicted upon him by the *Chef de Poste* of the State,

---

* *Bulletin Officiel de l'Etat Indépendant du Congo.* June, 1903 (No. 6 Translation).
† These are, in each case, literal translations from the French (Belgian) text.
‡ State officials.

sought me out to inform me that the chiefs of the Mongwandi villages had been secretly informed by the State station that all who sold me ivory and rubber would no longer be the friends of Bula-Matari* (the State), and would have war. . . . The natives have been forbidden by the State to sell cassava bread to my men. I have sent an official letter protesting against this. . . . The people of the villages of Etiaka wish to settle in the neighbourhood of my factory. This would be a great advantage to us. The State have informed them that if they come and settle near the enemies ('Mukondje') of Bula Matari, the State would know how to punish them one way or another. . . . Thanks to the proceedings of the State, we cannot travel three hours in a canoe without coming across a hostile village! That is the way they go on. They go to a village and say to the chief, 'If by noon three tusks of ivory are not here for us *to buy*, you are no longer our friend.' At noon the chief arrives, and says, 'I have only two,' or one as the case may be. 'If that is the case,' replies the representative of the State, 'we will see.' The whole party then spring on shore, Hausas† and Bangalas,‡ and endeavour to make prisoners. That having been accomplished, the chief is told : 'Come with so many tusks, and your men and women will be returned to you !' That is how the State protects trade. These facts have been certified before me by the very men who took part in the palaver and by the chiefs.

"E. B."

"Equateurville, January 21, 1892.

"I think it necessary to give to you a rapid summary of the principal facts which have inspired my complaints. . . . (1) The day after my arrival I found that our men, instead of being employed looking after the craft, had been in the service of the State, had made palavers with the Mabali and Popouli ; *and that they were receiving* 40 *mitakos per man, and* 25 *mitakos for every woman they succeeded in making prisoners of. These men and women were afterwards bartered by the State against ivory.* (2) Men coming from the village of Buata to my factory with rubber to sell had to pass in front of a branch of the Ebala (?) River, which was situate exactly opposite to my factory. The *Chef de Poste* informed Chief Esiaka that if he did not take the rubber to him, he would block the route. But the Buata people continued to sell me their rubber, so that the *Chef de Poste* blocked the route and arrested four natives with rubber on their way to me. (3) A boy in the service of the State, named M'Boli, having been accused of stealing two bananas, was shot, the next morning, and his body flung into the river. This event made such an impression upon the Bangalas that seven of them deserted.

"E. B."

"Equateur, April 22, 1892.

"The State has put on rubber taxes. One chief alone has to furnish 1500 kilos. . . . Under the circumstances, we cannot hope to *buy* rubber.

"A. S."

"Equateur, July 7, 1892.

"The Government has sent fresh instructions to the Equateur concerning the purchase of ivory. . . . As for rubber, M—— sticks to his circular. He is acting by Government orders. No one, native or white, has

---

* Corruption of Bula-Matadi.
† State troops. (The British Government subsequently prohibited the recruiting of Hausas by the State.)
‡ State troops.

THE DESTRUCTION OF COMMERCE 41

the right to exploit the domains of the State ! . . . Nearly a ton of rubber belonging to the State has arrived at Equateur from Bassankusu, while we have not 10 centimes' worth. The reasons are, the rubber taxes, and that the natives are forbidden to sell any rubber to the trading firms.

"A. P."

"Bassankusu, September 17, 1892.

"I have given instructions to M. R—— to buy all rubber, and to foster purchases as much as possible. Unfortunately, the villages are compelled to pay heavy taxes on rubber ; they are compelled to furnish so many kilos to the State every week, and it is only by chance that we can buy any now and then. To give you an idea, the State has received 1060 kilos in one month and a half. The State has made war upon the villages from Lulonga to Bassankusu. All the villages in the Maringa suffered the same fate. On the other hand, it seems that Arabs have been observed in the Upper Maringa. The *Commissaire* of the Equateur district has taken the following decision (September 7th) :

" ' Considering that the presence of Arab bands in the Maringa creates a danger, proved moreover by the capture of a man armed with a snyder belonging to the Belgian house, the *Commissaire* of the district orders :

" ' The Maringa shall be provisionally closed to all expeditions other than those of the State.'

"The river is, therefore, closed to us. The real motive is not the presence of Arabs, but the incessant palavers with the natives who will not open up relations with the State.

"T. S."

" Likini, October 15, 1892.

"These gentlemen of the State Post of Mongwandi have set their hearts upon the destruction of trade in this country. After the wars with the Mombatis and the Boucoundu, where the State people took many prisoners, which the Mombatis redeemed with ivory, they have begun the same proceedings again. To buy ivory in this way does not require many goods, and has the merit of simplicity ! Four days ago, then, they started making war again : 13 killed, 6 prisoners, 100 spears and as many knives —that was a day's work. Not content with this, they threatened and even detained for some hours people from Businga and Moungoumbouli on the pretext that these villages did not produce ivory and rubber. That is true enough, because these villages have always *sold* me their produce. The result is that two-thirds of the whole country dare not come to our factory, and not a ball of rubber is brought to us for sale. The equivocal proceedings of the State have destroyed all confidence in the native towards the white man, and have led to the big villages near the State Station being abandoned by the inhabitants. At Boucoundu, where the State has just established itself, the people of the village, which was a very important and actively producing one, have emigrated two days' journey into the forest of Monboika.

"E. B."

"Likini, October, 1892.

" The frequent wars upon the natives, undertaken without any motive by the State soldiers sent out to get ivory and rubber, are depopulating the country. The soldiers find that the quickest and cheapest method is to raid villages, seize prisoners, and have them redeemed afterwards against ivory. At Boucoundje they took thirty prisoners, whom they released upon payment of ten tusks ! There is trade for you ! Brilliant trade! Two villages used to sell me a good deal of rubber, so war was made upon them, and we get no more rubber. Everywhere the State is exercising formidable pressure to compel the natives not to sell us their produce. . . . Each agent of the State receives 1000 francs commission per ton of ivory secured, and 175 francs per ton of rubber.

"E. B."

"Zongo, November 30, 1892.

"The Independent State, which is aiming at the destruction of trade by men who can see clearly all its inconceivable and nameless deeds, has taken the most outrageous measures against the *Société Anonyme Belge*, which has become its *bête noire*. I do not speak of the instructions given out to its agents to have nothing to do with us under the threat of censure, a measure which I regret more for them than for us, because they stand more in need of us than we of them, but the prohibition to allow us to settle in the only places where any results can be obtained, under the fallacious pretext of a state of siege, or military expeditions, when the sole reason is to have the field to itself, is a proceeding of so arbitrary a nature as to call forth energetic protest, which, however, will be ineffectual unless made from higher quarters. . . . The actual position of affairs is as follows : Explicit prohibition to trade with the natives above Cetema (?) —there is ivory above that place ; permission, on the other hand, to settle below that place where hardly any trade is to be done, and where, if there still remains a tusk or two left, the natives dare not bring it in for sale for fear of being punished. We are not forbidden to settle or buy *there ;* but if the sellers are seen, they are told their village will be burnt. . . . Please note, in passing, that, having just arrived, I have as yet *seen* nothing except a few strings of slaves which are very *mal à propos* called 'libérés ;' but I have enough reports to fill a volume of the scandalous proceedings of this singular Government.

"E. B."

"Banzyville, December 30, 1892.

"The so-called freedom of State in four or five villages placed under the active supervision of the State appears ridiculous to me, because, as I wrote you from Zongo—when I only knew of it from hearsay—the State terrorises any natives who might feel inclined to trade with merchants. I have now the proof of this. During my voyage from Zongo to Banzyville, when in the evening hailing the villages on the Belgian Banks where we had been advised there was ivory for sale, we found the natives fearful and undecided, first saying they had nothing, then saying they would bring a tusk the next day, and then the next day saying they did not dare to bring it for fear of having their village burnt. And from what I have seen *de visu* it is only too obvious that such things do take place. Under these conditions, which will be the same at Yakoma, I do not see that it is any use our going there, because we should be just near the State *Poste*, and would have no facilities for buying produce at night.

"E. B."

"Equateur, January 29, 1893.

"The 19th January, I learnt that the State's agents, Peters and Thermolle, had been massacred near the Station by the natives. . . . The motive was the following : they were tired of the various taxes levied by the State, especially the rubber tax.

"T. S."

THE DESTRUCTION OF COMMERCE 43

"Yambuya, March 23, 1893.

"The trade in rubber becomes more unfavourable every day. The natives say there is very little of it left. Some chiefs had promised to collect some, but after fourteen days' journey in the neighbourhood, I have not been able to obtain a single ball. Moreover, the reason is clear enough. The majority of natives in every village are fleeing to the forests on account of the perpetual troubles with the State.

"J. N."

Thus was trade destroyed in the Upper Congo, and thus did forced production and slavery take its place. The latter system has now endured for twelve years, with the result that vast stretches of country are depopulated, that tens of thousands of natives have been killed, that emigration on a huge scale has taken place, and that the natives that remain have been reduced to the condition of miserable slaves, poverty-stricken and helpless, a prey to sickness and despair.

CHAPTER VI

THE ECONOMIC TEST OF CONGO STATE RULE

"Thanks to trade, all this produce will enter into circulation; *the counterpart of its value will return to Africa,** for which it will prove a source of prosperity."—Manifesto of the International Association, October, 1884.

"The system of the State at the same time that it hastens the economic development of the country has *given rise** to a considerable *commercial** movement, since the exports now show a value of two millions sterling, and that there are sold at Antwerp every year 5000 tons of rubber, taken from the forests of the Congo."—Bulletin Officiel de l'Etat Indépendant du Congo, 1903 (No. 6 Translation).

THERE are several ways of testing the conclusions advanced in the last chapters—ways which are particularly valuable inasmuch as they exclude the element of hypothesis and merely deal with figures recorded in official publications.

Now, one of the principal tests which can be applied by the impartial investigator to the characteristics of Congo State administration lies in an examination of the Commercial Statistics—so called.

The difficulty facing those who are contending in the cause of the Congo natives—in which cause is bound up the honour of the white races in tropical Africa—is that of making people not entirely familiar with the subject understand the INEVITABLENESS of the misrule reported from the Congo territories so long as the legislative and economic basis of the Administration remains what it is to-day; that is to say, so long as the Congo State, as at present constituted and managed, is allowed by civilised mankind to exist.

Ninety-nine per cent. of Englishmen, who have even casually investigated the subject, have, it is safe to say, been convinced for a considerable time past, and before reading Consul Casement's report, that the Congo territories are the scene of gross misgovernment and oppression. How profound is the feeling engendered by the mass of evidence which has been accumulating for years, was seen in the famous House

* Italics the author's.

of Commons debate on May 20 of last year, when the House, without a single dissentient voice, passed a resolution pledging the Government to approach the other signatory Powers of the Berlin Act, with a view "that measures should be adopted to abate the evils prevalent in that State."

It is seldom that Governments display enthusiasm in matters of this kind, even though their members may be convinced, as they were in the present case, of the shame of this Congo business, and the present Government has certainly not erred in that direction. Nevertheless, Mr. Balfour admitted that if the resolution, even as originally proposed, were pressed, it would be impossible for the Government to vote against it, "BECAUSE IT INDICATED A POLICY THE GOVERNMENT DESIRED TO FOLLOW;" and the Prime Minister recognised that an "overwhelming case" had been made out.

The language used by members was eloquent of the depth of feeling aroused, as may be judged by the following passages :

"If the administration of the Congo State was civilisation, then, he asked, what was barbarism?"—Mr. HERBERT SAMUEL, M.P.

"It was obvious that here was a complete enslavement of the whole population, and that it could lead to nothing but a system of horrors."—Right Hon. SIR C. W. DILKE, Bart., M.P.

"Surely we, who were responsible for the Berlin Act, had a perfect right to take such steps as would bring this terrible state of things to an end."—Right Hon. SIR JOHN GORST.

"Judged by any decent standard, what were they to say of the Congo State?"—Mr. ALFRED EMMOTT, M.P.

"Atrocities had been committed which curdled the blood and made civilisation ashamed of its name."—LORD EDMUND FITZMAURICE.

It is well to recall these deliberate statements ; especially is it necessary to accentuate the fact that a unanimous House of Commons endorsed them, and that the Prime Minister endorsed them, *eight months before Mr. Roger Casement, H.M. Consul at Boma, verified their accuracy on the spot.* The verdict of the House of Commons was a striking justification of the deliberate and unanswerable charges made outside the House of Commons by those who had studied the subject. The contents of the Congo White Book containing Mr. Casement's report, and Lord Cromer's scathing allusions, were a complete justification of the verdict of the House of Commons, which verdict it has repeated in accents even more emphatic this year (June 9).

So much for the British House of Commons. But it is the people, not only of Great Britain, but of America and the Continent of Europe, whose hearts and whose thinking capacities must be reached before we can hope to rouse feelings sufficiently intense to complete the work begun so well on May 20, 1903.

What are the arguments with which one becomes most familiar in endeavouring to educate the public to a true appreciation of the "evils prevalent" in the Congo State? They may be briefly summed up thus: "We know that evils exist, evils on a large scale. But we are told that the Congo Government is doing its best to eliminate them. We read of trials and punishments of guilty agents. Are not these evils in a measure inseparable from the early stages of a vast colonising enterprise? Should they not be regarded as acts of individual wrongdoing, terribly blameworthy in themselves, but attributable, perhaps, to the indifferent class of officials selected, and calculated to right themselves in time? And again, how comes it that men are to be found who believe that these evils are no greater than those which exist, or have existed in the possessions of other Powers, when the conquering white race is opposed to primitive people in a low state of civilisation? Are there not two sides to this question? Are there not means, outside conflicting testimony and individual statements on both sides, whereby the ordinary man can test the accuracy of these grave charges for himself on general principles, and find out definitely whether the entire system is at fault, or whether the Congo Government is, more or less, inefficient, and the victim of circumstances?"

Such, in brief, is the substance of the objections which are raised, not infrequently, by those—and they are the vast majority still—whose knowledge of the Congo question is necessarily incomplete. They are perfectly legitimate objections. The last point covers them all. "Are there not means, outside conflicting testimony and individual statements on both sides, whereby the ordinary man can test the accuracy of these grave charges for himself on general principles, and find out definitely whether the entire system is at fault, or whether the Congo Government is, more or less, inefficient, and the victim of circumstances?" There are several such means. The one I propose to treat of now is, perhaps, the most convincing, if the facts can be brought with sufficient clearness to people's minds.

For purposes of simplicity in exposition we will begin our inquiry, with the reader's permission, by a series of questions and answers, elaborating by this means, as briefly as is possible, the grounds upon which the relationship between the white and black races in tropical Western-Central Africa is based.

ECONOMIC TEST OF CONGO STATE RULE 47

Q. What is primarily the explanation of European activity in tropical Africa?
A. Trade relationship.
Q. What does trade in tropical Africa consist of?
A. The exchange of produce collected by the natives, and bartered by them against merchandise of Europe imported into their country.
Q. What is that produce composed of?
A. Palm-oil and kernels, ground-nuts, cabinet woods, rubber, piassava, gum-copal and gum-arabic, cocoa, cotton, shea-butter, and various other vegetable products.
Q. How is this trade regulated?
A. By ruling market prices in Europe.
Q. You mean that if the selling price in Europe of palm oil or rubber falls, the native producer will receive proportionately less in merchandise of Europe, and *vice versa*?
A. Precisely.
Q. Then this collection of produce by the natives represents their purchasing capacity in European goods—that is to say, in goods which they cannot otherwise procure?
A. Precisely.
Q. And it also represents the labour of the country?
A. It represents a portion of the labour of the country.
Q. Why do you say "a portion"?
A. Because, in addition to the labour expended by the people in collecting produce with which to purchase European goods, there is the labour required to provide for their own sustenance in food-stuffs; that is to say, agricultural labour, cattle-rearing where cattle can live, hunting, fishing, and so on. Then there are also local industries, developed to a greater or lesser degree according to circumstances, such as cotton-growing, the manufacture of cotton cloths, the dyeing of cotton cloths, the manufacture of leather ware and brass ware, the extraction of salt and potash, basket, and sometimes pottery work, smelting, the manufacture of weapons for war and the chase, and many other things, including the search for precious metals, where such exist. These industries supply the ordinary wants of the people, and provide material for the vast internal trade of Western Central Africa between native communities, often at very great distances apart.
Q. So the collection by the natives of produce for the European markets is a self-imposed task, over and above their usual avocations, in order to acquire articles of European manufacture?
A. That is so. The natives are not in their natural state

in any way impelled to collect produce for the European markets, being able to supply their positive requirements at home. If they collect palm-oil and rubber, cultivate cocoa, cotton, and ground-nuts, it is because they desire to purchase European manufactured goods.

Q. Does the produce thus collected by the natives amount to much?

A. The British possessions in West Africa have, in the last five years, exported produce to Europe amounting to 11 millions sterling; in the similar period the French possessions in West Africa have exported produce to Europe amounting to 9 millions sterling, and the German possessions in West Africa have exported produce to Europe amounting to $4\frac{1}{2}$ millions sterling.

Q. Then the export to Europe of this produce, voluntarily collected and cultivated by the native, constitutes the export trade of the possessions of the various Powers in West Africa?

A. Yes.

Q. And the export of manufactured goods from Europe to those possessions represents the price paid to the natives for their produce, and constitutes the import trade of those possessions?

A. That is so. But bear in mind that, in addition to the manufactured goods imported by those possessions to purchase the produce collected and cultivated by the natives, the local Administration imports material for its own use.

Q. So the value of the imports of a West African possession exceeds the value of its exports?

A. As a rule, yes; and sometimes very greatly, as, for instance, where there is a large white population to cater for, railways and steamers requiring replenishment of material and coal, public works in course of construction requiring material for building purposes, and hired native labour—where, in short, there is considerable capital expenditure, but not necessarily. Some years there may be a large increased quantity of merchandise imported to replenish stocks, and the value of trade goods thus imported may exceed the value of the produce exported, while the following year the reverse may be the case.

Q. In a general way, the margin over a number of years covering genuine trade, imports and export, will, I suppose, represent the profit of the importing and exporting merchant, who is presumably the middleman between the native producer and the manufacturer at home, and who makes his profit, after paying the expenses of his establishment, on the transaction?

NATIVES OF THE NSONGO DISTRICT (ABIR CONCESSION)

(With hands of two of their countrymen, Lingomo and Bolengo, murdered by rubber sentries in May, 1904. The white men are Mr. Stannard and Mr. Harris, of the Congo Balolo Mission at Baringa. See letter from Mr. Stannard in the Appendix.)

ECONOMIC TEST OF CONGO STATE RULE

A. Yes.

Q. To resume, then; if I understand you aright, the native is a voluntary collector and cultivator of produce for the European markets. That produce, which represents a portion of the labour of the country, represents also the purchasing capacity of the native in European goods. He disposes of his produce to the merchant, who sells him European goods in exchange at rates depending upon ruling market prices, and allowing a fair profit—the profit being large or small according to prevailing conditions at home and locally. This native production constitutes the export trade of the country, and the goods imported to pay for it constitute the true import trade, in addition to which the Administration imports goods and material for its own uses; sometimes, when much capital is being invested, to a considerable extent. The greater the native production, the larger the quantity of trade goods required to pay for it?

A. Precisely.

I trust that, put in the above form, the principles underlying the relationship between the white and black races in tropical Africa will be made quite clear to the reader.

We will now examine the import and export returns of three British West African colonies for the four years, 1899-1902.

SIERRA LEONE.

Imports (less specie and Colonial stores).		Exports of produce.	
1899	£566,067	1899	£288,584
1900	478,462	1900	297,332
1901	451,800	1901	242,024
1902	528,197	1902	299,455
Total	£2,024,526	Total	£1,127,395

The total exports of all kinds amounted to £1,406,006, the balance between this figure and the export of produce consisting partly in the re-exportation of imports.

GOLD COAST.

Imports (less specie).		Exports of produce.	
1899	£1,066,503	1899	£1,074,205
1900	1,099,041	1900	852,368
1901	1,595,965	1901	534,423
1902	1,832,857	1902	715,551
Total	£5,594,366	Total	£3,176,547

It has not been possible (owing to the construction of the Blue Book) to separate Government imports from trade imports.* The large excess of imports over exports is an illustration (touched on in the questions and answers) of a colony spending large sums in capital expenditure, connected in this case largely with a nascent gold industry.

LAGOS.

Imports (less specie).		Exports of produce and manufacture.	
1899	. £800,472	1899	. £804,174
1900	. 751,362	1900	. 726,679
1901	. 717,996	1901	. 768,150
1902	. 895,231	1902	. 1,220,338
Total	. £3,165,061	Total	. £3,519,341

The same remark applies to Imperial and Colonial stores, as in the case of the Gold Coast. Here we have one of those comparatively rare cases in a tropical African possession administered on civilised lines, where the exports exceed, to a limited extent, the imports in a given period, the excess being almost wholly accounted for by the exports in 1902, which was a big produce year in Lagos, and when much of the stock of 1901 was raised in paying for 1902 produce: 1902 being also an abnormal year in other ways. The railway to Ibadan opened that year, and tapped accumulations of palm-kernels especially, which otherwise would probably never have been marketed, because of the cost of transport.

Passing from the British West African possessions to the possessions of foreign Powers in West Africa, we may examine in the first place the two French Colonies of Senegal (which includes the vast territories in the Upper Niger and Western Soudan attached thereto) and Dahomey.

SENEGAL.

Imports.		Exports.	
1899	. 50,059,834 francs.	1899	. 23,546,425 francs.
1900	. 46,805,147 ,,	1900	. 32,932,142 ,,
1901	. 64,073,960 ,,	1901	. 38,205,361 ,,
1902	. 38,205,361 ,,	1902	. 25,562,781 ,,
Total	. 199,144,302 ,,	Total	. 120,246,709 ,,

Thus, in this French Colony, which in many respects—in the sense of possessing a considerable white population,

* I understand that the Colonial Office has now given instructions for a common form to be adopted in all the British West African Colonies, which will certainly be an improvement upon the existing system.

ECONOMIC TEST OF CONGO STATE RULE 51

two railways, large military forces; and in the sense, too, of produce from the interior being subject to railway charges— is on all fours with the Congo State, the imports in the four years, 1899–1902, have been £7,965,772, and the exports £4,809,868, which is what we should expect to find. It should be noted, in passing, that Senegal is a prosperous and expanding Colony, and is to-day the largest vegetable-oil producing country in the world, the natives cultivating their *lougans* (fields) in freedom, owners of their land, and of the product of their labour. From Senegal we turn to Dahomey, where conditions are somewhat similar to Lagos, it being chiefly a palm oil and kernel producing country, with a single line of railway, but of more recent construction, and still incomplete.

DAHOMEY.

	Imports.			Exports.	
1899 .	. 12,348,970	francs.	1899 .	. 12,719,189	francs.
1900 .	. 15,221,419	,,	1900 .	. 12,755,894	,,
1901 .	. 15,752,650	,,	1901 .	. 10,478,916	,,
1902 .	. 17,090,386	,,	1902 .	. 13,669,216	,,
Total	. 60,413,425	,,	Total	. 49,623,215	,,

We find, therefore, Dahomey importing in four years articles of a value of £2,416,537, and exporting articles to the value of £1,984,928.

Let us next examine the two German West African Colonies, Togoland and Cameroons.

TOGOLAND.*

	Imports.		Exports.
1898 .	. £124,546	1898 .	. £ 73,524
1899 .	. 151,480	1899 .	. 100,785
1900 .	. 175,840	1900 .	. 152,945
1901 .	. 236,145	1901 .	. 184,525
Total	. £688,011	Total	. £511,779

CAMEROONS.†

	Imports.		Exports.
1898 .	. £464,829	1898 .	. £230,081
1900 .	. 712,250	1900 .	. 294,300
1901 .	. 462,557	1901 .	. 299,229
1902 .	. 663,785	1902 .	. 313,204
Total	. £2,303,421	Total	. £1,136,814

Capital expenditure is the main explanation of this large disproportion. Finally, we may turn to the old Portuguese

* Not having the figures for 1902, I take the four years 1898–1901.
† Not having the figures for 1899, I have incorporated those for 1898.

West African possession of Angola, where capital expenditure is not much in evidence. I have the figures for three years.

ANGOLA.

	Imports.			Exports.
1899 . .	£953,941	1899 . .	£1,105,323
1900 . .	973,611	1900 . .	1,084,707
1901 . .	981,635	1901 . .	813,825
Total .	£2,909,187	Total .	£3,003,855

In nearly all the colonies of the Powers in Western Africa we find, therefore, that the value of the imports largely exceeds the exports. In the case of Sierra Leone we observe that, even after deduction of Imperial and colonial stores, the value of the trade goods imported is largely in excess of the produce exported. That, no doubt, is partly attributable to the fact that stocks have needed replenishing, in view of the destruction which took place during the troubles of 1898, and also that a considerable proportion of trade goods imported are sold to the natives of Freetown and suburbs against cash, the balance going to the Protectorate natives to pay for produce.

In the Gold Coast there is a large import of machinery—capital expenditure for the mines; Imperial stores; rolling stock for the railway and other colonial stores; and the needs of a large European population to cater for.

In the case of Lagos we find, with the exception of the year 1902, trade more or less in its normal conditions, the margin between exports being accounted for by colonial stores, and the profits of the importer.* In Dahomey and Cameroons there has been a large import of what we should term Imperial and colonial stores—in other words, large development works going on—to swell the total of imports.

In all these colonies we have the native voluntarily collecting and cultivating produce for the European market, which produce is PURCHASED from him with European goods.

And now let us examine the statistics of the Congo State. What do these trade statistics tell us?

In the four years 1899–1902 the natives of the Congo State have collected raw produce to the value of £7,360,130 sterling, the vast majority of which consists of rubber (which, like ivory and gum-copal, comes from the vast Upper Congo) valued at £6,146,974.

---

* The figures for 1903, which I have now received, show trade to be recovering its normal equilibrium compared with the abnormal year 1902; the exports have decreased £334,734, while the imports only show a fall of £31,743.

ECONOMIC TEST OF CONGO STATE RULE

Here are the figures—

1899	£1,442,718
1900	1,895,096
1901	2,019,535
1902	2,002,756

That is a large export of produce, and represents, or should represent, a very large purchasing capacity in European goods—a purchasing capacity which we may fairly reckon at £6,500,000. If, then, produce to that amount had been collected by the natives of a British, French, or German tropical African possession, we should have this result—

Export Trade.	Import Trade.
Raw produce collected by the natives in four years. Value in sterling: £7,360,130	European merchandise import to pay for produce in four years. Value in sterling: £6,500,000

But there are the wants of 2400 white men to be catered for in the Congo State, in the shape of food-stuffs, liquors, clothing, linen, haberdashery, drugs, hardware, soap, manufactured tobacco, and so on. There is a long line of railway and a shorter one, both constructed, requiring large imports of patent fuel, railway waggons, rails, and machinery of various kinds. There is also a third railway under construction, necessitating large import of material. There are more than forty steamboats of various kinds on the upper river necessitating a large import of machinery, boilers, sectional parts, anchors, chains, and so forth. There is an army of nearly 20,000 regular troops, requiring a large import of military equipment; and there is, in addition, an irregular army, estimated by H.M. Consul in the Congo at 10,000, likewise necessitating a large import of war material. There is an enormous number of military and other stations, depôts, and what not. These require a considerable import of furniture, paints, varnish, crockery, and building materials of all kinds. Finally, articles are required, and imported, such as camping materials, coffee, candles, seeds, scientific instruments, note-paper, desk fittings, live stock and fodder, and many others.

From a careful computation of the officially published import returns of the Congo State, we can ascertain that the minimum average value of the various articles enumerated above, imported into the Congo territories during the period of four years under review, has amounted to £450,000 per annum. If, then, we were dealing with a British, French, or

German tropical possession, we should be able to extend our previous table thus—

EXPORT RETURNS.

	Value in sterling.
Raw produce collected by the natives in four years	£7,360,130

IMPORT RETURNS.

European merchandise imported to pay for produce in four years	£6,500,000
Articles imported for administrative needs and local European consumption	1,800,000
Total	£8,300,000

Over and above the articles mentioned, however, the Congo State Government, and the Great Trusts dependent upon it, require large quantities of cloth and brass rods, the only currency in the Upper Congo, to pay the services of their native military staff. Thus we find from an examination of the statistics that the Congo State pays a minimum yearly average in articles other than cash (cloth almost entirely) to its soldiers of £45,000, which in four years would amount, therefore, to £180,000. The sums paid by the Trusts for these irregular troops are necessarily not given, but on the basis (already established) that the irregular troops number half the regulars, we may estimate the value of the payment made to the irregular troops in articles other than cash at the low yearly average of £20,000, deducting, as will be seen, a yearly sum of £5000 from our average, on the assumption that the regulars are, perhaps, more highly remunerated. This, in four years, will amount to £80,000. But apart from these military necessities, both the Congo State and its trusts require very large imports, principally of cloth, to pay the tens of thousands of natives they employ all the year round in various capacities. In Leopoldville alone 3000 workmen in State employ—as we learn from H.M. Consul's report—are kept busy: maintaining telegraph lines, keeping roads clear, supplying up-river steamers with fuel, building stations, and attending to Government plantations —these are some of the uses to which native labour is put. And we must not forget the perennial supply of food-stuffs demanded from the natives all over the country, usually in fortnightly instalments. In endeavouring to estimate the sum expended in this manner, we shall, of course, be entering for the first time in our calculations the region of hypothesis; but as we are informed that the natives are "adequately remunerated" for their labour, we can hardly suppose that

ECONOMIC TEST OF CONGO STATE RULE

they receive on the average less than, say, ten francs, or 8s. 4d., per month in goods; and in view of the enormous number of stations—both State stations and those belonging to the various Trusts—the large *personnel* to feed, and so forth, we can hardly suppose—it is a very moderate estimate—that less than 50,000 natives are kept continuously employed as workmen, carriers, suppliers of food-stuffs and wood fuel. Let us, however, for purposes of argument, allow that only 30,000 natives are thus continually employed; this would give us 30,000 natives at 10 francs per month, payable in goods, 300,000 francs; multiply by 12—to get at the yearly expenditure—3,600,000 francs, or, say, £144,000 per annum—in four years, £576,000. Our completed table would thus appear as follows:—

EXPORT RETURNS.

	Value in sterling.
Raw produce collected by the natives in four years	£7,360,130

IMPORT RETURNS.

European merchandise imported to pay for produce in four years		£6,500,000
Articles imported for administrative needs and local European consumption in four years	£1,800,000	
Trade goods imported to pay soldiers, regular and irregular, in four years	260,000	
Trade goods imported to pay for hired native labour in four years	576,000	2,636,000
Total		£9,136,000

A British, French, or German tropical African possession whose inhabitants collected raw produce in four years amounting to £7,360,130, which had a white population of 2400, a large river flotilla, two railways constructed and one in course of construction, and a regular and irregular native army of 30,000 men, would, therefore, possess a total import trade of, at the very least, in round figures, £9,000,000, of which £6,500,000 would be composed of trade goods wherewith to purchase the raw produce from the natives.

What do we find when we refer to the import returns of the Congo State? We find that the total imports in the four years under review only amounted to £3,529,317!

Here are the figures for each year—

1899	£893,033
1900	988,964
1901	924,084
1902	723,236

Imagine! Here is a possession, whose rulers inform the world that their policy is not only just and humanitarian, but positively philanthropic; and whose subjects collect in four years raw produce to the value of £7,360,130 (£6,146,973 being indiarubber)—which has a value in European goods of £6,500,000—while the TOTAL IMPORT into that possession only amounts to £3,529,317, of which articles of a minimum value of £2,636,000 never reach the native producer at all!

I have taken the four years 1899-1902 because, at the time of writing, the figures for 1903 were incomplete in the case of most of the tropical African possessions of the civilised Powers. But by taking the quinquennial period, 1899-1903, of the Congo State's statistics, an even better case could be made out. In that period the total exports have amounted to £9,544,043, and the total imports to only £4,365,170, a difference in favour of the exports of no less than £5,178,873. In 1903—last year—the exports were £2,183,913, the imports only £835,853! The figures are even more striking when placed side by side in francs—

Year.	Imports.		Exports.	
1899	22,325,846	francs.	36,067,959	francs.
1900	24,724,108	„	47,377,401	„
1901	23,102,064	„	50,488,394	„
1902	18,080,909	„	50,069,514	„
1903	20,896,331	„	54,597,835	„
Total	109,129,258	„	Total . 238,601,103	„

In other words, the Congo State, which should have imported a strict minimum of £11,500,000 in five years, to pay for an export of raw produce valued at £9,544,043, *plus* the material required for the Administration, only imported material and goods valued at £4,365,170, of which articles to the value of £3,295,000 were not intended for the native producer, thus leaving a balance of £1,070,170 to *pay* for produce of a value of £9,544,043! But it should be borne in mind that these figures are worked out on a basis eminently favourable to the Congo Government. They represent the conclusions which may be arrived at by a study of the Congo State's economics available in Europe. From the numerous and detailed particulars we now possess of the *modus operandi* in Africa, it is morally certain that goods to the value of not one half of the balance above indicated have found their way into the hands of the native collector of nearly ten millions sterling of forest produce.

What does it all mean? But need we ask? Here is a test which all men can apply to the Congo State, its Government,

ECONOMIC TEST OF CONGO STATE RULE

and its methods. It means that the indiarubber, collected by the natives, and exported in vast quantities, is not paid for, or paid for in such a way as to constitute a farce of payment.* It means not only that the native producer does not obtain the intrinsic value for his produce in European goods, but that he is not even paid for his labour in collecting it.

And what in turn does that mean?

The native of tropical Africa under natural conditions is, as we have seen, a collector and cultivator of raw produce for the European markets whenever such markets are made accessible to him; voluntarily adding to such labour, which may be fairly considerable, or light according to circumstances, as is necessitated for his own sustenance and comfort, and in doing so responding to that commercial and trading instinct inbred in his race. But does this additional labour to supply the European market remain a voluntary labour, where the producer obtains—after, as is the case with rubber, for instance, very considerable labour, exposure, and hardships—nothing for his produce? Of course it does not.

The lesson derivable from a study of the export and import returns of the Congo State is a plain and simple one. It proves conclusively that the vast indiarubber output of the Congo territories is not a voluntary production, but that it is a production FORCED UPON the natives. It proves that the system itself is "at fault."

And in practice this forced production necessitates that whole tribes—a rubber output of over £6,000,000 in four years means the unceasing labour of tens of thousands of men—must be subjected to a condition of abject and impotent submission; that whole tribes must be virtually enslaved, living on from day to day, from week to week, from month to month, from year to year, only to serve the behests of their taskmasters; that slaughter and gross and perpetual oppression must be the accompaniments of such a system; that depopulation, disease, neglect, apathy, and despair must be its endemic concomitants.

* Here is a practical instance of "payment" as reported by H.M. Consul (White Book, Africa, No. 1, 1904).

"Production."	"Payment."
Per basket of pure rubber, £1 1s. 8d.	Knife worth 6d. (after adding 100 per cent. transport charges).
Rubber brought in by three men, 7 kilos, at 7 francs per kilo = £2.	Goods worth under 1s.; local valuation, 1s. 10d.
Process repeats itself every fortnight, or twenty-six times a year —£52 per annum.	Goods worth 24s. or 25s.; local valuation, £2 7s. 8d.

We know—those of us who have followed the atrocious records of the Congo State for many years—we know that these things are. We knew them long before their irrefutable confirmation by H.M. Consul in the Congo.

A study of these figures enables every man to be persuaded of them.

And if we seek amidst all the cant and the perennial outpourings of hypocritical falsehoods, which, like some poisonous stream, wells forth from the headquarters of those concerned in the maintenance of this system of African enslavement—if we seek amidst all this to find here and there, uttered at odd times and in some unguarded moment, a cynical revelation of the established fact, where shall we find a more striking illustration than in the words of M. de Smet de Naeyer, pronounced in the Belgian House in July of last year, in the course of the famous three days' Congo debate—

"THEY (THE NATIVES) ARE NOT ENTITLED TO ANYTHING : WHAT IS GIVEN THEM IS A VERITABLE GRATUITY"—words which should be bracketed with the quotation at the head of this article. The promise in 1884: the performance in 1903!

In four years the natives of the Congo territories have been robbed, in the name of philanthropy and civilisation, of produce collected by them to the tune of nearly £6,000,000. And that is the least count in the indictment. The number of human lives that have been sacrificed directly and indirectly in the process is appalling to contemplate. One of the largest of the Trusts, Mr. Roger Casement tells us, expended in three years 72,000 cartridges "in the production of indiarubber," and he quotes a diary shown him testifying to the usage by the Government of 6000 cartridges in six months on the Mamboyo River, "which means that 6000 are killed or mutilated, because for every cartridge used the soldiers must bring back a right hand." The diary adds, " It means more than 6000, for the people told me repeatedly that the soldiers kill the children with the butt of their guns." The Mongalla Trust imported—as we know from the Caudron case—40,000 ball cartridges last year, and the murder of 122 inoffensive natives was brought home to one of its agents only in March, 1904.

CHAPTER VII

THE FINANCIAL TEST OF CONGO STATE RULE—THE BENEFICIARIES BY GOVERNMENT SLAVERY

"In less than twenty-five years, acting under the impulse of a persevering and tenacious will, immense territories have been explored, the basin of a vast Empire established, and considerable natural riches exploited, which, however, are of very small importance to the general trade of Belgium, but which bring enormous profit to the Congo State and its associates. . . . To collect rubber or ivory to-day in the Congo, one must either be the Sovereign-King, or one of the Companies of the Domaine Privé. . . . There is no doubt that the economic results of this *régime* have been very brilliant for the Sovereign of the Congo State, and for the Companies of the Domaine Privé, but not to Belgium. Belgian trade in the Congo does not represent even 1 per cent. of the general trade of Belgium. A few people make enormous profits out of the sale of the rubber and ivory which fall into their hands. . . . Considerable sums are invested by the Congo State in Eastern, and especially in Chinese undertakings. Moreover, the Congo State has latterly taken to buying land in the Commune of Laeken and elsewhere. Property is also being bought up by the Congo State in Brussels, representing a value of several millions of francs. . . ."—M. VANDERVELDE, in the Belgian House, July, 1903.

"The administrative *régime* of the State is an absolute despotism."—Professor CATTIER,* Brussels University.

"All the Powers emanate from the Sovereign, who exercises them personally or through his delegates. If he deems it advisable he consults the Superior Council sitting in Brussels. He personally drafts the most important measures. . . . The Sovereign manifests his will in the form of decrees countersigned by the Secretary of State."—M. A. J. WAUTERS.†

"The success secured for the benefit of one person, and that person's immediate *entourage*, has been at the price of the enslavement of millions of men."—M. LORAND, in the Belgian House, July, 1903.

"It is a danger, it is an abuse, it is a thing contrary to the principles of our Constitution, that the King, to whom is allotted emoluments by the nation, should become a merchant and a speculator."—M. JANSON, in the Belgian House, July, 1903.

THE figures set forth in the previous chapter are in themselves sufficient to condemn the whole fabric of Congo State rule in Africa. They are the fitting background to the Leopoldian

* *Op. cit.* † *Op. cit.*

conception of tropical African development as defined in the typical exclamation of M. Smet de Naeyer, the Belgian Premier and faithful henchman of the Sovereign of the Congo State. Producer, under compulsion, of £6,146,974 sterling worth of rubber (let alone ivory, and other articles having market value in Europe, and without counting, of course, the vast quantities of food-stuffs for the up-keep of officials and the army), in four years, the native must still consider himself lucky—according to M. Smet de Naeyer—if he gets anything at all for his arduous labour in collecting these products, while he gets nothing at all for the intrinsic value of the articles which his labour produces, on the ground that the said articles do not belong to him either before or after collection, but to the State which compels him to gather them, either directly, or indirectly through the corporations to which it delegates its ownership, and in the profits of whose operations it is the largest participant.

And who in the last resort benefits by this Government slavery? On whose behalf are these natives robbed of the fruits of their toil? This is a matter which requires careful investigation. The ground we shall cover will be found to provide us with the second test, the financial test, of Congo State rule. I have shown that the rulers of the Congo have destroyed, throughout the vast territories assigned to them in trust for civilisation, the basis of commercial relationship between the European and the African by appropriating the elements pertaining to the African which constitute commerce, viz. the raw produce of the soil which the African alone can gather. I have shown that, notwithstanding this elimination of the commercial or natural relationship between the European and African in tropical Africa, the natives of the Congo State have nevertheless collected in five years for the European markets raw produce valued at over nine and a half millions sterling. And I have shown that such a condition of affairs can only be the outcome of a *régime* of coercion persistently and pitilessly applied.

As every act of man, good or bad, is the outcome of motive, so every policy, affecting the lives of many millions of men, must have behind it, whether it be beneficial or the reverse, purpose. The "development" of the Congo territories is pointed to by apologists of Congo State methods as a triumph for what is called the "colonising aptitudes" of the Belgian people; as an enormous moral asset to Belgium, and a material one to boot; as a vivifying and instructive example of what a small nation can do by energetic effort. Persons who argue in this way have a most pronounced

FINANCIAL TEST OF CONGO STATE RULE 61

objection to face facts, and either through ignorance, as, personally, I believe is the case in many instances, or through deliberate and interested misrepresentation, seek to blind, if not themselves, at least the public.

For example, are we not repeatedly told of the great increase in the "trade" of the Congo territories; when it is palpably obvious, when the facts are gone into, that there is no "trade" in the Congo territories at all, if we except the infinitesimal Lower Congo, where a miserable turn-over of some £200,000 per annum takes place, a large proportion of which is not an Afro-European transaction, but a retail business for local European consumption? That is but one specimen of the hollow contentions put forward. Is it not continually repeated that the admirable civilising work performed by the Sovereign of the Congo State in Africa is enriching the Belgian people? Could anything be more fallacious, when the facts are looked at? True, the whole of the indiarubber and most of the ivory obtained from the Congo find their way, in the first place, to Belgium, brought thereto in the steamers of the Compagnie Belge Maritime du Congo, of which Sir Alfred Jones is a director and an important shareholder, and so give employment to a certain amount of Belgian labour. But this is a very small matter. Consider, on the other hand, the opportunities of extending his business of which the Belgian manufacturer is deprived, owing to the methods adopted on the Congo. If this indiarubber and ivory were *purchased* from the native producer in European goods, as would be the case if it came from a British, a German, or a French West African possession, and some sort of privilege over his competitors were conferred upon the Belgian manufacturer—which, we can hardly suppose would be beyond the ingenuity of a sovereign who has driven a coach-and-four through the Berlin Act—look at the enormous export trade with the Congo which Belgium would be able to boast of! If in the four years we have reviewed, Belgian manufacturers had only supplied £4,500,000 out of the £6,500,000 of manufactured goods required to *purchase* the £7,360,130 of raw produce exported from the Congo, it would have represented a trade of 12s. per head for the population of Belgium. "King Leopold seems to have realised the crowning importance of acquiring a colony as a trade outlet," says Major St. H. Gibbons in his recent book,* in which we find much that is sound on the subject of Congo misrule coupled with a great deal which shows that the author is not acquainted with the essentials of Congo State policy and

* "Africa from South to North through Barotseland," 1904.

knows little of the European aspects of that policy.* And
he speaks of the object of King Leopold as having been "the
reservation of nearly a million square miles as a protected
field for Belgian commerce." That the Congo territories
may with accuracy be termed a "protected field" is not to
be disputed; but that they are "a protected field for Belgian
commerce," or that they can be spoken of as a "trade outlet"
for Belgian industry, facts disprove conclusively. Commerce
there is none, and trade there is none, and if we compare the
turn-over of Belgium's connection with the Congo after
twenty years of misplaced "energy," we find that it only
represents 1 per cent. of the total trade of Belgium!

And that is why, outside the small and noisy clique which
runs the Congo and those who benefit indirectly from its
operations, the Belgian people are absolutely indifferent to
the African undertaking of their Sovereign. One has only
to travel in Belgium and converse with Belgians of all classes
to see how true this is. Often and often have I, in endeavouring to interest Belgians in the Congo question, come across
this brick wall of indifference and ignorance: "The Congo—
why should we trouble about the Congo? We are not responsible for the Congo. It is no use to us. We get nothing
out of it. It only interests the King and a few financial
groups who hold shares in the Companies." That is the
substance of statements repeatedly made to me by Belgian
individuals. To an important member of an international
Jesuit college which numbers many Belgians among its adepts,
to whom I was deploring the silence of the Belgian Priest-
hood on the Congo in the face of the atrocities and oppression
endemic in that unhappy land, the answer was: "Our brothers
know that these things occur, and I have read many private
letters from some of our Belgian workers on the Congo which
more than confirm your statements; but what can they do?
Belgian public opinion is indifferent, and they are the subjects
of their King, and would be at once disavowed if they spoke
or allowed their letters to be published."

But the Congo clique, however numerically small, is
financially extremely powerful; the King can always count
upon the support of the Catholic Right in his African undertaking as the price paid for keeping the Socialists out of
office; the old Liberal party is an agglomeration of inchoate
atoms; the majority of the Belgian newspapers are, I am
sorry to say, easily purchasable; and the Belgian ambassadors
and consuls in foreign countries obey, as they needs must do,

* Major St. H. Gibbons has since declared that he was driven to the
conclusion that the "general system of government is bad."

FINANCIAL TEST OF CONGO STATE RULE 63

the royal *mot d'ordre*. The consequence is that Europe is altogether misled as to the real sentiments or lack of sentiments of the Belgian people, among whom King Leopold is not at all respected, let alone liked. The real condition of the Congo, for which Belgium is made to appear responsible by her Constitutional monarch, and is, in effect, morally responsible beyond all other Powers, is studiously kept from the nation, which is not one naturally given to philanthropic impulse. I do not think, however, that this state of things can last for ever. The high standing and European reputation of several Englishmen, known as the defenders constitutionally of small peoples, who have allied themselves with a movement for the reform of the abominations of Congo misrule, must have an effect, before very long, which will be heightened by the splendid labours of Belgians like Vandervelde and Lorand. Even now it is beginning to be apparent that, despite the incessant efforts of the King and his *entourage*, the Belgian people are becoming aware that the condemnation pronounced upon Congolese methods by civilisation—with England, I am proud to say, in the van—is not a condemnation of themselves as a people, but of those who are dragging the fair fame of Belgium in the mire.

Before dealing in specific fashion with the query set forth at the commencement of this chapter, it may be advisable to give some little-known particulars as to the condition of Congo State finances—"*finances véreuses*," as their Belgian critics say. In point of fact, the Congo State is pretty heavily mortgaged, as the following figures of loans contracted tell :—

	Francs.
1904	30,000,000
1902 (balance of 1888 loan) .	80,000,000
1901 (Great Lakes railway) .	25,000,000
1901	50,000,000
1896	1,500,000
1888	70,000,000
1885 (balance) . . .	422,200
Total . .	256,922,200

In addition to this indebtedness of £10,276,880, of which France is understood to hold stock amounting to £3,200,000, there is a capital of £1,200,000 (30,000,000 francs) lent by the Belgian State, of which neither capital nor interest is repayable, Belgium having renounced both in 1901, provided she annexes the Congo. If she should not annex the Congo, then her loan would have to be paid off. Much of this money has been borrowed ostensibly for works on the Congo; in reality, to allow King Leopold to meet some of his other engagements, notably in China. His Majesty found it necessary recently to put up 55,000,000 francs (£2,200,000) in this connection. He endeavoured to do so by issuing a loan in February, 1904. That loan did not, however, come off. There were openly expressed opinions that it was illegal in its form and conception, and, at any rate, it has not "proceeded." Valuable light is thrown upon the peculiar part played by the Sovereign of the Congo State in connection with the sinking fund of the 1888 Congo loan, the American Chinese Development Company, l'Asiatique, and the National Savings Bank of Belgium (*Caisse d'Epargne*), by the proceedings of the Belgian House of Representatives in March, 1903.*

These loans, I may remark, are, as a rule, devised in the seclusion of Ostend, remote from the control or advice of the Belgian Finance Minister. They have even been known to be put into being over a dinner-table. There is not the least doubt that the true reason no lands are now sold on the Congo, but only leased, is to be found in the conditions of the Belgian renunciation in 1901, of both the capital and interest of her loan. By the terms of that loan all sums derivable from the sales of land were to be devoted to paying off the capital. In other words, the proceeds of the sales would go to Belgium, and not to the Congo State. The Sovereign of that State finds he can obtain quite as much for leasing land as for selling it, and as in the former case the proceeds go towards that mysterious compilation, the Congo State "budget," and not to Belgium, it is seen to be preferable to lease land instead of selling it. The advantage of being Constitutional monarch of a country whence you can obtain a loan on such terms, and Sovereign absolute of another country where 2,000,000 kilometres square of Domaine Privé are leasable on such terms, is not to be reckoned lightly.

Passing from these under-currents of Congolese high finance, the full depth of which I do not profess to have yet

* "Annales parlementaires." In 1889 the Société Asiatique, one of the King's Chinese ventures, "the King and the creatures of the King," to quote M. Vandervelde, was successful in getting the Committee which has charge of the Sinking Fund of the 1888 loan to invest in the Chinese concern; the game was tried again in 1902, when the Asiatique made a bid for 10 million francs out of the same fund. Two of the members objected. Thereupon the Committee was increased from three members to six, and the 10 millions were secured. A still bolder move was made in the spring of 1903 to involve the Caisse d'Epargne in the undertaking, and the debate which took place on that occasion was most instructive.

Photograph by ALFRED EMMOTT, ESQ., M.P. *Elliott & Fry*

Has taken a prominent part in denouncing Congo misgovernment and in creating the Congo Reform Association.

FINANCIAL TEST OF CONGO STATE RULE 65

sounded, the Congo State's yearly budgetary returns offer a field of equally revealing investigation. First of all, the true revenue and expenditure returns are never published. In this respect the Congo State enjoys a unique distinction among civilised states. The only returns which see the light of day are "estimates." These "estimates" are drafted, apparently, with the clear and definite purpose of causing the world to believe that, administratively, the Congo State is a losing concern, or at best barely meets expenses. The expenditure is either shown as exceeding the revenue, or providing a very small margin on the right side. This is, however, like so much which pertains to that anachronism, the Congo State, excessively fallacious. For instance, the "taxes in kind" paid by the natives figure as the principal item in the revenue returns, which *per se* is perfectly accurate. If it were not for these "taxes" the Congo State, as at present managed, would be bankrupt to-morrow. The "taxes" in question are supposed to represent the value of the india-rubber and ivory thus "paid" by the natives for the great benefits conferred upon them by civilisation, *viâ* King Leopold and his agents. It is rather amusing to note, by the way, that the values of the articles thus obtained by *impôt légitime* are incorporated in the trade returns! They are included in the exports under the designation of *statisques commerciales!* So, on the one hand, we are invited to express admiration at the growth of the export "trade" which includes the product of "taxation." When, however, we point out the extraordinary difference in the respective values of the exports and imports in the case of a country whose purchasing capacity in European goods lies in its exports alone; and when, going further, we are uncharitable enough to remark that the Congo State, by its own legislation, by the utterances of its officials, by its own diplomatic documents, admits that the entire products of economic value throughout the Congo territories have been appropriated by the State, and that consequently the element of "trade" has disappeared with the elimination of the right of possession on the part of the native to the very articles which constitute trade; the reply is, "You are confusing trade with taxation!"* And, to crown all, the Congo Government points to the growth in the exports as proving the economic development of the country in the shape of a "considerable *commercial* movement!"

The published figures of this estimated "taxation" between 1894 and 1902 are as follows:—

* *Bulletin Officiel*, June, 1903.

F

		Francs.
1895	.	1,250,000
1896	.	1,200,000
1897	.	3,500,000
1898	.	6,700,000
1899	.	10,000,000
1900	.	10,500,000
1901	.	17,424,630
1902	.	15,452,000

But these estimates are much below the actual amounts realised by the Congo State on the Antwerp market for the sale of the products of these "taxes." The realisations between 1895 and 1900 are as follows:—

		Francs.
1895	.	5,500,000
1896	.	6,000,000
1897	.	8,500,000
1898	.	9,000,000
1899	.	19,130,000
1900	.	14,991,300

Since my publication of the 1899 and 1900 figures the sources of information have been more jealously guarded than ever, and so far it has not been possible to ascertain the figures for 1901, 1902, and 1903.

Let us take the year 1899 as an example, and see how it works out.

The budgetary estimates of revenue and expenditure for that year were published as follows:—

Revenue.	Expenditure.
19,966,500 francs	19,672,965 francs.
(of which 10,000,000 francs derived from "taxes" as per estimate).	

According to the official figures, therefore, the excess of revenue over expenditure was only 293,535 francs. But the "taxes," as we see by the second column of figures given above, exceeded the budgetary estimates by no less a sum than 9,130,000 francs, and with this important correction (I cannot imagine that the compilers of the "estimates" would under-estimate the expenditure, but you cannot check them!) the revenue and expenditure returns figure out as follows:—

Revenue.	Expenditure.
29,096,500 francs	19,672,963 francs.
(of which 19,130,000 francs derived from "taxes").	

The excess of revenue over expenditure, therefore, was

FINANCIAL TEST OF CONGO STATE RULE 67

not a paltry 293,535 francs, but amounted to the very substantial sum of 9,423,535 francs.

Take the year 1900, according to the budgetary estimates:

Revenue.	Expenditure.
26,256,500 francs (of which 10,500,000 francs derived from "taxes" as per estimate).	27,731,254 francs.

Here we have an apparent excess of expenditure over revenue amounting to 1,474,754 francs, whereas, in point of fact, the figures should read—

Revenue.	Expenditure.
30,747,800 francs (of which 14,991,300 francs derived from "taxes").	27,731,254 francs.

A New York newspaper published last year an interview with a personality on the subject of the Congo to whom was attributed royal prescience and knowledge, and in that interview the royal person interviewed remarked upon the confusion which was being made between gross and net revenue; unhappily for the enlightenment of the community the interviewer did not attempt a differentiation as between gross and net expenditure.

Where do these surpluses go? We shall certainly not find the explanation in the budgetary "estimates," and nothing beyond them is ever published on Congo State finances. We must therefore look further afield, which brings us to a consideration of the Domaine Privé and its various branches.

The Domaine Privé covers, theoretically, the entire area of the Congo territories above Leopoldville, with the exception of a few tracts along the banks of some of the rivers which are nominally open to trade, but where, as in the case of the La Lulonga Company, the "traders" have the right to exact rubber *à titre d'impôt*. But the Domaine Privé is split up into sections. There are the areas given over to the great Trusts, and there is the Domaine de la Couronne, of which very little was heard prior to the debate in the Belgian House in July, 1903. What is not incorporated in the Domaine de la Couronne or absorbed by the Trusts is the area in which the black subjects of King Leopold are "taxed" in order to provide revenues for the Government.

Lord Cromer tells us that the Congo Government, so far as he could judge, is conducted "almost exclusively on commercial principles," and even judged by that standard, added his Lordship, those principles appeared to be "somewhat short-sighted."* In his Note to the Powers, Lord Lansdowne, basing himself upon—

"information which has reached His Majesty's Government from British officers in territory adjacent to that of the State, tends to show that . . . no attempt at any administration of the natives is made, and that the officers of the Government do not apparently concern themselves with such work, but devote all their energies to the collection of revenue." †

Many are the records to the same effect in Consul Casement's report,‡ and, apart from such testimony, there is a mass of irrefutable data from unofficial sources beyond suspicion, proving that the chief, if not the main, solicitude of the authorities is the acquisition of indiarubber for revenue purposes, which, in practice, means getting as much indiarubber as possible out of each rubber-producing district in the Domaine Privé by way of "taxes." This anxiety is, moreover, so conspicuously evident in the *pronunciamientos* of the Congo State authorities themselves, that we really need not go beyond them. Take, for example, the memorandum of Governor-General Wahis to the Commissioners of Districts and Chiefs of Zones, a copy of which is given in the White Book.§

The memorandum is all about rubber from beginning to end. It concludes as follows:—

"A cette cause de la diminution de la valeur du caoutchouc, il faut ajouter celle provenant de l'emballage défectueux du produit, qui par suite voyage souvent pendant plusieurs mois dans les plus mauvaises conditions. L'on peut dire qu'a cause de cette négligence une notable partie des efforts qui ont été faits pour obtenir une production en rapport avec la richesse du pays, doivent être considérés comme perdus, puisque la valeur du caoutchouc peut diminuer de moitié par suite de ce manque de soin. J'ajouterai que la valeur du caoutchouc, même pur de tout mélange, a diminué depuis quelque temps sur tous les marchés ; il faut donc que les chefs territoriaux fassent non seulement disparaître les deux causes de pertes qu'ils peuvent éliminer, mais encore qu'ils compensent la troisième en faisent des efforts continus pour augmenter la production dans la mesure prescrite par les instructions. Mon attention sera d'une façon constante, fixée sur les prescriptions que je donne ici."

Here we have the Governor-General himself abjuring the high officials under him to make "continued efforts" to increase the output of rubber. As Mr. Casement sarcastically remarks—

"The instructions this circular conveys would be excellent if coming from the head of a trading house to his subordinates, but addressed, as they are, by a Governor-General to the principal officers of his Administration, they reveal a somewhat limited conception of public duty."

---

* Africa, No. 1, 1904, *op. cit.* † British Note to Powers.
‡ Africa, No. 1, 1904, *op. cit.* § Idem.

FINANCIAL TEST OF CONGO STATE RULE 69

It must not be forgotten, however, that the "conception of public duty" held by the Governor-General of the Congo State is the conception required and prescribed by a higher authority than he. The brain which directs the Congo machine is not in Africa, but in Brussels, and the Governor-General is the "personal mandatory," as the Congo text-books tell us, of the Sovereign King. What, again, could be more significant than the memorandum of M. Felix Fuchs, the Governor-General *ad interim* to Commandant Verstraeten, the Commissaire of the Rubi-Welle zone, coupled with the latter's instructions to the subordinate "administrators" of that district, as quoted by M. Vandervelde in the course of the Congo debates in the Belgian House last year?

"Je terminerai," wrote M. Felix Fuchs, "en vous disant que le gouvernement a le ferme espoir que, vous inspirant des considérations exposées en tête de la présente, vous fournirez une nouvelle preuve d'activité et de dévouement, en faisant produire à la zone que vous commandez le maximum de ressources qu'on en peut tirer."

And the faithful under-strapper to those placed under his authority—

"MESSIEURS LES CHEFS DE POSTE DE LA ZONE DE RUBI-OUELLE,

"J'ai l'honneur de porter à votre connaîssance qu'a partir du Ier Janvier 1899, il faut arriver à fournir mensuellement 4000 kilogrammes de caoutchouc. . . . Vous avez donc deux mois pour travailler vos populations," etc.

The outcome of those particular instructions we shall read of in Chapter XIV.

"Du caoutchouc, encore du caoutchouc, toujours du caoutchouc!"—that is the insistent demand, and might well be adopted by the Congo State as its motto, with a severed hand as its emblem; but we will come to the emblem presently. These words, so pregnant of meaning for the unhappy peoples of the Congo, whispered at the Place du Trône, consigned in confidential memoranda (which sometimes see the light of day) at Boma, thence despatched all over the vast Congo State, even unto the Great Lakes, to be passed from Commissaire de District to Chef de Zone; from Chef de Zone to Chef de Factorerie; from Chef de Factorerie to the humblest sub-agents of the great Machine, the latter to be sacrificed when local risings and the cause thereof have become too intensive and too notorious to be hushed up, to answer for the crimes of their employers. India-rubber, first discovered in Africa by a Minister of God, has, on the Congo, become synonymous with oppression, outrage, and massacre; gathered at the point of the bayonet, hurried down river to the ocean, sweating in the hold of the great steamer, flung upon the quay at Antwerp; the theme of every sordid tale of crime unfolded before the Boma Courts; the constant preoccupation of every State official from the day he lands in the sphere reserved to the process of "moral and material regeneration"—how many lives are sacrificed for each ton of it!

The right of a European Government to tax directly its subjects in tropical Africa will not be queried (although there may be differences of opinion as to the wisdom of a European Government desirous of building up a healthy, happy, and prosperous dependency for future generations in applying direct taxation to peoples among whom a recurring impost is, in the majority of cases, unknown in native custom), provided that the taxation bears a reasonable relationship to the capabilities in labour and wage-earning capacity of the tax-payer. It may be remarked in this connection that whereas England, France, and Germany are content to tax their African subjects once or at most twice a year, the Congo Government, in its laudable zeal to inculcate to a sufficient degree the dignity of labour, prefers to tax its subjects once a week or once a fortnight, with the not infrequent result that from year's end to year's end the Congo native is employed in meeting demands which, apparently, remain stationary, or even increase with the corresponding decrease of the population—the infallible consequence of such a continuous strain.*

So much for the Domaine Privé *stricto sensu*, the portion of the Congo territories exclusively set aside for purposes of acquiring indiarubber for Government "taxation." †

Until the debates of 1903 in the Belgian House, public opinion in Belgium and outside of it was made to understand that the taxation of natives in the Domaine Privé represented the *summum* of "taxation" exacted from the natives of the Congo. The Congo Government, in official documents, its apologists, official and unofficial, and its paid writers in the Press, have declared over and over again that the whole amount derived from the "taxation" of the natives appeared in the Budget, a statement in itself manifestly misleading, if

* See *inter alia*, Africa, No. 1, 1904, *op. cit.*; the letters of Mr. Weeks in the *West African Mail*, etc. The statement put forward by the Congo Government and its apologists to the effect that the native of the Congo is only required to give forty hours' labour per month is a fair example of a mendacity whose shamelessness is only equalled by its absurdity.

† The word "taxation" is placed in inverted commas because it is the word used by the Congo Government. Personally, I do not think that the word is applicable to the process whereby Government revenues are acquired.

not positively untrue, since, as we have had occasion to observe, only "estimates" are published, never actual returns. The author of the present volume had consistently maintained the contrary,* viz. that large sums were obtained from "taxation" which figured nowhere, not even as "estimates." To dismiss the author as "a calumniator," the epithet reserved for those who disagree with the methods of the Congo Government, and more particularly, it would seem, for the individual against whom the choicest compliments of the Congo State's defenders are directed, was a sufficiently easy task until the afore-mentioned debate. The revelations made on that occasion have, however, corroborated my previous statements up to the hilt. It was then made clear for the first time that, in addition to the Government "taxes" required of the natives "for benefits rendered," in the Domaine Privé *stricto sensu*, "taxes" were imposed upon the natives in a special section of the Domaine Privé, called Domaine de la Couronne, not for Government purposes, but for account and on behalf of the Sovereign-King. It transpired that the Domaine de la Couronne, of which many members of the House had never heard, was "a civil personality" ruled by a special staff, and the proceeds of whose revenues were managed for the Sovereign-King in Europe by a committee of three persons, two of them attached to the Court (Baron Raoul Snoy and Baron Goffinet), and the other the Finance Minister of the Congo State (M. Droogmans). The extent and the disposal of these revenues, it also transpired, figured in no public accounts and were nowhere specified. This scandalous *exposé*, forced out of the official defenders of the Congo Government in the course of an extraordinarily heated discussion, was received with loud protests and expressions of indignation from the Left, and in slavish silence by the Right.†

Thus is partially explained the wide margin between the revenue "estimates" and the actual returns from "taxation" in the shape of produce sold by the State's brokers on the Antwerp market, and thus is finally disposed of the contention that the Congo State is, administratively, a losing concern. It has now been made abundantly clear that the budgetary "estimates" bear but the faintest relation to truth, and that, in addition to "taxation" imposed for Government requirements, the natives of the Congo are "taxed" for the benefit of, shall we say, in the language of the *Bulletin Officiel*, "a civil personality"?

* "Affairs of West Africa," and notably the "Congo Slave State," 1903, chap. ii. p. 22.
† "Annales parlementaires," *vide* Part V.

The query at the opening of these pages is partly answered. The answer will be complete when we have examined the constitution and the nature of the great Trusts. I should say here that, apart from the Domaine Privé, the Domaine de la Couronne, and the areas allotted to the Trusts, there exists what is known as the Thys group of companies, of which the Société Anonyme du Haut Congo is the principal company. So far as these companies act independently, I have not a word to say against them. The enterprise originated as a genuine commercial undertaking, as we have already noted. For years the Société Anonyme du Haut Congo carried on a legitimate trade, and was well served by honourable agents, until the Congo Government violently interfered, destroyed a trade which had been built up, and forced the company to its knees. I cannot think that the men connected with the Thys concerns, bad and demoralising as has been the example set them, have altered their original methods, and adopted the policy of compelling the natives *vi et armis* to produce for nothing that which there had been no previous difficulty in purchasing from them on fair terms. They were pursuing a legitimate trade prior to 1891. That they have been conducting their business on the same lines in such restricted areas as the stand they then made has enabled them in some degree to retain, I would fain hope. But I confess to have but little information on the subject of those companies, save, of course, that which is public property, to wit, the open rupture which has come about once more between the King and Colonel Thys—a rupture that may yet have far-reaching results. The turnover of the Société Anonyme is very small compared with that of the Trusts; its profits are reasonable, and such as one would expect from trading operations so far inland, and it is not under present conditions a factor with which we need concern ourselves very greatly in reference to the query, "Who are the beneficiaries under the slave system which prevails in the Congo territories?" It should be stated that in many respects the interests of the Thys group are bound up very closely with the Congo Government, notably in the Katanga country, and in connection with the Matadi-Stanley Pool Railway.

The Trusts are eight in number. Two of them, the Lomami (in which the Thys group is concerned) and the Société d'Agriculture et de plantations, are relatively unimportant. The following list provides their titles, and the financial and administrative relationship between them and the Government :—

FINANCIAL TEST OF CONGO STATE RULE 73

Titles.	Relations with the Government.
L'Abir (A.B.I.R.).	Congo State holds 50 per cent. of shares.
L'Anversoise	Congo State holds 50 per cent. of shares.
Kasai	Congo State holds 50 per cent of shares; appoints president, manager, and majority of administrators.
Kwango	Congo State gets one-third of profits.
Grands Lacs	Congo State holds 100,000 dividend-paying shares; approves nomination of administrators, and appoints three delegates.
Katanga	Congo State gets two-thirds of the profits; appoints the president in Europe, the manager in Africa, and two-thirds of the administrators.

The men who participate in controlling these Trusts are virtually the King's bodyguard, financiers and others without whose good-will even Leopold II. might find it difficult to manage satisfactorily his African undertaking.

Most of these Trusts, their operations, their profits, the dull routine of oppression and atrocity which characterises the management of their estates, are dealt with in Part III.

Our query is now answered. It is not to serve a national interest that the Congo natives have been enslaved. The egotism which has imposed upon the inhabitants of the vast Upper Congo a burden more crushing than ever applied by Arab half-caste, is not even a national egotism. It is far more restricted than that! If people will only realise that the chaos and destruction which the Policy put into practice a dozen years ago has wrought in the Congo territories is the work not of a misguided and misled nation, but of a few individuals working for their own ends and their own pecuniary benefit, they will be in a position to solve what has been a puzzle to so many, viz. the apparent short-sightedness of the conception. How often has it not been said to me, in effect, " The stupidity, the crass stupidity of this system which is killing the goose that lays the golden eggs, is such that, despite the overwhelming proofs afforded of its existence, and of its effects, the mind retains an element of doubt, it being seemingly impossible that the Belgian people can be so blind to their own most obvious interests."

If the Policy were one pursued as a deliberate national end; if the Congo territories were colonisable by a white race; if its vegetable riches were obtainable by any other race but the race indigenous to its forests and its plains, and which moral and material regeneration is fast exterminating —then the Policy from top to bottom would indeed be incredibly stupid. But as it is not, and has never been, a national enterprise, but a private one, it is really the reverse of stupid. Why should the present rulers of the Congo care for posterity? Their objects are wholly of the momènt, and the havoc which has been caused already in the acquirement of the fortunes they have made by battening upon the misery of an entire people, will take generations of patient effort on the part of their successors—successors, whoever they may be, to a heritage of woe—to remedy, if, indeed, the mischief has not gone too deep for remedial measures.

For millions of African men, women, and children, oppression, despair, wretchedness appalling and unimaginable; for Belgium, moral bankruptcy; for a handful of callous and selfish men, enormous wealth;—that, in brief, is the result of twenty years of King Leopold's rule in tropical Africa.

CHAPTER VIII

THE "PROPERTY" PLEA—THE CONGO STATE'S MAIN LINE OF DEFENCE

"But beyond the special stipulations of Article IV., we have recognised and sanctioned a certain number of principles which assure the application of freedom of commerce in the Basin of the Congo against all infraction in the future."—Protocol No. 8, Berlin Act.

"Celles-ci (les communautés indigènes) toutefois telle est l'observation qui mérite d'être recueillie, n'ont point été considérées commes des agglomérations assez dépourvues de fixité et de consistance pour que le sol qu'elles habitent lors même qu'il n'est pas utilisé put être qualifié de terre inappropriée . . . toutes les fois qu'un vote ou qu'une simple proposition a mis en cause les intérêts des peuples africains, l'assemblée de Berlin a demontré qu'elle ne voyait pas en eux des associations purement accidentelles, sans personalité juridique et en dehors de la communauté du droit des gens."—RAPPORT ENGELHARDT (a French Delegate at the Berlin Conference).

"L'Acte général de la Conference de Berlin fait partie du droit public de l'Etat Indépendant du Congo, il lie celui-ci vis-à-vis des autres Puissances et les dispositions législatives du nouvel Etat ne pourront jamais se trouver en contradiction avec les résolutions de l'Acte général."—Pandectes belges.*

As the knowledge of Congo State methods has gradually extended, and the criticism of those methods taken specific form and substance, so the Authorities of the State have gradually fallen back upon their main line of defence. So far as this country, which since 1896 has led the van in censuring the proceedings of the State, is concerned, no very clear conception of the root of the evils prevalent in the Congo territories appears at first to have been formed. Attention was directed mainly to the *symptoms* of mal-administration in the shape of constantly recurring reports of ill-treatment of natives in connection with the rubber and ivory tribute; to the perpetual warfare waged all over the country, and to the fearful slaughter and cannibal festivities which characterised the extermination by the State troops of the Arab half-castes, who, if they were slave-raiders, also possessed the monopoly of the ivory trade, of which they held enormous stocks,

* The *Pandectes belges* are a collection of Belgian laws; a sort of standard legal code of great weight and importance.

subsequently seized and disposed of by the Congo State authorities on the Antwerp market. It is only little by little, perhaps within the last two years, that the full significance of the economic policy embodied in the decrees and circulars of 1891 and 1892, and the relation borne by those decrees and circulars to the *symptoms*, have become apparent, even to those who have studied the Congo State and its ways for a much longer time. I am quite sure that the majority of the British people have not yet grasped the situation; but until the economic policy of the Congo State *is* grasped, the Congo problem and the much larger problems, present and future, bound up in it can never be properly understood. It is the crux of the whole matter.

But there were men who did understand from the start. Those men were Belgians, and their leaders were Messrs. Thys, Brugmann, and Urban, the founders of the Belgian Trading Companies in the Upper Congo, the men who built the Matadi-Stanley Pool Railway, the men who represent the only legitimate Belgian enterprise of which the Congo Basin has been the scene. They saw plainly the immediate effect of the decrees and circulars, and with equal perspicacity, borne of acquaintance with Equatorial African conditions, they foresaw the resultant effect. The immediate effect was the *elimination of trade.* The resultant effect was the *enslavement of the population.* In the clearest terms did they assert these incontrovertible facts, and their statements are on record. Truly deplorable is it to look back at that crisis in the modern history of Africa, and to realise that its gravity was totally underrated. The Belgian Trading Companies, as we have seen, were compelled after a hard fight to give way. Had they been efficaciously backed up from without, the history of the Congo territories would have been very different. Had but one signatory Power to the Berlin Act protested officially against the violation of the Act which the newly promulgated policy of the Congo State entailed, the Authorities of the State would to-day be deprived of a useful weapon; the plea of the accomplished fact. If England had protested she could have rebutted the Continental taunt of insincerity of motive by the strongest of all arguments, the argument of consistency in censure. But alas! no one in England realised the great issue which had been raised, nor the vital principles at stake, and two years later the British Government concluded with the Congo State a Treaty which has brought us nothing but perplexities and embarrassments.*

* This Treaty was publicly acknowledged as a mistake, by one of the Cabinet Ministers concerned, three years after it was signed.

THE "PROPERTY" PLEA

The earlier criticisms against the State were met successively by blank denials and indignant repudiations; by high-sounding expressions of philanthropic motive; by perfervid allusions to the noble work of suppressing the internal slave-trade; by promises of inquiry which never came to anything; by the enumeration of sundry laws drafted to ensure the protection of natives;* by admitting the existence of individual abuses common to the Colonial enterprise of all nations; by the constitution of a "Commission for the Protection of Natives;" by asserting the existence of a perfected judicial establishment which ensured the punishment of all evil doers; by the actual punishment of a few sub-agents; by pointing to sundry legislative measures calculated to confer "moral and material regeneration" in a variety of ways upon the natives; by emphasising the material improvements introduced into the country, such as steamers, brick houses, fine stations, telegraph lines, even automobiles; by accentuating the enormous increase in "trade;" by imputing the basest motives to the critics.

Nearly all these lines of defence are still put forward. Thus in the special Bulletin issued early this year the old familiar claims of benefits conferred upon the natives are recapitulated, down to the inevitable suppression of polygamy among the native troops (!) and prophylactic measures against small-pox.†
Again, in reply to the British Note issued September 18, we read that the Congo State has proved itself a "faithful servant" of the Berlin Act; we note that "isolated acts are invoked under humanitarian pretences in order to conceal the true object of a barely concealed covetousness;" that "the same charges of alleged violence to natives are continually dished up," and so on and so forth. But now these old counters in the game of bluff, played so long and so successfully, are merely subsidiary to the main line of defence. As the attack is pressed home, the masked batteries come into action. The instruction of the public has gone on apace, and more serious weapons are needed to check the assault. It has even been found necessary to abandon some of the outer lines. The claim to philanthropy, for instance, is not nearly so accentuated as formerly. In its place the contention is put forward that the native of Western Africa is a slothful creature, and that compulsion is absolutely essential to make him produce. We are also informed that in matters of internal administration the Congo State has no account to render to any one. But all

---
* The same farce is now being repeated.
† The subscription given by King Leopold to the expedition sent by the Liverpool School of Tropical Medicine to the Congo to study sleeping sickness will no doubt be invoked in the next edition.

this is by the way. These various arguments are useful insomuch as they are calculated to give rise to discussion, and to help to obscure the main issue. They are incidental to the grand theory of PROPERTY, the battle-ground upon which the Congo State has concentrated all its forces for the supreme resistance.

Briefly stated, the contention amounts to this. All land not built upon by natives, nor under cultivation by natives for food-stuffs, is "vacant." The official Decree of July 1, 1885, provided that "vacant land must be considered as belonging to the State." Hence all land not built upon, nor under cultivation by natives for food-stuffs, is the property of the State. For six years the State made no attempt to develop its property. It allowed natives living upon it (the contradiction implied in "vacant" land being inhabited does not trouble the Congo State dialectians) to tap the rubber vines and sell the latex to European merchants; it allowed European merchants to buy that latex from the natives; its foolishness in doing so being doubtless a manifestation of the philanthropic spirit. But at a given moment the State saw the folly of its ways, and issued a series of regulations forbidding the natives to collect and sell rubber * or ivory to merchants, and forbidding merchants to buy those articles from natives. In doing so it was merely exercising its rights as a land-owner. It has done nothing more than that ever since; and the assertion that trade is thereby interfered with reposes upon no judicial foundation whatever, the State disposing, as it is entitled to do, of the products of economic value yielded by its PROPERTY.

Thus epitomised, and epitomised, I think, quite accurately, the contention of the Congo State appears so absolutely puerile that it seems a perfect waste of time to discuss it. I must confess that I take that view of it myself. But I am told that I am a very ignorant person, and that, clothed in all the trappings and paraphernalia of legal dissertations, the contention looks quite different to what it really is. Let us, then, see the appearance it presents with the needful embellishments. We will turn, first, to the official defence of the Congo State published in the *Bulletin Officiel* of June, 1903. In it we find the following :—

"When the State, in the regulation of July 1, 1885, decreed that 'no one has the right to occupy without title vacant lands; vacant lands must be considered as belonging to the State,' it referred to a principle

---

* Which, let it be repeated for the twentieth time, the natives had been doing long before King Leopold conceived the wish to regenerate them.

of law universally admitted, without its being intended, as had been said, as the first stake in a premeditated policy of exclusiveness. This principle was inscribed in the codes of all civilised countries, it had been established by all Colonial legislations. Its consequence—that is to say, the right of the State to dispose to the best of the *general interest** of the lands of which it has the proprietorship—is not less legitimate. The Berlin Act, in its text or in its protocols, does not restrain either the right of property on the part of individuals, or on that of bodies, or the free exercise of its use or its effects. Liberty of commerce, such as it has been defined, is in nothing exclusive of the right of property, that not being a 'commercial monopoly' of the kind which the Berlin Act prohibits."

The contention is repeated in much the same words in the Congo State's reply to the British Note.

"The Government of the independent State of the Congo," says the Official Reply, "denies that the way in which the State is administrated involves a systematic *régime* of cruelty and oppression ; or that the principle of free trade can modify rights of proprietorship such as are universally admitted, when there is not a word to that effect in the Berlin Act. The Congo State notes that there are no clauses in that Act tending to restrict in any way the right of property. . . . The British Note does not demonstrate that the economic system of the State is opposed to the Berlin Act. It does not meet the arguments of law, and of a fact by which the Congo State has justified its land laws and its concessions, with the clauses of that Act. It does not explain how, or in what way, the freedom of trade-terms, which the Berlin Conference used in their usual, grammatical, and economic sense, is not complete because there are owners of property in the Congo. The Note confuses trade with the development of his property by a landlord. The native who gathers products for account of the owner † does not become owner of the harvested products, and can naturally not dispose of them to others, any more than the workman who extracts ore from the mine can defraud the owner by disposing of it himself. These rules are law, and are propounded in a multiplicity of documents."

The official defenders of the Congo State in the Belgian House on the occasion of the great Congo debate last July—which will be found in Part V.—naturally adopted the same line.

"It is, therefore, solely as regards trade," said M. de Favereau, the Belgian Minister for Foreign Affairs, "that monopoly and privilege were forbidden by the Berlin Act. But no one can argue that such stipulations can be interpreted as signifying the claim to interfere with the sovereign right of the State to regulate its property as it chooses. . . . In what legislation in the world will it be found that to sell the products of one's domain constitutes a commercial act?"

---

* Italics the author's—the words should be borne in mind : "general interests" includes, necessarily, the interests of the *native producer* of raw material in the Upper Congo.

† That the native is the "owner" himself is a detail unworthy of notice, apparently !

After M. de Favereau, M. Woeste, leader of the Catholic party:

"In appropriating for itself the fruits of the *Domaine*, the State was justified. . . . The argument which attributes to the Congo State a violation of the commercial clauses in the Berlin Act is a sophism. Trade is confounded with the right of the State to exploit its own Domaine."

After M. Woeste, M. Smet de Naeyer, the Belgian Premier:

"The appropriation of vacant lands is the first inevitable and necessary step in constituting property in a country which is being opened to civilisation. . . . It has been twenty times demonstrated that realising the fruits of a 'Domaine' is not commerce or speculation."

In the learned treatises of Professor Descamps, Maître Nys, and Maître Barboux there is a repetition in degrees of varying eloquence of the same thesis.

The Congo State finds much consolation in pointing a *tu quoque*. Other Powers, it seems, have declared "vacant" lands to be State property. A regulation passed in German East Africa declares that "the Government alone has the right to take possession of vacant lands." The *Bulletin Officiel* of the Congo State (June, 1903) also quotes from agreements made in 1890 and 1894 between the German Government and the *Deutsche Ostafrikanische Gesellschaft* with regard to vacant lands, but naturally omits to indicate the modifications which experience has, since that date, led the German Government to make; and similarly as regards the Cameroon *Concessionnaire* Companies, likewise referred to in the *Bulletin Officiel*. The French Congo regulation of 1891, declaring that "*waste lands and abandoned lands, to the ownership of which no one can legitimately lay* claim, will be considered as belonging to the State," is quoted in the *Bulletin Officiel*, as also the circumstance that some forty concessions have been granted in that colony by the French Government. Finally, an extract from a report by Sir Harry Johnston, dated 1900, is given in connection with waste land in British East Africa. After this enumeration, the Congo State triumphantly points out in indifferent English:

"If it was true that the Congo State had, in proclaiming its ownership of waste lands, expropriated natives, this reproach should be addressed to all these different legislations."

In short, the Congo State argues, "If we have done wrong, so have you; and you are not one whit better than we are." It will not hold water for a moment. That the Congo State's

Photograph by   MR. ROGER CASEMENT   *Stuart, London*

Decree of July, 1895, might have remained as innocuous as similar decrees issued by the European Powers having possessions in tropical Africa, is an assumption which has never been disputed. The enunciation of a theoretical right of sovereignty over uninhabited wilderness is a paper measure perfectly harmless and legitimate in itself; it may, indeed, become useful to protect at some future date the Colony from the schemes of adventurers attracted by mineral or other natural wealth. But when these theoretical rights of sovereignty over territory in Africa, having been satisfactorily inscribed on thick parchment, signed, sealed, and put away with due pomp, in European archives, are made a pretext for subsequently treating all territory not actually built upon or in cultivation as "vacant," followed by a claim to ownership over every product of commercial value which the territory in Africa supplies, then it is a very different matter. The Congo State did not stop at the enunciation of a harmless platitude. By a succession of decrees it broadened those "vacant" lands, until the point was reached when everything had become "vacant," save where the native had built his village, and was cultivating his plantations for food consumption.* All land, "which the natives do not occupy in the sense which must be given to that word"—the Leopoldian "sense," of course—became *terre domaniale*. And still the Congo State remained in the "domaine" of theory, and still its decrees were so much waste paper, and as ineffective as a wasp without its sting. The Congo State had not "expropriated natives" in proclaiming "its ownership of waste land." It had not "expropriated natives" by a series of decrees which, on paper, deprived them of all ancestral tenure outside the clearings round their villages. But by those decrees *it had paved the way for expropriation if ever these decrees came to be applied in practice*. In 1891 the time came, and the Sovereign of the Congo State drafted secret instructions, and in secret despatched them to his Commissioners, ordering those decrees to be applied; and applied they were, with the results which we have seen in the previous chapters. The instructions bade the Commissioners "take urgent and necessary measures to

* That the Congo State has any more regard for the natives in their villages than outside of them, or respects native plantations any more than rubber forests, is, of course, absurd. The whole argument is a piece of bluff, draped in legal phraseology, from beginning to end. The evidence adduced, in Consul Casement's report, is overwhelmingly conclusive on the point. In theory, the native has some sort of right to his village and plantations; in practice, their village grounds are no more theirs than any of the grounds of that vast country, and the produce from their plantations belongs to the State.

preserve the fruits of the Domaine, especially ivory and rubber," or, in other words, to preserve the products of economic value which the "vacant lands" contained. A crop of circulars drafted locally followed the receipt of the instructions; forbidding the natives to hunt elephants, unless they brought the tusks to the State stations; forbidding the natives to collect rubber, unless they brought it to the State stations; and warning European merchants "purchasing such articles from the natives, whose right to collect them the State only recognised provided that they were brought to it," that they "would be looked upon as receivers of stolen goods, and denounced to the judicial authorities." The policy laid down in those regulations in the Congo State has followed ever since. Therein have the actions of the Congo State differed from the actions of the European Powers on whose level it ventures to place itself. Unhappily, a still later feature of the Congo State's policy—to wit, its delegation of proprietorship over "vacant" lands and over the articles of commercial value contained therein to financiers with whom it had contracted debts, and others—has, within the last few years, found imitators in France and Germany. But there is a brighter side even to that picture, because of those two Powers one has already recognised, and the other is fast recognising, that the *Concessionnaire* conception is an impossible and imbecile conception if it be not accompanied by the forced enslavement of the native, which neither of these Powers is disposed to tolerate within its over-sea possessions.*

It now behoves us to examine in closer detail, in the light of the principles embodied in the Berlin Act, the claim of the State as to its rights of proprietorship over the territories of the Congo Basin entrusted to the stewardship of King Leopold. In the first place, where are such rights to be found? In the Berlin Act? I defy any Belgian jurist to quote them. It is not enough to repeat, parrot-like, that the Congo State has adhered to the Berlin Act, because the Berlin Act did not forbid the Congo State from appropriating everything of any commercial value in the Congo territories! But that is precisely what the Act of Berlin did forbid, not in so many words, perhaps—no more than it forbade in so many words the taking of hostages from native tribes in order to enforce taxation, nor the chaining up of women to accelerate the production of food-stuffs, nor a dozen other concomitants of the "moral and material regeneration" policy. The Act of Berlin laid down categorically that commerce should be free and unrestricted in the Congo Basin, that no monopolies or privileges

* *Vide* M. Dubief's report on the French Colonial Budget for 1904.

in matters of trade or commerce should be granted therein, and that the rights of the natives should be respected. Those were the three main co-ordinate requirements, and although indicated in the briefest fashion in the Articles of the Act, the protocols show clearly what the Powers meant when they authorised their representatives to attach their signatures to that document. The Congolese jurists have sought to establish that all that was intended by "freedom of trade" was the non-imposition of differential duties. But that is a narrowing down of the commercial clause of the Act, for which no justification exists.

"The Berlin Act—to quote once more the passage in the Congo State's defence—in its text or in its Protocols does not restrain either the right of property on the part of individuals, or on that of bodies, or the free exercise of its use or its effects.*
"Liberty of commerce such as it has been defined, is in nothing exclusive of the right of property, that not being a 'commercial monopoly' of the kind which the Berlin Act prohibits."

The above should be bracketed with two other passages from the same publication:

"The field of action in trade open to individuals in the Congo has never been, and is not restricted; throughout the whole territory this commerce can be carried on in what is legitimate. . . ."
"In law and in equity no one can be deprived of his property except for a just and previously-agreed-upon indemnity."

Before analysing these passages, may I ask the reader to bear in mind this, that, owing to the heavy cost of transport from the far interior of Africa, only two articles can at present be dealt with—ivory and rubber †—these two articles forming, as has been previously shown, practically the entire export of the Congo State, with the exception of a little palm-oil and kernels from the Lower River, and a few thousand pounds' worth of "oddments" not worth considering.

Therefore, when we talk of "commerce" in the Congo territories, the term refers virtually to rubber and ivory, and to ivory in a relatively small and rapidly diminishing quantity.

Now, when the Congo State tells us that liberty of commerce, as defined in the Berlin Act, is "in nothing exclusive of the right of property," the only possible reply to the contention is that whatever value it may contain to minds saturated in a sort of fourth-class legal jugglery, to the plain man who sees the interpretation placed by the Congo State on the word "property," it conveys nought but a contradiction in terms, and

* *Vide* Chapter I.
† Gum-copal would also pay carriage, and a little is being exported under circumstances detailed in Consul Casement's report, *op. cit.*

amounts, in practice, to a transparent and dishonest absurdity. Did the plenipotentiaries of the Berlin Act know what constituted "trade and commerce" in Equatorial Africa? What impartial inquirer can doubt it? Can it be seriously maintained that when they stipulated that trade or commerce should be allowed to follow its natural developments, they were talking about something they did not understand? It is simply ridiculous to suggest such a thing. Besides, the speech of Baron Lambermont, the Belgian delegate, is specific. Said Baron Lambermont, ". . . Mr. Woerman, the most competent authority on these subjects, has explained to us how, in these countries, commerce is carried on *exclusively by barter* . . .," that is to say, by bartering European merchandise against raw material, against produce collected by the native of the country. That is the only trade which exists in Western Africa. What other trade could exist,* or has ever existed, except the slave-trade?

Then how, in the name of common sense, can liberty of commerce remain either for the European or the native when the Congo State has declared that the elements which constitute that commerce *are its* PROPERTY? when the very decrees of the Congo State prove that it allows no freedom to the native to dispose of those elements of commerce whose ownership of the same the State does not admit, either before or after they are gathered, but *which claims them for itself?* when, in point of fact, it has destroyed commerce in the Congo territories † and has substituted for it a system of Government slavery, carried out either directly or by proxy? The words "commerce" or "trade" applied to transactions between the European and the African in tropical Africa necessitate two entities, and involve two conditions—a seller, a purchaser; the possession by the seller of articles to sell, the possession by the purchaser of articles wherewith to purchase. If we eliminate one or other or both these entities, one or other or both these conditions, the commercial relationship is itself eliminated. If, notwithstanding the elimination of this commercial relationship, the African continues to produce in large quantities those articles which are required by European industrialism, and which, let it be repeated, he alone can gather, then must it be obvious to the meanest understanding that the relationship between the European and the African in tropical Africa has altered, and that, whatever it may be, it is not, and cannot by any possibility be, "commercial."

* The introduction of currency merely duplicates transactions.
† The Lower Congo excepted. There the Congo State has indirectly almost destroyed it by taxation and by depopulating the country.

THE "PROPERTY" PLE...

The sophistry of the Congo State is equall[y...]
second passage I have quoted.

Individuals, it asserts, can trade on the C[ongo]
only in "*what is legitimate*," the truth being, o[f...]
only two articles such individuals could by any [chance deal]
in at all are rubber and ivory, and trade in th[ose, of]
course, illegitimate, because rubber and ivory [in those]
territories *are the property of the State!*

The Act of Berlin forbade commercial monopoly or privilege. The Congo State attempts to elude that point in similar fashion. The elements which constitute trade *having become the property of the State*, it virtually follows that whether the State's Department of the Interior compels the native to collect those "elements"—that is, rubber and ivory—or whether it delegates its powers to the Trusts it has formed, which it controls, and in whose profits it shares, the State cannot be accused of having granted a "commercial monopoly!" Was there ever such a series of palpable subterfuges?

The Congo State now claims to have appropriated, not in theory, but in fact, the entire Congo territories. It says so explicitly in its reply to the British Note.* It thereby excludes many millions of natives from the slightest proprietary rights, not only in their land, but in the raw material which their land produces, treating them in effect as degraded serfs, wherever it can establish its authority by the help of its 30,000 soldiers, and in the same breath protests that "law and equity both forbid deprivation of property except by just and previously-agreed-upon indemnity!" Indeed, its claim to proprietorship extends to the very bodies of the people themselves!

At the same time the Congo State keeps up its double-faced attitude in Africa with quite remarkable ingenuity. The occasion may arise when its representatives on the spot, in portions of the territory adjoining the territory of other Powers, may be formally asked by some new arrival in, say, British or German territory, what regulations a merchant must conform to in order to trade in the "Congo Free State." If such an individual were to receive a communication telling him he was not allowed in the country, it might find its way to some European Foreign Office or pestilent journalist, and give rise to unpleasant questions; so, although the Congo State advances in Europe, as a piece of diplomatic arrogance, the preposterous claim that "no unappropriated" land is left in the Congo territories (while urging *inter alia* that the land is "vacant" so far as native rights are concerned), the State is quite ready to play an outwardly

* "Quoique le système ainsi préconisé ne puisse avoir d'application dans l'Etat du Congo puisqu'il ne s'y trouve *plus de terres inappropriées*."

erent game in Africa. I have before me the reply, dated June, 1903, sent by one of the officials of the Katanga Trust to a merchant established in Northern Rhodesia, enumerating the conditions under which the applicant might open trade in the Congo territory. The official in question quotes the laws of November 21, 1896, and May 17, 1898. Here is a summary of the requirements of the Congo State. To trade in rubber (that and ivory, as I have already explained, are the only two articles which *can* be traded in) a licence must be obtained from the Governor-General in Boma (3000 miles away); if answered at once, and in the affirmative—which we may feel pretty sure would not be the case either way—three months at the very least would elapse before the reply would reach the applicant. "Such a licence costs 5000 francs." *The applicant would therefore have to pay, provided he got his licence, a preliminary sum of £200.* On all goods imported, other than spirits, articles for Divine Service (*sic*), agricultural tools, and one or two other specifically mentioned things, the import duty is 10 per cent., and "to this the customs officer adds 20 per cent. for transporting expenses to the frontier." So there is a 30 per cent. import duty to begin with on cottons, brass wire, handkerchiefs, and other genuine trading articles, plus the £200 licence. But the export duties "lick creation," as the American would say. *On rubber there is an export duty of 90 francs per 100 kilos., or £3 12s. for every 200 lbs., or £36 per ton.* In other words, trading, in the most important article of trade, is made just as absolutely prohibitive as if the applicant were informed point blank that he was not allowed in the country. And this is the Congo *Free* State.

I am told by those whose opinions I am bound to treat with deference that this is a legal question. For the life of me I cannot see it. The defence of the Congo State appears, the more one looks at it, as nothing but a feeble attempt to justify the most vulgar swindle perpetrated at the expense of the European Powers, and with the most terrible effects upon the natives. It is with facts—with facts arising out of specific causes—not with judicial dissertations and theoretical rights of sovereignty, that we are called upon to deal. The one paragraph in the British Note which lacks in conciseness is the paragraph referring to the partition of land by the Congo State. It gave the Congo State a rare chance for the exercise of that tortuous political Jesuitism in which it excels. Nevertheless, the meaning of the British Government, though needlessly involved, is clear enough. Here is the passage:

"His Majesty's Government in no way deny either that the State has the right to partition the State lands among *bonâ fide* occupants, or that the natives will, as the land is so divided out among *bonâ fide* occupiers, lose their rights of roaming over it and collecting the natural fruits which it produces. But His Majesty's Government maintain that until unoccupied land is reduced into individual occupation, and so long as the produce can only be collected by the native, the native should be free to dispose of that produce as he pleases."

Now, it is obvious from the above that the actions which H.M. Government do not disapprove of are subject to the existence of a given state of things which in point of fact does not exist, and, what is more, *never will exist.* " So long," says the Note, "as the produce can only be collected by the native, the native should be free to dispose of that produce as he pleases." Precisely; but why the preamble? The produce of the forests of Equatorial Africa can never, until the end of time, be collected by any one but the native. The paragraph would have been better *minus* the padding.

Solely on its merits, and presuming that the defence were not the last resort to justify, by pitiful legal quibbles, the committal of the most systematic outrages of modern times, we should have to admit an absolute revolution in all our preconceived notions of good and evil, of morality and immorality, of the knowledge of African conditions and requirements, of the entire principles guiding European effort in Africa, before the Congo State's apologies could even be discussed. Have the economic conditions of Equatorial Africa changed so wholly and completely since the Berlin Act was signed, that what was considered right then is wrong now? Has the African native ceased to be a being whose life and property the Powers of Western Europe, in 1885, thought it necessary, in their own ultimate interests, as well as in common decency, to protect, and become a being so low that it were fantastic foolery to credit him with rights of any kind whatsoever, a slave so debased that only forced labour at the end of the lash or the point of a bayonet can make of him even a docile beast? Have the material elements which constituted trade eighteen years ago become, by the touch of a magician's wand, something entirely different? Has commerce, which used to be regarded as a civilising medium, become an agency of evil so great that forced production must be accepted as a panacea? Has the act of purchasing certain articles from the native on a fair basis of exchange become an outrage against international usage in the relations between peoples of the higher and lower "culture"? Have those gloomy forests of the Congo, so rich in certain vegetable products required by modern industry, so stupendously vast in extent, so virgin of anything approaching "occupation" by the white man or his soldiers, suddenly become suitable to the enforcement of rules and regulations applicable only to the Western world, and then only after twenty centuries of development under the Christian creed? Is the basis of relationship prevailing between European and Negro to sink back, at the opening of the twentieth century, to the level of the over-sea Slave-Trade epoch?

This is not a matter for lawyers, but for enlightened statesmanship and civilised public opinion to settle once and for all, by an unhesitating negative reply to the above questions, followed by speedy, positive action.

CHAPTER IX

NATIVE LAND-TENURE, TRADE, AND LABOUR

" I admit that labour is imposed upon the natives (le travail est imposé), but it is in the interest of all, and when the work is done, the native is paid."—M. DE FAVEREAU, Belgian Minister for Foreign Affairs.*
" They are not entitled to anything : what is given to them is a pure gratuity."—M. SMET DE NAEYER, Belgian Premier.†

THE twistings and wrigglings of Congo State diplomacy, whatever attraction they may have for learned gentlemen like Professor Descamps, who recently devoted a volume to proving "judicially" and to his entire satisfaction that the Congo State represented the perfectibility of human foresight and goodness in the treatment of native races, can only inspire the plain man with contempt and repulsion. Stripped of its trappings, the policy of King Leopold stands naked before the world, a loathsome thing. It is the old, old story : the story of evil and greed and lust perpetrated upon a weaker people, but never before, assuredly, has the hypocrisy with which such deeds have been cloaked, attained to heights so sublime. Never before has hypocrisy been so successful. For nearly twenty years has the Sovereign of the Congo State posed before the world as the embodiment of philanthropic motive, high intent, humanitarian zeal, lofty and stimulating righteousness. No more marvellous piece of acting has been witnessed on the world's stage than this.

And let us remember that if the story in itself is old, it nevertheless contains distinctive features of peculiarity. The *conquisitadores* of Peru were, after all, the repositories of the national purpose, and their ruthless cruelties were but the concomitants of the national policy. The over-sea slave-trade, first started by Portugal under the plea of religious zeal, and afterwards continued by her, and adopted by other Powers for frankly material reasons, was acquiesced in by the national conscience of the times, and was put to national ends. But what nation is interested in the perpetuation of the system

* Congo debate in Belgian House, July, 1903.   † Ibid.

which has converted the Congo territories into a charnel-house? Not Belgium, whose Congo turn-over, as we have noted already, amounts, after nearly twenty years, to 1 per cent. of her total trade!* Such a thing has never been known as one man with a few partners controlling, for his benefit and that of his associates, one million square miles of territory, and wielding the power of life and death over many millions of human beings.

And what has rallied to his side the support of a certain class of latter-day colonial politicians and amateurs of all that is bad in the frenzied expansionism of the hour? I do not speak of paid journalistic or legal hacks. How can one explain the fascination which a policy absolutely selfish has nevertheless exercised over the minds of many? To those whose business it has been to follow the evolution of European thought concerning tropical Africa during the last decade, the answer to the question need not be sought for. The Sovereign of the Congo State is the living personation; and the administrative system he has conceived and applied is the working embodiment, of the theory that the Negro will not produce without compulsion; and that if tropical Africa can ever be developed, it must be through a *régime* of forced labour. Thus has the Sovereign of the Congo State become a sort of *point d'appui* for the thoughtless, the inexperienced, the inhumane. He has been the one strong man, resolute in his views, inflexible in carrying them out. His would-be imitators have never been deceived by the " Property " quibble. They have known what his policy meant, although they may have conveniently shut out some of its unpleasant details from their mental vision. As Mr. Stephen Gwynne has justly remarked, " This new servitude has in it the worst of all elements, in that the slave-owner no longer sees the slaves at work, but sits at home and receives his dividends." † But the success of the Sovereign of the Congo State in maintaining with marvellous ability and resource the New African Slave Trade has enlisted the support and the sympathies of all those who, in their haste to get rich, would to-morrow convert the black man throughout Africa, if they could, into a tenant

---

* It must not be supposed that the Belgian newspapers have always followed the slavish attitude towards the Congo State which prevails among them to-day. Thus the *Réforme* of September 14, 1896, wrote: " Si l'Etat persiste dans son systeme actuel, il pourrait bien voir les gouvernements mêmes qui ont été ses complices ou ses dupes, forcés par l'opinion publique de l'Europe à se réunir en une Conférence qui ferait, elle, l'enquête sérieuse que Belges et Congolais n'auraient pas voulu faire, même pour laver leur honneur."

† *Fortnightly Review*, March, 1903.

NATIVE LAND-TENURE, TRADE, ETC.

on his own land, a serf doomed to ceaseless and unremunerated toil, in the interests of cosmopolitan exploitationists in Europe.

The peculiar conditions under which the Congo State was created has greatly intensified the mischief, already considerable, of the existence of such a focus of pernicious influence. Its neighbours in Europe and Africa—for if the arms of the Congo State are in Africa, its brain, it cannot be too often stated, is in Brussels—have |seen within the last decade the growth of a great revenue through direct "taxation," so-called: the sudden upspringing of an enormously valuable export of raw material which the unremitting labour of literally millions of men could alone have produced; the acquisition of colossal profits by nominally trading Companies—and this while their own possessions were advancing but slowly. They have seen Belgian colonial securities leap to heights undreamt of; fortunes made in a few hours; huge dividends earned after a year or two's working;—all these striking results accomplished by Belgian tyros at colonisation, by a so-called State run to all intents and purposes by a single man. And so, greatly in ignorance, urged on by designing men who had their own ends to serve, two of the Congo State's neighbours in Africa thought they would try their hands at a system which could yield such magnificent material returns. But being civilised nations, they have found, or are ascertaining, that the system cannot be carried out in practice without unending barbarity, and they have but added to their difficulties.

The doctrine of forced production is based upon data deliberately falsified. The whole thing, to put it bluntly, is a lie—a mere excuse to palliate the exploits of the buccaneer. The two essentials of this doctrine are, denial to the native of any rights in his land and in the products of commercial value his land produces; to which is added physical force to compel the native to gather those products for the European.

It is simply untrue that the native of Western Africa will not work unless compelled. Experience, facts, the existence of which cannot be disputed because they are there palpably and unmistakably before us, disprove the assertion, which is not believed in by those who make it.

Experience, reason, common sense, and justice tells us that it is as wrong as it is foolish, and as foolish as it is wrong, to treat native rights of land-tenure as non-existent. "In dealing with the natives," says Sir William MacGregor, one of our most experienced West African administrators, "one must never touch their rights in land." Similarly we find Doctor Zimmerman, an eminent German colonial authority, declaring that the "protection of property is the surest means" to develop Africa rationally. No student of African questions needs to be reminded of the passionate insistence with which the late Mary Kingsley urged the conservation of native land-tenure, with a force of conviction and a scientific perception of the needful which has never been equalled. Wherever native law and custom have been studied in tropical Africa, we find the same doctrine preached, "If you want to govern successfully and justly, respect native land-tenure."

Says M. Bohn, one of the ablest Frenchmen who have handled West African affairs :

"Land laws exist in these countries as they do in Europe, and have not been overthrown by wars of conquest or change of rulers. There is nothing more antagonistic to the native mind, whether in the case of Chiefs or subjects, than to have their rights of land-tenure discussed, let alone taken from them."

Or take another experienced Frenchman, M. Fondère :

"The right to sell his products to whomsoever he may please cannot be denied to the native, because he has always possessed it. Moreover, all stipulations to the contrary notwithstanding, it would be quite illusory to think of taking this right away from the native. That could only be done by force of arms."

The best school of Colonial thought in France is coming to the same conclusion, witness recent published statements by M. Cousin, M. Chailley Bert, and M. Dubief. One could give pages of quotations to the same effect from Dennett, Ellis, Clozel, Delafosse, and many others,* but it is unnecessary. Every Governor of a British West African Possession knows that land-tenure is, as a recognised authority has aptly put it, perhaps the "greatest ruling passion of the negro ;" and knows that in every legislative measure he adopts, this factor of the internal politics with which he has to deal is the paramount factor. The most distinguished amongst French Government officials in Western Africa are absolutely of the same opinion ; for example, the present Governor-General, M. Roume, the late Governor-General, M. Ballay, the late Governor of the French Ivory Coast, M. Binger (now head of the African Department of the French Colonial Office), and also the present Governor of that Colony, M. Clozel. The only two West African natives who

---

* "We must leave to the native his land, and no longer attempt any direct means to alienate him therefrom."—Chailley-Bert in *La Quinzaine Coloniale*. "The Belgian system, which is the apotheosis of monopoly, and consequently of arbitrariness, . . . has as its object the rapid accumulation of dividends, and leads to the exhaustion of the country."— Lucien Hubert in *La Politique Africaine* (Dejarric et Cie., Paris). See also the pamphlet by Gaston Bouteillier published by Pezous, Albi, France.

NATIVE LAND-TENURE, TRADE, ETC.

have established themselves as authorities, Sarbah,* the great Fanti lawyer, and Blyden, who though American born has lived the greater part of his life in West Africa, and traces his descent to the Ibo tribe, are naturally of the same opinion. Better far is it for European Governments to respect native land-tenure even to the point which, to its credit be it said, the British Colonial Office has followed in the matter of the Gold Coast mining industry, much to the annoyance of various estimable people; than to abandon a principle which, if once set aside, paves the way for a whole crop of legislative abuses, and puts us on the path which must lead to denying to the native any proprietary right over the articles of value which his land produces, and consequently to slavery.

Wherever their forms have been examined, native laws of land-tenure † have been found to repose upon just principles, to be thoroughly well understood, recognised, and adhered to by the people of the land, and to be worthy of serious and sympathetic study. Tropical Africa is an immensity, and much of it has never been trodden by the white man's foot, let alone observed by the white man's brain, and consequently native laws of land-tenure in a very small portion of it only have been gone into. The results of such study as has been made are on record, and not only do they exclude the idea that native land-tenure is the imaginary product of certain so-called negrophiles in this country, but they prove that it is part and parcel of the social organisation of the people, a knowledge of which, as every competent official knows, is essential to good government in tropical Africa. Such knowledge, however, is not essential to slave-driving, and we need not be surprised that the Congo State dismisses the idea that such a thing as *native* rights in land can by any possibility be held to exist at all, and affectedly ignores any other proprietary rights to land but the ones which it has vested in itself or in its associates.‡

* See "Fanti Customary Law" in particular. Blyden's works are numerous.

† Roughly stated, the laws of most tropical African peoples with regard to land are very similar. The land laws of the old native kingdom of Congo are given by Mr. Dennett in his "The Laws and Customs of the Bavili."

‡ "Dans l'un comme dans l'autre cas, il ne se conçoit pas que les fruits du sol puissent être reservés à d'autres qu'au propriétaire sous le prétexte qu'il n'est pas apte, en faite, à recolter ces produits de son fonds" (*Congo State's reply to British Note*). The "propriétaire" here is, of course, either the State or the *concessionnaire;* and again, "Jamais au Congo que nous sachions les demandes d'achat des produits naturels n'ont été adréssées aux légitimes propriétaires" (*Ibid.*). Here, once more, the "propriétaires" are not the natives, but the *concessionnaires*—the Government, acting by proxy. And even this passage of the reply is

A European Government may be justified in evolving theoretical paper rights of sovereignty over land which—and such land does exist in many parts of tropical Africa—is, through pestilence, inter-tribal warfare, emigration, or some such cause, really and truly "vacant." It is the clear duty of the European over-lord in tropical Africa to draft such laws and regulations affecting land duly held under native tenure, which shall make it difficult, if not impossible, for the native owner to be cheated out of his land by adventurers and swindlers. But to treat native land-tenure as a factor of no account in Afro-European relationship, on the plea that native ownership disappears with the simple enunciation of a theoretical right of proprietorship in Europe, or by signing a piece of parchment conveying the proprietorship of some thousands of square miles of African territory and all that therein is to a group of financiers, is merely an attempt to cover spoliation, robbery, and violence under legal *formulæ*.

To sweep away native land-tenure is the preliminary step to forced labour, and forced labour in tropical Africa means the enslavement of the African by the European-armed and European-directed African; and that, in tropical Africa, spells the coming destruction of European effort.

And so, from denying the rights of the natives to their land, we come by natural sequence to the doctrine of forced production. The Congo State claims that, by its system—

"it is permissible for the native to find by work the remuneration * which contributes to augment his well-being.† Such is, in fact, one of the ends of the general policy of the State to promote the regeneration of the race, by instilling into him a higher idea of the necessity of labour.‡ It can be imagined that Governments conscious of their moral responsibility do not advocate among inferior races the right to idleness and laziness with, as their consequence, the maintenance of an anti-civilising social state."

Could hypocrisy reach serener heights? The Congo State's consciousness of "moral responsibility" compels it to keep on a war footing an army of nearly 20,000 men,§ so that the "regeneration of the race" shall not be hindered by this inbred "idleness and laziness."

---

untrue, because Rabinek, the Austrian trader, had obtained from the *concessionnaire*, and from the State itself, licences to trade for which he had paid, and yet he was persecuted and condemned to a year's imprisonment! (See Part IV.) The contention is, therefore, doubly dishonest.
    * Mark the word "remuneration," and turn back to Chapter VIII.
    † Mark the word "well-being," and read Part III.
    ‡ "Our only programme, I am anxious to repeat, is the work of moral and material regeneration."—*King Leopold*.
    § And to allow its Trusts to arm at least half as many irregulars.

NATIVE LAND-TENURE, TRADE, ETC. 95

The Congo State authorities, however, do not appear to have been particularly impressed with the "laziness and idleness" of the native when, in June, 1896, they attached to their own *Bulletin Officiel* the report of an agricultural tour undertaken by M. Emile Laurent, *before the completion of the Matadi-Stanley Pool Railway*. This gentleman was sent on an extensive survey to report upon the "agricultural" possibilities of the country, the characteristics of the various tribes, etc. His testimony to the "idleness" of the native is emphatic. Referring to the region of the Cataracts (Lower Congo, between Matadi and Stanley-Pool), he says :

"It is here that the natives often build their villages; they plant the palm tree and the *sofa*, which grows well. In this neighbourhood they cultivate sweet potatoes, manioc, and ground-nuts. . . . There is also sandy ground in the district; they form rather large plains, often utilised for the cultivation of the ground-nut. This plant gives abundant crops. Formerly the natives brought the ground-nuts to Matadi to the Dutch factory, in exchange for salt, which they in turn sold to the people of the interior."

Not much sign of "idleness" there, at the time that particular report was penned, apparently. A little later on there was "idleness;" but it was the inertia of death, for death and depopulation had stalked through the land in the shape of forced labour and forced porterage. The published narratives of M. Pierre Mille and Baron de Mandat Grancy may be consulted with advantage in that connection.* The ground-nut trade of the Lower Congo region, it is useful to remember, was a very large one before the Congo State assumed the reins of government in the river. It has now virtually disappeared. The Congo Government has recently inaugurated a system of forced labour in the Cataracts region, in order to revive the cultivation of this nut. Reference is made to the subject in Chapter XX.

We will follow M. Laurent on his journey. Of the Stanley-Pool and Eastern Kwango region he writes as follows :—

"From what Messrs. Costermans and Deghilage, two officials who have visited this district, tell me, the ground rubber covers vast extents of sandy soil, and the natives exploit it on a large scale. Not long ago the rubber from this region was exported to Portuguese Angola, and there was a considerable trade in it. M. Deghilage tells me that he has seen on the native markets of Kenghe-Diadia thirty tons of this rubber exposed for sale every four days."

That was before the Congo State was paramount in the land; the days when the native could *sell* his produce on

---

* Or Mr. Fox-Bourne's book, "Civilisation in Congoland," which contains many useful extracts from those two works.

legitimate commercial lines ; the days when the native either bartered his rubber with other native traders from Portuguese territory, who afterwards sold it to the Portuguese on the coast, or direct with European merchants established in Portuguese territory. Compare the above passage—which, mind you, is an official report—with the claim of the Congo State put forward to-day, to have taught the native of the Congo territories how to collect rubber! "The policy of the State," says the official reply to the British Note, "has not, as has been asserted, killed trade ; it has, on the contrary, created it." It did not create the ground-nut trade of the Lower Congo, or the rubber trade of the Kwango, on the testimony of its own expert! But it has certainly killed the former ; and as for the latter, the rubber which used to *belong* to the native, and which the native *sold*, is now the *property* of the Kwango Trust, for which the native is expected to collect it, on the usual regenerating lines. One fails to detect any signs of "idleness" in the Kwango region at the time of M. Laurent's report.

From the Kwango district, M. Laurent takes us to Lake Leopold II. district. Here we learn that :

"I saw a rubber vine which was ten centimetres in diameter and bore numerous transversal incisions, which is a proof that the natives know and practice the right method of extracting rubber. . . . I also noticed the large quantities of gum-copal which is to be found in the neighbourhood of the lake, and which the natives extract from the ground at the foot of the trees along the river."

Always the same peculiar form of "laziness." The district of Lake Leopold II. is now the centre of the secret revenues department, the *Domaine de la Couronne*, the scene of the horrors and desolation so graphically described by Consul Casement and the Rev. A. E. Scrivener, *vide* Chapter XV. In the Kasai and Lualaba region the "idleness" of the native becomes still more apparent from this report :

"The population is comparatively dense, and is distinguished for its truly remarkable trading and labour capacities."

The feeling of "moral responsibility" entertained by the State towards these particular tribes may be estimated from Morrison's account, which is given in Chapter XVII. The "idleness" of the native, "from the Sankuru River to Nyangwe," is simply deplorable, for, according to M. Laurent :

"Around these truly negro towns the bush is cultivated for a distance of an hour and a half's walk, and the plantations are often as carefully cultivated as they are in Flanders. The natives cultivate manioc, maize, millet, rice, *voandzou*, and ground-nuts. The latter yield magnificent crops."

Photograph by MR. H. R. FOX-BOURNE *Elliott & Fry*
(Secretary of the Aborigines Protection Society)

NATIVE LAND-TENURE, TRADE, ETC.

So much for the "idleness" of the Congo native, as observed by a trained "agriculturist" employed by the Congo State and as embodied in an official report. It is always well to confound the Congo State authorities with their own published documents; but men who traded with, or travelled among, the Upper Congo natives in many parts of the territory before the grip of Africa's regenerator tightened upon the land, know well that these unfortunate people are no more idle than any of the tropical African peoples, among whom labour other than the labour required for the supply of food-stuffs is not an economic necessity; that their commercial instincts were very highly developed, that they were eager to trade with the white man, and did trade indirectly with the white man; and that, given a fair chance, a large and legitimate trade would have sprung up there, as it has everywhere else in West Africa, when the native has been given markets and decent treatment.

Is this a general statement easy to make, but difficult to prove, so far as the Congo natives are concerned? Let us see. Well, in the first place, we have the official report of M. Laurent. But, after all, that is one man's statement. One of the earlier pioneers of the Congo was M. Herbert Ward. Here is a passage from his book, which rather bears out M. Laurent:

"The rocky banks and tree-hidden bays concealed no worse foe than the keen Bateke or Byanzi trader, thirsting, not for the white man's blood, but for his cotton cloths and bright brass rods, and anxious only to get the better of him in bargaining, when his natural timidity and suspicion had been lulled to sleep by the exhibition of such 'inconsidered trifles' of this description as my fast-failing and scanty stock enabled me to display whenever my own wants or the necessities of my men induced us to call at any of the villages we might pass."

There we have the picture of a riverain population of keen trading instincts.

With Mr. R. E. Dennett, whose ethnological studies are well known, and who is probably an unrivalled authority on the commercial capacities of the Congo tribes, among whom he has lived for some twenty years, I have exchanged occasionally a friendly correspondence. Some few weeks ago I wrote to him—he was then in Africa—pointing out the State's claim to have introduced commerce in the Upper Congo, and asking him what he thought of it. His reply is now before me.

"Certainly most of the trade," he writes, "done in the Lower Congo came from the Upper Congo from beyond the Kasai. In 1879 I assisted —— to trade in Kinsembo, and we bought quite a lot of ivory and rubber coming in from the Upper Congo. In 1880 I was in Ambrizette, and we bought large quantities of the same produce coming from the same district and passing through 'Moaquita's' town. About 1881 most of the traders on the South-West Coast opened up above Musuku, at Noki, Ango-Ango, Kola-Kola, and Matadi,* and as a proof that the Coast trade came, for the most part, from the Upper Congo, it may be stated that as soon as these firms commenced buying at these places great quantities of rubber and ivory, the Coast trade fell off enormously. This can again be proved by the fact that as soon as the Belgian Companies went into the interior (*i.e.* the Upper Congo, above the Cataracts, which divide the Upper from the Lower Congo, now connected by a railway) the factories below Matadi (*i.e.* in the Lower Congo, below the Cataracts) fared very badly, only getting that trade which came from the Portuguese Upper Congo."

So, on this evidence—the competency of which no one acquainted with West African affairs will presume to discuss—we find that long before M. Laurent went on his tour of inspection, long before Mr. Ward recorded his experiences, the natives of the Upper Congo were selling large quantities of African produce to the Ba-Congo peoples—ivory and rubber—who in turn carried that produce to the Lower Congo along the caravan road of 200 odd miles, which their feet had trodden and made. And this testimony, let us bear carefully in mind, is amply corroborated in the Protest drawn up by the Belgian companies alluded to in Mr. Dennett's letter (and whose treatment at the hands of "Bula Matadi" are fully set forth in Part II.) when they declared :

"To forbid the natives from selling the ivory and rubber from their forests and plains, which constitutes their hereditary birthright, and in which they have traded from time immemorial, is a violation of natural rights."

Is any more proof needed to confirm the accuracy of my contention, that the natives of the Upper Congo, if they had been decently treated, would have built up a trade of infinitely greater volume, so far as the export of raw material is concerned, than the quantity wrung from them to-day by massacre and outrage ; while that produce, legitimately acquired, bartered for, traded for, would have necessitated an import "the counterpart of its value," bringing prosperity to the producer, progress, and development? Whether the reader considers additional proof to be necessary or not, I propose to adduce it, and from no less an authority than the late Sir Henry M. Stanley. Speaking at the London Chamber of Commerce in 1884, Stanley remarked :

"The fixed and permanent way (he was referring to a railway) which would be such a benefit to the Cataract region just described, would be of still greater benefit to the Upper Congo and its plain-like lands, and

---

* Places up the Lower Congo River.

NATIVE LAND-TENURE, TRADE, ETC. 99

to the keen, enterprising, high-spirited * peoples who occupy them. Even now many a flotilla descends the great river 500 miles down to Stanley-Pool,† to wait patiently for months before their goods can be disposed of to the Lower Congo caravans."

That was before a single European merchant had established himself beyond Matadi, and, therefore, long prior to the rubber "taxes" of "Bula Matadi"!

I began with a Belgian authority to drive my point home. I will end with another. In an official publication printed in Brussels in 1897 (in connection with the Brussels Exhibition of that year), under the auspices of "M. le Commandant Liebrechts," one of the principal Secretaries of State of the Congo Administration in Brussels, I find the following reference to the trading instincts of the great riverain tribe of the Batekes ‡ above Stanley-Pool:—

"To this incessant movement produced for long years is due that, much before the arrival of Europeans, the Congo river tribes as far even as the Aruwimi had European goods which had passed from hand to hand from the Coast, and had acquired extraordinary value."

That is a true statement, and the European merchandise was paid for by the native producer in rubber and ivory. Purchased from the factories in the Lower River by natives, transported by them for 200 weary miles along the Cataracts to the Upper River; sold by them to Upper River natives at the Pool against rubber and ivory, which rubber and ivory was carried down to the factories by the native middlemen who had brought up the goods to buy those articles; while the native middle-men in the Upper River, who, Stanley tells us, sometimes waited "for months," having disposed of their rubber and ivory, started off with full canoes to their customers along the banks of the mighty river and its branches. Such the trade—viewed in its native aspect—which "Bula Matadi" has wiped out by declaring the rubber and ivory of the Upper Congo to be its property, and by compelling the natives to produce it for nothing; such the natural commercial instincts of a people that it has crushed; such the commerce which the Berlin Act was intended not only to preserve, but even to keep unhampered by vexatious customs dues. What are we to think of the honesty

* Will any one who was acquainted with those peoples in 1884, and who has seen them recently, apply those adjectives to them now? Mr. Casement's report is peculiarly illuminating on this point. Will the reader bear also carefully in mind the word "occupy," and compare it with that convenient term "vacant" so dear to Congolese jurists?

† At the head of the Cataracts.

‡ These Batekes have now nearly all emigrated to the French Congo, abandoning Congo State territory. See Official White Book, *op. cit.*

of a Government which can declare in 1903 that it has "created trade" and taught the natives the art of collecting rubber, when it has destroyed trade which European enterprise and native energy had established?

Leaving the Congo, the commercial proclivities of the Negro meet us wherever we care to pursue our inquiry, and his alleged idleness vanishes into the mists of mendaciousness whence it originates. Every year the voluntary labour of the West African Negro supplies Europe with nearly four millions sterling of palm-oil and kernels alone, requiring infinite time, infinite toil, and infinite trouble in their preparation ;* employing hundreds of thousands of African men and women. The voluntary labour of the natives of the French Colony of Senegal and the British Colony of Gambia supplies Europe every year with ground-nuts to the tune of over one million sterling.

Last year the voluntary labour of the natives of the Gold Coast supplied Europe with £100,000 worth of high-class cocoa, and they and their relatives on the French Ivory Coast sent us £500,000 worth of mahogany. From West Africa the Negro sends us every year thousands of tons of precious cabinet woods, involving the expenditure of an enormous amount of physical labour in felling and squaring the logs, and floating them down the rivers and creeks to the sea. Europe, and especially Great Britain, rely to-day upon the voluntary labour of the Negro to relieve the intolerable strain of the cotton industry, groaning under the dead weight of dependence upon America for the source of the raw material, and the Negro is responding right gallantly to the demand. After only a few months' effort, Lagos is beginning to send us cotton, and Nigeria will do so just as soon as we can give her the light railway that she needs. In the five years ending with 1900 the trade of the British West African Possessions amounted to 43 millions sterling.

These are facts, and they are not got over by calling a man who points them out a "sentimentalist." But the apostles of coercion, and the upholders of the New Slave Trade, do not care for facts ; they prefer legal conundrums in which to wrap their selfish creed, and give it an appearance of respectability. Now, as in the days when the conscience of the world awoke to the iniquities of the over-sea slave-trade, we are flooded with hypocritical arguments drawn from false premises, with specious pleadings and judicial compositions designed to confuse the

* For a detailed description of the palm-oil and palm-kernel trade of West Africa, see " Affairs of West Africa " (London : William Heinemann, 1902).

NATIVE LAND-TENURE, TRADE, ETC. 101

judgment, cloud the understanding, and distort the teachings of history. The Congo State, as I have said before, is the incarnation of all this callous and pernicious humbug. We have fought it, a handful of us, from different standpoints for many a long year, and at last we have dragged the Government and public opinion along with us. We must go on fighting it until the diseases it has introduced into Africa and the virus with which it has temporarily saturated a portion of European thought are utterly destroyed. The one bulwark of the Negro in tropical Africa against the worst excesses of European civilisation is the determination of Europe to conserve his rights in his land and in his property. In helping him to develop his property on scientific lines ; in granting him internal peace ; in proving to him that he is regarded not as a brute, but as a partner in a great undertaking from which Europe and Africa will derive lasting benefit—Europe will be adopting the only just, right, and practical policy.

That was the policy laid down by the Powers in Berlin in 1885. Any other policy is doomed to ultimate failure and disaster to Europe,* and must result in untold misery to the peoples of tropical Africa. Any other policy must be resisted to the uttermost by all those who believe in the great future which is in store for tropical Africa wisely administered by the white man, and who have some regard for the honour of Europe and the just and humane treatment of the races of Africa.

* Just as the Van den Bosch "culture-system" in the Dutch East Indies perished amid universal execration after almost ruining the country.

CHAPTER X

THE THIRD TEST OF CONGO STATE RULE—MILITARISM, MURDER, MUTILATION, AND THE TRAFFIC IN ARMS

> "The wretched negroes, however, who are still under the sole sway of their traditions, have that horrible belief that victory is only decisive when the enemy, fallen beneath their blows, is annihilated. The soldiers of the State, who are recruited necessarily from among the natives, do not immediately forsake those sanguinary habits that have been transmitted from generation to generation. The example of the white officer and wholesome military discipline gradually inspire in them a horror of human trophies of which they previously had made their boast."—KING LEOPOLD, in a letter to his Agents.

THE indispensable instrument of a policy which denies to the native of tropical Africa all rights in land, and in the products of economic value the land produces, but which requires, in order to maintain itself, vast quantities of those products, is an army of very large dimensions. The late Governor-General of the West African Possessions of France put the truth in one, fierce— M. Ballay was opposed to the New Slavery—terse expression. "The system," he said, necessitated "an armed soldier behind every producer." This the Sovereign of the Congo State thoroughly understood from the beginning. In the words of Pierre Mille,* another Frenchman of much African knowledge and experience, "The basis of the King's economic policy has been the formation of an army sufficiently strong to force the native to pay the rubber and ivory tax."

The International Association was born in an atmosphere of virtuous philanthropy. Philanthropic aspirations presided over its entry into the "family of nations," under the title of the "Congo Free State," in charge of a ruler dedicated "from his cradle to the exercise of every kind of freedom." † The ruler, upon whom fell the choice of the Powers, laid claim to the loftiest of human motives. To-day, the Congo State keeps on a war-footing a regular native army of nearly 20,000 men, armed with repeating rifles, while the Trusts it has created,

---

* "Au Congo Belge."
† Baron de Courcel. Protocol No. 9, Berlin Act, *op. cit.*

whose policy it controls, and in whose profits it shares, raise their own troops, which may be estimated at a further 10,000 to 15,000.* To-day, munitions of war pour into the Congo territories in one continuous stream. To-day, from almost every part of the Congo territories, the tale of fighting, more fighting, and again fighting comes with monotonous persistency.

When M. Georges Lorand declared in the Belgian House a few months ago that the Congo State's "work of civilisation" had been "an enormous and continual butchery," he was not exaggerating. The carnival of massacre, of which the Congo territories have been the scene for the last twelve years, must appal all those who have studied the facts. From 1890 onwards the records of the Congo State have been literally blood-soaked. Even at that early date, the real complexion of Congo State philanthropy was beginning to appear, but public opinion in Europe was then in its hoodwinked stage. It is instructive to quote from one or two of the earlier accounts which filtered through. In 1889, Mr. E. Sowerbutts, Secretary of the Manchester Geographical Society, published letters from the Lower Congo to the effect that "the Belgians' methods of trade were to employ 100 armed soldiers round each station to terrorise the natives into bringing them produce"—all, as the writer added bitterly, "in the name of philanthropy and no slavery." In March, 1891, further correspondence of the same nature from the Lower Congo was read at a meeting of the same Geographical Society.

"I would to God," ran one of the letters, "we had a population able to cope with these so-called philanthropists in the summary way they should be dealt with ; but alas ! the poor creatures are unarmed against the Snider rifles and machine-guns of the holy philanthropists."

Another letter speaks of atrocities committed upon young children by the State's soldiers ; of women and children being seized as prisoners in order to obtain carriers, and so on ; and the "prime-movers," continues the writer, "in this diabolical and unholy so-called civilising Power are actuated, we are told, by holy motives, by a sincere love for their fellow-men and black brothers."

Mr. R. Cobden Phillips, who presided over the meeting, gave it as his opinion that the whole question wanted investigating. "If an inquiry were made," he said, "it might be possible to

* From the accounts which reach me from one of these Trust's territories alone, where the non-regular troops are said to number nearly 10,000, I am inclined to think that the total number must be even greater. The British Consul (Africa, No. 1, 1904) estimates the figure at 10,000. I am inclined to think that had his travels carried him as far as the Katanga country, his estimates would have been higher.

obtain some guarantees against the continuance of the atrocities which had marked the history of the Congo State from the beginning." That was in 1891! The year previous, at the gathering held in London, on November 4, 1900, under the chairmanship of Sir Albert Rollit, M.P., to protest against the proposed imposition of import duties and to denounce the hypocrisy which attributed to philanthropic motives the desire of the Congo State to so impose them, it was shown on the testimony of Europeans on the spot, such as Mr. Herbert Ward and Colonel Williams, that the Congo State was exchanging natives captured by its soldiers in raids against ivory. Colonel Williams' letter to King Leopold was read to the meeting by Mr. Phillips, representing the Manchester Chamber of Commerce. Here is an extract from it :

"Your Majesty's Government has been, and is now, guilty of waging unjust and cruel wars again the natives, with the hope of securing slaves and women to minister to the behests of the officers of your Government. In such slave-hunting raids one village is armed by the State against the other, and the force thus secured is incorporated with the regular troops. I have no adequate terms with which to depict to your Majesty the brutal acts of your soldiers upon raids such as these."

The army was very small then compared with its numbers now.

The war of extermination against the Arabs begun in 1886, more or less postponed until 1891, renewed and on a graver scale in October of that year, and brought to an end in January, 1894, occasioned as much positive slaughter probably as during the forty years of Arab dominion round the Great Lakes and the eastern districts of the Congo. The Congo State employed thousands of cannibal auxiliaries, and thousands of auxiliaries fought on the side of the Arabs. The Arabs fought for their independence, their ivory markets, and to keep their bodies from *post mortem* desecration at the teeth of the cannibal troops opposed to them. The Congo State fought for its prestige and the ivory stores and markets which it hoped to capture, and did. The opening of the Arab campaign was more or less synonymous with the application of the Congo State's new policy embodied in the decrees and regulations already referred to, and the unhappy native passed from the bondage of the Arab, which, brutal as it was, had something to recommend it—gave the native some hope in his life, at any rate—to the bondage of the Congo State, which has nothing to recommend it whatsoever, except dividends for the few men who pull the strings in Belgium.* It is perfectly safe to say that ever since

* Since the above passage was written I have perused Major W. St. H. Gibbons' book (*op. cit.*), and I find therein the following confirmatory appreciation : "Under Arab influence the freedom of organised native

THE THIRD TEST OF CONGO STATE RULE 105

the annihilation of the Arab power, warfare has never ceased for a day in some part or other of the Congo territories. It takes a long time to kill 20 million souls, so, notwithstanding the frightful depopulation of many of the get-atable regions, the whole country is not yet "vacant." But there is abundant evidence to show that in parts the native is simply being wiped out. Here are passages from private letters written home from the Upper Congo in 1896. Let the reader compare them with the evidence given in Chapter XXI., which brings us down to the present time. The similarity is eloquent.

"It is impossible for you to understand how bitterly all are in power of the unscrupulous men in office. Law, truth, and justice are only names or instruments to serve the cause of tyranny and oppression. Their soldiers are the worst and vilest savages, and they are let loose upon the unoffending population. So that rubber may be extorted. ..."

"Every week we hear of some fighting, and there are frequent rows even in our village with the armed and unruly soldiers. God save poor hunted Africa from the iniquitous rubber traffic! During the past twelve months it has cost more lives than native wars and superstition would have sacrificed in five years. ..."

I merely touch upon one or two of these old records by way of illustrating the truth of the words "enormous and continual butchery" used by M. Georges Lorand. In Mr. Fox-Bourne's book will be found numerous and authenticated testimony covering all that earlier period, such as the published diary of that fine man, E. J. Glave; the revelations of the Swedish missionary Sjöblom, also a splendid character; the statement of Murphy, etc. With the growth of the regular army, with the appearance of the Trusts and their soldiers, the area of oppression and devastation has rapidly spread, and is making fresh strides every year. The "civilised native troops" —to use Sir Hugh Gilzean Reid's delicate euphemism *—are doing their work well.

Let us consider for a moment the significance of this admitted army of 20,000 † regular troops, to say nothing of the armed bands raised by the Trusts, which, at the very lowest computation, we may place at 10,000.

This armed force is considerably larger than that which

communities was not interfered with. These people came to trade—to give and take, not to take only. Morally speaking, I will content myself here with the bare assertion that the natives are not the gainers by the Belgian occupation."
   * *Speaker*, April, 1900.
   † The *Officiel Bulletin* of 1900 speaks of 15,000. In the debate in the Belgian House the number was spoken of as between 16,000 and 17,000. A decree issued at the close of 1903 puts the number to be recruited in 1904 at 2600.

France, England, and Germany put together maintain in the whole of their West African possessions. The troops and police of England in West Africa* number 8000. The Governor-General of French West Africa disposes of 9400 men in troops and police, including the European element; the French Congo troops (including the Chad territories) number 2700—a gross total of 12,000. The German forces in the Cameroons and Togo number 1800.

The significance of the Congo State's military strength is the greater when we bear in mind that, ever since the overthrow of the Arabs, it has been faced by no native combination, and has persistently, and of set purpose, destroyed all organisation in native communities susceptible of containing the seed of possible combination. Unhappily for themselves, and happily for their oppressors, the unfortunate tribes of the Congo territories appear to be unable to combine—at least, the bulk of them cannot. The day when a Bantu leader of men, in one of the larger and more powerful tribes, such as the Batetla or Asande, can direct a true combination against the State, might well see the end of Belgian domination in the Upper River, despite the disintegrating effect of Congo State rule. Yet, notwithstanding this fact, although the only weapons possessed by the Congo natives have been spears, bows and arrows, and knives, and, in some parts, axes—notwithstanding the network of fluvial communication; in the absence of the fanaticism which Islam inspires (together with the capacity of combination and organisation), and which France and, to a lesser extent, Great Britain have had to face in Western Africa —the regular army of the Congo State, nursed in philanthropy, and whose watchword is "moral and material regeneration," owns to a regular army of nearly 20,000 men, while the irregulars raised by its Trusts number at the very least half that figure! And the Congo State tells us that it *controls* its soldiers, when the *total number of white men*—not merely *white officials of the State*, but the total number of white men in the Congo territories—is 2400! It controls them so well that they raid the territories of their neighbours† in search of loot, committing havoc and atrocity. It controls them so well that in the remoter districts, at any rate, they are absolutely out of hand, and assault Europeans as soon as look at them,‡ which is not to be wondered at, for the Congolese officials have shown their soldiers on several occasions the amount of respect with which Europeans unconnected with the State or its Trusts

---

* Exclusive of the West Indian garrison (300 men) at Freetown.
† See Part III.
‡ *Ibid.*

are treated by the Government.* It controls them so well that it has had two great rebellions, and that a considerable portion of the South-Eastern District, and also the Kivu District, is still, after eight years, in the hands of the rebels.† It controls them so well that but three years ago they seized the fort outside the capital itself, upon which they rained shell for a day and a half.‡ It controls them so well that it allows them—because its policy renders such things inevitable and necessary—to plunder, rape, murder, and mutilate to their hearts' content. The Congo State army, regular and irregular, with its leaders—often non-commissioned officers of the Belgian army, or civilians in the employ of the Trusts—poorly paid, brutalised, and degraded by a policy to which they have become bound as in fetters of steel, and which is a direct incentive to the worst elements in their character, sweeps like a destroying breath across the equatorial forests, and no chance Arab slave-trader left more ruin and desolation in his track —ruin from which there is no recovery, desolation for ever desolate. It is called in Brussels, and on the Congo, " restoring order."

Not only is the policy which the officials are paid to carry out by means of the tens of thousands of black mercenaries which have been raised for the purpose, a policy demoralising to the officials, and tending to accentuate the fiercest instincts of the fighting Bantu tribes of the Congo territory whence the majority of the soldiers are drawn, but the way these soldiers are recruited constitutes in itself a system little, if at all, removed from slavery.

The authorities of the Congo State describe it, indeed, in very different terms.

" Military service no more constitutes slavery in the Congo State than it does in any country where the system of the conscription exists. The recruiting and the organisation of the public force are the subjects of minute legislative enactments to prevent abuses. After all, military service does not weigh heavily on the population from which it asks only one man in every ten thousand."

The latter paragraph is delicious. The population of the Congo territory is believed to be somewhere about twenty

* The hanging of Stokes, and the despatch of Rabinek, a prisoner under native escort from Albertville to the Congo, are cases in point.

† See Part III. In the Congo State's official report for 1900 it was admitted that the rebellion had lasted then three years, and had not been put down. The rebellion referred to was that of 1897, but the rebels who hold the Lake region of Katanga are probably the rebels of 1896.

‡ Had they known the secret of the time-fuse, Boma would have been levelled to the ground.

million;* but no positive data, of course, exist, because, speaking generally, the officials have no authority within a mile or two of the river banks. The Congo State's regular army, as already stated, is close on 20,000, without counting the irregulars raised by the Trusts; yet we are told that only one man in every ten thousand men is taken! The "minute legislation" is on a par with the minute calculation. The bald facts are—

1. That the Congo recruits are taken for twelve years, seven in active service, and five in the reserve.
2. That the levy is a compulsory levy.
3. That recruits used to be, and may, for aught we know to the contrary, be now, in many districts secured by raids upon villages.†

How many soldiers are there in the Congo State army to-day whose mothers and fathers have been slaughtered in connection with the rubber traffic?

I have referred to the term of service already. With regard to the levy being a compulsory levy, even when no actual raiding goes on, there is an abundance of evidence.

At one time—before the proceedings of the Congo Government became known—Congo State agents were allowed to enlist Hausas in Lagos, and also recruits in the Gold Coast and Sierra Leone, as so-called "labourers." These labourers were promptly impressed as soldiers when they got to Boma, and sent up country on military expeditions lasting for years, and whence many of them never returned. The survivors suffered terrible hardships, and were sometimes most brutally treated by their officers.‡ Finally, the British Government stepped in, and absolutely forbade any further recruiting. In a letter to the author, received a few months ago from a native of Lagos who had "served twelve years as a soldier in rubber and ivory collecting districts such as Equateur, Bangala,

---

* Probably very much overstated even in 1884; since then it has, of course, dwindled enormously.

† "It is reported that . . . the method of obtaining men for labour or for military service is often but little different from that formerly employed to obtain slaves."—*British Note to Powers*, 1903.

‡ Judging from its own published declarations, the British Government possesses much evidence of the mal-treatment of its subjects which has not yet been made public, although Parliament has pressed for it. It would seem to be the clear duty of the British Government, in view of the proved incompetency of the Congo Courts to secure justice for British coloured subjects, to exercise its rights of Consular jurisdiction secured under the Convention of 1884. I say nothing, for the moment, on the subject of British, and also American, missionary enterprise, which is being hampered in many respects, and, from that point of view alone, the exercise of our Consular rights is greatly to be desired.

THE THIRD TEST OF CONGO STATE RULE 109

Basoko, Stanley Falls, and Kasongo," the writer thus describes the duties of the Congo soldiery:

"To 'trade' with Albini rifles; to collect rubber and ivory without payment; to flog women in the hot African sun—100 lashes on their naked backs; to murder children on their mothers' breasts for refusing to show where food is stored; to take the natives' goats, sheep, fowls; to take their land and burn their villages."

Shortly afterwards the French Government prohibited the recruiting of Senegalese in its own Colony of Senegal. Efforts were then made to entice Senegalese over the Gambia border, and embark them at Bathurst. The attempt succeeded on one occasion, when several hundred men were so shipped; but a proclamation was subsequently issued by the Gambia Government which put a stop to that. On one occasion Congo agents secured several hundred West Indian blacks, in Barbadoes, as "labourers." When the vessel arrived at Boma, the men learned that they were to serve as soldiers, and being seized with panic, refused to land. They were actually fired upon from the shore, and several of the poor fellows were killed and wounded. This shocking outrage was never properly shown up. Some two years later, I met one of the survivors in a northern port, and I have a letter from him in my possession now which he wrote me after reaching his own home in Barbadoes.*

The methods which characterise recruiting operations in the Congo territories; the fact that the "recruiting" synchronises in many cases with the loss to the recruit of all beings for whom he may have entertained affection; that the recruit knows, in any case, he will probably never see his people or his village again; the natural tendency of the African, if placed in possession of weapons which give him an immeasurable advantage over his fellows, to oppress and bully—these things, combined with the deplorable example given by his officers and the horrible tasks he is called upon to perform,† convert the Congo soldier into a man-hunter of the most accomplished type. Perpetual warfare makes him desperate and ferocious; unlimited authority of life and death, and unlimited opportunities to kill, violate, plunder, and rob, make him the fit

* In it he says he complained to the agent who shipped him under false pretences, but got no redress.

† Mr. Casement had some conversation with a Government soldier (p. 36, Africa, No. 1, 1904). "This was," he said, "his third term of service with the *Force Publique*. As his reason for remaining so long in this service, he asserted that, as his own village and country were subjected to much trouble in connection with the rubber tax, he could not live in his own home, and preferred," he said, laughing, "to be with the hunters, rather than with the hunted."

instrument of an inhuman and callous policy, of which his officers, himself, and the natives are alike the victims in different degrees of suffering. The Nemesis of such a state of affairs is certain. Either grievances or a sense of power will lead to a rebellion on an even larger scale than the Batetla and Bakusu revolts; or, some day, a more than usually intelligent native corporal, with the characteristic of leadership, will suddenly realise that the black man is on the wrong tack in continually slaughtering his brother for the sake of the white interloper. And then . . . the deluge.

Meanwhile, the Congo soldier is kept busy at the game of murder and outrage, in order that the supplies of rubber shall not fall short of the appointed quantity, that the revenues of the *Domaine Privé* shall be maintained at their proper level, that the "Committee of Three" * shall not fail in attending to certain artistic longings attributed to the Belgian people by the State apologists,† and that the Trusts shall pay good dividends.

One of the most atrocious features of the persistent warfare of which year in year out the Congo territories are the scene, is the mutilation both of the dead and of the living which goes on under it, and of which ocular demonstration is given in this volume. In connection with this rather ghastly side of the "moral and material regeneration" policy introduced into the Congo territories, the time has come for straight speaking. I have used the word "introduced" advisedly, and I propose to explain why. Meanwhile it is necessary to examine carefully, and in detail, the available evidence on the subject.

The first intimation that Congo State troops were in the habit of cutting off the hands of men, women, and children in connection with the rubber traffic reached Europe through the Rev. J. B. Murphy, of the American Baptist Missionary Union, in 1895. He described how the State soldiers had shot some people on Lake Mantumba ‡ (Tumba), "cut off their hands, *and took them to the Commissaire.*" § The survivors of the slaughter reported the matter to a missionary at Irebu, who went down to see if it were true, and was quickly convinced by ocular demonstration. Among the mutilated victims was a little girl, not quite dead, who subsequently recovered. In a statement which appeared in the *Times*, Mr. Murphy said,‖ "These hands—the hands of men, women,

---

* See Part V. † See Part V.
‡ Situated within the *Domaine de la Couronne.*
§ Quoted from Fox-Bourne, *op. cit.*
‖ *Times*, November 18, 1895. *Ibid.*

THE THIRD TEST OF CONGO STATE R

and children—were *placed in rows before the Comm*
counted them to see that the soldiers had not wasted
The second intimation was conveyed in the dia
(one of the fine type of Englishmen connected wit
in the early days), and published in 1896 after his
Century Magazine. Glave wrote that the Rev. J. Clarke, a
missionary at Mantumba, reported that he had seen "several
men with bunches of hands, signifying their individual skill.
These, I presume (Glave), *they must produce to prove their
successes.* . . . I have previously heard of hands, among them
children's, being brought to the stations. . . ."*

Mr. Sjöblom, a Swedish missionary, confirmed, in 1897,
the statements of Murphy and Glave. He reported having
seen a native shot by a soldier before his eyes. After the
murder the soldier

"told a little boy . . . to go and cut off the right hand of the man who
had been shot. . . . The boy after some labour (the native was not quite
dead) cut the hand off and laid it by a fallen tree. A little later the
hand was put on a fire to smoke *before being sent to the Commissary.* . . .
If the rubber does not reach the full amount required, the sentinels
attack the natives; they kill some *and bring the hands to the Commissary.* . . . The sentinels, or else the boys in attendance on them,
put these hands on a little kiln, and after they have been smoked, they
by-and-by put them on the top of the rubber baskets. I have many
times seen this done. . . . From this village I went to another, where
I met a man, who pointed to a basket, and said to me, 'Look, I have only
two hands!' He meant there were not enough to make up for the rubber
he had brought. . . . When I reached the river, I turned round and saw
that the people had large hammocks in which they were gathering the
rubber to be taken to the Commissary. I also saw smoked hands and
prisoners to be *taken down to the Commissary.* That is only one of the
places. . . . When I crossed the stream, I saw some dead bodies
hanging down from branches in the water. As I turned my face away
from the horrible sight, one of the native corporals who was following us
down said, 'Oh, that is nothing; a few days ago I returned from a fight,
and I *brought the white man* 160 *hands*.' . . . Two or three days after
a fight, a dead mother was found with two of her children. The mother
was shot, and the right hand taken off. On one side was the elder child,
also shot, and the right hand also taken off. On the other side was the
younger child with the right hand cut off, but the child still living was
resting against the dead mother's breast. This dark picture was seen
by four missionaries. On December 14 a sentinel passed our mission
station and a woman accompanied him, carrying a basket of hands.
Mr. and Mrs. Banks, beside myself, went down the road, and they told
the sentinel to put the hands on the road that they might count them.
We counted eighteen right hands smoked, and from the size of the
hands we could judge that they belonged to men, women, and even
children. . . . I have seen extracts from letters in which the writers
have freely told about *hundreds of hands being brought by the sentinels.*
Another agent told me that he had himself seen a State officer at one of

* Fox-Bourne, *op. cit.*

the outposts pay a certain number of brass rods to the soldiers for a number of hands they had brought. One of the soldiers told me the same. . . . '*The Commissary has promised us, if we bring plenty of hands, he will shorten our service.* . . . *I have brought in plenty of hands already, and I expect my time of service will soon be finished.*'"*

The confessions of the agents of the *Anversoise* are fully dealt with later on. In that same year we had the debate in the Belgian House, in the course of which M. Lorand cited a Belgian officer who had admitted in writing to him that his soldiers had brought in hundreds of hands.

M. Lorand : "It is so true that, as a result of what I have stated here, the particular officer whom I challenged to deny the facts has written giving me information, in which he admits that these 'war trophies' were brought in. That is Congo civilisation! On all sides war, massacre, crimes." M. de Smet de Naeyer : "The exploitation of the *Domaine Privé* is conformable with jurisprudence. . . . Why suspect the Congo State of cruelty?" M. Lorand : "Remember the 1300 severed hands." M. de Smet de Naeyer : "Faults have certainly been committed."†

Again, in 1900, the particulars sent home by the American Baptist Missionary Society at Luebo were published for the first time, and will be found at length in Chapter XVI. The native affidavits published in Chapter XVII., dealing with the South-Eastern District tell the same tale, as also the letters from my correspondents in British territory adjoining that district of the State, and received in 1902 and 1903.

The following passage from a letter received by the author from a correspondent in the Bangala District in 1901 may be quoted :—

"*Re* cutting off of hands. I do not know from whom the order emanates, but this I do know : there are victims who have survived this cruelty in every district, in some more than others. I know white men who have seen the baskets of hands being carried to the central State station, and others have told me of the hands being put in line or lines. State soldiers themselves give us their reason for this barbarous deed, that they have to account for the use of their cartridges in this way. The cutting off of hands for this reason is a common report on the Upper River, and is generally believed by all who live there."

Personally, I had always thought, until the early part of 1901, that these mutilations were carried out upon *dead* people only—natives slain in connection with the odious raids upon villages, for not bringing in a sufficiency of rubber, and that the idea was at once to strike terror into the hearts of other

* The whole of Sjöblom's evidence is quoted from Fox-Bourne, *op. cit.*
† Debate in the Belgian House, July, 1900 (not to be confounded with the debate of 1903).

IKABO LOKOTA EPONDO

CHILDREN MUTILATED BY CONGO SOLDIERY

(For particulars of Ikabo and Lokota, refer to Appendix; for particulars of Epondo, see concluding chapter)

THE THIRD TEST OF CONGO STATE RULE 113

villages, and to justify, in the eyes of the Congo State officer, the expenditure of the cartridges by soldiers whom he had sent out upon the work of slaughter, to prove to the satisfaction of their superiors that a village behindhand in its tribute of rubber or food-stuffs had been really and effectively wiped out.

But it was only towards the end of 1901 that I ascertained, by receiving photographs and letters from the Upper Congo, that mutilations were frequently practised by the Congo soldiery upon *the living*, upon men, upon women, upon poor little innocent children of tender years. The information I then received has been, alas! but too amply corroborated since from various sources, and notably by Mr. Roger Casement. Consul Casement's evidence is abundant and precise. In the Lake Mantumba District he saw two mutilated natives, whose cases, authenticated beyond doubt, proved the committal of the deed by Government soldiers "accompanied by white officers." The Government official in this district said men still came to him who had been victims of the practice while the rubber *régime* was in force; in that particular district it seems to have been abandoned a year or two ago, probably owing to the enormous depopulation which had ensued from its application. The Consul was given by the natives the names of six other persons mutilated in a similar way. Many statements were also given to him, and are printed in the report, showing on what a colossal scale these mutilations were carried out, by instructions, in that district. The day he left the Lake five men crossed it from another direction to see him, all being mutilated in the same manner. When informed of the fact by a messenger, the Consul was on his return journey, and did not, therefore, meet them. The estimate of a Government officer that 6000 people had been killed or mutilated in six months in the Mamboyo District of the *Domaine de la Couronne* is referred to in Chapter XIX., as is also the sexual mutilations inflicted by the Government soldiers upon the people of L——, which the Consul obtained from the lips of the refugees from Lake Leopold II. On the Lulongo River a boy of sixteen whose right hand was missing was brought to the Consul. This boy, the natives said, had been first shot in the shoulder, and then mutilated by a soldier. Here, two boys not older than seven were also brought to him in a similar condition—both mutilations perpetrated by sentries, as part of the "punishment" to which the village they belonged to was subjected for not bringing in enough rubber. A fourth case of mutilation, which had occurred a few months previously in the same neighbourhood, was personally investigated by the Consul. It was that of a boy of fifteen years of age, "whose left arm was wrapped up in a dirty rag. Removing this, I found the left hand had been hacked off at the wrist." He declared that a soldier of the La Lulanga Company had done the deed, "on account of the rubber." The boy was confronted with the soldier, whose statements were quite unsatisfactory, and at the Consul's insistent request he was arrested. The Consul, after pointing out that it was impossible for him to visit all the villages whence similar complaints come pouring in to him, adds :

"In that one case the truth of the charges preferred was amply demonstrated, and their significance was not diminished by the fact that, whereas this act of mutilation had been committed within a few miles of Q——, the head-quarters of a European civilising agency, and the guilty man was still in their midst, armed with the gun with which he had first shot his victim, not one of the natives of the terrorised town had attempted to report the occurrence. They had in the interval visited Mampoko each fortnight with the indiarubber from their district. There was also in their midst another mutilated boy, X., whose hand had been cut off by this or another sentry. The main waterway of the Lulongo River lay at their doors, and on it well-nigh every fortnight a Government steamer had passed up and down stream on its way to bring the indiarubber of the A. B. I. R. Company to Coquilhatville. They possessed, too, some canoes ; and, if all other agencies of relief were closed, the territorial tribunal of Coquilhatville lay open to them, and the journey to it down stream from their village could have been accomplished in some twelve hours. . . . The fact that no effort had been made by these people to secure relief from their unhappy situation impelled me to believe that a very real fear of reporting such occurrences actually existed among them."

Comment is needless.

Now, the question arises, who is responsible for these atrocities? I do not mean responsible in a general sense, of course, because the Congo Administration is obviously and palpably responsible ; I mean in a much more specific and direct sense. Let us see what the attitude of the authorities in Brussels has been in connection with the matter. So long as it could, the Congo State denied that mutilations were inflicted by its soldiers upon the natives when those soldiers were sent against them. When denial became no longer possible—since the confessions of the *Anversoise* agents and the Belgian Parliamentary Debates of 1900—the official defenders of the Congo State declared that these terrible practices had been immemorially rife amongst the natives themselves, and that, as the soldiers were locally recruited, they would naturally be imbued with such habits, which could only be eradicated by degrees. At the head of this chapter will be found King Leopold's version, which is much the same as the above, only clothed in the exalted language with which the world is so perfectly familiar.

A Roman Catholic priest, the "Superior" of the "Upper Kasai Mission," while demurring at the idea that "a young soldier animated with a desire to show his prowess" should be forbidden to "bring back war trophies,"* professed, similarly, to see in the practice merely the continuation of an old order of things. M. Woeste, the leader of the Catholic party in Belgium, made a sort of apology for the existence—after eighteen years' administration—of such horrors when referring in the Belgian House last July to the disclosures of Morrison. He said they would disappear "little by little."

Now, I assert deliberately that the employes of the Congo State in Africa have themselves introduced these practices— that is to say, the bringing in of "trophies" by their men as a sign of prowess in war; that they were unknown until the policy of "moral and material regeneration" was introduced; that they are the direct outcome of that policy; that they have attained widespread notoriety from the example set by these agents and officials; that what was first intended to be confined to mutilation of the dead has by continuous usage come to mean, not infrequently, mutilation of the living, and that, far from disappearing "little by little," they will increase if the blood-stained and barbarous *régime* to which they are attributable is not swept out of existence. The charge is a serious one, and is not lightly made. I may say that I had made it before reading the Consul's report, the present chapter having been written before that report appeared. As the Consul brings a similar charge against the Administration, I cannot do better than preface my observations by quoting the words used by the Consul in the same connection.

"Of acts of persistent mutilation," says Mr. Casement, "by Government soldiers of this nature, I had many statements made to me, some of them specifically, others in a general way. Of the fact of this mutilation and the causes inducing it there can be no shadow of doubt. It was not a native custom prior to the coming of the white man; it was not the outcome of the primitive instincts of savages in their fights between village and village; it was the deliberate act of the soldiers of a European Administration, and these men themselves never made any concealment that in committing these acts they were but obeying the positive orders of their superiors."

The subject is such an important one that I feel it should be dealt with at some length.

The whole evidence which has come to hand points

* "The Truth about the Civilisation in Congoland," by a Belgian (Sampson Low, Marston & Co., 1903).

conclusively to this—that the soldiers, in mutilating the dead bodies of the natives whom they have been sent to punish, have acted under definite instructions, although, needless to say, such instructions have probably not been committed to writing. Why should they have brought the hands to the State posts unless instructed to do so? Apart from the several positive statements to that effect elicited from the soldiers themselves, the mere circumstance of the preservation of these "trophies," the counting of them, the placing of them in baskets, and so on, is, in my opinion, conclusive proof. The frequency and extent of the occurrence and the systematic procedure adopted is also overwhelmingly significant. Admitting that a peculiarly brutal soldier should be addicted to the habit, and admitting (for the sake of argument only) that many soldiers should be addicted to it, how explain the trouble and care taken to keep such relics? Why should soldiers campaigning, travelling light, burden themselves with hundreds of severed human hands, which in the aggregate must weigh fairly heavy? Why this provision of baskets?

On two occasions, Belgian agents of the State and one of its Trusts have publicly confessed to (1) soldiers bringing in severed hands, (2) ordering mutilation.

I have read, I think, nearly all that is to be read of Congo literature, and, eliminating the recent bald official statements —statements unsupported by a shadow of proof—I have come across nothing which tends to show, or even to suggest, that the native tribes of the Congo territories mutilate their enemies either dead or living. In cases of serious crime against native law, it is the habit of many native tribes all over Africa to mutilate the culprits. In one or two of the eastern districts of the State the existence of that habit has been reported.* Adultery among some of the Upper Welle peoples is punished, in the case of the men, by mutilation. Where Arab influence has predominated for many years, the practice of castration may, to a very limited extent, have been adopted by certain powerful native kings. But of a wholesale, or even partial, system of mutilating the dead body of the foe, there is no trace anywhere in the Congo territories. Many of the tribes, being cannibals, would eat the dead bodies of the slain, like the Batetla allies of the State devoured the corpses of natives fighting on the Arab side; but of a system of cutting off of hands or the sexual members of males as a sign of prowess in war, much as a Red Indian would take a scalp, there is absolutely no trace in Congo native custom, that I have been able to discover. Neither have I found any positive traces of the recorded mutilation of living

* In Urua, and among the Bakusus on the Lomami.

THE THIRD TEST OF CONGO STATE RULE 117

women, by the cutting off of hands, even for offences which might have been committed against native law; and certainly nowhere any trace of *little children* undergoing such torture.

Yet there are women and little children who have survived that mutilation in the Congo territories to-day, and the mutilation can only have been inflicted by the Congo soldiery, regular or irregular.

So far as my own individual researches go, they tend to accentuate the reasons already given for believing that the practice of mutilation in war is an exotic so far as the Congo natives are concerned.

On the other hand, the Arab half-castes have not, that I am aware of, been accused of having mutilated the bodies of the natives they fought against, although they did, on occasion, revenge themselves on individual chiefs, and sometimes mutilated prisoners in that way. The Congo State would surely not have neglected to bring forward such a charge when calling upon high Heaven to bear witness to its philanthropic motives in exterminating those inconvenient competitors!

I have endeavoured to obtain corroboration or refutation of the result of my researches among published records, by soliciting the opinions of Englishmen who saw service in the Congo territories "in the old, humane days," *i.e.* between 1884 and 1889. The testimony is clear and unhesitating. To my question as to whether the custom of mutilating in war was a native custom, so far as their extensive experience went, Mr. Herbert Ward writes as follows:

"In answer to your question I would say at once that I have never seen an instance of such a thing on the Congo, and, moreover, have never heard of such a thing as mutilating foes. I would say emphatically that during the period between 1884 and 1889 no instance was known of the Congo natives mutilating their foes by cutting off their hands."

I have not the honour of Mr. Joseph Conrad's acquaintance, but I am permitted to quote the following letter to a friend of his on the subject. He speaks, needless to say, with *de visu* experience:

"During my sojourn in the interior, keeping my eyes and ears well open too, I've never heard of the alleged custom of cutting off hands among the natives. I am convinced that no such custom ever existed along the whole course of the Congo River to which my experience is limited. Neither in casual talk of white men, nor in the course of definite inquiries as to the tribal customs, was ever such a practice hinted at. My informants were numerous, of all sorts, and many of them possessed of abundant knowledge."

Mr. Theodore Hoste, for thirteen years a missionary on the

Congo, and a noted scholar of Congo languages, writes this year as follows, privately to a friend:

"*Re* mutilation. During my thirteen years' residence in Congoland, I never from any source, native or foreign, heard any report that mutilation was practised by natives of the Congo country."

Dr. H. Grattan Guinness, of the Congo Balolo Mission, writes as follows:

"I entirely reprobate the suggestion made by the officers of the State that it is a native custom to cut off the hands of their foes. To the best of my knowledge, speaking after careful discussion on this subject with our missionaries who were in the country before the advent of the rubber concessionnaires, no such mutilations ever took place. . . . I believe that this was the invention of the white man purely and simply, and introduced in the first instance as a proof that cartridges were not being wasted by the native soldiers of the Trust. Unfortunately, the custom thus introduced and practised on so wide a scale has evidently become a recognised form of indignity, and is now carried on by the native sentries upon the living as a sheer act of cruelty and tyranny."

Theodora McKenzie, Daniel Hayes, Emily Banks, Peter Whytock, and William Wilkes, all missionaries belonging to the Congo Balolo Mission and American Baptist Mission, have made sworn declarations to the effect that the custom is entirely unknown amongst the natives, and detailing instances where they saw soldiers in the possession of these ghastly trophies. Mr. Hayes says: "The truth is that the Administration is doing its best to bring this practice about. . . ." These declarations, which have been published by Dr. Guinness, cover experiences between 1890 and 1898. The evidence of Mr. Charles Bond, another member of the Congo Balolo Mission, is more recent. Writing in September, 1903, he says:

"I have the evidence of a number of men, working for us at the present time, that at their town—on the Bosamba River—numbers of men have been killed outright, and others have died from having their hands cut off because they would not submit to demands. However, all the mutilated people do not die, as the State officials have had ocular demonstration quite recently."

The Rev. A. E. Scrivener, of the British Baptist Mission, whose experiences in the *Domaine de la Couronne* are detailed in Chapter XIX., in a private letter accompanying his notes of that journey, written to myself, says:

"I heard at Bongo (soldiers told the evangelists who were with me) confirmation of a report common amongst the refugees that the soldiers took the organs of the men they had killed to ——,* to show that they were men and not women who were being killed."†

---

* The native name of a Congo State official.

† Confirmed by the statements made to Mr. Casement (Africa, No. 1, 1904).

THE THIRD TEST OF CONGO STATE RULE 119

In conclusion, I can vouch for the truth of the following incident, although I cannot in this particular instance, not having the necessary authority, the informant being in Africa at the present time, give any names. Some years ago, two English missionaries came across a Hausa soldier in the employ of the State (the British Government had not then stopped the recruiting of Hausas in Lagos by Congo State Government agents) with a bag full of human hands. The bag was deposited at the foot of a tree, and the stench arising from it was so horrible that the missionaries could not count the hands it contained. The soldier being interrogated replied in *English*, "Those are hands I am taking to the *Commissaire*, to show that we have done what we were ordered to do." I merely give that story to point out that here was a case where a *semi-civilised, English-speaking* native from a *British Colony* had to commit these atrocities acting under orders! Here was no "debased primitive instinct," but a sample of the effect of Congolese civilisation. Even the official defenders of the Congo State would not venture to suggest a predisposition to mutilate on the part of the *Hausaman!* And now, to crown all, we have the deliberate statement of Mr. Roger Casement, to which I have already referred.*

The systematic hand-cutting and worse forms of mutilation which for over a decade have been practised all over the Congo territories—mutilation of dead and living—must be assigned to the direct instigation of State officials and agents of the Trusts appointed to terrorise the rubber districts. The soldiers, let loose throughout the country with the object of reducing, by perpetual and repeated slaughter, the people of a specific district to abject and absolute submission, have been required to bring back tangible proof that proper punishment was inflicted, and the hands of slain, or partly slain, people were the readiest and most acceptable form of proof. Many of these victims have survived, and the soldiery, grown callous by years of this moral example; absolute masters of the villages and townships upon which they are quartered; themselves brutalised and degraded, have probably long since ceased to distinguish between the motives which inspired the earlier instructions they received and the exercise of their own particular quarrels with the people among whom they are sent. Not one in a thousand of the dark deeds performed under such a *régime* can ever, in the nature of things, become publicly known.

The charge has surely been made out; and are we not

---

* As this book is going to press further detailed, specific, and abundantly corroborative information is to hand, and will be found among recent letters received in the Appendix.

entitled to ask, why, in God's name, should a so-called Administration, which tolerates—nay, which incites, and by its officers, whom its policy converts but too often into incarnate fiends, orders the perpetration of—such practices as these, be permitted any longer to pollute the earth with its abominations and bestialities? I cannot write down here many things I have heard by word of mouth, from men whom I know to be truthful, as to what goes on in the Congo territories, and which would only be fit for a treatise on European criminology under the African sun.

The term "cannibal troops" has been used in reference to the Congo soldiers; I have used it myself. It is, perhaps, open to misconstruction. It is not suggested that the Congo soldiers are *all* active cannibals at the present time, and feed upon recalcitrant rubber-collectors, as well as mutilate them, or indulge in the same cannibal orgies as the Batetla allies of the State did in 1893-94, as graphically told by Dr. Hinde. But a considerable portion of them are recruited from tribes which are still notably cannibalistic, such as the Asandes, Batetla, Manyema, etc. Cannibalism clings, and if you stick a rifle into a cannibal's hand, and put a uniform on his back, you don't thereby convert him into a vegetarian. In the more accessible regions of the Congo the troops of the State may have been drilled out of it, but that in districts further afield some of them still indulge in a human steak is not to be doubted. The testimony of various travellers (Wright, Grogan, etc.) is given in Part III.

Moreover, it would appear that, even in proximity to the main stream and under the eyes of their European officers, the practice is by no means unknown. Only a few months ago Messrs. John Howell, S. O. Kempton, R. H. Kirkland, and W. B. Frame, all experienced members of the British Baptist Missionary Society, were the horrified witnesses of a cannibal orgie which rivals Dante's inferno. They were coming down river in the steamer *Goodwill*, and landed near a village well known to some of the members of the party, to camp for the night. They speedily ascertained that fighting was going on. The rest had better be given in the words of the account itself:

"The s.s. *Goodwill*, of the Baptist Missionary Society, with four missionaries on board, put into the village of Yandjali below Yakusu on the Upper Congo on the 28th November. Yandjali is a native town in the Basoko district, and the mission steamer had frequently put into that locality for stopping the night and obtaining fuel. On this occasion the town was found to be occupied by a party of Government soldiers under two white officers. The four missionaries on board were horrified to find the native soldiers of the Government under the very eyes of their officers engaged in mutilating the dead bodies of the natives who had just been killed. The senior missionary on board, the Rev. John Howell, of Bolobo, reported to the *Commissaire* of the Aruwimi district, and later to the Governor-General of the State, what the party had witnessed. Three native bodies were lying near the river's edge as the *Goodwill* put into the bank, and human limbs were lying within a few yards of the steamer, as she sought to make fast to the bank. One of the slaughtered natives was a child. A State soldier was seen drawing away the legs and other portions of a human body. Another soldier was seen standing by a large native basket in which were the viscera of a human body. The missionaries were promptly ordered off the beach by the two officers presiding over this human shambles; and as the *Goodwill* steamed away from the bank firing was renewed, and one bullet struck a fleeing native in a canoe just ahead of the steamer. The *Goodwill* proceeded to Basoko, where the missionaries entered an instant protest against these horrible proceedings. Their statements were taken down in writing, and a 'trial' is promised. The ground covered by the military operations is described by the missionary spectators as very small—a narrow stretch of cleared river bank where the village of Yandjali stood, measuring some three hundred yards long, but not more than twenty yards deep. It might have been thought that two European officers could effectively control their savage troops over so tiny a field of action."*

To speak of the "cannibal" troops of the Congo State does not appear, therefore, to lend itself to the epithet "exaggerated." †

In Mr. Roger Casement's report also, on p. 74, there is the distinct statement made on native testimony that the Government soldiers asked their white officer " C. D." for permission to eat a prisoner taken by them, which permission was given, and the deed performed.

The Congo State, which in five years has imported, according to the official figures, £65,000 of guns and £45,000 of cartridges and caps into its territories, directly and indirectly, does not appear to be in the least chary of distributing them to the natives, or rather to important chiefs, when it suits its convenience to do so. The Belgian papers inform us that the Asande chieftains in Congo State territory (Upper Ubanghi-Welle), under the authority of Sultan Semio, possess many guns : " Bondono and Semio have 350 guns ; Djeme has 50 ;

---

* I have since heard from Mr. Frame personally on this subject. He confirms the horrible details given in the published account. He says he will never forget the sight as long as he lives. Imagine that it should be possible for an incident of this kind to take place on the *main river* after twenty years' European rule ! *Vide West African Mail* (Organ of the Congo Reform Association), letter from Mr. Frame, May, 1904.

† The reader is referred to the recent letters of Mr. Harris and others in the Appendix, giving atrocious instances of cannibalism by soldiers of the *Abir* Trust which have occurred this year.

Gatanga, 100; Yapato, 64; Kipa, 50; Biamboro, 60, etc."*
Of course, the policy will in the long run prove as suicidal a one as it is dangerous for the Congo State's neighbours. Of course, it is in flagrant violation of the Berlin Act. But what does the Congo State care for the Berlin Act, or the future? M. Leon C. Berthier's † notes enable us to understand why the big Asande chiefs are being armed by the Congo State. He writes as follows:

"The M'Bomu River (at Bangasso) is very wide here, and forms the southern basis of the square; it is the route through which the ivory passes, under our noses and beneath the eyes of our Post, to be sold on the other bank (Belgian), where it is paid for in Albini rifles, despite all the Acts of Berlin and Brussels forbidding even the sale of cap-guns. On all the convoys of rifles and ammunition which are sent there, the representative of the Congo State declares by *procès verbal* in good and due form the disappearance of a few cases of rifles and cartridges, which are not lost for every one, by virtue of the adage that nothing is lost and nothing is created in nature. They are stolen. By a new magic, the secrets of which I know, these quick-firing guns thus 'virtually lost' become transformed into ivory, at the rate of a rifle and a small quantity of cartridges for about 50 kilos. of ivory."

M. Berthier calls the attention of his Government to this affair. That Government has received (and, I believe, our own has also) similar information direct. The official report of M. Bonnel de Mézières ‡ on the Upper Ubanghi, M'Bomu, and Bahr-el-Ghazal regions, confirms M. Berthier's statements and the cheerful admissions of the Belgian newspapers up to the hilt. M. Bonnel de Mézières is, indeed, most specific. Describing the relations of the Belgians with these Asande or Niam-Niam § sultans, he says:

"These Belgians pay for ivory like princes. They give the petty Sultans muskets and repeaters; yea, even cannon and ammunition figure among their generous presents, so effective in these parts is the International Agreement forbidding weapons of precision to be supplied to the African peoples. . . . The Belgians get 35 to 40 kilos. of ivory for a musket worth 20 francs, which works out at about 50 centimes a kilo., and 100 kilos. for a repeater worth 20 francs, which is about 20 centimes

---

* *Tribune Congolaise*, May 21, 1903. "This form of rule," adds that Congophile organ, " gives excellent results."

† A Frenchman; travelled on the Ubanghi and Welle in 1899-1901. "Notes de reconnaissance et d'exploration économique au Congo Français. Annales de L'Institut Colonial de Marseilles."

‡ "Rapport de M. A. Bonnel de Mézières, Chargé de Mission." Paris. Imprimerie V^{re}. Albony.

§ The word "Niam-Niam" means cannibal. The word occurs also in the Chad District. The Bornuese legends speak of their struggles against "Nyam-Nyams"—meaning cannibals.

THE THIRD TEST OF CONGO STATE RULE

a kilo.* If they use beads, the bargain is not so profitable; a kilo. of beads worth 4 francs will fetch 2 kilos. of ivory, which brings the ivory up to 2 francs a kilo., that is to say, eighteen to twenty times dearer than it can be got for guns, which are, in fact, the only medium of exchange for ivory. . . . The guns most highly prized are repeaters, Albini, Remington, Gras, etc. . . . The result of all this must be that the period of prohibition of guns is over so effectually that Europeans and negroes will soon be marshalled for the fray equally armed with weapons of precision."

The Congo State would thus appear to be deliberately arming the big Asande chiefs, whom it does not feel itself powerful enough to crush, in order to obtain ivory! The Asandes, it may be remarked, are great fighters, and although cannibalism is rampant among them, they are progressive, and were able to combine against Dervish raids. About half the tribe live in the Congo State territories, a considerable number in the Anglo-Egyptian, and the remainder in the French sphere. It is in the hands of these people that the Congo State is placing weapons of precision and cap-guns. A pretty task will lie before the Anglo-Egyptian Government one of these days! What the Congo State officials † may be doing elsewhere, it is impossible, in the absence of accessible information, to say; but there is no reason to believe that they would act more scrupulously in other cases than they are doing with the Asandes.

Apart, however, from subsidies in quick-firing guns to powerful chiefs, it is beyond question that the Congo Government and its Trusts are instructing tens of thousands of fierce black men in the usage of rifles and cap-guns (which, at short range, are very deadly weapons), and are supplying them freely with these weapons. The Congo State may say that in its "Codes congolaises" is to be found legislation controlling the issue of cap-guns from the depôt. But are the authorities of that State prepared to prove—not to assert, but to prove—that any of these decrees were put into effective force before the middle of 1902, when, for reasons best known to itself, greater stringency was shown? Will the Brussels authorities explain the ultimate use to which the contents of those hundreds of *ballots fusils*, which prior to the middle of 1902 were shipped out with punctual regularity from Antwerp, were put? Did they go into store, as the law provides, unless issued to individuals on a licence given by authority of the Governor-General, and at a cost of 20 francs per licence; or were they allowed to go up country to arm the *gardes forestiers* maintained by the

* Or, say, 1*d*. per pound.
† In doing so, of course, they are merely agents of a policy, as fixed and unalterable as the pyramids—we must never forget that.

Trusts in violation of the law?* If, on the other hand, the authorities enforced the law, then they stand convicted of having armed by licence the irregular levies of the Trusts which have committed, as the prosecutions of the Boma Courts prove, and are committing, as recent correspondence shows, abominable outrages under the direction of the sub-agents of the Trusts, victimised to save their superiors, and with their superiors "Bula Matadi" itself.

The authorities of the Congo State are putting these black men to tasks which must for ever stifle in their breasts all sentiments other than mere blood-letting and lust. On a natural and, in many cases, very much exaggerated savagery, which does not exclude many good qualities, as Belgian travellers and official reports admit themselves, the authorities have grafted the vices of the European savage and the power to minister to them. By this detestable policy, by the inculcation of horrible practices not previously known in the country, in their greed for gain, in the furtherance of the unutterably egotistical ambitions prevalent at the fountain-head, the authorities of the Congo State have converted the Congo territories into an earthly hell for African humanity, and have raised a monster which is already outgrowing, and will one day entirely outgrow, their control.

   *   *   *   *   *

With this chapter closes Part II., in which the author has endeavoured to explain the fundamental basis of King Leopold's rule in Tropical Africa, wherein it differs from the policy of civilised Powers having possessions in that part of the world, wherein it is opposed to morality and common sense. Treated on its economic side, its financial and its military aspects, the colossal egotism and wickedness of the whole conception has, the author hopes, been made manifest. The disease has been diagnosed. We have now to study more particularly the inevitable effects of that disease by its recent manifestations.

* In this connection the reader is invited to study carefully the Caudron case in Chapter XII.

PART III

THE NEW SLAVE-TRADE IN BEING

The Working of the System as it affects the Natives

CONGO STATE CONTROL IN THE CENTRAL DISTRICT
  The Mongalla—I.

CONGO STATE CONTROL IN THE CENTRAL DISTRICT
  The Mongalla—II. (The Caudron Case)

CONGO STATE CONTROL IN THE CENTRAL DISTRICT
  In the Lopori-Maringa Country, and in the Lulanga District

CONGO STATE CONTROL IN THE NORTHERN DISTRICT
  The Welle-Rubi, Welle-Makua, and Lado Enclave

CONGO STATE CONTROL IN THE DOMAINE DE LA COURONNE

CONGO STATE CONTROL IN THE WESTERN DISTRICT
  Basin of the Kasai

CONGO STATE CONTROL IN THE EASTERN DISTRICT
  From the Lomami to the Eastern Frontier: the Aruwimi, Lakes Tanganyika, Kivu, Albert Edward, and Albert

CONGO STATE CONTROL IN THE SOUTH-EASTERN DISTRICT
  Katanga

CONGO STATE CONTROL ON THE RIVER BANKS

CONGO STATE CONTROL IN THE LOWER CONGO

THE GENERAL CONDITION OF NATIVE LIFE UNDER CONGO STATE CONTROL

CHAPTER XI

CONGO STATE CONTROL IN THE CENTRAL DISTRICT

THE MONGALLA

"Mr. Morel's indictment is one of the most terrible things ever written, *if true.*"—Sir HARRY JOHNSTON, Dec. 20, 1902.*
"*If Mr. Morel is accurately informed* . . . the sufferings of which the picture is given to the world in 'Uncle Tom's Cabin' are as nothing to those which he represents to be the habitual accompaniments of the acquisition of rubber and ivory by the Belgian Companies."—*Times*, Dec. 19, 1902.†

THE *Abir* and *Anversoise* Trusts being situated on the main highway of the Congo River system, it naturally follows that their performances have attracted more publicity. For atrocious, and well-nigh incredible oppression, it would be difficult to award the palm between them.

In 1892 was founded the *Société Anversoise du Commerce au Congo*, under Belgian law. It was dissolved in January, 1898, and reconstructed under Congo law. Its sphere of operations is the Mongalla district, and the area is understood to be twice the size of Belgium, or over 22,000 square miles in extent—all "vacant" territory, of course! The administrators of this Trust are (or were) Baron Goffinet, E. Bunge, and C. de Brown de Tiège. After its reconstruction, the principal shareholders were:

1. The Congo State, 1000 shares;
2. A. de Brown de Tiège, 1100 shares;
3. Bunge and Company, 100 shares;
4. E. P. Grisar, 130 shares;
5. Deyman-Druart, 100 shares.

The capital of the *Anversoise* was, after reconstruction,

* Sir Harry Johnston's review of "Affairs of West Africa" in the *Daily Chronicle.*
† The *Times* review of "Affairs of West Africa." A brief epitome—conveyed in three chapters—of Congo State rule was given in the volume referred to. The italics are the author's. I quote these passages with some diffidence, but with frank egotism. It is difficult to refrain sometimes from referring to the scepticism of a recent past.

declared to be 1,700,000 francs, or £68,000, in 3400 "privileged" shares of £20 each, the State being, therefore, holder to the extent of 50 per cent. The State receives (or received), moreover, 300 francs per ton of rubber "collected" by the Trust, and 5 per cent. on the market value in Europe of ivory " collected " by the Trust. The concession was a renewable one of 50 years' duration.* The year of its reconstruction (1898) under Congo law, the net profits of the *Anversoise* leaped from 120,697 francs in 1897 to 3,968,832 in 1898 ; or considerably more than twice as much as its total capital. In 1899 its net profits amounted to 3,083,976 francs. In 1900, owing to the determined opposition of the natives to the process whereby these profits were obtained, the figure fell to 84,333 francs.

In 1902 the profits were 1,080,247 francs. Major Lothaire, the hangman of the unfortunate Stokes, was, shortly after his farcical trials and acquittal, appointed manager of the Trust in Africa—that is to say, at the end of 1897. He was permitted to leave that post and return to Europe, at the time of the scandals of 1900. The *Anversoise*, like the *Abir*, has its own levies, which it arms with Albinis and cap-guns ; and its operations are assisted by the regular army when necessary, which appears to be pretty often. That this frequently denied state of affairs still existed at the end of 1903 is seen from the findings in the Caudron case, to which allusion will be made.

The first stories of really heavy fighting in the *Anversoise* concession reached Europe about the autumn of 1898, when it transpired that the *Anversoise* station at Dundasame had been attacked by natives of the Budja tribe, and the two European agents, Bardard and Gydens, killed, together with their soldiers. This was followed by the intelligence that two other agents, Ceulemans and Kessels, on their way to relieve Dundasame, had also been cut up, together with their force. Fighting appears to have gone on intermittently during the whole of 1898 and 1899, developing towards the end of that year in an attack upon the Yambata station by the natives, and in a very serious and general uprising. The usual explanations were given as to the causes which had led to this long series of struggles, when suddenly a bombshell fell at the feet of the worthy administrators of the Trust, and greatly disturbed that equanimity which large profits and steady dividends may be presumed to cultivate.

One of the Trust's agents, Lacroix by name, sent a confession and explanation to the *Nieuwe Gazet*, of Antwerp, in which paper it appeared on April 10, 1900. It then became

* A. J. Wauters, *op. cit.*, 1899, p. 395. Under present arrangements, it would appear to receive the whole !

apparent why the natives of the Mongalla district had shown themselves so refractory to civilisation. Lacroix asserted, amongst other things, that in November, 1899, he was instructed by his chief to massacre all the natives of a certain village. Twenty-two women and two children were killed, and two other women who were fleeing in a canoe were drowned. The massacre had been ordered *because the village had been slow in bringing in rubber.* On another occasion Lacroix's chief had put sixty women "in chains," nearly all of whom had been allowed to die of starvation *because the village to which it belonged, Mummumbula, had not brought in enough rubber.** Lacroix wound up his letter with the following flourish:—

"I am going to appear before the judge (1) for having assassinated 150 men, and cut off 60 hands; (2) for having crucified women and children, and for having mutilated many men and hung the remains on the village fence; (3) for having shot a native with a revolver; (4) for having murdered a native." †

This very inconvenient confession was promptly followed by the publication in *Le Petit Bleu*, also of Antwerp—then a courageous free-lance, now a most devoted organ of "Bula Matadi"—of sworn affidavits by soldiers in the employ of the Trust, to the effect that, acting by order of another European agent of the Trust, who wished to "make an example" of several villages for failure in the rubber supply, they had proceeded to carry out their mission. The substance of the declarations was this. The doomed villages were surrounded, every man, woman, and child butchered without mercy, their remains mutilated in the most fiendish manner, and the villages then burnt. A statutory declaration by Moray, another of the Trust's sub-agents, was also published in *Le Petit Bleu*, from which the following is a brief extract:—

"At Ambas we were a party of thirty under X——, who sent us into a village to ascertain if the natives were collecting rubber, and in the contrary case to murder all, including men, women, and children. We found the natives sitting peaceably. We asked them what they were doing. They were unable to reply, thereupon we fell upon them all, and killed them

---

* Corroborated by Cyrus Smith, a Lagos sub-agent of the Company, *Vide* White Book—Africa, No. 1, 1904.

† The full list of crimes which formed the basis of the prosecution of the agents of the *Anversoise* was as follows: Killing 150 persons and cutting off 60 hands; crucifying women and children; cutting off the sexual members and the heads of men, and nailing them on the palisades of the village; shooting a native with a revolver; killing a native chief; shooting 22 women and 2 children of the village of Manbia, and shooting 3 women outside it; shooting a native soldier; imprisoning 60 women and putting them "in the chains," where all but five died of starvation.

without mercy. An hour later we were joined by X——, and told him what had been done. He answered, 'It is well, but you have not done enough!' Thereupon he ordered us to cut off the heads of the men and hang them on the village palisades, also their sexual members, and to hang the women and children on the palisades in the form of a cross."

Several other statements of a similar nature were published in the Belgian Press. The extent of the military operations which became necessary to cope with the infuriated natives had caused such a commotion, and the "revelations" in Belgium were so explicit, that the legal paraphernalia of the Congolese Courts had been set in motion, and a number of the sub-agents of the *Anversoise* were arrested, as Lacroix's confession indicates. He and some of the others seemed to have determined that if they were to suffer for having carried out the instructions of their superiors, the least they could do by way of revenge was to communicate what had been going on to the Belgian newspapers. Those newspapers were not so subservient at that time as they have become since; hence the unusual publicity given to these particular atrocities which, however, were not specially remarkable, and did not differentiate from others.

Official explanations and excuses were speedily forthcoming. M. Liebrechts, one of the Secretaries of the central Administration of the State in Brussels, was positively astonished.

"A customs officer," he declared, "recently made a tour of inspection in the district, and found everything in such an excellent state, the people so well disposed, order so perfect, that he reported to us officially: Ah! you can rest assured, light will be forthcoming, complete, striking." *

Stormy scenes took place in the Belgian Chamber, the gallant opponents of the new dispensation, Vandervelde and Lorand, protesting in the name of humanity against a system which could allow of such barbarities. M. de Favereau, the Minister for Foreign Affairs, was virtuously indignant, but declared that Belgium could not ask explanations of the Congo State, to which the *Mouvement Géographique* retorted that, while M. de Favereau's thesis might be "judicially accurate," it was contrary to common sense to affirm that Belgium "had not the right to concern herself with the administrative methods of the Congo State," a line of argument which that excellent organ appears to have forgotten when M. de Favereau made a similar statement in the course of the Congo debate in July, 1903.†

An explanatory statement was also issued by the Congo

* *Mouvement Géographique.* Brussels, April 29, 1900.
† See Part V.

IN THE MONGALLA

State to the effect that the Budja region had been occupied in September, 1899, the natives appearing at that time "favourably disposed." "But," continued the official statement, "when they were asked to furnish food-stuffs to the newly formed stations, they became suspicious, and abandoned the neighbourhood, trying by starving out the *postes** to compel the Europeans to evacuate them"—a rather ingenious way of putting it. To accentuate the unreasonableness of the natives, M. de Cuvelier, another of the Congo State Secretaries, issued a lengthy statement describing the *modus operandi* followed by the *Anversoise*. This statement appeared almost simultaneously with another by Moray, the incriminated agent already referred to, in the *Messager de Bruxelles*, and yet another by an ex-agent of the Trust, in the *Petit Bleu*. The three versions may be usefully placed side by side:

M. de Cuvelier's version.	Moray's version.	The ex-agent's version.
"Each factory makes a census of the men inhabiting the adjacent villages. Nominative lists are thus formed, and the natives inscribed thereon are summoned to the factory, where they are made to understand the benefits which will accrue to them through collecting rubber, by showing them merchandise, which they greatly covet. The Company, from the start, paid the natives in a fair manner, and acquired their confidence. The natives inscribed on the list have got into a habit (*ont pris pour habitude*) to go each week to the factory to exchange their produce. The means employed by this Company are of the most legal and pacific nature."	"When natives bring rubber to a factory, they are received by an agent surrounded by soldiers. The baskets are weighed. If the baskets do not contain the five kilos. required, the natives receive 100 blows with a *chicotte*. Those whose baskets attain the correct weight receive a piece of cloth or some other object. If a certain village contains 100 male inhabitants, and 50 come to the factory with rubber, they are retained as hostages, and a force is sent to bring the 50 unruly natives and burn their village."	"At first the blacks generally promised what they are asked for —1000 kilos. monthly for every village of 100 persons—but they hardly ever keep their word. Then it is necessary to use coercion. The refractory village is attacked, a certain number of hostages are seized, and only released upon the payment of so many baskets of rubber for every hostage. Sometimes the outbreak extends to the neighbouring villages, and then the entire region is in revolt, and the troops of the State placed at the disposal of the Company have to put it down. In this manner a condition of war exists almost continuously in one portion or another of the Mongalla district."

---

* Stations.

M. Liebrechts had promised light "complete" and "striking," but the manager of the Company, Lothaire,* was allowed to return to Europe "*sans être inquiété*," as a Belgian newspaper put it, while his miserable subordinates were being tried. M. Liebrechts had promised light "complete" and "striking," but the minutes of the trials never saw the light of day, with the exception of one passage—a very significant one—from the verdict on Mattheys quoted by M. Vandervelde in the Belgian House in July, 1903.† Lacroix was released after four years. Van Eycken was acquitted. Moray, whose testimony at the trial would, for special reasons, have been of great importance, died mysteriously just as the trial was coming on. He was found dead in bed. Mattheys was condemned to twelve years' penal servitude, and after serving three years was liberated last October (1903). He appears to have been fêted in Boma on his release, and *La Tribune Congolaise*, an Antwerp newspaper

* The *Petit Bleu* published, in connection with this person's home-coming, the following remarks from its diminutive and courageous—his courage has not been equally conspicuous of late—correspondent in the Lower Congo, Paul Conreur:
"The precipitate return of M. Lothaire to Belgium is the subject of general discussion. He arrived (at Matadi) the day before the steamer sailed, went on board immediately, and left in the steamer the following morning. People do not understand how, after having handed over to justice seven of his agents, who accuse him of having instructed them to act as they did towards the natives, Lothaire should not have been retained by the Public Prosecutor of Boma to facilitate the inquiry. Is it really true that in the Congo justice specially works to hush up the responsibility of a powerful agent, thus showing itself less severe for the great than the small? We have, in the Mongalla affair, terrible accusations against agents, who claim *that they acted under orders*. As chief, Lothaire is responsible for the acts of his agents. At least, he should be interrogated at Boma, and confronted with his accusers. Instead of that, he returned to Belgium, where he explains the massacres as he chooses, accuses the agents of being the cause of same, together with the savagery of the Budjas, who prefer to rebel rather than be shot in the process of 'making rubber.'"
It is useless to refer to the mutual accusations bandied about in the Belgian Press by Lothaire against his accusers, and *vice versâ*. It need only be said that Lothaire has again visited the Congo in his position as Director-General of various enterprises more or less connected with the Government; and in spite of the fact that he has been "wanted" by Congolese justice to render an explanation in connection with these scandals, he has flouted their "invitations," and treated with derision the "requests" of the Director of Justice. His appointment by *the Sovereign of the Congo State* to the directorship of the *Anversoise*, subsequent to the murder of Mr. Stokes, accounts perhaps for the way in which Lothaire has laughed at the efforts of Congolese "law" to examine him in connection with the Mongalla massacres.

† See Part V. Here is part of it: "Seeing that it is also just to take into account the example which his superiors gave him, in showing no respect for the lives or the rights of the natives."

IN THE MONGALLA

dealing wholly with Congo affairs, published in its issue of November 19, 1903, a eulogistic article on "*le pauvre Garçon.*" Of such is the kingdom of Congo. So much for the revelations of 1900 from exclusively Belgian sources.*

An ex-agent of the Trust stated in 1903 that fully ten thousand natives must have been done to death in the Mongalla country since the advent of the *Anversoise*.

During 1902 and 1903, the efforts to teach the Mongalla natives the dignity of labour do not appear to have much relaxed, as the following extracts, taken from the Belgian Press, show :—

February, 1902.—Fighting in the Mongalla district. M. Mardulier, *Commissaire* for Bangala, captures three of the most important Budja chiefs, and 450 cap-guns, 50 Albinis, 4 revolvers, and much ammunition.

April.—Of the three Budja chiefs captured by M. Mardulier, one was hanged, one exiled, and one escaped.

May.—Mongalla district quiet. The paramount Budja chief Eseko, condemned to transportation, is at Banana. Two other chiefs are in prison at Nouvelle Anvers.

October.—A partial uprising has taken place in the Bangala district (the Mongalla concession is within the " Bangala district ").

May, 1903.—" Complaints have been received that a white agent has murdered many people in the Mongalla district, and burned several villages."

June.—Annual meeting of the Trust, reports the Company's work now proceeds on "normal lines, and it is very prosperous." The President declares that the debate in the House of Commons does not trouble him in the least. An agent of the Trust expected at Boma to answer charges of " exactions and *faits d'armes*."

August.—" We learn that the Tribunal of the First Instance has condemned to ten years' penal servitude on August 28, M. G——, who attacked without any motive the village of Boli and massacred 45 Budjas." †

October.—" Perfect calm " in the Mongalla district.

November.—" The position is not precisely agreeable in the Mongalla. Agent E—— has disappeared. He is said to have been massacred. Fifteen soldiers who accompanied him have been killed."

November.—" A force of 700 soldiers is proceeding to the Ebunda district (Budja country)."

No editorial comment ever accompanies these statements. They are noted—and accepted.

In May, 1904, a document was published which, while

---

* In any civilised country, at the hands of any civilised government, these men would have been shot out of hand. But if such drastic measures had been adopted, public opinion in Belgium might have insisted upon the production of the minutes of the trials ! Compare the treatment of these men with the summary execution of Stokes by Lothaire. Yet the apologists of the State declare that agents guilty of atrocity are punished with " rigour " !

† *Le Patriote*, October, 1903.

completing the link in this chain of misery and wickedness, dealt the State one of the most staggering blows it has ever received. It deserves a chapter to itself.*

* In July, 1904, a further outbreak was reported, an agent of the Trust being killed, together with many soldiers. A column of 200 men was to be sent against the "rebels." As this book goes to press, it is announced that the "rebels" have compelled the "column" to retreat.

CHAPTER XII

CONGO STATE CONTROL IN THE CENTRAL DISTRICT—
THE MONGALLA—THE CAUDRON CASE (*continued*).

> "It is unfortunately true that acts of violence have been committed against the natives in the Congo, as everywhere else in Africa: the Congo State has never sought either to deny *or to conceal them*. The detractors of the State show themselves to be prejudiced when they quote these acts as the necessary consequence of a bad system of administration, or *when they assert that they are tolerated by the higher authorities.*"—Congo State's reply to British Note, Sept. 17, 1903. Africa, No. 1, 1904.
>
> "No agreement can be entertained to the effect that acts of violence are improbable or impossible under a system such as that revealed by the judgment pronounced by the Court of Appeal at Boma in the Caudron case."—The Marquess of LANSDOWNE to Sir C. PHIPPS, June 6, 1904. Africa, No. 7.

BEFORE May of this year, the world had never been placed in possession of the minutes of a single judgment of the law courts of the Lower Congo. In one case only—that of the Mongalla atrocities of 1900—had a few extracts from the findings of the judges filtered through to Europe.

On May 4 * I published the complete text of the judgment of the Court of Appeal at Boma—the supreme tribunal of the Congo State's judicial establishment. The publication of this document caused an immense stir, and forced King Leopold to the issue of a singular manifesto. By common accord the publication of the judgment has been regarded as the most damaging blow ever received by the Congo State. Why was this? Why should the verdict of the highest judicial court in the Congo State, in a specific case, have such an effect, or be regarded as so momentous an event? Should it not rather have strengthened the position in Europe of an institution which boasts of the independence of its judicature, which places on record its unalterable determination to pursue evil-doers; the inevitable and rigorous punishment which follows crime on

---

* Congo Supplement of the *West African Mail* for May. The Congo Supplement of the *West African Mail* is the official organ of the Congo Reform Association. Six weeks later, the judgment was published in the White Book—Africa, No. 7, 1904.

the Congo; the impartiality of the judges who prosecute, regardless of the position of offenders, those guilty of reprehensible acts towards natives?

A backward glance is required to appreciate the situation. The annals of European dealing with the races of Western Central Africa are stained with individual acts of wrong-doing. Instances of barbarity towards natives have, I am afraid, been frequent; acts of brutality amounting to atrocity have been far less common. But isolated instances of the sort have occurred, and, so far as my knowledge goes, they have been dealt with by the civilized governments concerned, whenever the facts have come to light. During the last ten years, the Congo State, according to the Belgian newspapers themselves, has been the scene of a perfect epidemic of such cases. Times almost without number has one come across a bald paragraph in the Congo correspondence of Belgian newspapers, announcing the arrest of Mr. So-and-So, for *sévices* against the natives. The penal code contains numerous provisions for safeguarding the native population.* Yet it is safe to say that in no part of Africa has European criminality in regard to natives in the remotest degree approached the proportion or the character recorded in the Congo State. And, curious to relate, the prosecution in the Congo of Europeans guilty of such outrages seems to have been marked by considerable increase of energy whenever the voice of protest in Europe has been loudest. Last year, for instance, the cry for reform was very emphatic, and the Boma courts were exceptionally busy. "Men are being brought to Boma every week," a correspondent wrote to me last summer, "from the interior on the charge of atrocities upon natives." Indeed, to such lengths was the Executive in Brussels willing to go, to convince the world of its determination to put down abuses, that it was semi-officially and somewhat disingenuously announced in the autumn of 1903 that no fewer than thirty-five † Europeans were at Boma awaiting trial!

* There is also an amusing body, in the Congo, going by the name of Commission for the Protection of the Natives. This Commission, upon which two Baptist missionaries are not ashamed to serve, was appointed in 1896 in response to the thrill of horror which went through Europe at Mr. Sjöblom's narration. During the first three years of its appointment it held two brief and ineffective sittings. It has held none at all since its reappointment in 1901. White Book Co. 1754, February, 1904. See also published correspondence between the Aborigines' Protection Society and the Baptists. May, 1904.

† More cautious in its diplomatic correspondence, the Congo State speaks of "a certain number of Europeans who at this moment are in the prisons of the State expiating their offences against the penal laws which protect the life and person of the native." Africa, No. 1, 1904. According to a letter dated July 25 of this year, received from a

THE CAUDRON CASE

Think of it! Think of the fuss which is made if one Englishman, German, or Frenchman, in an English, German, or French possession in West Africa, is accused of a crime of this nature! All the world is apprised of the facts, and many are the solemn leading articles devoted to discussing the ill effects which contact with the Negro in his natural surroundings produces upon European *morale*. But on the Congo it all seems to be a matter of course. That there should be thirty-five, or even three, Europeans, involved in acts of atrocity upon the natives, awaiting trial in Boma at one time, does not, apparently, cause the flutter of an eyelid in Brussels or Antwerp. It provokes no public comment, *and the minutes of these trials never see the light of day! unless by chance, and despite the Government!*

It was, no doubt, owing to the publicity given to the Mongalla massacre of 1900, thanks to Lacroix's confession, the despatches of the *Petit Bleu's* correspondent in the Congo, and the controversy which arose over the personality of Lothaire, that brief extracts from the findings of the Boma courts eventually reached Belgium.

Such as they were, they possessed considerable interest, because they appeared to point to the complicity of local officials in the rubber raids conducted by the accused. But it was not until long afterwards, that is to say, until the issue of the White Book—Africa, No. 1, 1904, that a quotation from the findings, in so far as the case of a British coloured subject (an agent of the *Anversoise* was also involved) was concerned, gave us a fuller acquaintance with the facts. From this quotation, it is quite clear that, in the mind of the judges of 1900, the complicity of the local authorities in specific acts of illegal violence towards the natives was established. Here is the quotation, given by Consul Casement:

> "That, above all, the facts that the arrest of women and their detention, to compel the villages to furnish both produce and workmen, was tolerated and admitted even by certain of the Administrative Authorities of the region."

None of the "Administrative Authorities" were troubled, however; and, as we have had occasion to notice, the manager in Africa of the *Anversoise* at the time was not "*inquiété.*" Further, with the exception of Moray, whose sudden demise gave rise to much speculation (doubtless a decree of Providence),

correspondent in the Congo who is thoroughly well informed, there were on that date thirteen Europeans in Boma prison, viz. Enbach, Goffat, Goyers, Dagot, Delatte, Caudron, Merrens, Haibel, Claus, Honart, Perilleux, Manquette, Sarmain. Four more had just arrived, and were awaiting trial.

the atrocious crimes of the subordinate agents—crimes which one cannot read without feeling that hanging was too good for the men guilty of perpetrating or ordering them—were visited nominally with long terms of imprisonment, in reality serving four and three years respectively.

At the time, be it noted, the Congo Government posed, albeit not very successfully, before the world as the resolute guardian of the natives' rights. Horror at the possibility of such deeds was openly expressed. The Commission for the Protection of Natives (see footnote, p. 136) was shortly afterwards reappointed. Justice had been vindicated. The guilty men had been punished. The immunity enjoyed by Lothaire was perhaps not quite satisfactory; still the matter blew over. Ever since, the Congo Government, as before, has loudly and insistently proclaimed its determination to prosecute evil-doers with all the rigour of the Law with a capital L; failing, of course, to explain why Belgians who slaughter men and impale their sexual remains on village palissades, because when living those men failed to bring in enough rubber to a company in which the State owned half the shares; who slaughter, crucify, imprison, and starve women by way of encouraging their male relatives to increase the production of that article;—are considered to have purged their crimes after, in one instance three, and in the other instance four, years of "imprisonment."

That, I repeat, was the *summum* of knowledge the European public—though not, I am sorry to say, some of the European Governments—possessed of the efficacy and procedure of the Congolese Courts in "safeguarding the lives and the property of the natives" in accordance with the Berlin Act, in cases of fiendish atrocity perpetrated upon the bodies of native men, women, and children by Europeans—until I published the verdict of the Appeal Court in the Caudron and Sylvanus Jones cases, which endorses not only the very worst charges ever brought against King Leopold's rule in Africa, but, in the condition of affairs it discloses, is alone sufficient to justify the immediate intervention of the civilised Powers. The Judgment is published in full in the Appendix. Its salient points may be given here.

Caudron was the *Chef de Zone Commercial* of the Melo district. Brought before the Court of First Instance on an indictment of eight counts, he was condemned on February 12, 1904, to twenty years' imprisonment. Appealing, he saw his sentence reduced to fifteen years' imprisonment, with extenuating circumstances, by the Appeal Court at Boma. The counts were, briefly, as follows: Attacking the village of

THE CAUDRON CASE

Liboke with the armed soldiers of the Company, whereby a "certain number" of natives were killed. Attacking a number of villages in the Banza country, whereby a "great number" of natives were killed. Shooting at and wounding a native woman. Arbitrarily detaining for nearly a month twenty prisoners taken from the Banza villages attacked. Indirectly causing the death of an escaping prisoner by having previously given instructions to his soldiers to shoot all who might attempt to escape. Ordering the murder of a Mogwande Chief when a prisoner at Bonga. Arming soldiers of the Company with rifles and cartridges taken from two police-stations of the State. Disposing of Government cartridges to his subordinates.

As regards the first count, the defence argued that existing documents proved that Caudron's superior was present at the spot whence the attack took place, and ordered it. Every single witness called denied this. The prosecution alleged the documents were forged subsequently, in the interests of the accused. In view of the fact, however, that the said documents were found at the police-station, that they were actually incorporated in the *dossier* by the examining magistrate, and that their existence was confirmed by the manager of the station at the preliminary inquiry, the Appeal Court concluded that the chief of police "was at Akula when the attack against the village of Liboke took place, and that he was aware of, and authorised that attack."

The Court decided, however, that the police officer at Akula was not Caudron's superior, and the latter could not shelter himself behind this officer, and that in attempting to do so he was merely trying to shield himself from the consequences of his own delinquencies.

Withdrawn from their ponderous legal phraseology, the facts thus appear:

The manager of the station of the *Société Anversoise* at Akula writes on October 12 to the neighbouring Government police-station at Binga, demanding "intervention" against the village of Liboke. In the night of the 15th-16th an expedition attacks the village, and a "certain number" of natives are killed. Caudron, of the *Société Anversoise*, was present at the attack, together with the Government official commanding the Government police-station at Binga and his subordinates. Irregulars belonging to the *Société Anversoise* armed with rifles, and Government troops co-operating, together deliver the attack. "All the witnesses," according to the minutes of the Court of Appeal, agreed that Caudron was the presiding genius at the affray. It would, perhaps, be more logical to assume that he commanded his own men, and that the State officials commanded their own troops. However, that is not a very important point. What is important is the admitted fact that Government troops and *Société Anversoise* irregulars co-operated in making a night attack, at the written request of the manager of the *Société Anversoise* station at Akula, upon an unfortunate village in the neighbourhood, which, as the Appeal Court found, had committed no hostile act, and was merely guilty of "failing to furnish the Company with the amount of labour exacted by it." On October 16, the day after the attack, the manager of the *Société Anversoise* station at Akula writes to the Government official commanding the Government police-station at Binga, whose "intervention" against the village of Liboke he had, as we have seen, solicited, thanking him for that "intervention," and telling him that the survivors of the attack had "come in the morning to the station, and had undertaken to furnish regularly the impositions." *

The story is instructive. Its sequel is more informing still. The defence put forward the plea, on this Liboke incident, as in the case of the expedition against the Banza, that the accused Caudron had "precedently and subsequently participated in other expeditions against the natives," accompanied by Government officials and officers. This the Appeal Court found established from the evidence of witnesses, and mention is made, in particular, of an expedition against the Gwakas—not forming part of the indictment. Yet on February 12, 1904, the accused is condemned, amongst other counts, to twenty years' imprisonment by the Court of First Instance for participating in such an expedition in October, 1902.

While justly condemning such practices in the abstract, the Appeal Court, admitting the existence of "toleration" towards them on the part of the "superior authorities," and allowing that such "toleration" might be held to constitute "extenuating circumstances in favour of the accused," rejected, on various grounds, the appeal of the accused, that he was merely carrying out his normal work in accordance with recognised practice. It did not, the Court held, "form part of his business as an agent of a company to co-operate in acts of repression." The Court did not pronounce as to whether it formed part of the business of the Company's manager at Akula † to invoke the

* Note this word in connection with the operations of a reputed "trading" company !

† The following description of Akula is supplied to me by one who has "been there": "The houses are built upon what is practically an island raised from the swamp by the unremitting and unrecompensed

co-operation of Government officials and troops in attacking a village solely guilty of failing in its labour supply, which was the origin of the affair. The Court also held, as already stated, that the Government official in charge of the police-station at Binga and his subordinate were not the superiors of the accused, and that, even if they had been, "obedience to one's superiors does not constitute an excuse when the illegality of the order is obvious."

In the expedition, or series of expeditions, against the Banza villages, carried out in January, February, and March of last year, a "great number of natives" were killed. These expeditions were undertaken "in order to force the natives of the region of Banza to increase their rubber supply." The *Société Anversoise du Commerce au Congo*, be it noted, is, as its name and constitution imply, a *trading* company! The accused was accompanied by twenty of the Company's irregulars armed with rifles, and by a non-commissioned officer of the Government—described as "Chief of Police Jamart"—with fifty Government soldiers.

The expeditions against the Banzas formed, as the Liboke incident, a count in the indictment under which the accused was condemned in February, 1904, by the Court of First Instance, to twenty years' imprisonment, against which he appealed. In rejecting that appeal, the Court found the fact of Government co-operation borne out, and all that remained to be examined was whether "the presence and the authorisation of these representatives of authority may be taken as justifying the action of the accused."

The Court found that the accused was acting in the interest of his Company, in order that the output of rubber might be increased; that no precedent act of hostility had been committed by the natives; that not a solitary casuality occurred among the attacking party; that "killing under such circumstances constitutes a crime which no law, which no necessity, authorises." Having reached these conclusions, the Appeal Court rejected the appeal. Many of the grounds for rejection adduced by the Court, in this case, were similar to those adduced by it in the case of the Liboke affair, and it is, therefore, unnecessary to repeat them.

The complicity of the local representatives of authority

work of labour of hundreds of native women, who are forced by the Company's agents to perform this work, in spite of their pitiful appeals to be allowed time to attend to their work, as many were starving through being forced to neglect it. When employed on this labour, the women either carry their young children or have to leave them in the villages."

was set aside, so far as the plea of justification set up by the accused was concerned.

The Court displayed great caution in respect to the demand of the defence in connection with the production of official documents. The defence demanded a supplementary inquiry with the object of including in the *dossier*, the political reports of the "superior authorities" of the region to the Government, which documents, the defence alleged, would show that the "authorities had known and approved of the action" of the accused. The Government declined to furnish them. The Appeal Court, after protesting its right to insist upon their production, explained why it forbore to do so, on the grounds, *inter alia*, that the greatest "circumspection" should be made use of in such matters, and that if toleration, or even positive orders on the part of the authorities, for the committal of the acts charged against the accused were proved, "facts contrary to law" could not thereby be justified, and all that could be urged therefrom in palliation of the charges against the accused would be "extenuating circumstances." The Court declared itself satisfied that a case for "extenuating circumstances" had been made out *inter alia* on the basis of such documents as the *dossier* already contained and the proved co-operation of Government troops, and concluded that "any supplementary inquiry on this subject, if it served to prove the responsibility of other persons, could be of no utility to accused."

The conclusion is interesting. Put briefly, the story as unfolded in the minutes appears somewhat as follows. An agent of the *Société Anversoise* conducts military expeditions in co-operation with Government officials and Government troops against various native villages. The operations last three months, and a large number of natives are killed. These natives, it is expressly admitted, had committed no hostile act, and there was no state of war. Their fault was that they had not supplied the *Société Anversoise* with a sufficient quantity of indiarubber, for which the Government, according to the constitution of the Company as stated by M. A. J. Wauters, the historian of Congo, received £12 per ton collected, and in which Company the Government held one-half the shares. A year after these expeditions, the agent of the *Société Anversoise*, who conducted, or participated in them, is condemned, for having done this and other things, to twenty years' imprisonment. He appeals. His appeal is rejected, but his sentence is lightened by five years, with extenuating circumstances. His defence is that the authorities knew and approved of these expeditions. The Appeal Court admits the co-operation of

THE CAUDRON CASE

Government official troops, and from this fact and from documents produced concludes that official "toleration" existed, and allows extenuating circumstances on that account. But the accused goes further. He demands the production of official reports, which he says will prove that the "superior authorities" themselves knew and approved of his actions. These reports are refused by Government, and the Appeal Court observes in effect that even if they were produced, and proved all that the accused says they would, even to direct orders given, the actions of the accused were themselves contrary to law, and could under no circumstances be considered justified.

The fourth count was the imprisonment of natives for being short in supplies of rubber. In addition to the "great number of natives" killed in the course of the three months' expedition against the Banzas, twenty natives (sexes not given) were imprisoned on the premises of the factory of the *Société Anversoise du Commerce au Congo*. Their detention, it was shown, "had no other object than to force their villagers to collect rubber." This arbitrary detention formed the fourth count in the indictment against the accused. The accused pleaded in his defence that the Government authorised the *Société Anversoise du Commerce au Congo*, in April, 1901, "to exact rubber as a tax from the people," and had decreed, in case of refusal, "the bodily detention of the defaulters." It was admitted by the prosecution that the Governor-General had written a letter authorising this procedure. The Court, however, decided in effect that the instructions of the Governor-General were invalid, and "that the right of establishing taxes on the people, and to fix punishments, can only belong to the Sovereign King, or by the authority legally delegated by him to that effect." The Court concluded that this letter could not "justify the wrong done to individual liberty;" but as the accused might have been led into error thereby, extenuating circumstances were allowable.

The findings of the Court in regard to extenuating circumstances are worthy of some little attention. The extenuating circumstances were made applicable only to the first, second, and fourth counts. The shooting of a native woman in a fit of temper (third count); the cold-blooded murder, committed by authority of the accused upon the person of a Mogwande Chief in prison (sixth count); and a breach of the fire-arms regulations (seventh count); these acts did not benefit by "extenuating circumstances." The fifth and eighth counts—alleged responsibility for the shooting of an escaping prisoner, and breach of the fire-arms regulations, were dismissed.

With regard to the first, second, and fourth counts, the Court held that "killing, under such circumstances, constitutes a crime which no law, which no necessity, authorises"—an assertion which will not be queried. But in concluding for extenuating circumstances, the President of the Appeal Court used remarkable language. To the reasons already given—and which we have passed in review—he added the "good antecedents of the accused, and the difficulties under which he must have laboured in the accomplishment of his mission," in the midst of a population "entirely refractory to all kinds of work, and which only respects the law of force, knows no other persuasion than terror" ("et qui ne respecte d'autre loi que la force, ne connait d'autre persuasion que la terreur"). And again :

"Although the acts are in themselves very grave, they lose a part of their gravity when taken into consideration with their environment, where, according to secular custom, human life had no value, and where pillage, murder, and cannibalism constituted, until yesterday, daily life."

The Appeal Court reduced the sentence upon Caudron by five years, making his sentence fifteen years instead of twenty years, which in view of the Lacroix and Mattheys cases, there is not the least likelihood of his ever serving.

Now, what in a nutshell does this verdict prove? It proves :

1. The existence of a system of *organised* oppression, plunder, and massacre, in order to increase the output of indiarubber for the benefit of a "Company," which is only a covering name for the Government itself.

2. That the local authorities of the Government are cognisant, and participatory in this system.

3. That local officials of the Government engage in these rubber raids, and that Government troops are regularly employed thereon.

4. That the Judicature is powerless to place the real responsibility on the proper shoulders.

5. That, consequently, these atrocities will continue until the system itself is extirpated.

Overwhelmingly clear as the above conclusions are, it is necessary to drive them home, in order that their full significance may be grasped. Let us take first, because it is, perhaps, the most important point, the proved complicity of the local authorities. What is meant by local authorities? The local authorities are the representatives of the Government scattered about the district of Bangala, of which the Mongalla forms a

NSALA OF WALA IN THE NSONGO DISTRICT (ABIR CONCESSION)

(Photographed by Mr. John H. Harris in May, 1904, with the hand and foot of his little girl of five years old—all that remained of a cannibal feast by armed rubber sentries. The sentries killed his wife, his daughter, and a son, cutting up the bodies, cooking and eating them. See letter from Mr. Stannard in the Appendix.)

part. They are under the direct orders of the Chief of the District, the Commissaire-Général of Nouvelle Anvers (Bangala), who is himself under the orders of the Governor-General. Is it likely that these local authorities would act on their own initiative? From the highest to the lowest, the main object of the "Administration," so called, is the increase of revenue, which means an increase in indiarubber. These men were merely carrying out the normal duties assigned to them by their own Government. Caudron's counsel stated in open court that Caudron's expeditions against the Banza and his attack on Liboke were ordered by the Commissaire-Général, *who required, by written orders, Caudron's presence with his deputies on these raids.*

Moreover, Caudron's counsel *demanded the production of the "political reports" of the district to make good his assertion.* Here was an opportunity for the Congolese Judicature, had it been independent, to confound, once and for all, the accusers of the State, who maintain that the Executive, and not its agents, is responsible for the abominations of the Congo. If it could have been shown that local officials alone were guilty, a case of individual wrong-doing—terribly scandalous, it is true, proving the culpable negligence of the supreme authorities, but not involving them as actual *particeps criminis*—could have been made out. But the risk, on the other hand, was great. The Commissaire-Général of a District is one of the highest officials of the State. If his direct responsibility were established by the reports asked for, proceedings would have had to have been taken against him, and where would they have ended? Where, indeed! I cannot pretend to surmise the nature of the discussions which may have passed between the President of the Appeal Court and the Public Prosecutor. Certain is it, that—acting according to the dictates of duty, as we should understand it—the former demanded from the Executive the production of the reports asked for by Caudron's counsel.

Their production was refused!

Here was an open defiance of the Judicature. Did the President of the Appeal Court resign? Not a bit of it. He declined to press the point. He declared that in such matters the greatest "circumspection" was necessary—" a certain toleration" on the part of the authorities was proved by the documents in the *dossier*—" consequently all supplementary inquiry on the subject, if it served to prove the responsibility of other persons"—that is to say, as is obvious on the face of it, higher officials than those already implicated—" could be of no utility to the accused." What could be more significant? The

Executive flouted the Judicature, and the highest representative of that JUSTICE which the Congo State declares to be absolutely independent, unimpeachable, and impeccable, bows his head.

The fact of the matter is, of course, that the President of the Appeal Court, nominated by the Sovereign, however wishful to do the right thing he may have been, could not enter upon a course of action which, if successfully and resolutely pursued through one labyrinth after another, would have pilloried the real and supreme offender, the Sovereign himself! As it was, the President was compelled to go uncommonly near doing so on one point—in dealing with the fourth count against Caudron. The existence of the Governor-General's letter authorising an illegal act had to be admitted, for Caudron's counsel cited both its number and its date (No. 548, April 11, 1900). That the act of the Governor-General *was* illegal could not be denied. But although the Governor-General is, according to the constitution of the Congo State, the "personal mandatory" of the Sovereign in Africa, the Appeal Court contrived to pass off that illegal act as a personal one, thus covering the responsibility of the Sovereign, who not only does not impeach his "personal mandatory," the Governor-General, but addresses the manifesto, to which we shall presently refer, to the "Governor-General"!

In the graver question of the murderous expeditions, however, it was palpably impossible to allow full light to be thrown thereon by insistence upon the whole truth being dragged out. How inconvenient such a proceeding would have been may be still further recognised by the statements of the very able counsel by whom Caudron was defended. That gentleman's pleadings may be epitomised thus :

The operations of the *Société Anversoise* were conducted on a portion of the *Domaine Privé* of the Sovereign, with the open assistance of the Government forces and their officers. The full responsibility laid with the Executive, which used the *Anversoise* as its tax-collector, which was itself a shareholder, and which took three-fourths of the profits of that alleged "trading Company."

The Executive had itself required by letter the agents of the *Anversoise* to collect indiarubber *à titre d'impôt* (as a tax), and had authorised them by delegation to imprison those who failed in complying with the demands.

The arms and ammunition permitted the *Anversoise* were in themselves proof that the Government recognised the right of the *Anversoise* to employ them, since they could by law only be placed in the hands of those specially authorised by the Governor-General under his licence.

THE CAUDRON CASE 147

The *Anversoise*—a "trading Company," let us never forget! —had imported close on 40,000 ball cartridges during the year 1903 by special permission of the Executive, whose own vessels carried this ammunition to its destination on the Upper Congo.

The commission Caudron received on indiarubber "collected" was paid to him with the full consent of the Congo Government, and was, indeed, paid by that Government out of the profits it made from Caudron's raids, and was a commission on the "taxes" he was deputed to collect; and that if Caudron went out on these raids, it was in company with State officials of the district and the Public Force, and that he was not responsible for the effects of those expeditions he was called on to accompany, or for the great loss of life they entailed. The Public Prosecutor in charge of the case against Caudron averred that he was guilty of murdering 122 natives in cold blood, that this number had been actually verified, but that it represented only a small portion of those who suffered death during the course of these rubber expeditions, on the proceeds of which Caudron reaped a commission of 3 per cent. But that for those results the Congo Government was itself alone responsible by the illegal methods it had adopted and enforced by prescription on its employees for compelling the natives to work for its profit and sole advantage.

It is obvious from the above, coupled with the findings of the Court, that the whole hideous fabric upon which reposes the personal rule set over the Congo territories would have been disclosed with the production of the reports demanded, and the consequences to which that production would have given rise could not be faced by a Judicature depending for its existence upon the Sovereign's will and pleasure. "Circumspection" was therefore essential.

Before we treat of the action of King Leopold, taken as a result of the wide publicity given to this case, it is necessary to touch upon one other feature of Congo State "administration," which this exhibition of Congolese JUSTICE accentuates. For bestial atrocities upon natives, two Belgians are sentenced, in 1900, to long terms of imprisonment, and released after three and four years respectively. For killing a minimum of 122 human beings in cold blood, the Congo Appeal Court sentences another Belgian, in 1904, to fifteen years' imprisonment; in other words, the sentence is in the proportion of eight human beings slaughtered to one year's imprisonment, and a purely nominal imprisonment at that—a term of imprisonment, moreover, which will never be completed. And the supreme representative of Justice, who thought a sentence of twenty years too heavy for such crimes, added to the causes I have already detailed as justifying the exercise of partial clemency, the fact that "until yesterday" the slaughtered people were a very bad people, only respecting the law of "Force," and amenable only to the persuasion of "Terror." I am not condemning the plea of "extenuating circumstances." To my mind, Caudron, scoundrel though he be, was in one sense as great a victim as the people he slaughtered by authority; victim of a system from which there is no escape when once in its clutches in the heart of Africa, where the agent must obey, or be—removed. But could any utterance be more revealing than this utterance of the President of the Court of Appeal of the Congo, not necessarily reflecting upon him personally, but reflecting upon the whole conception of what should constitute the duties of the European in his relationship to the African? "Until yesterday," he tells us in effect, these people had every vice under heaven. But "yesterday" implies a past state. Are we to infer that the President of the Appeal Court was referring to the period immediately preceding their murders? But if so, why was the murder of these poor people—the Judgment itself says they were peaceful, inoffensive, and too helpless even to offer resistance to their hired murderers—a "crime which no law, which no necessity authorises"? And what is the ideal put before those who have future dealings with the survivors of these "cold-blooded" massacres? That FORCE and TERROR alone can prove adequate in dealing with them! What does the application of "force" and what does the inculcation of "terror" imply in tropical Africa, when those deputed to apply and inculcate those morally and materially regenerating sentiments are themselves savages armed with weapons of precision, trained to outrage and slaughter, commanded by men drilled in this conception of the nature of a trust entrusted them by civilisation—the trust of caring for the "well-being" of the native population? In those expressions of the President of the Boma Appeal Court is embodied the whole history of the Congo State, past, present, and future, whatever further prolongation of records blood-stained to the core is allowed to it by civilisation.

It would need a particularly vivid imagination to discover in the Caudron case any elements of a humorous character. But only Mr. W. S. Gilbert could hope to rival the humour displayed in the Manifesto drafted in hot-haste by King Leopold and his secretaries, when the effect of the publication of the Judgment in the *West African Mail* began to be apparent. The occasion was serious. Here was no "odious calumniator" to be reckoned with: but the deliberate Judgment

THE CAUDRON CASE

of the highest tribunal in the land; the first one of a long, long series, upon which the eye of the world had been allowed to rest. And what did it disclose? And what did it stop short of disclosing? Plainly, the sublimest heights of altruistic epistolary effort could alone meet the case. And so a declaration was issued—a declaration full of melancholy dignity, clothed in language of sonorous reproof, breathing through every sentence the unadulterated essence of philanthropic motive, struggling with the natural viciousness of man. In the first place, we have the familiar note of profound astonishment. No fairy princess falling asleep at night in an enchanted palace, with the murmurs of splashing fountains, the sweet odours of flowers, and the song of the nightingale floating through the open windows of her perfumed and sumptuous chamber, and awakening amid the sordid surroundings of the lowest slum in London, could have exhibited more surprise, more pained, more poignant sorrow than the "Godefroi de Bouillon of the Nineteenth Century Crusade," when apprised of the conduct of his knights in Africa. Some of them had positively "tolerated" abuses, had been found "sufficiently forgetful of their duties to associate themselves directly or indirectly in acts of maltreatment." Disgraceful! Such acts were "contrary to the principles of superior order which guide the State in its policy towards native peoples," and so on. Does the Sovereign of the Congo State really imagine that he can deceive public opinion in Europe or in America by such obstetrical pedantries, and dishonest trifling? The crimes of Caudron, committed by authority and in co-operation with the officials of the Government and the regular army, were not marked by such ghastly incidents as the massacres perpetrated in the very same region, and under the very same circumstances in 1899–1900. But on the former occasion no copy of the Judgment reached Europe, and King Leopold left one of his secretaries to display the required "astonishment." As for the "duties" of Congo State officials, their association "in acts of maltreatment" is but the obvious indication of their devotion to duties they are called upon to perform—duties consigned in innumerable circulars from the highest authorities in the State, some of which have been published, and of which the refrain runs somewhat thus—

"Rubber, rubber, rubber,
Mind you get the rubber.
It really does not matter
How you get it.

"But be careful to remember
That your principal endeavour
Must be rubber, rubber, rubber
All the day.

"On this the Government relies
And abundantly supplies
The necessary allies
For the purpose.

"The *chicotte*, the cartridge, and the gun
The more easily to dun
(While providing extra fun)
'*A titre d'impôt.*'

"The *Force Publique*, the chain, the prison
Must be the limit of your vision
When making adequate provision
For the Domaine.

"To this confidential information
We draw your strict attention.
Just as well not to mention
It outside.

"For the world, another tale
We have perpetually on sale
Which can never, never fail
To be effective.

"Regeneration, moral and material
From the daily to the serial
Is preached in tones ethereal
To the universe.

"But pray once again remember
That your principal endeavour
Must be rubber, rubber, rubber
All the day."

The Manifesto goes on to positively abjure the Judicature to "seek out" the agents who accompanied Caudron, and "to fix the responsibilities of those who have really been found to be implicated in the incriminating practices"—"*no matter who they may be.*" It is likewise stated that the Government intends that "no indulgence" shall be displayed "towards any of its agents participating in blamable acts towards the natives." That is a clear issue.

In the first place, then, the Governor-General, the "personal mandatory" of the Sovereign in Africa, must arrest himself. There is no help for it. He is indicted by the President of the Appeal Court with the perpetration of an illegal act: to wit, the issue of instructions in writing, authorising by delegation

THE CAUDRON CASE 151

the exaction of indiarubber from the natives, on the part of the agents of a "commercial" company "as a tax," to be accompanied in case of default by the bodily detention of the recalcitrant taxpayers, which implies—as we know from the incidents of 1900—the detention of women and children, who are sometimes allowed to die of neglect and starvation during their confinement in the "*maison des ôtages*," as these modern black-holes of Calcutta are termed. The President of the Appeal Court will then have to judge between the personal guilt of the impeached "mandatory" of the Sovereign, and certain persons in Brussels who transmit to him the orders of his Sovereign! Doubtless the Governor-General will be adequately defended, and he will produce documents in his defence of the highest historical value. On the occasion of such an interesting trial, representatives of the world's Press will, of course, be invited. Pending that trial, the substitute for the impeached Governor-General will doubtless order the immediate arrest of (1) the Commissaire-Général of the Bangala District, the supreme authority of Government in the Mongalla region; (2) the official who participated in the attack on the village of Liboke; (3) the officials who participated in the series of expeditions against the Banza people; (4) the official who sanctioned the arrest of the twenty natives whose villages had failed in their rubber supply, as authorised so to do by the letter of the impeached Governor-General; and (5) finally all the officials who participated in the similar expeditions for similar purposes undertaken "precedently and subsequently" to the Liboke and Banza incidents, in the course of which the forty thousand rounds of ball cartridges imported last year with the knowledge of the Government were presumably utilised. The prison at Boma will have to be enlarged, that is quite certain, and an entire new staff appointed to the Bangala district. Most people will think that there is even more pressing need for a change in the European Directorship of this Equatorial African slaughter-house. Of course the Manifesto from top to bottom is a farce *de premier ordre*. The instructions are *instructions pour rire*. The fact that they are addressed to the Governor-General himself, whom the Court has indicted for the committal of an illegal act, renders it superfluous to labour the point. The glory of Pecksniff is for ever dimmed. Thou wast but a tyro, oh worthy Pecksniff!

There is just one last matter concerning this Manifesto which should be touched upon. It concludes with the announcement that the territory assigned to the *Anversoise* is now taken over by the State, replacing a "private enterprise" in which the State holds 50 per cent. of the shares, controls the machinery, appoints the directors, and gets heavy royalties on all produce exported. What does that mean? In the eyes of the world it is *meant* to mean this: "Appalled and grieved at the misdoings of a commercial company as disclosed by the Judgment in the Caudron case, We have dissolved it. Observe, read, mark, and learn this further proof of Our determination to put down abuses." What it means, in reality, is this: The *Anversoise* was the "tax-collector" for the Sovereign of the Congo State in the Mongalla region of the *Domaine Privé*. It now ceases to be so, and the Government which formerly obtained a large portion of the yield of such "taxes," will now obtain the entire yield. No doubt the handful of financiers, principally concerned in the *Anversoise*, will receive royal compensation. How will the change work out in practice? The following quotation from an Antwerp newspaper supplies the answer. This statement, apparently sent to the newspaper in question from the spot, and appearing almost simultaneously with the royal Manifesto in Brussels, may be usefully compared with the latter—

MANIFESTO (*June*).	"LE TRIBUNE CONGOLAISE" (*June*).
"The Government which has taken over the exploitation of a concession made to this Society, repeats its inflexible will that the whole of the *personnel* in the Congo, whether belonging to the State or the Companies, shall be inspired with its views, and shall reconcile, with the necessary firmness towards the natives, the absolute respect of the rules of the law."	"It is announced from the Mongalla that, with the assistance of the Government police, four new factories (*sic*) have just been established in the Mandika* region. Last April preparations were complete for the establishment of a police-station at Yalombo, the result of which will doubtless be the pacifying (*sic*) of this district, which is peopled by the Budja. Ten factories (*sic*) will then be erected, *i.e.* one in each group of villages. Captain V——† commands the police."

It would seem from the above that the rubber required of the natives of the Mongalla is not likely to diminish in quantity under the new *régime*. What he has been compelled hitherto to bring in in the form of a "trade" to the factories of the *Anversoise*, the native will now be forced to bring in to the "factories" of this singular Government *à titre d'impôt!* And

* Moray, the agent concerned in the massacre of 1900, and who died at a most convenient moment, was in charge of the Mandika factory.
† This Captain V—— is now reported by the Belgian newspapers to be suppressing a "rebellion" in the district mentioned! (August.)

if he is too slow; then, in addition to those indispensable moral elements in dealing with a primitive people, according to the President of the Appeal Court, "Force" and "Terror"; there is, as we also learn from the same authority, a brand-new law authorising his corporal detention—the corporal detention of his women-folk would appear to be the procedure which commends itself more especially to the regenerating representatives of "Bula Matadi"—for default, and proceedings which might have been "illegal" when performed by a "trading company" will, of course, be strictly legal when performed by a Government.

What the natives will gain by the re-absorption of the *Anversoise* into the *Domaine Privé, stricto sensu,* may be judged by their treatment in other regions of that *Domaine*, and its *annex*, the *Domaine de la Couronne*. But the *Domaine Privé*, as already pointed out, will certainly gain. It is an unpleasant story, is it not? But then it has its rosy side too, for, as Chateaubriand tells us, "Les mendiants vivent de leurs plaies: il y à des hommes qui profitent de tout, même du mépris." *

* "Melanges et Poésies."

CHAPTER XIII

CONGO STATE CONTROL IN THE CENTRAL DISTRICT (IN THE LOPORI-MARINGA COUNTRY, AND IN THE LULANGA DISTRICT)

"Our refined Society attaches to human life (and with reason) a value unknown to barbarous communities."—Letter from KING LEOPOLD to his agents in the Congo.

THE region drained by the Lopori and Maringa Rivers is situate between the Congo River and the Equator. The rubber it produces is said to be of excellent quality, and it appears to command very high prices on the Antwerp market. This is the district which is "exploited" by one of the most powerful of the Congo State's Trusts, viz. *L'Abir*.

Originally, the Anglo-Belgian Indiarubber Company, founded in August, 1892, and in which Colonel North was at one time largely interested, it was like *L'Anversoise* reconstructed under "Congo Law" in 1898, with a capital of 1,000,000 francs, divided into 2000 shares without designation of value, "giving right of $\frac{1}{2000}$ of the "Avoir Social." From that date it has been known as *L'Abir*. At the time of reconstruction, the following were the principal shareholders:—

	Shares.
Alex. de Browne de Tiège, as Mandatory of the Congo State	1000
Societe Anversoise du Commerce au Congo	150
Alex. de Browne de Tiège	60
Horace van den Burch, as mandatory of A. van den Nest	125
Horace van den Burch	58
C. de Browne de Tiège	50

The foregoing particulars are taken from the official Statutes of the "Company" (*Abir : Société à responsabilité Limité*), printed by Ratinckx Brothers, at Grande Place, Antwerp. It is interesting to note that M. A. de Browne de Tiège is the famous Antwerp banker, with whom in 1892, 1893, and 1894, the Congo State secretly contracted loans "bearing interest at 6 per cent., and reimbursable on July 1, 1895, by 5,287,415 francs." These secret loans the Congo State was compelled to reveal early in 1895, for it appeared that, failing payment, M. de Browne de Tiège would have become owner of the "greater portions of the Basins of the Aruwimi, Rubi, Lomami, Lake Leopold II., the Lukenye, and Manyemba . . . equal to sixteen million *hectares*." So King Leopold cried *peccavi* to the Belgian Government, and the Belgian Government obligingly paid M. de Browne de Tiège the 5,287,415 francs! * That gentleman, however, managed to remain one of the foremost partners in the Belgian Clique, which runs the Congo for the good of humanity in general, and the Negro race in particular. Besides the important part he plays as shareholder in *L'Abir*, he is President of *L'Anversoise*,† which is the second largest original shareholder in *L'Abir*, and, in addition to being President, is the original shareholder of 1000 shares (out of 3400) in the former concern. To all intents and purposes, then, the fate of the natives of the Lopori and Maringa districts would appear to be primarily in the hands of King Leopold; M. A. de Browne de Tiège; a near relative of the latter, presumably, in the shape of C. de Browne de Tiège of that ilk; M. A. van den Nest, a Senator and Ex-Sheriff of Antwerp, who is also President of the "Company"; and Count Horace van den Burch, an ex-artillery officer, who is also one of the administrators of the "Company"— or, say, five men. M. A. van den Nest is reported to have declared at a meeting in Brussels shortly after the debate in the House of Commons of May 20, 1903, that "Europe would do full justice to the civilising efforts of Belgians in Central Africa." Possibly the speaker was thinking primarily of the efforts of *L'Abir* in that particular line. Let us, then, first examine the material aspects of this "civilising" process, and then pass to its moral aspects —for has not King Leopold repeatedly declared that the "moral" as well as the "material" regeneration of the natives of Africa is the one end and aim of Congo State administration?

Its "material" effects—from the point of view of M. A. van den Nest and his friends—have certainly been most remarkable. In the five years, 1898-1903, the net profits of the "Company" have amounted to no less a sum than 15,078,805 francs, and each full share has received dividends in that period aggregating an enormous amount. In 1903 the dividend per share was £48. In 1901 the Antwerp Stock Exchange drove up the shares to 27,000 francs per share; at that time, therefore, the value of the thousand shares held by the "Congo State" was *twenty-seven million francs*—or, say,

* June 27, 1895. See A. J. Wauters, *op. cit.*
† The *Anversoise* is said to have been now reincorporated in the *Domaine Privé*. (See previous chapters.)

£1,008,000. For some time past the shares have been quoted in *tenth shares.* Owing to certain disclosures beginning in 1901, anent the "moral" side of this "civilising process," and also, no doubt, to the criticisms of wicked Englishmen, the value of the shares has fallen considerably: the shares only stand now at about 13,000 francs per share—a truly deplorable figure, and each *one-tenth* part of a share is quoted at about 1300 francs. It is instructive to look at these figures in tabular form—

Number of shares.	Capital in francs.	Each share value.
2000	1,000,000	500 francs.

Net profits on four years' working.
15,078,805 francs.

Market value of 2000 shares in 1901.	Market value of 2000 shares in June, 1904.
54,000,000 francs.	26,000,000 francs.
Market value per 500 francs share in 1901.	Market value per 500 francs share in June, 1904.
27,500 francs.	13,000 francs.

Thus in five years the profits of this "Company" have been fifteen times greater than its capital, and the market value of its shares to-day is twenty-six times greater than its capital. Is it surprising that the President of *L'Abir* should expatiate on the "civilising effects" of his countrymen on the Congo?

Now, it does not require more than a very general knowledge of African conditions to enable one to declare emphatically that these colossal profits have not been legitimately acquired. There is no need to refer to any reports, from whatever source, to arrive at that conclusion. One has only to consider that the centre of this "Company's" operations is situate 1000 kilometres above Stanley Pool, that all its rubber has to be transported over 1000 kilometres of waterway, transhipped at the Pool, embarked on a railway which charges excessively high rates of freight, carried on that railway from the Pool to Matadi (the limit of ocean steamer navigation on the Congo), there shipped on board a steamer which conveys it to Antwerp at a charge of 52s. 7d. per ton freight: one has only to consider those facts, and the further point that the "Company's" imported goods—supposing that it *traded* with the natives for rubber on commercial lines—would have to go through the same enormous transport difficulties and expenses, to realise that no *commercial* undertaking could by the wildest stretch of imagination be able under such circumstances to make such profits. But then we have to remember that *L'Abir* is not a *commercial* undertaking; it is merely a factor in the regeneration of the African native. And that brings us to a consideration of the "moral" aspect of the "civilising effort" put forth in the Lopori and Maringa District of the *Domaine Privé.*

The exact privileges obtained by *L'Abir* were, according to M. Wauters—*

"the full proprietorship of the vacant lands belonging to the Domaine in the basins of the Lopori and Maringa, around eight stations (*huit postes d'éxploitation*) and within a perimetre of five leagues ; moreover, it obtained for a period of thirty years the right of exploiting all the products of the forest in the Basins of the Lopori and Maringa, starting from Basankusu."

Judging from the reports to hand since 1900, it would seem that these "vacant" lands, whose inhabitants have been civilised up to the point of producing during the last four years enough rubber to enable the worthy shareholders of *L'Abir* to reap a net profit of over fifteen million francs, will really and truly become "vacant," in the sense of being uninhabited, long before the thirty years are up.

In October, 1901, the Belgian papers published particulars, of which the following are extracts :—

"The *Abir* is a Company in which many bigwigs were, or are interested. . . . The enormous quantities of rubber sold on its account, and on account of the *Anversoise*, caused astonishment. But people thought that the territories conceded were very rich, and that the Companies having received—from all-powerful sources—certain privileges and advantages, all was well."

The papers then went on to refer to the scandals attending the *Anversoise* operations, speaking of the crimes committed on behalf of the shareholders "as exceeding in horror and cruelty anything that can be imagined." As to that, the reader can form his own opinions from the previous chapters. It was thereupon stated that "three months ago" reports "giving absolutely precise details" had been furnished to the Council of Administration of the *Abir*, as to the atrocities taking place upon its concession.

"1. A sub-agent of the *Abir* ordered a native who had not made enough rubber to receive fifty blows of the *chicotte*. After the punishment the agent pulled out his revolver and shot the man, breaking his shin-bone.

"2. The head of a factory, dismissed for brutality towards the natives, had tied up for a whole day several rubber collectors, in a state of nudity, to stakes, in the full glare of the sun.

"3. In September, 1899, all the Upper Balombo region was put to fire

---

* *Op. cit.*

and sword by the Dikila factory, to force the natives, with whom the Company had not yet come in contact, to make rubber.

"4. On August 24, 1900, passing by Boyela (in the *Abir* concession) I met in the said village two young girls, one of whom was *enceinte*, with their right hands cut off. They told me that they belonged to the village of Bossombo, and that the soldiers of the white man of Boyela had cut off their hands, because their master did not make enough rubber."

Stirred by the publicity given to these reports, the Company or the State—there is not much difference—ordered an inquiry, and the Belgian papers announced the year before last, with complacency, that Judge Rossi had looked into the charges, which he had found "much exaggerated"—naturally. The worthy judge apparently did more. The Belgian papers of October, 1902, reported him to have said that the "English missionaries were inciting the natives to complain."

Now I happen to have before me the copy of the minutes of the examination by Judge Rossi of Mr. Ruskin, one of the representatives of the Congo Balolo Mission ("Regions Beyond") with reference to these and other atrocities. The examination of Mr. Ruskin took place at Bongandanga, which is on the *Abir* territory, and where the Congo Balolo Mission have a station, on April 12, 1902; the minutes were taken down in shorthand at the time by M. Jeffrey, who accompanied Mr. Ruskin, and acted as witness to his statements. As the report of the proceedings cover twelve type-written pages, I cannot reproduce them *in extenso*, much as I should like to do so. Here are some extracts—

"*Mr. Ruskin.* In the early months of 1899 M——* had a large number of prisoners at the factory.† *They were improperly fed and cared for, so much so that they died at the rate of three, five, and sometimes as many as ten a day.* These were dragged by a piece of *ngoji*, tied to the foot, out into the bush, and only a little earth and a few sticks thrown on top of them. Hands and feet were left sticking up, and the stench was awful. . . . On Sunday, June 10, 1899, four were released. An old man was found on the Mission Station. We gave him food and water, which he ate ravenously; but he was too far gone to recover. He died, and was buried by our own people. Another died at Boyela; the other two were never heard of again. They were Nsumgamboyo people. . . . On July 18, 1899, M——, the director, came up with M——, and after making inquiries, he went back to the factory, and released *one hundred and six prisoners. We saw them pass our station—living skeletons. Some were so much reduced that they had to be carried home. Among them were old*

---

* One of the agents of *L'Abir*. I see no necessity to reproduce the actual names of these fiends.

† Note this in connection with Consul Casement's report four years later, when he found *precisely the same state of affairs prevailing!* And compare with similar practices revealed by the Boma Law Courts in 1900 and 1904, by Scrivener, Consul Casement, and others, to which should now be added recent letters given in the Appendix.

grey-headed men and women. Many children were born in prison. One poor woman was working in the sun three days after the child was born.

"*Mr. Ruskin.* (*Balua.*) Early in 1899, M. F—— sent a number of his workmen into Bongandanga to arrest some men for not bringing in sufficient meat. They also seized Balua, the wife of Bontanga, and M. F—— had her flogged, giving her two hundred chicotte. So severely was she dealt with that urine and blood flowed from her. Just as they were dragging her away to the prison, her husband appeared with twenty fowls to redeem her. He took her home, but she died shortly after from the effect of the punishment she received. Bokato is the name of the sentry who inflicted the punishment, and he is at present at Bosidikolo in the service of the *Abir*. Botanga, who now resides at Mpona, afterwards appeared before the judge, and verified these statements relating to his wife Balua.

"*Mr. Ruskin.* M. F—— thought that his men were not strong enough, and therefore could not compel the people to bring in what he considered sufficient rubber. Once when he was away, his men stole some rubber, and for this he had them tied up, right in the sun, to stakes for a day and a night. Mrs. Cole (now Mrs. Harber), when passing on her way to the schools, saw the men tied there from a distance. They were naked and without food and water all day, and so great was their agony that their tongues were hanging out. Mrs. Cole having seen it herself, came and reported it to me. The names of the men who were thus tied up were Lokilo, Lokwa, Bateko, and Lomboto. (Lokilo and Lokwa both appeared before the judge and reported all they knew.)

"*Judge.* What do you know of the G—— palaver?
"*Mr. Ruskin.* I know it well. In December—near Christmas—1899, M. G—— went to Bosidikolo. . . . One man had bad rubber. M. G—— compelled him to lie down on the ground, and Ilunga, one of his sentries, gave the man *chicotte*. G—— then struck the man with the flat of a machet, and he jumped up. G—— drew his revolver and shot him through the leg, breaking the tibia. Ilunga asked whether he should shoot him, but G—— said no. Three days afterwards, I went to Bosidikolo and saw this man myself. Ekuva, one of our workmen, who was at that time boy to the sentry, saw it all. Ilunga is a native of Bongandanga, and is at Bosidikolo now. (Ekuva afterwards went before the judge, and reported all that he knew about the above palaver.)

"*Mr. Ruskin.* Mpanza palaver. Some months previous to the Botilosombo attack, the natives of Mpanza had killed five *Abir* 'gardes forestiers '* out of revenge for brutality. I spoke to the director, who was passing down country at the time, about this affair, pointing out that it was the result of the *Abir* 'gardes forestiers' having killed many of the Ngombe people. He went on to Basankusu, and a short time after a State officer went in behind Boyela with a company of soldiers, and a lot of innocent people were killed. The State soldiers afterwards came to Bongandanga selling spears and other loot|from the fight. . . . I wish to make a general statement about the *Abir*. The sentries often make pretence; they go to villages, seize a number of spears, come back and say they have been attacked. The natives are too much afraid of the *chicotte*

---

* These 'gardes forestiers,' or sentries, are native soldiers armed with rifles or cap-guns despatched by *L'Abir*—and the other trusts—into the villages to terrorise the inhabitants into producing rubber.

to come out and report, and should they come, the sentries (gardes forestiers) would punish them on the road.

"*Judge.* What about the Van B—— * affair?

"*Mr. Ruskin.* This is from the natives. They say that Van B—— went to a village called Lendo, in the Ngombe country, and attacked it; and the report reached us that he had been wounded by a spear. M. Gamman went with Mr. M. B—— † to the *Abir* factory at Ngwire, M. B—— to make inquiry, and M. Gemman to attend to Van S——'s wound. M. B—— questioned the 'gardes forestiers,' and they said that fourteen had been killed. M. Van B—— said it was not true, as only a few were killed. He also said that he sent the Gardes to one village, and as he was returning from another, a man attacked him with a spear and wounded him. . . . On January 14, 1902, M. B—— told me, in the presence of Mrs. Ruskin and Mr. Gamman, that 38 cartridges had been expended in that one fight. He also said that 90 Albini cartridges had been expended at Ngwire in December, 1901, also 200 caps and 120 cartridges—piston—native name *pataki*. M. B—— only told me about the cartridges. There are various native reports.

Re M. Van S——, Bokecu ‡ and Lulama affair.

"*Mr. Ruskin.* On March 27, 1902, Ivasu and Bangenge, of Lulama, came to Mr. Jeffrey and myself and reported that Bokecu, one of the *Abir* gardes, had killed Ivasu and badly wounded Bonyoma. The body of Ivasu was brought here at 11 o'clock the same day, and we (M. Jeffrey, Mrs. Ruskin, and myself) saw where the bullet had entered the upper part of the left lung. Bonyoma is now very sick. As far as we know the palaver, Bokecu did it on his own responsibility. He and some others had been sent to arrest the Chief, because the Lulama people had not brought in their meat (they were compelled to bring in four animals—fresh meat—every week). . . . This is a case in point, showing that the policy of the *Abir* is bad. They engage as 'gardes,' savages, cannibals, and fools, and supply them with guns without discrimination."

These reports which were read, interpreted, and signed by the judge and Mr. Ruskin, and then forwarded to Boma on April 13, 1902, have been placed at my disposal by Dr. Grattan Guinness. Mr. Ruskin, it seems, had promised the judge that if satisfaction were given and justice done he would "not make these things public in Europe." Nothing was done, of course. Nothing ever is, except the occasional imprisonment of individual offenders—and then always sub-agents.

Nothing ever will be, until the Congo territories are freed from the rapacious and callous scoundrels who are fattening upon it. It is not upon the men in Africa that the chief blame must be laid, bad as many of them are; but upon the men in Brussels and Antwerp, whose policy the usually low type of agent sent out has perforce to carry through.

It will be observed that these ordinary incidents in the

* Agent of *L'Abir*.   Ibid.
‡ Ibid.

IN THE MISSION VILLAGE AT LULANGA (CONGO BALOLO MISSION)
(Showing improved type of native houses built under missionary supervision by converts)

process of "trading" in rubber occurred in 1899, 1900, 1901, and 1902.

We have seen that in October, 1902, the Belgian papers reported that Judge Rossi had declared after investigation that the reports had been "much exaggerated." The judges of the Congo State, as I have stated before, are appointed by the Sovereign of the Congo State, and are revocable at the Sovereign's will; and the "Congo State" is the holder of 1000 shares in *L'Abir*. The Judicial Establishment of the Congo State is distinctly Gilbertian in nature.

In April, 1903, Dr. Grattan Guinness sent the author a letter just received from one of the representatives of the Congo Balolo Mission in the territory of *L'Abir*, from which it appeared that, far from Judge Rossi's investigations in April, 1902, proving efficacious, matters were worse than ever—

"'The Trading Company,' says the letter, 'have now a different system in order to get rubber. Ten soldiers, with rifles, are apportioned to Sungamboyo; ten also to Banlongo, two to Boseke, Ilinga, Lumala, Boyela, and Bavaka respectively. This means, as you understand, that the country is in the hands of these merciless fellows, who abuse, oppress, rob, and kill at their pleasure. M. L., who is here, . . . told me that he was only producing five and a half tons per month, and that although M. —— had promised him another agent, he writes now that he cannot do so unless seven and a half tons are forthcoming per month. This is impossible, as every available man is working rubber, and that with a gun behind him. The laws that appeared to come into force just before you left here are now considered *nil*, and we have the terrors of the gun; the wretched prison life and work; the *chicotte;* the chain; the transport down river; and other offshoots of oppression too numerous to mention. The place is greatly changed. They have made a new line of towns, but the houses are scattered and poor. The people are tyrannised over by the sentries, and therefore spend most of their time in the bush.'"

The extract given in Dr. Guinness's letter brings the picture of the "civilising effort" of the Company directed by Messrs. A. van den Nest, Alex. de Browne de Tiège, C. de Browne de Tiège, Van den Burch and the "Congo State" in the Lopori and Maringa District down to the early part of 1903.

Mr. Charles Bond, of the same Mission, in a letter dated from Lolanga, September 28, and published in the *Daily News*, in December, speaks of the measures employed by the *Abir* to "compel the natives" to bring in the rubber by the wholesale arming of the "Company's" black agents. Writing from a point south of the *Abir* concession, in the direction of Lake Mantumba, he says—

" I have the evidence of a number of men working for us at the present time, that at their town, on the Bosomba River (Lake Mantumba), numbers of men have been killed outright, and others have died from having their hands cut off, because they would not submit to demands. . . ."

The profits of *L'Abir* in 1903 were 2,975,915·09 francs, nearly three times the amount of its capital, and the dividend paid per share was, as already stated, £48, or more than double the original value of a full share.

Consul Casement has shown us, in detail, the habitual conditions prevalent under which these legitimate trading profits are being earned at the present time.

I have shown the elements of *L'Abir* in Europe. Consul Casement gives us the elements in Africa. A staff of 58 Europeans, managing "at least" 20 "factories"; each factory has, with the permission of the Government, of course, 25 rifles; two steamers, each carrying 25 rifles; total number of rifles 550; number of cartridges unlimited; a "moderate computation" gives 150 cap-guns to each "factory"; total number of cap-guns 3000; total, 3500 armed men—all for the "exploitation" of indiarubber! Dr. Guinness thinks that the figures are considerably below the actual. I have shown the connection between the Executive and *L'Abir*, so far as that connection is ascertainable in Europe. Consul Casement gives us its aspects in Africa, first, as regards the arming of the "sentries" which is directly authorised by Government, and could not, in any case, be carried out without Government sanction and approval; secondly, in the fact that the rubber brought down from the waterways of the concession is transhipped at Bassankusu on a Government steamer, "which plies for this purpose between Coquilhatville and Bassankusu, a distance of probably 160 miles"; thirdly, in the fact that the "transport of all goods and agents of the Company, immediately these quit the concession, is carried on exclusively by the steamers of the Congo Government, the freight and passage money obtained being reckoned as part of the public revenue."

Such is the healthy basis for "trading" operations, described by one of the agents to our Consul in these terms, "We do not buy the indiarubber. What we pay to the native is a remuneration for his labour in collecting *our* produce on *our* land, and bringing it to *us*." * The "remuneration"—what M. de Smet de Naeyer would call a "veritable gratuity," since, according to that gentleman,† the native is "not entitled to anything"— Mr. Casement found upon working it out *de visu*, and by actually purchasing from the natives their fortnight's "pay" for five teaspoonfuls of salt, amounted to the ratio of 25*s.* worth of goods with a local market value of £2 7*s.* 8*d.* for £52

---

* Italics mine.   † The Belgian Premier. See Part V.

worth of pure rubber! On these lines the modest profits of *L'Abir* are not difficult to understand.

Rifles and cap-guns for stores, arsenals for "factories," robbery in guise of "payment"—so much is clear. But what of the *modus operandi?* Perfectly simple. "Sentries" in the villages, in the "factories" prisoners as "hostages," and *la chicotte* for slothful workers.

I cannot forbear quoting the Consul's description of a typical rubber "market" scene on the territory of *L'Abir*. In reading it, the reader will do well to have before him just a few of King Leopold's explanations on this subject, intended for European consumption. Perhaps I had better put them and the Consul's description in parallel columns.

"Freedom of trade is complete in the Congo, and is restricted neither by monopoly nor privilege."

"The law protects this freedom by forbidding any interference with the freedom of business transactions."

"The State has been at much pains to prevent the natives from being robbed."

"Steps have been taken to safeguard the individual liberty of the blacks, and especially to prevent labour contracts between blacks and non-natives degenerating into disguised slavery."

"The native is free to seek by work the remuneration which contributes to the increase of his well-being."

"One of the objects of the general policy of the State is to aim at the regeneration of the race by impressing them with the high idea of the necessity of work."

"The system which the State has followed while forwarding the economic development of the country has at the same time caused a considerable commercial movement."

"Whatever may have been said, this prosperity has not been at-

"I arrived at Bongandanga on August 29, when what was locally termed the rubber market was in full swing. The natives of the surrounding country are, on these market days, which are held at intervals of a fortnight, marched in under a number of armed guards, each native carrying his fortnight's supply of indiarubber for delivery to the agent of the Company."

"At Bongandanga the men of the district named E——, distant about 20 miles, had been brought in with the rubber from that district. They marched in in a long file, guarded by sentries of the Abir Company, and when I visited the factory grounds to observe the progress of the 'market,' I was informed by the local agent that there were 242 men actually present. As each man was required, I was told, to bring in 3 kilog. nett of rubber, the quantity actually brought in on that occasion should have yielded about three-quarters of a ton of pure rubber. The rubber brought by each man, after being weighed and found correct, was taken off to be cut up in a large store, and then placed out on drying shelves in other stores. As considerable loss of weight arises in the drying, to obtain 3 kilog. nett, a dead weight of crude rubber, considerably in excess of that quantity, must be brought in. There were everywhere sentries in

tained to the detriment of the lot of the natives."

Ad infinitum et nauseam.

the Abir grounds, guarding and controlling the natives, many of whom carried their knives and spears. The sentries were often armed with rifles, some of them with several cartridges slipped between the fingers of the hands ready for instant use; others had cap-guns, with a species of paper cartridge locally manufactured for charging this form of muzzle-loader. The native vendors of the rubber were guarded in detachments or herds, many of them behind a barricade which stretched in front of a house I was told was the factory prison, termed locally, I found, the *maison des ôtages*. The rubber as brought up by each man under guard, was weighed by one of the two agents of the Abir present, who sat upon the verandah of his house. If the rubber were found to be of the right weight its vendor would be led off with it to the cutting-up store, or to one of the drying stores. In the former were fully 80 or 100 natives who had already passed muster, squatting on raised cane platforms busily cutting up into the required sizes the rubber which had been passed and accepted. At the corners of these platforms stood, or equally squatted, sentries of the Abir with their rifles ready.

" In another store where rubber was being dried, seven natives came in while I was inspecting it, carrying baskets which were filled with the cut-up rubber, which they then at once began sorting and spreading on high platforms. These seven men were guarded by four sentries armed with rifles.

" Somewhat differing explanations were offered me of the reasons for the constant guarding of the natives I observed during the course of the 'market.' This was first said to be a necessary precaution to insure tranquillity and order within the trading factory during the presence there of so many raw and sturdy savages. But when I drew attention to the close guard kept upon the natives in the drying and cutting sheds, I was told that these were 'prisoners.' If the rubber brought in by its native vendor were found on the weighing-machine to be seriously under the required weight, the defaulting individual was detained to be dealt with in the *maison des ôtages*. One such case occurred while I was on the ground. The defaulter was directed to be taken away, and was dragged off by some of the sentries, who forced him on to the ground to remain until the market was over. While being held by these men he struggled to escape, and one of them struck him in the mouth, whence blood issued, and he then remained passive. I did not learn how this individual subsequently purged his offence, but when on a later occasion I visited the enclosure in front of the prison, I counted fifteen men and youths who were being guarded while they worked at mat-making for the use of the station buildings. These men, I was then told, were some of the defaulters of the previous market day, who were being kept as compulsory workmen to make good the deficiency in their rubber."

This "considerable commercial movement" which "contributes to the well-being of the native" is supplemented by another sort of movement, what might be described as the Victualling Department. The theory in this case is to "aim at the regeneration of the race" in another form. Indiarubber is not in itself a sufficient regenerator. Moreover, it is surely right that the fifty-eight European regenerators in this particular district, and their crowd of armed and unarmed retainers—also regenerators, of course *—should be abundantly supplied with adequate means of sustenance during the exhausting process of regeneration? No one, save perhaps some "prejudiced detractor of the work of civilisation in the Congo," would argue that a profit in five years of over £600,000 is sufficient reward for the labour entailed in such work. To pretend that so

* "... Ces gardes forestiers ont pour mission de veiller à ce que la recolte du caoutchouc se fasse rationnellement et d'empêcher notamment que les indigènes ne coupent les lianes." This extract is not from *Comic Cuts*, or *Le Journal Amusant*. It is from the Congo State's "Notes" issued in reply to the British White Book !

paltry a sum is commensurate with the immense debt of gratitude owed by the natives to their regenerators, affords palpable evidence of the gross partiality of the Congo State's critics. But any kind of gratitude, like any kind of work, is, of course, quite unknown among the natives, so a little pressure has to be exercised occasionally. The gentle and humane forms which such persuasion takes is thus described by our Consul from the standpoint of an eye-witness :

"On a Sunday in August, I saw six of the local sentries going back with cap-guns and ammunition pouches to E——, after the previous day's market, and later in the day, when in the factory grounds, two armed sentries came up to the agent as we walked, guarding sixteen natives, five men tied neck to neck, with five untied women and six young children. This somewhat embarrassing situation, it was explained to me, was due to the persistent failure of the people of the village these persons came from to supply its proper quota of food. These people, I was told, had just been captured 'on the river' by one of the sentries placed there to watch the waterway. They had been proceeding in their canoes to some native fishing-grounds, and were espied and brought in. I asked if the children also were held responsible for food supplies, and they, along with an elderly woman, were released, and told to run over to the Mission, and go to school there. This they did not do, but doubtless returned to their homes in the recalcitrant village. The remaining five men and four women were led off to the *maison des ôtages* under guard of the sentry.

"An agent explained that he was forced to catch women in preference to the men, as then supplies were brought in quicker; but he did not explain how the children deprived of their parents obtained their own food supplies.

"He deplored this hard necessity, but he said the vital needs of his own station, as well as of the local missionaries, who, being guests of the *Abir* Society, had to be provided for, sternly imposed it upon him if the people failed to keep up their proper supplies.

"While we thus talked, an armed sentry came along guarding four natives—men—who were carrying bunches of bananas, a part of another food imposition. This sentry explained to his master that the village he had just visited had failed to give antelope meat, alleging the heavy rain of the previous night as an excuse for not hunting.

"The agent apologised to me for his inability to give me meat during my stay, pointing out the obvious necessity he now was under of catching some persons without delay. He should certainly, he said, have to send out and catch women that very night.

"On leaving the *Abir* grounds, still accompanied by this gentleman, another batch of men carrying food supplies were marched in by three armed guards, and were conducted towards the *maison des ôtages*, which two other sentries apparently guarded.

"At 8 p.m. that evening, just after the Sunday service, a number of women were taken through the Mission grounds past the church by the *Abir* sentries, and in the morning I was told that three seizures had been effected during the night. On September 2, I met, when walking in the *Abir* grounds with the subordinate agent of the factory, a file of fifteen women, under the guard of three unarmed sentries, who were being brought in from the adjoining villages, and were led past me. These women, who were evidently wives and mothers, it was explained in answer to my inquiry, had been seized in order to compel their husbands to bring in antelope or other meat which was overdue, and some of which it was very kindly promised should be sent on board my steamer when leaving. As a matter of fact, half an antelope was so sent on board by the good offices of this gentleman.

"As I was leaving Bongandanga, on September 3, several elderly headmen of the neighbouring villages were putting off in their canoes to the opposite forest, to get meat wherewith to redeem their wives, whom I had seen arrested the previous day. I learned later that the husband of one of these women brought in, two days afterwards, to the Mission station, his infant daughter, who, being deprived of her mother, had fallen seriously ill, and whom he could not feed. At the request of the missionary, this woman was released on September 5."

The effect of these sights upon our Consul would appear to have been quite contrary to that which the philanthropic monarch of the Congo territories in Brussels had a right to expect. Mr. Casement, extraordinary to relate, was painfully affected. In an extremely courteous letter to the "supreme authorities" in the Congo, chiefly concerned with certain well-founded complaints on the part of British subjects, Mr. Casement says:

"I am sure your Excellency would share my feelings of indignation had the unhappy spectacles I have witnessed of late come before your Excellency's own eyes. I cannot believe that the full extent of the illegality of the system of arbitrary impositions, followed by dire and illegal punishments, which is in force over so wide an area of the country I have so recently visited, is known to or properly appreciated by your Excellency, or the central administration of the Congo State Government. I have seen women and young children summarily arrested, taken away from their homes and families, to be kept in a wholly illegal and painful detention, guarded often by armed sentries, because, as I was informed by their captors, their villages, or their male relatives, had failed to bring in antelope meat or some other commodity desired by the local Europeans. . . . On September 2, I encountered at Bongandanga fifteen women and girls, one with a baby at the breast, being led to the prison (termed, I find, the *maison des ôtages*) and guarded by three sentries of the *Abir* Company ; and in answer to my inquiry as to who these women were, and why they were being thus led away, I was told by the acting representative of that company, a M. Peters, that they were arrested, and would be kept in detention, until their husbands or male relatives had redeemed them in antelope or other meat, which was required from their village for the use of the white man's table. . . . This method of obtaining supplies, I am informed, is in frequent operation, and I saw, during my brief stay at Bongandanga, several other cases of arrest and detention by the local agent of the *Abir*, which were, I believe, equally illegal. The effect produced on my mind from a very limited inspection of the system, revealing itself in such painful incidents as these, was that that system, and not the agents who are forced to keep it at work, was wrong in the extreme. . . . I gather, too, that Bongandanga is, perhaps, noteworthy among the stations of the *Abir* concession for the forbearance and discretion shown by its agent, M. Lejeune, in his manner of imposing these exactions upon the local inhabitants ; but I must confess with pain and astonishment that, instead of a trading or commercial establishment, I felt that I was visiting a penal settlement."

The lot of the natives of the Lopori-Maringa region does not appear to be much brighter now than it was when "Judge Rossi" made his tour of inquiry. But what matter; have not the dividends of *L'Abir* been fat and comely? Was not the native of Africa created for the especial purpose of contributing to the well-being of Messrs. A. Van den Nest & Co.? As the Congo Note says:

> "It is intelligible that Governments (*sic !*) conscious of their moral responsibility, should not advocate the right of the inferior races to be idle, which would entail the continuance of a social system opposed to civilisation."

Let "civilisation" flourish, then, and down with the "sentimentalists"!*

The "civilisation" of the Lulonga district has been taken in hand quite a number of times. After being subjected to "comprehensive handling" by two of the large Concession Companies — possibly one of those mentioned by Consul Casement as having expended in "three years 72,000 rounds of ball cartridge" in the production of indiarubber—"who only abandoned it when, as one of their agents informed me, it was nearly exhausted," the district has been handed over to a small "company" known as the La Lulanga. The stock of rubber vines is nearly exhausted, and "it is only with great difficulty that the natives are able to produce the quantity sufficient to satisfy their local masters." Oppression, outrage, murder, and mutilation supply the stimulus to their exertions in this respect. This "Trading Company," we infer from Consul Casement's report, is entitled to claim its indiarubber from the natives *à titre d'impôt*. That the inference is correct, we have since learned from the document issued by the Congo Government as a "reply" to the British White Book, wherein we are informed, *inter alia*, that the natives of the Lulonga lied to the Consul (in connection with the mutilation of Epondo, see Chapter XXX.) in order to escape from "*l'obligation de l'impôt!*" Singular form of "trading"!

The following extract from our Consul's report describes more eloquently the condition of the people of the Lulanga district than any words of mine:

> "At a village I touched at up the Lulonga River, a small collection of dwellings named Z——, the people complained that there was no rubber left in their district, and yet that the La Lulanga Company required of them each fortnight a fixed quantity they could not supply. Three forest

---

* For still more recent and more appalling details from the *Abir* territory, the reader is referred to the letters in the Appendix, received since this volume was completed.

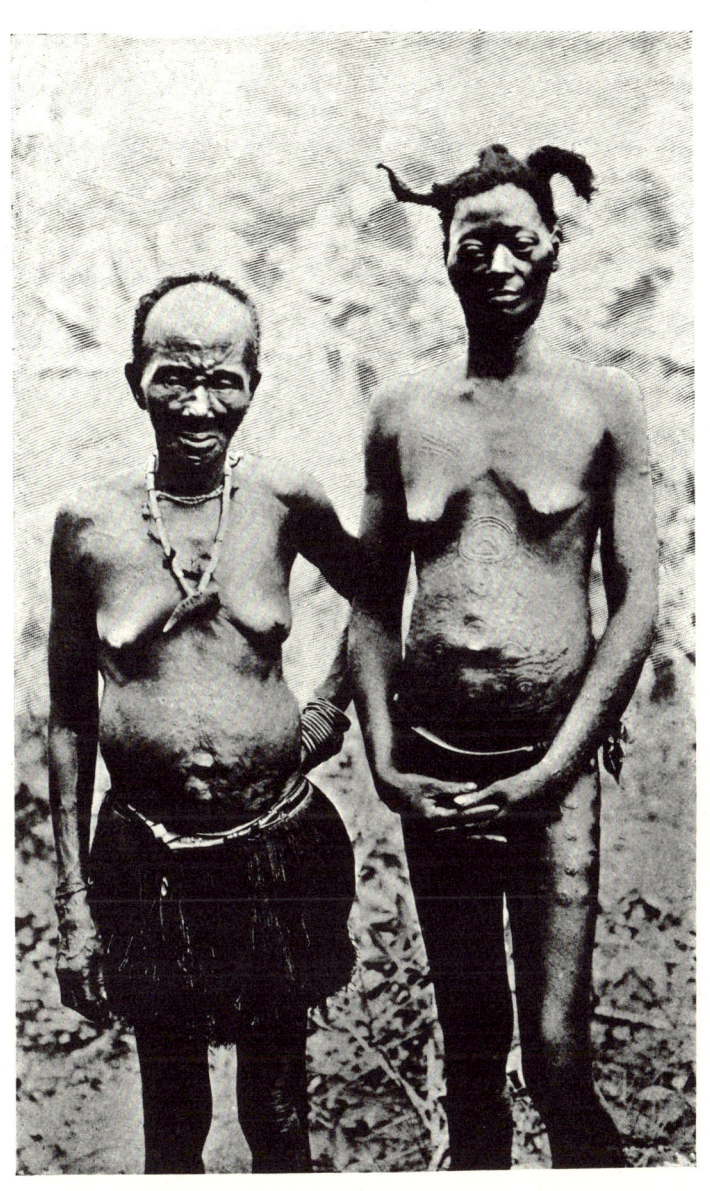

TWO WRETCHED MONGO WOMEN FROM THE ABIR CONCESSION.

guards of that Company were quartered, it was said, in this village, one of whom I found on duty, the two others, he informed me, having gone to Mampoko to convoy the fortnight's rubber. No live stock of any kind could be seen or purchased in this town, which had only a few years ago been a large and populous community, filled with people and well stocked with sheep, goats, ducks, and fowls. Although I walked through most of it, I could only count ten men with their families. There were said to be others in the part of the town I did not visit, but the entire community I saw were living in wretched houses and in most visible distress. Three months previously (in May, I believe), they said, a Government force, commanded by a white man, had occupied their town owing to their failure to send in to the Mampoko head-quarters of the La Lulanga Company a regular supply of indiarubber, and two men, whose names were given, had been killed by the soldiers at that time.

"As Z—— lies upon the main stream of the Lulongo River, and is often touched at by passing steamers, I chose for the next inspection a town lying somewhat off this beaten track, where my coming would be quite unexpected. Steaming up a small tributary of the Lulongo, I arrived, unpreceded by any rumour of my coming, at the village of A——. In an open shed I found two sentries of the La Lulanga Company guarding fifteen native women, five of whom had infants at the breast, and three of whom were about to become mothers. The chief of these sentries, a man called S——, who was bearing a double-barrelled shot-gun, for which he had a belt of cartridges, at once volunteered an explanation of the reason for these women's detention. Four of them, he said, were hostages who were being held to ensure the peaceful settlement of a dispute between two neighbouring towns, which had already cost the life of a man. His employer, the agent of the La Lulanga Company at B—— near by, he said, had ordered these women to be seized and kept until the Chief of the offending town to which they belonged should come in to talk over the palaver. The sentry pointed out that this was evidently a much better way to settle such troubles between native towns than to leave them to be fought out among the people themselves.

"The eleven remaining women, whom he indicated, he said he had caught and was detaining as prisoners to compel their husbands to bring in the right amount of indiarubber required of them on next market day. When I asked if it was a woman's work to collect indiarubber, he said, 'No; that, of course, was man's work.' 'Then why do you catch the women and not the men?' I asked. 'Don't you see,' was the answer, 'if I caught and kept the men, who would work the rubber? But if I catch the wives, the husbands are anxious to have them home again, and so the rubber is brought in quickly and quite up to the mark.' When I asked what would become of these women if their husbands failed to bring in the right quantity of rubber on the next market day, he said at once that then they would be kept there until their husbands had redeemed them. Their food, he explained, he made the Chief of A—— provide, and he himself saw it given to them daily. They came from more than one village of the neighbourhood, he said, mostly from the Ngombi or inland country, where he often had to catch women to ensure the rubber being brought in in sufficient quantity. It was an institution, he explained, that served well and saved much trouble. When his master came each fortnight to A—— to take away the rubber so collected, if it was found to be sufficient, the women were released and allowed to return with their husbands, but if not sufficient they would undergo continued detention. The sentry's statements were clear and explicit, as were equally those of several of the villagers with whom I spoke. The sentry further explained, in answer to my inquiry, that he caught women in this way by direction of his employers. That it was a custom generally adopted and found to work well; that the people were very lazy, and that this was much the simplest way of making them do what was required of them. When asked if he had any use for his shot-gun, he answered that it had been given him by the white man 'to frighten people and make them bring in rubber,' but that he had never otherwise used it. I found that the two sentries at A—— were complete masters of the town. Everything I needed in the way of food or firewood they at once ordered the men of the town to bring me. One of them, gun over shoulder, marched a procession of men—the Chief of the village at their head—down to the water side, each carrying a bundle of firewood for my steamer. A few chickens which were brought were only purchased through their intermediary, the native owner in each case handing the fowl over to the sentry, who then brought it on board, bargained for it, and took the price agreed upon. When, in the evening, the Chief of the village was invited to come and talk to me, he came in evident fear of the sentries seeing him or overhearing his remarks, and the leader, S——, finding him talking to me, peremptorily broke into the conversation and himself answered each question put to the Chief. When I asked this latter if he and his townsmen did not catch fish in the C—— River, in which we learned there was much, the sentry, intervening, said it was not the business of these people to catch fish—'they have no time for that, they have got to get the rubber I tell them to.'

"At nightfall the fifteen women in the shed were tied together, either neck to neck or ankle to ankle, to secure them for the night, and in this posture I saw them twice during the evening. They were then trying to huddle around a fire. In the morning the leading sentry, before leaving the village, ordered his companion in my hearing to 'keep close guard on the prisoners.'"

In conclusion, the reader should be reminded that "whatever may have been said," the "prosperity" of the Congo State "has not been attained to the detriment of the lot of the native."

CHAPTER XIV

CONGO STATE CONTROL IN THE NORTHERN DISTRICT
(THE WELLE-RUBI, WELLE-MAKUA, AND LADO ENCLAVE)

"When our directing will is implanted among them ('barbarous communities') its aim is to triumph over all obstacles, and results which could not be attained by lengthy speeches may follow *philanthropic* influence."—KING LEOPOLD, in a letter to his agents.

" Je terminerai, en vous distant que le gouvernement a le ferme espoir que, vous inspirant des considérations exposées en tête de la présente, vous fournirez une nouvelle preuve d'activité et de dévouement en faisante *produire à la Zone que vous commandez le maximum de ressources qu'on en peut tirer.*"—Governor-general *ad interim* FELIX FUCHS to District Commissioner of the Rubi-Welle Zone.*

"It appears to me that the facts which I have stated above afford amply sufficient evidence of the spirit which animates the Belgian Administration, if, indeed, administration it can be called."
—Lord CROMER (Africa, No. I., 1904).

BETWEEN the Welle and Rubi rivers, and immediately south of the former, is the country of the Aba-Buas. Early in 1901, these people rose, attacked, captured, and sacked the Congo State Station of Libokwa, killing forty-five soldiers, and carrying away many rifles and nearly 50,000 rounds of ammunition. For nearly a year the State was powerless to regain control of the country, and its communications with the Lado Enclave were cut off. However, in January, 1902, the Belgian Press announced that "the revolt of the Aba-Buas was ended" by Commandant Lahaye, who had recaptured 107 rifles and much ammunition from the rebels. Whether the victory was the crushing one it was represented to be, may well be doubted. At any rate, the Belgian papers announced, in November, 1902, that trouble had again broken out in the Welle district, and that Commandant Lahaye had been killed by Chief Kodja, who then committed suicide ; and in December a further announcement was made that a European sergeant of the Force Publique had been killed by the natives in the Welle

* Congo Debate, Belgian House, July, 1903.

region. Of course, the Welle region is very large, and these occurrences may have referred to other portions of it.*

The reader who has followed up to this point the unravelling of the Congo problem, as attempted in the present volume, will not presumably entertain much doubt as to the origin of the Aba-Bua rising. He will put it down to the same causes which have led, for the last thirteen years, to those innumerable risings of natives, tormented beyond endurance by the grinding oppression of which the Congo territory has been the scene. And he will be right.

Here, however, is what the Belgian public was told, and the European public outside of Belgium invited to believe, in regard to this particular revolt. In May, 1902, Commandant Chaltin, in charge of the Congo State forces in the Lado Enclave, and whose comfort, in the absence of fresh supplies, may have been interfered with by the Aba-Bua rising which closed the route for a time, returned to Belgium and was interviewed by the Belgian Press. The world was informed by the gallant officer—he was, at any rate, reported thus to have said—that the reason of the Aba-Bua revolt "is the same as that which provokes nearly all the uprisings, viz. the laziness of the negro and his opposition to civilisation."

We have discussed both the "laziness" of the Negro and the particular brand of civilisation which is offered to him under the "blue banner with the golden star," so it is unnecessary to go into that again. But by the merest chance the facts as to this specific "revolt" have come to light; they do not altogether fit in with Commandant Chaltin's *dictum*. They constitute what has since become known as the Tilkens case, which will be found fully set forth in the speeches of M. Vandervelde in the Belgian House (Part V.). Meanwhile here, in brief, is a summary of the events which led to the Aba-Buas' "opposition to civilisation."

Captain Tilkens, a non-commissioned officer of the Belgian army, but a commissioned one in the Congo army, having already spent some time in the Congo in the State's employ, returned to Africa in November, 1897, and was given command of the Government station of Libokwa in the Rubi-Welle Zone, in the country of the Aba-Buas. His station was on the route which supplies for the Congo State "posts" on the Nile had to take. At that period the State was organising heavy transport for its Nilotic stations, and the Aba-Buas had to furnish carriers. The official in charge of Libokwa had to find the men. He was the *only European* in the station, and he

* The Aba-Buas are once more reported to be in revolt, by the Belgian Press (August).

had eighty native soldiers under him, over whose actions he, being the only white man, could in any case have had little or no control. The people were much oppressed by this continual drain upon their resources. Tilkens wrote home to a military friend about this time, telling him of the state of affairs, and mentioning that, to make matters worse, he had just been instructed by the official of the neighbouring post that he would be expected to produce 1500 carriers, as very large transport was coming up. He wrote to his friend in a despairing tone. Three times, he said, he had had to make war upon the people, to force them to come in as carriers; his soldiers raped the women and stole the children; the people were wretchedly paid for the work; the road was a very bad one, and numbers of carriers used to die of exhaustion and privation. Notwithstanding these heavy calls upon their "laziness," the Aba-Buas at that time apparently produced some little rubber, in the usual form, of course, viz. taxation, "for benefits rendered." But, early in 1898, the Rubi-Welle Zone was placed under the *régime militaire spécial*, and a new District Commissioner was appointed. To this man, the acting Governor-General of the Congo, M. Felix Fuchs, wrote on March 28 of that year, instructing him to increase the rubber yield of the region, and assuring him that he could best serve his interests and those of the Government "*en faisant produire à la Zone que vous commandez, le maximum de ressources que l'on en peut tirer.*" The District Commissioner, acting upon his instructions, promptly informed by letter his subordinates who were scattered about the country that their stations must produce 4000 kilos. of rubber per month, and that they could use force if required.* By October, 1898, Libokwa was producing 1500 kilos. compared with 360 kilos., the average of the previous months! In a letter to his relatives, Tilkens wrote in high spirits, explaining the system of bonuses whereby his earnings were to be proportionate to the quantity of rubber produced. At the same time, Tilkens was unbosoming himself in letters to his military friend in Belgium. It is important to note that they were written at the time Tilkens was actually displaying that "activity," and earning rewards, distinctions, congratulations, and military stripes.

They are a strange mixture, these letters, of the sort of dull ferocity of a man rendered callous and desperate by the knowledge that he is placed between the devil and the deep sea, and of one who is appalled at the task which he has to perform. They afford in themselves a psychological study of

* *Vide* Vandervelde in the course of the debate referred to.

no little interest.* The writer warns his friends over and over again that the natives will rise. They have to furnish rubber, food-stuffs, carriers. He has been raiding and fighting them for three months; several of his soldiers have been killed; he has 152 "hostages" † which he is taking back to his post. Chiefs come to him saying that they cannot fulfil his requests, as they are ruined, and their people are abandoning the country; he puts them in "the chains." On one occasion he is ordered to attack Chief Beretio, who is not supplying enough rubber; he cannot use his own soldiers, for fear of weakening his station, so invites auxiliaries, who join on the understanding that they get a woman apiece as their share of the loot! For two years this butchery and misery goes on. Then he is ordered to leave Libokwa and take charge of the larger station at Jabir.

That was in September, 1900. On November 17 the Governor-General of the Congo writes him a letter bestowing good-conduct stripes, and "sincerely congratulating" him on his labours! Then the dreaded rising takes place. The natives attack Libokwa and sack it; the whole country is up. "*La boutique saute,*" writes Tilkens to a military friend on February 3, 1901, "the native is tired, worn out, and in every mouth are heard complaints and recriminations against this cursed rubber which will bring the State to ruin."

The main thing to bear in mind is (1) the entire similarity between the revelations of Tilkens and the proved atrocities of the Mongalla in 1900 and 1903; the condition of the Abir territories as disclosed by Judge Rossi's interrogatory, by Consul Casement in 1903, and by the resident missionaries in 1903 and 1904; the revelations of Scrivener from the Domaine de la Couronne, Morrison from the Kasai, Campbell and others from Katanga, etc., identical results ensuing from the same system. But the Tilkens case in another respect is unique, being the first instance where a Belgian officer, condemned in default in the Congo, returns to Belgium and begs to be allowed to clear himself, and to prove that what he did, he did because he was

* They recall vividly to mind the powerful picture of Congo life drawn by Mr. Joseph Conrad in the "Heart of Darkness."
† One of the counts of the indictment against this man, read out to the Belgian House by the Minister for Foreign Affairs, was that of ill-treating and starving prisoners, to which Tilkens replied through M. Vandervelde that the fact of his keeping hostages was perfectly well known to his superiors. Compare in this connection Consul Casement's references to the case of the British subject in the Mongalla Concession, the Consul's references to the *maison des ôtages* in the Abir concession, etc. It is the same all through. Whenever a ray of light pierces the clouds, the same system is seen at work, producing the same results.

IN THE RUBI-WELLE

a soldier compelled to obey instructions. He begs the boon earnestly and repeatedly, and it is refused, because—the facts are absolutely conclusive—because the Congo Executive no more dare prosecute in open court in Belgium than it would dare to assent to an international commission of inquiry unless certain beforehand of being able to pack it.

However greatly we may reprobate the acts of a Tilkens, a Caudron, a Mattheys, or a Lacroix, it must never be forgotten that they are victims of a murderous system of organised extortion. What can these men—seldom of a high type—do in the heart of Africa but what they are told? They cannot get out of the country save by the Congo ports; they would not be allowed to leave; they are at the mercy of the Executive; half their salary is detained in Europe, and nine times out of ten, even if by exceptional good fortune they managed to reach Matadi, they would not have sufficient money to pay their passage home. That there have been occasions when a young fellow of good instincts, realising upon reaching his destination the full horror of his duties, has unbosomed himself and begged piteously to be allowed to return, I know, and also that the request has been refused. That officers of humane feelings have been rebuked on occasion by their superiors for "softness," I know. That several of the recently recruited Italian officers, who are on a different footing, have resigned, and sent home burning letters of protest, I know. The responsibility before God and man is not theirs, but that of the barbarous and disgraced "Government" into whose clutches they fall, and through which they are debased.

Thus was brought about the "opposition" of the Aba-Buas to "civilisation." But the Rubi-Welle "Zone" of the *Domaine Privé* has produced much rubber for two years; and, for still longer, many carriers to transport those munitions of war with which the Sovereign of the Congo State has been filling the Lado Enclave these many years past. And that is only one small item of Congolese history, one bloody page alone in the Book of the Dead.*

The Belgian papers reported in 1901 and 1902 fighting in the Niam-Niam country bordering the Bahr-el-Ghazal, and in the Welle-Makua "Zone" against a branch of the Asande people. *La Tribune Congolaise*, of Antwerp, referring to the Makua "Zone," published in 1902 a letter from a correspondent to the effect that, *after the fighting,* " all the rich Southern region has submitted; it is making rubber. It brings in enormous quantities, and will bring in more," etc. One can

---

* For a full account of the Tilkens affair, and the various aspects of the Congo problem which it raises, see Part V.

only imagine what the condition of affairs must be in this region, by what one knows it to be where particulars have come to hand. But one cannot but be struck by the cheerfulness or the indifference with which the Belgian papers make periodical announcements such as these: "The Asandes have risen. A column is being sent against them." "The Dinkas, who live on the Congo State frontier, have revolted." "Reinforcements have been sent to the Welle district." No questions are ever asked; no editorial comments ever indulged in! It seems the most natural thing in the world. It is all part of the "pacification" of those vast regions; necessary accompaniments of "social development;" the resistance of "primitive nature" to the "pressing appeals of Christian culture." * In September, 1903, the Belgian papers announced another "revolt" of the Asandes.

The political intrigues of the Sovereign of the Congo State in respect to the Bahr-el-Ghazal territories were more or less fully set forth by the author in the *Nineteenth Century* for August, 1901.† As we are dealing in this section of the present volume solely with the results of the application of the New African Slave Trade upon the natives of the Congo territories, it would be out of place to refer either to the political history of the Bahr-el-Ghazal, or to that portion of it known as the Lado Enclave, since the thrice unfortunate Agreement of 1894, one of the most unhappy diplomatic entanglements in which this country ever found itself inveigled. For the same reason, it is unnecessary to deal with the more recent developments of the question.

The small Lower Congo and the Lado Enclave are on a somewhat different footing to the enormous territory of the Congo State outside of them. In the Lower Congo it has not been thought worth while hitherto to put the "Domaine" theory in "execution," but, from what I hear, the Lower Congo will not escape much longer, as the Executive is said to be filling the Mayumbe with troops, and the condition of affairs is steadily worsening.

On the other hand, the occupation of the Lado Enclave has been a political move throughout on the part of King Leopold. He did not go there, and has not maintained himself there at fabulous expense, and at the cost of thousands of lives (for the Sovereign of the Congo State's Nilotic ambitions not only led to one of the two great military rebellions, but have necessitated the enslavement and death of innumerable natives forced into carriers to keep the Government

* King Leopold, in a letter to his agents.
† "The Congo State and the Bahr-el-Ghazal."

MANYANGA NATIVES, CATARACTS REGION (LOWER CONGO)

officers, soldiers, and forts in the Lado Enclave supplied for nearly a decade, to say nothing of the expense and the consequent rubber "taxes"), in order to obtain rubber and ivory out of a very restricted area, such as the Enclave covers. To extend the State's sphere right over the Bahr-el-Ghazal province, with its huge supplies of ivory and enormous herds of cattle, was no doubt one of the main ideas of King Leopold in filling the Lado Enclave with troops and war material. That he had others, and even more ambitious ones, there is no doubt, nor of their nature; but Dhanis's failure,* and the timely information sent home by Colonel Pulteney, wrecked his plans, to the great good of Africa. So we find that the duties of the officials in the Lado Enclave, which the Sovereign of the Congo State continues to occupy, and it is said with much appearance of truth, to fortify, have been mainly military. They have not, so far as can be gathered, had to play the part of "farmers of the taxes" levied upon the inhabitants. The consequence is that the policy of "moral and material regeneration" has been less conspicuous. Several British officers have testified to the fine military stations and the smart equipment of Congo State soldiers in the Enclave, and as on several occasions British officers, whose business brought them either permanently or temporarily in touch with the Congo State officers, have been courteously treated by the latter, one or two British military observers have rather rashly jumped to the conclusion that the Lado Enclave is a typical example of Congo State administration in Africa. They have been the more prone to judge thus hastily, as the British Treasury has not been so lavish in its expenditure of money on the British stations facing the Congo State side of the river as the Sovereign of the Congo State has been to embellish the State posts. But although the territory of the Lado Enclave is virgin of the worst aspects of Congo State policy, the treatment of the native population appears to be tainted by the general disregard of elementary native rights, which is the characteristic feature of that policy all through.

Thus M. Didier of the (French) du Bourg de Bozas expedition, which passed through the Lado Enclave in October, 1902, reports that the neighbourhood of the Congo State fort at Dufile "has been deserted by its former inhabitants." Along the whole course of the route followed by the expedition no villages were found; the natives, he reports, had fled, "fearing the white man's impositions."

Lord Cromer's allusions to the administration of the State, as observed and gathered by him, in the Lado Enclave, are given in the White Book (Africa, No. 1, 1904):

* See Chapter XIX.

"The reason of all this (deserted condition of country, oppression, etc.) is obvious enough. The Belgians are disliked. People fly from them, and it is no wonder they should do so, for I am informed that the soldiers are allowed full liberty to plunder, that payments are rarely made for supplies. . . . I understand that no Belgian officer can move outside the settlements without a strong guard. It appears to me that the facts I have stated above afford amply sufficient evidence of the spirit which animates the Belgian administration, if indeed administration it can be called. The Government, so far as I could judge, is conducted almost exclusively on commercial principles, and even judged by that standard it would appear that those principles are somewhat short sighted."

A polite condemnation and, in view of the high position and experience of the writer, a weighty indictment, root and branch, of the "administration" in a part of the territory where its evil methods are least conspicuous.

CHAPTER XV

CONGO STATE CONTROL IN THE DOMAINE DE LA COURONNE

> "I may add that the value of rubber, even when free from all admixture, has gone down in every market for some time. Territorial chiefs must, therefore, not only remove the two causes of loss which they can eliminate, but they must also try to neutralise the third by making unceasing efforts to increase production to the extent laid down in the instructions."—Governor-General WAHIS, March 29, 1901 (Africa, No. I., 1904).
>
> "The personnel of the district of Lake Leopold II. increases progressively with the exploitation of those vast territories; there are now thirty-five Europeans therein. From the commercial point of view, the situation is most prosperous; the natives continue to cultivate, and labour, with regularity. The most perfect calm does not cease to exist in all parts of the district which have submitted to the authority of the State."—*Tribune Congolaise*, Antwerp, Feb. 18, 1904.

"IN the Name of Almighty God," the great Powers met in Brussels in 1890, and with that invocation—as at Berlin five years before—they closed their sittings on July 2. They declared themselves to be "equally animated by a firm intention of putting an end to the crimes and devastations engendered by the traffic in African slaves, of protecting effectually the aboriginal population of Africa, and of ensuring for that vast continent the benefit of peace and civilisation." The Congo State, to whom was chiefly committed the conduct of this campaign of light against darkness, launched many crusaders into the night of Central Africa. The dawn has broken; the work these champions of Christendom have accomplished grows slowly clear.

To aid in this noble project the Sovereign of this high order even gave a special portion of his Royal Domain—carved from the ampler whole—which, as the *Domaine de la Couronne*, constitutes a "civil personality," administered by a special board of civil knights composed of three persons, all high in His Majesty's confidence. The revenues of this region were devoted to the cause of Right—so we were told. Virtue, true virtue, is ever modest. No public account has ever been given of the revenues of the *Domaine de la Couronne*. The truly great, and truly generous man, does not care that his neighbours shall know the full extent of his private charities. He prefers to distribute alms in silence and secrecy, lest the extent of his benefactions, becoming common property, should lead the vulgar to declare, "See the gifts of this fellow. They are but conceived in ostentation and distributed as an indication of self-constituted righteousness." So to this day, the world ignores the amount of the revenues yielded up yearly from the mysterious depths of the *Domaine de la Couronne*.

But here, if anywhere, this holy cause, the world felt, was at home ; here, if anywhere, "the lilies of eternal peace" must be springing from the blood-stained soil of heathendom ; here, if anywhere, through the blackness of the long African midnight, had shone the bright armour of Galahad.

But that "divinity which doth hedge a king" set a thicket of thorns—or bayonets—around this divine demesne ; here no curious philanthropic eye might invade the sacred enclosure where the Master Philanthropist devised peace for the benighted African. These were the home-lands of material and moral regeneration ; sweetness and light reposed upon their threshold, across which the knights of the holy quest alone were permitted to tread. Afar off the missionary might look with wonder at the smoke he saw issuing from the lips of a thousand rifles which built up that sacred barrier. It was the smoke of peace—so we were told.

In 1899 a party of missionaries ascended the Ruki, a great central affluent of the Congo, which drains a portion of this mystic domain of the Crown. They laboured under the delusion that here, if anywhere, they might found a temple to the Christian God. But the Knights of the Grail willed otherwise. They were pursued by some of the chivalry of the region, and, under a strict guard of thirty rifles, were barred from all intercourse with the regenerated heathen. They were not allowed to speak, or even to buy food from their nearest native neighbours. After a month of vain effort to enter into relations with the natives, whose lips were sealed to them, as were theirs, with their message of good-will, by that potent barrier of rifles, they had to descend the Ruki in canoes, and in a state of semi-starvation.

That was the sole effort outside Christendom had made to see the knights of the anti-slavery crusade in the inner house of their order . . . until last year. It was reserved for another missionary, this time alone, and on foot, across 150 miles of wasted desolation whence all human life has been extirpated, to at length penetrate this innermost sanctuary of Congo State rule; where theory has given place to practice, and where moral regeneration has laid its bloody grip upon the entrails of Africa. It has been reserved also for a British official, of experience and repute, to gather from the lips of some of the fugitive tribesmen from this holy of holies the tales of horror and bestial savagery to which their poor bodies have been subjected. Mr. Scrivener is an Englishman who has been a missionary in the Congo since 1888. He entered and traversed a tract of the *Domaine de la Couronne* in July, August, and September, 1903. Mr. Roger Casement is an official of tried experience, of great and peculiar knowledge of Africa and African conditions. Moved by a worthy impulse, Mr. Scrivener placed his journal of notes at my disposal. Mr. Casement's account figures in the official report recently published.

I append the following extracts from Mr. Scrivener's journal:

"Leaving Bombenda on the 12th August, we struck inland, making a somewhat circuitous route to Mpoko. Here I heard of several men * who were wishful of seeing their old home near Lake Leopold II. Sent for them to come. . . . Started on Tuesday, 18th August, for the lake, caravan mustering in all thirty-two, including a widow who wanted to see her mother near the lake. Six hours' walking took us to Kebembe, a rather miserable group of villages on the side of a low hill. Country through which we passed only sparsely populated. . . .

"On the 21st we came to some cassava plantations, and we saw a man running away. He was called to, but would not stop. A little later we saw a few little huts. When we got into the village, we found it to consist of four wretched huts with three men, four women and a few boys and girls, all looking as miserable as they could be. . . . At six in the morning woke up to find it still raining. It kept on till nine, and we managed to get off by eleven. All the cassava bread was finished the day previous, so a little rice was cooked, but it was a hungry crowd that left the little village. I tried to find out something about them. They said they were runaways from a district a little distance away, where rubber was being collected. They told us some horrible tales of murder and starvation, and when we heard all we wondered that men so maltreated should be able to live without retaliation. The boys and girls were naked, and I gave them each a strip of calico, much to their wonderment. . . . The broad road we had seen was a relic of the days when the rubber war was in full swing, and the people of that district had been compelled to collect it by the ton. The country had been depopulated, hence the difficulty in finding roads, the unburnt grass, and increase in buffaloes. . . . In the afternoon we passed a ruined mud house, and were told that this had been a rubber post with soldiers in charge, but that since all the people had run away it had been given up. Later on we saw still more numerous sites where only recently thousands of people had been living. Cassava was still growing in the plantations, and bananas were rotting on the trees. Here and there a few blackened sticks showed where the huts had been, and sometimes

---

* Refugees.

huts were seen fairly well preserved and with cooking utensils lying about; but never a man, woman, or child : all as still as the grave. A little further on we found another deserted rubber post. This one had evidently been quite an imposing affair, and although I heard it had been abandoned for over two years, it still looked as if at one time it had been a place of considerable importance. But I was assured that at no time had a white man been resident here, but only a soldier with a few raw helpers. The white man had made occasional visits, and yet the whole district was practically cleared of every vestige of population. Just as the sun was setting we reached a large and imposing State post. A large quadrangle, say 300 yards square, surrounded by wattle and daub erections. I expected at least two white men would be resident, but was surprised to find only a retired soldier with a few nondescripts to assist. There was a long house which I was told had been the residence of a white man they called ———. I had heard before of this white man from the refugees in the neighbourhood of Bolobo, and was naturally curious to know more about him. But there was no need to probe or question. From the work-people about the post, and the few miserable people in the wretched village adjoining the post, came spontaneously stories of the most atrocious deeds, and of murders of such a wholesale character that it was difficult to believe them. All round the post, which was splendidly situated and commanded fine views in all directions, were plentiful signs of the former population. This place, Mbolo, had been the home of some of the people near Bolobo, and I heard many stories of the big villages and the many chiefs. But, alas! I could only hear of three very small villages, and later I heard from a white official that the total remaining population did not number 100 all told. . . . On the Monday (24th) we made an early start, and with a well-cleared road, through a fine open country, made good progress. . . . Here and there on both sides were frequent signs of a recent population, but for hours we walked through a deserted country, and not once did we see the slightest sign of human habitation, excepting the road over which we walked. . . . Four hours and a half brought us to a place called Sa. . . . On the way we passed two villages with more people than we had seen for days. There may have been 120. Close to the post was another small village. We decided to stay there the rest of the day. Three chiefs came in with all the adult members of their people, and altogether there were not 300. And this where, not more than six or seven years ago, there were at least 3000! It made one's heart heavy to listen to the tales of bloodshed and cruelty. And it all seemed so foolish. To kill the people off in the wholesale way in which it has been done in this lake district, because they would not bring in sufficient quantity of rubber to satisfy the white men—and now here is an empty country and a very much diminished output of rubber as the inevitable consequence. . . . Next morning when we started again we had to be ferried over a small river. We began to think we must be getting near the lake. We passed a deserted post with fine houses all in good repair, and a little farther on we went through another village. On for another good spell of walking through fairly open country to a very large and flourishing-looking post, with several big villages close by. This place must formerly have been a very large settlement of the Basengele or Bakutu. We passed through miles and miles of deserted sites, and on all sides were groves of palms, and bananas, and many other evidences of a big people."

Finally, Mr. Scrivener emerged in the neighbourhood of a "big State station." He was hospitably received, and had many chats with his host, who seems to have been a very decent sort of man, doing his best under very trying circumstances. His predecessor had worked incalculable havoc in the country, and the present occupant of the post was endeavouring to carry out the duties assigned to him (those duties consisting, as usual, of orders to get all the rubber possible out of the people) with as much humanity as the nature of the task permitted. In this he, no doubt, did what was possible as one whom the system had not yet degraded to its level—one of the rare few; and one cannot wonder that they should be rare, seeing the nature of the bonds, and the helplessness in which an official is placed who does not carry out the full desires of his superiors. But he had only succeeded in getting himself into trouble with the district commander in consequence. He showed Mr. Scrivener a letter from the latter upbraiding him for not using more vigorous means, telling him to talk less and shoot more, and reprimanding him for not killing more than one man in a district under his care where there was a little trouble! *

Mr. Scrivener had the opportunity while at this State post, under the *régime* of a man who was endeavouring to be as humane as his instructions allowed, to actually see the process whereby the secret revenues of the *Domaine de la Couronne* are obtained. He says:

"Everything was on a military basis, but so far as I could see, the one and only reason for it all was rubber. It was the theme of every conversation, and it was evident that the only way to please one's superiors was to increase the output somehow. I saw a few men come in, and the frightened look even now on their faces tells only too eloquently of the awful time they have passed through. As I saw it brought in, each man had a little basket, containing say, four or five pounds of rubber. This was emptied into a larger basket and weighed, and being found sufficient, each man was given a cupful of coarse salt, and to some of the headmen a fathom of calico. . . . I heard from the white men and some of the soldiers some most gruesome stories. The former white man (I feel ashamed of my colour every time I think of him) would stand at the door of the store to receive the rubber from the poor trembling wretches, who after, in some cases, weeks of privation in the forests, had ventured in with what they had been able to collect. A man bringing rather under the proper amount, the white man flies into a rage, and seizing a rifle from one of the guards, shoots him dead on the spot. Very rarely did rubber come in, but one or more were shot in that way at the door of the store —'to make the survivors bring more next time.' Men who had tried to run from the country and had been caught, were brought to the station and made to stand one behind the other, and an Albini bullet sent through them. 'A pity to waste cartridges on such wretches.' On —— removing

---

* See also "Africa," No. I., p. 63. This official has since died, and his predecessor has apparently gone out to the Congo once more.

from the station, his successor almost fainted on attempting to enter the station prison, in which were numbers of poor wretches so reduced by starvation and the awful stench from weeks of accumulation of filth, that they were not able to stand. Some of the stories are unprintable. . . . Under the present *régime* a list is kept of all the people. Every town is known and visited at stated intervals. Those stationed near the posts are required to do the various tasks, such as the bringing in of timber and other material. A little payment is made, but that it is in any respect an equivalent it would be absurd to suppose. The people are regarded as the property of the State for any purpose for which they may be needed. That they have any desires of their own, or any plans worth carrying out in connection with their own lives, would create a smile among the officials. It is one continual grind, and the native intercourse between one district and another in the old style is practically non-existent. Only the roads to and fro from the various posts are kept open, and large tracts of country are abandoned to the wild beasts. The white man himself told me that you could walk on for five days in one direction, and not see a single village or a single human being. And this where formerly there was a big tribe! . . . From thence on to the Lake we found the road more and more swampy. Leaving Mbongo on Saturday (29th) we passed through miles of deserted villages, and saw at varying distances many signs of the former inhabitants. . . . Leaving the plain, we entered a forest and found the road followed for three-quarters of an hour the course of a fast-flowing, swollen stream. Then for half an hour through some deserted gardens and amongst the ruins of a number of villages, then a sharp turn to the left through another low-lying bit of grassland. . . ."

In due course Mr. Scrivener arrived at Ngongo, where the surviving relatives of the refugees whom Mr. Scrivener had brought with him, as already mentioned, met after their long parting:

"As one by one the surviving relatives of my men arrived, some affecting scenes were enacted. There was no falling on necks and weeping, but very genuine joy was shown and tears were shed as the losses death had made were told. How they shook hands and snapped their fingers! What expressions of surprise—the wide-opened mouth covered with the open hand to make its evidence of wonder the more apparent. . . . So far as the State post was concerned, it was in a very dilapidated condition. . . . On three sides of the usual huge quadrangle there were abundant signs of a former population, but we only found three villages —bigger indeed than any we had seen before, but sadly diminished from what had been but recently the condition of the place . . . Soon we began talking, and, without any encouragement on my part, they began the tales I had become so accustomed to. They were living in peace and quietness when the white men came in from the Lake with all sorts of requests to do this and to do that, and they thought it meant slavery. So they attempted to keep the white men out of their country, but without avail. The rifles were too much for them. So they submitted, and made up their minds to do the best they could under the altered circumstances. First came the command to build houses for the soldiers, and this was done without a murmur. Then they had to feed the soldiers, and all the men and women—hangers-on who accompanied them. Then they were told to bring in rubber. This was quite a new thing for them to do. There was rubber in the forest several days away from their home,

DOMAINE DE LA COURONNE

but that it was worth anything was news to them.* A small reward was offered, and a rush was made for the rubber; 'What strange white men to give us cloth and beads for the sap of a wild vine.' They rejoiced in what they thought was their good fortune. But soon the reward was reduced until they were told to bring in the rubber for nothing. To this they tried to demur, but to their great surprise several were shot by the soldiers, and the rest were told, with many curses and blows, to go at once or more would be killed. Terrified, they began to prepare their food for the fortnight's absence from the village, which the collection of the rubber entailed. The soldiers discovered them sitting about. 'What, not gone yet!' Bang! bang! bang! And down fell one and another dead, in the midst of wives and companions. There is a terrible wail, and an attempt made to prepare the dead for burial, but this is not allowed. All must go at once to the forest. And off the poor wretches had to go without even their tinder-boxes to make fires. Many died in the forests from exposure and hunger, and still more from the rifles of the ferocious soldiers in charge of the post. In spite of all their efforts, the amount fell off, and more and more were killed. . . . I was shown round the place, and the sites of former big chiefs' settlements were pointed out. A careful estimate made the population of, say, seven years ago, to be 2000 people in and about the post, within the radius of, say, a quarter of a mile. All told they would not muster 200 now, and there is so much sadness and gloom that they are fast decreasing. . . . Lying about in the grass, within a few yards of the house I was occupying, were numbers of human bones, in some cases complete skeletons. I counted thirty-six skulls, and saw many sets of bones from which the skulls were missing. I called one of the men, and asked the meaning of it. 'When the rubber palaver began,' said he, 'the soldiers shot so many we grew tired of burying, and very often we were not allowed to bury, and so just dragged the bodies out into the grass and left them. There are hundreds all round if you would like to see them.' But I had seen more than enough, and was sickened by the stories that came from men and women alike of the awful time they had passed through. The Bulgarian atrocities might be considered as mildness itself when compared with what has been done here. . . . In due course we reached Ibali. There was hardly a sound building in the place. . . . Why such dilapidation? The Commandant away for a trip likely to extend into three months, the sub-lieutenant away in another direction on a punitive expedition. In other words, station must be neglected and rubber-hunting carried out with all vigour. I stayed here two days, and the one thing that impressed itself upon me was the collection of rubber. I saw long files of men come as at Mbongo with their little baskets under their arms, saw them paid their milk-tin-full of salt, and the two yards of calico flung to the head men; saw their trembling timidity, and in fact a great deal more, to prove the state of terrorism that exists, and the virtual slavery in which the people are held. . . . So much for the journey to the Lake. It has enlarged my knowledge of the country, and also, alas! my knowledge of the awful deeds enacted in the mad haste of men to get rich. So far as I know I am the first white man to go into the *Domaine privé* of the King, other than the

---

* The district now under review is, of course, a remote district, and consequently had not entered into relationship with the white man, either before or after the State inaugurated its 1891 policy of general appropriation and slavery. The first contact of these people with the white race is a grisly satire on the alleged blessings of "civilisation."

employés of the State. I expect there will be wrath in some quarters, but that cannot be helped."

Mr. Scrivener is quite right. There will be wrath—such enduring wrath, let us hope, as will rescue the inhabitants of the *Domaine de la Couronne*, or what may be left of them, from these modern Knights of the Grail, and from the gigantic infamy which is being perpetrated " In the name of Almighty God " by the legatees of the Berlin and Brussels Acts.

From Mr. Srivener we turn to the report of Mr. Roger Casement. On pages 60, 61, 62, and 63 of the Appendix to that appalling document we have full and detailed reports of the Consul's conversations with some of the refugees of the *Domaine de la Couronne* region.* A few extracts will give the nature of the revelations made to the Consul by these hunted beings.

" I asked first why they had left their homes, and had come to live in a strange far-off country among the K——, where they owned nothing, and were little better than servitors. All, when this question was put, women as well as men, shouted out, ' On account of the rubber tax levied by the Government posts.' I asked particularly the names of the places whence they had come. . . . All had fled from their homes for the same reason—it was the 'rubber tax.' I asked them how this tax was imposed. One of them who had been hammering out an iron neck-collar on my arrival spoke first. He said, '. . . From our country each village had to take twenty loads of rubber. . . . We had to take these loads in four times a month.' Q.—' How much pay did you get for this?' A. (Entire audience)—' We got no pay ! We got nothing !' And then NN, whom I asked again, said, ' Our village got cloth and a little salt, but not the people who did the work. Our Chiefs ate up the cloth ; the workers got nothing. The pay was a fathom of cloth and a little salt for every basketful, but it was given to the Chief. . . . It used to take ten days to get the twenty baskets full of rubber. We were always in the forest, and then when we were late we were killed. We had to go further and further into the forest to find the rubber vines, to go without food, and our women had to give up cultivating the fields and gardens. Then we starved. Wild beasts—the leopards—killed some of us when we were working away in the forest, and others got lost or died from exposure and starvation, and we begged the white man to leave us alone, saying we could get no more rubber ; but the white men and their soldiers said ' Go ! you are only beasts yourselves, you are nyama (meat).' We tried always going further into the forest, and when we failed and our rubber was short, the soldiers came to our towns and killed us. Many were shot, some had their ears cut off, others were tied up with ropes round their necks and bodies, and taken away. . . .' Q.—' How many days is it from N—— to your own country ?' A.—' Six days of quick marching. We fled because we could not endure the things done to us. Our Chiefs were

---

* Scrivener, it will be observed, met and spoke with the survivors on the spot. Mr. Casement interrogated an entirely different set of individuals, viz. refugees who had fled into another district.

hanged, and we were killed and starved and worked beyond endurance to get rubber.' Q.—' How do you know it was the white men themselves who ordered these cruel things to be done to you? These things must have been done without the white man's knowledge by the black soldiers.' A.—' The white men told their soldiers, "You kill only women; you cannot kill men. You must prove that you kill men.' So then the soldiers when they killed us——' Here he stopped and hesitated, and then, pointing to the private parts of my bull-dog—it was lying asleep at my feet—he said, ' Then they cut off those things, and took them to the white men, who said, "It is true, you have killed men."* Q.—' You mean to tell me that any white man ordered your bodies to be mutilated like that, and those parts of you carried to him?' A. (PP, OO, and all, shouting)—' Yes, many white men.' Q.—' You say this is true? Were many of you so treated after being shot?' A. (All shouting out)—' Nkoto! Nkoto!' (Very many! Very many!). There was no doubt that these people were not inventing. Their vehemence, their flashing eyes, their excitement was not simulated. Doubtless they exaggerated the numbers, but they were clearly telling what they knew and loathed. I was told that they often became so furious at the recollection of what had been done to them that they lost control over themselves. One of the men before me was getting into that state now."

"An old woman soon came and joined, and another man. The woman began talking with much earnestness. She said the Government had worked them so hard, they had no time to tend their fields and gardens, and they had starved to death. Her children had died; her sons had been killed. The two men, as she spoke, muttered murmurs of assent. The old chief said, ' We used to hunt elephants long ago, there were plenty in our forests, and we got much meat; but Bula Matadi killed the elephant-hunters because they could not get rubber, and so we starved. We were sent out to get rubber, and when we came back with little rubber we were shot.' Q.—' Who shot you?' A.—' The white men . . . sent their soldiers out to kill us.' Q.—' How do you know it was the white man who sent the soldiers? It might be only these savage soldiers themselves.' A.—' No, no! Sometimes we brought rubber into the white man's stations . . . When it was not enough rubber the white man would put some of us in lines, one behind the other, and would shoot through all our bodies. Sometimes he would shoot us like that with his own hand; sometimes his soldiers would do it.' Q.—' You mean to say you were killed in the Government posts themselves by the Goverment white men themselves, or under their eyes?' A. (emphatically)—' We were killed in the stations of the white men themselves. We were killed by the white man himself. We were shot before his eyes.'"

The initials of several white men guilty of these murders are given in the Government report.

It would really be interesting to know the value of the rubber got out of the *Domaine de la Couronne,* say within the last few years, if only to attempt a calculation as to the number of human lives taken per ton of that useful article exported.

* For a *confession* of similar practices the reader is referred to the Mongalla Massacres of 1900 already referred to.

Both Mr. Scrivener's account * of what he personally witnessed, and the statements made to the Consul, merely cover, be it noted, a very small portion of the area specially set aside as the home-land *par excellence* of the philanthropic efforts of Africa's regenerator.

* A further and more recent letter from Mr. Scrivener, in which he describes another journey taken by him this year in a different district of the Domaine de la Couronne, is given in the Appendix.

CHAPTER XVI

CONGO STATE CONTROL IN THE WESTERN DISTRICT
(BASIN OF THE KASAI)

> "The produce of the Domain, including the taxes in kind, out of a budget of £1,120,000 figures therein for a total of £640,000. ... The State has thus found itself able to apply itself to the realisation of the humanitarian views of the Berlin and Brussels Conferences. The results obtained in the material and moral spheres could not be entirely overlooked, so evident are they, despite a systematic *partipris*. ... No matter what has been said, this prosperity has not been attained by any detriment to the lot of the native."—*Bulletin Official de l'Etat Indépendant du Congo*, No. 6 Translation, June, 1903.

To follow the developments of Congo State control in the Basin of the Kasai, it is necessary to indulge in an historical retrospect.

When the New Slave Trade was introduced into the Congo territories, the Belgian Trading Companies, as we have seen, objected very strongly; and one of the measures taken to pacify them was a temporary arrangement to leave the Kasai Basin open to trade. This did not mean, of course, that the State forbore applying the "rubber tax" in that immense region, when and wherever it chose, and was powerful enough to do so. King Leopold's gracious permission to allow merchants in the Kasai was eagerly seized upon, and between 1893 and 1899 a considerable number of firms opened factories along the Kasai and its tributaries. The Basin of the Kasai remained, therefore, nominally at any rate, open to free trade. Competition between the merchants became keen, and their transactions were not assisted by the "tax-gathering" operations of "Bula Matadi," complaints, especially in recent years, being forthcoming from the merchants, that the natives were told by the State officers to bring *them* their rubber and ivory, under pain of chastisement—a repetition, in short, of the tactics pursued in 1891 and 1892 in other parts of the Congo territory, and pursued in the Kasai, as on the Congo and Ubanghi, with a definite object which has since become apparent. At this stage it is necessary to refer to an event of considerable importance, as it subsequently led to an alliance fatal in results to all the natives of the country, between "Bula Matadi" and a fierce tribe of pronounced cannibals, the "Zappo-Zaps."

The eastern portion of the Kasai District was in 1895 the scene of the explosion of one of the two great military uprisings which have nearly brought the State toppling to the ground. Gongo Lutete, the famous Batetla Chief, without whose aid the State forces would probably never have got the better of the Arabs, having been murdered—legally, of course, much as Stokes was at a later date promoted to the majority by Lothaire —on a false charge by a State officer at Gandu, as a reward for the military and sanitary* assistance rendered by his soldiers; his picked body-guard, numbering 350 men, "were removed as a matter of precaution" † to Lusambo, and afterwards to Luluabourg. Here they were enrolled as regular soldiers. In 1895 they mutinied, killed their officers, defeated several detachments of State troops, captured one or two stations, and marched eastwards till they arrived at Gandu exactly two years after their leader's execution. Here they were met by Lothaire at the head of a large force, the ranks of the mutineers having been swelled meanwhile by sympathisers to double the number they originally started with, and defeated. Some days afterwards they repaid their defeat with interest, and cut up a State column, killing four European officers. They were, however, followed by Lothaire, and again beaten in November, 1897. By this last action the State claimed to have "wiped out" the rebellion. It was speedily undeceived. In 1900 and 1901 further fighting took place, and in March of the latter year, the State announced their utter destruction by Major Malfeyt. In point of fact, these Luluabourg mutineers, joined probably by remnants from the still greater mutiny which occurred two years later, and the members of which worked their way down from the frontiers of the Bahr-el-Ghazel to the banks of the Luapula, are to-day the apparently uncontested masters of a region about the size of Belgium (see map, p. 466) in the Western Katanga country.

In 1898 and 1899, terrible tales of oppression reached Europe from the Kasai region, sent by the representatives of the American Baptist Missionary Society at Luebo. We may pause here to give a Belgian estimate of some of the largest and most important native tribes inhabiting the Kasai Basin,

---

* Gongo's men kept the neighbourhood of the State camps fairly healthy by devouring the dead bodies of the natives who had fought on the Arab side.

† "The Congo State," D. C. Boulger, page 242.

to whom M. A. J. Wauters, the historian of the Congo State, applies the following general estimate. "The inhabitants of the Kasai are justly regarded as the most industrious in the State." Of the Balunda, we are told that they are "a peaceful and hospitable people." Of the Bakuba, that they are "great traders and workers in iron." But it is over the great Baluba nation and its various branches—the Bashilange, the Bambue, Bakolosh, Basonge, Beneki, etc.—that the Belgian authorities wax enthusiastic. "Sous le rapport," says M. Wauters, "de l'étendu du territoire et de la densité de la population, comme aussi de la beauté physique et morale de la race," the Bakuba nation is "la plus importante et la plus intéressante du basin méridionale du Congo." The German von Wissmann dubs them "great thinkers." They are clever agriculturists, hardly darker in colouring than the Fellaheen, and have regular features.* Here, if anywhere in the Congo, one would have thought was a grand field open to the exercise of the regenerating influences of "Bula Matadi;" fine material to work upon, calculated to stir the imagination and stimulate the efforts of an honest Administration. We shall see presently to what usage the State has put its opportunities.

At the close of 1901 the Congo State threw off the mask, and inaugurated a new policy in the Kasai Basin, a policy calculated to bring "prosperity" without "any detriment to the lot of the native."† The State had been directly exploiting the fruits of its Kasai "domain" *en régie* before. Henceforth it would also exploit it indirectly. The independent trading companies were converted into a Trust on the lines of the *Abir* and *Anversoise*, controlled by the State, and 50 per cent. of whose shares the State retained. Thus did the sole remaining region of the Upper Congo, not previously closed to trade, become monopolised. The Trust received a huge concession "more than twelve times the area of Belgium."

It is worth while studying its composition a little closely. The capital of the Trust is 1,005,000 francs (£40,200), of which the State contributes 502,500 francs, or a little over a third, the remainder being subscribed by the fourteen firms previously trading in the district, the largest amount subscribed by any one firm being 85,000 francs, and the smallest 5750 francs. The above capital is represented by 4020 shares of 250 francs each. In addition to these shares, 4020 more dividend-paying

---

* The Batetla and Bakusus inhabit partly the Kasai and partly the Lomami Basin. Physically very fine peoples, they are great fighters, and, like the Zappo-Zaps, inveterate cannibals—choice subjects for the State army.

† *Bulletin Officiel.*

shares were issued (*parts bénificiaires*), of which the State holds 2010, the balance being distributed amongst the fourteen firms. So far as the control of the Trust is concerned, the State has matters all its own way. One-half of the administrators are subject to the State agreeing with their nomination (Article 13). A permanent committee exists to which the Administrative Council delegates its powers. This committee is composed of four members, two of whom the State appoints, while the nomination of the other two must be submitted and agreed to by it (Article 15). The State appoints the Chairman in Europe and the manager in Africa (Article 15). The Administrative Council and the permanent committee cannot meet unless a majority be present, and the chairman has the casting vote (Article 15). Or, in other words, the Kasai Trust is a " State institution." " The policy of the State," declared the now defunct *Gazette Coloniale* of Antwerp, in January, 1902, is the " absorption of the Trading Companies ; the State has absorbed the fourteen companies which previously existed, leaving them only a purely nominal autonomy."

The *Gazette Coloniale* went on—

"There will be in the Congo nothing but vast organisations placed under the direction and control of the Government. Private initiative will disappear. . . . To employ an expression which appears accurate under the circumstances, the Congo State will soon be nothing but a vast farm, exploited either directly or for joint account by a few officials. The interests of Belgian trade have nothing to gain by such a state of affairs. The *Domaine Privé* will probably increase its rubber production, but, save for a few rare shareholders holding " parts," the Congo State will become, in the eyes of the majority of the Belgians, a Colony more and more foreign to them."

That is a very good description of the condition of affairs to-day. The newspaper I have quoted from was a resolute supporter of the State, but the Kasai Trust was too much for its digestion, and it is since deceased. Candid friends are not appreciated in Congolese circles ; they either disappear, or —well, they cease to be candid.

In 1899 and 1900, as before stated, the American missionaries at Luebo sent home detailed accounts of terrible atrocities committed by State troops in that neighbourhood. They appealed to the President of the American Republic, and the Congo State promised an inquiry—as usual. However, things went on just the same, and early in 1903 the Rev. W. M. Morrison,[*] who had just returned from the Congo, addressed a

---

[*] I would like to say here that the Rev. W. M. Morrison impressed all those who heard him or conversed with him, including the author, by his honesty and straightforwardness. The attempts of the State to

NATIVE PRISONERS AT BOMA TAKING THE AIR

(The mortality among native prisoners in Boma gaol is enormous, the normal death-rate being 50 to 70 per cent., under favourable conditions)

public meeting at the United Service Institution, Whitehall, on May 5, in the course of which he amplified the reports previously forwarded to his Government by the Mission, of which he is the principal representative. The events recorded cover roughly a period of four years, from 1898 to the time of the Rev. W. M. Morrison's return. The following is an epitome of his experiences, and those of other members attached to the Mission. They are confined to the immediate vicinity of Luebo, the head-quarters of the Mission. Luebo is situate at the confluence of the Kasai, Lulua, and Luebo rivers, is the centre of a populous district inhabited by the fine Baluba race, already referred to, and its branches; while north of Luebo, between the Kasai and its great eastern tributary the Sankuru, the Bakuba people predominate.

Prior to 1902, the Luebo District, as I have explained, was nominally open to trade, although the rubber tax remained in force,* so that it was until that time in a measure a "favoured section." The people suffered occasionally from periodical visitations of State troops. "Even when an officer is present, we have had the greatest difficulty in keeping the soldiers from looting and otherwise abusing the native population. The latter know from bitter experience that it is useless to resist the soldiers." †

In 1898 a State officer arrived at Luebo, "followed, as usual, by a squad of native soldiers, together with carriers and camp followers." As he entered the town, "natives came running into the Mission house to report that the soldiers were pillaging their villages." Morrison immediately went to the scene of the disturbance, "found the villagers fleeing to the forests, and the soldiers in full possession of a village which they were busy looting, having already severely wounded an innocent woman." Morrison sought out the officer, who was at the house of a trader, "only a few yards distant, and demanded protection for the people. He professed ignorance as to what the soldiers were doing." A few days later the natives reported —the report being confirmed by one of the European traders —that the State officer intended to "compel the entire Baluba population of Luebo, consisting of several thousands, to remove to Luluabourg, the State post, five days distant." ‡ Morrison

discredit him because he made the tactical error of going to Brussels and asking for a grant of land to build a school upon—which, indeed, he had every right to do under the Berlin Act—is a fair specimen of the State's methods.
 * All the rubber vines in the Congo territories belong, of course, to the State and the latex within them. See Part II.
 † Morrison.
 ‡ Such wholesale expropriation is by no means unusual. It has been carried out at Irebo, round Lake Mantumba, and elsewhere.

called upon the officer, who admitted his intention, "but gave as an excuse that the people of Luebo did not work"—the same people, be it noted, described by M. Wauters, who has access to all the reports of Belgian explorers, in the highest terms—and that he wanted to take them to Luluabourg, "where they would have to work." Morrison pointed out that, on the contrary, the natives worked for the traders, and that "many of them had even gone far away down the Kasai River, where they had willingly accepted contracts to work." Morrison protested against such action being taken, threatened to report the matter to Boma, and to "publish the facts to the world." Impressed by the attitude of Morrison, the State officer gave up his plan.

In July, 1899, the American missionaries at Luebo heard that a large band of Zappo-Zaps, under a famous warrior chief named Mlumba Nkusa, "was proceeding into the Bena Pianga country, not far from one of the Mission stations, in order to collect tribute and get stores for the State." The Zappo-Zap chiefs appear to be * used by the State much in the same way as the so-called Arab Chiefs of the Manyema, the local "capitas" on the Mongalla by the *Anversoise*, and on the Lopori-Maringa by the *Abir*, that is to say, as auxiliary tax-gatherers. They rendered some assistance to the State posts in 1895, when the mutiny of Gongo Lutete's bodyguard took place, which has, no doubt, partly accounted for the friendly relations existing between them and the State, while their qualities of "fierce warriors and cannibals" doubtless commend themselves to "Bula Matadi" rather than the "physical and moral beauties" of the Baluba race, upon whom they prey on the State's account. Morrison describes the Zappo-Zaps as "cannibals, the greatest slave-dealers and slave-raiders of the district." He says—

"Perhaps half of the 7000 or 8000 people at Luebo who have been, or are now slaves,† have been caught by Zappo-Zaps in their numerous

---

* According to Morrison, the Zappo-Zaps were imported into the Luluabourg district by Lieutenant Le Marinel in 1890, or thereabouts.

† The word "slaves" used in this connection being somewhat obscure, I have written to Mr. Morrison, who is at present in the United States, for a clear explanation. His answer reads as follows :

"The slave in the Congo State may be divided into four classes, as follows :

"(1) Those caught in raids made by one village upon another. This form of slavery is not now allowed by the State ; the latter evidently prefers that all such slave-raiding shall be done under its own auspices, in a proper, systematic way.

"(2) Those caught by the State either in formal, or informal, raids for this purpose. Many of this class are caught by Sepoys or friendlies raids. . . . The State must of necessity know of the many thousands of slaves who have passed, and are now passing, through the hands of these Zappo-Zaps. The only possible explanation is that the State and the Zappo-Zaps are in alliance in the matter. Up to the time I left Luebo, slaves caught in the regions to the east of Luluabourg and Lusambo are almost daily exposed for sale, and always by the Zappo-Zaps. Either the latter themselves have done the raiding, or it has been done by some of the State soldiers about Lusambo, who sold the slaves to the Zappo-Zaps."

Soon after the arrival of the tribute-collecting Zappo-Zaps into the Bena Pianga country, news reached the Rev. W. H. Sheppard, F.R.G.S., in charge of the American Mission House at Ibanj, that the Zappo-Zaps had made the village of Chinyama, which they had stockaded, their headquarters, and were looting and slave-raiding in every direction. Five days off, at Luluabourg, was the State-post! "Great terror prevailed throughout the whole region," and thousands of people deserted their homes and fled to the forest. Sheppard then heard that the Zappo-Zaps had "treacherously invited a large number of the prominent chiefs of the region to come inside this stockade, and had there shot them down without quarter." Mr. Sheppard, who knew many of the Zappo-Zaps, thereupon set off for Chinyama (a singularly courageous act, by the way), taking "reliable natives with him, who could serve as witnesses. Along the way to Chinyama, Sheppard saw several burnt villages, also some wounded persons. He was received

who act under surveillance of the State. Out of this number the State selects what it wants for labour or military purposes; the remainder are left in the hands of the soldiers, or Sepoys, to be sold to other native free men.

"(3) Those who are forced into the labour and military service of the State by levies made upon the villages by the State.

"(4) Those held in domestic slavery, having been caught in one or the other of the ways above-mentioned.

"The majority of the slaves at Luebo belong to this latter class; they have been caught for the greater part by the soldiers of the State, or by some of the State Sepoys. Most prominent among these Sepoys in our district are the Zappo-Zaps, and a large chief near Lusambo called Mpenya Mutombo. It is simply puerile of the State to deny that they know nothing about the raids by the Zappo-Zaps and Mpenya Mutombo. They are right near the State post, and have long been known to be friendlies of the State. A fifth class might be added to the others, those who, though living in their own villages, are yet compelled to bring in tribute of ivory and rubber. These latter, perhaps, suffer more than any others, because they are absolutely at the mercy of the soldiery and the Sepoys."

The above very valuable description shows the system of Government slavery and slave-raiding, introduced by the "Administration" of the Congo State by way of regenerating the natives of the Congo territories.

in a friendly way by Mlumba Nkusa, and "his five hundred or more followers," inside the stockade. Sheppard "saw and counted" eighty-one human hands slowly drying over a fire; outside the stockade he counted "more than two score" bodies piled in a heap. The flesh had been carved off some of the bodies, and eaten, as Mlumba Nkusa cheerfully admitted. Several Albini rifles—which the natives not employed by the State are forbidden by law to possess—and a pistol and cartridges, were seen by Mr. Sheppard in the stockade. "Mlumba Nkusa said plainly that he had been sent by the State officer at Luluabourg."

The same year (1899) a State officer visited the village of Chief Lukenga, five days from Luebo. The chief knew the American missionaries, and sent messages to them to come at once. They went, and found the community "in the greatest excitement." The State soldiers, they were told, had fired upon the villages, killing fourteen. The villagers had defended themselves with bows and arrows. A year later a further visit was paid to Lukenga's village by a State officer. Lukenga was killed, and "from native reports, which we have every reason to believe to be true, also a great number of men, women, and children."

In June, July, and August, 1902, another "reign of terror" took place at Luebo, "and in fact throughout the region between Luluabourg and Luebo." But here I will quote Morrison's statement in full—

"A new officer named Deschamps had just come into power at Luluabourg. During my absence he came to Luebo, and there, without warning to the chiefs or villagers, sent out his soldiers to catch men by force wherever they could be found. The people fled at once to the forests for safety; some of the women and children, as is their custom in such times of fear, found refuge about the Mission premises. He went away with a number of men thus caught. Upon my return to Luebo, only a few days after the departure of the officer, and finding the whole community naturally in a state of unrest, I made complaint to the authorities about the matter. Scarcely had my letter been despatched when another officer, named Ducès, sent by Deschamps, came to 'recruit' soldiers, as he said. I went to him, and in person demanded protection for the natives, that none be taken by force. This, M. Ducès promised, and I in turn told the natives what he had said. Within a few days, however, he received imperative orders from his chief, Deschamps. Consequently he began catching the people by force. They fled to the forests for safety, but day by day, for perhaps a week or ten days, the soldiers scoured the woods in search of men. They succeeded in catching about eighteen or twenty, and these I saw taken away under guard, tied about the necks with ropes. When I began to make trouble about the matter, some of the men were returned, but some were never given up. Only the day before I left Luebo, the old Chief of the village came to me and begged me to try to find and send back his boys whom the State had taken away. This whole affair I reported to the Native Protection Commission, appointed by the King some years ago, to see that the natives were protected in their rights! The only answer I received was that the State had established laws for forced labour, and that doubtless the officers were acting entirely within their powers, the Commission thus sheltering itself and the officers guilty of these outrages under a form of legality.*

Vague statements of fighting and uprisings in the Kasai district were published by the Belgian Press in 1901 and 1902. But the next positive statement we have had concerning the Kasai district was that published by the Belgian papers in June, 1903. The information given referred to the results of the first year's operations of the new Trust, and were to the following effect:

"The cargo brought by the last steamer, the *Philippeville*, brings the amount received up to the present by the Kasai Company to 330,000 kilos. The rubber collected is of two kinds, one fetches 9 francs 10 centimes per kilo., the other, 7 francs 75 centimes per kilo. The sales have produced two million and a half francs (£90,000), without counting 50,000 francs (£2000) of ivory. At the last sale the Company's rubber import fetched nearly half a million francs (£20,000). The total rubber collected during the year ending December 31 (that is, the first years's working) is estimated at 565 tons. From the above an opinion can be formed of the Company's operations."

I do not guarantee the above figures; I merely quote them. In September, 1903, the Belgian newspapers reported a fight between the State troops in the neighbourhood of Luluabourg, in which Lieutenant Liar was killed; and as this book goes to press a further "revolt" is reported from the same quarter. The civilising of the Baluba nation would appear to be proceeding satisfactorily.

The most ingenious attempts, of course, have been made by the Congo State and its agents to discredit the testimony of the American missionaries on all the counts of their indictment. That is a fixed policy which has been pursued for many years with signal success. "Discredited missionaries," "untruthful travellers;" and as for Mr. Fox-Bourne and Mr. Morel, the Belgian vocabulary is long since exhausted!

I propose to deal with only one of these counts, the

* The story current on the Congo about this farcical Commission——reports from which have been vainly asked in the Belgian House—is that the two things which the Commission must never inquire into are (1) the rubber traffic; (2) the forced military and labour service. One can quite understand that, those two items being responsible for all the atrocities which occur! I have already referred to the active performances of this Commission.

massacre at Chinyama. I think the respective versions may be compared at greater advantage in parallel columns—

MORRISON. (Head, and legal representative of American Baptist Missionary Society).	CONGO STATE ACTION IN AFRICA.
1899. Morrison makes report of Chinyama massacre to State officer at Luluabourg, demanding immediate recall of Zappo-Zaps. (Reports also to Congo State Government at Brussels in a letter dated October 21, acknowledged February 29, 1900.* Morrison's account of the "inquiry is as follows:—" Upon my arrival at Ibory, the so-called investigation was begun, but it was from the first painfully evident that the Judge, who was writing down the evidence to send to Boma, was doing all in his power to free his fellow-officer, even attempting to influence witnesses by making an argument in favour of the officer charged. I was permitted to hear some of the evidence on this case, but I was told by another judge that the Government had reprimanded his colleague for permitting me to hear the evidence."	1899. 1. State officer at Luluabourg writes Morrison denying having anything to do with the matter. 2. Judge arrives at Luebo and summons Morrison to Ibory to establish his charges. "Inquiry takes place." Result: State officer at Luluabourg exonerated from all blame, Mlumba Nkusa declared at fault. 3. Mlumba Nkusa said to have been kept in confinement a short time at Luluabourg, but a few weeks only after the massacre "*he was back at Luebo.*" Natives reported the "Zappo-Zaps had been treacherously dealt with, were on the eve of revolting, and it would have been a most serious affair, seeing that their number is estimated at about 25,000 or 30,000, and that they have many guns, and know from long experience how to use them." 1900. (In Europe.) 1. Father Cambier, a Roman Catholic priest at Luluabourg, endeavours in *La Métropole* of June 3 to discredit the report of the American missionaries, but as his statement admits that "with respect to the behaviour of the Zappo-Zaps—for which they alone are responsible—if the facts are as stated, I will not discuss them. I have no personal knowledge of the facts;" and further on, as regards the mutilations, admits that "they are still carried on," his evidence may be taken as rather confirmatory than otherwise.

---

* Morrison to Baerts, *Chef de Cabinet*. Letter dated May 9, 1903. Published in the *West African Mail, Morning Post,* and *Daily News.*

IN THE KASAI

1903.
Morrison returns home and recapitulates before a public audience the Zappo-Zap incidents, together with more recent events.

1903.
2. Belgian papers admit the accuracy of the American missionary's report, but explain that the atrocities "were perpetrated by the Zappo-Zaps, who had been armed by the State in order to protect the Catholic Missions, and who through oversight were allowed to retain the arms given to them. *The guilty parties had been severely punished.*"

1903.
1. M. Jules Houdret, Consul-General of the Congo State in London, writes to the papers pointing out that a judicial inquiry had exonerated the State Officer at Luluabourg, and that Mlumba Nkusa was alone to blame. It was "conclusively proved" that the Zappo-Zaps had not acted on the State's instructions.

Morrison replies as follows:—
1. Had reported Zappo-Zap affair locally. Nothing had been done, and "you will also bear in mind that up to this time I have received no official notification of the result of the Zappo-Zap affair reported to you in my letter of October 21, 1899, the receipt of which was duly acknowledged in yours of February 23, 1900."

2. Had reported events of 1902 to the Governor-General of Boma, and was in due course informed that after "investigation," the charges were found to be "much exaggerated."

3. Felt it to be simply useless to refer to such matters in Brussels, so long as the present system of forced labour and forced military system prevails; "to be perfectly candid, I cannot bitterly condemn the subordinate officials who have to put such laws into operation."

2. M. Jules Houdret sends to the British Press a letter from M. Baerts, *Chef de Cabinet* of the Congo State's administration in Brussels, reminding Morrison that he had been in Brussels asking for a grant of land for his mission, that he had not referred to atrocities. "The administration of the Congo Free State takes note that you have kept silence towards the administration with respect to the alleged offences which you afterwards publicly denounced."

The above furnishes a concrete instance of the State's methods when the miserable effects of its policy in one particular spot are brought to light. It needs no comment, only an addition which will serve as an instructive and illuminating moral. The addition is an extract from the speech of M. Woeste—more fully reported in Part V—the ardent defender of the Congo State in the Belgian House last July:—

> "In the House of Commons, an old fact* was brought up, that of the cut hands. . . . M. Samuel made use of the following words: 'In one place an ocular witness saw slowly drying over a fire eighty human hands.† Is the fact true? I do not know. But I will admit that it is. What should have been added, however, is that, anyhow, they were not the hands of living men.'"

M. Woeste is easily satisfied! I have shown that the cutting off of hands, from *living and dead men, women, and children, is not a native custom*—and what is more important, M. Roger Casement, H.M. Consul on the Congo, has shown this also—but is an exotic introduced by the regenerators of the African. With this knowledge, with photographic evidence of living victims, with the published confessions of Belgian agents, with the testimony already available from many parts of the Congo, —with all this before us, it is only possible to come to one conclusion, viz. that the eighty severed hands on the stockade of Mlumba Nkusa, and his band of armed ruffians, some with Albini quick-firing rifles, were intended to show the Congo State officials that the work given to Mlumba Nkusa to perform had been well and effectively performed. It is only possible to come to the conclusion that Mlumbo Nkusa did not lie when he told Mr. Sheppard that he was in the employ of the State. How much "physical and moral beauty" will be left to the Baluba natives after a few more years of "Bula Matadi"?

* Note the words "old fact," and refer to Chapter X., and to recent letters in the Appendix.
† The Chinyama incident.

CHAPTER XVII

CONGO STATE CONTROL IN THE EASTERN DISTRICT (FROM THE LOMAMI TO THE EASTERN FRONTIER: THE ARUWIMI, LAKES TANGANYIKA, KIVU, ALBERT EDWARD, AND ALBERT)

> "Our only programme, I am anxious to repeat, is the work of moral and material regeneration, and we must do this among a population whose degeneration in its inherited conditions it is difficult to measure. The many horrors and atrocities which disgrace humanity give way little by little before our intervention."—KING LEOPOLD, in a letter to his agents.

FROM the accounts, all too few, unfortunately, which have reached us of late years, from the Eastern district, it appears that the Congo State officials have replaced the rule of the Arabs, which they destroyed, by something quite as bad, and in many respects worse. The Arab committed many atrocities, but he had a certain constructive faculty: he did not merely destroy, he also built up. Dr. Hinde, in his famous *Fall of the Congo Arabs*, bears witness to this.

"Despite their (the Arabs) slave-raiding propensities during the forty years of their dominion," he writes, "the Arabs had converted the Manyema and Malela countries into some of the most prosperous* in Central Africa."

Mr. Arnold Malet, an official in the employ of the Congo State, who is, or was, in charge of some of the State's coffee plantations, wrote to a friend of mine from Stanley Falls on December 4, 1901, as follows—

"Here we are in the midst of the 'Arab Zone,' and all around us we see the results of their industry in the shape of immense tracts of land planted with rice, manioc, etc., and flocks of goats and sheep. The most interesting part of the Congo perhaps."

---

* No country—certainly no country in tropical Africa—can be described as "prosperous," if the people of the land whose cultivation induces that prosperity are not well-off, settled, and contented.

Major Gibbons has recently remarked *—

"To say that the status and lot of the native population have been in any way improved by the Belgian occupation seems to me more than doubtful. The Arab traders have been exterminated, and Western civilisation has been substituted for that of the East; but by how much has the change benefited the natives? Certainly it has resulted in their subjugation to the yoke of 'civilisation,' that is to say, it has reduced once homogeneous communities to countless impotent groups from which taxes, just or unjust, can be conveniently squeezed with the alternative of a punitive expedition to enforce the law †—and we all know what that means when native soldiery under a certain type of white man is employed. *Under Arab influence the freedom of organised native communities was not interfered with. The people came to trade—to give and take, not to take only.*‡ Morally speaking, I will content myself here with the bare assertion that the natives are not the gainers by the Belgian occupation. . . ."

The results of the State's "industry," on the other hand, we may gather fairly comprehensibly from the account given by Mr. A. B. Lloyd (latter part of 1899); Mr. Ewart Grogan (1899–1900); Mr. Robert Codrington (1902); and various information from different sources, to date.

The state of affairs in the Tanganyika region is partly covered by the particulars given in Chapter XVIII.

From the latter region, two recent reports may be cited. Mr. Robert Codrington (1902), now a British official in Nyassaland, writes—

"There is no trade, properly so-called, on the Congo coast of Tanganyika, but all rubber and ivory is regarded as the property of the State, and has to be surrendered in fixed quantities annually. The natives are, however, continually in rebellion, and the country is unsafe, except in the immediate vicinity of the military garrisons, and within the sphere of influence of the missionaries."

In a letter received by the author from a correspondent in Nyassaland, the following passage can be quoted. The letter is dated Abercorn, February 10, 1903, and the passage reads as follows—

"The latest news we have of the Belgians in Congo State territory is to the effect that they are building a new fort at Uwiri (north end of

---

* *Op. cit.*

† The method of enforcing these taxes in the Congo State is in itself wholly illegal, even according to the State's own "law."

‡ Italics mine. That is precisely the point. The Arab rule was bad, but it was not wholly destructive, it was marked by the species of rude statesmanship which looks ahead, albeit through faulty glasses. Congo State rule *is* wholly destructive, and its effects are one long demoralisation; the breath of the pestilence from which recovery is either hopeless or terribly protracted, rather than the whirling Harmattan, which is followed by sunlight giving play for the exercise of internally recuperative forces.

Lake Tanganyika), only women being employed in its construction. These women are said to be slaves by a European who has visited the fort. They have probably been forced into service or hired somewhere in the interior. They work all day, and at night are at the disposal of the soldiers, of whom there are about 800 in the neighbourhood. These particulars are known to the German authorities at Ujiji (east shore of Lake Tanganyika)."

Mr. Ewart Grogan, whose remarkable journey from the Cape to Cairo *via* Lakes Tanganyika, Kivu, Albert Edward, and Albert, will be fresh in every one's mind, published his experiences and those of his companion, Mr. Arthur H. Sharpe, in an exceedingly attractive book.* Prior to its appearance, Mr. Grogan lectured before the Royal Geographical Society, and was interviewed by several newspapers. Judging from Mr. Grogan's emphatic remarks, he does not appear to have been particularly struck by the "civilising" methods of the Congo State. I may venture to observe that Mr. Grogan's evidence is specially valuable, insomuch as his ideas of labour necessities and the treatment of natives are so drastic that no one would venture to accuse him, in his references to the Congo State, of being influenced by any feelings remotely approaching sentimentalism, a charge sometimes levelled at those who urge that the natives of Africa have rights after all, and that it is generally wiser in the long run for the white man not to treat the native as a species of anthropoid ape. Here is what Mr. Grogan has to say on Congo State methods *along the whole Eastern frontier* region—

"From the north of Lake Albert to Lake Mweru there is a perfect state of chaos. Whole districts are administered by incompetent officials, often non-commissioned officers, and the troops are the lowest type of natives, almost invariably cannibals."

In *British territory*, in the neighbourhood of Lake Albert, Mr. Grogan found that—

"The people were terrorised and were living in marshes . . . the Belgians have crossed the frontier, descended into the valley, shot down large numbers of natives—British subjects—driven off the young women and cattle, and actually tied up and burned the old women.† I do not make these statement without having gone into the matter. . . . I remarked on the absence of women, and the reason for this was given. . . . It was on further inquiry that I was assured by the natives that white men had been present when the old women had been burnt. In each village I heard the same tale. The natives said that the troops had come from the adjacent Belgian posts—the nearest was only a few miles across

---

* "From the Cape to Cairo." London : Hurst & Blackwell, Ltd.

† For a somewhat similar incident in a widely removed part of the country, see Consul Casement, Africa, No. I. (1904), p. 73.

the frontier—and they even described to me the personal appearance of the white officers with the troops. . . . For days the natives left me to starve, until I hit upon the idea of calling myself Lugard's brother, and of producing Colonel Lugard's photograph, which I happened to have with me. Then the wretched people came to me and asked me why the British had deserted them."

Here is a description of the Mushari district, near Lake Kivu, in Congo territory, which had been attacked by Congo State revolted soldiery, and then ravaged by a cannibal tribe.

" Every village had been burnt to the ground, and as I fled from the country, I saw skeletons, skeletons everywhere; and such postures, what tales of horror they told ! . . .* I would not have entered into these revolting details, but that I think it advisable that those who have not the chance of seeing for themselves should know what is going on every day in this country. A beautiful yellow covers this spot on the map, with a fringe of red spots with flags attached, denoting (as the map informs you) stations of the Congo Free State. And yet a peaceful, agricultural people can be subjected to horrors like this for months (*without any one knowing*). And why ? Because the whole system is bunkum—the so-called partition of Africa. The stations marked do not exist; and read, mark, learn, and inwardly digest this fact : I have to pay a licence to shoot game, or to *carry a gun* in the country. . . . Thus a tract of country about 3000 square miles in extent has been depopulated and devastated. I do not believe that 2 per cent. of the thousands of the inhabitants have survived the massacre and famine ; in Kishari and Kameronse † there is not one single soul. And all this is directly attributable to the revolted *Askaris* of the Congo ; they led the attack, with thirty guns, took all the cattle, and then departed. . . . Rapid movements alone could save us from annihilation, and we travelled from sunrise to sunset, camping in patches of forest, and concealing our route by leaving the paths and forcing our way through the grass. Mummies, skulls, limbs, putrifying carcases, washing to and fro in every limpid stream, marked the course of the fiendish horde. An insufferable stench filled the land, concentrating round every defiled homestead. This was the Congo Free State, and I thought with bitterness on the vast sums recently expended in sending filibustering expeditions up the Nile.‡

Mr. Grogan's observations in the Semliki valley (between Lakes Albert and Albert Edward) and Kavalli's country, south-west of Lake Albert, are in contradiction with Sir Harry Johnston's—both men apparently visited the Semliki the same year. Sir Harry Johnston § penetrated " for about thirty miles west of the Semliki." Grogan appears to have

* " From the Cape to Cairo," p. 156, *op. cit.*
† So far as Kameronse is specifically mentioned by Dr. Kandt, Mr. Grogan's account confirms the former explorer's story. Dr. Kandt passed through Kameronse early in 1899. He says of it, " All is destroyed ; all is burnt ; the population is in flight."
‡ Mr. Grogan refers no doubt to the Congo State's Bahr-el-Ghazal expedition under Dhanis, wrecked by the mutiny of his troops.
§ *Daily Chronicle*, September 28, 1903.

THE EASTERN DISTRICT 205

travelled right through the region the river traverses on his way northwards from Lake Albert Edward to Kavalli's country on the south-west of Lake Albert, and would naturally have seen a great deal more of the country than Sir Harry Johnston. Here is Grogan's account :

"I asked him why all the people were so frightened, and where they had all gone; whereupon he proceeded to recount the same tales of misery and oppression that I had heard the day before, from which I gathered that a Congo Free State (I like the title 'Free State'—so suitable!) official, rejoicing in the name of 'Billygee,' had suddenly swooped down on the country a year ago, and after shooting down numbers of the natives had returned west, carrying off forty young women, numerous children, and all the cattle and goats. . . ."

After recapitulating in greater detail the burning of the old people in their villages, which has been touched upon already, Mr. Grogan continued :

"When in Mboya, the Balegga told me similar tales : here I was repeatedly given accounts that tallied in all essentials, and further north, the Wakoba made the same piteous complaints ; and I saw myself that a country apparently well populated and responsive to just treatment in Lugard's time is now practically a howling wilderness."

Mr. A. B. Lloyd, who crossed the Semliki on his way from Uganda to the west coast through the Congo State in the latter part of 1899, did not form a high idea of Belgian administration in that particular region either, judging from the following passage in his book :*

"In the afternoon I was walking through the potato fields when I came upon sixty or a hundred women, all with hoes, cultivating the ground, and close at hand was a native soldier with a rifle across his shoulder, acting as guard. I inquired where all the poor creatures had come from, and I was told a sad, sad story—alas ! not an uncommon one in the Belgian Free State. A Wakona chief had been told to do some work for the Belgians, and when he refused soldiers were sent, and upon the least resistance the men were shot down, and the women were captured as slaves and made to work. It was a sad sight to behold these poor creatures, driven like dogs here and there, and kept hard at their toil from morning to night. One of the Belgian soldiers told me that there had been many killed, including the chief, and when I said what a terrible thing it was, he merely laughed and said, 'Washenzi Bevana' ('They are only heathen ')."

About the middle of 1902, Lieutenant Tondeur, an official of the Congo State, and his escort were killed by natives near Lake Kivu. In December of that year, the Belgian papers announced that an expedition left in October to avenge his

* "In Dwarf-land and Cannibal Country." Albert B. Lloyd. (T. Fisher Unwin.)

death, and defeated the natives, several of whom were hanged. The latest news available from that district was published on October 25, 1903, in the *Morning Post*, from an English sportsman in the north of Lake Kivu. The extracts published by the *Morning Post* from this gentleman's letters, read as follows:

"The natives are not actively hostile, but they run away to the top of the hills, and refuse for a long time to sell anything or give any assistance. The Belgian Government does not inspire a liking for white men, and I am not surprised, for their *askaris** up there do anything they like."

The opinions formed by Mr. Grogan from his *de visu* experiences of the "moral and material regeneration" theory—otherwise stated, the theory of the *Domaine Privé*—as it works out in practice were strong, and he does not mince his words—

"... The participation or occupation of Africa "—he writes—" with a view to sound colonisation, is the obvious duty of the nations that form the vanguard of civilisation.... But what can be said in favour of committing a vast tract of country to be run merely as a commercial speculation without more legitimate objective than that of squeezing as much rubber and ivory out of the natives as possible; of arming large numbers of savages, and entrusting them to inexperienced exports from a land of untravelled commercials, to whom expatriation is akin to disgrace; of making the administrators of districts to all intents and purposes farmers of the taxes?"

And further on, after describing the Congo State territory from Mweru to the Nile as "chaos, hopeless abyssmal chaos," he concludes:

"I have no hesitation in condemning the whole State as a vampire growth, intended to suck the country dry, and to provide a happy hunting-ground for a pack of unprincipled outcasts and untutored scoundrels."

The Congo State Administration, it may be useful to remember, is directly concerned in the regions covered by Mr. Grogan and Mr. Lloyd, and referred to above. There are no trusts in that portion of the country. It forms part of the *Domaine Privé—stricto sensu*.

After crossing the Semliki (end of 1899), Mr. A. B. Lloyd, already referred to, struck the Aruwimi, and followed it through the great forest and beyond. Early in the same year, an Englishman, Captain Bell, in the State's service, was killed by the natives on this river, and Lieutenant Andrews, another

* *Askaris* is a word commonly used in Central and East Africa, meaning soldiers.

British officer who returned to England also that year, gave it as his opinion that the "zone of safety, and so-called civilisation" did not extend a mile back from the river side.

Perhaps that was not altogether surprising, for we find Mr. Lloyd writing of "the smouldering fire at the heart of the people (Bangwa)" with whom he spoke at Avakubi, Banelya, and elsewhere, owing to the brutality of the Congo State officials. Mr. Lloyd's version of the procedure of the State's representatives in that region is the familiar one : the same story, which in a continuous and barely diversified form, and from every district whence information has filtered through, has come to us for the last decade down to the report of the official representative of his Majesty's Government, Mr. Roger Casement.

"A Chief of the district"—writes Mr. Lloyd—"where some European of the Congo Free State is stationed, is called up and told to send his people out for rubber, so many pounds' weight are required and *must* be brought in. The chief, perhaps, has but a small following, and cannot produce what is asked of him ; he is given another chance to get it, and again fails and must be punished. A native officer is instructed to take a number of soldiers and destroy the Chief's village. Then follows the most bloodthirsty wickedness that is anywhere recorded—men, women, and children ruthlessly murdered, and the whole place destroyed."

On January 4, 1902, the *Compagnie des chemins de fer du Congo supérieur aux grands Lacs Africains* was started. It has received large concessions * in the Aruwimi country. Its object is to build a railway—preliminary work on the line is understood to be going on with somewhat feverish haste—from Stanley Falls to Ponthierville and Lake Albert. In most countries the construction of a railway is the forerunner of progress, civilisation and development. In the case of the *Domaine Privé* in the Congo, a railway is merely an instrument for the extension and aggravation of a crushing and perpetual tyranny. The lot of the Aruwimi natives is not an enviable one. Their forests, hardly tapped as yet, are understood to be very rich in rubber ; and the railway can only accentuate the merciless exploitation to which they will presently be subjected. It is a remote region, and it will be probably a long time before anything more definite than the usual vague reports of risings, followed by "repressions," reach the civilised world. It will then be no great consolation to the victims to pillory the shareholders of this newest Trust, which includes a member of the present Government of the French Republic, and unhappily a considerable portion of French capital. We are likely to

* Some 22,000 square miles.

hear a good deal about the "vacant lands" of the Aruwimi, the scene of the operations of the Trust. At present our information is limited to the knowledge that an American engineer was killed a few months ago by the natives; that "labour troubles" were reported from Basoko * last August, that in September last the Belgian newspapers published the following:

> "The situation is grave in the Basoko District. Commander Van Werdt is establishing order. The natives complain of the heavy transport work (*portage intensif*) to which they are subjected."

and finally, that the Trust is already exporting no inconsiderable quantities of rubber, coupled with the intelligence that the State "is now exploiting" its domains in the district.

THE LOMAMI DISTRICT.

The Lomami Company belongs virtually (although the State shares in the profits to the extent of 25 per cent.) to the Thys group, and, like the *Société Anonyme Belge* is, there is reason to hope, run on different lines, as I have remarked already. Founded in July, 1898, with a capital of 3,000,000 francs, its profits in 1898–99 were 130,605 francs; 1899–1900, 152,000 francs; 1900–01, 155,000 francs. Belgian reports to hand during the latter part of last year, announce uprisings in the district, although whether in the Company's sphere or outside it is not yet apparent.† M. Langeld, an agent of the *Société Anonyme Belge*, reported in 1898 of the people on the Lomami banks, as follows:—

> "... Numerous and populous villages, inhabited by a very fine race (*de grande beauté*), a superb people, most intelligent in appearance, quite inclined to welcome the white men, and with whom the latter will do good business, *on condition that they treat them well*."

---

* At the mouth of the Aruwimi.

† The Belgian newspapers have since given the following version. Lieutenant Vandevelde was sent to a Chief who "had not submitted to the State, to make him hear reason" (*sic*). Lieutenant Vandevelde attacked the Chief and was taken prisoner. The natives made him labour continuously for many days, and then released him. Evidently another "rubber palaver" of the State.

NATIVE METHOD OF MENDING A BROKEN LEG.

THE NATIVE AT HOME
(French explorer enjoying the hospitality of a village in French Congo)

CHAPTER XVIII

CONGO STATE CONTROL IN THE SOUTH-EASTERN DISTRICT (KATANGA)

> "Each step forward made by our people must mark an improvement in the condition of the natives."—KING LEOPOLD, in a letter to his Agents on the Congo.

THE specific case of the treatment meted out to a white merchant by the Congo State Authorities in this district is fully set forth in Part IV. We may now examine the general condition of affairs in the Katanga District, where the persecution of the Austrian trader, Rabinek, took place. Since 1896, or thereabouts, a portion of the South-Eastern District has been entirely in the hands of mutineers from the State army, remains of the force which mutinied at Luluabourg in 1895, and Dungu in 1897. The State Authorities have claimed on many occasions to have wiped out these people. This is far from being the truth, according to many independent reports. The rebels of 1897, who had gradually made their way eastward, inflicted three successive defeats upon the Congo State forces in 1898 at Agusa, Hubari, and Kabambare. The last disaster was the most serious of all, as Kabambare was one of the strongest military posts in the Eastern Districts. It was captured, and the whole of the munitions it contained, "enough—as a participant in the rout informed one of my correspondents shortly afterwards—to arm 2000 Batetlas," fell into the enemy's hands. The mutineers, instead of following up their successes, retreated southwards into the Katanga District proper, where they joined,* apparently, the rebels of 1895, who were in occupation of the Katanga Lake country. At the present time they are said to be absolute masters of the regions around Lakes Kisale and Kabele, and one or two feeble efforts to evict them on the part of the authorities have entirely failed. They have

* It would seem, however, that some of the rebel bands still exist in the neighbourhood of the Eastern frontier about Lake Kivu. See in this respect Major Gibbons (*op. cit.*).

appointed, it is said, their own War and Finance Ministers, and have reared a sort of State, modelled upon that of their former masters. Mr. Dugald Campbell, who has ten years' experience of the country, writes from Johnstone Falls, May 19, 1904, that the rebels are "to-day, May, 1904, as busy and lively as ever in the districts round the Lubudi river."

Outside the "Rebel Zone," as it is usually termed, the sway of the officials and their murderous auxiliaries is more or less in evidence, and is accompanied by the usual incidents. Here, as elsewhere in the territories of the State, the officials, to use the term of the British Note of August 8, 1903 (which, by the way, has special application to the South-Eastern District of the Congo State, for it is from officials in North-Eastern Rhodesia and Nyassaland that the particular reports referred to by the British Government have been received), "do not apparently concern themselves with such work (administration), but devote all their energy to the collection of revenue." We know what the "collection of revenue" means in the Congo State! It means the systematic pillaging of native villages for ivory by bands of soldiery despatched throughout the country from the various State stations, and the levying of the eternal rubber tribute.

"The Congo State stations," continues the Note, "are shunned, the only natives seen being soldiers, prisoners, and men who are brought in to work"—a polite formula for slaves. "The neighbourhood of stations which are known to have been populous a few years ago, is now uninhabited, and emigration on a large scale takes to the territory of neighbouring States, the natives usually averring that they are driven away from their homes by the tyranny and exaction of the soldiers."

Precisely similar information, only given in more detail, has reached me for some time past from non-official European residents in North-Eastern Rhodesia and Nyassaland. I have before me at the present moment a statement by a former agent of the Katanga Company,* sworn before a British official at Karonga (Nyassa), bearing the seal and stamp of the British Central Africa Protectorate, and dated March 9, 1903. It contains the following passages :

"At the different Congo State Government stations women are kept for the following purposes :—

"In the daytime, they do all the usual station work, such as carrying water for the Government officials, cleaning their rooms, etc., and during the night they are obliged to be at the disposal of the soldiers. The soldier must live with the women as long as he is at the station ; should he be removed, the woman must remain at the station whether

---

* Who left the Company upon its amalgamation with the Congo State.

he has children by her or not. The women are slaves captured by the Government soldiers when raiding the country, they are there to facilitate the ordinary requirements of labour, and to prevent the soldiers from their usual customs of raping in the native villages."

Two affidavits, the one made by two British protected natives (apparently recruited by a Congo State official in British territory), the other by a native woman before a British official in Nyassaland, in each case in the presence of European witnesses, and bearing the official seal and stamp, are also before me. The first affidavit contains the following passages descriptive of the powerlessness of the Congo State officers to control their soldiery:

"On our arrival in the Congo State, we learnt from the inhabitants and the Government soldiers that there always is war between the white man, the soldiers and the natives. . . . The white men are so afraid of the soldiers that they let them do whatever they like. They rape, murder, and steal everything of the inhabitants, and if the Chief or villagers object, they are often shot dead on the spot. The officers all know this, but they never take any notice of it, as they are afraid to punish their soldiers. Another officer called by the natives Kaputisnasinga . . . punished the natives by cutting off their hands, ears, etc., or hanged them according to the crime."

The second affidavit describes a characteristic raiding expedition on the part of the Congo State officials.

"They (the Belgian soldiers with four white men) came from Lukafu and made war with our Chief Chiwala, many people were killed, but the Chief and his wife escaped to the English side of the Luapula. I, together with other women, and many tusks of ivory, were captured. . . . When we were transported to Lukafu we were fastened together by a rope round our necks, and at night time our hands and feet were tied together to prevent us from escaping. . . . After one month at Lukafu I and the three other girls were sent to Mpueto; we were tied together the whole way. . . . At Mpueto I witnessed the killing of two natives who had stolen rubber from the Government stores. By the order of the white man called Lutina,* the two natives were beaten by his soldiers with hippo-hide whip, after this they were made to stand up, the soldiers then threw bricks on them till they died. One native was from Chewerchewera's village, very near Mptueo, and was buried by his relations, the other, who had no relations so near, was thrown into Lake Mweru." †

An official of the African International Flotilla Transport Company, Ltd., writes from Kambwe (Nyassa) on November 18, 1892, as follows—

"There are many, many atrocities and cruelties which have taken place in the Congo (Free?) State which have not yet come to light, but

---

* Native name.
† I may mention that all these affidavits have been communicated by the author to his Majesty's Government.

which I sincerely trust and hope will be shown up now, although there are many which never will be shown up. If people at home only knew the disgraceful way in which the natives are treated and the Congo Free State run, the Belgians would be dispossessed of the territory immediately. While I was stationed at Chienji, Lake Mweru, from April 1890 to April 1892, I had ample opportunities of meeting the officials of the Comité Spécial du Katanga. . . . I also knew Mr. ——— * of the ——— Mission, stationed for many years at ———. I spoke to him of the abominable way in which native soldiers were armed and let loose over the country, to the curse of all other native men and women, facts which he, of course, knew to be true, and told him that he, as a missionary, ought really to report and expose; but he was afraid his mission would be turned out of the country."

A correspondent in Nyassaland, writing under date of January 17, 1903, after giving a long description of the state of affairs in the Katanga territory, as taken down before two European witnesses from the lips of a native merchant in British territory, which fully bears out the statements of other correspondents, says :

"For the last six years, English and German traders have been establishing their *dépôts* as far as the Congo boundaries, but the Belgians will not allow them to trade in Congo State territory. . . . You can form a pretty good idea from this of the way that our natives are treated by the Belgians. If they go into the Congo State territory at all, they do so in fear of their lives. I suppose the profits tempt them. What we traders want to know is, why the great Powers—and especially England, who signed the Berlin Treaty—stand this sort of thing. From all we hear, all that goes on in the Congo territory itself beggars description. There are not hundreds, but thousands of mutilated natives all over the Congo. . . . I am trying to get some photographs of these cases, with a fully certified statement of the facts in each case. It is difficult to bring home these mutilations to the State soldiers. To take down what the native says is not considered sufficient proof, without another European being present; and for white men to go into the Congo territory, or to bring a native out of the Congo, is always very risky and expensive."

From another letter, received in 1903 from the same correspondent, I give the following extracts :

"The rebels," he writes, "in the Katanga country are well armed, and not at least afraid of the Belgians; and this makes a very bad impression on the whole of the native population of these parts. The Belgians are also, as a rule, in the hands of their soldiers, and in many cases the officers have been threatened by them, to such an extent that the future of the country will be in the greatest danger for the development of Europeans. The Belgians do not allow any white men in the Katanga territory. It is thus very difficult to actually witness the daily reports of disgraceful treatment of the inhabitants by the Belgians and

---

* The name is suppressed because I have no authority on the part of the missionary named to give it, and without his authority I do not wish to expose him to unpleasantness.

their soldiers, and the way the soldiers treat their officers. The reports are, usually, that several soldiers are sent out to collect rubber in the interior, and have a free hand to do so, so long as they bring in long caravans of rubber. The natives are forced to collect rubber, otherwise their villages are burnt, and in many cases people mutilated or killed. This is what I hear of every black man, and from white men who know what goes on. The soldiers are generally selected from warlike tribes far in the interior, and as long as those soldiers have the right to treat the inhabitants as they like, large quantities of rubber are got, which is what is required. The natives, knowing the soldiers act for the white men, are all the more frightened. In addition to this, the soldiers are supplied with good guns and plenty of ammunition; they are uniformed, and lead an independent life; are not troubled with military instructions, have plenty of women, slaves, beer and food, and the right of disposing of life and death at their option. Any one who knows natives will agree that the danger of such a state of matters is very great. That such a policy on the part of the Belgians makes a bad, dangerous impression upon all the natives is without question. The increasing hatred and terror of the natives against Europeans is proved by the fact that both peace and welfare, and also the population, are decreasing wherever the Belgians take possession. With the exception of half-a-dozen villages, the whole Belgian Luapula, from Mweru to the Falls, has been abandoned by the natives. They have all crossed to the British side, simply on account of the Belgians and their soldiers."

The above testimony, coming from a variety of sources, is conclusive. It bears out, moreover, the declarations of M. Lévêque, the Director of the Katanga Company, as to the condition of affairs in the territory assigned to his Company by the Congo State authorities.* Extracts from the diary of an English representative of the Katanga Company, which has come into my possession, will put the finishing touches to the picture of Congo State "Control" in the South-Eastern District, in so far as the treatment of natives and general administration are concerned.

The writer of this diary was despatched by his Chief, M. Lévêque,† along the Belgian bank of the Luapula, in order to build trading stations for the Company. The very briefness of the extracts accentuates their significance. They are the hurried jottings, written down *de visu*, of an ordinary unemotional individual. He has set down just what he saw roughly, and with no attempt at literary embellishments.

"Johnston Falls, October 20th, 1900.

"*October 14th.*—Paid the canoes off and we left for our journey up river at 6 a.m., and reached the village of Kawine at 4 p.m. Here we heard that the Lufoi soldiers had been again shooting, and have killed one man,

---

* See Part IV.
† It may be useful to mention, by the way, that I have never held any communication of any kind with this M. Lévêque, who is only known to me by name.

also badly wounding another. This took place above here, and there is fighting, in fact, along the whole river (when I say fighting, I mean stealing, and taking women prisoners for their own use). The people have all gone across to the English side for safety.

"*October 16th.*—Left at 6 a.m., and passed a small village on the English side. . . . 3.45 p.m. we passed a great many small villages on the English side, but could get no labour, as they are afraid of this side.

"*October 17th.*—Left at 6 a.m., and about 8 a.m. we passed a great many people on the English side, about, I should say, two to three hundred men, women, and children. I stayed and spoke to them, also telling them to wait till we could arrange for their return to their own villages again. It is really sad to see these poor hungry people, whose food crops have all been destroyed and their property stolen.

"*October 18th.*—Left at 4 a.m., and we stuck on a small sandbank for about one hour. We passed the villages of 'Musoka,' who have had to flee to the English side for protection. Here the soldiers have taken away women as prisoners, all because these people have no rubber for the Lufoi station. Again I have told these people to wait, and all will be well when we have our steamer on the river to assist them and their troubles.

"*October 19th.*—Left at 5.30 a.m. and reached the falls at 11 a.m. Got our baggage on shore and camped on the Katanga Company's territory at the foot of the falls. Here we find also all the people gone over the river. I shall have to arrange about getting men from the English side.

"Mr. Milstead came across * to see us, and he tells me that no less than seven chiefs from this side † have been to see him, saying that they wish to build on the English side. The reasons given him by these chiefs are that the Lufoi *askaris* have robbed and molested their people to such an extent that they find it impossible to live on this side any longer. I have told some of them that we would give them protection soon.

"Johnston Falls, October 23rd.
"I find that owing to the impossibility to obtain carriers for us both to proceed at once, I must go on ahead and procure men. . . . This has been caused by the devastation of the country, and also the ravishing of native women by the Lufoi soldiers.

"*October 24th*, 9 *a.m.*—Left Johnston Falls with only sufficient men to take myself and loads to Chinamas. We went along a ridge for about two hours, and came to a large number of temporary huts of people who had fled from inland. I understand that between the river and Lufoi the people have now settled on the English side of the river.

"*October 25th.*—Left camp at 9 a.m., and after two and a half hours' walk we passed a small village of some ten huts, but the people had all fled. We then went on until 11.30 a.m., and camped. There was a large village on the English side of the Luapula, but we could not get them to come to us, as they were afraid we were from the Lufoi station.

"*October 27th.*—. . . The road to-day has been through forest, and only once did we pass water *en route*. We also passed a village deserted. The large gardens show there must have been a very large population, and that they had not long left the place.

"*October 30th.*—Left camp at 7 a.m., after another bad night of rain. We reached Chinamas at 10.30 a.m. I find that, owing to so many

---

* That is, from the English side of Luapula.
† That is, the Congo State side.

IN KATANGA

difficulties, I must give up the idea of going any further south. The people are a poor hunted race so far; and, further south, we should only have the blame of the mischief put on our shoulders for what the Lufoi soldiers have done to destroy the natives.

"*October* 31*st.*—The men I sent yesterday to call 'Chinamas' returned, and the chief is now on his way to see me. He arrived at 11 a.m., and we held a meeting. The old chief was a very intelligent old man, and it seems he has been hardly dealt with, and hunted about for his wealth of ivory. He says most of his cattle and ivory have been taken from him at odd times."

The treatment of M. Teixeira de Mattos, a trader of Dutch extraction, long established in Nyassaland, a representative of Sharrar's Zambesi Traffic Co., Ltd., and Zambesi Trading Co., at the hands of the Congo State people may, in conclusion, be briefly touched upon. M. Teixeira de Mattos it should be mentioned, is a creditor on the late Herr Rabinek's * estate, which may account in some measure for the action of the *Comité Spécial du Katanga*—the name of the Trust under which the Congo State now conceals its operations in the South Eastern District.

I understand from M. Teixeira de Mattos that the Dutch Government is concerning itself in an endeavour to obtain compensation from the Congo State for the outrage of which its subject has been the victim, at the hands of the *Comité's* agents.

The main facts of the case are these:

In September, 1901, M. Teixeira de Mattos went down the Luapula from Chienji to Fort Rosebery, in the African Lakes Corporation Steamer, *Scotia*. The steamer took in firewood at the English village of Kampalla-Luapula. Two natives employed by M. de Mattos were at Kampalla, whither they had been sent by M. de Mattos' agent on Lake Tanganyika to buy rubber in British territory. They reported the need of cloths to pay carriers to bring the rubber they had bought to Chienji. Two canoes were hired by M. de Mattos from the chief of the village at Kampala to convey the rubber by water to Chienji. The task was undertaken by the son of the chief and three other natives. M. de Mattos then proceeded to Chienji in the *Scotia*. Four days after his arrival at that place his two rubber buyers turned up, reporting that all the rubber had been loaded into one canoe, and as they did not know how to paddle, they had travelled overland. The canoe, however, did not arrive. Some three days later the Katanga Company's steamer arrived, and upon inquiry being made, M. de Mattos ascertained that his canoe had been

* See Part IV.

seized on the Luapula, when on its way to Chienji, and confiscated, together with its contents, by the Katanga Company's agent. The captain of the Katanga Company's steamer, challenged by M. de Mattos, admitted the fact, adding that upon seeing the Belgian steamer bearing down upon them, two of the natives in the canoe had sprung into the water, but that one remained, and the canoe with the remaining native on board had been towed to Mpueto, the Congo State station on Lake Mweru. M. de Mattos lost no time in going to Mpueto and confronting the "Commandant" in charge. The latter replied that he was on board the Belgian steamer when she captured the canoe, and that the native who had remained on board was in gaol. He refused to answer any questions, declined to give the weight of the rubber seized, and behaved in an insolent manner generally. M. de Mattos thereupon left Mpueto and laid his complaint before Dr. Blair Watson, British Magistrate for the Mweru District. The latter communicated with the "Commandant" at Pueto. This individual replied that the rubber had been collected from the Congo State side of the Luapula, from territory belonging to the *Comité Spécial du Katanga*—otherwise stated, the Katanga Trust—that the seizure was perfectly legal, and that the native would be dealt with by *la justice*. This reply showed once again that the Congo Authorities, contrary to the Act of Berlin, do not allow the natives of the Congo State territory to sell rubber to European traders, or to any one. *But the statement in itself was also totally untrue, because, as already stated, the rubber was gathered by British natives in British territory, and was being conveyed to a British port in a British canoe, manned by British natives.* There were several witnesses, white and black, to testify to this, and sworn declarations by the native buyers of M. de Mattos were made before Mr. J. L. Green, the British native Commissioner. Owing to the energetic representations of Dr. Blair Watson, the Katanga Trust was subsequently compelled to change its tune. W——, the Trust's chief representative, discredited his "Commandant," and on April 29, 1902, six months after the seizure occurred, M. de Mattos received the following letter from M. Chesneye, acting administrator at Fort Jameson.

"Administrator's Office, Fort Jameson, N.E. Rhodesia,
"April 29, 1902.

"SIR,—I have the honour to inform you that I have received a letter from Dr. Blair Watson, Civil Commissioner, Mweru District, to the effect that W——, representative of the *Comité Spécial du Katanga*, of the Congo Free State, had discredited the action taken by M. C—— in seizing a canoe containing rubber belonging to you. At Dr. Watson's request, the rubber in question is being sent to Chienji, to be delivered to yourself or your agents. Dr. Watson informs me that he has communicated with me on this subject. Representations are now being made to the Congo Free State Authorities with a view of effecting the immediate release of the canoe and the native of Kampallas, which were illegally seized by order of M. C——. Should you claim any compensation for illegal detention and seizure on the part of the Katanga Company, I will be glad to receive your claims and the reasons on which these demands are based.

"I have the honour to be, sir,
"Your obedient servant,
"C. J. CHESNEYE.

"M. Teixeira de Mattos, Esq.,
"Acting Administrator, Katonga."

The amount claimed by M. de Mattos amounted to about £500. All he has received, however, at the time his latest communication has reached me, is the value of three bags of rubber, all that the canoe contained according to the agents of the Katanga Trust! Possibly, however, M. de Mattos may still get adequate compensation, for a passenger on board the Belgian steamer when the seizure took place, has signed an affidavit (copy of which is in my possession) before M. C. MacKennon, Magistrate at Murongo, N.E. Rhodesia, and dated January, 1903. In this affidavit, it is stated that the quantity seized was very much larger than the "three bags" allowed by the Katanga Trust. The circumstances of the seizure and the treatment of the unfortunate *British native* are minutely described in the affidavit. The native was tied up to the steamer rail, and was left there for two nights and one day. The native, as already explained, was finally handed over to *la justice* at Mpueto. Whether he ever escaped from the clutches of Congo "justice" does not transpire.

The following extract from Mr. Owen Stroud's diary, published in the *Bournemouth Guardian* in 1903, adds another touch to the condition of the South-Eastern District. Mr. Stroud was recently entrusted with the task of placing a monument on the spot where Dr. Livingstone died. The extract is dated September 9, 1902:

"Left early, and after travelling for about three hours, I met a Mr. Wright, a hunter and trader, and as I had known him years ago at a place called Blantyre, in the Shire highlands, I stopped my loads, put the kettle on, opened tinned meats, etc. . . . He told me to look out for the Belgian police of the Congo territory, as they were *now raiding in British territory*,[*]—*all cannibals; having just killed and eaten seven men of the African Lakes Corporation, Ltd.* . . . He said I had better keep my eyes open, and have my revolver and rifle always by the side of me."

---

[*] That would be in the neighbourhood of Lake Bangwelo.

The latest information from this part of the Congo comes in the form of a letter to my friend, Mr. Fox-Bourne (received in February of this year), from the Rev. Dugald Campbell, who has spent nearly eleven years in the Katanga country. This gentleman goes through his experiences since 1894 down to November of last year. He speaks of the raids for ivory, in the course of which "baskets of human heads" were brought in to the State's post, and "long strings of captives, mostly women and children, who were made to serve seven years as 'prisoners of war.'" The usual shooting and torturing of women is reported by the writer. Upon one occasion when he protested against the summary shooting of natives, and referred to "rules and regulations," the officer concerned replied, "Ah, monsieur, je n'ai ni livre de règlements, ni de lois de l'Etat. Que puis-je faire moi? Je suis la seule loi. Moi, je suis le seul Dieu dans le Katanga." He graphically describes the arrival at his mission station of an expedition commanded by a Captain X—— and Lieutenant Z——, returning from an "ivory and head hunting expedition round the populous Chivanda District and Lubaland," which they had reduced to "beggary and ashes."

"They filed into the mission town, with flags flying and bugles blowing, and came up the long street to my home at the top of the mountain, where I entertained them for two days. Long strings of old women and children tied together, mere skin and bone, and numbers of long, deep baskets filled with human heads (hair shaved off) were emptied, and the heads counted and put to dry in the sun."

In another case, mentioned in considerable detail by the writer which occurred about 1898:

"The heads were counted at the officer's feet, and then returned to Mukandu Bantu * and his people, with a barrel of gunpowder, for a war dance to celebrate the victory. I sat by and saw the dance with heads, which was also witnessed by about five hundred people, three Congo flags flying high over the proceedings."

After enumerating other instances of frightful oppression, injustice, and murder, the writer adds a postscript, dated November 9, 1903:

"I must add a postscript to what I have written above, as news came to hand yesterday from Mweru (Congo Free State side) of a Belgian officer, who was sent to hunt up carriers in the district of Tambe. He shot six natives on no known pretext whatever; my informant, who lives near the place of the murders, suggests 'prestige.' Along with the above,

---

* Who had been raiding on the State account, much like the Zappo-Zaps in the Kasai. See Chapter XVI.

my messengers tell me of the brutal murder of a native, *a British subject*, who had unfortunately crossed over into the Congo Free State, and, being a hunter, had killed two hippopotami. He was caught by the same officer, and, lagging behind, was knocked on the head with the butts of the soldiers' rifles. When the soldiers reported to the officer that the man was unable to travel—'Shoot him,' was the prompt reply. Thereupon he was tied to a pole stuck in the ground at the cross-roads, and shot dead, his body being left fastened to the pole, to be carried off and eaten at night by hyenas."

Some of these statements would appear incredible were it not that similar incidents—the head-hunting (although the proved Mongalla atrocities of 1900 included the placing of severed heads on village palisades) excepted—are reported on every hand; the same cause in every case, rubber, and ivory raids, and officials demoralised by a policy which impels them to acts that after a certain time become, as it were, second nature.*

Thus do the agents of the Congo State in Africa pursue their mad course, oblivious of all law and international usage; dealing with the natives as the beast of prey deals with its victims; arming and letting loose cannibal troops all over the country to pillage, outrage, and murder; breeding hatred and fury against the white man in tens of thousands of dusky breasts; unable to control the excesses of their savage allies; not hesitating to go to almost any lengths against Europeans who inconvenience them; callous of human suffering, and drunk with self-importance—worthy representatives of the European institution which calls itself a medium for the "moral and material regeneration" of Africa, and whose diplomacy consists for the most part in opposing to the crushing weight of evidence accumulated against its POLICY and procedure, the miserable legal quibbles of a handful of cosmopolitan jurists.

* Mr. H. R. Fox-Bourne has now received a further and much more detailed letter from Mr. Campbell, wherein the writer gives a brief history of the thirteen years of Congo misgovernment in Katanga. It is a story of incredible horror, and will be found in full in the Appendix.

CHAPTER XIX

CONGO STATE CONTROL ON THE RIVER BANKS

". . . grand State stations with wide roads, fine avenues, large gardens and solid brick houses—regular show places—that testified to the energy of some of the Belgian officials, and one could not help but admire them until one remembered that they were built, and are now maintained at the cost of the heart's blood of the neighbouring tribes. . . . To one who sees only the telegraph, the railway and the State stations, the progress seems wonderful, and they cannot withold exclamations of admiration; but to one who can compare the condition of the natives to-day on the Upper Congo with their condition thirteen years ago, I say without fear of contradiction by any one able to make the comparison impartially, that the condition of the people, to put it mildly, is one hundred per cent. worse now than then."—Rev. J. H. WEEKS, for twenty-four years a representative of the British Baptist Missionary Society on the Congo, in a letter to the author, dated Monsembe, Upper Congo, July, 1903.

THE endeavour is being made in this volume to localise, as far as possible, the records of Congo State misrule which have reached us of late. The actual effects of the application of this policy vary in intensity, and correspond with the character of the people, and the nature of the productive power of the country. Districts which are rubber-producing suffer most, for they are bled unmercifully for that valuable product. Other districts which do not produce rubber are mulcted in heavy food taxes; in other districts, again, taxation takes the form of levies upon the population for soldiers and for workmen. But everywhere there is the same disregard of the laws of humanity and decency, the same everlasting oppression and outrage; for although abuses in the Congo territories take many forms, there is only one *policy*—the policy devised in 1891, and applied with relentless determination ever since. It is important for the reader to bear this in mind. The system I have adopted of localising reports has its disadvantages. But what it may lack in picturesqueness, it gains, I think, in precision, and one cannot be too specific in exposing the recorded results of a conception, the general nature and inevitable consequences of which have been dealt with early in the volume on broad lines.

THE RIVER BANKS

The first and fullest particulars which are available in regard to effects of Congo State rule on the great arteries, refer to the banks of the Congo itself between Stanley Pool and Bangala (Nouvelle-Anvers). Both Stanley Pool and Nouvelle-Anvers are important administrative centres of the Congo State. Before the State was powerful enough to make its baneful influence felt, the banks of the river between those two places were very populous. On a portion of that distance —50 miles only—from Bokongo to Likunugu, Stanley estimated in 1888 the population at 80,000 souls. In 1891, the Belgian Lieutenant, Lemaire, Commissaire of the Equateur District, reported as follows :

"The truth is, that from Stanley Pool onwards, one meets with nothing but large centres of population, thus Chumbiri 10,000, Bolobo 25,000, Lukolela 5000, *Irebu* 10,000—N'Gandas, Wangatas, Bandakas, Burukis, Loliva (30,000 souls on 30 kilometres of river), etc."

About the same period the Belgian, Captain Coquilhat, estimated the population of other towns along this stretch of river, such as "Monsembe at 3000, Bolumbo 3000, Lulanga 8000, Lobengo 3000," etc.

The depopulation of this region of late years through administrative exactions, in the form of crushing taxation, and military levies, has been terrible in the extreme. Take, for instance, the town of Irebu, now a military station. Mr. Hall, a West Indian member of the American Baptist Missionary Society of Boston, tells me that when he left Irebu, after eight years' residence, 1889-1897, "The population only amounted to about three or four hundred." Mr. J. H. Weeks, one of the oldest and most respected members of the British Baptist Missionary Society, with an experience of the Upper Congo of almost a quarter of a century, writing from Monsembe, in July, 1903, says that in Irebu "there are not now 50 persons"! In a letter to the Commissaire of the Equateur District, written at Monsembe, in June, 1903 (and a copy of which is in my possession) Mr. Weeks says :

"When we came to settle in Monsembe, in 1890, there were over 7000 people between here and Bokongo. In 1901 there were very few over 3000, and now there are not many above 1000. If the decrease continues at the same rate, there will be no people left."

The population between Bokongo and Likunungu, Mr. Weeks now estimates at only 9400, from 80,000 in 1888, and he adds :

"Of the 9400 now on the banks in this district, quite half have just been driven from the bush to repopulate the river banks, for we found that if we had gone up only six weeks earlier than we did, we should have scarcely found 5000 people."

Mr. Weeks continues:

"Starting from Stanley Pool, Bwemba has about a hundred for every thousand it once had; Bolobo has not a third of its former population; Lukolela had about 4000 people and now it has not 300; Bolenge has not half its former population; Lulanga had over 3000 people in 1890, but now there are not 800."

One stands aghast at these figures; but the story is universally the same, whether the Upper Ubanghi is in question, or the Luapula in the Eastern District, or even the Lower Congo, the north bank of which used to be crowded with villages in the pre-Congo State days, and which are now virtually deserted, except in the immediate neighbourhood of Banana, Boma and Matadi.

From whatever part of the Congo territories information filters through, the tale is repeated: one monotonous round of oppression, depopulation, emigration, dying out. Occasionally species of *battues* are organised, and villages from the interior are compulsorily evacuated, their inhabitants being driven to the water's edge, there compelled to reside until food taxes, labour taxes, and military taxes have reduced them to vanishing point, when the process is repeated.

In the particular region which we are examining at present, Mr. Weeks has supplied detailed explanations of the reasons for the depopulation. He has protested to the officials. Thus in his afore-mentioned letter to the Commissaire of the Equateurville District, a copy of which he forwarded to the Governor-General, Mr. Weeks writes:

"Many things have conduced to this deplorable decrease in population. Will you pardon me if I presume on my thirteen years' residence in this district and my twenty-two years' residence on the Congo, to point out to you what appear to me to be the principal reasons for this sad and alarming diminution of one of the finest tribes of the Congo Free State?

"They are, I think, as follows:—

"1. The continual deportation of young men (and in a lesser degree of young women) to serve as soldiers and workmen for the State, and the very few that ever return home. As a consequence of this drainage of the young blood and strength of the district, there is a marked paucity of children, so that the deaths are far in advance of the births. Had the demand for men been levied in a fixed and regular manner, it might not have been so harmful. But it has been levied (so it appears to us) at the caprice of the authorities for the time being, without any regard to the population.

"2. The flight of the people from the river to get away from oppressive taxation. As an example of this, I would mention the towns of Lobengo and Mantele, which, a few years ago, were large and prosperous towns, but are now simply grass and bush, with not a single person living in them.

"3. Sleeping sickness has undoubtedly carried off many, but from careful observation of this and other parts of the Congo where I have resided,

I think that this disease would never have taken such a hold on the people if they had not had their spirit crushed out of them by an ever increasing burden of taxation that has taken the heart out of them and made life not worth living.

"4. The heavy burden of taxation, which for each person is becoming heavier and heavier, because fewer are left to share it. It was some time in 1896 that the people in this district were first taxed, and the tax was then fixed, I presume, according to the population of the district. Since then three-fourths of the people have been deported, fled, or died, yet the tax has not been reduced one iota to relieve a broken-spirited, diminished, and dying people. Again, in 1890–95, goats exchanged for 100 to 150 rods;* from 1896 to 1901 the price rose steadily to 800 rods; and now, in 1903, the price ranges from 1500 to 2500 rods. Yet, notwithstanding the high price of goats and the decrease in population, the tax on goats and fish, which was doubled in 1897, has remained the same ever since. I think you will see from this that the burden of taxation has become more than a dying people can bear, if you wish to have any people left to govern.

"5. The imposition of whimsical fines, out of all proportion to real or supposed offences, is sapping the life of the people. As an example of this, take the recent visit of 'Mabata'† (I regret that I can only give his native name) to this town. He quartered himself, with over twenty soldiers and many paddlers, twice on a people that had broken no law and refused no demand of the State. The second time he came, because food for his increased crowd was not forthcoming at once, he took the chief Mangumbe, appointed by the State itself, and carried him as hostage to his sleeping camp some miles up river until the food arrived. He also demanded from this Monsembe district of 300 people 8000 rods, and although he was frequently asked the reason for such a demand, he never deigned to give one. Among the 800 people that comprise the districts below us, viz. Bongwele, Malele, Bokomela, Mungunbu, and Bokongo, he quartered himself and his men for over a month, which sadly taxed their resources, and in addition demanded and tied up‡ people until he obtained nearly 50,000 rods from them. Surely, if no proper explanation of this is given, we shall be within our rights in referring this matter to the authorities at Bona.

"Have the delinquencies of these people been tried in a properly constituted court? Is 'Mabata' a judge that he has power to impose these so-called fines? In addition to a tax that presses sorely, these unfortunate people are subjected also to irregular and capricious demands. We pray you, for humanitarian reasons, to lighten the burdens of these people and to bring their taxation within their limited and decreasing means. It is heart-rending to compare this district now with what it was in 1890. At that date, in the Mungala Creek, there were more than 1500 people, now there are scarcely 200; and thus one can take district after district with the same sad tale to tell.

---

* The currency of the district.

† The native name of a Congo State official.

‡ This "tying up" of people the reader may not quite understand. The meaning is this: Ever since 1891 this system of taking "hostages," that is to say, capturing prisoners and tying them up until redeemed either for ivory, rubber, food-stuffs, or what not, has been regularly practised. In this connection, too, the reader is referred to many instances of the practice given in this volume, and to the admissions of General Wahis himself, mentioned in the Congo Debate, Part V.

"In 1890 the towns were well kept, clean, and tidy, with neatly built houses; now they are ill kept and very slovenly, because at any moment the inhabitants fear they may have to flee to the bush for refuge, or have their towns looted and burned through inability to meet some heavy demand. Then, also, there was some security for life and property, for men defended them by the strength of their arms, now there is no security for either.

In reply to some of the above statements, it may be said that the State pays for what the natives take to Bangala, but the remuneration paid is less than one-tenth of the real value. And the natives are forced to take produce to the State under threat of having their towns burned down, and have to accept for their goods what is given them.* Again we pray you to do all you possibly can for the amelioration of these unfortunate people, that the remnant may not die out, but rather be fostered again into a strong tribe."

Mr. Weeks speaks of the people who are thus suffering as one of the "finest tribes of the Congo," whom, owing to their splendid physique, the State uses largely for military service. The system of military recruiting by the State is on a par with its other methods of "moral and material regeneration," notwithstanding the oft-repeated official assurances that the men are eager to enlist, and that recruiting is entirely voluntary.† The very nature of the terms of service precludes the possibility of the levy being otherwise than coercive and forced. *The men are taken on twelve years' contracts.* Imagine any native acquiescing in a twelve years' contract! By no one has this abominable system been so warmly denounced as in Belgium by Professor Cattier,‡ of the Brussels University, in his remarkable book on the Congo, published in 1898—a book which, by reason of the many excuses which it contains for sundry aspects of the State's policy, only makes his indictment the more telling. "For twelve years," he writes, "they are deprived of their liberty, removed from their centres, taken away from their villages. In fact, they become foreigners to their tribe; after such an absence, how could they return? This military imposition is excessive.... Such practices must be fought in the name of humanity."

Times without number has this military "tax" been denounced in the Belgian House. A high French official, recently returned from the Congo, has declared that it is one

* In a letter published by the *Daily News*, in December, 1903, from Mr. Charles Bond, and referred to in Chapter XI., the writer says that at the State station of Coquilhatville on the river, capital of the "Equateur" district, the Commandant "regularly" imprisons men "for weeks at a time," and puts them "in the chain," because sufficient supplies of rubber are not forthcoming.

† See in this connection Mr. Campbell's letter in the Appendix.

‡ "Droit et Administration de l'Etat Indépendant du Congo." By F. Cattier. Brussels, 1898.

INDIA-RUBBER "HOSTAGES" CHAINED BY THE NECK. COLLECTING GRASS

(Photo by Mr. Herbert Frost, Baringa, 1903)

(When the forest has been cleared and left for some time, tall, rank grass grows which requires uprooting before anything can be planted. "Hostages" are placed in a line or row and scrape away at the roots with hands and watchets)

"HOSTAGES", SHARPENING STICKS IN PALM-AVENUE, BARINGA

(Photo by Mr. Herbert Frost)

of the most fruitful sources of the perpetual uprisings in the State.* From the Upper Congo, between Stanley-Pool and Nouvelle-Anvers, we pass to the Ubanghi, the great northern branch of the Congo. The Colonial Institute of Marseilles has recently published the diary of M. Leon C. Berthier, who spent two years—May, 1899, to June, 1901—in that neighbourhood. M. Berthier speaks of the hatred and fear of the white man which Belgian oppression has caused among the natives in the entire region he passed through. He speaks of the difficulties experienced by merchants on the French banks of the Ubanghi, on account of these proceedings. "The terrifying example of the Belgians is the cause," he writes, "that the natives from Brazzaville to Banghi retreat before the white man, and that, notwithstanding their intense desire for European goods, they will not come in to acquire them against rubber, fearing that the Moloch of European rapacity will oppress them as in the territory of Bula Matadi." And again, "The Belgian bank is far less inhabited than the French bank; the natives leave the Belgian bank in masses to take refuge with us." Here is a further typical passage from his notes:

"*Belgian Post of Imesse*, well constructed. The chief of the Post of Imesse (Belgian Congo) is absent. He has gone to punish the village of M'Batchi up river, guilty of being a little late in paying the rubber tax imposed by Bula Matari.

"Nine o'clock in the evening. A canoe full of Congo State soldiers returns from the pillage of M'Batchi. And yet this Free State was created in order to civilise the black races!

"*Post of Ibenga*, in the river of that name, affluent of the Congo. Before arriving, we passed the canoe of the *Chef de Poste* of Imesse, who gave us details of the punishment of M'Batchi: thirty killed, fifty wounded!

"At three o'clock, *M'Batchi*, the scene of the bloody punishment of the *Chef de Poste*, of Imesse. Poor village! The *débris* of miserable huts, and of canoes covered with a bark which resembles birch; in the huts, above the smoking embers, one or two human skulls. The natives have taken refuge in the bush, and the blandishments of Shaw, who speaks to them in Bangala, cannot induce them to approach. One goes away, humiliated and saddened, from these scenes of desolation, filled with indescribable feelings. How can these negroes be really blamed if one fine day they surprise one of their white oppressors and exterminate him? Probably it will not be one of those guilty of the destruction of the village, but an innocent person who will suffer for the guilty."

In the South-Eastern District, as will be found recorded in fuller detail in Chapter XIV., the Belgian banks of the Luapula River are deserted, the natives having emigrated in large numbers to the British bank, owing to the raids of Congo

* M. Gentil.

State soldiery, for rubber and ivory. The migration from the Congo State bank of the Congo to the opposite side is also referred to by M. de Lamothe, ex-Governor of the French Congo. From the Kasai District, and Lakes Leopold II. and Matumba, comes the same tale; the people seek refuge from the accursed white man and his soldiers in the solitudes of the forest, leaving homes, plantations, fisheries, anything and everything to get away—if they can—from the oppressor.

Mr. Weeks' letter to the Governor-General, to which I have alluded, was apparently taken no notice of whatever, until it appeared in the *West African Mail.* Then the action of the Congo State followed its invariable precedent. Monsignor von Ronslé was put up to answer it, and the answer was incorporated in the Congo State's "reply" to the British White Book.* But the answer was no answer at all. Mr. Weeks had cited specific facts with regard to the effect of oppressive taxation upon the Bangalas. Monsignor von Ronslé's answer is almost entirely concerned with Mr. Weeks' casual allusion—not of his own investigation—to the Bobangis. Yet the Roman Catholic Prelate's "answer" was trumpeted abroad as a conclusive reply to Mr. Weeks' "misrepresentations." Such as it was, the "answer" has been subsequently riddled through and through by Mr. Weeks.† The amusing part of this particular controversy is that, in a further letter, one dated December 24, 1903, Mr. Weeks specified at great length, and with considerable detail, the nature and extent of the taxation in food-stuffs levied upon the population of the "four native sections of Malela, Bokomela, Mungunda, and Bokongo," showing that a small native community of 820 persons, including both sexes, infants, children, and sick persons, was compelled to contribute food-stuffs amounting in value to £1605 16s. 8d. per annum. The publicity given in Europe to these outrageous instances compelled the Congo Executive, while *denying* the facts in Europe, to "inquire" into them in Africa (let it be borne in mind that the taxation was applied by the Government itself), with the result that a further letter from Mr. Weeks announced an enormous reduction in this "taxation." Mr. Weeks again took a specific instance, comparing the just instituted new tax with the old as levied upon the "Creek towns" immediately above his own station of Monsombe. In 1890 the population of these towns was estimated by Mr. Weeks and his colleagues at 1500. In

---

* Notes sur le rapport de M. Casement, Consul de Sa Majesté Britannique du 11 Décembre, 1903.
† Special Congo supplement, *West African Mail,* June, 1904.

June, 1903, there were 67 men, women, and children left. The "tax" was first levied in 1896, and doubled in 1897. It remained at its 1897 figure down to this year, notwithstanding the decrease in population almost to vanishing point. In December, 1903, these 67 men, women, and children were paying a paternal government £387 18s. 10d. per annum in food-stuffs. It has now been reduced to £25 3s. 8d., yet, to its European hearers, the Congo Executive was loudly proclaiming the unreliability of Mr. Weeks' 23 years' experience on the Congo!* There is an example of what can be done by courage on the Congo, and by publicity at home.

Now take the reverse side of the picture, or rather, I should say, that portion of it which refers to the value of publicity in these matters. In July, 1903, Mr. Gilchrist, belonging to the Congo Balolo Mission, and consequently to a different mission from that to which Mr. Weeks is attached, writes to the Governor-General from Lolanga, describing the fearful oppression visited upon the riverain population of that neighbourhood, far removed, of course, from Mr. Weeks' sphere. On August 26, the Governor-General replies that the state of things "signalised by the Rev. Gilchrist's letter will be the object of serious inquiry." In January, 1904, Mr. Gilchrist writes to the head of his mission in England to the effect that "the measures promised to put an end to these things have either not been taken, or else they have proved ineffective, for the same order of things continues practically the same as they were." Correspondence is subsequently exchanged between Dr. Guinness (the head of the Congo Balolo Mission) and the Congo Executive in Brussels, and the reply of the latter is to the effect that Mr. Gilchrist's charges were unfounded. They had not been published, that is all; but it made all the difference. The full text of Mr. Gilchrist's letter is given in the Appendix, as also Mr. Gilchrist's version of the "inquiry" made. I will merely quote here its conclusion:

"Eight years ago there was a population in these towns of at least 5000 people compared with the 1200 of to-day. The impositions then were not nearly so heavy as at the present time. In conclusion, I would draw your attention to the money value of the taxes and fines, over and above the nominal value of price they receive for their supplies—*it is at the rate of £60 per month for the last eighteen months.* I also would like you to know that the people themselves are *literally starving* to keep up these supplies. In becoming acquainted with these facts, I cannot but

---

* Meantime the oppressive "taxation" *has done its work*, and the reduction, as a result of publicity in Europe, will not bring back to life those who have died under it.

think you will feel it your duty to take steps to remove these oppressive measures, under which the people are groaning—and dying."

In dealing with the Congo State control on the river banks, one might easily fill half a dozen chapters alone. Our own Consul's observations on this point have been referred to, although quite inadequately. With few exceptions—the immediate neighbourhood of Stanley Falls for one, and in that case there are very tangible existing causes enjoining greater caution on the Executive and its allies—the tale is everywhere the same. Mr. Whitehead at Lukolela,* Mr. Whitmore and Mr. Clark at Ikoko, Mr. Billington at Bwanbu, Mr. Layton on a large stretch of river, and especially at Bolangi, all have the same story to tell, and all consist of recent testimony, which can be perused (Mr. Whitehead's excepted) in the American Memorial to Congress.† Nor does that exhaust the list, for we have Mr. Frame describing his recent trip (in the course of which he came upon the cannibalistic orgie at Yandjali, to which reference is made, *inter alia*, in Chapter X.) to me, where he says:

"On a single trip one sees enough and hears enough to convince him that the lot of the native is that of a harassed and crushed slave." ‡

There are others, who prefer not to give their names, and whose testimony, while equally true, is, therefore, less valuable for our purpose; and finally there is the most recent testimony of all, letters received this year, in the Appendix. Against this crushing mass of testimony from almost every part of the banks of the great river and its affluents, who but those who are directly or indirectly interested in concealing the truth, and acting as " devils "—a term used in law, I believe, to indicate a paid collaborator—to a "Government" which has befouled Christendom in tropical Africa, and has caused the very name of "civilisation," in its application to the races of Africa, to stink in the nostrils of every honest man, would venture to oppose their word?

* Africa, No. 1, 1904, *op. cit.*
† Document 282.
‡ *West African Mail*, Congo issue, May, 1904.

CHAPTER XX

CONGO STATE CONTROL IN THE LOWER CONGO

"My aim throughout life has been to find the truth, and make the truth known to others."—KING LEOPOLD, as quoted by Sir Hugh Gilzean-Reid.

THE portion of the Congo territories known as Lower Congo includes the north bank of the river below Matadi and the Cataracts region, or virtually the Congo State up to Stanley Pool. Until this year no rubber tax had been applied in the Lower Congo, and, therefore, there have been no organized massacres, and probably no mutilations; only the milder forms of "Bula Matadi's" oppression prevailed. Happy Ba-Congo peoples!

In this chapter I deal mainly with the condition of affairs down to December, 1903. At the close of the chapter the new *régime* is briefly indicated. Although there have been no murders on a large scale, the country has been sadly depopulated by forced labour, forced military service, seizure of live stock, and so on. For nearly twenty years the Ba-Congo have known the blessings of "Bula Matadi," and the result is seen in emigration to Portuguese and French territory on the north bank, and to Portuguese territory on the south bank; and in the decay of trade, and notably the ground-nut trade, which at one time, in the pre-generating days, was considerable. The north bank of the Lower Congo, where twenty years ago numerous villages existed, is to-day virtually silent and deserted; the Cataracts region, which used to be thickly populated, is but sparsely so, for the breath of "Bula Matadi" has passed over the land. It has brought ocean steamers and workshops, a railway, a couple of piers, fine houses, a public library, a prison,* and a fort; useful things in their way, admirable and necessary things, especially the prison (for "Bula Matadi's" servants). But these eminently desirable accompaniments of civilisation have not come alone, and the

* Where the mortality of the native prisoners is terrific.

Ba-Congo have suffered much. Here are some typical instances of their suffering.

Unkind European critics had pointed to the circumstance that the output of the Ba-Congo people—the only *trade* output in the whole of the Congo territories—was largely on the decrease, and in particular that the great ground-nut trade which existed prior to 1885 had virtually disappeared. The petition of the merchants established in the Lower Congo—there are still a few merchants left in the Lower Congo—had also reached Europe, and had been published in a wicked book called "Affairs of West Africa." That petition, after pointing out the heavy import and export duty on goods and produce (20*s.* per ton on palm-oil, for instance), and showing how small the existing export trade had become, owing to the taxes and the emigration of native labour, due to the "means employed in raising native levies," went on to say :

> "We do not disguise from ourselves that business in the Lower Congo is practically *nil*. . . Each of us consistently hopes for an increase in trade ; but these hopes appear to be more and more unreliable. . . "

So "Bula Matadi" hit upon an excellent plan. The ground-nut *trade* should be revived and the critics confounded. The last "commercial" *Bulletin Officiel* chuckles softly over the revival of the "collection of this useful product." But the authorities of the Congo State, who are able to conceal their practices in the vast Upper Congo to no little extent, do not fare quite so well in the Lower Congo, which is more accessible to inquiry. I am in a position to explain under what circumstances the Ba-Congo are again producing ground-nuts. Two words express the *modus operandi*—forced labour. Each village is compelled to produce a given number of bags of ground-nuts in the shell. Each of these bags—which have to be carried by the producers, in many cases for a distance of eighty miles, to *Tumba*, the head-quarters of the Cataracts District—weighs 120 lbs. A nominal payment is given of 5*s.* 10*d.* per bag. This munificent sum is divided as follows. The two natives who carry the bag—it takes two natives to do so—get 1*s.* 8*d.* apiece at the end of their eighty miles' journey, the balance of 2*s.* 6*d.* being remitted to the Chief of the producing village. If the requisite number of bags is not forthcoming in the stated period, "punishment" is inflicted ; the said punishment consisting of the seizure of men and boys, who are made to work, without food or pay, at the State post of Luozi, or at other Government stations, until the offending village is considered as having wiped off its debt. The natives would like to *sell* their produce to the merchants at Matadi, as they used to do in the old days, and from whom they would get a price commensurate with the trade value of the article. But "Bula Matadi" forbids; the nuts must go to the Government as a slight, a very slight contribution for benefits rendered! The natives vainly plead that the compulsory transport imposed by the State before the railway was completed has decimated them in numbers—in point of fact, the population of the Cataracts region alone has gone down seventy-five per cent. in the last ten years—and, nevertheless, they are now expected to furnish more compulsory transport, at lower rates, than under the former *régime*. It follows as a natural sequence that the "punishments" are more or less perpetual, and as the units which each village behindhand in its tribute of nuts has to furnish get neither food nor pay, as already stated, these unfortunate people have to depend upon their relatives in the neighbourhood of Luozi to keep them supplied with food-stuffs, which, of course, is a tax upon the latter also. Indeed, the system works so well that, owing to the food difficulty, many of the "labourers" fall ill and die, while those who survive, reach their homes in a broken-down condition.

Another outcome of the system is this. Human nature being what it is, and the natives of the villages in the Cataracts region dreading and hating the forced labour at Luozi and elsewhere, the full-grown men and able-bodied youths shirk it, and the boys and immature youths have to expiate the sins of the village. Early in the present year it transpired that the Acting-Governor General's attention had been called to the sickness among the boys who had been working at the Government stations. It also became known that the receipt of these complaints had been immediately followed by the despatch of a large body of troops into the Luozi District. By chance a copy of the Acting-Governor General's letter—to a member of the farcical "Commission for the Protection of the Natives"—has come into my hands. It is characterised by the superlative hypocrisy and guarded respect for appearances which invariably distinguish the official communications of "Bula Matadi."

"In reply to your letter of January 25th last," writes M. Fuchs, "I have the honour to inform you that I have asked the *Commissaire* of the Cataracts Districts to kindly give me some information as to the work of children at Luozi. That official has told the head of the region to only accept in future for that work adults in good health. It is, in point of fact, the latter who, by showing themselves refractory to work which is imposed by their village Chief, must undergo constraint (*la contrainte*).

The "contrainte" consisted in the quartering of soldiers

upon the villagers, and doubtless the natives of that district are now in a position—or would be if they knew how to read French and were furnished with a copy of the *Bulletin Officiel* —to appreciate the full humour of the "encouragements (in the words of the *Bulletin*) which have been lavished upon them (the natives) for the active resumption of planting and gathering this useful product."

The pretence which is made in the official letter to ignore the existence of unremunerated and unfed child labour at Luozi until attention was called to it, is equalled by the remark that the labour of cultivating ground-nuts in the form of taxation was "imposed by the village chief"; as if "the village chief" had any freedom in the matter! Such are the features of the "revival" of the ground-nut industry in the "free" Lower Congo:—1. Compulsory production, remunerated at a price that enables the State to assert that it "pays" its people, but which does not even pay the producer for transport, let alone trouble of cultivation or the trade value of the article itself. 2. Punishment by forced labour, unremunerated and unfed, if villages fall short in production. 3. Result, sickness and death. 4. On its being pointed out that boys and immature youths are employed at this forced labour, soldiers are quartered upon the villages. So much for the Cataracts region.

In the Mayumbe District, immediately north of Boma, the capital of the State, the benevolent policy of "Bula Matadi" is again apparent. The experiences of the Rev. A. R. Williams of the Christian Missionary Alliance of New York, who returned from that district in 1903 after a four years' residence, as related to the author, are notable.

Mr. Williams' remarks may be given in his own words:

"The inhabitants of Mayumbe are Fjorts, very peaceable folk, and naturally friendly towards the white man. The State post of Tshala is 3½ hours' march to the west of my station at Kinkonse. It is garrisoned by about eighty soldiers from the Upper Congo. The existing taxation in this district takes the form of labour. The pay is utterly inadequate both for labour and victuals with which the natives are compelled to furnish the State posts. The men are employed in carrying loads of rice from the neighbourhood of Tshala to rail-head (Mayumbe railway). So heavy are these loads that the men come back utterly played out, and not infrequently die from the effects of over-fatigue. If proper wages were paid, and the loads more fairly adjusted, there would be no difficulty in getting carriers. Moreover, cases have come to my personal knowledge where the men have not been paid at all. The soldiers are a perfect terror to the whole place, and the bad characters of the neighbourhood are enlisted to help them. They rape the women and clear the villages of live stock, and generally behave in a most oppressive and unjust way. I have taken soldiers red-handed in acts of oppression, and complained to their officers; but, as a rule, they are never punished, although promises are made. A day or two after such an event has occurred, the soldier has passed by me grinning. The result of this wholesale levying of a tax on foot-stuffs is that towns become almost destitute of animals. This means, of course, the impoverishment of the people. Natives are continually complaining to us. When news arrives that the soldiers are going to visit a particular district, all the women take refuge in the bush, and live there shelterless, homeless, and half-starved with their children until the soldiers have gone, to escape being raped or seized. I have seen with my own eyes streams of women and children, with such household utensils as they could carry, flying to the bush, or to villages close to our stations, where they were sure of not being molested. I was at our own out-school last December when about 100 women and children came in, flying from the soldiers."

Mr. Hall, a West Indian missionary of good family, trained at the Calabar College, Kingston, Jamaica, attached to the Baptist Missionary Society of Boston, and conveying in a visit he paid to the author in 1903 the highest testimonials as to his uprightness and veracity from Dr. E. Wilmot Blyden, General Director of Mohammedan education in Sierra Leone, and from the Rev. J. H. Weeks (whose reports in respect to the Upper Congo have been quoted), gives the following account of his observations after an eight years' residence in the Lower Congo ending in December, 1902:

"There is no progress whatever among the natives of the Lower Congo. In fact, except in the immediate vicinity of the Mission Stations, they are going back. There is no rubber tax there; but towns and little hamlets have to supply labourers for the State for three months at a time. After three months' work they have, of course, nothing left out of their earnings, and they go home again with nothing with which to support their families or better their position. The result is they simply live on from year to year in the same condition, getting more impoverished every year. In many parts of the Lower Congo there is much depopulation. In what is now Congo State territory, near the Portuguese frontier, there used to be very large towns and villages. They are now quite abandoned, the natives preferring the rule of the Portuguese, which is not of the best, to the rule of the Belgians, which is far worse. . . . In conclusion, I can assert, after my long experience, that the State rule has in no way benefited the natives. On the contrary, they are being utilised for the pecuniary benefits of the State, while the State does nothing to benefit their condition."

But the relative elysium of the Ba-Congo will not, I am afraid, last very much longer. Mr. Frame, who did not believe the reports of native ill-treatment, writes me under date of March 16 of this year as follows:

"As I traversed the old caravan route to the Pool, my eyes were opened. Crowds of people passed me every now and then, bearing heavy loads of Kwanga (Cassara puddings), and all were for the State. Some were little girls of twelve years of age, carrying eight or ten; some were women converted into sweating beasts of burden, for besides the twelve Kwanya on the head, they often had a baby on the back; some were men, and some were little boys. No one will accuse me of exaggeration if I say each Kwanga weighs 3½ to 4 lbs., and that the women often carry loads varying from 42 to 50 lbs. It is quite true that the State does not fix the loads that the women should carry. What it does demand is that such and such a town shall bring in, say 250 Kwanga every fourth, eighth, or twelfth day, according to distance, and if the people fail to do it, then punishment follows. What it means to the people is nothing to the State, and the cry of the poor women who have to grind on from morning to night to provide, and often to carry, is not heard by the State officers. The labour is forced. If in reply it be said that the people are paid for it, let it be understood that the payment is very small compared with local rates, and, as a matter of fact, if a man pays another to carry his load of Kwanga, he has to pay all he gets from the State and something on top. Some have to carry three days' journey. These have to bring in every twelfth day. That means they spend five days on the road and seven in their towns, which have to be spent in planting and cooking for the State. They have time for nothing else. They are slaves."

That account refers to the northern part of the Lower Congo. Now here is a letter which reached me in June from a British trader (one of the few left) at Matadi, describing the new *régime* in the southern part:

"In the Mayumbe country behind Boma, the State has begun collecting rubber by force from the natives. We were supposed to have 'free-trade' below Stanley Pool, but even that narrow belt is now to be invaded by the 'tax-collector.' . . . The oil and kernel trade has almost died out at Boma, as a consequence of these Mayumbe prestations. The State are founding a camp * of 1000 soldiers—independent of the one already at Luki, seventeen miles inland of Boma, where Mr. Meyer and the Sierre Leone men were arrested, and so many of them done to death. This new camp is at Boma Sundi, or rather between that place and the Lukula river, about 35 or 40 miles from Boma, in the heart of the Mayumbe country, where the people have brought oil and kernels from time immemorial to the Boma factories. This invasion of these ancient trading rights will damage considerably the old-established trade in the Chilango District, and the exports there, through the Portuguese provinces, will also fail. Everything in the country is for the Government. The traders, who are not concession holders, but who made such trade as exists are only to be taxed and thwarted, and the poor natives are to pay the piper. Of course, as soon as this new camp is established, the State will begin to force the people in the usual way to bring in food, etc., for the soldiers. I see no possible future for the country, or the poor people, unless something is done by the Powers."

The Ba-Congo people have evidently got a rosy time in store for them.

* Confirmed by the Belgian Press.

CHAPTER XXI

THE GENERAL CONDITION OF NATIVE LIFE UNDER CONGO STATE RULE

The persecution of the Netherlands in the Sixteenth Century under Philip II.

"The country was absolutely helpless.... The most industrious and valuable part of the population left the land in droves.... The Venetian envoy, Navigiero, estimated the victims in the provinces of Holland and Friesland alone at thirty thousand.... The tide swept onwards with such rapidity that the Netherlands seemed fast becoming the desolate waste which they had been before the Christian era."—MOTLEY, "The Rise of the Dutch Republic."

The persecution of the Congo territories in the Twentieth Century under Leopold II.

"The population during the continuance of these wars ('consequent on the attempt to levy a rubber tax') diminished I estimate, by some 60 per cent., and the remnant of the inhabitants are only now, in many cases, returning to their destroyed or abandoned villages."—CONSUL CASEMENT, describing Lake Mantumba region, 1903.

"The southern shores of Stanley Pool had formerly a population of fully 5000 Batekes. These people decided to abandon their homes, and in one night the great majority of them crossed over into French territory . . . where formerly had stretched populous native African villages. I saw to-day only a few scattered houses.—"CONSUL CASEMENT at Leopoldville, 1903.

"Here and there, on both sides, were frequent signs of a recent population, but for hours we walked through a deserted country, and not once did we see the slightest signs of a human habitation. . . . Large tracts of country are abandoned to the wild beasts."—SCRIVENER, describing the Domaine de la Couronne, 1903.

"The population has in thirteen years dropped from about 50,000 to less than 5000. . . . At this rate of decrease you will have nothing down there to govern but palm trees and bush."—WEEKS, describing the Bangala District, 1903.

WE have now examined successively the effects of Congo State control during the last few years in various distinct portions of the vast territory assigned to King Leopold II. in trust for civilisation. Some of the regions reviewed are as far apart as Paris from St. Petersburg, and the peoples inhabiting them differ almost as much as the Gaul from the Slav. Yet everywhere we see the same policy at work, with the same results. What are the chief symptoms of the effects of that policy upon native life?

Outwardly the most striking effect is depopulation: slaughter, mutilation; emigration; sickness, largely aggravated by cruel and systematic oppression; poverty, and even positive starvation, induced by unlimited taxation in food-stuffs and live stock; a hopeless despair, and mental depression engendered by years of grinding tyranny; neglect of children by the general maltreatment of women, one of the most odious and disgraceful features of the system—these are some of the many recorded causes of depopulation which, in certain districts, has assumed gigantic proportions. Mr. Casement tells us how 5000 Batekes—spoken of in official Congo State publications as the greatest native pioneers of the Upper Congo trade, which existed prior to the advent of " Bulu Matadi "—crossed, in one night, from the Belgian to the French shore; M. de Lamothe,* ex-Governor of French Congo, speaks of the emigration of 30,000 Congo State natives to the French bank of the river; M. Berthier also refers to the visible depopulation of the Belgian banks of the main river, and its tributary, the Ubanghi; the Congo State side of the Luapula is to-day a desert for many miles inland from the river side, the entire population having emigrated to the British bank; missionaries and other eye-witnesses speak of the constant emigration of Congo State natives in the Lower Congo to Portuguese and French territory—the instances might be easily multiplied. There we have depopulation through emigration consequent upon maladministration and terrorism.

Mr. Casement found the population of the Lake Mantumba region reduced in seventeen years by 60 to 70 per cent. Mr. Scrivener gives a terrifying account of the depopulation of part of the Western portion of the *Domaine de la Couronne* (Lake Leopold II. District); the reduction of the population of the Mongalla Basin in connection with the continual fighting, connected with the rubber *battues*, which has been going on for the past seven years without intermission, must be enormous; a Belgian deputy asserts, on the strength of reliable information from the Congo, that the Equateurville District has been thinned to the extent of 9000 people from the same cause; a "gentleman of experience" shows Mr. Casement a diary indicating that some 6000 people have been killed or mutilated in a period of six months in the Momboyo region;

* Examination before Cotelle Commission: on the advisability of extending the *Concessionnaire régime* to all French West African Colonies.

an officer "of the highest standing in the interior" tells our Consul that he has seen correspondence between the head agent of one of the Trusts, and his directors in Europe, to the effect that in three years 72,000 cartridges have been expended, in the production of indiarubber; it is averred in open Court in the Caudron proceedings, that the *Anversoise* Trust imported on Government steamers, and with Government sanction, 40,000 rounds of ball cartridge in 1903; Mr. Grogan finds the country of Mboga a "howling wilderness"; missionary evidence from the Katanga country points to Congo State military exploits reducing the populous Chivanda District and Lubaland to "beggary and ashes." In fact, from almost every part of the Congo State comes abundant evidence of depopulation by wholesale slaughter, irrespective of depopulation by emigration. It is impossible, unfortunately, to present reliable statistics on this subject, but the following table will give a fair idea of the scale in which depopulation is going on :—

TABLE SHOWING ROUGHLY DEPOPULATION WHERE DATA ARE AVAILABLE.

RIVER BANKS (CONGO RIVER AND AFFLUENTS).

			Causes.
Between (1) Bokongo and Likunungu, 150 miles along north bank; (2) Bokatalaka Creek and Bolombo, 70 miles along south bank	1890 Pop. 50,000 (J. H. Weeks)	1903 (July) Pop. 9400, 5000 of whom, driven in from bush to populate river banks; actual depopulation from 50,000 to less than 5000 in 13 years (J. H. Weeks)	Deportation of young men and women to serve (1) as soldiers, (2) labourers; resulting decrease in birth-rate by withdrawal of virile elements; flight from oppressive taxation; sleeping sickness aggravated by misery caused through "an ever increasing burden of taxation; outrageous demands for food-stuffs and live stock; fines and punishment; murders by soldiers" (J. H. Weeks)
Bwemba	1890 Pop. (J. H. Weeks).	1903 Pop. decreased by 90% (J. H. Weeks)	Same causes—last one not specified (J. H. Weeks)
Bolobo	1887 Pop. 40,000 (Consul Casement)	1903 Pop. 7000-8000 (Consul Casement) Decrease of 75% compared with 1890 (J. H. Weeks)	Oppressive taxation; forced labour; sickness, partly due to insufficiency of food and mental depression; emigration. (Consul Casement)
Lukolela	1887 Pop. 5000 (Consul Casement)	1896 Pop. 719 (Whitehead) 1903 Pop. "less than 600" (Consul Casement) Pop. 300 (J. H. Weeks). Pop. 352 (Whitehead)	Sleeping sickness; general ill-health; insufficiency of food; forced labour methods and oppressive taxation (Consul Casement) Sleeping sickness, aggravated by constant pressure by authorities; terrorism and brutality; insufficiency of food required by people, but demanded by Administration. (Whitehead)

NATIVE LIFE UNDER CONGO STATE RULE 239

Location	Earlier data	Later data	Cause
Mongalla Creek Towns	1900 Pop. 1500 (J. H. Weeks)	1904 Pop. 67 (J. H. Weeks)	Oppressive taxation in food-stuffs (J. H. Weeks)
"O—— villages"	1887 Pop. 5000 (Consul Casement)	1903 Pop. disappeared (Consul Casement)	
Irebu	1890 Pop. 8000–10,000 (J. H. Weeks) 1897 Pop. 300–400 (Hall)	1903 Pop. 50 (J. H. Weeks)	Expropriation to make way for military camp; emigration through oppression
"F—— villages"	1887 Pop. 4000–5000 (Consul Casement)	1903 Pop. 500 (Consul Casement)	Sleeping sickness; emigration; interference with ordinary avocations (Consul Casement)
South shore of Stanley Pool	1887 Pop. 5000 (Consul Casement)	1903 Pop. 500 (Consul Casement)	Emigration (Consul Casement)
Bolenge	1890 Pop. — (J. H. Weeks)	1903 Decrease of 50% compared with 1900 (J. H. Weeks)	Same causes as between Bokongo and Likunungu, save last, not specified (J. H. Weeks)
Mongalla concession			Many thousands killed since 1897 in rubber wars undertaken with assent and co-operation of authorities
Abir			,,

TABLE SHOWING DEPOPULATION, ETC.—continued.

	1890	1895		1903	
Lulanga	Pop. 3000 (J. H. Weeks)	(Lulanga and neighbourhood) Pop. 5000 (Gilchrist)		800 (J. H. Weeks) (Lulanga and neighbourhood) 1200 (Gilchrist)	Same causes as between Bokongo and Likunungu save last, not specified (J.H. Weeks). Extortionate food-taxes leading to poverty, starvation, and selling into slavery. (Gilchrist)
Luapula (banks of)			1900-1902 Deserted; natives crossed over to English bank. (Government reports; private advices; statements by agents of Katanga Company; statements by Rev. Dugald Campbell)		Raiding by Congo soldiery for rubber and ivory
Lado Enclave			1902-1903 Deserted appearance owing to oppression and misrule (Lord Cromer, Paul Didier)		Oppression
Ubanghi			1899-1900 Deserted appearance of banks; emigration to French banks (Berthier)		Raids and murders for rubber
Congo-Portuguese frontier			1901-1902 Disappearance of large towns and villages on Congo State side (Williams, Hall)		General oppression; raiding for women and live stock
			1894-1896 Many unpublished atrocities. Terrible charges brought against State officers by Senhor G. Ribeiro, Portuguese Resident at Landana. Commission appointed by Governor of Cabinda to investigate, under S. Gomez de Sousa. Depositions taken down by Ernesta Morgueira. Records held by Portuguese Government (Private advices)		

TYPICAL BARRACK HOUSE UNDER CIVILIZED ADMINISTRATION!

POLICE BARRACKS AT MATADI

(Within twenty yards of the Judge's official residence, after twenty years' "civilization")

	1896	1903	
Upper Congo in general			Governor of French Congo declares that owing to ill-treatment 30,000 natives have crossed over to French bank
Domaine de la Couronne	Pop. —	Pop. 100	Slaughter in connection with rubber tax. Desolation universal for a distance of 150 miles traversed in July, August, and September, 1903. (Scrivener.) Confirmed to Consul Casement from the lips of refugees
Mbolo; one time a big village and many chiefs			
Villages unnamed	3000	300	
Ngongo	2000	200	

	1893	1903	
Lake Mantumba district (Consul Casement)	Pop. 500	Pop. 80	
Botunu	500	80	
Bosende	660	—	
Ngombe	500	40	Slaughter in connection with rubber tax; insufficient food supply; forced labour
Bokaka	500	30	
Lobwaka	200	30	
Boboko	300	35	
Mwenge	150	30	
Boonga	120	50	
Ituta	300	60	
Ikenze	320	20	
Ngero	2500	300	
Mweba	700	75	
Ikoko	2500	800	

But depopulation, after all, is only an outward and visible sign of inward causes. What a sum total of human wretchedness does not lie behind that bald word "depopulation"! To my mind, the horror of this curse which has come upon the Congo peoples reaches its maximum of intensity when we force ourselves to consider its everyday concomitants; the crushing weight of perpetual, remorseless oppression; the gradual elimination of everything in the daily life of the natives which makes that life worth living. Under the prevailing system, every village is a penal settlement. Armed soldiers are quartered in every hamlet; the men pass nearly the whole of their lives in satisfying the ceaseless demands of the "Administration," or its affiliates the Trusts; whether it be in the collection of rubber, of gum-copal, of food-stuffs, or forced labour in Government plantations, or in the construction of those "fine brick houses" on which the apologists of the State are for ever harping. Women and children do not enjoy as much protection as a dog in this country. They are imprisoned, flogged, left at the mercy of the soldiery, taxed beyond endurance, regarded as lower than the beasts. Native industries die out. Intercommunication between native communities ceases. The people who are taxed in what may be termed sedentary taxation can never leave their homes, where they reside under the vigilant eye of a sentry, loaded rifle or cap-gun in hand, the real king of the village, omnipotent and insolent. Monstrous fines are inflicted for the slightest shortage in taxes, and punishments varying in degree from murder and mutilation to the chain-gang, the "house of hostages," and the *chicotte.* If the taxation involves long journeys, such as the fish tax, the natives' whole time is taken up in journeyings to and fro from the fishing grounds and the State stations. "It would be hard to say how the people live," says Consul Casement of the Bolobo tribe, famous in the old days for their trading abilities. Floggings are perpetual; for insufficient supplies of rubber; for inadequate supplies of food; as a punishment for lack of activity or ability in forced labour; on the most trivial pretexts, sparing neither age nor sex. *La chicotte,* like the *collier national,* otherwise the "chains," is regarded as an indispensable adjunct in production—a sort of trading asset.* It is one unending, heartrending story of odious brutality from first to last.

* Mr. Whitehead, in his letter to the Governor-General (Lukolela, Sept. 7, 1903), mentions the case of a Chief who had been so frightfully flogged and cut about the feet "that he despaired of walking again, and those who had seen him last said he got along by dragging himself along on his buttocks."

Mr. Casement refers to men "so severely flogged, in one of the *maison des ôtages,* that they were seen being carried away by their friends."

Chiefs are shamelessly degraded in the eyes of their people; made to fetch and carry for the soldiers; cast in the chains, and flogged for remissness in village taxes; flung into the "prisons" often to die of neglect, ill-treatment, and starvation; forced to the commitment of unspeakable bestialities * by their "moral and material" regenerators. Mr. Whitehead † mentions the case of a Chief—Mabungikindo from Bokobo—who was actually wearing his "State Chief's medal" when Mr. Whitehead (who knew him) met him "returning from the chains in which he had been detained to get three more baskets of rubber." He had also been beaten. He took his medal in his hand and asked Mr. Whitehead to look at it, remarking bitterly upon his treatment. "I cringed with shame," says Mr. Whitehead. And no wonder! Such things are an ineffaceable blot upon the white race in Africa; and every white man who has a soul, whether brought into contact with them on the spot, or acquainted with them from a distance, cannot but "cringe with shame" for his race. I have before me the translation of a pathetic statement ‡ drawn up by the people of Monsembe concerning the death of their Chief "in the chain" which took place a few months ago. It is worthy, it seems to me, of reproduction:

"Afterwards, M—— (native name of the local Congo State official) called Mangumbe (that was the name of the Chief of Monsembe) and said to him, 'Your tax is very good; however, because you do not come with the tax every time, you must go to prison for eight days.' Mangumbe said to him, 'I did not come because I went to seek a goat (goats are part of the tax levied, and being now very scarce, have to be fetched at long distances) at Malele.' When M—— heard that, he called soldiers to tie the Chief up, and to put him in prison. And the soldiers seized him, and beat him with the butt end of their guns on his chest and side and loins, because M—— himself spoke to them thus, 'It does not matter, if he dies, no palaver.' And the soldiers cast him into prison. And on account of this persecution and beating, Mangumba suffered in his back, chest, and sides. When the time appointed by M——, eight days, was passed, we went up river to embark Mangumbe. On arrival at Nouvelle Anvers, we went to L—— (another State official), and we said to him that the time appointed by them for our father (the natives call their Chiefs ' our father ') having ended, we had come to fetch him away. Then L—— said, 'But he will not be released just now, because he does not understand tax collecting. He constantly delays, and does not bring his tax quickly, he despises me. He will not be released until 22 days are over. At present I shall punish him, and if he does not obey them afterwards I shall hang him.' And we replied, 'Commissaire, if hitherto

---

* The Chief Lisanginya, of Mbenga, was compelled to drink from the white man's latrine.—Whitehead to Governor-General, Africa, No. 1, 1904, *op. cit.*
† Letter to Governor-General, *op. cit.*
‡ For which I am indebted to Mr. Charles Dodds. Mr. Weeks writes me the wretched man was only 20 days in the chains.

he has not been energetic (cunning) enough, how dare he do so again? As regards the tax, he will bring you, everything you want he will give you. When is there anything he has refused you? You say he despises you.' We besought him passionately again and again, but he would not hear, until at last we grew weary, and returned to our town. We had been home just over a week, when we saw some men coming with our father's corpse. We asked them if they had brought his body. They said, ' He died in prison, and we begged his body from the Commissaire, just as we bring it to you.' We received the body and buried it."

Of the treatment of women and children by King Leopold's " agents of civilisation " it is difficult to write calmly. You will find nothing worse in the pages of Motley. And the agents of Phillip of Spain had this much in their favour that, in their eyes, every woman killed meant the elimination of unborn or unconceived heretics. It was clearly the Lord's work from their point of view, if we saturate our minds so far as we can with the spirit of those distant days. But on the Congo, in the twentieth century, where is the ghost of an excuse to be found? Talk of the exploits of the Arab! The exploits of the Arabs pale beside these, and Civilisation, stirred to its depths by Livingstone's revelations, still hearkens to the blasphemies and hypocrisies of Brussels. Civilisation, which held up its hands in horror at the thought of Tippu-Tib, is content to do no more than look somewhat askance at Leopold II. The former was a rough, uneducated Arab half-breed; the latter is a product of Christian culture, and wears a crown.

The European defenders of the conception of tropical African " development " which the Sovereign of the Congo State has so logically and ruthlessly carried out, allege that in his natural condition, the native of tropical Africa is content to smoke and drink all day, while his wife labours. It is either grossly exaggerated, or totally untrue; but even were it true to the very letter, then the male African is an angel of light by comparison with those who, on the Congo, profess (in Europe) to lead him into better ways. Under the aboriginal African system women are not flogged to death, and there are no " prisons "—*maisons des ôtages*—for the detention of women for faults, or alleged faults committed by their husbands, where such things, as these are the habitual accompaniments thereof:

"Women, often big with child, or with babies at their breast, tied neck by neck, in long files, are imprisoned at the 'factory' until redeemed by a large quantity of rubber. In the 'prisons' can always be seen men and children, and women in all stages of pregnancy, all herded together."*

---

* Report from a missionary on the spot. Equateurville District, 1903. In a letter communicated to the author.

"Men are first applied for, and if they do not present themselves, a soldier, or soldiers are sent, who tie up the women or the chiefs until the workmen are forthcoming." *

"I have seen men and women chained together by the neck, being driven by an armed soldier." †

"They also seized Balua, the wife of Botanga, and M. F—— had her flogged, giving her 200 *chicotte*.‡ So severely was she dealt with that urine and blood flowed from her. Just as they were dragging her away to the prison, her husband appeared with 20 fowls to redeem her. He took her home, but she died shortly after from the effect of the punishment she received." §

"On July 8, 1899, M——, after making inquiries, went to the factory, and released 106 prisoners. We saw them pass our stations—living skeletons . . . among them grey-headed old men and women. Many children were born in prison. One poor woman was working in the sun three days after the child was born." ‖

"Imprisoning 60 women and putting them in the chain, where all but five died of starvation." ¶

"This man himself, when I visited him in Boma goal, in March, 1901, said that more than 100 women and children had died of starvation at his hands, but that the responsibility for both their arrest and his own lack of food to give them was due to his superiors' orders and neglect." **

"That, above all, the facts that the arrest of women and their detention, to compel the villages to furnish both produce and workmen, was tolerated and admitted even by certain of the Administrative Authorities of the region." ††

"Upon the least resistance the men were shot down, and the women were captured as slaves and made to work. It was a sad sight to behold these poor creatures, driven like dogs here and there, and kept hard at their toil from morning to night." ‡‡

"At the different Congo Government stations, women are kept for the following purposes. In the daytime they do all the usual station work . . . at night they are obliged to be at the disposal of the soldiers. . . . The women are slaves captured by the Government soldiers when raiding the country." §§

"Here the soldiers have taken away women as prisoners all because these people have no rubber for the Lufoi station." ‖‖

"Long strings of captives, mostly women and children," brought in after raids by State troops, "made to serve seven years as prisoners of war." ¶¶

---

* Rev. A. Billington, Bwanbu, 1903. American Memorial, *op. cit.*
† Rev. Joseph Clark, Ikoko, 1903. Ibid.
‡ 200 blows this means.
§ Mr. Ruskin's evidence before Judge Rossi in 1903. Incident in 1899. ‖ Ibid.
¶ One of the counts in the indictment drawn up against the agents of the *Anversoise* in the Mongalla massacres of 1900.
** Cyrus Smith to Consul Casement. Incident in the Mongalla atrocities of 1900 (Africa, No. 1, 1904).
†† Findings of the Boma Court in the above case. Arguments for "extenuating circumstances" towards Cyrus Smith.
‡‡ Semliki region. Lloyd, 1899.
§§ Katanga region. Affidavit. March 1903.
‖‖ Johnston Falls neighbourhood. Diary.
¶¶ Katanga region. Missionary evidence received by Mr. H. R. Fox Bourne in 1903—covering period from 1894 to 1903.

"On —— removing from the station, his successor almost fainted on attempting to enter the station prison, in which were numbers of poor wretches so reduced by starvation and the awful stench from weeks of accumulation of filth, that they were not able to stand."*

"The accused detained arbitrarily a large number of men and women, many of whom died owing to the insanitary condition of the prison where the accused incarcerated them, and through the fearful misery in which he left them."†

"In an open shed I found two sentries of the La Lulanga Company guarding fifteen women, five of whom had infants at the breast, and three of whom were about to become mothers. . . . The remaining eleven women, whom he indicated, he said he had caught, and was detaining as prisoners to compel their husbands to bring in the right amount of india-rubber required of them on the next market day. When I asked if it was a woman's work to collect indiarubber, he said 'No;‡ that of course it was man's work.' 'Then why do you catch the women and not the men?' I asked. 'Don't you see,' was the answer, 'if I caught and kept the men, who would work the rubber? But if I catch their wives, the husbands are anxious to have them home again, and so the rubber is brought in quickly and quite up to the mark.' When I asked what would become of these women if their husbands failed to bring in the right quantity of rubber on the next market day, he said at once that then they would be kept there until their husbands had redeemed them.' . . . At nightfall the fifteen women in the shed were tied together, either neck to neck, or ankle to ankle, to secure them for the night, and in this posture I saw them twice during the evening. They were then trying to huddle around a fire."§

"Later in the day . . . two armed soldiers came up to the agent as we walked, guarding sixteen natives, five men tied neck to neck, with five untied women and six young children. This somewhat embarrassing situation, it was explained to me, was due to the persistent failure of the people of the village these persons came from to supply its proper quota of food. . . . I asked if the children also were held responsible for food supplies, and they, along with an elderly woman, were released. . . . The remaining five men and four women were led off to the *maison des ôtages* under guard of the sentry. The agent explained that he was forced to catch women in preference to the men, as then supplies were brought in quicker; but he did not explain how the children deprived of their parents obtained their own food supplies."‖

"I met, when walking in the Abir grounds with the subordinate agent of the factory, a file of fifteen women, under the guard of three unarmed sentries, who were being brought in from the adjoining villages, and were led past me. These women, who were evidently wives and mothers, it

---

* Domaine de la Couronne region. Scrivener.

† Rubi-Welle region. M. de Favereau reading out to Belgian House charges against Tilkens. Tilkens' defence is that "these hostages were inscribed each month on the reports sent to my Chiefs. If there was mortality amongst them my Chiefs knew it, and never made of the fact a cause of complaint against me."—*Annales parlementaires*, Part V.

‡ Mr. Scrivener writes me that he hears that women are also about to be compelled to collect indiarubber in his district. He does not mention it as a fact, but as a rumour.

§ Lulonga district. Consul Casement, 1903. Africa, White Book, No. 1, 1904.

‖ Lopori-Maringa District. Consul Casement, 1903. Ibid.

NATIVE LIFE UNDER CONGO STATE RULE

was explained in answer to my inquiry, had been seized in order to compel their husbands to bring in antelope or other meat which was overdue.*

"The Commissaire had visited P—— and had ordered the people of that town to work daily at Q—— for the La Lulonga factory. W—— had replied that it was too far for the women of P—— to go daily to Q—— as was required; but the Commissaire in reply had taken fifty women and carried them away with him." †

"In addition fifty women are required each morning to go to the factory and work there all day. They complained that the remuneration given for these services was most inadequate, and that they were continually beaten.‡

"A considerable number of children necessarily engaged in this work, and, moreover, were often held by the State as 'hostages' because of delinquencies or defects." §

If this is not the slave trade, what is it? How much longer will the civilised world tolerate these things? ||

It would need a volume in itself to deal in a thorough manner with the exotic abominations introduced into the Congo territories under King Leopold's sway. One labours under the weight of well-nigh overpowering testimony. These short extracts I have quoted can give no adequate account of the full misery upon the people which such measures entail.

The cumulative effects of depopulation and infantile mortality by dragging women away from their homes for forced labour requisitions—seizing them as "hostages," and "tying them up," whether virgins, wives, mothers, or those about to become mothers, in order to bring pressure to bear upon brothers, husbands, and fathers for the adequate supply of rubber or food taxes; flinging them into "prison," together with their children, often to die of starvation and neglect; flogging them, sometimes even unto death; leaving them at the mercy of the soldiers; distributing them after punitive raids among hangers-on—must be enormous. There we have depopulation through the infamous torture of women —often enough shot outright or mutilated ¶—and the neglect

* Lopori-Maringa District. Consul Casement, 1903. Africa, White Book, No. 1, 1904.
† Lulonga District. Consul Casement, 1903. Ibid.
‡ Lulonga District. Consul Casement, 1903. Ibid.
§ E. A. Layton. Coquilhatville District. American Memorial, *op. cit.*
|| It will be observed that I have left out of account all records of a similar character, of ancient date, such as Glave's, Sjöblom, Murphy, etc.
¶ Referring to the depopulation of the Lake Mantumba towns, Consul Casement says : "War in which children and women were killed as well as men. Women and children were killed, not in all cases by stray bullets, but were taken as prisoners and killed. Sad to say, these horrible cases were not always the acts of some black soldier. Proof was laid against one officer who shot one woman and one man, when they were before him as prisoners with their hands tied, and no attempt was made by the accused to deny the truth of the statement."—Africa, No. 1, 1904, p. 70.

and the mutilation of young children and boys; most of whom, it may be presumed, when so mutilated do not survive the operation, in order to have "the bad taste to show their stumps to the missionaries," as one of the Belgian deputies said in the course of the Congo debate in the Belgian House last year.

What has come over the civilised people of the globe that they can allow their Governments to remain inactive and apathetic in the face of incidents which recall in aggravated form the worst horrors of the over-sea slave trade, which surpass the exploits of Arab slave catchers? What could be worse than scenes such as these, which can be culled by the dozen from Consul Casement's report, and from the testimony of a score of independent, non-official resident observers, scattered throughout the country:

"Then the soldiers came again to fight us. We ran into the bush. ... After that they saw a little of my mother's head, and the soldiers ran quickly towards the place where we were, and caught my grandmother, my mother, my sister, and another little one younger than us. Several of the soldiers argued about my mother, because each wanted her for a wife, so they finally decided to kill her. They killed her with a gun, they shot her through the stomach and she fell, and when I saw that I cried very much, because they killed my grandmother and my mother, and I was left alone. My mother was near her confinement at the time. And they killed my grandmother too, and I saw it all done..."

Offence: villages slow in the production of rubber!

"While they were both standing outside the soldiers came upon them and took them both. One of the soldiers said, 'We might keep them both, the little one is not bad looking.' But the others said, 'No, we are not going to carry her all the way; we must kill the younger girl.' So they put a knife through the child's stomach, and left the body lying there where they had killed it...."

Merely an incident in a rubber war!

Take the case of the twenty poor wretches belonging to the villages of Bokongo and Bongondo, murdered for being behindhand in their supply of goats. Eleven of the victims of this outrage, which occurred last May twelvemonth, were women, and one was a girl. The crime has gone unpunished, although I have published the full list of names.* That is a

* This atrocity was brought to my notice by Mr. Weeks, who denounced it to the authorities on November 30, 1903. See *West African Mail*, January 22, 1904; also Congo issue, June. The crimes were perpetrated by State soldiers under a Government officer, who, if not actually present, was in the neighbourhood, and who has been allowed to return with this charge hanging over his head. Several weeks after he was allowed to leave, a judicial officer was sent to investigate and found the statements fully proved!

NATIVE LIFE UNDER CONGO STATE RULE 249

recent case. The massacre of 120 natives in "cold blood" in the raids against the Banza (Caudron case) is another recent case. How many of the victims were women and children, I wonder? Let the reader never fail to bear in mind that it is only by accident we ever hear of any of these deeds of darkness which, as I pen these lines, are going on all over the Congo unchecked and unpunished, a necessary and endemic effect of the new slave trade which has replaced the milder one of the Arabs.

The Congo Government boasts that, in stopping intertribal warfare, it has stopped the selling of tribal prisoners of war into domestic slavery. The condition of the domestic slave under the African system is blissful beyond words, if you compare his lot with that of the degraded serf under the Leopoldian system.*

But, in point of fact, the State, having violently reduced free communities to agglomerations of broken-spirited bondsmen, is deliberately encouraging the slave traffic in another form. Individuals in a village are frequently compelled to sell themselves, and each other, to neighbouring tribes, in order that the village as a whole may not suffer from one or other of the fearful punishments inflicted for non-compliance in that filling of a bottomless sack which the Congo Executive describes as "taxation"—the light, extremely light, "taxation" of "40 hours per month"! We have reports of this from various widely removed parts of the Congo.

"A close acquaintance with the conditions," writes Dr. Lyon,† "shows the cogency of the natives' contentions that they are no less than slaves to the State. And as slaves, I have observed they must sometimes 'make bricks without straw,' as when one must furnish fish nearly the year round, and he can catch fish only at certain seasons. Then one is forced to buy in other parts, paying in this way ten to forty times what will be received in return at the State post. To meet these obligations A——, of W——, one of the remaining few of a once large family, had to pawn, i.e. sell into slavery, a younger member of his family."

Mr. Weeks gives me the names of twenty-one persons, with their villages, whom their relatives were compelled to sell into

---

* If it be objected that in certain instances the lot of the domestic slave was apt to be cut short for culinary purposes in the pre-regenerating days, it may with equal point be retorted that, after 20 years of "regeneration," Government soldiers and auxiliaries are found in the plentitude of their civilising mission, and under the eyes of Government officials, disembowelling and cutting up the recently slaughtered bodies of recalcitrant native taxpayers for similar purpose.—*Vide* Yandjali massacre, 1903. And further, that instances of cannibalism by soldiers in the Abir territory have been openly committed—the facts clearly established—many times during the last few months. See letters in Appendix.

† American Memorial, *op. cit.*

slavery, in his district last year in order to supply the goats required as part of the food tax levied upon their villages.* In his letter to the Commissaire-General of the Bangala District (November 30, 1903) protesting against this occurrence, which letter was published in the *West African Mail* of January 22 1904, Mr. Weeks says : " Thus to supply your table at Bangala the life of these people is being slowly crushed out, and many sold into slavery."

Mr. Gilchrist, in his letter † to the Governor-General (July, 1903), explains how in order to meet an exorbitant fine levied for shortness in the supply of food-stuffs : " Some of the men had to sell their wives and children into slavery, and some sold themselves to the river people."

Consul Casement reports similar incidents. A village near Coquilhatville, for instance, is fined 55,000 rods (£110) for failure in supplying food-stuffs in sufficient quantities :

"This sum they had been forced to pay, and as they had no other means of raising so large a sum, they had, many of them, been compelled to sell their children and their wives."

And again :

"A father and mother stepped out and said that they had been forced to sell their son, a little boy called F——, for 1000 rods to meet their share of the fine. A widow came and declared she had been forced, in order to meet her share of the fine, to sell her daughter, G——, a little girl, whom I judged from her description to be about ten years of age."

Our Consul remarks that he was not able to verify all these statements, but the one he was able to do turned out correct. It was the case of two little children. One of them was, by his intervention, restored to her parents, but the other had " again changed hands, and was promised in sale to a town on the north bank of the Congo named Iberi, whose people are still said to be open cannibals." Charming picture of moral and material regeneration !

Again, I ask, if this is not the slave trade, what is it ?

Pages could be given to the evidence available proving that workmen and soldiers are obtained by methods differing in very little, if at all, from open slave-raiding, but it will be

---

* A few years ago every village in the Congo had its goats. Now very few villages, which are not too remote from the State posts to be got at, have any left. But the natives are still expected to provide the officials with these animals, as part and parcel of the food tax. The result is that the price of goats has reached a phenomenal figure. These particular twenty-one poor people were sold to other tribes—29,000 rods, for thirty-one goats !

† Appendix.

NATIVE LIFE UNDER CONGO STATE RULE 251

sufficient to give a translation of the following order for Government workmen drawn up by "Le Capitaine-Commandant Sarrazyn,"* a former Commissaire of the Equateur District, surnamed by the natives "Widjima," or "Darkness":

> "The Chief Ngula of Wangasa is sent into the Maringa to buy slaves for me. The agents of the Abir are instructed to be good enough to let me know of the ill-deeds (*les méfaits*) which he may commit on the road."

Comment is needless. †

Once more—if this is not the slave trade, what is it?

We have many sad glimpses of the inward effect produced upon the people by this system of organised murder, robbery, and oppression. The women, Consul Casement tells us, are deliberately practising abortion, because, as they say, "If war should come, a woman big with child, or with a baby to carry, cannot well run away and hide from the soldiers." The Rev. Joseph Clark has the same tale to tell:

> "The native mind is not at rest. He has no desire for the improvement of his surroundings. He will not make a good house or large gardens, because that will give the State a greater hold on him. His wife refuses to become a mother because she will not be able to run away in case of an attack. Twice this week the people of Ikoko have been rushing off to the 'bush' to hide on the approach of a large canoe with soldiers." ‡

Weeks, writing of the effect of a yearly taxation of £1605 16s. 8d. on a miserable population of 820 persons, of both sexes, says:

> "I need scarcely point out that young children, very old people, and invalids cannot earn a wage, or even farm or fish; consequently the burden falls heavier on those who can, and the vision before them is one of unceasing toil in order to comply with the demands of the State. Is it any wonder the natives die under the burden? The wonder to me is that so many are alive after these seven years of oppression and taxation. Were this tax a yearly, or even a half-yearly one, it would not be so bad; but it is a fortnightly one, and consequently an ever-present nightmare. No sooner is one tax sent off in canoes than they have to worry about collecting materials for the next. Thus it is a constant grind, grind, grind, that is sapping the spirit and strength of these people, and causing them to succumb. Death is kinder than this kind of living." §

---

* White Book, Africa, No. 1, 1904.

† "I have had several cases brought to my knowledge lately of the mode of slavery adopted at the post. Briefly it is as follows: a man for some reason . . . commences work at the post. He completes his term, and he is told he cannot have his pay unless he engages himself another term or brings another in his place. I know of those who have left their earnings in the hands of the Chef de Poste rather than begin again. Such compulsion is contrary to civilised law, and is rightly termed slavery, and is utterly illegal."—Whitehead to Governor-General, Sept., 1903.

‡ American Memorial, *op. cit.*

§ Weeks to Author, Dec. 24, 1903.

"Death and decay in all around I see," was the impression of a colleague of my friend Mr. Weeks in returning last December from a visit to the Ndobo towns, whose inhabitants live on the banks of streamlets and lakelets about twenty miles from Monsembe and the main river. "A policy"—to quote Weeks once more—"that is impoverishing these people, sapping their strength, and sending them to the grave."* "Surely this is slavery," writes Mr. Frame, describing the usual tale of brutal oppression, and adds: "The slavery of the people on this side of Stanley Pool to the Nkissi River is fairly complete, with no hope of improvement." † "Oppressive measures under which the people are groaning and dying," writes Mr. Gilchrist.‡

"The people are regarded as the property of the State for any purpose for which they may be needed. That they have any desires of their own, or any plans worth carrying out in connection with their own lives, would create a smile among the officials." §

"The poor people of this section" (Bolengi near Coquilhatville, one of the most important State stations on the Upper River) "are broken-spirited and poverty-stricken by an arbitrary and oppressive system of taxation." ‖

"In the village of W——," writes Consul Casement, "extortionately fined for being in arrears, one of the natives, a strong, indeed a splendid-looking man, broke down and wept, saying that their lives were useless to them, and that they knew of no means of escape from the troubles which were gathering round them." ¶

Our Consul's report abounds in incidents showing the utter misery and demoralisation of the people. Some persons seem to think that rubber falls off the trees in Africa like apples in autumn, and all that the "lazy native" has to do is to pick it up. In point of fact, rubber collecting is, even under normal conditions, dangerous to health—any one acquainted with the South American rubber business will bear me out. What must it be under the compulsory conditions prevalent in the Congo? Hundreds, if not thousands, of natives on the Congo must die every year merely through fatigue, exposure, chills, ill-health, engendered by working in fœtid swamps, the attacks of wild animals, and privations of all kinds. Rubber collecting in the tropical African forests is the most ultimately exhausting of all forms of labour voluntarily undertaken by the African; but he knows the product is of value, and that he

* Weeks to Author, Dec. 23, 1903.
† W. B. Frame to Author, March 16, 1904.
‡ S. Gilchrist to Governor-General, Sept. 1903.
§ Scrivener to Author, Oct., 1903.
‖ Dr. Lyon, 1903 or 1904, American Memorial, *op. cit*
¶ Africa, No. 1, 1904, *op. cit.*

NATIVE LIFE UNDER CONGO STATE RULE

will get many more goods for a couple of pounds of pure rubber than for most other things that the white man requires. On the Congo, however, the native is *driven* into the forest. He is not a trader, but a beast. If he brings in the stipulated quantity after days of absence from his family, he gets a few teaspoonfuls of salt, or a handful of beads, and immediately he must begin again, and so on, until he dies or manages to escape to remoter regions.

Here is a typical insight into native life in a rubber district, under the gloriously humanitarian system beneath the "blue banner with the golden star," so dear to the severely impartial hearts of Sir Hugh Gilzean Reid, Mr. Demetrius C. Boulger, Sir Alfred Jones, and his crowd of obedient followers:

> "I went to the homes of these men, some miles away, and found out their circumstances. To get the rubber they had first to go fully a two days' journey from their homes, leaving their wives, and being absent for from five to six days. They were seen to the forest limits under guard, and, if not back by the sixth day, trouble was likely to ensue. To get the rubber in the forests, which, generally speaking, are very swampy, involves much fatigue, and often fruitless searching for a well-flowing vine. As the area of supply diminishes, moreover, the demand for rubber constantly increases. Some little time back I learned the Bongandanga District supplied seven tons of rubber a month, a quantity which it was hoped would shortly be increased to ten tons. . . . In addition to these formal payments, they are liable at times to be dealt with in another manner, for should their work, which might have been just as hard, have proved less profitable in its yield of rubber, the local prison would have seen them. The people everywhere assured me that they were not happy under this system, and it was apparent to a callous eye that in this they spoke the strict truth."

"They were not happy." Mr. Casement has never forgotten in the course of his report that he was a machine sent to record in a spirit of calm, judicial impartiality the sights he witnessed, and he performed his task with marvellous self-restraint; for, though an official, he may be presumed to have the feelings of an ordinary mortal, and his "they were not happy" conveys, under the circumstances, a story of abject and unspeakable wretchedness. Enough has been said to show that under this system of "moral and material regeneration," constituting a monstrous invasion of primitive rights which has no parallel in the whole world, the family life and social ties of the people are utterly destroyed. Another horrible aspect of Congo State rule is touched upon by Mr. Dugald Campbell in the letter which will be found in the Appendix, viz. the spread of syphilis through promiscuous "forcing into lives of shame" of women and young girls to pander to the lusts of

* Africa, No. 1, 1904, *op. cit.*

the ceaselessly shifting and enormous army. Under native conditions, he says, strict measures are taken to circumscribe the area of this disease, but under the Congo Government system it is everywhere extending and infecting whole districts.

Within the last few weeks detailed and specific accounts, clearly established, have come to hand from Messrs. Stannard, Harris, and Frost, all in the Baringa district of the *Abir* concession, painting a picture of native misery at the hands of the servants of that insatiable rubber-hunting corporation which would touch a heart of stone. They will be found in full in the Appendix. What is the reply which King Leopold flings to the world?* It consists in the appointment to the Board of Administration of Count John d'Oultremont, Grand Marshal to the Belgian Court, and Baron Dhanis, an ex-Governor-General of the Congo State! This measure is accompanied by a statement from the worthy Senator who nominally presides over the destinies of this Trust, to the effect that its rubber-producing capacities have not nearly attained their zenith, for the labour of the natives may be easily requisitioned to produce one hundred and twenty tons of that article a month, whereas the present output is only sixty tons!

I will conclude with an extract of a letter I have recently received from my friend Mr. Weeks, who has rendered such invaluable service during the past year, in helping the cause of these oppressed people. The letter is dated Monsembe, Dec. 26, 1903.

"What does the native receive in return for all this taxation? I know of absolutely no way in which he is benefited. Some point to the telegraph. In what way does that benefit a native? Those who live near the line have to keep the road clear for nothing, and in tropical Africa that is not an easy task. Others point to the scores of steamers running on the Upper Congo. In what way do they benefit the native? Here and there along the river, natives are forced to supply large quantities of firewood for an inadequate remuneration. Others, again, point to well-built State stations. In what way do they benefit the native? They are largely built, and are now largely maintained, by forced labour. Then others point to the railway. It is a splendid achievement of engineering skill, and is paying large dividends to shareholders, but in what way does it benefit the thousands of natives on the Upper Congo? It certainly takes the rubber they are forced to supply so cheaply, more rapidly than otherwise possible, to the European markets. Is there more security for life now than under the old *régime?* It does not appear so when a white officer of the State allowed his soldiers last May to shoot down 22 men and women for the paltry offence of owing a paternal State a few groats. Is there more security for property now than under the old *régime?* No, for then men defended his goods by his spear; now their goods are open to the depredations of State messengers and soldiers. And there is no redress."

---

* The Congo Government, as already shown, holds half the shares of the *Abir*.

If Gladstone had been alive he would perhaps have found a phrase adequate to describe the revival of the slave trade under the ægis of a European Sovereign in Equatorial Africa, and the forms which that revival takes. But I doubt if even he could have found one more fittingly characterising it than that he so truly applied to other quarters. The "Negation of God" erected with a system—yes, indeed!

Why are these people allowed to suffer thus cruelly? What crime have they collectively committed in past ages that they should undergo to-day so terrible an expiation? Are they "groaning and dying" under this murderous system as a great object-lesson to Europe? What price, then, will Europe later on have to pay for the teaching? Inscrutable are the decrees of Providence. One wonders whether the deepening horror of this colossal crime will end by a reaction so violent that an era of justice will, for the first time in the history of Caucasian relationship with the Dark Continent, arise, never to be eradicated, for the peoples of Africa. Or that some day tropical Africa may breed brains as she breeds muscles, and then . . . ? But it bodes little to dwell among the mists of conjecture. The future is closed to us. We grope in the dark, puzzled, incensed, impatient. The future is with God. To the past man may look and gather consolation in the knowledge that evils such as these bring their own Nemesis upon the nation whose moral guilt is primarily involved. Belgium, technically unconcerned, is morally responsible, and Belgium will suffer. Strange that it should be the seceded Southern Provinces of those very Netherlands, so terribly served five hundred years ago, which are allowing another foreign Monarch of theirs to plagiarise in Africa, exploits formerly visited upon themselves. Strange too, perhaps, that a descendant of one of the victims of Philip II. should have been driven by Fate to participate in the movement directed against his latter-day prototype, in all respects save religious fanaticism. We are powerless as to the future, and if in past history we may find a partial solace, it is the present that concerns us. And here we are neither blindfolded nor impotent for action. Action it is we claim; action there must be.

If the policy of the Congo State were a national policy; if the Congo tribes were being systematically bled to death either through distorted zeal, as the population of the Netherlands were harried with fire and sword by Philip and his lieutenants, or through lust of conquest; if the Congo Basin were capable of being colonised by the Caucasian race, the policy we condemn and reprobate would still be a crime against humanity, an outrage upon civilisation. But the Congo territories can never be a white man's country; the "Congo State" is naught but a collection of individuals—with one supreme above them all—working for their own selfish ends, caring nothing for posterity, callous of the present, indifferent of the future, as of the past, animated by no fanaticism other than the fanaticism of dividends—and so upon the wickedness of this thing is grafted the fatuous stupidity and inhumanity of the Powers in allowing the extermination of the Congo races to go on unchecked, barely, if at all, reproved.

Surely the time has come to cease the usage of kid gloves and rose-water in dealing with this Congo question? For eight years that process has been adopted, and it has yielded nothing—absolutely nothing. Things are infinitely worse to-day than they were eight years ago. Anyhow, it is time some one called a spade a spade in this infernal business, even if the tender susceptibilites of certain estimable people are hurt by so unfashionable a method.

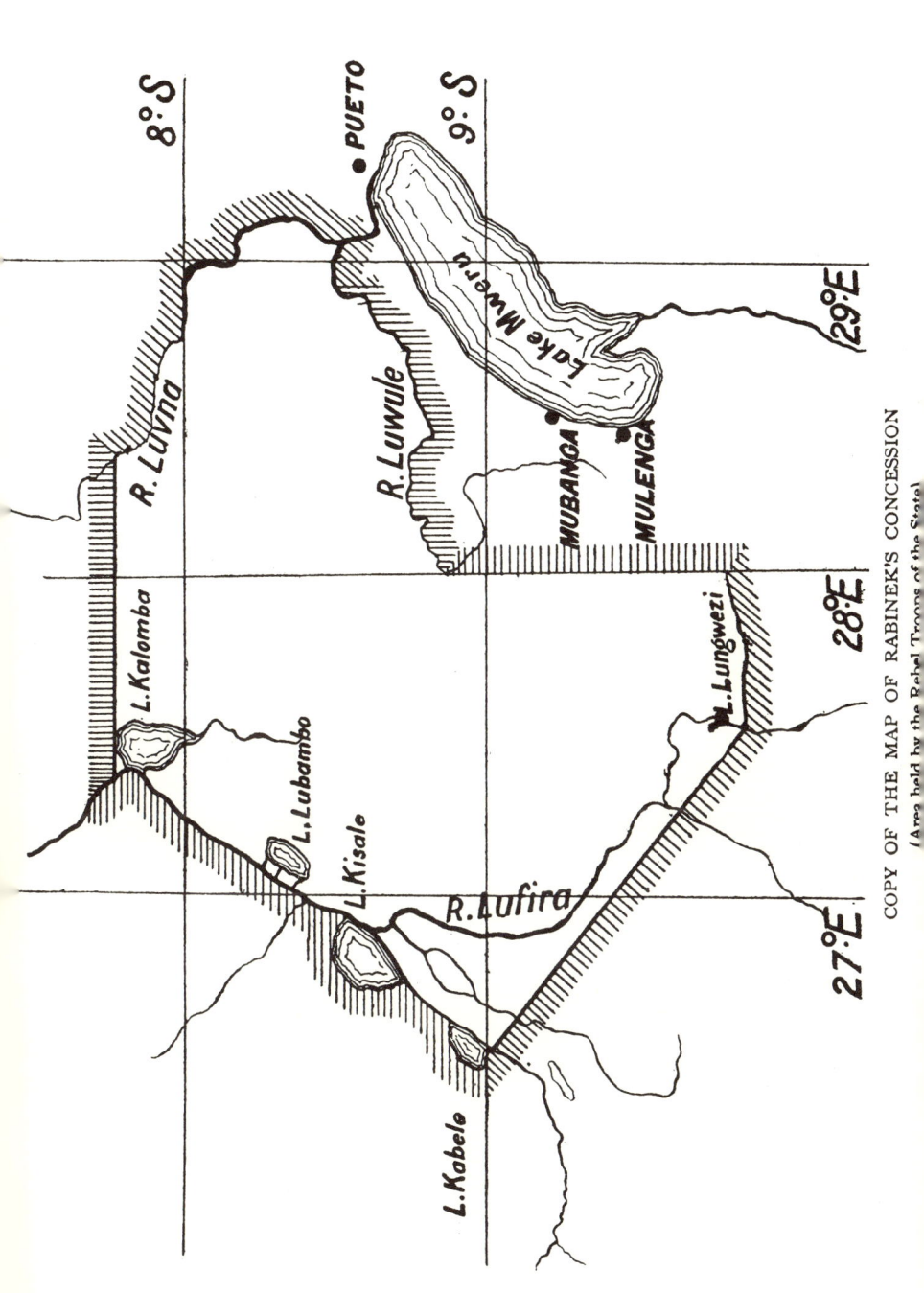

COPY OF THE MAP OF RABINEK'S CONCESSION
(Area held by the Rebel Troops of the State)

PART IV

THE WORKINGS OF THE SYSTEM AS IT AFFECTS INTERNATIONAL COMMERCIAL INTERESTS

THE CASE OF GUSTAV MARIA RABINEK

RABINEK'S PERSONALITY AND HISTORY

THE KATANGA COMPANY AND THE CONGO STATE: RABINEK'S RELATIONS WITH BOTH

THE PLOT AND THE ARREST

THE TRIAL, THE SENTENCE, AND THE END

CHAPTER XXII

THE CASE OF GUSTAV MARIA RABINEK—I. RABINEK'S PERSONALITY AND HISTORY.

"The trade of all nations shall enjoy perfect freedom."—Article 1, Berlin Act.
"So complete is this restriction that only recently—without attending to other cases which might be cited—an Austrian subject, Herr Rabinek, was sentenced to one year's imprisonment and to a fine, for no other crime than that of daring to purchase rubber from the natives; and this in a district solemnly guaranteed to be open to unfettered commerce."—Memorial to the peoples of Europe signed by seventeen Members of the House of Commons, July, 1903.

HAVING gained, under false pretences, an introduction among the family of States, the Congo Government proceeded—as I have shown—by a series of carefully planned and interrelated acts, to translate the freedom to which the "Congo Free State" was dedicated by making free of everything the African possessed, including his body and his life.

Having imposed this conception of "freedom" upon his African subjects, the Sovereign of the Congo issued instructions that the European, equally with the African, must be forced to recognise his unquestioned personal right to every article of economic value the Congo territories possessed.

The first European victim to this unpublished decree * was the British subject, Stokes.

Accused of trading with the natives, of having arms in his possession, and even of selling these to native traders, Mr. Stokes was invited by Captain Lothaire, the Sovereign's representative, to visit his camp. Mr. Stokes, nothing doubting and conscious of no wrong-doing, accepted this invitation, and arrived as Captain Lothaire's guest in the latter's camp at 4 p.m. one hot African afternoon. Instead of an invitation to dinner, he found his host awaiting him with a drawn revolver and a band of armed cannibal soldiers. At once seized, in

* The circulars issued by the various Commandants on the strength of that unpublished decree have been made public. *Vide* Part II.

violation of all decency and in the face of strenuous protest, and charged with an offence which, even had he been guilty, entailed a sentence of imprisonment and fine only, Mr. Stokes found himself condemned to immediate death. At four in the morning of the night of his arrival in Captain Lothaire's camp as a guest, he was taken out to the forest and hanged.

When the news of this summary method of dispensing Congolese justice reached Europe, some comment was excited, and both the German * and British Governments took diplomatic steps to ensure a " proper " trial of the murderer.

In the face of the remonstrances of Her Majesty's Government, the "trial" of Captain Lothaire at Boma by the Congo Courts constituted an even more flagrant violation of decency than the original act of Lothaire himself, for which act the Congo Government had hastened to disclaim responsibility by declaring it, in the most specific terms, to have been illegal.

Refusing to accept the finding of the " High Court " at Boma as final, Lord Salisbury pressed for a further trial in Belgium. Lothaire was indicted before a tribunal in his own land ; and again an offensive exhibition of " patriotism " induced the Public Prosecutor to throw down his brief in dramatic pose, and to declare that it was impossible for him, as a Belgian, to impeach " this brave Belgian officer."

Lothaire was again triumphantly acquitted, his trial being but an ovation. Brussels rang with his triumphs.

Her Majesty's Government of the day dropped the matter in contemptuous disgust. Stokes lay dead in his Central African grave. His murderer, whose illegal action in trying and sentencing him, the Congo Government had been prompt to disown by despatch, was rewarded for his " breach of law " by being promptly appointed by the Sovereign of the Congo State director in Africa of the *Société Anversoise du Commerce au Congo*, with whose history the reader is now familiar. At the end of a three years' administration, characterised by the series of tragedies termed the Mongalla scandals, the director of this Company returned to Belgium.

The second European to fall a victim to this unpublished decree has been an Austrian subject, Rabinek. It is the history of this second tragedy, this second example of the working of the Congo State system as it affects international commercial interests, that I am about to relate.

In unfolding the story of the circumstances connected with the arrest of Herr Gustav Maria Rabinek, an Austrian

---

* The defenceless porters of Stokes' caravan were shot down in cold blood, subsequent to the murder of their leader, to the number of fully one hundred. They were natives of German East Africa.

merchant trading in Katanga, by the Congo State Authorities, and the various incidents which preceded and followed that arrest, the reader is asked to bear in mind that it is to an even greater degree, perhaps (for reasons which will appear in the narrative), than the murder of Mr. Stokes, a test case as illustrative of the Congo State's interpretation of articles 1 and 5 of the Berlin Act where *white men*, unconnected with the Government, or the corporations it controls, are in question.

Who was Rabinek? How did his life's tragedy reach the ears of Europe?

Towards the end of July, 1902, I received a letter dated Blantyre, May 8 of the same year, and signed by a name quite unfamiliar to me, viz: "M. T. de Mattos." The letter paper bore the following printed description: "M. Teixeira de Mattos & Co., Chiromo (this word crossed out), British Central Africa, Nyassa Land, Agent for Sharrar's Zambesi Traffic Co., Ltd., and Zambesi Trading Co." Under the above, the words "Karonga, Lake Nyassa *via* Chinde," were written. The writer, after referring to an article * of mine in the *Contemporary Review* for March of that year, and corroborating the strictures passed therein upon the administration of the Congo State, went on to say that a friend of his, Rabinek, an Austrian merchant, trading in the vicinity of Lake Mweru, "with full permission" from the Katanga Company had been arrested on a British steamer and in British waters by the Congo State Authorities, and handed over to an escort of Congo soldiery to be taken to Boma, and "had died on the road." My correspondent made a vague allusion, explanatory of Rabinek's arrest, to "the alteration" of the Katanga Company, into the "Comité Especial (*sic*) du Katanga," † and referred to Messrs. Ludwig Deuss & Co., ‡ of Hamburg, who supplied Rabinek with trade goods. It was due, therefore, to the fortuitous circumstances of a copy of the *Contemporary Review* falling into the hands of a European trader, (a subject of Holland) in the wilds of Central Africa, that the Rabinek tragedy first became publicly known. §

* " The Belgian Curse in Africa."
† Comité Spécial du Katanga.
‡ I subsequently ascertained that Messrs. Ludwig Deuss & Co. were a highly respectable firm of German merchants, established since 1886 in Hamburg and East Africa ; factories at Chinde, Quelimane, Tete, Chicoa, Chiromo, and Luangwe ; own a steamer and lighters on the Zambesi ; agents for German East Africa Line at Chinde, and for Aberdeen Line at Quelimane.
§ The reptile Congophile Press of Brussels and Antwerp was good enough to suggest subsequently that the Rabinek case had been raised by a gang of blackmailers, of which I was at once the most distinguished

Gustav Maria Rabinek was born at Olmutz and was thirty-eight years of age when he met his death. Vienna is the residence of his nearest relatives, and Rabinek was well known in that city. M. Leonard Rabinek, the brother of the deceased merchant, is a bank clerk; two sisters are living, one married to a captain in the Austrian Army, the other to an official of the Northern Railway Company. For some years Rabinek was employed as a clerk in the Northern Railway Company, but he was of a roving, adventurous disposition, and after visiting Constantinople, Cairo, and German East Africa, he finally settled down to business as a rubber and ivory merchant in the neighbourhood of Lakes Mweru and Tanganyika. His commercial ability and integrity appear to have been conspicuous. He was trusted by European and native alike, and firms * established in Nyassaland advanced him practically all the credit in goods he asked for. From several written documents in my possession testifying to the esteem in which Rabinek was held, I may quote two opinions: that of Mr. E. A. Young, Native Commissioner, Mirongo, N. Shuangwa, N. E. Rhodesia, and of Mr. L. Deuss, head of the firm of that name. Mr. Young says †:

"You wish to know what I know about the late G. M. Rabinek; well, I made his acquaintance in 1897, when he came here from Karonga, to trade in rubber and ivory. He stayed here for some time, and on several occasions he and I travelled together over the greater part of this district, also of the Awenba District, for weeks together. I always found the late M. Rabinek a gentleman in every way. He was anxious to learn the ways of the country concerning his business, and never gave me any trouble in trying to avoid what was required of him by the Government. . . . I never had any complaints from natives about the late M. Rabinek's treatment of them. He, I knew from personal observation, when travelling for weeks together, was very good to natives, paying them well and treating them well in every possible way. . . . As far as my experience goes, M. G. M. Rabinek always did his best to conform to the laws of this country, and the natives to-day speak of him as a good man."

M. Ludwig Deuss, writing to his firm from Karonga in 1900, gives the following impression of M. Rabinek:

"Rabinek interests me by his enterprising character. He is a man of good education and learning, and has the valuable capacity to earn the confidence and affection of the natives."

---

member and the docile instrument—a somewhat contradictory statement, by the way.—" Une affaire de gros sous," *Tribune Congolaise*, August, 1902.

* Among these firms may be mentioned the African Lakes Corporation; Keiller's African Trading Co., Ltd., Glasgow; Ludwig Deuss & Co.; Teixeira de Mattos & Co.; E. H. C. Michahelles & Co.; and Prins & Stuerken.

† In a letter written to a correspondent, and published in the *West African Mail*.

THE CASE OF GUSTAV MARIA RABINEK

Some six years ago Rabinek paid a visit to Europe, stayed with his relatives in Vienna, and gave a lecture on Central African trade before the Chamber of Commerce of that city.

Rabinek's head-quarters, and the centre of his trading operations, were at Kazembe, in the British Central Africa Protectorate. He seems to have had agents travelling about in various directions, amongst others in the South-Eastern District of the Congo State, commonly known as the Katanga Country—directing that portion of his trade from Kamambas on the British side of the Luapula, which river forms the boundary between British and Congo State territory. That district was absolutely closed to the Congo State Authorities, being largely in the power of numerous bands of revolted soldiery,* with whom apparently the natives of the country were in sympathetic co-operation.† But if the district was closed to the Belgians, it was not closed to Rabinek, to whose legitimate trade neither the "rebels" nor the natives offered any opposition. How were Rabinek's trading operations viewed at first by the officials of the Congo State in the nearest stations to the scene of his commercial activity, and what was the former's attitude towards them? In view of the fact that the Congo State Authorities were incapable of exercising any influence whatever in many parts of the Congo State's sphere where Rabinek was pursuing his legitimate business, the Austrian trader might have been excused had he ignored their existence. But he did nothing of the kind. He showed himself on the contrary, as solicitous of regularising his position with the Congo State Authorities, as he had been in conforming to the regulations in vogue in the British Protectorate. The first available official record of his relations with the Congo State Authorities dates back to September 10, 1899, in the shape of a licence for trading in the Congo, dated September 10, 1899, signed Cerckel,‡ official in charge of the Congo State Station at Kilwa, and reading as follows :

"Le porteur de la présente patente ayant acquitté la taxe annuelle de *dix francs* établie par l'ordonnance de M. le Gouverneur-Général, en date du 29 Aout, 1896, est autorisé à opérer sur le téritoire de l' Etat.

---

* A portion of it is still held by them. See Chapters XVII. and XVIII.
† *Vide* published testimony of M. Lévêque, Director of the Katanga Company. Appendix.
‡ As showing the excellent terms existing between this Congo State official and Rabinek, I may quote the following sentence from a letter written to the latter by the former on September 10, 1899: "Vos capitaos sont partis ce matin vers le sud : je leur souhaite beaucoup de chance dans leur entreprise." The writer signs, " Your devoted " ("Votre dévoué ") Cerckel.

"Nom et prénoms du porteur de la patente : Rabinek G. M.
"Qualité ou profession : commercant.
"Signalement : {Taille :
{Signes particuliers :
"Date de la délivrance de la patente : 10 Septembre, 1899.
"Id. de l'éxpiration de la validité de la patente : 9 Septembre, 1900.
"A. Kilwa, le 10 Septembre, 1899.
"Le receveur des impots ff^{ons},
"CERCKEL, LEON."

To this trading licence, Rabinek added two others. One dated February 4, 1900, involving a charge of 500 francs, and reading as follows :

"ÉTAT INDÉPENDANT DU CONGO

"PERMIS DE PORT D'ARMES.
"No. 17.
"(1) M. Rabinek, Gustave Maria.
"(2) Commerçant.
Est autorisé à porter les armes renseignées ci-dessous dans le territoire de l'État Indépendent du Congo pendant un terme de cinq années consécutives à dater du présent permis.

Nombre (en toutes lettres).	Désignation et Description.	Lettre et Numeros.
deux	Lee-Metford	Tan No. 1 et 2
un	Jeffreys-Metford	i No. 3
un	Mauser Mod. 88	i No. 4
trois	Martini-Henri	i No. 5, 6, 7
un	Mauser Mod. 71	i No. 8
deux	Martini-Henry	i No. 9, 10
un	Express rifle calibre 461	i No. 11
un	Fusil du chasse	i No. 12
vingt-cinq	Fusils a piston	i No. 13 à 37

"Recu 500 frcs.
"O. HENNEBERT.
"Albertville, le 4 Fevrier, 1900.
"Le fonctionnaire délégué par le Gouverneur-Général,
"(L.S.) O. HENNEBERT."

The other of equal date, and reading as follows :

"ÉTAT INDÉPENDANT DU CONGO.

"PERMIS DE PORT D'ARMES Provisoire.
"Pour la chasse à l'Eléphant.
"No. 18.
"(1) M. Rabinek, Gustave Maria.
"(2) Commerçant.
Est autorisé à porter les armes renseignées ci-dessous dans le territoire de l'État Indépandant du Congo pendant un terme de cinq années consécutives à dater du présent permis.

THE CASE OF GUSTAV MARIA RABINEK

Nombre (en toutes lettres).	Désignation et Description.	Lettre et Numeros.
deux	Lee-Metford	Tan No. 1 et 2
un	Jeffreys-Metford	i No. 3
un	Mauser Mod. 88	i No. 4
trois	Martini-Henri	i No. 5, 6, 7
un	Mauser Mod. 71	i No. 8
deux	Martini-Henry	i No. 9, 10
un	Express rifle calibre 461	i No. 11
un	Fusil de chasse	i No. 12
vingt-cinq	Fusils a piston	i No. 13 à 37

"Recu 500 frcs.
"O. HENNEBERT.
  "Albertville, le 4 Fevrier, 1900.
  "Le fonctionnaire délégué par le Gouverneur-Général,
    "(L.S.) O. HENNEBERT."

Both these licences refer apparently to one lot of guns: one licence allows him to carry them, the other to shoot elephants with them. In addition to the cost of licence, Rabinek paid 1950 francs customs duty on their importation.

Thus Rabinek went out of his way to conform to the regulations of the Congo State, although no Congo State official dared show his face in the district where the Austrian was trading. Similarly, when the Katanga Company in the person of M. Lévêque, its manager, subsequently appeared upon the scene, Rabinek—having already paid pretty heavily for official licences—came to an understanding with the former, whereby, in exchange for the recognition by that Company of his right to trade in territory assigned to it (which, as may be gathered from M. Lévêque's testimony, consisted, partly at any rate, of a district where Rabinek had been trading for years previous to that Company's resuscitation) he agreed to pay the Company £10 per annum for a licence for each European engaged by him "to collect ivory in the territories of the Katanga Company, which are situated within the rebel zone," * plus one franc tax per kilo on rubber and ivory, "bought and remitted in our hands before leaving the Congo, and the obligation to plant 150 plants of rubber for every ton exported." The agreement was signed on September 23, 1900, in ignorance, of course, that the Katanga Company, as such, had meanwhile ceased to exist, owing to the absorption of that Company by the Congo State Government, as detailed in the next chapter.

Such was the character and such the proceedings of the man whom the Congo State Press has called a "filibuster," and whom the Congo State Authorities illegally sentenced to one

* *Vide* Agreement between Rabinek and the Katanga Company. Appendix.

year's imprisonment; despatched across Africa in charge of native soldiers, and treated * from beginning to end with cynical, calculated cruelty, which lays the moral responsibility for his death directly at their door.

* " Treated as a common criminal," as Major Gibbons puts it, *op. cit.*

CHAPTER XXIII

THE KATANGA COMPANY AND THE CONGO STATE—
RABINEK'S RELATIONS WITH BOTH

"Foreigners, without distinction, shall enjoy protection of their persons and property."—Article V., Berlin Act.
"No doubt exists on the strict and literal meaning to be assigned to the word, 'Trade.' It means exclusively 'Traffic'—*the unlimited option for every one to sell and to buy : to import and to export products and manufactured articles.* In this respect no privileged position can be created; business remains open and unrestricted for free competition on commercial lines."—BARON LAMBERMONT (Belgian representative at the Berlin Conference).
"Liberty of commerce is complete in the Congo and is not restricted by any monopoly or privilege. Every one is free to sell all produce in which THE TRAFFIC IS LEGITIMATE."— Official defence of the Congo State, "Bulletin Officiel," No. 6, June, 1903.

ON April 15, 1891, the parent of the Thys group of Belgian Congo Companies, *La Compagnie pour le commerce et l'Industrie,* founded the Katanga Company, *Compagnie du Katanga,* with a capital of 3,000,000 francs in 6000 " privileged " shares of 500 francs each : 18,000 ordinary shares were also issued "without designation of value." * The mineral value of the Katanga District was supposed to be considerable, and preferential rights over all the mines were granted to the Company, by the Congo State Government for twenty years, with further privileges, on condition that, *inter alia,* two steamers should be launched on the affluents of the Upper Congo or the adjacent lakes, and at least three stations established within the district. The object of the Company was that of conducting " all industrial enterprise, public and private works, *commerce,* agriculture, etc." Article 1 refers to the Company " exploiting " the regions allotted to it " from the point of view of colonisation, agriculture, *commerce,* and mining." Article 3 authorises the Company to "*constitute* by its own resources, or by special companies, enterprises of colonisation or *exploitation of the soil,* and subsoil, etc." The Congo State received under this agreement 600 of the " privileged " shares, and 1800 of the

* *Bilans Congolais,* Alphonse Poskin, Brussels, 1900.

ordinary shares. The Katanga Company received from the Congo State, in full proprietorship, a third of the territories, "belonging to the Domaine of the State, situated in the territories referred to in the present Convention"; and the concession for 99 years of the mining rights in the conceded territories."* Thus the Katanga Company received from the Congo State in full proprietorship a third of the so-called "vacant" territories of the State situated in the Katanga region.

So little were these territories "vacant," that the Katanga Company, which lost no time in despatching an expedition to explore and open up its concession, found therein a ruler, Msiri, who, proving recalcitrant—that is the right word, I think —was promptly shot while the "blue banner with the golden star" was run up at Bunkeia, his capital, December, 1901. So little were they "vacant" that the Company's second expedition was entirely wiped out † in May, 1892. But that is by the way—merely an illustration of the appropriateness of that charming word "vacant."

Just about this time, the famous circulars and decrees embodying the new policy of the Congo State came out, and as the Congo State Government, through the obliging intermediary of Sir Hugh Gilzean Reid, has recently taken the opportunity of reminding us, ‡ "The exploitation of india-rubber was forbidden in the territory of the Katanga by virtue of the decree of October 30, 1892"; § or, in other words, the Katanga territory was by that decree closed to merchants. The Katanga Company then virtually became moribund, and so remained until July, 1899, when it was galvanised into life again. On December 18 of that year (1899) M. Georges Brugmann,‖ presiding over the annual meeting of the *Compagnie du Congo pour le Commerce et l'Industrie*, made the following statement:

"The Katanga Company has at last emerged from its period of inactivity which circumstances, foreign to its wishes, had imposed upon it.

---

* *Bulletin Official*, September, 1891, and *annexe* to same. The Convention was signed in March, 1891.

† By Arabs under a misapprehension. The Arabs took them for State people! (Wauters), *op. cit.*

‡ *Vide* the Congo State's official reply, *viâ* Sir Hugh Gilzean Reid to my articles on the Rabinek affair in the *Morning Post*.

§ *Vide* Appendix.

‖ M. Brugmann, it may be remembered, protested against the circulars and decrees of 1891 and 1892, together with Messrs. Thys, Urban, etc., "To forbid the natives selling their ivory and rubber from their forests and plains, which constitute their hereditary birthright and in which they have traded from time immemorial, is a violation of natural rights," etc

KATANGA COMPANY AND CONGO STATE 269

In execution of its convention with the Congo State on March 12, 1891, the Company has sent two steamers and four lighters to the Tanganyika region, to be launched on Lakes Tanganyika and Mweru. . . . Let me add that the extraordinary meeting of the shareholders of the Katanga Company, held on July 12 last, approved the resolution adopted by the Company's Directorate, in consequence of the correspondence exchanged with the Congo State, following upon which a mixed commission to delimit the conceded territories has been sent to Africa." *

The Katanga Company was thus at last to benefit by its original arrangement with the State—that is to say, conduct all industrial enterprise, to *trade*, to develop its property by (*inter alia*) *commerce*, to create (*inter alia*) subsidiary *commercial* enterprises. It is important to bear this in mind.

So a manager was appointed by the Company and sent out, a M. Gustave Lévêque, an engineer and a Frenchman, I believe. M. Lévêque, who was handed a power of attorney of the most extensive kind,† did not, we gather from his statement ‡ made at a later date, find matters in a very pleasant condition when he got out there. The natives were up in arms against the State, more or less everywhere, owing to the organised raiding carried on by the Congo State soldiery. § Some parts were in the hands of the rebels, the officials had no power outside gunshot of their stations, there was no rubber in the neighbourhood of Lake Tanganyika, and the quantity procurable in the Lake Mweru District did not suffice to pay the Company's expenses. It may be readily understood, therefore, that the manager of the Katanga Company was very pleased to make an arrangement with Rabinek to work a portion of the vast and, under the circumstances, unprofitable territory made over to his Company. "Rabinek," remarks M. Lévêque in his published declaration, ‖ "reckoned to be able to collect 100 tons of rubber per annum, which would have brought in a profit of 100,000 francs (£4,000) *per annum*, to the Company without any risks, or disbursements, all the more so, as we

---

* The resuscitation of the Katanga Company "in consequence" of the correspondence above referred to by M. Brugmann, appears to have had a marked effect upon the Company's shares, for in July, 1899, we find the 500 francs "privileged" shares (of which, be it remembered, the State held 600) quoted on the Antwerp Stock Exchange at 1250 francs, and the ordinary shares (of which, be it remembered, the State held 1800) of undesignated value, quoted at 895 francs, giving a total capitalisation at these valuations for the 6000 privileged and 18,000 ordinaries, of 23,610,000 francs, or close upon £1,000,000 sterling.
† *Vide* Appendix.
‡ *Vide* Appendix.
§ The condition of affairs is eloquently described by Mr. Dugald Campbell (Appendix).
‖ *Vide* Appendix.

were not sufficiently strong to enter the territories of the rebels." The arrangement was one which would naturally commend itself to a man in the position of the manager of the Katanga Company. Here was a trader, well known throughout the country, upright and highly thought of, who had been doing business for some years with the natives in a district which now formed part of the Company's territory, but which no Belgian dared enter owing to the detestation in which they were regarded by the inhabitants,* and to the circumstances that it was held by mutineers, whom neither the State nor the Company were strong enough to tackle. This trader volunteered to pay the Katanga Company certain royalties from which the Company stood to benefit largely, without going to any expense or trouble. Clearly the manager would have displayed singular neglect of his Company's interests had he refused an offer which had everything to recommend it. He appears, moreover, to have exercised particular care in defining the agreement. The privileges conferred upon Rabinek were very modest, when the considerable royalties he was expected to pay are borne in mind. They consisted in a licence conferring upon Rabinek the right, for five years, of trading in rubber and ivory, in the portion of the Company's territories, *which was held by the rebels.* That was all. No territorial rights were granted of any description. It was further stipulated in the agreement that over and above the royalties to be paid, Rabinek should undertake to plant 150 rubber trees for every ton of rubber he exported; that he should pass all his goods through the custom-house (which he had been regularly in the habit of doing before Lévêque came on the scene †), and conform generally with the laws of the country. The agreement, then, was nothing more than a trading licence, pure and simple, and one extremely favourable to the licensor, for it involved the acquisition of a revenue from territories which the licensor could not enter! ‡

The agreement was signed on September 23, 1900, as already stated, and after M. Lévêque, apparently at Rabinek's

---

* So ignorant were the Belgian officials even of the state of affairs in the "revolted district," that they asked Rabinek for information on the subject.—*Vide* M. Lévêque's testimony.

† We find him importing in April, 1900, *inter alia*, 22,080 yards of Bombay cloth; 11,360 yards of printed cottons; 1,276,000 kilos of beads, etc. Total value, 29,165·52 francs: customs duty levied, 1749·93 francs, signed as received by " Le Receveur, f. fons C. Haubroe" at the " Bureau de Pweto, No. 63·85." In May, 1900, at the same place, *inter alia*, 800 yards printed cottons, etc. Total value, 1278·60 francs: customs duty levied, 77·26 francs, etc.

‡ *Vide* Agreement, Appendix.

KATANGA COMPANY AND CONGO STATE

request as a business precaution, had submitted his power of attorney for inspection to a British official in the adjacent territory.* It is important to remember the date. It is also important to bear in mind, before we leave Central Africa for Europe, in order the better to piece together the different parts of the narrative, that before obtaining his licence from the Katanga Company, Rabinek, as I have already explained, had obtained hunting and trading permits and licences *from the officials of the Congo State Government*, for which permits and licences he had paid the sum (including import duty) of 2450 francs. Rabinek was, then, in the position of having fulfilled every formality which could possibly be required of him.

Meanwhile, events were occurring in Brussels, the effect of which was to alter profoundly the status of the Katanga Company, and to convert it from a more or less private concern of the *Rue Bréderode* (Colonel Thys) group of genuine trading Companies into a State institution on the lines of the other Trusts of the *Domaine Privé*, but, if possible, with an even greater official complexion. On June 15, 1900—a little more than three months before the Katanga Company, in the person of its manager in Africa, granted Rabinek his licence—a Convention had been signed in Brussels between the Katanga Company on the one part, and the Congo State Government on the other. The first article of the Convention provided for the creation of a "Special Committee" to ensure and direct a joint exploitation of all the territories belonging to the Domaine of the State, and to the Katanga Company, "between the 5th degree of south latitude to the 24 degrees 10 min. of longitude east of Greenwich, a straight line joining that point at its intersection with the 6th degree of south latitude, with the 23rd degree 54 min. of longitude east, with the 23rd degree 54 min. of longitude, and the southern and eastern frontiers of the Congo State." According to Article 1, the Committee had "the most extended powers of administration, gestation, and alienation, without exception or reserve." Article 2 provided that the Committee should be composed of six members, "four of these members, and amongst them the president, *who will have the preponderating voice, will be named by the Congo State*, and two by the Katanga Company." Article 5 reads as follows: "All advantages and profits obtained from the exploitation mentioned in Article 1, and all expenses, charges, or losses, etc., will be distributed by the Committee of Management, as to two-thirds for the Congo State, and as to one-third for the Katanga Company." The *Compagnie du Katanga* became transformed into the *Comité Spécial du Katanga*. Its

* *Vide* Agreement, Appendix.

management and directorship were established on the following lines: The interests of the Congo State were represented by M. H. Droogmans, General Secretary of the Finance Department of the Congo State, President;* Messrs. N. Arnold, Director of the Service of Agriculture of the Domaine, and of "Central Book-keeping"; E. de Keyser, Director of the Finance Department; R. Lombard, Director of the Department of the Interior—all "members." The Katanga Company's interests were represented by two directors of that Company.† The *Comité Spécial du Katanga* was authorised to raise, arm, and equip its own soldiers.

Thus the "exploitation" of the Katanga country became to all intents and purposes vested in the State, and the State was to retain two-thirds of the proceeds of the sale in Europe of the rubber and ivory obtained therefrom *à titre d'impôt*—which is what "exploitation" signifies! There appears to be some good ground for the presumption that the Katanga Company was forced against its will into absorption by the Congo State,‡ but that in itself is not a matter of peculiar interest, except for the additional evidence it provides of the intention of the Congo State to be the absolutely supreme "exploitationist" throughout the Congo territories from Leopoldville to the Great Lakes. §

Although the Convention was signed on June 15, 1900, it was only on August 9 of that year that the Katanga Company advised its manager in Africa of the fact, the advice reaching him on November 7, not quite two months *after* the conferring of the licence upon Rabinek. ||

Meanwhile, the manager of the Katanga Company had written home to his directors, informing them of the Rabinek agreement. It was repudiated in a letter dated January 12, 1901, which reached the manager on April 11, and was communicated by him on April 20 to Rabinek in the presence of

---

* One of the "Committee of Three" for the unpublished revenues derived from the *Domaine de la Couronne*, from the labours and the slaughter of the natives within that sanctuary.

† Messrs. Gambier and Delcomunne.

‡ *Vide* Lévêque's published declaration. Appendix.

§ Of which we now have further evidence in the absorption of the *Anversoise*.

|| By this means, of course, a legitimate barter trade in rubber conducted by third parties in the Katanga territory would become "illegitimate" on the strength of the decree of 1892—itself internationally illegal—prohibiting the sale and purchase of rubber in the State's "Domaine," to which the Katanga territory had reverted with the disappearance of legitimate trade within it, represented by the Katanga Company. That such a contention is in flagrant violation with the Berlin Act, goes without saying.

GUSTAV MARIA RABINEK
As a student. Aged 18

GUSTAV MARIA RABINEK
As a cadet. Aged 22

KATANGA COMPANY AND CONGO STATE 273

M. Weyns, a retired Belgian officer sent out by the *Comité Spécial du Katanga* to take M. Lévêque's place—Rabinek declining to admit the validity of the refusal. Rumours had about that time, seemingly, reached Africa that something was in the wind, because on April 8 we find Rabinek writing to a friend as follows:

"You will have heard that serious complications have arisen between the Katanga Company and the Congo Free State Government, which may have some influence on my concession. I have not so far though received any official information,* but I learn from my agent in the Congo Region that the Belgian Government will not allow the export of rubber and ivory."

To his relatives in Austria he writes: "The ex-major Weyns has, I learn, succeeded Lévêque. It is rumoured he will not respect the concessions made by former directors."

He little knew when he penned those lines that a warrant had been out for his arrest since December, 1900, on the ostensible charge of violating the rubber law of 1892!

This chapter may be fittingly concluded by quoting from M. Lévêque's published declaration made at Abercorn on August 12, 1901:

"Weyns sent Rabinek with the Company's steamer to Kasanga † to buy provisions for his officers, who were short of provisions at Sumbu.‡ These provisions have not even yet been paid for, although they were consumed at Sumbu, as the Europeans at that place will easily corroborate. As soon as the steamer returned from Sumbu, Weyns left on April 23 for Mtoa,§ and came back on May 4 to Mvoa, informing us that a warrant for arrest, which had been applied for some time before from Boma by Commandant Hennebert, had just arrived. . . . He then spoke of Rabinek, pretending that the latter had furnished the rebels with weapons by sending armed *capitaos* to hunt the elephant in that country. On May 17 Major Weyns left Sumbu for Mpueto, and on June 7 M. Richard came back to Sumbu. I learned from the latter that he had seen Rabinek a free prisoner at Mpueto, and that he had been able to speak to him. On June 18, 1901, the German steamer *Von Wissman* arrived at Sumbu: bringing us the news that Rabinek at Mtoa had been

---

* Major Weyns wrote to Rabinek repudiating on behalf of the *Comité Spécial du Katanga* the agreement concluded by the Katanga Company with Rabinek. The letter is dated March 30, 1901, but it is obvious from Rabinek's above quoted letter that he had not received it on April 8. A copy of Major Weyns' letter is before me. It contains the following sentence, a significant comment upon the Berlin Act! "Seul le Comité peut récolter les produits de son domaine, dans toute la région qui lui est concédée."

† In German territory, east shore of Lake Tanganyika. Weyns and his party had come out by the East African route *viâ* German East Africa.

‡ Weyns' first step, therefore, was to utilise the services of Rabinek!
§ M'Towa.

condemned to one year's imprisonment and a 1000 francs fine, and that he was being compelled to undertake a journey from Mtoa to Boma to be judged once more, the charges against him being very serious, *illegal introduction of weapons and ammunition into the Congo*. . . . Such a journey from Mtoa to Boma certainly means death (*est certainment la mort*)."

That there was not a word of truth in the charge of supplying the rebels with arms and ammunition, and that the charge was never officially preferred by the State authorities on the spot, and has never been officially preferred by the Executive in Europe, will presently be shown. That Rabinek would never reach Boma alive appears to have been the belief entertained by other local Europeans besides M. Lévêque.

CHAPTER XXIV

THE PLOT AND THE ARREST

"Never in the Congo, so far as we know, have requests to buy natural products been addressed to the rightful owners. Up to now the only attempts made have been to buy the produce which has been stolen, and the State, as was its duty, has had those guilty of these unlawful attempts prosecuted."—Congo Government's reply to British Note.

"The State can hardly be blamed because, in face of the almost universal inaction on the part of private individuals, it endeavoured to turn its territories to account by working its domain lands, either on its own account or through others."—Ibid.

"The commercial field open to private persons on the Congo never has been and is not limited."—Ibid.

IT has been previously stated that Rabinek, before the Katanga Company appeared upon the scene, had obtained a licence for "trading on the Congo" from the Congo State official in charge of the Kilwa Station (September 10, 1899), and two licences from Commandant Hennebert, the District Commissioner of "Tanganyika-Katanga," one for "hunting elephants for five years," the other for carrying thirty-nine guns" (February, 1900). Similar licences appear to have been granted to other Europeans, such as Mr. G. T. Hilpert, a German trader, who had also obtained a licence from M. Lévêque, the manager of the Katanga Company, in July, 1900, for purchasing and gathering rubber in the Katanga Company's territory. Indeed, it would seem to be well established that prior to the absorption of the Katanga Company by the Congo State Government in June, 1900, *becoming known in Africa*, the officials of that Government, being powerless to exercise any influence outside the immediate vicinity of their stations, were not loath to collect revenue from traders in British and German territory out of such licences, and for the time being tacitly allowed independent merchants to carry on a legitimate barter trade within Congo State territory.

The substitution of the *Comité Spécial du Katanga*—or, in other words, the State—for the Katanga Company however, involving as it did the clearly declared intention of the Government to itself "exploit" the Katanga territory, introduced an entirely new element into the situation. It was not likely that the Congo State Government, which, according to some accounts, had forced the Katanga Company to "amalgamate," would tolerate lesser fry interfering with its plans, and it became necessary, therefore, to repudiate the trading and hunting licences its agents had issued, and to clear these smaller fry out of the country. The ingenuity of the Authorities of the Congo State is never at fault in matters of this kind, whether the undertaking it is desirable to slide out of is international or personal in nature. In this case the means lay ready at hand, for did not the Decree of 1892 declare that the exploitation of rubber was prohibited in the Katanga region?* True, the "law" had remained by force of circumstances somewhat of a dead letter in that portion of the Katanga territory neighbouring the British possessions! But now that the Congo State, in the shape of the *Comité Spécial du Katanga* had decided to send out an expedition for the purpose of "exploiting" it in the interest of the "Government," it was obviously necessary to revive the law, or rather, to act as if it had always been in force. Thus could a legal basis † be devised in order to justify the expulsion of the inconvenient "third parties."

That Rabinek should have been singled out as an example to the "others"— to quote the statement attributed by M. Lévêque to Major Weyns—is not altogether surprising. He was the principal independent merchant doing business in the country, and his downfall or disappearance would serve as a salutary example.‡

* In violation of the Berlin Act.
† Although manifestly illegal, internationally.
‡ Mr. G. T. Hilpert, writing to the *West African Mail*, from Sumbu, Bismarkburg, Tanganyika (German territory), May 21, 1903, gives the following account of his treatment at the hands of the Congo State Authorities in the South-Eastern District. He obtained a licence in July, 1900, from the manager of the Katanga Company to trade in rubber in the Katanga territories. On the strength of his agreement, he entered the Katanga country with £1000 of trade goods. He paid Customs duties on his goods at Moliro in September of the same year. Some of his native traders were arrested by Congo soldiery. He started off to M'Toa to protest to the Belgian Commandant. Meanwhile the Congo soldiers broke into his factory, stole many of his effects, and seized 75 loads of his property, which they took to M'Towa. The Commandant at M'Towa, after seeing Hilpert's papers, apologised, and restored the loads. In November, Hilpert returned to Moliro with some rubber, leaving his head men and goods at his factory. At Moliro the *Chef de Poste* produced the letter from the Commandant at M'Towa, ordering the confiscation of all Hilpert's rubber. Hilpert then went to M'Towa again, and was told he had better wait, as the Congo State and the Katanga Company would "amalgamate." He placed his case before the

What passed between the Congo State and its agents we shall probably never know, but we are justified in assuming—and the presumption, moreover, is a common-sense one—that the representatives of the Congo State Government in the Katanga region received orders from Brussels, that they knew of the contemplated absorption of the Katanga Company by the State, and that they were instructed in consequence.

A month after Rabinek obtained from the Congo State official, Cerckel, his licence to trade, it was withdrawn, so far as trading in *rubber* was concerned, and the caravans which Rabinek had sent into the country on the strength of that licence were seized. In July he seems to have got a letter from a Commandant Verdick, in which the following passage occurs:

"It is forbidden in the most formal manner, and until the Government has adopted measures on the subject, to exploit or buy rubber in the region which I administrate."

A nice sort of communication for the representative of a Government which, in Europe, asserts that "trade is free" on the Congo! The letter further says: "Your obstinacy in not conforming to the existing rules and decrees renders you liable to the most serious repressive judicial measures." In his reply (July 8) Rabinek expresses surprise at the communication. "Up to this moment I have done nothing against the existing regulations which gives you the right to call me obstinate." He says that his agents have been told not to buy *rubber*, but only to buy ivory, and he concludes by hoping that "all differences of opinion may be arranged upon my arrival at your station." *

We gather from these communications that some of the Congo State officials were seeking to deprive Rabinek of the rights under his trade licence to trade in rubber, that Rabinek disputed their right to do so, and was prepared to discuss matters of "opinion" on a convenient opportunity, meanwhile instructing his agents only to buy ivory, which, apparently, was not objected to.

Now, setting aside for a moment the Protocols and the Act of the Berlin Conference which prohibited any obstacle to

German Government. So far he does not appear to have got any compensation or satisfaction.—*West African Mail*, September 4, 1903.
  Since penning the above, I have heard from a correspondent in Central Africa that the German Government has succeeded in getting £1000 compensation for Mr. Hilpert. I do not guarantee the information, but I think it is likely to be accurate. There are obvious reasons for King Leopold to keep on good terms with the German Foreign Office.

* I am indebted to Dr. Rudolf Hertz, of Hamburg, for the documents from which the above extracts are taken.

freedom of trade, it is exceedingly doubtful whether the local authorities in the Katanga District had any legal grounds whatever for interfering with the free exercise of the Austrian's business, seeing that, at the time they were so interfering, the Katanga country had been handed over to the Katanga Company. Unquestionably they had no such right from the moment that M. Lévêque, the Katanga Company's manager in Africa, arrived on the scene, prior to that gentleman being officially apprised of the absorption of the Katanga Company by the Congo Government.

However, to cut short such matters of "opinion," and to further regularise his position, Rabinek, as we have seen, made an arrangement in September of the same year—1900—with the representative of the Company which had received "full proprietorship" of the territory, involving the right to develop its property by *trade*, to conduct *trading* enterprise, or to create subsidiary *trading* enterprises.

It is quite beside the mark, therefore, for the Congo Government to argue, as it has done, that repeated warnings "were addressed to Rabinek by the officials of the State that his trade was 'illegal.'"

What is not beside the mark are the facts that Rabinek applied to local Government officials for permits to trade, to carry thirty-nine guns, and to shoot elephants, for which licenses he paid pretty heavily; that he conducted his trading operations in a legitimate manner, which is proved by the Custom House returns of the port of Mpueto; and, finally, that when Lévêque came out as supreme authority in the country, he made the necessary arrangements with that gentleman for the continuation of his business.

So much for the Austrian's relations with the local Government Authorities, and subsequently with the manager of the Katanga Company, prior to the news of the fresh alteration in that Company's affairs, which had occurred in Brussels, reaching either Rabinek or Lévêque.

As we have seen, the news of the absorption of the Katanga Company by the Congo Government only reached that Company's manager in Africa on November 7, not quite two months after the arrangement with Rabinek had been concluded.

The technical effect of that fresh alteration in the Katanga Company's affairs was, of course, to vest once again in the Congo Government—disguised under the name of *Comité Spécial du Katanga*—the products of the soil in the Katanga country, which for a short period had been made over to the Katanga Company, and consequently to revive once more the Decree of 1892 forbidding trade in rubber, which decree had

THE PLOT AND THE ARREST 279

technically lapsed during the period when the rubber of the country was vested in the Katanga Company.

Henceforth the one end and aim of the officials of the Congo Government was to eliminate Rabinek, who, *paying* for that rubber which both *commerce* and morality recognises as belonging to the man who gathers it, appeared as a formidable competitor to a Government which claims to ownership over that article both prior and subsequent to its collection.

The story of the proceedings of the Congo Government officials towards this desired end is really almost incredible. A warrant for Rabinek's arrest was applied for. The document reads as follows :

"MANDAT—D'ARRÊT.

"*Pro Justitia.*

"Nous Officiers du Ministère Public près le tribunal territorial d'Albertville.

"Vu les pièces de la procedure instruite à charge de Rabinek, négociant de nationalité autrichienne sans résidence connue, prévenu de contravention aux articles 3 et 10 du décret du 30 Octobre, 1892, sur l'exploitation du caoutchouc ou tout au moins de recel, fait prévu par l'article 29 du code pénal.

"Attendu que le prévenu n'est pas présent et qu'il est signalé comme continuant à contrevenir aux articles précités. Vu l'article 28 du décret du 27 Avril, 1869.

"Mandons et ordonnons que le susdit Rabinek soit arrêté et conduit à la maison de détention d'Albertville.

"Requerons tous agents de la Force Publique auxquels le present mandat sera exhibé de prêter main forte pour son exécution, à l'effet de quoi nous avons signé le présent mandat.

"Fait à Albertville, le 17 Decembre, 1900.
"L'Officer du Ministère Public,
(Sig.) "DUPONT."

Major Weyns and Captain Tonneau, both of the *Comité Spécial du Katanga*, told Mr. Alfred Sharpe H.M. Commissioner for British Central Africa, that the warrant for Rabinek's arrest had been issued by the State Procurator at Boma (Africa, No. 4, 1903), and Major Weyns told Lévêque the same thing. But the document itself is signed as above and dated as above. It is, of course, possible that Dupont was acting upon instructions from Boma, but it is at least curious that the Congo State, in its communication to the *Morning Post*, distinctly states that " M. Dupont issued on December 17, 1900, a warrant against Rabinek," and makes no allusion to a warrant from Boma.

What is more important is to note that the warrant accuses the Austrian of one offence, and of one offence only, viz.

violation of the rubber laws.—Decree of October 30, 1892. The judicial formulas necessary to Rabinek's ruin being thus complete, all that remained to be done, one might have supposed, was to arrest him. Not so, however.

Article 10 of the Decree of October 30, 1892, under which the warrant of arrest was issued, provides that violation of the law shall be visited by a fine of 10 to 1000 francs, and to *imprisonment ("Servitude pénale") of one day to a month, or to one of these penalties only.** *Had Rabinek been indicted on this charge alone, he could have got out of the clutches of the State, and made himself uncommonly unpleasant afterwards on the strength* (1) *of the free trade clauses of the Berlin Act,* (2) *of the official licences granted him, for which he had paid, and* (3) *of the licence granted him by the Katanga Company to benefit by which he had opened large credits with European firms.*

So, with truly devilish ingenuity, a charge of gun-running was concocted against Rabinek, which should be made to appear all the more plausible since his trading relations with the "rebels" was known to every one, and, indeed, expressly recognised in his agreement with the Katanga Company.† This charge, locally made, might or might not be afterwards officially endorsed; *but in the meantime it would serve its purpose*—and it did so serve, as we shall see. That these charges were secretly made, we learn from M. Lévêque's testimony, who mentions having received on December 6 a note from the Congo State official at Mpueto, asking if a certain gun taken from a native headman had been given to the latter by himself (Lévêque) or by Rabinek; and again that the newly arrived manager of the *Comité Spécial du Katanga* had "insinuated before him (Lévêque) that Rabinek had sold arms to the rebels." ‡

It may be as well to state now, before dealing with the

* See Penal Clause, Appendix.
† *Vide* Agreement, Appendix.
‡ The *Central African Times*, Blantyre, of February 21, 1903, publishes an interview with Major Weyns, in which the latter is reported as having said, " I might tell you that it is a matter of common knowledge that Rabinek and some of his agents *had been found* to have supplied arms and ammunition to the rebels in the Congo Free State, and as this portion of the country referred to was under martial law, he could have been tried for this and executed. The officials did not wish to do this, however." In the same interview, Major Weyns is reported to have declared, " I may say that the *Comité Spécial du Katanga*, is an entirely private Company "—a fair sample of that gentleman's veracity ! *Vide* text of agreement, Appendix, and Weyns' letter to Rabinek. See also Lévêque's published declaration, which, in this respect, at any rate, is amply corroborated by Weyns' own reported declarations to the *Central African Times*.

THE PLOT AND THE ARREST

irregular proceedings which characterised the trial of Rabinek, that no jot or tittle of evidence has ever been publicly produced by Rabinek's persecutors to substantiate the charge. Apart from the specific nature of the accusation made in the warrant for arrest, viz. that of violating the Decree of 1892, in respect to the collection of rubber, the judgment itself, to which I shall subsequently return, explicitly repeats the accusation mentioned in the warrant; while the Congo State, in its communication to the *Morning Post*, justifies its proceedings towards Rabinek solely on the same ground. In addition to this amply sufficient *official* testimony, we have an abundance of outside evidence. Several men acquainted with the nature of Rabinek's business affairs flatly deny that he ever traded in arms. M. Lévêque does the same, and Mr. Robert E. A. Young, Native Commissioner for Northern Rhodesia, in a letter to a correspondent, dated November 15, 1902, and published in the *West African Mail* of September 11, 1903, says:

"A great part of the late G. M. Rabinek's goods for the Congo Free State passed through my hands,* and if I had seen any importation of rifles or ammunition, I would have detained such until I received orders in writing from the Civil Commissioner to allow such to be sent on."

The evidence of Mr. Alfred Sharpe, H.M. Commissioner for Central Africa, is equally conclusive:

"I could ascertain nothing," he says, "to show that Rabinek traded in firearms or ammunition; these could, I think, only have been obtained by the Nyassa route, and he appears to have received none from this direction." †

The charge may therefore be summarily dismissed. It had not the slightest foundation, and was merely used locally at that time to gain an end which, it is obvious, must have been deliberately planned.

And now we approach the moment when the drama about to be enacted gathers in the intensity of its human interest. Lévêque's declaration shows us that Rabinek was in April, 1904,—four months after the issue of the warrant for his arrest—actually assisting Major Weyns to revictual his expedition in German territory! It is difficult to believe that he would have acted thus had he been aware at the time that a warrant was out for his arrest; but he evidently knew about it shortly afterwards, if we are to believe the agent at Chienji of the African Lakes Corporation. ‡

* That is to say, were imported through British territory.
† Africa, No. 4, 1903, page 3.
‡ Africa, No. 4, 1903, enclosure 5.

On May 14, 1901, Rabinek embarked at Chienji,* together with one of his agents, on the *Scotia*, a small steam launch plying on Lake Mweru and belonging to the African Lakes Corporation. The *Scotia* had cargo on board for the *Comité Spécial du Katanga*, consigned to Mpueto, and Rabinek had apparently arranged to charter the *Scotia* to convey him to Kazembe (British territory) after discharging the *Comité's* cargo. At half-past eleven on the morning of the 15th the *Scotia* anchored in British waters,† forty yards from the Congo State port of Mpueto. The captain landed after discharging the cargo, and went up to the station to get his papers signed; Rabinek remaining on board. ‡ The Congo State official asked the captain if Rabinek was on board, and, being answered in the affirmative, demanded that he should be handed over to him. § The captain declining, M. Chargois, the official in question, threatened to refuse to take delivery of the cargo, and said he would take steps to withdraw all the *Comité Spécial du Katanga's* transport work from the hands of the African Lakes Corporation—the captain's employers. The captain replied that he could do as he liked. Thereupon M. Chargois sent a lieutenant on board to arrest Rabinek. The name of this officer was Louis Saroléa, and on his way down to the boat he remarked to the captain, "That he did not think it a pleasant job to arrest a white man before natives." The party having boarded the *Scotia*, Lieutenant Saroléa descended into the cabin, and read out the warrant to Rabinek. We have two versions of what then took place, both supplied by Captain Milne. ||

The earlier version reads as follows:

"As it (the warrant) was in French, I did not understand what it contained. However, Rabinek said to me, 'I am arrested. What are you going to do in the matter, as I am on a British steamer?' I answered that I did not know international law on the subject, and did not see what I could do, as Mr. Chargois might have the right to arrest in a Congo State port. Rabinek then said he would go on shore and see the matter through. For the meantime, the lieutenant had been turning

---

* British territory.
† Africa, No. 4, 1903, page 3.
‡ According to the agent of the African Lakes Corporation at Chienji. Africa, No. 4, 1903.
§ *Vide* sworn declaration of A. J. C. Milne, in charge of the *Scotia*, before the British Consulate-General at Zomba. Africa, No. 4, 1903, page 5.
|| Captain Milne made two declarations, one before the British Consulate-General at Zomba (*op. cit.*) on February 16, 1903, and the other two months after the event took place, viz. August 24, 1901, before three witnesses. The latter was published in the *Morning Post*, in an article contributed by the author on the subject.

sick, as the steamer had been rolling a good deal, so he went on shore and waited till Rabinek came also. Then the two of them went up to the house together."

The latter version reads as follows :

"Rabinek, after hearing the warrant read, turned to me and asked me what I would do. The warrant was written in French, and I did not know more than a word or two. In reply to Mr. Rabinek, I stated it was for him to decide, and that he could either stop on board and allow them to take him by force, or else go on shore as he pleased. The officer at this point said he felt very sea-sick, and asked us to excuse him, and went on shore in the canoe. Mr. Rabinek, after some reflection, said, 'They evidently want to deprive me of my concession in the Katanga territory. I will go on shore, and see the matter through, even though they send me to Mtowa.'"

Thus did the unfortunate Austrian place himself in the hands of his enemies, conscious of the strength of his case, and little reckoning on what was in store for him. He appears to have spent a few days at Mpueto, a prisoner on parole unmolested, and lulled into a sense of false security. While there, he formally protested by letter against his treatment. He says in his letter that the first representation made to him by the Government since his arrangement with M. Lévêque has been the warrant of arrest. His letter contains the following important sentence: "I came by the *Scotia* to see M. Chargois *with the authority of Major Weyns.*"

He was then conveyed to Mtowa. Rabinek's state of mind at that time, his fearless determination to face his accusers, and to insist on having his rights respected, his unconsciousness of danger, or that anything more than an attempt to jockey him out of his agreement with the Katanga Company was on the *tapis*, is clearly shown in the following extract from a letter he wrote from Mpueto to one of his agents—a Mr. Hastings—the original of which is in my possession.

"Mpueto, May 16, 1901.

"I have been originally yesterday formally arrested, but am now free and I consider it the best to go through this mock trial, and to settle once and for all the pending questions."

And from the following letter written to the same person, which, in view of its interest, I reproduce.

"Mpueto, May 18, 1901.

"There is no need for anxiety, as I am at liberty, but I do not want to leave here till everything is settled. The best is, you come over here and see for yourself how matters stand. I shall give you instructions and power of attorney here, and then I intend to go to Mtowa to finish once for all this unbearable situation. Within four weeks everything will be decided, and I wish to answer the charge brought against me. There can be no serious punishment ; even if I am found guilty of having bought rubber in my concession, I can only be fined with a fine amounting from 10 francs to 1000 francs. *If I refuse to attend the court, I probably shall lose all my claims on the Government and the Katanga Company*, so I am determined to fulfil all formalities ; even by the officials here there is no doubt as to my final success."

Whether or no the subordinate officials and the representative of the Comité Spécial du Katanga at Mpueto were ignorant of the plot to effectually prevent Rabinek from troubling either the Congo State or the Katanga Company with his future claims it is difficult to say. But that his treatment at Mpueto, was designed, as I have said, to lull him into a sense of false security is, when we consider subsequent events, very obvious.

CHAPTER XXV

THE TRIAL, THE SENTENCE, AND THE END

"With consistent enterprise he (Rabinek) had within the last two or three years founded the basis of a monster trading scheme for the exploitation of rubber and ivory. He had established himself in British Central Africa, where he was qualifying for naturalisation. His agents worked in that protectorate, in North Charterland, and in German East Africa, and he had recently purchased trading rights in Katanga, which, by the treaty conferring existence on the Congo State, is, in common with the rest of Congoland, open to the trade of the world; he therefore merely purchased rights which were his already. . . . He was then treated as a common criminal, and transported, under escort for Boma, after being fined and sentenced to a year's imprisonment . . . for apparently standing on the rights he had acquired in good faith."—Major A. St. H. GIBBONS, F.R.G.S. ("Africa from South to North through Marotseland," 1904.)

"Mtowa, June 15, 1901.

"MY DEAR MR. HASTINGS,

"The most unexpected thing happened here,* and I have been condemned by court-martial to one year's imprisonment, against which judgment I have launched an appeal before the High Court at Boma, so I am compelled to make a very involuntary traverse of Africa. The court-martial consisted of *the Commandant* and a judge. The judge proposed to fine me with £40, but the *Commandant of his own added one year prison*, against which judgment even the judge protested, and has also made an appeal in my favour to the Court in Boma. . . . The judgment pronounced here *by the Commandant* has no foundation,† and I have not even been told for what reason I am condemned. I asked to-day the judge about it, and he also declared not to know what for I am condemned, as the *Commandant did not give explanation or reasons for his judgment*, and therefore the judge himself has also launched an appeal in my favour.‡ . . . Although I don't consider my

---

* Rabinek telegraphed to a friend of his early in June, that he would have to go from Mpeuto to Mtowa, 150 miles, *under an escort of native soldiery.*

† Meaning, presumably, "no foundation" in law—which, of course, is true, because the sentence was a violation of the law in so far as the law related to the only specific count upon which the warrant for arrest was issued, and judgment passed.

‡ In a letter to a friend of his dated June 18, Rabinek repeats this statement. "Mr. Codrington will have told you, I hope, that even the

condemnation serious,* and am absolutely convinced to find full justice in Boma, I am depressed in my mind. . . . Please accept my sincere thanks for what you have done up to date, and my best wishes for the future.

"Yours faithfully,
(Signed) "G. M. RABINEK.

"P.S.—Please send this letter to M—— and copy to Mr. ——. Just received notice that I have been condemned *by the Commandant* for nothing else but for *exploitation of rubber* in the *Katanga country* generally."

The dead man's original letter to his agent in British territory, from which the above extracts are reproduced, is before me as I write. It is a very long letter, and portrays the writer's feelings at the unexpected blow fallen upon him. Yet it is full of dignity and business-like considerations. He leaves directions as to the management of his affairs during his absence; begs that a personal friend, whom it is unnecessary to name, will sell some of his (Rabinek's) personal effects in order to send a sum of money to his brother in Vienna, so that the latter may engage a lawyer to go to Boma to assist him at the coming trial: laments that his prolonged absence will jeopardise the interests of the firms who have credits open with him, and, a characteristic note, begs that one of his employes whose wages are overdue shall be paid. He expresses the hope that his friends and agents will not abandon him in his hour of trial.

Let us examine the bald facts.

The nature of the offence with which Rabinek was charged, and for which he was *condemned to one year's imprisonment*, and a fine of 1000 francs, was for "illegal" TRADING IN RUBBER in the Katanga country generally. The warrant for arrest, the dead man's letter, the communication which the Congo State Government sent to the *Morning Post* (in reply to my articles), the reply given to Mr. Alfred Sharpe (Commissioner for British Central Africa) by Captain Tonneau, are all conclusive and concordant on the point, AND SO IS THE VERDICT OF THE COURT MARTIAL. Here it is:

Belgian judge made an appeal in my favour, and that I shall certainly be set at liberty immediately on arrival in Boma." Codrington was then administrator for N.E. Rhodesia. That the prosecuting judge did appeal is true, and is *proved* by the minutes of the Boma Appeal Court, October 23rd, 1901 (G. Nisco, President).

* I think the word used here must be read in the sense in which the French use it—Rabinek was a French scholar—"ce n'est pas sérieux," would in the above connection signify, "it is all nonsense," or "it is a farce," or again, "it carries no weight; it is not valid."

THE TRIAL, THE SENTENCE, AND THE END

"JUGEMENT.

"CONSEIL DE GUERRE D'ALBERTVILLE.

"Audience publique du 14 Juin 1901. En cause du Ministère Public " *Contre* Rabinek, négociant, sujet autrichien.

"Vu par le Conseil de Guerre séant à Albertville, la|procedure à charge du prévenu ci-dessus pour avoir :

"A. exploité le caoutchouc dans les terrains réservés par l'art. 3 du décret du 30 Octobre, 1892, subsidiairement recelé du caoutchouc obtenu à l'aide d'une infraction.

"Vu l'assignation en date du 13 juin, 1901 ;
"Oui le Ministère Public en ses requisitions ;
"Oui les temoins dans leur dépositions ainsi que le prévenu dans ses dires et moyens de défense ;
"Le Conseil de Guerre.

"Attendu que les faits mis à charge du prévenu sont établis, *le condamne à une servitude pénale de un an,* à une amende de mille francs et à defaut de paiement à une servitude pénale de six mois, à un quart de frais du procès et à defaut paiement à une contrainte par corps de deux mois ; ordonne la restitution à l'Etat du caoutchouc saisi, prononce la confiscation des marchandises saisies, ordonne l'arrestation immédiate.

"Ainsi jugé et prononcé à l'audience du 14 juin, 1901, où siègeaient
" MM. Morisseau Juge Levévre, Ministère Public,
"Van Staegen, Gréffier,
" Le Juge du Conseil de Guerre,
(sig.) " MORISSEAU.

" Le Gréffier
(Sig.) " VAN STAEGEN."

There can be, therefore, no doubt or question on the point. Yet the Austrian was condemned to one year's imprisonment —an absolutely illegal sentence according to the law under which he was chargeable!

His "immediate arrest" was ordered.

It seems inconceivable ; but it is true.

In a letter describing the "trial," written to Mr. Codrington, on June 16, 1901, Rabinek says :

"As everybody knows, I got my concession to trade in rubber and ivory from the Manager of the Katanga Company. *In my trial before the Conseil de Guerre, this fact was not even mentioned. The whole trial did last* (sic) *only about 40 minutes.*"

He goes on to say that certain of his agents were accused by the judge of buying rubber, and that he "as their employer, is responsible for their illegal actions." In reply to this charge, he refers *inter alia* to his agreement with the Katanga Company, that the manager—M. Lévêque—had produced his power of attorney when making the arrangement, and that he,

Rabinek, had acted in good faith. The prosecuting judge then declared that "I have certainly been guilty of buying rubber; but as I was in the believe (*sic*) of having a right to do so, he proposed to fine me £40." Rabinek again speaks.

"Then the Commandant rose and said something which I did not understand—it were (*sic*) only a few words—and I am sentenced to one year prison, when I was arrested. There was no reason given for this judgement by the Commandant, and I asked the judge and the uchor of the Court, who both declared that the Commandant did not explain the judgement. I cannot say more as that I have been condemned, without any witnesses or proves (*sic*) of my guilt." *

Such is JUSTICE to independent Europeans under the blue banner with the golden star!

Rabinek seems to have been under the impression that Judge Levèvre was the judge. He says that the "judge"—meaning Levèvre—"proposed" to fine him £40. In other words, the judicial officer acting as public prosecutor demanded the maximum *fine* under law. It is significant to note that this official (who protested † against the illegal sentence of a year's imprisonment, pronounced by the President of the Court Martial) did not even urge the *full penalty* against the Austrian provided by the law, that is to say, 1000 francs fine, *and* one month's imprisonment. That official was evidently not privy to the plot—at first, at any rate—for Rabinek tells us that he did not "understand the sentence."

In the belief that Levèvre was his judge, Rabinek was, of course, mistaken. It was a Court Martial sitting upon him, and the President of the Court Martial was Commandant Morisseau, by whom the minutes are signed.

This illegal sentence was the consummation of the plot.

The President of the Court Martial knew the sentence was illegal, and imposed it. The acting Public Prosecutor knew it was illegal, and, to his credit be it said, protested against it. The Congo Government knows it was illegal, and has upheld it.

The violent interference with Rabinek's business, the seizure of his caravans, the warrant issued for his arrest, and the arrest itself—these constituted so many outrages against the International Treaty under which the Congo State was admitted into the family of States. His trial was a mockery,

---

* I am indebted to Dr. Rudolf Hertz, of Hamburg, for the document from which the above extracts are made.

† "Vu les appels interjetés contre le dit jugement par le prevenu et le *ministère Public*." "*Tribunal d'Appel de Boma séant en tribunal repressif. Audience Publique du Octobre* 22, 1901."

SCENE IN THE CATARACTS REGION, LOWER CONGO

THE TRIAL, THE SENTENCE, AND THE END 289

and the sentence passed upon him was a judicial outrage according to the Congo State's own laws.

The Congo authorities meant to get Rabinek removed, and to achieve their purpose they stopped short of nothing, save actual murder, fearing perhaps that a second Stokes affair might stir even the torpid conscience of Europe.

The offence charged against the Austrian was illegal trading in rubber, and the verdict lays no other charge at his door.

But the sentence pronounced was the sentence which would have been pronounced had Rabinek been convicted of illegal traffic, not in rubber, but in weapons of war !

The decree of March 10, 1892, which provides for the latter offence, stipulates that :

"Whoever shall commit or allow to be committed by his subordinates an infraction of the present decree ... will be punished by a fine of 100 to 1000 francs, *and to* imprisonment not exceeding one year, or to one of these punishments only. *The sentence of imprisonment will always be pronounced.*"

Is the word "plot" too strong, and is the qualifying expression "devilish ingenuity" I have applied to that plot too emphatic ?

From the moment the verdict was pronounced, Rabinek was a prisoner under sentence of one year's imprisonment. He appealed, and was sent away "a prisoner" under escort.

The Congo State being hard put to frame a defence (for the attitude of its representatives which it endorsed) when I first brought this case to public notice, not knowing its full history ; sought to found one upon the dead man's appeal.

In its communication to the *Morning Post* of July 22, 1903, the Congo State argues as though the fact of Rabinek being allowed the faculty of appealing against the sentence passed against him, was in itself a proof of the *admirable manner in which the judicial organisation of the State is carried out !* The passage reads as follows :

"It is, in short, the simple matter of a foreign trader carrying on operations in the Congo State, who has committed an offence against common law. Being proceeded against and condemned by the local court, he appealed as was his right, and *undertook* the voyage to Boma, to present himself before the higher court which sits there."

Could the attitude of a Government be more despicable ? Note the statement "offence against common law." Note the words "local court." Rabinek having been *condemned by Court Martial,* and sentenced to a term of imprisonment which violates the provisions of the very law he was accused of breaking ! Note also the "undertook," which suggests willingness on the part of the individual—as if the unfortunate man had any other course open to him. Note the words "to present himself" when he left a "prisoner" under escort!* Does a man undertake a journey of 2000 miles to *present himself* to such and such a party, when he leaves a Court House as a "prisoner," as the official document records:

"Etat Indépendant du Congo. Feuille de route pour l'agent nommé ci-après qui se rend d'Albertville à *la prison* de Boma."

A mere enumeration of such documents as are available will now suffice to enable the reader to follow Rabinek to his lonely, nameless grave in the African forest.

I

From the *Feuille de route* already referred to it appears that Rabinek left Albertville on June 17, three days after the trial; arrived at Kabambare June 29: left Kabambare June 30: arrived at Kasorigo July 6: left Kasorigo July 7: arrived at Nyangwe July 8. That would mean a 21 days' land journey as a prisoner under native escort.

II

In a letter written by Rabinek directly after his trial to his relatives, he expressed anxiety as to his personal fate. The postscript contains the following sentence:

"Rumours have it that Europeans who have been taken are poisoned, so if I disappear without any further news you may guess what has become of me."

He added that he had made his will, and would post it home. It has not, I believe, been received. This letter was published in the Viennese papers.

III

In a letter written by Rabinek directly after his trial, to a friend at Karonga, he says: "I will send you from the next post-office the whole account of my illegal condemnation." This letter was never received.

* Under "an escort of 50 Askari" (Africa, No. 4, 1902).

THE TRIAL, THE SENTENCE, AND THE END

IV

From the *Feuille de route* we gather that Rabinek left Nyangwe on July 9; arrived (after several days) at Ponthierville, July 16; arrived at Stanleyville, July 17. Here there was a delay of nearly a month, for, according to the *Feuille de route*, Rabinek did not leave there before August 18. Of his physical condition when he arrived, and his treatment during his stay,* we know practically nothing, the only allusion being contained in the declaration of Mr. C. Fuhler, agent of the Tanganyika Concession, Limited, who writing from Ujiji, January 14, 1903, says:

"I was told by Captain Anderson, of the Katanga steamer, when coming up the Lake Tanganyika, from the West Coast, that he saw Rabinek carrying his own food under an escort of Congo soldiers. *If that is true, I then come to the conclusion that his death is only due to the hardships of the voyage, which would be enough to kill any European.*"

But although we can only guess as to his physical condition, we have the last despairing cry of the broken-hearted man, before he vanishes from the mortal ken of all save that of his tormentors. It is conveyed in two letters which he wrote to the judicial officer of the State at Stanleyville the day after his arrival, imploring to be allowed to continue his journey. They are written in French.†

"Stanleyville, July 19, 1901.

"MONSIEUR LE JUGE!

"I have the honour to refer to my respectful demand of yesterday, and I beg you to procure for me an audience of the President of the Appeal Court. It is a month to-day since I left Mtowa, and I hastened in the hope of having the good fortune of finding the President here, and now I am naturally impatient to make my statement. I beg you, Monsieur le Juge, to take into account my state of nervous excitement, and to give me the opportunity of listening to the opinion of an impartial judge, because at Mtowa I was sentenced without any witnesses and without any evidence, and I was not able to produce my witnesses or to undertake my defence. I hope you will not take my importance (*sic*—importunity?) as arrogance, and that you will agree to my request. I have the honour to remain,

"Your very devoted servant,
(Sgd.) "G. M. RABINEK."

---

* I reject a statement made long afterwards on oath by his cook, that he repeatedly asked to see a doctor and was denied one; because the cook's statement contains many flagrant inaccuracies.

† I am indebted to Dr. Rudolf Hertz, of Hamburg, for a copy of these two letters.

"Stanleyville, July 30, 1901.
"Monsieur le Juge!
"I take the liberty to make once more an appeal to you to let me *leave on this occasion* (read by this steamer?—E.D.M.) I do not want more room than a native, and I submit myself under those conditions absolutely; only let me go, because I am in a condition of despair.
"Your devoted servant,
(Sgd.)   "G. M. Rabinek."

He knew too well how "Bula Matadi" treats its black subjects, yet he only asked to be treated as one of them, so long as he could continue his journey!

Did they keep him at Stanleyville hoping that he would die—as he subsequently did—before getting to Boma, where his case would be pleaded by counsel?

V

The *Feuille de route* ends abruptly as follows: "Décédé le 1er Septembre, 1901, à bord du *Hainaut* à Black River."

VI

But we have a fuller document,* and from no less a person than Commandant Hennebert. The following is a literal translation: †

"Boma, September 18, 1901.
"M. le Gouverneur-Général,
"On August 20, I embarked at Bumba on the *Hainaut*. The boat coming from Stanleyville had several passengers on board, amongst them Rabinek.‡ I noticed that the latter had access to the bridge, and to the saloon in the same way as the passengers. I remarked (*Je fis observer*) to the purser the irregularity of this situation. He replied that the *Substitut du Procureur d'Etat* at Stanleyville had declared, when Rabinek embarked (*en faisant embarquer Rabinek*) that he could be treated like an ordinary passenger, because he desired to plead his case before the Appeal Court. I refrained from modifying these instructions. During the voyage Rabinek showed himself in a careless mood (*insouciant d'humeur*). Most of the passengers were on good terms with him, and he was generally among the group speaking loud and gaily. I will mention among his usual companions, the captain of the steamer *Otto*, purser Pahaunt, Sub-lieutenant Rosendale, the agriculturist Wen Waert, and the non-commissioned officer Rovers, the engineer Carey, etc. Rabinek

---

* A copy of this document was communicated to the Austro-Hungarian Government by the Congo State.
† The original extract is given in the Annex (Appendix).
‡ It was Commandant Hennebert who, it will be remembered, originally issued two licences to Rabinek.

THE TRIAL, THE SENTENCE, AND THE END 293

became ill on the 27th or 28th of August. He had fever attacks and bile vomitings. On the 29th the doctor attached to the camp at Irebu * examined him, diagnosed bilious fever, but did not manifest any fears. The illness followed its course until September 1. The patient was looked after by the purser; several passengers, and especially Mr. Carey, often visited him. Sunday, September 1, about 8 o'clock at night, the condition of Rabinek, which had never been alarming (inquiétant), became worse, and I was informed that his temperature was very high. I recognised, indeed, the urgency of administering a hypodermic injection of quinine. This medicine (médicament) had not the hoped for results, the temperature of the patient increased, and half an hour afterwards he expired. I heard the general opinion passed that Rabinek, by his long sojourn in the Tropics, and by the passion for morphia which dominated him, was not in a condition to resist a violent access of fever. Everything that he left was enclosed in his trunks, which were sealed up as far as Leopoldville. Next morning Rabinek was interred at the woodingstation at Black River, where the *Hainaut* had stayed during the night. I followed the corpse with nearly all the passengers.

(Signed) " COMMANDANT HENNEBERT."

I will confine myself to two comments on this document. One will be an expression of opinion, the other a statement of fact.

The expression of opinion is one which, I think, most of my readers who have followed this tale of wrong will agree with. The statement attributing sprightly cheerfulness to Rabinek, in view of his letters to his relatives and his pathetic communications to the official at Stanleyville, appears to me to be as odious as the rest of the proceedings of the agents of the Congo Government. The suggestion that the dead man was a morphomaniac has been emphatically repudiated by four persons who knew Rabinek, viz. Messrs. Robert Young, C. L. Greer, M. Leyer, and C. Fuhler, the first three being Native Commissioners, and Justices of the Peace in North-East Rhodesia.†

An affidavit dated September 2, 1901, by the captain of the *Hainaut* states that Rabinek died on board, and was

---

* One of the calling places. There was, apparently, no doctor on board.

† Major St. H. Gibbons, now writes me in that connection: "I certainly never saw anything in the manner of Rabinek to lead me to suspect that he was addicted to morphia-taking. On the contrary, it seemed to me that a man of his energy and ambition was extremely unlikely to be at the same time a morphomaniac, and the statement in the Press to that effect caused me much surprise. Of course a traveller like myself, on the strength of a short acquaintance, cannot give *positive* evidence in such a case; but in this instance I see more reason for taking the charitable view than the reverse."

The Congo State has published a statement by an ex-employé of Rabinek, confirming Commandant Hennebert's accusation, but seeing that this man is in the employ of Rabinek's persecutors, no attention need be given to the said statement, especially in view of the independent and emphatic testimony of so many witnesses.

buried at Black River Station; and a further affidavit made on May 24, 1902, before "L'officier de l'Etat Civil" at Leopoldville (countersigned as valid by the *Directeur de la Justice* at Boma on June 10, 1902) by S. Pruddhomme and Emile Pecklers, declaring that "Rabinek Gustave, aged 38 years, merchant, living at Ungarish-Ostra (Moravia), died at Black River the first day of September, 1901," completes the list of available documents concerning the unfortunate Austrian from the time of his condemnation to his death.

Although I had proposed to give a detailed account of what in Europe and in Africa has followed the wished-for disappearance of Gustav Maria Rabinek, I feel on consideration that the simple narrative here set forth is sufficient for my purpose. I will add merely this, that all the deceased's effects in Congo territory have been seized * by the agents of the *Comité Spécial du Katanga*, to the value, it is estimated, of £12,000; that neither the heirs nor the European creditors of the deceased have received a penny piece compensation, notwithstanding interminable legal proceedings which are still going on; that, owing to the apathy of the German and Austrian Governments, the Congo Executive has been allowed to continue its game of chicanery and deceit; that Rabinek's persecution and death remain unavenged and unresented, save by the few who have interested themselves in his sad and unmerited fate. May these chapters assist in some small degree the efforts of the handful of men—my friend Ludwig Deuss† amongst them—who are endeavouring to break the Chinese wall of indifference which for some occult reason the German Foreign Office has of late built up between itself and the dictates of duty and honour on the Congo. May they stimulate public opinion in

* There is an enormous amount of documentary evidence to prove this. Much of it Dr. Hertz, the extremely able solicitor for the creditors of Rabinek, has published. The following extracts from letters written at the time by an English sportsman in the country, Mr. Poulett Weatherly (the gentleman is referred to, by the way, in Major St. H. Gibbons' volume, *op. cit.*) may, however, be given here. The first letter is dated Nymbwa Kunda, Urua, 9/7/01. It says, "I am *awfully* sorry to hear things have come to such a pass with Rabinek for whom I have the most sincere liking. . . . As regards getting damages out of the Katanga Company—hopeless—not the ghost of a chance. As to the rubber caravans—none will come back. All will have been seized by now." In a subsequent letter, the writer says: " Rabinek's caravans are being seized all over the country." He adds the following note: " The new Katanga Company seem to have a rooted objection to anything English, except £ s. d. I have been informed that no one not connected with the Company can remain in their territory, so C—— and I must part."

† Whose acquaintance I have been privileged to make since I first heard of his name through poor Rabinek's tragedy.

THE TRIAL, THE SENTENCE, AND THE END 295

Great Britain and America to the contemplation of this monster which those Powers have helped to raise in Central Africa, and which, like Frankenstein, they are, apparently, unable to control.

First an Englishman, now an Austrian have fallen victims to the insatiable greed, the disreputable avariciousness, the brutality and illegality of the system of "moral and material regeneration" in Africa. Who will be the next European to suffer?

Once more has King Leopold with impunity said in effect to civilisation, "The Congo is *my* property; its people are *my* slaves; its products belong to *me*. Whoever enters that territory without my approval will be dealt with according to *my* laws." The fact is, it is "hands off" to the natives in one sense, and "hands off" to the Western world in another! This situation may also commend itself to Mr. Gilbert, although its humour is not precisely genial.

The Congo forests now cover the remains of two Europeans (and most probably others)—one actually, the other morally murdered by the representatives of King Leopold.

In an abandoned clearing, where once stood a Government wooding-post, at the mouth of Stanley Pool, lies all that is left of Gustav Maria Rabinek. A grave hastily dug and roughly closed; the body flung there like a dog, with not even a stone to mark its resting-place—only the grim African forest mounting guard.

*   *   *   *   *   *

Twenty-five miles from the spot is the port of Leopoldville, boasting two churches (a Catholic and Protestant Mission) and a cemetery, where at least the common decencies of Christian interment might have been rendered. But no . . . alive, Rabinek was a competitor in "trade." Long before he died "Bula Matadi" had rifled his goods, and stolen his produce in faraway Katanga. When he breathed his last his body could not be left on board the *Hainaut* for the two hours' further steaming required to convey it to Leopoldville! As though with unquiet consciences they thrust it into the shadows . . . and then pursued the even tenor of their way. I agree with Dr. Berthold Reif, the solicitor for the Rabinek family, who in a letter to me remarks: "Such a deed offends the law of nations, and will find its retribution."

I said at the beginning of the narrative which now closes *that the Rabinek scandal was a test case,* and on that account I have deemed it necessary to deal with it at considerable length. Let the reader bear well in mind that had Rabinek not happened to have the support of friends among Europeans in

Nyassaland, and had he not been connected in business relations with several European firms, the history of his treatment at the hands of the Congo State Government might never have transpired. If that Government can behave as it has done where a European is concerned, what must be its habitual methods of handling natives who have no one to inquire into their wrongs and expose, except on rare occasions, the outrages of which they are the victims?

PART V

THE GREAT CONGO DEBATE IN THE BELGIAN HOUSE OF REPRESENTATIVES*—JULY, 1903

FIRST DAY'S PROCEEDINGS
SECOND DAY'S PROCEEDINGS
THIRD DAY'S PROCEEDINGS
LESSONS OF THE DEBATE

* From the Annales Parlementaires—Chambre des Représentants Séance du 1er Juillet, 1903.

CHAPTER XXVI

FIRST DAY'S PROCEEDINGS

(M. Vandervelde opens the Debate)

ON July 1 of last year, at the afternoon sitting of the Belgian House, on the interpellation by Messrs. Vandervelde and Lorand, Congo affairs coming up for discussion, M. Lemonnier proposed that the debate stand adjourned. The proposal being resisted by Messrs. Vandervelde and Lorand, M. de Favereau, Minister for Foreign Affairs, announced that the Government were prepared to accept the debate. M. Lemonnier having given way, M. Vandervelde opened the debate. He began by saying that he had never denied the greatness of the effort accomplished by some of his compatriots in Africa.

"In less than twenty-five years, acting under the impulse of a persevering and tenacious will, immense territories have been explored, the basis of a vast empire established, and considerable natural riches exploited which, however, are of very small importance to the general trade of Belgium, but which bring enormous profits to the Congo State and its associates." M. Vandervelde then proceeded to explain why the Belgian Parliament could not disinterest itself from the resolution recently adopted by the British House of Commons.*
"The object of the discussion," he said, "is solely the question of knowing if the Congo State has fulfilled its international obligations, if it has faithfully carried out its stipulations in accordance with Articles 1, 5, and 6, of the Act of Berlin.
"Belgium had the right and the duty to intervene, because Belgium was a signatory party to the Berlin Act; because the responsibility of a certain number of Belgians was involved; because Belgium had put 15,000,000 francs into the Congo railway, had lent 35,000,000 francs to the State, had given money and men to the Congo State; and, therefore, possessed in the administration of the Congo State moral and material

* Resolution of May 20, 1903.

interests which it was essential for Belgium to safeguard, notwithstanding the fact that no official link existed between the Government of Belgium and the Congo State. After referring in some detail to the Congo debate in the House of Commons, and emphasising the fact that the feeling of the House was absolutely unanimous in respect to the grave charges made by members against the Congo State, M. Vandervelde went on to criticise the reply of the Congo State to these charges as published in a special issue of the *Bulletin Officiel*.* Beginning with the commercial aspect, the speaker said that he would only touch upon it lightly, were it not for the fact *that the commercial question was closely and inseparably linked to the question of the treatment of the natives.*

M. Vandervelde pointed out that if the policy pursued by the Congo State up to 1892 had been continued, there would have been no complaints.† "At that time the rights of the natives were recognised, not only over the land they cultivated, and over the land upon which they had built their habitations, but also over the forests which form the markets of their villages; the forests where, from time immemorial, they and their ancestors hunted the elephant and the antelope, collected palm-oil and kernels, and gathered rubber either for the purposes of sale or for home usage. During that period the Congo State acted as Sovereign and not as merchant."

M. Vandervelde then sketched out the new policy, showing how, by decrees and regulations,‡ the Congo State had appropriated to its own exclusive uses all the products of commercial value throughout the country. He quoted the protests made at the time against this policy, by the Belgian Trading Companies established in the Upper Congo, under the managership of Messrs. Thys, Brugmann, and Urban.§ "To forbid, declared these gentlemen, the natives from selling the ivory and rubber from their forests and plains which constitutes their hereditary birthright, and in which they have

* *Op. Cit.*

† Up to 1892—*i.e.* prior to the Decree of September, 1891, and the decrees and circulars of 1892—the theoretical right of the Congo State to declare all lands not built upon or under cultivation for food-stuffs, "vacant," and to declare all such so-called "vacant" land State property, which theoretical right was first laid down in July, 1885, *had not been carried out in practice*. The assumption of State proprietorship over land, logically carried with it a claim to the produce of the land, or "fruits of the soil;" but that claim was allowed to lie fallow until 1892 as aforesaid.

‡ Decree of September, 1891; Circulars of December 15, 1891; February 14, 1892; May 8, 1892; Decree of October, 1892, etc.

§ Refer to early reports by agents in Africa of these companies, in Chapter V.

traded from time immemorial, is a violation of natural rights. To forbid European merchants exchanging this rubber and ivory with the natives against goods; to compel them to pay for concessions to 'trade' with the natives, is contrary to the spirit and the text of the Berlin Act, which proclaimed the unrestrained freedom for every one to buy and sell, and forbade monopoly and privilege." M. Vandervelde proceeded to taunt those who to-day professed indignation at British attacks:—"You are indignant at the speeches made by Englishmen when those speeches are nothing more than the almost textual reproduction of those which were formerly made by Belgians, and which received the unanimous approval of the shareholders of the Belgian Trading Companies." Going into facts and figures, and dissecting the areas of the various "Trusts," M. Vandervelde showed that the whole of the Congo State, with the exception of an infinitesimal proportion, had been split up between the Government and its various *concessionnaires.* "The *Domaine Privé*," declared the speaker, "is forty-six times the size of Belgium; the area farmed out to 'Companies' managed by the State is twenty-nine times the size of Belgium; the area farmed out to 'Companies' in which the State is interested, is six times the size of Belgium; and the area in which trade is free is only once again as large as Belgium!" The statements made by the State that freedom exists under such circumstances, either for merchants or natives, was scathingly denounced by the speaker. "To trade in rubber and ivory, to-day, in the Congo, one must either be the Sovereign-King, or one of the Companies of the *Domaine Privé*. The only things which will bear cost of carriage to Europe are rubber and ivory; according to the Congo State's decrees, neither of these objects can be sold to traders. They must either be handed over to the State, or to the *Domaine Privé* Companies. On that basis, we have the right to assert that the Congo natives have been absolutely expropriated. The common market which surrounded their farms has been taken from them; freedom of trade has been taken from them; and they are compelled, by measures which I shall refer to, to deliver produce of the soil to the State and its nominees. There is no doubt that the economic results of this *régime* have been very brilliant for the Sovereign of the Congo State, and for the companies of the *Domaine Privé*, but not for Belgium. Belgium trade in the Congo does not represent even one per cent. of the general trade of Belgium!*

* It is King Leopold's object to make European and American public opinion believe that our condemnation of his personal rule in Africa, is a condemnation of the people over whom he rules as

A few people make enormous profits out of the sale of the rubber and ivory which falls into their hands, and these profits explain the patriotic ebullitions which are taking place. As for the Congo State itself, *only the estimated receipts are ever published;* it is perfectly obvious that the State is making large sums. Considerable amounts are placed by the Congo State in Eastern, and especially in Chinese undertakings.* Moreover, the Congo State has latterly taken to buying up land in the *Commune* of Laeken and elsewhere. Property is also being bought up by the Congo State in Brussels, representing a value of several millions of francs.

"Let us now examine the social aspect of this affair. We shall find a painful contrast between the patriotic enthusiasm and the humanitarian sentiments of Congo State apologists and the condition of the unfortunate natives. It is asserted that the Congolese institutions are beyond criticism. To refute constitutional monarch. The game can only deceive the superficial investigator. In this connection it is somewhat pertinent to quote the following extracts from a very well-known Belgian newspaper, *La Belgique financière*, of August 18, 1904:

"Speaking economically—says *La Belgique financière*—the system of the *rue de Namur* (*i.e.* the Congo Government) is worse than the famous Van den Bosch system. . . . It is so universally condemned that its adoption can only be explained by one motive; the aim is to make the Congo State—the word is a hard one, but we do not find any other—into a paying farm for the Sovereign-King, and the object is nearly attained already."

This surprising outburst is, apparently, not unconnected with the rumours prevalent that King Leopold intends to absorb wholly the *Abir* Trust. What *La Belgique financière* says is in all respects true, but it is certainly news that the "economic system" of the Congo State is "universally" condemned . . . in Belgium! *La Belgique financière* continues:

"Belgium has no interest in the Congo, as administered to-day. This is a surprising statement, but one which is profoundly true. . . ."

Undoubtedly true, but why then does Belgium allow her fair fame to be dragged in the mire?

* Through the Société Générale Africaine (one of the *Domaine Privé* Companies in whose name the rubber and ivory coming from the *Domaine Privé* and the *Domaine de la Couronne* was, until quite recently, shipped) or, in other words, the Congo State Government, or, in other words, the King; a large amount of money has been invested by the "Congo State" in China. This Belgian undertaking is known, or was known, as the *Société Asiatique;* it is connected with the American Chinese Development Company, an American Company founded in New York in 1897 (capital, 600,000 dollars). In this way, King Leopold has managed to secure the sympathy and interest of an American financial group, of which the principals appear to be "General" Wittier and Messrs. Pearson, Belmont and Willrich. M. Mali, Belgian Consul in the States, is, or was, also one of the Directors of the Company.

these sophistries, let us examine the fiscal and military organisation of the Congo." M. Vandervelde went on to point out, in the first place, that an army of 16,000 to 17,000 men * existed; that these men had to undergo a total military service of *twelve years*, and, chosen for the most part from the slave element † of the population, were placed in authority over free men. The speaker next examined the principle and system of taxation, and how the soldiers were used as tax-gatherers by the Congo State. He quoted official documents to show that the State not only recognised, but actually encouraged, the capturing of hostages,‡ and the use of force when the natives did not produce a sufficiency of rubber. Thus, M. Wahis, Governor-General of the Congo State, had, in 1897, in a circular to the District Commissioner of the district known as Lake Leopold II., made use of the following language:

"'Where natives obstinately refuse to work, *you will compel them to obey by taking hostages. You will not make use of your arms unless you meet with resistance....*' Thus," exclaimed M. Vandervelde, "treat the natives with kindness, but compel them to work; if they obstinately refuse,§ take hostages, take their children, take their wives. If they resist, use armed force. And to think that it is in the name of civilisation, and of humanity, that a Government which professes never to have inflicted bad treatment upon natives, tells us that to collect rubber and ivory, to furnish to the owner of the *Domaine Privé* and his friends, the requisite millions, it is legitimate to capture hostages, and to shoot those who resist such a demand!

"Think what these soldiers are—cannibals, belonging to other tribes than those over whom they are set, imperfectly and superficially trained to military discipline! Think that this *Force Publique* is commanded by non-commissioned officers intoxicated with self-importance; free, or practically so, from all control, demoralised by the pernicious effect of the climate, exasperated by resistance. How can any one dare to maintain that such a *régime* must not fatally, inevitably

---

* Since increased. These figures, of course, only refer to the regular army.
† That is to say, domestic slave element.
‡ For capturing of hostages see direct testimony in Part III.
§ It should be carefully borne in mind that the word "work," as used on the Congo, has a peculiar and special significance of its own. The Government has expropriated the natives from their land, and from the products of economic value which grow therein—the natives not being allowed to dispose of those products—which constitutes their sole wealth —by barter; but, on the contrary, being compelled—by force, if they object—to bring in the said products (rubber principally) to the State in the form of taxation. That is "work" as understood in Congoland.

lead to innumerable atrocities? How can it be pretended that these atrocities do not involve the responsibility of all those who practise, or order these acts of exploitation and oppression?" M. Vandervelde thereupon referred to the Mongalla atrocities of 1900 and 1901, and brought out a new fact throwing a singular light on Congo "justice." One of the sub-agents of the Mongalla Trust (*Société Anversoise du Commerce au Congo*) was condemned to imprisonment for "abominable tortures" perpetrated upon the unfortunate natives. But the rider of the Court, explaining the lightness of the sentence, had never previously been published. M. Vandervelde read it over to the House: "Seeing that the accused should benefit by attenuating circumstances in view of the nervous troubles to which he is subject, and to the critical circumstances in which he found himself in the midst of hostile tribes; that it is also just to take into account the example which his superiors gave him, in showing no respect for the lives or the rights of the natives; and from the fact that, instead of trading, he had been told to make war and punish the natives who would not work for the Company." "Thus," continued M. Vandervelde, "while the subordinates went to prison, their superiors were covered with honour and glory."

Passing rapidly in review the Rev. W. M. Morrison's disclosures,* M. Vandervelde brought forward another case—not previously recorded. "Since the Congo State affirms that it is prepared to pursue all those who are found guilty of acts of cruelty and oppression upon the natives, I bring forward specific facts, and I demand, in the name of Captain of the *Force Publique*—Tilkens—that he should be brought before the Assize Court of his own country.†

"I shall, no doubt, be told: 'Do you propose to quote as a witness an officer who himself has been condemned for having committed acts of cruelty and oppression?' If I were only bringing forward here a report compiled subsequent to condemnation, in order to lay the burden of responsibility upon other shoulders, the above contention would be sound; but, during his period of service in the Congo, at a time when the Congo State was lavishing upon him advancement and favours, M. Tilkens wrote letters periodically to a senior officer of the Army—retired Major Lenssens. These letters constitute a diary, and their very text is a proof of their sincerity. It is those letters which I shall refer to, and not to subsequent statements. In 1893, Tilkens, Sergeant of the 9th Regiment

* In the territories of the Kasai Trust. (See Part III.)
† That is Belgium. The Congo State Courts constitute "a separate judicial entity," to use a phraseology so dear to the Descamps School.

THE AGENTS OF THE MODERN AFRICAN SLAVE TRADE
THE "FORCE PUBLIQUE" OF THE CONGO STATE

of the Line, applied to go to the Congo; upon the expiry of his first term of service, he returned as a sub-lieutenant with service medal with one stripe. On November 6, 1897, he left for the second term of service, and was sent to the Rubi-Welle zone, to take charge of the station of Libokwa. For many months he was there alone, or with an assistant, in the equatorial forest, with seventy to eighty black soldiers under his command, and with the duty of imposing a very heavy burden upon one of the most savage tribes in the Congo State—the Aba-Buas. His station was on the line of transports to the Nile; and as long as Commandant Meeus, who was then chief of the district, occupied his post, the exploitation of rubber was only a secondary consideration, and the energies of the native population were directed towards supplying the Bahr-el-Ghazal Expedition with food-stuffs. The natives threatened over and over again to rebel. Tilkens, as I have said, was condemned by default at Boma to ten years' penal servitude; but, as I propose to show the House, he asks to be brought before the Assize Court, in order to justify himself and to prove that he acted upon the orders of his superiors, and was merely an instrument in their hands. This, moreover, is shown clearly by these letters, the originals of which are before me, and which one cannot read without being convinced that Tilkens, having at that time no interest in lying, and still less in accusing himself, rather under-stated than over-stated the case. Here, for instance, is what he wrote to Major Lenssens on July 20, 1898 :—

"'The *Chef de Poste*, of Buta, announces the arrival of the steamer *Vande Kerkhove*, which is to be floated upon the Nile. He will require the colossal number of 1500 carriers. Unhappy blacks! I do not like to think of it. I ask myself where I can find them? If the roads were good, it might be different, but they are barely cleared, crossed repeatedly by marshes, where many will find a certain death. Hunger, and the fatigues of an eight-day march, will account for many more. What blood this transport has not made to flow! Already, three times have I been forced to make war upon chiefs who refuse to co-operate in the work. Unfortunately, they are but poorly paid for such arduous labour, 5d. (50 *centimes*) worth of cowries for the outward journey, and a piece of American cloth for the homeward journey. If a Chief refuses, it is war; and that atrocious war—perfected weapons of destruction against spears and lances! . . . A native Chief has just come to tell me : " My village is a heap of ruins: all my wives have been killed. Yet, what can I do? I am Chief, because my father was Chief, but I have not his strength and power. When I tell my people to carry the white man's transports, they flee to the woods, and when your soldiers come to recruit, I can give them no one, because my people prefer to die of hunger in the woods rather than do transport work. . ." Often am I compelled to put these unhappy Chiefs in the chains, until some 100 or 200 carriers are obtained, which procures their liberation. Very often my soldiers find the villages deserted; then they seize women and children, and capture them.'

"Such was the condition of things," continued M. Vandervelde, "in the Rubi-Welle zone, when Commandant Meeus was in charge. In due course, Commandant Verstraeten, District Commissioner, replaced Commandant Meeus, and rubber taxes were added to transport work. By the decree of July 22, 1898, the Rubi-Welle district had been placed under special military law. At this time the station of Buta only furnished two tons of rubber monthly, and the post of Libokwa 360 kilos. But, in a letter dated March 28, 1898, M. Felix Fuchs, *ad-interim* Governor of the Congo State, wrote to the new District Commissioner Verstraeten to emphasise the necessity of an immediate increase in production.

"'It will end,'" the letter concluded, "'by telling you that the Government has the strong hope that you will give a new proof of your activity and devotion by making the district under your command provide the *maximum* of its resources.'

"To arrive at this result, it was indispensable to take energetic measures. Commandant Verstraeten, shortly after taking up his new duties, sent a circular letter to the different *Chefs de Poste* of Libokwa, Jabir, and Buta—a letter relating to the exploitation of rubber, which is copied, according to M. Tilkens, in all the station books of the Rubi-Welle district. Here is the letter, reconstituted from memory by M. Tilkens, and the accuracy of which can easily be verified.

"'To the "Chefs de Poste" of the Rubi-Welle District.

"'I beg to bring to your notice that from January 1, 1899, it is necessary that 4000 kilos (4 tons) of rubber be furnished every month. To ensure this result, I give you *carte blanche*. You have two months in which to *work* your people. Use gentleness, first of all, and, if they persist in not accepting the State's taxes (*impositions*), employ armed force.'

"I have said that the existence of this document is easily verifiable. I would add that, in the event of its being decided to prosecute M. Tilkens—a step which I maintain should be undertaken—I hold at the disposal of the Minister of Justice a long list of witnesses who can affirm the existence of this document. And now, gentlemen, let us see the results of this rubber exploitation in the Rubi-Welle district, commanded by District Commissioner Verstraeten. But first of all a parenthesis."

M. Vandervelde thereupon proceeded to refer to the subject of the payment by the Congo State of bonuses to its agents, proportionate to the amount of rubber sent home from their respective stations. M. Vandervelde quoted the denials which the Congo State have constantly formulated against this charge; and particularly the well-known correspondence exchanged between Count Alvensleben, Ambassador for Germany, in Brussels, and M. Van Eetvelde, Congo State secretary, shortly after the Stokes affair.*

"Here," continued M. Vandervelde, "are precise and categorical statements. The Congo State does not give bonuses either on rubber or ivory, and the Congo State has no intention of establishing them. Very well, gentlemen, I would ask how these statements can be reconciled with the following letter which the commandant of the Libokwa station wrote to his mother, in 1898, and the original of which is before me:—

"'Commandant Meeus, my District-Commissioner, is about to return, and Commandant Verstraeten, the friend of Major Lenssens, replaces him. It is he who inspected my station, and who complimented me highly upon the discipline and exactness with which I accomplished my duties. He told me that the nature of his report would *depend upon the quantity of rubber produced.* When he left, he told me to employ myself actively in collecting rubber, and from 360 kilos in September my production rose to 1500 in October, and this month, I trust it will be over two tons. Here is the way it is divided cent. per cent. (*sic*) ten points (*sic*) are granted by the Government to the collecting agent. Of these ten points (*sic*) Commandant Verstraeten said that he would take five and leave me five, which represents 12½ per cent. per kilo (125 francs per ton). By January 1, I shall be making 4000 kilos per month, which makes 500 francs profit over and above my salary... I really am a lucky fellow, and if I play at rubber (*joue caoutchouc*) for two years, I shall make 12,000 francs over and above my salary.'

"Tilkens also wrote home to say that as soon as he got back he would buy a house. After that he would return and do another term of service, then he would marry and settle down comfortably with the profits of his African campaign! However, it seems that the system of 'points' resembled too closely the system of bonuses, because, instead of giving Tilkens what he was promised, Commandant Verstraeten thought out another system. On January 26, 1899, he wrote to the Governor-General at Boma the following letter:—

"'MONSIEUR LE GOUVERNEUR-GÉNÉRAL,
"'I draw the Government's attention to Lieutenants Tilkens, Landeghem, and Verslype. These agents have specially distinguished themselves in putting in train the exploitation of rubber. To them is

---

* The correspondence is given in full in M. Demetrius C. Boulger's book on the Congo State. See also "Affairs of West Africa."

due the honour of the surprising results obtained in the area allotted to their action. It is, I think, useless to suggest their advancement, or increase in their wages, seeing that advancement in the Congo is similar to that in the Belgian army, that is to say, by seniority. Deeming however that the aforesaid officers deserve *special favours*, I ask that they shall receive, either an honorific recompense or some gratuity.

(Signed) "'VERSTRAETEN,
"'Bembo, January 26, 1899.'

"This gratuity was given them, in the shape of a retiring grant of a nominal capital of 5500 francs. Gentlemen, I ask that the denial of the Congo State, as regards the system of bonuses, be envisaged in the light of the letter of Tilkens, concerning the 'points' granted to agents, and the particular bonus which was granted to him for having produced 4000 kilos per month; and I should like to be told if the Government of the Congo State spoke the truth when questioned by the German Minister.*

"I will now show by what means, and under what conditions an output of 4000 kilos of rubber per month has been obtained from several stations in the Rubi-Welle district. To arrive at this result, it was necessary to bring such coercive measures to bear upon the natives that keen resentment was occasioned. I find the proof of this in a series of letters written by M. Tilkens to Major Lenssens, on May 12 and 25, July 11, and August 10, 1899.

"'I expect a general uprising. I think I warned you of this, Major, in my last. The motive is always the same. The natives are tired of the existing *régime*—transport work, rubber collecting, furnishing live stock for whites and blacks. . . For three months I have been fighting, with ten days' rest. . . I have 152 prisoners. . . '†

"In another letter, written to a Belgian officer, Tilkens said :

"'For two years I have been making war in this couhtry, always accompanied by forty or fifty *Albinis*.‡ Yet I cannot say I have subjugated the people. . . They prefer to die. . . What can I do? I am paid to do my work, I am an instrument in the hands of my chiefs, and I obey the orders which discipline exacts.'

"Such, gentlemen, are the facts."

M. Vandervelde then went on to describe the sequel. He first read to the House letters to M. Tilkens, from his District Commissioner, and even from Governor-General Wahis, complimenting him on the services he had rendered. But

---

* Alvensleben.—Van Eetvelde correspondence, *op. cit.*
† More "hostages"!
‡ That is to say, soldiers armed with the *Albini* rifle.

FIRST DAY'S PROCEEDINGS

Nemesis was approaching. The natives of the Rubi-Welle district, goaded to frenzy by this long oppression, rose, attacked the station of Libokwa, sacked it, capturing many rifles and much ammunition. Then the high officials of the State, probably to save their "face," turned upon their too docile instrument. The very acts which the instructions given to Tilkens rendered inevitable, were brought up against him. He was accused of various crimes. He returned to Europe. The Congo State declined to re-engage him, but he obtained an appointment with the Upper Kasai Company. He went back, landed at Boma in September, 1902, was arrested, and let out on bail of £200. The amount of this bail elicited a fine passage from M. Vandervelde:

"You will admit, gentlemen, that Congolese justice does not take much account of the lives of the natives, when a man accused of the most terrible crimes is allowed his liberty on a bail of £200."

Tilkens stowed away on board a steamer, and was condemned in default to ten years' penal servitude.*

Concluding his speech, M. Vandervelde said: "I submit that, in the face of these facts, the Congo State must prosecute Tilkens.... But the Tilkens incident is only an instance. What has taken place in the Welle is merely a reproduction of what has taken place in the districts of Mongalla, Equateur, Luebo, etc. The revolt of Libokwa is the repetition of other native uprisings, which have been endemic for over ten years, and which necessitate the up-keep on the war footing of 17,000 men. It is only with the help of this army that the Congo State succeeds in forcing upon the natives a Government which constitutes, perhaps, the most perfect form of absolutism in the world. Is there any other sovereign in the world who disposes to this extent of men and land? It is he who possesses or concedes the land, who assigns duties, who fixes the price of labour, who specifies the number of recruits, who incarnates the only source of legislative and executive power. To execute his orders he borrows from the Belgian army officers and non-commissioned officers habituated to passive obedience. He puts them in the presence of savages who yesterday were cannibals, and perhaps are still. Is it not sufficient to think for a moment of the inevitable consequences of such a *régime* to understand the charges which are accumulating from all sides against the Congo State?"

M. Vandervelde finally concluded with an eloquent appeal

* The whole truth of the circumstances under which Tilkens left the Congo has yet to be disclosed. It is virtually impossible that he could have left the Congo *unknown to the authorities.*

that the Belgian Government should approach the Congo State with a view to a thorough, searching inquiry.

M. De Favereau then rose to reply, He remarked that M. Vandervelde had invited the Belgian Government "to make representations to the Independent State, so that it may constitute an inquiry, an inquiry on a vast scale offering all the guarantees of impartiality for the purpose of throwing the most complete light on its own administration." But, argued M. de Favereau, an inquiry was impossible. The reasons given by the Minister were as follows: "There is in international law an essential principle, of which all Governments have with reason shown themselves particularly jealous. This principle consists in no Government possessing the right to interfere in the administration of another State."

M. de Favereau expressed surprise that "a member of the Belgian Parliament should seek to force us into a breach of this principle, and ask us to mix ourselves up even indirectly in the affairs of a *Foreign State*." *

Several speakers here interrupted, saying that the Congo State was affiliated to (*une filiale*) Belgium, and was frequently called Belgian Congo.† The Minister took no notice of the interruptions, and, after declaring that the Congo State was an independent Sovereign State, remarked that M. Vandervelde "has not told us whence the Belgian Government would derive the right to intervene in the affairs of the Independent State."

M. Vandervelde: "In its friendly relations with the Independent State, and by reason of the practical links (*liens de fait*) which exist between the two Governments."

M. de Favereau retorted that what they had to go on was international law, and therefore "from the point of view of the individual relations of Belgium and the Congo State, the hon. member has himself recognised that we have no right of intervention." ‡ As to the Berlin Act, the Act would have to have been violated for Belgium to intervene. "And this flagrant violation, where do you see it? We have heard the hon. member mention certain abominable acts committed by an agent of the Congo Independent State. But has not the Congo Independent State prosecuted and punished him?"

M. Vandervelde: "You arrested him, and afterwards let him go."

* M. de Favereau gave the same reply in 1901, in the course of the debate on the Mongalla atrocities.
† Usually so by Belgians themselves.
‡ Refer to Vandervelde's opening statement.

FIRST DAY'S PROCEEDINGS

M. Huysmans having said that crimes were also committed in civilised countries, M. Anscele exclaimed, "Yes, but the Belgian Government does not give *carte blanche** to its agents to steal and assassinate."

M. de Favereau contended that no proof had been furnished that the Congo State had violated the Act of Berlin. The Congo State had "done a great deal for the protection of Missions." It had also organised scientific expeditions. As regards Article 6, respecting the treatment of the natives, the Congo State had "punctually observed" its engagements. It had destroyed the Arab Slave Trade, of which the speaker gave details.

The House then rose.

* Refer to instructions of Commandant Verstraeten, quoted by Vandervelde.

CHAPTER XXVII

SECOND DAY'S PROCEEDINGS

(M. de Favereau continues his reply to M. Vandervelde)

THE debate being resumed (July 2),
M. de Favereau said: "The hon. member (M. Vandervelde) asks the Government to approach the Congo Government with a view of throwing light upon everything that takes place on the Congo. Yesterday I said that the Belgian Government has no right to do this. The special Convention between Belgium and the Congo State no longer exists, and on that ground we have no right. The hon. member quotes the Berlin Act, but we have no right to interfere in the internal affairs of the Congo State. Moreover, the Congo State has fulfilled all its duties under the Berlin Act." M. de Favereau thereupon enumerated sundry laws of the State for the protection of religion, the lessening of the liquor traffic, the safe-guarding of the natives, the abolition of cannibalism, etc. In particular, M. de Favereau contended that the judicial system of the Congo State was admirable. "Congolese legislation is complete, and the penal code reaches all evil-doers. In thirty different places there are tribunals."

M. de Favereau proceeded to read laws and decrees * affecting the judicial establishment and the "Commission for the Protection of the Natives." He then spoke of the work of the religious missions in elevating the natives; "instructing

---

* The laws and decrees of the State fill many volumes of the *Bulletins Officiels*. The language in which they are clothed, the sentiments they in many cases display, are philanthropic to the most extreme degree. Underneath this monument of hypocrisy lies the great foundation-stone, the primary law of the founder of the Congo State, that the land and the products of the land belong to the State, and that the natives have no right to gather those products for the purposes of sale. Add to this primary law the bald fact that the financial existence of the State, and the wealth accruing to a few men out of its exploitation is obtained from the sale of the products of the land which the natives are compelled to bring in to the posts of the *Domaine Privé* and the Trusts; and Congo legislation will be understood.

SECOND DAY'S PROCEEDINGS   313

them in all kinds of craft, and conducting them progressively in the path of civilisation, that supreme object of the founder of the Congo State."

As regards the native army, M. de Favereau asserted that 10 per cent. of it was composed of recruits who had voluntarily re-engaged themselves.* He admitted that the Congo soldiers served seven years on active service, and added, " But, gentlemen, these soldiers ask to remain on the expiry of their first term." † "Slavery," declared M. de Favereau, "does not exist on the Congo."

M. de Favereau then continued at great length to argue that the Congo State had not violated the Berlin Act in the matter of freedom of trade. The thesis developed by M. de Favereau has been fully discussed in Part II. Having quoted the various declarations of the plenipotentiaries at the Conference in respect to the interpretation of the commercial clause of the Berlin Act, M. de Favereau exclaimed, "And yet no one would think that provisions of that kind could be interpreted as diminishing the Sovereign rights of the State to regulate its property as it chooses." As a proof that trade was free in the Congo State, M. de Favereau enumerated 403 "commercial factories ‡ existing in the Congo State, many of which were in no way connected with the administration." § After this enumeration, M. de Favereau triumphantly exclaimed, " That is my reply to M. Vandervelde, who says that everthing, or nearly everything, is in the hands of the State, and that it is only the State which disposes of the produce of the land." And once more the Minister put forward the "juridical" basis of the Congo State's conception: "In what legislation in the world would it be found that to sell the products of one's domain constitutes a commercial act ? "

Proceeding, M. de Favereau maintained that some of M. Vandervelde's statements regarding the *Domaine Privé* Companies were wrong. "The Lomami Company," he explained, "is the owner of the land it exploits. The *Société*

* The assertion was not backed up by any attempt at proof.
† Ibid. No attempt to prove this assertion was made. It remains a mere assertion, and no one who knows how lightly domestic slavery—which, be it noted, is a national institution—weighs upon the natives, in comparison with an active military service of seven years, plus five years in the reserves, can credit for one moment M. de Favereau's statement. To describe a conscription which removes natives from their homes and their relatives for twelve whole years as voluntary, is, of course, transparently absurd.
‡ See Chapter XXIX.
§ Ibid.

Anonyme Belge is the owner of the land it exploits, the *Campagnie du Katanga* is the owner of one-third of the territory it exploits. The *Campagnie du Kasai* is not managed by the Congo State, but is composed of fourteen firms. The *Campagnie des Chemins de fer du Congo Supérieur aux Grands Lacs Africains* possesses 4,000,000 hectares for a subscribed capital of 25,000,000 francs. The *Société d'Études des Chemins de fer du Stanley Pool au Katanga et de l'Itimbri à l' Uellé* had 20,000 *hectares* to choose among vacant land, plus 5,000,000 *hectares* for every 25,000,000 francs subscribed."* After this enumeration, M. de Favereau repeated once again the formula that the Congo State "has never contravened the stipulations of the Berlin Act with regard to freedom of trade. It has, I repeat, kept all its engagements. How can we justify the intervention asked? How can the Belgian Government bring about such an intervention when it is convinced that the Congo State has done its duty and kept its engagements?"

Passing to the Tilkens case, M. de Favereau said, "M. Vandervelde finished his discourse by a long plea for M. Tilkens."

M. Vandervelde (interrupting): "It was a prosecutor's address, because I demanded that M. Tilkens should be prosecuted."

M. de Favereau: "M. Vandervelde supported him, as he supports the campaign abroad against the Congo State. He lacks in patriotism." (Murmurs.) "This is a national question. It is not only the august founder of the Congo State who is attacked, but a Belgian work. . . . I admit that labour is imposed upon the natives (*le travail est imposé*), but it is in the interest of all, and when the work is done, the native is paid.† What is there to object to?"

M. Lorand: "It is forced labour."

M. de Favereau: "Moreover, the peasants of parts of our country have to keep the roads in good order. It is the same thing as in the Congo——"

M. Vandervelde: "Do you suggest that there is any resemblance between road-clearing in the *communes* of this country, and the rubber *régime* in the Congo?"

M. de Favereau: "It is an impost applied by the authorities. . . . I do not think that I shall be contradicted when I assert that all progress in the path of civilisation is subordinate to the appropriation of the soil, and that——"

---

* See Part II.

† Fivepence for an eight days' march, carrying heavy cases, and a piece of American cloth on returning. *Vide* Tilkens' letters. For the so-called "payment" to the natives, see also various testimony in Part III.

M. Lorand: "The Congo State's conception is a collectivism of the worst kind."

M. Vandervelde: "A collectivism for the profit of one, or a few."

M. de Favereau: "You say that in the Congo it is one, or a few. No; the Congo is useful to every one in Belgium. The Congo State ordered 7,000,000 francs (£280,000) from Belgian industries last year."

M. Lorand: "But that is uncommonly little compared with our enormous trade——"

M. de Favereau (interrupting): "No doubt M. Lorand thinks it little."

M. Lorand: "Of 700,000,000 francs (£28,000,000), it is the millionth part of our general trade."

M. de Favereau: "I return to the Tilkens incident." The speaker then gave a list of the charges of atrocities against M. Tilkens, and reproached M. Vandervelde for undertaking to defend such a person. M. de Favereau sought to destroy the effect of Tilkens' letters in connection with bonuses for rubber. The Minister's statements were so lame and incomprehensible that they are here given textually:

"M. Vandervelde has spoken of 'the points' granted to the State agents. He commits an error when he establishes a correlation between the 'points' granted to the State functionaries, and the quantity of rubber collected by them. The 'points' are used to graduate the agents—all the agents of the State—whether they are given up to the collection of rubber or not. Tilkens," M. de Favereau declared, "was sentenced because he deserved to be, because he had broken the State instructions, because he had violated the provisions of the penal code. The Independent State acts thus each time that a reprehensible deed is brought to its knowledge. The severity shown is great,* and I may say that never, when it is a question of outrages on the blacks, are the sentenced pardoned."

M. de Favereau wound up his speech by quoting Sir Harry Johnston's declaration that in the very small portion of the Congo territory he had visited, he had seen nothing to complain of. He also quoted M. Mohun † as an impartial witness, and finished with the usual peroration of which this is the concluding sentence: "I end, gentlemen, by expressing my unmistakable conviction that the neighbouring nations will appreciate, as it deserves, the great work of civilisation."

M. Vandervelde, rising upon the conclusion of the

* Matthys' and Lacroix's punishment, for instance ! *Vide* Part III.
† This individual is, or was, in State employ.

Minister's speech, said that M. Lorand and himself would reply in due course to the same. Meanwhile, he wished to make a personal explanation. "The hon. Minister has reproached me," said M. Vandervelde, "with being anti-patriotic, of associating myself in a campaign against our country. Let us, however, understand one another. It is inadmissible that in one part of an oration it should be declared that the Congo State Government is a foreign government, so far as we are concerned, of whom we may not ask explanations; and that in another part of the same oration, we should be told that the Congo is so closely identified with Belgium, that to criticize the former is to attack the latter! The truth is, that Belgium, happily, is not the Congo, but that the acts committed by Belgians in the Congo may be of a kind to compromise our international good name. *Therefore we cannot disinterest ourselves from the question.* It was on that *account specially that I spoke of the Tilkens affair, and all* the details brought forward by the hon. Minister for Foreign Affairs do but confirm and aggravate the information which I myself gave to the House. The judgment pronounced by default against Captain Tilkens (rightly or wrongly, the future will decide) has been read to us. This judgment sets forth that Tilkens committed crimes, raided for slaves, caused carriers to be killed, and so on. Now, this man who has been condemned on these counts—this man is in Belgium! His whereabouts are known. The Congo State has merely to give official notice to the Minister of Justice to ensure his being brought before the Assize Court. Tilkens wants that; he only asks to be allowed to defend himself. As I have already stated, he certifies that he acted upon the instructions of his superior officers. He asks to prove it in open Court. I say you have no right to refuse this man, judges: and I await the official notice of the Congo State to the Minister of Justice to prosecute Tilkens. As for myself, I think that in bringing these facts before the House, I acted with a much truer patriotism than that which is concerned in trying to prevent scandals instead of suppressing abuses."

M. Woeste * then continued the debate.

M. Woeste began by characterising Mr. Herbert Samuel's and Sir Charles Dilke's speeches as "passionate and violent." The attacks abroad were "dictated by envy and malice." He sought to justify the Congo State in its appropriation of "vacant lands," alleging that the onus of proving that the

* M. Woeste is the leader of the Catholic party in the Belgian House. He is the King's ally in all Congo affairs by virtue of an understanding with which students of Belgian politics are thoroughly familiar.

lands were not "vacant" fell upon those who criticise the system. The natives, he said, had no knowledge of gathering forest products before the Congo State went there.*

[M. Vandervelde here referred the speaker to the protest of the Belgian Trading Companies in 1892, against the appropriation policy of the State, in which the petitioners asserted that the natives had been in the habit of collecting forest products for the purposes of trade "from time immemorial."]

M. Woeste, taking no notice of the interruption, said, "The decree of the Congo State, of September 29, 1891, mentioned yesterday, declares that the 'Administration will take the necessary measures to preserve for the State the fruits of the Domaine, notably, ivory and rubber.' You hear, gentlemen, 'the fruits of the Domaine.' That is the main point, and from the fact that the *forests, like the other territories, belong to the State, it follows that the State in appropriating what belongs to it, that is to say, the fruits of the Domaine, did not interfere with private property.*" †

"The argument," continued M. Woeste, "which attributes to the Congo State a violation of the commercial clauses of the Berlin Act, is a sophism. Trade is confounded with the right of the State to exploit its own domains."

The only remarkable part of the speech was that in which M. Woeste gave his views on what might perhaps be called the economy of severed hands. "Mr. Samuel," said M. Woeste, "speaking in the House of Commons, said, 'In one locality an eye-witness saw eighty human hands slowly drying over a fire.' Is the fact true? I do not know. But I will admit that it is. What Mr. Samuel ought to have added was that, at any rate, the hands had not been cut from living men. . . ." M. Woeste then referred to the Fiévez incident of 1896, and read an extract from the statements ‡ of that individual (a Congo State Official): "'Do not tell me that these practices do not still occur. Hands are still cut off . . . and other things. § Evidently, soldiers who have served three, four, and five years, respect our instructions; but can you forbid a young soldier, anxious to exhibit proofs of his bravery, bringing back war trophies?' Commandant Fiévez,"

* An obviously faulty statement, as I have shown. *Vide* Part II.
† This passage should be carefully noted. It explains the *policy* of the Congo State in the clearest possible manner, from the mouth of one of its principal apologists in Belgium.
‡ The statements of M. Fiévez were confirmed by Father Cambier, and his statement is to be found in the collection of cuttings issued as a defence of the Congo State this year, and entitled, "The Truth about Civilization in Congo-land," by a Belgian. See Part II.
§ See Parts II, and III.

continued M. Woeste, " was talking common sense.* He put matters in their true light, and showed that it was possible that cruelties take place in this great territory, but that the State suppresses them when it found them out."

M. Vandervelde : " Did the State punish the 'young soldiers' when they brought back the trophies of their valour ? "

M. Woeste : " You had better ask the State." (Ironical laughter from the Left.)

M. Vandervelde: " You ask it. You are the King's Postman. Take him my letter." (Laughter.)

M. Woeste : " But what I contend is, that if the practice of cutting off hands still continues, it must not be forgotten that those who practise it are blacks, yesterday barbarous, to-day still semi-barbarous ; and that it is only by degrees that the custom can be eradicated." †

M. Vandervelde : " And it is those very blacks who compose the *Force Publique* of the Congo State ! "

Concluding, M. Woeste declared that he was convinced if there was a new Conference of the Powers, the Conference would result in paying a well-deserved homage to the work which had been accomplished by the Congo State, and that England would associate herself in that homage. He proposed the following order of the day : " The Chamber, confiding together with the Government in the normal and progressive development of the Congo, under the ægis of the King-Sovereign of the Congo State, passes to the order of the day.' " (Loud cheers.)

M. Huysmans violently criticised M. Vandervelde and Lorand for their anti-patriotism in attacking the Congo State at home when it was being attacked abroad. As regards the " juridical " rights of the Congo State to " vacant lands," the question, he considered, was settled.

M. Vandervelde : " The question is : What do you mean by ' vacant lands ' ? "

M. Huysmans : " If you say lands have been appropriated which were not vacant, it is your business to prove that they were not vacant. You tell us that the natives were owners of enormous forests, from which they took a little rubber to put

---

* Evidently a very paying "common sense," for in the *Bulletin Officiel* for June, 1896, we read, " The results obtained by M. Fiévez are unrivalled. The district produced in 1895 more than 650 tons of rubber, bought at 25 centimes per kilo (about 1⅛d. per pound), and sold in Antwerp at 6 francs 50 centimes per kilo." £170,000 a year from one district. That was really good business !

† The mendacity of this argument is fully exposed in Chapter X.

on their drum-sticks." (Laughter.) "It is just as though someone in this country, by picking a few nuts in the wood, declared himself owner of them." (Laughter.)

M. Vandervelde: "You do not refute an argument by caricaturing it."

M. Huysmans, continuing, said that "the attacks upon the Congo State in Belgium and elsewhere were exaggerated. It was abominable that such attacks should be made in Belgium. The Congo was a national work . . ."

M. Bertrand: "International!"

M. Carton de Wiart: "It is a Belgian work."

M. Vandervelde: "The Minister himself (M. de Favereau) has declared it to be a foreign work."

M. Huysmans: "I repeat it is a Belgian work. The Congo State will emerge triumphant from this struggle."

M. Lorand: "Gentlemen, when I associated myself with my hon. friend, M. Vandervelde, in his interpellation, I expected to hear these objurgations and patriotic counsels such as have been addressed to us by M. Huysmans. I thank him for the trouble he has taken to censure me, but I do not in the least regret my action. . . ." M. Lorand went on to say that he did not think the English Government was conducting an intrigue against the Congo State, but that there was a movement of public opinion in England against the Congo. "In our opinion," declared the speaker, "the facts which have been given, and which are of undeniable importance, both by their numbers and their seriousness, are the direct, immediate, and necessary outcome of the commercial exploitation of the Congo State. I say that the Congo State began by general and absolute denials of such facts long before they were taken up in England. All the facts we brought forward in this Chamber were, I repeat, denied at first most energetically, and in general terms; but later, little by little, they were proved by documents and by official texts. Now they are admitted, but it is said that they are isolated incidents. The Minister (M. de Favereau) spoke for two hours yesterday without meeting a single one of the arguments and facts brought forward by M. Vandervelde. It is always the same system. We bring forward specific facts, weighty arguments, and the reply is, 'It is not our business to ask the Congo State for information'! But, immediately afterwards, a whole series of assertions, of details, and documents are produced, which emanate directly from the offices of the Congo State Administration; which shows that when the Minister for Foreign Affairs cares to take the trouble, he obtains from the Administration of the Congo State all the information he requires."

M. de Favereau: "All the information and documents I quoted I got from the publications of the Bureau for the Suppression of the Slave Trade."

M. Lorand: "You certainly did not seek your information about the Tilkens affair there."

M. de Favereau: "I suppose that there were matters in your interpellation beyond the Tilkens affair?"

M. Lorand: "Since yesterday you have put yourself in such close communication with the Congo State on the subject, that to-day you know all the details of the Tilkens affair, and you bring your judgment to bear upon it with an assurance which astonishes me."

M. Van den Heuvel (Minister of Justice): "You are narrowing considerably the debate in concentrating it upon the Tilkens affair."

M. Lorand: "I am not narrowing the debate, because, incidentally, I am compelled to refer to an affair which is assuredly important, since it concerns a Belgian condemned in default abroad * for very serious offences, and to whom judges are refused in Belgium, when he asks to be prosecuted."

M. Van den Heuvel: "It was his look out not to be condemned by default."

M. Lorand: "It was also his look out if he preferred to be judged in Belgium; and that is easily understood. When we consider that this man, accused of such crimes, is walking about freely in Belgium, because it was considered sufficient, notwithstanding the gravity of the accusations against him, to exact a bail of only £200 (fcs. 5000), which enabled him to take passage to Belgium; when we consider that others are in Belgium—where they are living at ease, although accused in the Congo of the gravest of crimes,—we have the right to ask, as they are not prosecuted, if it be true that the State punishes facts of this kind with that severity it would have us believe? How is it in that case that the Congo State does not send a Note to the Belgian Government, whereby these men would be at once prosecuted in Belgium, and if guilty, as is said, would no longer walk about amongst us with impunity?"

M. Vandervelde: "As long as that question has not been answered, everything that we have said remains unchallenged." †

* That is to say, in the Congo State, which has separate laws, and which the Belgian Government declares to be a foreign country when asked to inquire into its actions, but asserts to be a national enterprise when those actions are attacked.

† It is a notable fact that no one on the Government side of the House attempted to take up this categorical challenge. That is one of the lessons to be derived from the debate, which is referred to later on.

Photograph by Géruzet Frères, Brussels

M. EMILE VANDERVELDE
(Leader of the Belgian Labour Party)
(The most prominent Belgian critic of Congo misgovernment)

SECOND DAY'S PROCEEDINGS

M. Lorand: "It is that which makes the importance of the Tilkens affair. The position of the Congo State is peculiar. The whole of its agents are foreigners, and amongst those foreigners the greater number are Belgians, and even belong to the Belgian army! They serve for three years and come back to Belgium. If non-prosecution in Belgium for crimes committed in the Congo is a system, it will often happen that guilty agents will be assured of impunity because it frequently happens that the punishable facts have only been ascertained after the return of the agent to Belgium. That is the case of Tilkens. M. Woeste—and I confess that I thought he would have advanced worthier arguments—tells us that abominable crimes are also committed in Belgium. Perhaps the Minister of Justice will tell us if abominable crimes are often committed in Belgium by officials, by agents of the Administration, by representatives of the powers that be, by police officials; if we often meet in this country with officers, officials, and magistrates who are torturers, assassins, and incendiaries, and who take hostages! . . .

"In the Congo, we are told, there are individual abuses. It is no longer denied that abuses exist; but it is said they are individual acts. It would, however, be extremely interesting to learn the extent and the nature of these individual abuses. Of what kind are they, and in what number have they been perpetrated? We know of two judgments in this connection which are of a nature to cause us anxiety. I read in the *Indépendance Belge* the judgment on the Mongalla affair, which condemned Lacroix and Matthys for the committal of acts which were brought before this House. The truth was on that occasion ascertained, save in one particular—that other agents were also guilty, and that they should be sought for higher up! Indeed, it is a curious circumstance that up to the present—to my knowledge—only non-commissioned officers or agents of the Companies have been punished; never an officer."

"There must be some very interesting things in those Boma trial cases, for those who wish to know all the truth about the abuses perpetrated on the Congo. We have a Belgian Consul on the Congo: why do you not ask your Consul to give you a detailed report of all trials in which Belgians are implicated? You smile, M. le Ministre, but we have the right to say that these judgments throw a sorry light upon the condition of affairs in the Congo. We should have a complete collection of these trials and judgments."

Referring to the commission for the Protection of the

Natives,* "which was entrusted with the important duty of seeing to the execution of measures—so admirable on paper—which have been drafted in favour of the Natives," M. Lorand remarked "that it has not yet published, to my knowledge, a report—a document of any kind, stating that these measures have been applied, telling us what are the abuses which have been recorded, and what are their gravity and extent; and that is necessary, seeing that, at last, it is admitted that abuses exist."

M. Lorand, continuing, referred to M. Woeste's revival of the Fiévez affair. M. Woeste, he said, had revived a document which he himself (M. Lorand) had read to the Chamber two years ago. This document constituted the defence of an accused officer in connection with the cutting off of hands, and denoted amongst Congolese agents "a mental condition which was really alarming." M. Lorand pointed out that it was precisely the phrase used by this officer, and also by a priest, when interviewed by a defender of the State, viz. " How can you forbid a young soldier, animated with a desire to show his prowess, from bringing back war trophies ? " which had wrung from Lord Cranbourne, notwithstanding his bias in favour of the Congo State, these words, "It was precisely such a passage as that which made him doubt whether the authorities of the Congo Free State realised their responsibilities as the white Governors of these barbarous regions." " Now, it is a curious thing," continued M. Lorand, "that the only incident which stirred Lord Cranbourne is the very one that M. Woeste brings forward again now. M. Woeste does not think it astonishing that young soldiers should bring in these war trophies either."

M. Woeste: "I said it was a practice † which must be uprooted 'little by little.'" (Exclamations from the Left.)

M. Lorand: "I take note of that 'little by little.' Now, this incident, which drew from Lord Cranbourne the only distinct statement which is to be found in his speech, is reproduced in this Chamber by M. Woeste without protest and without reserve ! It is precisely against this way of looking upon such abominable practices that we protest, notably against the toleration of this practice of counting the number of people killed in war by the number of hands which the conquerors cut from the fallen enemy and bring back to

---

* See in this connection, the Rev. W. M. Morrison's experiences *re* this farcical commission. Part III.

† It is a practice which has been *introduced* by the Congo State officials. *Vide* Chapter X.

justify the number of cartridges given out to these soldiers, who, yesterday cannibals, have now become agents and inculcators of civilisation. It must not, in point of fact, be forgotten that the instructions given to the agents of the State, and which appear to be drafted with a singular humour, remind them that they have the part of teachers to fulfil." (Laughter.) "No doubt the practice of cutting off hands is not approved; it is said to be contrary to instructions. But you are content to say that indulgence must be shown, and that this bad habit must be corrected 'little by little;' and you plead, moreover, that only the hands of fallen enemies are cut off; and that if hands have been cut off enemies not quite dead, and who, after recovery, have had the bad taste to go to the missionaries and show them their stumps, that it was due to an original mistake in thinking that they were dead. What strange ideas are possessed by the inculcators of civilisation! In the face of such declarations, are we not entitled to assert that the civilisation of the Congo State is not a brilliant one? And it is easy to understand that people whose eyes are not blinded, as yours are; people who do not speak of the Congo with an evident bias and with the intention of praising everything,—it is easy to understand that people not in your condition look upon Congo civilisation as detestable. I, therefore, exaggerate nothing when I state that, as regards European public opinion—and especially British public opinion, which honours itself by its passionate interest in such matters—the Congo State is judged and condemned; and neither do I exaggerate when I say that that is a serious position for Belgium to be in—for Belgium is continually being made conjointly responsible with the Congo State, which tolerates such practices, and whose Belgian admirers—even statesmen in the position of M. Woeste—develop a mental condition which makes them the apologists of this toleration—and I repeat that it is all the more to be regretted that the official representatives of our country should identify themselves so completely with the Congo State."

Dealing with the charges of anti-patriotism, M. Lorand said: "When we speak of patriotism, I have the right to say that, in his speech of yesterday, and in his speech of to-day, the Minister for Foreign Affairs seemed to forget that he was a Belgian Minister, and spoke absolutely as though he were Minister of Foreign Affairs for the Congo State, accepting, without the least reserve, responsibility for all the assertions and all the views of the Congo State. He brought to the Chamber the official Congolese version of all the facts given in the debate, and which were being discussed."

M. Bethune *: "The official version is the true one."

M. de Favereau: "I began by saying that there was no longer any legal link between Belgium and the Congo Free State."

M. Lorand: "But you spoke all along as a Minister for the Sovereign of the Congo, accepting, without the least reserve, without the least discussion, all the theses which it pleases the Congo State to put forward. So much so, that when you receive the British Note, you will have replied to it in advance, and you will have replied that you are always and in everything of the same opinion as the Congo State. As was said at my side during your oration, you deposit your conclusions without having received the promised summons. Even before England has spoken officially, you reply that England is in the wrong on all points. Well, I consider you are wrong in taking up that attitude, from the point of view of Belgian interests. Amongst the questions raised is the question of atrocities committed, frequent, proved, and which, with much appearance of reason, are said to be the result of the system of exploitation adopted by the Congo State. Then there is the question of Free Trade. Again you have adopted the Congo State's view with a strange enthusiasm. I understand M. Woeste doing that—he has no official position; I understand M. Bethune doing that—he is a Congolese magistrate. But I do not understand why the Minister for Foreign Affairs of Belgium should say, as you say, that there is no foundation in the complaints put forward from the point of view of commercial liberty. I am all the more astonished, when we are accused of being anti-patriotic in interpellating you, that you should have taken the direct part of the Congo State against Belgian interests, in favour of which one of your predecessors had to make representations to the Congo State. For this thesis that commercial liberty is violated by a monopoly over the land—which, according to you, has been pulverised by Messrs. Woeste, Nys, Barboux, Picard, and other Congo State jurists—has been defended by other jurists. It is an arguable thesis. But far from being a British thesis; it is a Belgian thesis,† brought forward ten years ago by the *Société Anonyme pour le Commerce du Haut Congo*—that is to say, by the very earliest pioneers of the Congo. . . . That association

---

* M. Bethune is a Congo State official.

† It is really a thesis maintained by every competent student of Africa, of every nationality. If you deprive the Native of his land and the fruits thereof, by virtue of a piece of paper signed in Europe, you make him theoretically a slave in his own land. And when you put that policy in practice, you make him a slave in fact.

and its subsidiaries protested against the land appropriation of the Congo State, and denounced it as a violation of the Berlin Act. The resolution, adopted unanimously on September 9, 1892, at the general meeting of the shareholders of the *Société Anonyme*, was energetically defended by Messrs. Thys, Urban, and Brugmann, Administrators of the Company, and approved by the managers, among whom was Mr. Sam Wiener, and now you refute their arguments and their position without discussion or reserve, without troubling whether, in refuting them, you may not be injuring Belgian as well as British interests. And it is us whom you accuse of lack of patriotism! Well, gentlemen, may not the debate of 1892 between the Belgian Companies and the Congo State be revived one day or another? Messrs. Thys, Urban, and Brugmann have declared that, provisionally, they reserve their opinions upon the violation of the Berlin Act, because they have received a portion of the monopolised lands. The Congo State conceded to them a portion of its domain thus appropriated, and then they suspended their claim in favour of Free Trade. But they may have to wage another conflict of interests with their all-powerful competitor. They know now that Belgian interests cannot expect to have your protection. Does not that prove that you are going too far in adopting, blindly and without reserve, the side of the Congo State, even against Belgian interests?"

M. de Favereau (Minister for Foreign Affairs): "The Belgian Government is entitled to have an opinion of its own on a specific subject."

M. Lorand: "Undoubtedly."

M. de Favereau: "You do not dispute that right?"

M. Lorand: "No; but I think it extraordinary that―――"

M. de Favereau: "We are asked to intervene in Congo State affairs. I have given the reasons why we cannot. I have naturally given reasons justifying our attitude. I have shown that the Congo State has not violated the Berlin Act, and that we are not entitled to intervene―――"

M. Lorand: "I repeat, M. le Ministre, that the Congo State is accused in England of having violated the stipulations of the Berlin Act by the *Domaine Privé*, but that the Congo State was accused of having done so in Belgium first; and while we are accused of want of patriotism, because we have instigated the debate in this Chamber, *you are refuting, without reserve, in the interest of the Congo State, the thesis to which are subordinated important Belgian interests engaged in the Congo*—interests which are always at the mercy of the autocracy of the Congo State. We have only to remember the instance of the struggle of 1892 by the Belgian private trading companies against the Congo State to understand that the renewal of that struggle is always possible, and I am compelled to recognise that if, in 1892, Belgian interests were protected and safeguarded by the Belgian Government, to-day the Belgian Government, in its zeal to defend—before everything else, and under any circumstances—the Congo State, is taking in advance the side of the Congo State against Belgian interests. I say that, after that, it is more than strange for us to be accused of lack of patriotism."

The House then rose.

CHAPTER XXVIII

THIRD DAY'S PROCEEDINGS

M. LORAND, continuing his speech, gave an extract from the protest drawn up in 1892 by Messrs. Urban, Brugmann, Thys, and Wiener, Administrators of the Belgian Trading Companies, against the land appropriation policy of the Congo State. This protest, as the hon. member explained in the second day's proceedings, was based upon precisely the same ground as the critics of the Congo State based their condemnation of the State's methods to-day, viz. that appropriation by the State of the land, and the products of the land, violated the Berlin Act, swept commerce, properly so called, out of existence, and reduced the Natives to the level of slaves. The Associated Companies, presided over by the gentlemen named, received in 1892—as M. Lorand pointed out—the support of the Belgian Government, with the result that the Sovereign of the Congo State was virtually compelled, by the pressure of public opinion, to cede a portion of the territory appropriated by the Congo State to these companies; which surrender had silenced them for the time being. But M. Lorand specially insisted on the fact that the truce might be only temporary; that the Associated Companies were at the mercy of the "autocracy" of the Congo State; that the present Belgian Government had wholly and absolutely thrown over the arguments originally employed by the Associated Companies, and now advanced in England and elsewhere against the Congo State; that in doing so the Belgian Government had adopted blindly the thesis put forward by the Congo State, and had thereby prejudiced eventual Belgian interests, and also placed itself in the position of having refuted the British representations even before those representations had been made. Here is the extract read to the Chamber by M. Lorand, from the protest drawn up Messrs. Urban, Brugmann, Thys, and Wiener, Administrators of the Associated Companies in 1892:

"To deny to the Natives the right to sell ivory and rubber produced by the forests and plains belonging to their tribes, which (forests and plains) form part of their hereditary natal soil, and with which (ivory and rubber) they have traded freely from time immemorial, is a veritable violation of natural rights. To forbid European merchants from buying ivory and rubber from the Natives, to compel them to purchase concessions in order to trade with the Natives, is contrary to the spirit and the letter of the Berlin Act, which proclaimed the unlimited freedom of every one to trade, and forbade the creation of all monopoly."

M. Lorand continued: "It is all very well for the jurists of the Congo State to say that the Congo State's appropriation of the land is in conformity with the theoretical principle of the sovereignty of States, combined with the principles of the Belgian Civil Code, which have been transplanted and applied wholesale to the Congo State, to primitive people; it is none the less true that when ninety-nine per cent. of the territory is monopolised and exploited like a farm, either by the Congo State or by companies to which the State has made concessions, there can no longer be in practice any freedom of trade, and there can only be in practice the enslavement of the unfortunate inhabitants of the territory. Every one, we are told, can carry on licensed trade freely in the Congo with the Natives. Yet almost the entire territory has been appropriated, and no one can find thereon an inch of land which has not been appropriated by the State and the *Concessionnaire* Companies.* Again, there are no commercial products of any importance except ivory and rubber. Now these products are looked upon as the natural products of the *domainial* forests, and are appropriated by the *Domaine Privé*, the *Domaine de la Couronne*, and the *Concessionnaire* Companies."

After pointing out the inferior type of agent sent out to the Congo, and referring to the humanitarian instincts which preceded the birth of the Congo State, M. Lorand continued: "As an exploiting enterprise it may be admitted that the State has been a success. Its revenues enable it to support the constantly increasing expenses and the innumerable military expeditions. The Congo State has not only become the greatest vendor of ivory and rubber in the world, but has been enabled with its surplus revenues to conduct enterprises in China and elsewhere, to purchase property in Belgium, and concessions at Hankow. But the methods which have procured this success are without precedent, save, perhaps, in the case of the Jesuits in Paraguay. The success secured for the benefit of one person, and that person's immediate entourage, has been at the price of the enslavement of millions of men † handed

* This statement was fully borne out subsequently by the terms of the Congo State's reply to the British Note (see Part II.).

† "L'esclavage de millions d'hommes livrés à une exploitation sans merci et à des horreurs malheureusement trop réélles qui doivent necessairement résulter d'un tel système."

over to merciless exploitation and to horrors—unhappily, but too true—horrors which are the inevitable accompaniment of such a system. A *Domaine Privé* of the extent of that of the Congo State the world has never known. Never has a private property, *a domaine*, been created of such a vast size, eighty-one times the size of Belgium, worked like a farm, but, like one of the tropical farms of the planters of long ago, where free labour does not exist, and where the population is organised into vast droves of slaves." *

M. Lorand then went on to discuss the nature of the taxes levied upon the Native, his scathing denunciations eliciting from M. de Smet de Naeyer a declaration which will assuredly remain historic, and will go down to posterity as the embodiment of the Belgian conception of tropical African colonisation. Here are the sentences of M. Lorand's speech which drew from the Belgian Premier the declaration referred to:

"It is said that this taxation (*impôt*) is remunerated! Because what distinguishes the system applied in the Congo is that the taxpayer is compelled to work for the State, but that his labour, which the State imposes, is paid for by the same State! It is true that the amount of labour which the Natives have to give is arbitrarily regulated at the pleasure of the European Administrator, and that the price paid to them in remuneration thereof is also regulated by the Administrator!"

M. de Smet de Naeyer: "They are not entitled to anything: what is given to them is a pure gratuity." ("Ils n'ont droit à rien: ce qu'on leur donne est une véritable gratification.")

M. Lorand: "What! You went there with the pretence of saving the Natives from the slave trade and barbarism—with the pretence of initiating them to the advantages of civilisation, and you take their forests, you forbid them to hunt and to collect produce, you drive them to military service and forced labour! They did not call you to Africa; they did not want you, never having felt a need of working for anything beyond their own very modest needs, which they supplied from their lands and forests, which you have appropriated by the right of the strongest, and to-day a Belgian Minister says that they are entitled to nothing! ... And is it under this form that the blessings of civilisation are given to them—forced labour? They used to be free to gather what they required in their forests. To-day these forests belong to a potentate they have never seen, who lives in Brussels; and to financiers whose existence they are ignorant of, who live in

* "Où le travail libre n'existe pas, et où toute la population est organisée en vastes troupeaux d'esclaves travaillant sous l'empire de la menace et de la contrainte."

Brussels, or in Antwerp, and who are represented in Africa by soldiers armed with weapons of precision."

M. Lorand proceeded to particularise the system of forced labour and terrorism existing in the Congo State, in order to collect the revenues which the Sovereign and his financial friends require; the taking of hostages, the chain-gangs, the floggings, and the perpetual massacres. "The work of civilisation, as you call it," exclaimed the Belgian Deputy, "is an enormous and continual butchery."*

M. de Smet de Naeyer, the Belgian Premier, rising to reply, spoke of the "anti-colonial passion" of M. Lorand. The attacks against the State abroad were "interested." There were fewer abuses than formerly. "The appropriation of vacant lands was the first inevitable and necessary step in constituting property in a country which was being opened to civilisation." The interpellation M. de Smet de Naeyer characterised as "inane." "In foreign countries," he added, "people would be delighted to see Belgians attacking a Belgian work." "It is stupid; it is odious," declared the Premier. "Common sense," continued M. de Smet, "indicates that this claim of the State upon unowned possessions is the first stadium in the constitution of property in a country opening itself to colonisation. Has not the collective appropriation of the soil at the origin of the formation of society been seen everywhere to precede individual appropriation?"† As for the *Domaine Privé*, the Premier contended that there was "no nation that does not have its private domain." Similarly, M. de Smet sought to justify the Congo State's shares in the Trusts it has created—which he termed "stock and share portfolio"—on the following grounds: "The Independent State exploits its private domain partly itself, and partly, indirectly by the intermediary of concessionnaire societies, and the part that the State reserves to itself is represented by the shares of those 'Companies.'" With regard to the *Domaine de la Couronne*, "The *Domaine de la Couronne*," said M. de Smet de Naeyer, "is not the private property of the King Sovereign;" it was an official instrument borrowed from English law, created by a decree of Congo State legislation. The *Domaine de la Couronne* was a juridical entity; it was managed under an organic decree of the Sovereign-King, and by three Administrators.‡

---

* "Une énorme et continuelle tuerie."

† Precisely, and all the more reason for respecting Native land tenure, which *is* a collective appropriation, destined, in course of centuries, no doubt, to become modified in the direction of individual ownership.

‡ For the names of these gentlemen and remarks connected therewith, see Chapter XXIX.

The object was to create out of the revenues derived from its works institutions of public utility. The purposes of the Sovereign-King in founding the *Domaine de la Couronne* partook of a "social, scientific, and artistic (*sic*) order." Founder and owner of the Congo State constituted by his care and at his expense, the Sovereign-King was master of its revenues; but he drew no personal profits. The *Domaine de la Couronne* was for public purposes. The revenues of the Congo, apart from the revenues of the *Domaine de la Couronne*, figured in the Budget; as for the latter revenues, "the Sovereign had abandoned them to works of social and public interests." (Applause.)

M. Vandervelde rose to reply. In the first place, he wished to refer to the speech of M. de Favereau the day before. He had, he said, endeavoured to show the House that practically the whole territory of the Congo State was divided between the *Domaine Privé* or the *Domaine de la Couronne*, 1,375,000 kilometres square; Companies controlled by the State, 865,000 kilometres square; Companies in which the State had interest, 180,000 kilometres square; which left only 30,000 kilometres square for independent traders. The Minister for Foreign Affairs had tried to contradict. He had argued that the *Compagnie du Lomami* and the *Cie. du Katanga* owned wholly or partly their property, and also that the *Kasai Company* was not managed by the State. To this he (M. Vandervelde) would reply by giving precise facts and figures. M. Vandervelde then gave a number of particulars of the Congo State and its Trusts, quoting from official returns.

M. Vandervelde concluded his speech with a fierce indictment of the King. "I am told," said M. Vandervelde, "'collectivism is appropriation by the State.' I agree. But what is 'the State' in Belgium? It is the representative of the people. And what is 'the State' in the Congo? It is the representative of one individuality. You tell me that no one draws personal profits. You make the apologies of the Royal giver. You assert that, personally, he spends nothing out of the personal revenues which he draws from the Congo. I ask, Where is the proof of the statement? Where are the revenue and expenditure returns? I only see budgetary estimates, which have always been exceeded. You tell me the King is not influenced by pecuniary considerations; I do not assert the contrary. At a given moment, riches become so enormous that they cease to be a means of enjoyment, in order to become a source of power and an instrument of corruption." (Applause on the Left.) "And when you come and tell me that, thanks to the revenues of the *Domaine de la Couronne*, of that 'domaine,' which is nine times as large as Belgium, the King sheds his favours not only upon the Natives of the Congo, but on citizens of Belgium, I reply that in Belgium we do not care to live under a *régime* of favouritism, or to see the prosperity of the State at the mercy of the powerful. What we demand is to govern ourselves, and not to be governed by a man who devotes a large portion of his revenues to buy consciences and to manufacture public opinion." (Prolonged applause on the Left.)

Concluding his speech, M. Vandervelde referred once more to the Tilkens affair, and accentuated again its deep significance. "It is a strange thing," remarked the Belgian Deputy, "that if we deal with generalities, we are told that our allegations are too vague; and if, on the other hand, we bring forward specific facts, we are told that we are restricting the debate. We are reproached also for quoting as a witness a man condemned for acts of cruelty, for having traded in slaves, for having killed carriers and tortured prisoners. But this is the man you let out on the absurd bail of 5000 francs (£200)! He is at the present moment on Belgian territory, and you do nothing to prosecute him! A simple official notification given by the Congo State in conformity with Article 8 of the Law of April 17, 1878, would suffice to put the Minister of Justice in the position of having to arrest Captain Tilkens, and bringing him before an Assize Court. Why do you leave this man, whom you call a criminal, unpunished? Why do you not give him the judges he asks for? So long as you do not abandon your inaction, we shall have the right to say that you fear the revelations that Tilkens might make; that you fear to involve the superior officer whom Tilkens accuses of having forwarded to his *Chefs de Poste* the order which I have already read to the House: 'I beg to bring to your notice that from January 1, 1899, you must furnish monthly 4000 kilos of rubber. To that effect I give you *carte blanche*. You have two months in which to work your people. Use gentleness first, and, if they persist in not accepting the taxes of the State, employ armed force.' There has been neither protest nor denial of this order. Where is the protest of M. Verstraeten? Where is the prosecution you ought to be making? To these pertinent questions you have no answer to give. Now, gentlemen, a word as to the order of the day. We have demanded an inquiry recognising that there is no official link between the two States, and that consequently all that we can ask the Government is to use its friendly relations with the Congo State in order to get the latter to bind itself to a serious and impartial inquiry. The Government refuses. It will not take advantage of the legitimate influence which it possesses owing to the subsidies granted by Belgium to the Congo State; to the officers which Belgium lends to the Congo State; by the advantages of all kinds which Belgium gives to the Congo State. We, therefore, can only decline to propose an order of the day, contenting ourselves with rejecting that proposed by M. Woeste. It is a curious thing that M. Woeste, after having contended that no official link exists between the two countries, should propose to the Belgian Parliament, to express confidence in a foreign Government! The hon. member may perhaps explain this singular contradiction; as for us, we shall limit ourselves with giving a resolutely hostile vote to his order of the day." (Applause on the Left.)

M. Buyl regretted that, seeing the gravity of the circumstances, he should not be able to vote in favour of the Government. He was an upholder of a Colonial policy for Belgium. But precisely on that account, he could not endorse the dangerous opinions given by M. de Favereau. The hon. Minister for Foreign Affairs had not hesitated to affirm that no link existed between Belgium and the Congo State. The rights of Belgium in Africa had, therefore, been allowed to lapse. If such were the meaning of the law which the Government induced the Chambers to vote in 1901, it had gravely neglected its duties in not explaining it to the representatives of the people. "You have disarmed Belgium in the face of other Powers," concluded M. Buyl.

M. Degroote thought that the Government had "victoriously" defeated the attacks upon the Congo State.

M. Janson said he thought the attacks upon the State abroad were directed from selfish and mercenary motives. He thought that the Congo was the scene of some abuses, but he could not admit that it should be the object of special suspicion. On the other hand, he rejected the idea that there was anything wrong for Belgians to point out abuses which they thought existed. England transported many hundreds of thousands of Negroes every year to America at one time, but an illustrious Englishman, Wilberforce, succeeded—thanks to his energy, his courage, and his perseverance—in suppressing the over-sea slave trade.

M. Vandervelde: "And Wilberforce was accused of lack of patriotism because he damaged the interests of the slave traders."

M. Janson: "I know, and I consider that charges of antipatriotism cannot be levied against people who point out abuses, and who honour themselves in so doing." (Applause on the Left.)

M. Janson went on to say that he wished the State itself would undertake to stamp out abuses. No one, he thought, could deny to the State the right of having a private domaine, a right which had been exercised by every State since the days of the Romans. But in this case, it was necessary to examine whether the theory of "vacant lands" had not been exaggerated. What were the "vacant lands" of the territory? In what way were they vacant? The first people who objected to the land appropriation of the State were Belgians; they were the Administrators and Directors of the *Société du Haut Congo*. They were not accused of lack of patriotism.

M. Huysmans: "The situation was not the same. The Congo State was not being attacked abroad."

M. Janson: "I am absolutely disinterested, and have no lessons on patriotism to receive from any one."

M. Huysmans: "Neither have you any to give."

M. Janson: "I do not give any, and I am showing you where you are leading to in accusing your colleagues, who are doing their duty, of lack of patriotism."

M. Huysmans: "All Belgians should have the patriotism to hold their tongues at the right moment." (Interruptions on the Left. Applause on the Right.)

M. Dufrane: "That is your theory; we may be permitted to have ours."

M. Janson: "It is your interpretation of patriotism."

M. Dufrane: "But it is not ours."

M. Janson: "In all Parliaments, men who denounce abuses are true patriots." (Applause on the Left.)

M. Frederick Delvaux: "If you do not see the difference, I am sorry."

M. Janson: "M. Delvaux and M. Huysmans are very excitable, and one might think that they are afraid of hearing arguments." M. Janson went on to repeat that Belgians had been the first to protest against the land appropriation policy of the State. He read the order of the day voted by the Belgian Companies in 1892:—"This general meeting of shareholders, after having heard the report on the operations of the last period, and the speech of the President of the Company on the position, protests emphatically against the violation of free trade, and of the stipulations of the General Act of the Conference of Berlin, by the Congo State." M. Janson continued his speech amidst frequent interruptions from the members of the Congo Party. At one point, M. Janson asked M. Huysmans, who interrupted him, whether he approved of taking Natives as hostages to insure the payment of the tax. "If your patriotism goes as far as that," added M. Janson, "I pity you."

M. Huysmans: "You are manifestly exaggerating."

M. Janson: "No; I allude to precise facts stated in official documents." M. Janson then went on to say that while he did not admit that the *Domaine Privé* was contrary to the Berlin Act, he was persuaded that abuses were connected with its exploitation—there was forced labour.

M. Vandervelde: "And uncontrolled."

M. Janson: "The representatives of the Government are expected to collect the tax by force of arms."

M. Anseele: "And they receive indirectly gratuities for so doing."

M. Janson: "It is also officially admitted that hostages are taken to ensure the payment of the tax."

M. Bethune: "To what documents do you allude?"

M. Vandervelde: "To the circular of M. Wahis (Governor of the Congo State) to the Commissioner of the Equateur District, which was published in the *Times* as a defence of the State."

M. Deans: "M. Bethune will not listen. He has been told so three times."

M. Janson: "This exploitation of the *Domaine Privé*, if it does not constitute a monopoly, is at least exaggerated, and the best proof of that is that it yields enormous returns. How the times have changed! We went to the Congo for purposes of humanity and civilisation. It was a fine principle. To-day, the spirit of 'lucre' is pushed to excess. Taxes are produced by forced labour; the budget is made to balance by the proceeds of forced labour. Side by side with the official budget there is a secret budget—the budget of the *Domaine Privé de la Couronne.*"

M. de Smet de Naeyer: "There is nothing secret."

M. de Favereau: "Absolutely nothing."

A Member of the Left: "Everything is secret."

M. Vandervelde: "Where are the expenditure and revenue returns?"

M. de Smet de Naeyer: "The receipts of the *Domaine Privé** figure in the budget."

M. Lorand: "Everything is secret in your institution."

M. Janson: "There are two *Domaines Privés*—the *Domaine Privé* properly so called, and the *Domaine de la Couronne.* The latter, exploited in the same way as the former, produces enormous returns, of which we are not advised. I

* Only the estimates are published. The receipts of the *Domaine de la Couronne* figure nowhere, even in estimate form.

am not one of those detestable flatterers, 'the most dangerous present which Divine wrath can give to kings.' I speak the truth, and I say the King has lost sight of his earlier intentions, and, it is undeniable, has become a merchant and a speculator." (Applause on the Left.) "That is the peculiarity of the Congo *régime*. As deputies, by virtue of the constitution, we cannot accuse the personality of the King. I admire him for what he may have done, which is great; but as regards the Congo question, we have no responsible ministers before us, and, unless we hold our tongues, we must challenge the King's action." (Applause on the Left.) "I give him a counsel and a warning: let him return to his original intentions, and work in the interests of Belgium. I am told that a portion of the revenues has gone to defray the expenses attendant upon the acquisition of land and property to establish in Brussels an institution to Art (*Le Mont des Arts*). I say I do not want that institution if it is to be constructed from revenues obtained by the forced labour of black men." (Loud applause on the Left.)

M. Bertrand: "And by their blood."

M. Janson: "I repeat that the *Domaine de la Couronne* is a secret affair, of which we have learned the existence to-day,* and is managed by three unknown persons."

M. de Smet de Naeyer: "Why do you say unknown?"

M. Janson: "Because their names have not been disclosed."

M. de Smet de Naeyer: "I am prepared to give you them."

M. Janson: "Now let us look at the Constitutional aspect of the matter. Under the *régime* of a Constitutional monarchy, considerable emoluments (*liste civile*) are allotted to the King, but on the distinct understanding that he shall not meddle in business affairs. The most humble official of the State is not permitted to embark in commercial undertakings without ministerial authorisation. The same rule holds good for the King. . . . It is a danger, it is an abuse, it is a thing contrary to the principles of our Constitution, that the King, to whom is allotted emoluments by the Nation, should become a merchant and a speculator. . . . I cannot give my vote to the order of the day proposed. I cannot say that all is for the best in the best of all possible Congos."

---

* This admission would almost lead one to hope that if the Belgian deputies were properly informed about the Congo, Messrs. Vandervelde and Lorand would be more widely supported. The existence of the *Domaine de la Couronne* was known to foreigners long before this debate. See the "Congo Slave State," page 22. There is even a decree on it in one of the *Bulletins Officiels*.

M. Huysmans declared that he heartily endorsed the order of the day proposed by M. Woeste. He again accused M. Vandervelde and his friends of being lacking in patriotism. This led to a stormy altercation between the two deputies, in which an interesting disclosure was made, viz. that M. Huysmans was a Congo State official.

M. Huysmans (to M. Vandervelde): "I say that your systematic attacks and your Republican ideals make your arguments suspicious, and deprive them of all authority."

M. Vandervelde: "I say that your systematic apologies make your arguments suspicious, and deprive them of all authority." (Applause on the Left.)

M. Huysmans: "I am familiar with that kind of charge. M. Vandervelde thinks that all who do not share his views are animated by courtesan and base feeling. . . ."

M. Vandervelde: "You are a Congo State official."

M. Huysmans: "Yes, I am a member of the Superior Council of the Congo Free State."

M. Vandervelde: "I do not reproach you with the fact; I take note of it."

M. Huysmans contended that his independence was not on that account compromised, and that he received no portion of the *Domaine Privé* revenues—a statement which was greeted with laughter. "I said just now," continued M. Huysmans, "that national interests were at stake. What is the object of the campaign against the Belgian Congo? The object pursued under a cloak of humanitarianism is really the destruction of the Congo State. Sir Charles Dilke admitted it himself, for after attacking the Congo State's colonial *régime*, he declared 'the day when this *régime* falls to the ground the Congo State will fall with it.' Such was the peroration of Sir Charles Dilke. That is why we say that national interests are at stake." M. Huysmans concluded by repeating that he would vote the order of the day of M. Woeste "with two hands."

M. de Smet de Naeyer said "he did not rise to reply to M. Vandervelde, because there were some things one did not reply to. He, however, protested against M. Janson's statements when he said that the King was a speculator and a merchant. It was untrue. 'The *Domaine Privé* is a normal institution, and what it yields merely serves to feed the budget.' * As for the *Domaine de la Couronne*, it was 'a creation,' the total revenues of which are expended in works of public utility, without the Sovereign-King retaining a *centime*. Its administration is confided to men well known

* But its true yield is never disclosed. What is the inference?

in Belgium, whose names are above suspicion, viz. Baron Goffinet, Baron Raoul Snoy, and M. Droogmans." M. de Smet de Naeyer continued that M. Janson's imputations as to the revenues of the *Domaine de la Couronne* were false, and he should loyally admit his error.

M. Janson: "The Minister has said that if I wish to be loyal, I should admit my error. I do not think that loyalty necessitates admitting an error when one has on the contrary asserted an incontrovertible fact. I affirm, and you have admitted, that the *Domaine Privé de la Couronne* produces considerable revenues."

M. de Smet de Naeyer: "I did not refer to their importance."

M. Janson: "They must be considerable, to judge by the investments made from them in Belgium alone. I cannot look upon this exploitation of the *Domaine Privé* or the *Domaine de la Couronne* otherwise than as a commercial exploitation, because to obtain revenues it is necessary to collect rubber and ivory, which, after collection, give rise to commercial operations in order to derive profit from them."

M. de Smet de Naeyer: "It has been twenty times demonstrated that realising the fruits of a 'Domaine' is not commerce or speculation."

M. Colfs declared his adhesion to the Woeste order of the day.

M. Denis said he could not vote the order of the day.

M. Neugean did not altogether approve of the Woeste order of the day; but, under the circumstances, he would vote for it.

M. Deans would not vote the order of the day. Belgium gave her money and soldiers to the Congo State, and Belgium had a right to know how it was managed. Belgium was responsible for the grave abuses committed there.

The debate was then closed.

The Woeste order of the day was carried by three to one.

CHAPTER XXIX

THE LESSONS OF THE DEBATE

The indictment—The antecedents of the Debate—The main counts of the indictment—Violation of the Free Trade principles of the Berlin Act—What followed the policy of 1892—How revenue is obtained—The treatment of the Natives under the existing system—Sub-agents punished as a sop to Public Opinion—A concrete instance, the Tilkens case.

WHAT the dominating impression of the non-Belgian, who has hitherto paid but little attention to the Congo scandal, may be, after perusing this historic debate, I do not pretend to determine. But some of us, who, after many years of study of the Congo State and its methods, have almost reached the stage when nothing surprises; astonishment is nevertheless the dominant feeling—astonishment that the Belgian people, in the face of the damning exposure which this debate provides, should be content to bear the burden of shame which the cowardly subservience of the great majority of their public men, and the purchasable conscience of the vast majority of their newspapers, is passing down to their children and children's children. It would seem as though some corroding and corrupting medium had eaten into the very vitals of the nation; the perversion, or indifferentism of the mass being all the more startling by contrast with the splendid protest of the very few. Of Messrs. Vandervelde and Lorand it may be truly said that they are reviving the noble traditions of the men of a hundred years ago, who fought the over-sea slave trade. They are fighting another species of slavery, more insidious, and more terrible in its effects—the slavery introduced into unhappy Africa by the foreign Potentate who rules the destinies of their country. All honour to them. How difficult their task is may be appreciated when it is borne in mind that, in the course of this debate, the leader of the Catholic Party made the *apologia* of atrocity, while the Premier and Foreign Minister showed themselves the eager and willing tools of the financiers who, with their royal head, have converted the territories of the Congo State into a shambles.

Let us now examine the principal features of the debate, and accentuate the lessons conveyed thereby.

The debate took place last July, rather more than a month after the British House of Commons had passed, with an unanimity rare in Parliamentary annals, the following resolution :—

"That the Government of the Congo Free State having, at its inception, guaranteed to the Powers that its native subjects should be governed with humanity, and that no trading monopoly or privilege should be permitted within its dominions; this House requests His Majesty's Government to confer with the other Powers, Signatories of the Berlin General Act, by virtue of which the Congo Free State exists, in order that measures may be adopted to abate the evils prevalent in that State."

MM. Vandervelde and Lorand, leaders of the Labour and Radical sections of the Belgian assembly, thereupon announced their intention of interpellating the Government. The interpellation was accepted by the Government, and on July 1 M. Vandervelde opened a debate which was to last three days, and in the course of which the Congo State and its ruler were to be exposed to an indictment even more crushing and more unanswerable—because more detailed and specific in the counts—than that inflicted by the House of Commons. After pointing out the special duty and right of Belgium to inquire into the management of the Congo State, M. Vandervelde went straight to the point. He showed that in 1892 King Leopold claimed that the products of the land belonged to the State, that the Natives had no right to gather or collect them unless they brought them to the State stations, and that the European merchants established in the country would be prosecuted if they attempted to buy such products from the Natives; the "judicial" basis for this step—the basis upon which it is defended—having been laid in 1885, when the State declared all land to be "vacant" that was not actually built upon, or under cultivation for food-stuffs by the Natives.*
He referred to the protests which this claim brought forth from the Belgian traders at the time, the latter invoking the clauses of the Berlin Act which proclaimed unrestrained freedom for every one to buy and to sell; and he reminded his hearers that those who in England maintained the injustice of such a claim in its effects upon the Natives, were urging the same considerations, which the Belgian trading companies in the Congo had urged in 1892.

* See Chapter XXVI.

THE LESSONS OF THE DEBATE 341

M. Vandervelde reviewed the policy of 1892 in its successive stages. The initiatory claim had been followed by the partitioning of the whole of the territories of the Congo State, with the exception of the infinitesimal Lower Congo, into a series of vast trusts. The "State" Trust—the *Domaine Privé** and *Domaine de la Couronne*—was forty-six times the size of Belgium ; the subsidiary trusts covered between them an area of twenty-nine times the size of Belgium, while the original Belgian trading companies, who had been compelled to abide by a *modus vivendi* which gave the State an interest in their business, had an area six times the size of Belgium. No one outside these groups could enter the Congo territories. This policy, M. Vandervelde contended, was a violation of the Berlin Act, both as regards the freedom of trade stipulated under the Act, and the prohibition of granting monopolies or privileges as stipulated under the Act.

The immediate consequence of the policy, continued M. Vandervelde, was the acquisition of enormous sums by the Sovereign of the Congo State and his financial associates. The sums drawn by the Sovereign could not be ascertained, because only the estimated revenues of the *Domaine Privé* were published, and the actual returns never; while the revenues of the *Domaine de la Couronne* were kept entirely secret. So large were they, however, that the "Congo State" was investing considerable amounts in property in Belgium itself, and was sinking important sums in sundry Chinese undertakings.

But how were these enormous sums obtained ? They were the product of compulsory taxation, of which it was sometimes sought to hypocritically disguise the effects, on the plea that the Natives were paid for their labour. The truth was that the Natives, having been officially expropriated from their land, and from all rights in the products of economic value growing therein, had been reduced to the level of slaves : forced to produce rubber and ivory in unlimited quantities at the bidding of the State and the trusts, which the State either managed or was financially concerned in. Such systematic coercion was only possible by the medium of a large native army of " 16,000 to 17,000 men," men recruited chiefly from the domestic slave element of fierce cannibal tribes of the interior ; stationed in districts other than those of their origin, and, therefore, not likely to have any feelings for the tribes against whom they might be sent,† and commanded by "non-

* *Stricto sensu : vide* Cattier and others.
† The curious absence of racial feeling and combination amongst African tribes is, of course, too much of a commonplace to need accentuating here.

commissioned officers intoxicated with self-importance, free, or practically so, from all control." The soldiers, M. Vandervelde incidentally remarked, were compelled to serve twelve years, seven in active service and five in the reserves. This vast machine simply existed for forcing rubber and ivory out of the people in the form of taxes. M. Vandervelde quoted the textual instructions of the Governor-General of the Congo, authorising the officers of the State to take hostages from the people if they were recalcitrant in carrying out the demands made upon them, and to use force if opposed.

Such a *régime*, argued the leader of the Labour party, led "fatally and inevitably" to the perpetration of innumerable atrocities. When they reached the ears of public opinion, a show was made of punishing the culprits. But the true culprits were those who maintained the system, otherwise the Congo State itself. For this reason the high officials of the Government in the Congo were never punished, a few sub-agents being made scapegoats, until such time as the effect of the particular disclosures had worn off. In the case of the Mongalla massacres, the local judge, more courageous than the rest, had not hesitated to explain the lightness of the sentence passed upon one of the sub-agents found guilty of nameless mutilations upon natives, from the circumstances that he had carried out the instructions of his superiors "in showing no respect for the lives or the rights of the natives." The judge's pronouncement—although three years old—had not previously transpired, but M. Vandervelde read out the actual wording to the House. After referring to other recorded atrocities, M. Vandervelde brought a new and specific case of considerable importance before the House.

Prefacing his observations by emphasising the oft-repeated assurances of the Congo State's desire to punish agents guilty of atrocity, M. Vandervelde demanded that Captain Tilkens, of the *Force Publique* (Congo Army), condemned by default in the Congo to ten years' imprisonment for atrocities, should be brought before the Assize Court of his own country (Belgium). Anticipating the usual taunt of the apologists of the State whenever the testimony of its former officials are given against it, M. Vandervelde took care to point out that the documentary evidence upon which he relied to bring his facts before the House were letters written by Tilkens himself, not *subsequent* to his condemnation, in order to throw the blame of his misdeeds upon others, but at a time when the Congo State "was lavishing upon him advancement and favours." It is useless to recapitulate the whole story here. It will be found fully set forth in M. Vandervelde's speech.

THE LESSONS OF THE DEBATE 343

Suffice it to say that these letters, written by this man Tilkens when engaged in carrying out his instructions, are symbolic of Congo State rule, and throw an inner light upon the working of the Congo State system which is not new, but which, nevertheless, is both instructive and informing. In brief, Tilkens was officially instructed (letters of instructions read by M. Vandervelde) that his district was expected to produce a certain quantity of rubber and a certain number of carriers per month. He and his soldiers were already working the people to death, so that in order to obtain more out of them, he had to strike such terror into their hearts as would crush out the last spark of resistance to outrageous demands. Faithful to his mandate, he and his soldiers shot and massacred wholesale; burning villages, looting, raping, torturing, murdering: making of his district a small but particularly bad hell in the big hell around him. And even so, he could not entirely break the people, "Yet I cannot say," he wrote to his military friends, "I have subjugated the people. . . . *They prefer to die. What can I do?*" But the method succeeded for a time: the requisite quantity of rubber was forthcoming. Tilkens was praised, promoted, and remunerated. The aftermath was, however, looming ahead. The people rose, attacked the State post, sacked it. A scapegoat had to be found. Tilkens was merely a subordinate after all—a non-commissioned officer of the Belgian Army. After a long interval he was arrested, and although the indictment drawn up against him included enough crimes to hang a whole regiment, *he was released on finding sureties for £200*. He promptly stowed away on a home-coming boat, and, upon arriving in Belgium, knowing that the Congo State laws could not touch him in Belgium (for such is the convenient legislation of the State), claimed to be brought to public trial by the Belgian law courts. "I have," he admitted in effect, "acted badly; but I acted upon the instructions of my superior officers. I was compelled to obey. The instructions are extant. Witnesses can be brought to prove it. Here are their names and addresses. Justice I knew I could not obtain in the Congo; I have come to Belgium. I demand to be tried before a jury in the light of day. I was a soldier: as a soldier I had to obey my chiefs." Such was the story brought before the House by M. Vandervelde, touching one small corner only of the vast Congo State.

M. Vandervelde concluded his speech by saying that the Tilkens incident was only a repetition of what had taken place in numerous other districts. The risings which were the outcome of the Tilkens atrocities were the reproduction of other risings, "which have been endemic for over ten years, and which necessitate the up-keep, on a war footing, of 17,000 men." The honour of Belgium demanded that the Government should order a searching inquiry into the whole system of Congo rule.

Such were the main counts of M. Vandervelde's indictment. They were subsequently amplified and driven home by M. Lorand, by M. Vandervelde (in a later speech), by M. Janson, and one or two other speakers. The speakers on the Government side were M. de Favereau, the Minister for Foreign Affairs, who spoke twice; M. de Smet de Naeyer, the Premier, who spoke once; M. Woeste, the leader of the Catholic Party, and often described as the "King's henchman;" M. Bethune, and M. Huysmans, who, although members of the Belgian House, are officially connected with the Congo State! The main body of the House was discreetly silent, like a regiment of well-drilled soldiers. To the most personal, the most direct, the most damaging onslaught and imputations upon the person of the Sovereign of the Congo State, the House remained impassive; which, if it proves nothing else, proves at least the amount of respect with which the despotic Monarch of the Congo is held in Constitutional Belgium! Belgians should really not complain of foreign strictures upon King Leopold, when the Belgian House rings with accusations and charges, couched in language, the emphasis of which has never been approached outside of Belgium! Apart from certain features which marked the speech of M. Woeste—which will be referred to separately—we need only concern ourselves with dissecting the defence of Congo State institutions, attempted by M. de Favereau and M. de Smet de Naeyer. M. Bethune and M. Huysmans being Congo State officials, their effusions may be left out of account.

How was the indictment met by the official defenders of the Congo State? Let us take M. de Favereau's speech first. In the first place, he declined to institute an inquiry, on the ground that—

I. The Congo State was a foreign State.

The facts that—

(*a*) King Leopold, the Sovereign of the Congo State, is also King of Belgium.

(*b*) Belgium has lent £1,400,000 to the Congo State, and sunk £600,000 in the Congo Railway.

(*c*) Belgium lends her army officers to the State.

(*a*) That the moral responsibility of Belgium for the management of the Congo State, in view of an obvious

solidarity of interest, is evident to the world—the
did not weigh with the Belgian Minister for Foreign
He did not even discuss them. He set them on
and met the demand for an inquiry, on the part of
with a direct negative.*

II. The demand that Belgium, *as one of the Signatory Powers*
of the Berlin Act, should inquire, M. de Favereau also
refused, on the ground that—

(*a*) The Congo State had not violated the Berlin Act
either in respect to its free-trade provisions, or the obligations
it laid upon King Leopold to safeguard the rights of the
Natives.

Here M. de Favereau deigned to give his reasons, which,
with two exceptions, consisted in the mere enumeration of the
usual platitudes, such as the Congo State protected religious
and scientific missions, and had put down the Arab slave
trade, etc. The speaker also gave quotations from numerous
laws passed by the State. There was positively no attempt
on the part of M. de Favereau to deal with the specific
points contained in M. Vandervelde's indictment in regard
to the working in practice of the Congo State's policy. The
policy itself, viz. appropriation of the land and the fruits
thereof, M. de Favereau endeavoured to reconcile with the
commercial clauses of the Berlin Act, by putting forward the
threadbare claim of the right of the State to constitute itself
the proprietor of both the one and the other.

On that point, M. de Favereau was definite enough. I
have dealt with the contention in Part II.

Passing from the question of inquiry to a discussion of
some of the points raised by M. Vandervelde, the utter
feebleness of M. de Favereau's defence is indeed remarkable.
Let us take, in the first place, his attempted refutation of the
charge of violation of Article 5 of the Act—the Free Trade
article. To begin with, his definition of the fundamental
basis of the Congo State policy should, if that definition had
any force at all, have been sufficient for his purpose. He had
told the House plainly that, in asserting rights of proprietorship over the land and its products, the Congo State had not
violated Clause 5 of the Act of Berlin, because the stipulations
of that Act, in respect to freedom of trade, were rendered
valueless and non-pertinent by the subsequent conversion of
the products of the soil (*i.e.* the elements of trade) into State
property. There was no necessity then to go into details. If
all the products of economic value yielded by the land belong

* This denial of any special *locus standi* on the part of Belgium in
1900, and again in 1903, should be carefully noted.

to the State, it is obvious that the State can do what it likes with its own; it can create and control "companies" to "develop" its property—in fact, it need not be required to give particulars of its own affairs. It is, however, significant of the doubt existing even in the mind of M. de Favereau, as to the tenability of that doctrine, that he felt constrained to attempt a demonstration *ad absurdum*, viz. that trade was free in the Congo State! And here the feebleness of M. de Favereau's argument was strikingly conspicuous.

M. de Favereau's procedure was this. He said, in effect, "You assert that trade is not free in the Congo State. Why, there are 403 trading factories there (*comptoirs commerciaux*)! As for what you always assert, that the State controls, or is interested in, the trading companies, I will cite one or two instances which show how erroneous your information as a whole must be."

With regard to the latter point, it will be observed that M. de Favereau was careful not to deny that the bulk of the companies so called *were* controlled by the State. He merely endeavoured, for Parliamentary purposes probably, to convict the critics of the State of general inaccuracy in the eyes of the House, by citing several companies, as to which, it is to be presumed, he imagined that the critics did not possess the requisite information. Mark what took place on the following day. M. Vandervelde gave facts and figures—which, for the matter of that, are simply taken from the Official Bulletins of the State for different years—showing that regarding the "companies" mentioned by M. de Favereau as being independent of the State, the Congo State holds in the first one, one-half of the shares, gets one-half of the profits, and appoints the chairman, the manager, and the majority of the directors; receives 25 per cent. of the net profits of the second one; receives two-thirds of the profits of the third, appoints two-thirds of the directors, the chairman, and the manager; receives 100,000 dividend-paying shares of the fourth, approves the nomination of directors, and appoints three delegates! *M. de Favereau was dumb.* As for M. de Favereau's "403 trading factories," it is only necessary to say that he included in his list all the factories of the trusts, including those above mentioned, plus the trading factories in the small Lower Congo, where, as I have already explained, the State's policy did not apply prior to January, 1904 (and which therefore was entirely outside the sphere of debate), down to the small grog-shops at Boma and Matadi, which exist for catering for European wants!

When a Belgian Minister for Foreign Affairs, in his

THE LESSONS OF THE DEBATE

endeavours to bolster up a bad case, can stoop to such frivolities, the value attaching to the denials and assertions of Congo State officials may be surmised. The treatment of the Tilkens affair by M. de Favereau is again illustrative of the methods of the Congo State defenders.

M. de Favereau admitted the atrocities committed by Tilkens, but exclaimed that he had been punished, because he was condemned by default in the Congo to ten years' imprisonment, which, of course, is nothing more than a judicial farce, because the sentence cannot be enforced in Belgium, and there is no law of extradition. Reminded of the fact that Tilkens, notwithstanding his deeds, had been let out on bail of £200, M. de Favereau had nothing to say. On the other hand, he dilated at great length upon the system of bonuses paid to Tilkens and other agents in proportion to rubber collected, endeavouring, by a laboured explanation, to show that the "points" referred to by Tilkens in his letters could only have meant good conduct marks! *He never attempted to deny the authenticity of the damning letters of the ad-interim Governor-General and of the District Commandant, read out to the House by M. Vandervelde.* He was, of course, unable to do so, and he knew it quite well.

Again and again M. Vandervelde and M. Lorand returned to the assault. The Belgian Government, they argued, declined to inquire into the Congo State's *régime*. They accepted everything on hearsay. The Congo State denied that its policy involved abominable cruelties to the natives, and boasted of its judicial purity Here, then, was an opportunity for the State to justify itself in the light of day.* Here was an opportunity for Belgium to prove that she was not an accomplice to atrocity. Tilkens was in Belgium. Tilkens demanded to be tried before a Belgian jury. The Congo State had merely to ask the Belgian Government to prosecute. The Belgian Government itself could prosecute, if it were willing (M. Vandervelde is a barrister, and presumably knows his law). The commandant of the district, whose instructions were cited by Tilkens, was also in Belgium. Why did not the Congo State Government—why did not the Belgian Government take action ?

M. de Favereau, and M. de Smet de Naeyer, the obedient Premier, sat mute.

"Then you are afraid of what Tilkens would reveal!" exclaimed M. Vandervelde. "You dare not prosecute?" The direct challenge was ignored. *A dead silence was*

* In a different form the Caudron trial, in 1904, provided another opportunity. We have seen the result.

maintained on the Government benches; proving only too well that neither the Congo State nor the Belgian Government dares to face a public prosecution, in Belgium, of one of the agents of King Leopold. No more deeply significant incident has in recent years been recorded in connection with the Congo scandal. If there were nothing else, this would be conclusive in itself. With regard to the treatment of the Natives, M. de Favereau's speech contained nothing which can be at all considered definite. He quoted sundry laws in existence, which, in view of the fundamental basis of Congo State rule already defined, can only remain a dead letter.

It is like a man who has set fire to a house helping to pass the bucket round to extinguish the flames. What use can any number of laws be, when grafted upon a central law which deprives the Native of his property, vests it in the State or the corporations to which the State may elect to convey it, and compels the Native to collect that property for the State or its corporations? Such laws can only be framed for the purpose of deception, because the framers of them know perfectly well they can never be applied. M. de Favereau did not, of course, deny the existence of the enormous Native army maintained by the State: but endeavoured to minimise the arguments derived from the fact by going off on a side issue—to wit, the alleged hardships of the method of recruiting adopted by the State, hardships which he denied by the simple expedient of assertions uncorroborated by any attempt at proof, which had nothing to do with the main point.

In summarising M. de Favereau's defence, one can only say that it left M. Vandervelde's general indictment of Congo State rule wholly unimpaired; strengthened, indeed, rather than weakened. When, passing from high-flown generalities, the Minister for Foreign Affairs dealt with specific facts, he cannot be said to have improved his reputation. The arguments by which he sought to demonstrate the existence of free trade in the Congo territories, after admitting the appropriation by the Congo State of the African elements of trade, were proved to be in essential particulars quite inaccurate. In the Tilkens matter he showed conclusively that neither the Congo State nor Belgium dares to prosecute in Europe officials who perpetrate atrocities in Africa; nor to publicly investigate in Europe the circumstances which lead to the committal of such atrocities. He based his whole case, indeed, upon the legitimacy of the fundamental law of the Congo State, to wit, State appropriation of land, and the products of economic value yielded by

THE LESSONS OF THE DEBATE 349

it. What mattered everything else? So much for M. de Favereau.

But if M. de Favereau lacked in precision, the same cannot be said of M. de Smet de Naeyer, for he made two admissions which were more damaging, perhaps, than any of the criticisms passed upon the Congo State by its enemies.

The first admission was of supreme importance as a revelation of sentiment.

The second admission was of supreme importance as a revelation of fact.

The revelation of sentiment was wrung from M. de Smet in a moment of irritation. M. Lorand was exposing the hollow pretence of payment made by the State to the natives in exchange for the produce of the forced taxation thrust upon them. He was ironically commenting upon this special peculiarity of the State's system of dealing with the natives, when M. de Smet exclaimed—

"They are not entitled to anything. What is given them is a pure gratuity."

That unlucky statement of M. de Smet's embodies to a nicety the ideas which prevail in Belgian, or perhaps we should say in Congolese, circles, as to the principles which should preside over the relations between a European Power and the African Natives. In short, it is the conception, revived to-day in aggravated form in Belgium, of the Spanish *conquisitadores* in Peru and in the West Indies, of the Portuguese adventurers on the West African coast, of the old Dutch culture system of the East Indies, and perhaps we might add of Warren Hastings in India. It is the spirit of the slave trade—the spirit which looks upon the "coloured" man as a brute, destined by nature and circumstance to be the slave of the white. Under the boasted philanthropic veneer of European civilisation, this spirit lurks in individuals. In Belgium a few individuals have acquired for themselves a million square miles in tropical Africa, and on the Congo this spirit has become the working policy. The difference between the application of this policy in the Congo and its old prototypes is, that the latter constituted a policy of national wrong-doing which in due time found its corrective, whereas in the Congo the policy is a personal one, and not in any sense national, and, so long as the personal element exists, will continue. One might quote innumerable passages from the documents issued during the past few months by and on behalf of the Congo State, in support of the contention. But the words of the present Belgian Premier, whose relations past and present with the Sovereign of the Congo State are well known, provide sufficient proof. The Native of the Congo territories, whose "moral and material regeneration" King Leopold professes to have at heart, having been deprived of his land and the fruits of his land by decree, is now declared to be entitled to nothing even for his labour in securing the products of economic value growing on his land for the benefit of his despoilers! The miserable pittance—about 1*d.* per lb.—for his rubber paid in rubbishy goods, or in brass rods, which are apparently refused not infrequently as currency by the payers, is a "pure gratuity," on the part of his philanthropic rulers!

The revelation of fact is a confirmation of the statement repeatedly made by myself, and as repeatedly denied by the Congo State authorities—until M. de Smet raised the veil, viz. that vast sums are annually obtained by the Sovereign of the Congo State in the shape of the proceeds of the sale of ivory and rubber derived from regions specially marked out for State exploitation, *which do not figure in the budgetary returns*. The importance of this admission by M. de Smet is twofold. First, no one, not even sceptics who have rejected the accumulated proofs of the last ten years as to the motives and true meaning of Congo State rule—can, after the declarations of M. de Smet, retain their illusions with any attempt at honesty. Secondly, it explains in the clearest possible manner the true reasons which actuate the Sovereign of the Congo State in refusing to allow any impartial inquiry into his affairs.

The Belgian Premier admitted, for the first time be it noted again, that a certain portion of the Congo territories produced revenues which did not figure in the revenue and expenditure returns, viz. the portion of the territories known as the *Domaine de la Couronne*. Many of the members of the House heard of the *Domaine de la Couronne* for the first time.

Needless to remark, M. de Smet declared that the King *personally* did not touch a *centime* of these unrecorded revenues. The debate, however, definitely established the fact that profits derived from the sale of the rubber and ivory of the region of the *Domaine de la Couronne*—a region notoriously rich in rubber—do not figure in the public returns even in the form of estimates; are unaccounted for in the budget. Where do these proceeds go? It seems from M. de Smet's declaration that they are dealt with by a committee of three, viz. Baron Raoul Snoy, Baron Goffinet, M. Droogmans.

Who are these men? Baron Raoul Snoy is the King's diplomatic adviser in Congo affairs. He accompanied King

Leopold to Paris the other day, and was present at the King's interview with M. Delcassé.

Baron Goffinet is attached to the King's court. One of the administrators of the *Société Anversoise du Commerce au Congo*, better known as the Mongalla Trust, the scene of massacres so numerous that it has been impossible to withhold them from the light of day—in which the Congo State holds 50 per cent. of the shares, and which it has now, it seems, entirely absorbed is a Baron Goffinet. I do not know whether the two are one or distinct persons.

M. Droogmans is Financial Secretary of the Congo State and chairman of the *Comité Spécial du Katanga* (Katanga Trust), from whose operations the State takes two-thirds of the profits, and the *Comité* one-third.

Apart from these declarations, M. de Smet's discourse was merely a repetition of M. de Favereau's arguments; like the latter, he left the main counts of M. Vandervelde and M. Lorand's indictment unchallenged.

The only other episode in the Government defence was a contribution by M. Woeste, referring to the mutilation of natives by the Congo State troops. In seeking to palliate these atrocities, and enunciating with affable self-satisfaction the *dictum* that they would disappear " little by little," M. Woeste merely afforded further proof of what M. Lorand rightly termed the " mental condition " of the defenders of the Congo State—or, as it might be put, the depths to which the interested Belgian backers of the Congo State have fallen.

I do not think I can more fittingly close this review of the famous Belgian debate than by giving the following quotation —which I am permitted to do—from a letter written a few weeks ago by Mr. Joseph Conrad to a personal friend. In it the well-known author, who has lived in the Upper Congo, expresses in a few admirable sentences the feeling which all who have studied King Leopold's rule in Africa share with him :—

" It is an extraordinary thing that the conscience of Europe, which seventy years ago put down the slave trade on humanitarian grounds, tolerates the Congo State to-day. It is as if the moral clock had been put back many hours. And yet nowadays, if I were to overwork my horse so as to destroy its happiness or physical well-being, I should be hauled before a magistrate. It seems to me that the black man—say of Upoto—is deserving of as much humanitarian regard as any animal, since he has nerves, feels pain, can be made physically miserable. But, as a matter of fact, his happiness and misery are much more complex than the misery or happiness of animals, and deserving of greater regard. He shares with us the consciousness of the universe in which we live—no small burden.

"Barbarism *per se* is no crime deserving of a heavy visitation; and the Belgians are worse than the seven plagues of Egypt, in so much that in that case it was a punishment sent for a definite transgression; but in this the Upoto man is not aware of any transgression, and therefore can see no end to the infliction. It must appear to him very awful and mysterious; and I confess it appears so to me too. The slave trade has been abolished, and the Congo State exists to-day. This is very remarkable. What makes it more remarkable is this: the slave trade was an old-established form of commercial activity; it was not the monopoly of one small country, established to the disadvantage of the rest of the civilised world in defiance of international treaties and in brazen disregard of humanitarian declarations. But the Congo State, created yesterday, is all that, and yet it exists. It is very mysterious. One is tempted to exclaim (as poor Thiers did in 1871), 'Il n'y a pas d'Europe.' ... And the fact remains that in 1903, seventy years or so after the abolition of the slave trade (because it was cruel), there exists in Africa a Congo State, created by the act of European Powers, where ruthless, systematic cruelty towards the blacks is the basis of administration; and bad faith towards all the other States the basis of commercial policy."

PART VI

THE ATTEMPT TO DISCREDIT CONSUL CASEMENT'S REPORT

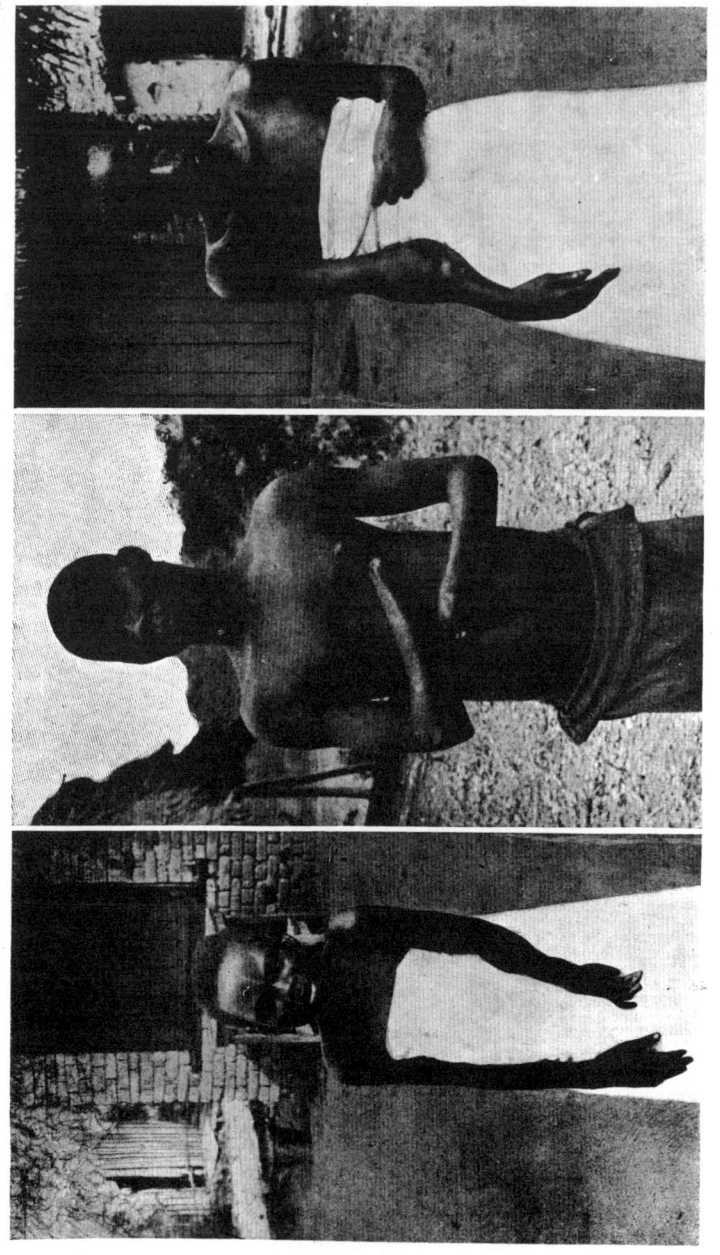

MONGALA MOLA EKULITI BIASIA

NATIVES SHOT AND MUTILATED BY CONGO SOLDIERY
(For particulars, refer to Appendix)

CHAPTER XXX

THE ATTEMPT TO DISCREDIT CONSUL CASEMENT'S REPORT

"Consul Casement's Report has been foully attacked."—Sir CHARLES DILKE (House of Commons, June 9th, 1904).

"There is one man who will probably soon become the target for profuse Belgian and Continental abuse, and that is the one Englishman who knows more of Belgium on the Congo than any other of my acquaintance. I refer to Mr. Roger Casement, His Majesty's Consul on the Congo. Mr. Casement was at Delagoa Bay when I landed there in 1896. . . . Roger Casement is the sort of man depicted in Jules Verne's novels, the man who is everlastingly exploring and extricating himself from every imaginable difficulty by superhuman tact, wit, and strength. He would wander away for weeks and months with merely a black attendant or two, trekking along the Swazi frontier, studying the language and the customs of the natives, establishing relations with the chiefs, and sounding them as to their feelings in matters interesting in Downing Street. . . . It is not saying more than the truth when I testify that Mr. Casement knew more of the Natives between Basutoland and the shores of Mozambique than any other white man. . . . It is not because Mr. Casement impressed me personally that I write. I went behind his back and made inquiries of others in South Africa."—Mr. POULTNEY BIGELOW. (*Morning Post*, Dec. 31st, 1903.)

To defend the report of a British official of the stamp of Mr. Roger Casement—a report, every page of which bears the hall-mark of truth; a report on which the British Government has placed implicit reliance; a report which has brought the most painful conviction to every unprejudiced mind that has perused it—to defend a document of this kind because it has been criticised by interested parties, would be a puerile superfluity.

But if to defend this historical document would be to assume a position derogatory both to dignity and common sense; to expose the tactics of those who have sought by every means which a sort of third-rate duplicity and a most ineffective mendaciousness could suggest, to discredit that report, and bespatter with the mud attaching to their own unclean fingers both the character and the capacity of its author—to do this, perhaps, will serve a useful purpose.

The conduct of the Congo State Authorities, of their paid allies in the Continental Press, of their contemptible handful of acolytes in this country, in the matter of Consul Casement's report, has demonstrated with greater clearness than ever the characteristic features of this fight, viz. that it is one between gentlemen on the one side, and a clique of adventurers on the other, remarkable for a species of low cunning, and utterly and absolutely shameless. The peculiar morality of the Congo Executive in eluding honest criticism by plausibilities and evasions, in laying down premises of its own creation, attributing them to its own critics, and proceeding to destroy them with unctuous elaboration, calling the while upon high Heaven to witness the overthrow of its adversaries; in concocting stories to pass muster in Europe, while secretly taking steps in Africa diametrically opposed thereto; in hurling calumnious charges at individuals in order the better to disguise its own turpitude and wrong-doing—of this abundant evidence has been given in the present volume, notably in the Rabinek tragedy, the Mongalla massacres of 1900 and 1903, the Rubi-Welle massacres, better known as the Tilkens case, the Kasai massacres denounced by Morrison, etc. But never have these features been so superlatively manifest as in the effort to demolish Consul Casement's report. Here, indeed, has the apotheosis of mendacity been reached.

To begin with, Consul Casement himself has been subjected to a stream of malignant abuse and cowardly insinuation. The Executive was outwardly content to make a superhuman effort to prove the incompetency of the Consul to deal with native evidence, varied at one point with the insolent suggestion that the "former employment of Mr. Casement had not entirely prepared him for Consular functions,"* whatever that may mean. That effort has recoiled upon its own head, as will presently be shown. The myrmidons of the State, taking their lead from head-quarters, have subjected our Consul to the foulest attacks (even various Consuls for Belgium, actually in this country, taking part in the fray), and I regret to say that they have been assisted—in Continental eyes at least—by a few obscure English prints, whose source of information is well known, and whose attacks upon their own distinguished countryman have been reproduced with much gusto in every issue of that remarkable publication, *La Vérité sur le Congo*.

It may be worth while, although certainly unnecessary, to devote a paragraph or two to Mr. Casement. Officially, an able and distinguished civil servant, with twelve years spent

* "Notes sur le rapport de Mr. Casement, Consul de sa Majesté Britannique du 11 Décembre, 1903."

ATTACKS ON CONSUL CASEMENT'S REPORT

in the Consular Department in various parts of Africa with twenty years' experience of tropical African peoples and conditions, whom Sir Claude Macdonald, our present Ambassador at Tokio, has described in the following words:* "It would be difficult to find any one in every way more suited" for his duties, and as having " considerable experience with Natives"; of whom Lord Lansdowne speaks as an official of "wide African experience." † Unofficially, a man almost worshipped by his friends, possessed of a personality inspiring respect and admiration, absolutely honest, absolutely fearless; saturated with Africa, the greatness, the grandeur of its wide expanse, the virgin depths of its vast forests, the natural kindliness and hospitality of its peoples. Writes one of his life-long friends to me—

> "He is a high-minded man, against whom there has never been a breath of any sort of scandal. To me, he has always represented what is meant by the words honour and courage. I have known him twenty-one years (five years of our friendship being spent together in Africa), and I cannot imagine a finer specimen of a man. He invariably wins the heart and confidence of all he meets. He is absolutely honourable, and without fear."

Of Roger Casement it may well be said, " Un Bayard sans peur et sans reproche." And it is a man such as this, whom the Congo crowd have with a subtlety designed to be Machiavellian, endeavoured to convict primarily of incompetence, and secondly of " mauvaise foi," the pet expression of these good people when their backslidings and foolish intrigues are remorselessly exposed. It is a man such as this upon whom Continental organs have exhausted the abusive epithets of their extensive vocabulary, while affecting pity for his incapacity. These personal insults to Consul Casement have had one good effect, at any rate. They have created deep anger in this country, while his detractors appear to have forgotten that from the moment the British Government issued that report, officially endorsed and defended it, the personality of its author was merged into the impersonality of his Government, and that every attack upon the honesty, truth, or integrity of H. M. Consul on the Congo has been an imputation upon the British Government.

* "Report on the Administration of the Niger Coast Protectorate," August 1891 to 1894. Sir Claude was then High Commissioner for that part of the world.
† Mr. Casement apparently entered the Consular service in 1892. From that date to 1895 he served in the Niger Coast Protectorate. From 1895 to 1898 he would seem to have served as H.M. Consul at Delagoa Bay.

And now let us consider the procedure of the Congo Government to discredit the report, apart from insinuation and insult.

They had in Consul Casement's report a document of thirty-nine pages and an appendix of twenty-three pages to deal with, or sixty-two pages in all; full of specific facts, of detailed and minute observations. They had in Lord Cromer's brief but scathing remarks the deliberate judgment of one of the most able statesmen and administrators in the world to upset. Deeming prudence the better part of valour, they decided that to attack a man of European reputation like Lord Cromer would be futile. So they left him severely alone—a silence at once significant and eloquent.

Their "Notes" in reply to Consul Casement's report cover eighteen pages, with an appendix of nineteen pages of small print. Out of this, seven pages of the "Notes"; and ten pages of the appendix—almost one-half the entire document—are devoted to a laboured effort to disprove *one single case of mutilation*—(the boy Epondo)—observed and inquired into by our Consul!

The other half of the document is composed in the main of the vaguest generalities, and of matters of only indirect reference to the indictment. The first three pages consist in an extremely feeble attempt to explain away the signs of appalling depopulation noted by our Consul since his previous visit to the country, seventeen years ago; the balance consists of mere padding in the shape of a *tu-quoque*, various rude remarks anent the incorrect attitude of our Consul in investigating matters of "purely internal administration," sneers at the Protestant missionaries, and various sonorous platitudes as to the inherent right pertaining to Governments of taxing their subjects. The balance of the appendix consists of a long letter from Monsignor Van Ronslé criticising the facts and figures given by Mr. Weeks in the *West African Mail*, respecting depopulation and its causes; one or two circulars with regard to the distribution of firearms, *et voilà tout*. Such, positively, is the "Reply" to the most terrific—and all the more terrific because drafted in language the most temperate—exposure to which a Government has ever been subjected!

The way they set about disposing of the case of Epondo is thoroughly typical, and their peculiar *mentalité*, as M. Vandervelde would say, clearly apparent. The supreme object is, to prove our Consul in the wrong in one instance of atrocity which he investigated. If they can do that, they can say to the world, with a shrug, "What can you make of this man?

Here is a sample of his accuracy." But that would not be quite enough. It is necessary to make the non-English speaking world believe that to this particular case our Consul attached quite special value. And this is the way it is done—

We are told (p. 5):

"It will suffice to . . . characterise the lack of value of his investigation, to examine a single case, *the one on which the entire effort of Mr. Casement was concentrated (celui sur lequel s'est porté tout l'éffort de M. Casement).* We mean the Epondo affair."

And again (p. 6)—

"Even had the facts been accurate, one would be struck with the want of proportion in the Consul's conclusions, deducted therefrom, in *generalising with emphasis* his system of criticism against the Congo State."

And yet again (p. 8)—

"If we have insisted on the details of this affair, it *is because it is regarded by the Consul himself as of capital importance,* and *because he bases himself upon this sole case to conclude as to the accuracy of all the other Native declarations he collected.*"

How do these statements accord with the facts?

It seems that our Consul founded upon this incident a general indictment of the system; he used this instance to " generalise with emphasis," etc.

If that be the case, how comes it that on September 4, when our Consul was 150 miles from Bosunguma (Epondo's village), of *whose very existence he did not then know,* he should have written the letter to the Governor-General given in the Appendix, in which the following passages occur?—

"I am sure your Excellency would share my feeling of indignation had the unhappy spectacles I have witnessed of late come before your Excellency's own eyes. I cannot believe that the full extent of the illegality of the system of arbitrary impositions, followed by dire and illegal punishment, which is in force over so wide an area of the country I have recently witnessed, is known to, or properly appreciated by, your Excellency, or the Central Administration of the Congo State Government. I have seen women and young children summarily arrested, taken away from their homes and families, to be kept in wholly illegal and painful detention, guarded often by armed sentries, because, as I was informed by their captors, their villages or their male relatives had failed to bring in antelope meat, or some other commodity desired by the local Europeans. I have seen recently, but not within the limits of the A.B.I.R. Concession, a number of native women (eleven in all) with five infants at the breast, and three of them big with child, who had been taken from their homes, and were tied together by the neck or ankle, guarded by two armed sentries, one of whom had a cap-gun, and the other a double-barrelled shot-gun."

These are samples of the sights witnessed by our Consul, and brought by him to the notice of the authorities, long before he knew that Epondo or his village existed. Yet the Congo Government has the disingenuousness to say that Mr. Casement "generalises" *from the Epondo case.* Then we are informed that on the Epondo incident the "entire effort of Mr. Casement was concentrated," that it was regarded by him as of "capital importance," and that "he *bases himself upon this sole case,*" etc. But what a singular thing if this indeed be so, that out of a document covering thirty-nine pages, Mr. Casement should only have devoted to it a single paragraph of thirty-seven lines, and less than two pages in an appendix of twenty-three pages!

Thus the Congo Government in Europe. Now let us study the Congo Government in Africa. The study will be equally instructive.

In the first place, what were the circumstances under which Consul Casement became acquainted with Epondo and his history? The report reads as follows—

"I proceeded in a canoe across the Lulonga, and up a tributary to a landing-place, which seemed to be about . . . miles from I——. Here, leaving the canoes, we walked for a couple of miles through a flooded forest to reach the village. I found here a sentry of the La Lulango Company and a considerable number of Natives. After some little delay, a boy of about fifteen years of age appeared, whose left arm was wrapped up in a dirty rag. Removing this, I found the left hand had been hacked off by the wrist, and that a shot-hole appeared in the fleshy part of the forearm. The boy, who gave his name as I I, in answer to my inquiry, said that a sentry of the La Lulanga Company, now in the town, had cut off his hand. I proceeded to look for this man, who, at first, could not be found, the Natives, to a considerable number, gathering behind me as I walked through the town. After some delay, the sentry appeared, carrying a cap-gun. The boy, whom I placed before him, then accused him to his face of having mutilated him. The men of the town, who were questioned in succession, corroborated the boy's statement. The sentry, who gave his name as K K, could make no answer to the charge. He met it by vaguely saying some other sentry of the Company had mutilated I I; his predecessor, he said, had cut off several hands, and probably this was one of the victims. The Natives around said that there were two other sentries at present in the town, who were not so bad as K K, but that he was a villain. As the evidence against him was perfectly clear, man after man standing out and declaring that he had seen the act committed, I informed him and the people present that I should appeal to the local authorities for his immediate arrest and trial. In the course of my interrogatory, several other charges transpired against him. These were of a minor nature, consisting of the usual characteristic acts of blackmailing, only too commonly reported on all sides. One man said that K K had tied up his wife, and only released her on payment of 1000 rods. Another man said that K K had robbed him of two ducks and a dog. These minor offences K K equally demurred to, and again said that I I had been mutilated by some other sentry, naming several. I took the boy back with me, and later brought him to Coquilhatville, where he formally charged K K with the crime, alleging to the Commandant, who took his statement, through a special Government interpreter, in my presence, that it had been done 'on account of rubber.' I have since been informed that, acting on my request, the authorities at Coquilhatville had arrested K K, who, presumably, will be tried in due course. A copy of my notes taken in K——, where I I charged K K before me, is appended."

The notes in the Appendix are too long to reproduce here.

Three Natives testified to seeing the act committed; one testified to seeing the severed hand and the blood lying on the ground. All the Natives present, to the number of "about forty ... nearly all men," testified to the sentry, Kelengo (K K. ... in the report), being the guilty person.

It is interesting to note that the sentry, in the course of his interrogatory, states that his predecessor, "who cut hands off," not himself, was responsible. *We have here an admission by the sentry Kelengo that hands are cut off by these regenerating agents.* The avowal is the more noteworthy when we consider a question afterwards put by M. Gennaro Bosco, the judicial officer, with whose subsequent "inquiry" we shall presently deal, to Epondo ("Notes," p. 29)—

Q. " Etes vous sur que c'est Kelengo qui vous a coupé la main ? *Ce n'est pas Bossole ?* "
A. " Non c'est Kelengo."

A somewhat disingenuous question, suggesting that *M. le Substitut* Gennaro Bosco would appear to be as equally familiar as Kelengo with hand-cutting incidents. But this is by the way. Consul Casement, we have seen, took Epondo down to the important State station of Coquilhatville on September 10, and afterwards sent him on to the Mission Station at Bonginda, in care of Mr. W. D. Armstrong. What happened after that?

The Congo Government tells us. There was an inquiry, as our Consul had asked there should be—" *a judicial inquiry, in normal conditions, free from all foreign influence.*" * The " inquiry " finally resulted in Epondo himself confessing that his hand had been torn off by a wild boar.† Naturally, the

* "Une enquête judiciaire dans les conditions normales en dehors de tonte influence étrangère."
† It shows the slovenliness with which the Congo Government prepares even its most amazing documents, that the passage in which this confession occurs (p. 3) reads as follows : " M'arrachant la main gauche au ventre et la hanche gauche," which may mean something in Congolese language, but does not make sense in any other language with which I am acquainted.

innocence of the much injured Kelengo being "completely proved," he was not prosecuted, and he has no doubt been busily employed since in tracking down wild boars, as his humble part in the grand scheme of his master—the regeneration of the Congo Native from barbarism.

How was this remarkable conclusion arrived at? It is a long story, and it is only worth going into because, as I have shown, Epondo's hand has been the *pièce de conviction* of the Congo Government against the British White Book, which, by the way, ought to have been translated into every European language.

Before M. Gennaro Bosco could grapple with the terrible problem of Epondo's hand, a preliminary inquiry was held by Lieutenant Bræckman, a Congo State officer. The only reference to this preliminary inquiry contained in the Congo Government's "Notes," is the following (p. 8)—

"Whereas the inquiry made by Lieutenant Braeckman, confirming partly the inquiry made by H.M. Consul, but contradicting it in part, and adding to the charges previously made against Kelengo, that of having killed a Native named Baluwa."

Presumably a wild boar was also responsible for Baluwa's death, because, as we have seen, Kelengo's innocence was "completely proved" to the satisfaction of M. Gennaro Bosco, and although we are led to infer from the text that this complete proof of innocence only refers to Epondo's hand, the death of Baluwa was doubtless accounted for in an equally satisfactory way. We are, however, left in doubt about it. Perhaps it was the same wild boar that disposed of Baluwa.

It is worth while noting that Epondo and the villagers corroborated to Lieutenant Braeckman the testimony they had given to our Consul. Although nowhere categorically affirmed in the "Notes," this is made quite clear by the following reference in M. Gennaro Bosco's finding—

"Attendu que tous les indigènes qui ont accuse Kelengo, soit au Consul de sa Majesté Britannique, *soit au Lieutenant Braeckman*, etc."

It is the more interesting to note this, insomuch as Mr. Gilchrist's letter, published in the Appendix, would seem to indicate a peculiar method of conducting his investigations on the part of Lieutenant Braeckman—

"The man to whom these people take their supplies at Coquilhatville, who, of course, acting on behalf of the Commissaire, received the fines levied on them, put them in the chain, when their supplies were short of the numbers demanded, and otherwise had dealings with them."

ATTACKS ON CONSUL CASEMENT'S REPORT

Mr. Gilchrist thus describes this official's methods of inquiry—

"Accompanied with seven soldiers armed with rifles and a full supply of cartridges, he took a daily excursion into the town. . . ."

But doubtless Lieutenant Braeckman's performances cannot be held to have formed part of that "judicial inquiry in normal conditions, free from all foreign influence," which was to come later under the *ægis* of *M. le Substitut* Gennaro Bosco.

Whether the thought that Lieutenant Braeckman and his seven soldiers, armed with rifles, were to be followed by a further inquiry terrified the unfortunate villagers of Bosunguma, or whether the Director of the incriminated La Lulanga Company—in whose service the sentry Kelengo was—and who appears to have been permitted to "arrest" one of the witnesses against his sentry *—an obviously improper proceeding—must remain a matter for conjecture. Anyway, M. Gennaro Bosco was, according to his own showing, deprived of the services of the principal witnesses in the case—the villagers of Bosunguma who were present on the Consul's visit, "all of whom," he says—"summoned by us—have fled!" † And he adds that that flight "evidently discredits their observations." ‡ Unhappily for *M. le Substitut's* reputation for accuracy, it is clear from his interrogatories that one at least of the witnesses had not fled—perhaps he had been also "arrested" by the incriminated director—for we find in another part of the notes § the following—

Q. "Why did you yourself declare to the English Consul that you saw the cut hand on the ground, the blood flowing, and the inhabitants fleeing in all directions?"
A. "I did not speak to the English. I did not even see them."
M. Gennaro Bosco: "You lie, because the English Consul says he spoke with you."
A. "Yes, it is true. *I was there.* I spoke like the others."

The comment of the British Government on this remarkable contradiction could hardly be improved—

"In view of a discrepancy of this kind, it is, perhaps, needless further to investigate the character of the evidence upon which a sustained effort is made to discredit Mr. Casement's testimony." ||

I trust the reader is not unduly fatigued, for we are about to reach the most entertaining portion of this inquiry, which might well be headed :

* See page 20, notes. Interrogatory of Kelengo.
† See page 8, notes. ‡ Ibid.
§ Page 30. || Africa, No. 7, page 66.

A NATURAL HISTORY TREATISE

The Congo Wild Boar in Normal Conditions free from all Foreign Influence.

A wild boar is associated with the very earliest stage of M. *le Substitut* Gennaro Bosco's "judicial inquiry," and we never lose sight of the strange beast until:

"L'enquête montre Epondo, enfin acculé retractant ses premières affirmations au Consul, et avouant avoir été influencé par les gens de son village."

The French word *acculer* means "to drive into a corner"—not, perhaps a very judicial term to use. It would appear to have an additional and special meaning in Congolese; but we will come to that presently.

The first interrogatory by M. Gennaro Bosco, recorded in the Notes, is that of the sentry Kelengo* on September 19, held, presumably, although the Notes do not say so, at Coquilhatville. Kelengo, naturally, has not only not cut off the hand of Epondo; he does not even know him. But, strange to say, there is one thing he does know, "that a wild boar bit him in the hand." It seems curious, to say the least, that the sentry had not remembered this very simple explanation of Epondo's lost hand when interrogated by Consul Casement, twelve days previously. On that occasion, it will be remembered, Kelengo's chief anxiety was to pass on the blame to his predecessor of hand-cutting fame. This singular circumstance did not, apparently, astonish M. *le Substitut*. There is nothing to suggest that he even found it remarkable. One might almost imagine that he had expected it.

The next interrogatories are also held at Coquilhatville. They consist in questions put to seven Natives, *three of whom are described as employees of the La Lulanga Company!*† With a touching unanimity they plump for the wild boar. Coquilhatville, as I have already remarked, is an important State station, where the might of Bula Matadi, in the shape of soldiers and rifles, is conspicuous. Singular to relate, however, their accounts of the way in which that wild boar behaved differ somewhat notably. According to Efundu, Epondo and a friend went wild-boar hunting. Epondo wounded the pig, *and tried to catch it by the ears*, but it bit him so severely that the hand "fell off after gangrening." ‡ Mongombe submits

---

* Notes, p. 25. † Ibid. ‡ Notes, p. 24.

that the wild boar "tore off" Epondo's hand.* Bangwala is sure that the hand was "lost on account of a wild boar's bite." † Momombo agrees with Bangwala. Ekumeleko declares that the wild boar "cut off" the hand.‡ Bungja and Bawsa agree with Ekumeleko.

This concludes the first portion of the "judicial inquiry in normal conditions free from all foreign influence."

By October 6, *M. le Substitut* has gone up river to Mampoko, still on the track of the wild boar. There he remains *as the guest of the La Lulanga Company*, itself primarily involved, *putting up at its stations, and travelling on its steamers with its agents!* That, I beg you to note is merely an incident in a "normal" judicial inquiry on the Congo. Here more natives are interrogated. They are really interesting, these interrogatories. There is not a question in them on the part of the Judge tending to elucidate whether the Natives are properly or improperly treated, duly or unduly worked; whether the armed sentries placed amongst them habitually treat them ill—nothing of that sort. Nowhere do we find the slightest evidence of astonishment on the part of *M. le Substitut* that a reputed "trading" company should find it part of its business to station armed sentries in the villages whence it draws its rubber supplies! On the other hand, we constantly find questions of this kind—

"How long were the English in the village?" §
"Did they write when they were in the village?" ‖
"Who went to speak with the English?" ¶
"When the English came to your village, what did they do?" **
"Who went to speak with the English?"
A. "Bodjengene."
Q. "Only Bodjengene?" ††
"Did you go to the Mission at Bonginda to complain?" ‡‡
"Did Ikabo go to the English?" §§
"Did they look for Ikabo?" ‖‖
"What time did they come, and what time did they leave?" ¶¶
"Who went to Bonginda to the English to speak?" ***
"Did the English tell you the rubber is finished?" †††
"Who went to Bonginda to call the English?"
A. "Bodjenje."
Q. "Only Bodjenje?" ‡‡‡

---

* Notes, p. 24.   † Notes, p. 25.   ‡ Ibid. (6).
§ Interrogatory of Eponge, p. 26.   ‖ Ibid.
¶ Interrogatory of Leboso.   ** Ibid.
†† Interrogatory of Etoko.   ‡‡ Interrogatory of Mafambi.
§§ Another mutilated boy.   ‖‖ Interrogatory of Mafambi.
¶¶ Ibid.   *** Interrogatory of Ekombo.
††† Ibid.   ‡‡‡ Interrogatory of Mondonga.

"What time was it the English came to Bosunguma ? " *
"Did they write at Bosunguma ? " †
"Who went to Bonginda to speak to the English ? " ‡
"Why did the English come to Bosunguma ? " §
"When the English came to Bosunguma, did they write ? " ‖

To any one ignorant of the special forms of Congo judicature, these questions would appear to have been framed with a very much more pronounced desire to find out something which might be brought up against "the English" than the truth about the mutilation. Needless to remark, all the natives interrogated declared with one voice that Epondo's hand was either bitten, torn off, or cut off by the extraordinary animal aforesaid. What a delightful story Mark Twain might make of this! Wild boars and cut hands would be a fitting pendant—albeit a somewhat ghastly one—to Blue Jays and acorns.

But to proceed, *M. le Substitut* arrives at Bonginda, where Epondo had remained since Consul Casement took him to Coquilhatville to testify before the Congo State official. He first of all interrogates Mr. Armstrong (who accompanied Mr. Casement to Bosunguma), and the latter repeats what took place on that occasion. Thereupon Epondo is brought in. *M. le Substitut*, in his opening notes to this interrogatory, says: "The deponent's left hand is *cut off*." It is extremely interesting to find *M. le Substitut* noting this in his interrogatory—the reader can arrive at the same conclusion from the photograph. It is all the more interesting as, in his "ordonnance de non-lieu" on the guilt of Kelengo,¶ M. Gennaro Bosco says: "Whereas . . . all the witnesses interrogated in our inquiry attest . . .** that Epondo lost his left hand because a wild boar *tore it off* . . ."†† ("le lui arrachée . . ."). Now, the hand cannot have been "torn off" as well as "cut off." No one outside a lunatic asylum or unconnected with the rue de Namur imagines that a wild boar could *cut* off a hand (or *tear it* off for the matter of that), and when *M. le Substitut* tells us that "the deponent's (Epondo's) hand is *cut off*," we believe him. But when this same official actually records in his "ordonnance de non-lieu" that Epondo's hand was *torn off*, we marvel greatly.

Epondo was equally precise in his statements before M. Gennaro Bosco as he was before Consul Casement and Lieutenant Braeckman.

* Interrogatory of Mondonga.   † Ibid.   ‡ Interrogatory of Lopenbo.
§ Ibid.   ‖ Ibid.   ¶ Page 7.
** These dots are in the original text.
†† Ibid

Q. "Who cut off your hand?"
A. "Kelengo."
Q. "Why?"
A. "For the rubber. He made war in our village, and killed Elua, and cut off a hand. I fell almost dead. I awoke after some time, and found myself without a hand."
Q. "Do you know Bossole?" *
A. "No! I know Kelengo."
Q. "Are you sure it was Kelengo who cut off your hand? It was not Bossole?"
A. "No; it was Kelengo."

  * * * * *

Q. "Did you not go at one time to the Bangalla?"
A. "No; I always lived in my village."
Q. "Was not your hand taken off (*enlevée*) by a wild boar?"
A. "No; Kelengo cut it off."

That was plain enough. Three times had Epondo been questioned by three different men, two of them Congo State officials. Three times he had explained the circumstances of his mutilation without deviating therefrom. Yet *M. le Substitut* Gennaro Bosco was not satisfied. So he *took the boy away from his friendly surroundings to the State post at Mampoko*. Here, at the mercy of Bula Matadi, Epondo was again interrogated, with the result on the second occasion that "enfin acculé" he, too, learnt the wild-boar story, and repeated it. His hand had been "torn off" by a wild boar in the course of a hunting expedition! We have M. Gennaro Bosco's opinion that it was cut off; but let that pass. Asked "How long since the accident took place," the boy replies, "I do not know. It is a long time ago." *And yet the wound was not healed, "blood showed still in two places over which the skin had not entirely formed, and it was wrapped up in a cloth"* † *when Mr. Casement examined it.*

This is the comic opera they call on the Congo "une enquête judiciaire dans les conditions normales en dehors de toute ingérence étrangère"! No sensible man needs Mr. Bond's letter to Mr. Armstrong, dated from Lulanga, in which he says—

"I hear through some Natives that they have found seven cases (of mutilation) on that river (Juapa), two of whom are stationed with a Chief near Coquilhatville, who has orders that the English are not to see them. This same man says he was at a State place when a white man made a soldier stand over the boy—who told the boar story—with a rifle, and told him he was not to tell the lie about a sentry cutting off his hand, but to tell the truth. The truth which the rifle brought out was the boar story;"—

---

* Kelengo's predecessor.   † Africa, No. 7, 1904, p. 65.

to be edified completely as to the methods followed by the Congo State's representatives in this case. All that need occasion surprise is the extremely clumsy way in which a desired conclusion was arrived at. It might have been done much more cleverly.*

Before I refer to the final phase of this "inquiry," it may be as well to mention the extremely disingenuous manner in which the Congo Authorities have sought to involve Mr. Faris in the case. In its "Notes" the Congo Government says: "Epondo reiterates his declarations and retractations spontaneously to a Protestant missionary, M. Faris, residing at Bolengi." "This reverend (*sic*) has given the Commissaire General of Coquilhatville the following written declaration." The written declaration reads as follows—

"I, the undersigned, E. E. Faris, missionary, residing at Bolengi, Upper Congo, declare that I questioned the child Epondo, of the village of Bosunguma, who was with me on September 10, with Mr. Casement, the British Consul, and whom I brought to the Mission of Bolengi, on October 16, 1903, according to the request of M. le Commandant Stevens, of Coquilhatville, and that the child told me to-day, October 17, 1903, that he lost his hand by the bite of a wild boar. He also told me that he told Mr. Casement that his hand was cut off by a soldier, or by one of the workmen of the white men, who made war upon his village to make it produce rubber; but he maintains that the last story he told me to-day is the truth."

Let us examine the circumstances. After the final and successful interrogatory at Mampoko, what would have been the natural course to pursue by a judicial officer desirous of ascertaining the real truth? Obviously to have taken the boy back to Bonginda—*which is only eight miles from Mampoko*—and there confronted him with Mr. Armstrong, in whose presence he had reiterated, when interrogated by *M. le Substitut*—*only the day before his "retraction" at Mampoko*—the original charge against Kelengo; either that, or else to have asked Mr. Armstrong to come to Mampoko himself. But—and nothing proves more clearly the singular nature of this "judicial inquiry in normal conditions," etc.—instead of adopting this simple course, Epondo was carried off eighty

---

* Side by side with the official version of Epondo's hand, we have had a whole crop of unofficial Congolese versions, made, apparently, in ignorance of M. Bosco's conclusions. One authority tells us that the boy was suffering from cancer, the loss of his hand being a mere "surgical operation." Another informs us that he has "personal" cognisance of the fact that Epondo lost his hand by the explosion of a gun. A third—a worthy bishop this time—has testified that he himself has seen Epondo, and that the mark of "a wolf's tooth, higher up," is plainly to be seen on the lad's arm!

miles away to Coquilhatville : no doubt to further refresh his memory with the cruel treatment he had met with at an unspecified date, in an unspecified place, from the pig. Having got him there, it seems to have occurred to the Authorities that, after all, their "inquiry" looked rather weak, and that it might be well to have some outside backing. So a week later Mr. Faris, whose residence was situated far from the scene of the occurrences, who had no knowledge of the boy's antecedents (he had only seen him for a few minutes on the previous occasion) or any means of testing his statement by cross-examination or otherwise, is sent for—not Mr. Armstrong, be it noted—to Coquilhatville, in order to obtain some independent testimony favourable to the official thesis. Mr. Faris' description of what took place is overwhelmingly significant.

"Commandant Stevens," he writes, "told me *he was anxious to learn the truth, and was not concerned about anything else.* HE TOLD ME THAT THE LAD HAD SINCE DECLARED, IN THE PRESENCE OF MR. ARMSTRONG, THAT HIS HAND HAD BEEN TORN OFF BY A WILD BOAR. I AM VERY POSITIVE ABOUT THIS STATEMENT, AS I WAS LISTENING VERY CAREFULLY AT THE TIME."

What does the reader think of *that*? As we have noted already, what Epondo *did* say in the presence of Mr. Armstrong, and replying to the interrogatory of *M. le Substitut* Gennaro Bosco, was this—

Q. "Who cut off your hand?"
A. "Kelengo."
* * * * * * *
Q. "Are you sure it was Kelengo who cut off your hand? It was not Bossole?"
A. "No; it was Kelengo."
* * * * * * *
Q. "Was not your hand taken off by a wild boar?"
A. "No; Kelengo cut it off."

After this evidence of Congolese humour—shall I call it ?—it seems superfluous to pursue the matter any further. Still, it may be just as well to give further extracts from Mr. Faris' letter—

"I had no objection at all to telling the Commandant, or the Judge, or the King, or any one else, what the boy said about his hand, but I objected till I could learn any reason why I should be sent for from Bolengi merely to make a statement as to the testimony of the boy. The Commandant represented to me thus : 'I am anxious to get at the real truth of the matter. The boy tells me that his hand was lost as the result of wounds resulting from the attack of a wild boar. The motive of his telling the other story to the Consul, he declares, was to excite sympathy, and thus to get the *rubber tax** removed. He says that the people of the town put him up to tell the story. Now, you take him and interrogate him, and tell me the truth as you think it is.' Upon my hesitating, and as it was getting late, Mr. Stevens proposed that I take the boy home with me and examine him at my leisure, and report the result to him. This I agreed to do; I felt sure of getting at some help in the difficulty. But not one thing could I do. The poor little fellow was listless, drowsy. He didn't seem himself at all. I tried to get out of him some details of when he decided to change his testimony, and why, and what inducements were offered; but he relapsed into a sleepy assertion that it was as he had said. I sent him to bed with a good supper, and allowed him to sleep all the next morning, so he would be refreshed; but I got nothing else out of him. If he had been threatened (and this could have been done without the Commandant's knowledge) it has been very effectual. . . . I sent the Commandant the statement and the letter."

In a subsequent letter Mr. Faris writes—

"As to the reasons that the State have in taking this line of defence, I suppose it is because they think they are sure to win in this way. The plan is to deny the fact. The Consul is to be represented in the defence as an honest inquirer, but too hasty, and therefore mistaken. The other white witness is to be discredited. A doctor's certificate is to be offered to prove that the wound was probably made by an animal, etc. I do not think that is the best way for them to proceed, but that is their affair."

The outside help of Mr. Faris to bolster up thoroughly discreditable tactics would not appear to be worth very much from the Congo State point of view; the pet witness of the Authorities does not seem to have a very high idea of those who sought, under the falsest of pretences, to use him for their questionable ends.

The final aspect of the Epondo "palaver" may be briefly dealt with.

The Natives, cited by the Congo Government, concurred in describing the accusation against the Lulanga Company's sentry as prompted by the wish of the Natives to escape from their rubber dealings with that Company.

If these dealings are commercial, as is repeatedly asserted by the Congo State, there would not appear to be any pretext for the accusations brought against that Company's sentry.

We find it stated that the "liberté du commerce" the men of Bosunguma enjoyed presented itself to them in the following guise—

" Pour ne pas faire de caoutchouc : Kelengo est sentinelle du caoutchouc. (Efundu, September 28, 1903, p. 24.)
"Oui ; j'ai entendu les indigànes se plaindre qu'ils travaillent

---

* Note this. Bosunguma is in the territory of the La Lulanga, a Company which is reputed to get its rubber through the medium of "commercial" transactions.

ATTACKS ON CONSUL CASEMENT'S REPORT 371

beaucoup pour rien ; que les Chefs s'emparaient des mitakos que les blancs payaient pour la recolte du caoutchouc ; enfin, qu'ils mouraient de faim. Ils ajoutaient qu'ils avaient reclamé plusieurs fois inutilement," etc. (Mongombe, September 28, 1903, p. 25.)

" Parce qu'ils étaient fatigués de faire du caoutchouc, qui n'était plus dans leur forêt. Ils ont cru qu'avec l'intervention des Anglais ils pourraient se soustraire à un travail très dur, etc. . . . Ils ont parlé avec les habitants qui se plaignaient de ce qu'ils devaient travailler beaucoup. Ils disaient que le caoutchouc n'était plus dans leur forêt, qu'ils voulaient faire un travail moins dur," etc. (Liboso, October 6, 1903, p. 27, " Notes.")

" Parce qu'ils trouvent que le travail du caoutchouc est trop dur, et ont cru de pouvoir s'en libérer, et pour les induire à s'en occuper ils sont allés leur conter des mensonges." (Bofoko, October 8, 1903, p. 30, " Notes.")

If, as the Congo " Notes " assert on p. 6, these " depositions sont typiques, uniformes, et concordantes, elles ne laissent aucun doute sur la cause de l'accident, attestent que les indigènes ont menti au Consul, et revèlent le mobile auquel ils ont obei "—they unquestionably leave no doubt that the relations of the Lulanga Company to the Natives of the surrounding country were not those of a trading Company engaged in commercial dealings, but of an organisation compelling, with the approval and support of the Executive, a widespread system of compulsory labour by armed force, for which no legal authority exists. The peculiar " trade " system prevailing is, indeed, revealed, and in characteristically clumsy fashion, by the Congo " Notes " themselves, for we are therein told that the Natives lied to the Consul in order to escape the "obligation de l'impôt." Thus, in a region repeatedly visited by Government officials, traversed weekly by Government steamers lying close to the capital of the district, the trading operations of a private Company are shown to consist in the enforcement of a tax in rubber upon the people, those to whom the duty is assigned of collecting that tax being armed soldiers !

Of such is the Kingdom of Congo.

* * * * * *

The tale is told—the tale of " King Leopold's rule in Africa." A piratical expedition on a scale incredibly colossal. The perfection of its hypocrisy ; the depth of its low cunning ; its pitiable intrigues ; the illimitableness of its egotism ; its moral hideousness ; the vastness and madness of its crimes— the heart sickens and the mind rebels at the thought of them. A perpetual nightmare reeking with vapours of vile ambitions —cynical, fantastic, appalling. A tragedy which appears unreal, so unutterably ghastly its concomitants, but the grimness of whose reality is incapable of superlative treatment. Destroying, decimating, degrading; its poisonous breath sweeps through the forests of the Congo. Men fall beneath it as grass beneath the scythe, by slaughter, famine, torture, sickness, and misery. Women and children flee from it, but not fast enough, though the mother destroy the unborn life within her that her feet may drag less heavily through the bush.

There has been nothing quite comparable with it since the world was made. The world can never see its like again.

Sufficient that it exists, that each month, each year, the terror of this Oppression grows, immolating fresh victims, demanding new offerings to minister to its lusts, spreading in ever wider circles the area of its abominations.

Sufficient that twenty years after solemnly and earnestly declaring their intentions to safeguard and protect the inhabitants of the Congo Basin, the Civilised Powers are content to let this thing be; that until the last few months, diplomacy had not even moved a little finger; and that action is still confined to the tentative, timorous efforts of one Government. Sufficient that after two thousand years of professed Christianity, the Civilised Peoples of the world can acquiesce in the indifferentism of their rulers.

Are the pessimists right, after all? Is the conscience of Christendom dead? Is it possible that the spirit which crushed the old African slave-trade is so impaired as to be incapable of dealing with the comparatively easy task of sweeping away the new African slave-trade? "It is very mysterious," as Mr. Joseph Conrad says. Have we gone back, and not forward, these last fifty years? Surely it cannot be.

In the name of humanity, of common decency and pity, for Honour's sake, if for no other cause, will not the Anglo-Saxon race—the Governments and the Peoples of Great Britain and the United States, who between them are primarily responsible for the creation of the Congo State—make up their minds to handle this monstrous outrage resolutely, and so point a way and set an example which others would then be compelled to follow?

In that hope, with humility, with an ever-present consciousness of inadequacy to portray the greatness of the evil, and the greatness of the responsibility, the author submits this volume to the Public.

E. D. M.

APPENDIX

MUTILATIONS

I. Biasia and Mongala.
II. Ikabo.
III. Lokota.
IV. Mola Ekuliti; Mokili and Eyeka.

OPPRESSION AT LOLANGA

I. Letter: Gilchrist to Governor-General.
II. Gilchrist to Dr. Guinness.
III. De Cuvelier and Guinness.

CONSUL CASEMENT'S PROTEST TO CONGO STATE AUTHORITIES.

ANNEXES TO RABINEK CASE.

JUDGMENT OF THE APPEAL COURT OF BOMA IN THE CASE OF CAUDRON AND JONES, MARCH, 1904.

LETTERS RECEIVED FROM THE CONGO THIS YEAR SINCE THE PRESENT VOLUME WAS COMPLETED:

In the Domaine de la Couronne: Rev. A. E. Scrivener.
In the Domaine Privé: Mr. John H. Harris.
In the Domaine Privé: Rev. J. H. Weeks.
In the Domaine Privé: Rev. W. B. Frame.
In the Lower Congo: A British Trader.
In the "Equateur" District: A Missionary.
In and around the Baringa District of the "Abir" Concession during the First Six Months of the Present Year:
  Mr. Herbert Frost's Diary.
  Letter from Mr. John H. Harris.
  Letter from Mr. E. Stannard.
Thirteen Years of Congo State Rule in Katanga.
Letter from the Rev. Dugald Campbell.

KING LEOPOLD'S PROMISES. MANIFESTO OF THE INTERNATIONAL ASSOCIATION.

MUTILATIONS

I

BIASIA (*grown man*).
MONGALA (*small boy*).

THESE two poor beings, whose arms, as will be seen, were terribly shattered by gun-fire at close quarters, were brought by their friends to the Mission Station at Bonginda, on September 7, 1903, during the visit of His Majesty's Consul.

These photographs were taken on that date by the Rev. W. D. Armstrong, the Chief of the Mission.

Both were natives of the Ngombe town Bosombongo, one of those which enjoy the privilege of contributing to the " obligation de l'impôt," which, with an extraordinary benevolence, the Congo Government assigns as its principal free trade perquisite to the trading company, called the La Lulanga Society. In order to carry on its trading " operations " on these generous lines, that company quartered a variety of sentries throughout the district of the lower Lulonga, who, being armed with weapons supplied to the company by the Congo Government, and ammunition, also issued from Government stores, were able to induce, by the most gentle means, the fortnightly payment of this unique form of " commercial dealing."

A sentry of the company, a man named Itela, considered that he, too, had a right to share in the " obligation de l'impôt "—and since his claims to participate in the profit of the system did not receive due recognition from the chiefs of Bosombongo, he seized four " hostages," in exact accordance with the " regulations " prescribed by the Governor-General of the Congo State, for the better civilising of the Mongalla region as exemplified in the Caudron case.*

Two of these " hostages," men named Ndekeli and Nabelengi, Itela tied up to trees and deliberately shot dead before the eyes of the villagers as " proof of his prowess," and to serve as warning of what should happen to all who refused to obey.

The horrified chiefs of the town hurried off to the factory of the company which had placed Itela in their midst, with the result that they were promptly made fast in the chain.

* See Chapter XII.

Being released on promise of "good behaviour," and under the customary bail of chickens for the white man's table, they returned to their town—only to find that, as punishment for their action in going to complain, the sentry had shot, in the way these photographs indicate, the other "hostages"—the man Biasia and child Mongala.

These trembling creatures, with shattered limbs, were still tied to the trees, bleeding and grievously wounded.

In order to obtain their release the chiefs had to pay to Itela a fine of 2000 brass rods (£4 sterling).

The report of these further proceedings of the representative of the organisation, which has opened up an account, "Central Africa in account with Civilisation," evoked no response from the employers of the sentry, other than commendation, retention at his post, and the injunction to the people of Bosombongo, that if their rubber was not promptly brought in each fortnight, " a worse thing" should happen.

Accordingly these living instances of the benefits accruing from the fatherly system of Government of the Congo State, sought His Majesty's Consul, in the hope that ocular demonstration of the infamies of that rule might move his heart, and might induce others than their benevolent regenerators to believe in the terrors of their oppression.

II

IKABO (*a native of the village of*).
BOSUNGUMA (*the same town as Epondo's*).

This boy was brought by his friends into the Mission at Bonginda, on Sunday evening, September 6, 1903, with the request that His Majesty's Consul, then in the Mission, should visit Bosunguma, to see there another mutilated boy (Epondo).

Ikabo had lost his hand, he averred, and all the men who accompanied him, by the act of one of the sentries of the La Lulanga Company.

This photograph was taken by the Rev. W. D. Armstrong, of Bonginda, on September 7, 1903.

In addition to the loss of his right hand, Ikabo was terribly wounded in the shoulder by a bullet wound. The shoulder-blade had been broken—and in setting had become distorted—so that the boy carried a veritable hump, which the photograph does not show.

The scar of the bullet was clear and plain across the flesh.

It will be observed from Mr. Faris' declaration to the Commandant at Coquilhatville,* that Epondo in his "retraction" assigned the loss of Ikabo's hand and that of another mutilated individual in his village of Bosunguma to the acts of the soldiers of the Government in the "wars."

While publishing that one of Mr. Faris' statements, which the

* See Chapter XXX.

APPENDIX 377

Congo Government thought might reflect on His Majesty's Consul, this damning testimony of their prize witness is carefully withheld from that extraordinary international document they have termed the "Notes sur le Rapport de M. Casement," but which a plainer intelligence would designate by a plainer and much simpler name.

III

LOKOTA OF MPELENGI.

This child—a boy—was brought by his friends to the Mission at Bonginda, on September 7, 1903, during the visit of His Majesty's Consul.

This photograph of the mutilated child was taken by the Rev. W. D. Armstrong, on the occasion of the visit to the Mission.

The village of Mpelengi lies only some three miles away from the Mission of Bonginda. This child was only able to run at the date of his mutilation, which is stated to have occurred under the following circumstances about four and a half or five years ago, at a period when the *régime* of the rubber blessing was being worked to its utmost in the lower Lulonga:—

Mpelengi was "attacked" for its failure to bring in enough rubber in the way described in March of this year in the Caudron case.* Sentries of the trading organisation appointed to the moral and material regeneration of Mpelengi were sent against it, with the usual supply of Government-distributed guns and ammunition.

The sentries, under a leader named Mokwolo, were named Ebomi, Mokuba, and Bomolo. These four well-armed men set out from a neighbouring town named Bolondo, and attacked Mpelengi at dawn. One of the first to fall was a principal chief of the town, a man named Eliba. The people fled to the forest, and the child Lokota toddled after. Mokwolo pursued and knocked the baby down with the butt of his rifle, and cut off its hand.

The hand of Eliba was also cut off and taken away in triumph, to attest that the sentries had done their duty and had punished the "rebel" town, which dared to fail in supplying the fixed quantity of indiarubber. These methods of tax-collecting are simplicity itself, and involve no formalities, such as receipt signing.

They are now so popular that the Congo State is believed to meditate a new Coat of Arms—or Hands.

The design will closely follow that in the Shield of Ulster—where the Red-Hand shines conspicuous; but in the Congo shield, I understand, the hands will be numerous and all black—while the motto to be substituted for the existing "Travail et progress," is, I am informed, to be "HANDS OFF!" Truly an appropriate motto for this poor little State, menaced by the intrigues of perfidious Albion!

* See Chapter XII.

IV

IN THE LAKE MANTUMBA REGION: MOLA EKULITI: MOKILI: AND EYEKA.

The correspondent * in the Congo who forwards me these photographs, accompanies them by the following explanations :—

"March 10th, 1904.

"DEAR MR. MOREL,

"In sending you the accompanying photographs of three mutilated natives who have come to my notice during my stay on the Congo, I wish to give you a few particulars of these cases.

"Reading from left to right these victims are—

"The youth standing up, with both hands gone—Mola Ekuliti.† This boy was a native of Mokili, a town of the Lake Mantumba district.

"His town was attacked by the soldiers of the Government post of Bikoro, in 1898, under the command of an officer whom I knew and often met.

"Several Natives were killed, but Mola was tied up and taken away to the lake-side, where, owing to the tightness of the thongs round his wrists, the flesh had swollen. The officer directed the thongs to be beaten off, but his soldiers translated that into beating off the hands—which they did with the butt end of their rifles against a tree. The officer was standing by drinking palm wine.

"Mola was shortly afterwards cared for by the Mission Station at Okoko. When Mr. Clark went there in 1901, he wrote to Governor-General Wahis, at Boma, a letter drawing his attention to the case of Mola, and begging that provision should be made for him by the Government. No reply was sent to this letter. Mr. Clark, on reaching Europe, wrote to the Central Administration in Brussels (this was in May or June, 1901), and sent a photograph of the boy in his helpless plight, begging that relief should be forthcoming.

"No notice was taken of this appeal—save by a paragraph in one of the Brussels papers insulting Mr. Clark.

"Mr. Clark returned to the Congo from America in 1903. Mola, meanwhile, having been always cared for at Okoko. He was seen there by our Consul, Mr. Casement, when he visited Lake Matumba last year, and the Consul took note of Mola's condition, and made a note of his statement as to how the mutilation occurred. Mr. Clark gave the Consul a copy of the letter he had written to

---

* The correspondent sent me two photographs, one of Mola Ekuliti by himself (which appears in this volume), the other of Mola Ekuliti in a group of three, a little boy (Mokili) and an old woman (Eyeka). The second photograph is not sufficiently clear for reproduction.

† See plate.

APPENDIX

Governor-General Wahis from Boma in 1901, and the Consul spoke to some of the State officers in the Lake about the boy's condition. They pretended to be shocked, and the Commissaire-Général, with the State Attorney's deputy, hurried down from Coquilhatville to hold an inquiry into the case of mutilation reported to the British Consul. They all assured the Consul they had known nothing of the case, and after holding a Court of Inquiry, as it was termed, Mola was provided for with a house, a wife, and twenty brass rods a week, as pension, in the State post of Bikoro. This was done in reality to hoodwink the Consul, who was assured that this was an isolated case, and they thanked him for bringing it to their notice and enabling them to make 'reparation.' The Consul told Mr. Clark that he was not satisfied at all—as it was quite clear to him that for two and a half years the Congo Government had known all about Mola through Mr. Clark's letters to them, and that they had done nothing, save insult Mr. Clark through the papers until he, the Consul, appeared on the scene. Then, in response to a few words he let drop in friendly conversation, the whole district was put in motion to convince him of their sympathy! The Consul said the case struck him as painfully significant, and that it was so fully corroborated by the other things he had seen and heard in Lake Mantumba—particularly from State officials there, themselves—that he had no option but to believe that the country had been systematically raided for rubber for several years.

"The woman sitting down was an old creature named Eyeka. I knew her well. She was the aunt of one of our best girls, who is now married to ——, and she often came here to visit her niece. She was the sister of ——'s mother—they came from the town of Mwebi, which is on the west shore of Lake Mantumba. Mwebi was attacked by the troops from Bikoro in pursuance of the customary punitive policy for not working rubber.

"Eyeka more than once told us in the Mission how she lost her hand. When the soldiers came to Mwebi, she said, they heard a bugle blow, and she and her son and many people fled. While they ran shots were fired, and her son fell by her side. She fainted, and fell down too. Then she felt some one cutting at her wrist, and she was afraid to move, for she knew that if she moved her life would be taken.

"When all was quiet she opened her eyes. Her son was lying dead beside her. His hand was gone, and hers was gone, and she was bleeding away.

"This story of Eyeka's I have heard from many others. A small boy up in Banto had just the same experience when —— led the soldiers from Wangata.

"There are still many more poor beings around the Lake without hands, and I have heard these poor men tell the present Government officer at Bikoro, in my hearing, that their hands had been hacked off against the sides of canoes to which they were clinging, by the State soldiers. No one was ever punished for all these barbarities—

that should be always remembered—and no attempt at providing for the mutilated victims of this rule of savagery, which, for nearly seven years, made Lake Mantumba a hell upon earth, has ever been attempted until the British Consul's visit last year, and his inquiry into Mola's case showed the authorities that the truth was at last likely to come out. Since the Consul's visit every effort has been made to discredit him, and to get up a case to show that he was misinformed, and we have heard of the efforts in this direction in the case of the boy Epondo, whom the Consul found mutilated up the Lulonga River and brought down to Coquilhatville.

"After Mola Ekuliti, which they could not deny, they thought the best way of dealing with Epondo's case was to deny the whole of the facts, to represent the Consul as entirely hoodwinked by the Natives, and so, if possible, discredit all he might say about the terrible wrongdoing which has gone on here for years.

"The accompanying letter* from Mr. Faris, at Bolengi, who was called in by the Authorities at Coquilhatville to testify to the retraction the poor little boy Epondo was forced to make after the Consul had gone away, is pretty clear evidence as far as it goes.

"But I am forgetting the photo of the mutilated people. The third figure—the little boy on the right, whose right hand is gone—was a poor little fellow named Mwanza.

"He was found by Mr. Clark, in 1897, over in Bikoro Station, and the Government officer there allowed Mr. Clark to bring him back to Ikoko, and to provide for him. The poor little chap was too sick to do much good, and he died about two years ago. There were three other children, all mutilated, at Ikoko, who were cared for by the Mission there at various times within my knowledge. They were—

"Ipembe—a little girl who was found lying beside the dead body of her mother, not far from the Mission Station. The mother had been shot by the State soldiers when they came over from Bikoro to raid Ikoko in 1895—in one of the punitive expeditions of that sad time. The mother's hand was cut off, and the child's also taken—but the poor little thing did not die, but lay beside its mother until some of the Mission boys heard of it and told Mr. and Mrs. Clark. A man called Moke, who was being taken back as a prisoner, told the Mission boys about Ipembe's mother being killed, and the child beside her, and so Mr. Clark sent out that evening and Ipembe was brought in to the Mission. At dinner-time that day Mr. Clark saw a soldier carrying a basket, which he laid down close to the verandah of the Mission while he went to get a canoe ready to go back to Bikoro in.

"Mr. Clark went out and looked in the basket, and found it had seventeen hands in it. Mr. Clark called Mrs. Clark to go out, and she told me she went and it made her feel sick. She stood over the

---

* This letter is referred to in Chapter XXX.

basket while her husband counted the hands—three of them were babies' hands.

"The soldier took the basket of hands away with him in the canoe to Bikoro, which lies in sight of Okoko across the lake.

"*The officer who was in command at Bikoro told Mr. Clark once that his dog used to eat some of the hands the men brought back from their raiding.*

"Ipembe, I know, was taken down to the State camp at Irebu by Mr. Clark to have her hand seen to, and Dr. Reussens, who was there then, dressed the stump and did what he could for her. She lived for about six months only. She was only about five or six years old.

"Then there was another small boy named Mwanza—who was brought in in the beginning of 1897, after a raid close to the Mission. He was in the school, but did not live long.

"Another boy was a little chap the late Mr. Sjöblom got from the State officer at Bikoro. This boy was called Ingwere, and he, too, only lived a short time.

"When the British Consul was here in August last year, I know he was told by one of the State officers in the neighbourhood—I heard the officer tell him myself—that there were still a lot of mutilated people in the lake-side country, and that they often came in and told the officer how his predecessors had given orders for their mutilation.

"The officer said that one of his predecessors, of whom he was speaking by name, had killed 'thousands' of the people around the lake, and that the mutilation of those killed had gone on for a long time, until the scandal in the Belgian Parliament and the outcry in Europe stopped it.*

"Just after the Consul had gone away, three poor men—some of those this officer had referred to—came over the lake to try to see the Consul, and tell him. They hoped that he might be able to help them, *as the State officers had not done anything for them.* Mutilation of the dead is not now permitted *openly*, to the Government soldiers; but it must be remembered that the long spell of murder and massacre and pitiless destruction of life, which went on from 1893 to 1900, *has done its work.*

"The people in the Lake *are entirely* broken, *and only a remnant of them remain.*

"It was not a wise policy, apart from all other considerations, for it has killed the goose that laid the golden egg, so far as this district is concerned, and it will take many years of peace and rest for the population to recover, while the native belief in the white man's truth, or justice, or decency, has gone for ever. They often say to me now, 'Will he never go home to his own country? Has not the white man got enough rubber yet?' Poor people! a strange

---

* In 1900. Stopped it locally, and in its intensive form, no doubt; but that mutilation of the *living* is still common—whatever may be the case as regards the dead—we know.

visitation—more dire than that which fell upon the Egyptians, for that was from above, with all its earthly plagues of loathsome nature; but who can say that what has come to the Congo people—whatever their faults may be—has been from above, or prompted by any love, but that of gain.

"Believe me, dear Mr. Morel,
"Yours faithfully,
"————"

OPPRESSION AT LOLANGA AND NEIGHBOURHOOD

I

LETTER OF THE REV. S. GILCHRIST TO THE GOVERNOR-GENERAL OF THE CONGO STATE ON THE CONDITION OF THE PEOPLE IN THE LOLANGA DISTRICT, JULY 1903.

"C. B. M., Lolanga, July, 1903.

"To His Excellency the Governor-General.

" As a member of the white community of this district, I beg to address you on a matter which, I feel, needs your interference. This matter is the State impositions laid on Lolanga towns.

" The town is composed of ten small sections. Six of these are on the up-river side of our station, three on the lower side, the remaining one is on an island near the opposite bank of the main river. This latter section was formerly the outlying one on the down-river end of the town, but moved to the island on account of the close proximity of the old site to the State wooding-post, where a soldier is stationed.

" After taking a very careful census, I find that the population of the sections on this side is 900. From my personal observation of the remaining section, I should say that a maximum estimate of the remaining section will be 50. Of these 1000 people 250 are children, 50 are working on the State steamers and elsewhere, and 150 are sick and infirm. Of the remaining 560—which is the working population—200 are men and youths, 360 are larger girls and women. The 560 of the working population is a very variable quantity, chiefly on account of the large amount of sickness due to continual exposure in getting fish, etc.

" The impositions consist of ' chikwanga,' dried fish, fowls, ducks, and firewood. Six of the sections supply the State post at Coquilhatville, and the Lolanga wooding-post; three sections are expected to supply us—the Mission (that is to supply chikwanga, fish, and fowls). They work the firewood for the State. The other section carries its supplies to Mampoko for the La Lulanga Company.

" In the sections which carry their supplies to the State there are, on an average, 110 men to supply 300 bunches of fish per week, and 220 women to supply—cultivate and cook—430 bunches of chikwanga, each bunch weighing about seven pounds, or a total of one ton seven cwt. There is also a slave town behind Lolanga (four miles away), which supplies Coquilhatville with another 280 bunches of chikwanga. This village has a population of 11 men, 180 women, and 89 children. All the above sections supply 110 fowls and 12 ducks per month to Coquilhatville. They also have each to keep 15 fathoms of firewood supplied to the wooding-post.

"In considering the amount of the tax, it must not be overlooked that a large number of men are employed three days each week in conveying the various supplies to Coquilhatville, whilst very frequently canoes are sunk, and if recovered the food is lost; sometimes lives are lost also. The market value of Lolanga of one week's supplies conveyed to Coquilhatville (of chikwanga and fish) is £9 10s.; the price actually paid by the State is £2 3s. Firewood, for which Commissaire Du Baw promised the people 10 mitakus per fathom—but for which they seldom get any payment—is worth (according to prices paid by us on the French Congo) 3 francs per fathom or 90 francs per week.

"In the three sections of the town which supply the Mission there are about 67 men to supply 38 bunches of fish—these bunches are about three times larger than those taken to Coquilhatville—and 130 women to cultivate and cook 140 bunches of chikwanga. These are also supposed to bring fowls weekly. They have, moreover, each to keep 15 fathoms of firewood supplied to the State wooding-post.

"The one section which supplies the La Lulanga Company at Mampoko has 13 men to procure 50 bunches of fish, and 22 women to get 100 bunches of chikwanga. They also supply fowls, and keep 15 fathoms of firewood supplied to the wooding-post.

"With regard to the labour involved in getting these various supplies, much more is involved than might at first sight be supposed. In the procuring of the fish the modes of fishing with which these people have been familiar are adapted to rising, seceding, or extreme low water. Before the State Imposition was laid upon them they never thought of doing any fishing except at these particular seasons, and then caught sufficient to keep themselves going till the next fishing season. These modes of fishing are ill-adapted to procure the quantities demanded of them—in fact, they buy a large quantity from another tribe whose surroundings and modes of fishing are adapted to other seasons. Of course they pay very much more for it than the price they receive for it from the State.

"With regard to the chikwanga: the land suitable for cultivation is in this district confined to a very limited area, on account of the lowness and consequent swampiness of the ground. They therefore have to go back frequently upon the land which has been excessively exhausted with manioc crops, and of course get small returns in quantity for the labour expended. This fact, coupled with the enormous quantity demanded, necessitates the buying of large quantities of the raw root (at a great monetary loss), and very often the chikwanga is short in quantity and bare in quality, the poisonous acid not being sufficiently eliminated. This is not calculated to be for the well-being of the consumer.

"Concerning the supply of fowls: besides the ordinary demand for fowls and eggs, there are extraordinarily heavy demands made, so much so that the people have no nucleus from which to rear.

"As respects the firewood: the number of steamers passing up and down the river is so great that they no sooner get their number of fathoms complete than the whole is taken away; and very frequently, although they work very hard to keep up the supply, there is not a complete store for a week at a stretch. The native implements by which the wood is cut are of such a primitive nature —little suited to cut the kind of wood required for the steamers— that the Native is badly equipped to get the quantities demanded. The expense also of these primitive knives is no small item in the amount of the tax. The time of the men is also so fully occupied in getting the fish that it is a matter of either neglecting that or the firewood.

"What with the variety of the taxes, the enormous demands, the small number of the people, and the difficulties encountered in attempting to procure the supplies, the people are continually falling short in quantities. The consequence of this is that some of the men are detained in chain at Coquilhatville until the quantities are completed. Another result is the people are exorbitantly fined. Only a few weeks ago Captain Hagstrom (acting in the name of the Commissaire of the district) imposed a fine of 5000 mitakus (45,000 in all) because their quantities of firewood had been short. They were given one night to gather the mitakus, or, failing to do so, a band of soldiers would be sent to sack the towns. During the last eighteen months fines amounting to over 100,000 mitakus have been imposed on Lolanga town, the white man's valuation of which is £200, but according to native value representing much more.

"One instance of exorbitant fines came to my notice two months ago at the slave town, Walla. Besides the (then) usual demand of fowls, a special demand was made, to be procured in a few days. These not being forthcoming, an under-officer—a white man—was sent with a band of about thirty soldiers to demand, not only the fowls, but 50,000 mitakus, and 20 people to be transported to the river wooding-posts—that is, away from the neighbourhood. When the officer and soldiers arrived, of course all the people ran away to the forest. The officer, however, took up his abode in the town, and, after a few days' waiting, was able to entice a number of the people back, amongst whom were several of the chief men. A number of these were tied to sticks in the open sun, and so kept for some days—for some time—until the majority of the people had returned. After staying in the town for a fortnight—the officer and soldiers being meantime supported by the people—the greater part of the mitakus were gathered, and the officer departed with these and most of the men demanded, but still keeping a number of people in the chain at the wooding-post till the demand was fully met. To procure these mitakus some of the men had to sell their wives and children, and some sold themselves to the river people.

"Eight years ago there was a population in these towns of at least 5000 people, compared with the 1200 of to-day. The impositions then were not nearly so heavy as at the present time.

"In conclusion, I would draw your attention to the money value of the taxes and fines, over and above the nominal value or price they receive for these supplies. It is at the rate of £60 per month for the last eighteen months. I would also like you to know that the people themselves are literally starving to keep up these supplies. In becoming acquainted with these facts I cannot but think you will feel it your duty to take steps to remove these oppressive measures, under which the people are groaning—and dying.

(Signed)   "S. GILCHRIST."

ADDITIONAL NOTE BY MR. GILCHRIST.

"P.S.—After the above letter was written to the Governor-General other fines were imposed which brought the amount up to close on 200,000 rods. One thing I omitted from that letter was to state that the women of the towns have to go down to work at the, or in the, coffee plantation three times a week. For this they get absolutely no payment; and, as Mr. Bond said in his letter, the coffee is allowed to fall on the ground and rot—it is never gathered."

II

How Mr. Gilchrist's Charges were "inquired" into. Letter from Mr. Gilchrist to Dr. Guinness, January, 1904.

"C. B. M., Lolanga, January 14, 1904.

"DEAR SIR,

"I beg to enclose a copy of a letter for your perusal and use which I sent to the Governor of this State in July of last year. My reason for appealing to him was that I thought it just possible the state of things indicated by the facts stated in the letter might be unknown to him, and therefore existing without his sanction and approval.

"The answer of the Governor to the letter, dated August 26th, transmitted through our legal representatives, was as follows: 'The situation of things signalised in the Rev. — Gilchrist's letter will be the object of serious inquiry, and measures will be subsequently taken to put an end to them.'

"This, of course, is a translation from the French.

"The measures promised to put an end to these things have either not been taken, or else they have proved ineffective; for the same order of things continues, practically the same as they were. The few improvements noticeable are—the fines have not been so frequent (only one or two having been levied since the letter was written), there have been no detentions in the chain since then, and now they have a book for each section of the town, in which the quantities are marked and the prices paid for them. But so far as lightening their burdens is concerned, nothing has been done.

"The only inquiry that we know of having been made scarcely merits the epithet of 'serious.' A day or two after our Consul, Mr. Casement, passed down, the Chef de Poste of Coquilhatville passed up on a district steamer with 25 soldiers to quell a rising among the people in the 'La Lolanga' territory, which had been instigated by the missionaries and the Consul! (so the report went which the Director of that Company took to the head-quarters of the district, but those living in the district never saw anything of it), and to inquire into the cases of hand cutting that had been reported. This officer called in on his way up to make some inquiries of us, the principal of which were: Where and when had we paid the taxes on the timber which we had used in the construction of our houses? How many goats and sheep had we on our stations? How many fowls did the people bring us? and how many would it take to supply all the white people on our station? and how many rations would be required to supply our workmen more than what we get from the towns or sections of the towns allotted to supply us?

"On the return of this officer from his inquiry up river he took up his abode at the wooding-post, which is about half an hour's journey below here at the bottom end of the town. Accompanied with seven soldiers, armed with rifles and a full supply of cartridges, he took a daily excursion into the town to make 'inquiry' in the various sections of it.

"One thing is to be noted about the 'inquirer.' He is the man to whom these people take their supplies at Coquilhatville, who, of course, acting on behalf of the Commissaire, receive the fines levied on them, put them in chain when their supplies were short of the numbers demanded, and otherwise had dealings with them. *His manner of making the inquiries* was noteworthy too. He selected one or two of the older men of the villages, who know very little of the State lingo, and are most easily intimidated by the sight of the 'Bini' (the rifle used by the State soldiers), and who thus are easily got into a frame of mind to make statements that are more calculated to please the inquisitor than those whom he represented, than to give the facts of the case. The younger men, who know the lingo used by the State and the traders, and who are less easily intimidated, and who have practically all the dealings with the State officials about the supplies and fines, were in most cases not listened to. Then, as regards the questions asked, and the manner in which they were asked, the principal aim in them seemed, so far as we could judge from them as they were stated to us by those who heard them, as well as their own conclusions about them, to try to find out something against the missionaries, and to lead them to make contradictory statements. In his inquiries about the number of brass rods they had been fined, some of those of whom the inquiries were made understood them to mean them as referring to their own section, some as referring to the whole district, some as referring to all the fines that had been imposed, and others as only to the later ones. Some of the questions asked were : What supplies they took to Coquilhatville; what prices they got for them; what prices they got in the towns for the same things; if any of their people had been tied up; if any had died in the chain; and such-like questions. *One man asked the officer if he was trying to make fun of him—he who had to do with the whole matter at Coquilhatville—asking them such questions.*

"That is the last we have heard of the inquiries, but it would seem, from the length of time that has elapsed, the last we are likely to hear.

"S. G."

III

THE CONGO STATE'S REPLY IN EUROPE TO MR. GILCHRIST. EXTRACT OF DR. GUINNESS' LETTER TO M. DE CUVELIER.

"April 21, 1904.

"In order to show you the kind of complaint that we make locally, I beg to send you a copy of the most recent letter we have received on this subject from the Rev. Somerville Gilchrist of Lolanga, together with the answer of the Governor-General, and a subsequent statement from Mr. Gilchrist. With regard to the latter, I need scarcely say that we should have been glad to note a substantial reduction of the taxation of the people, so that the actual pressure of taxation should correspond with the letter and spirit of the laws on this subject published in November last, by which it was arranged that forty hours a month should be the limit of labour demanded from the natives. I should be glad to hear from you as to whether or not you consider the existing conditions at Lolanga, as indicated by Mr. Gilchrist, correctly represent the forty hours' effective work that the Government considers it has a right to demand from the people. May I ask for an answer to this latter question at your earliest convenience."

EXTRACT OF M. DE CUVELIER'S REPLY.

"Bruxelles, Mai 21, 1904.

"Dans une lettre au Gouverneur-Général, M. Gilchrist semble se référer à des dires d'indigènes. L'on ne saurait être assez en garde contre cette source d'informations, et c'est sous cette réserve que je vous signale entr'autres que des indigènes des villages de Bokanza et de Bossumba ont déclaré qu'ils ne recevaient pas des missionnaires le paiement complet des vivres qu'ils leur fournissaient, et que ceux du village Bokele se sont plaints de ce que les missionnaires de Lulonga détenaient des femmes sous prétexte qu'elles étaient trop jeunes pour travailler et devaient rester à la mission pour recevoir l'enseignement. C'est ainsi encore que l'incident de Walla, dont parle M. Gilchrist, lui a été mal rapporté, cet incident ayant été provoqué par un acte de rébellion des indigènes de ce village qui avaient attaqué le représentant de l'autorité et l'avaient transporté, ligotté, à la mission anglaise."

CONSUL CASEMENT'S LETTER TO THE CONGO STATE AUTHORITIES IN AFRICA PROTESTING AGAINST TREATMENT METED OUT TO MISSIONARIES, AND DRAWING ATTENTION TO ABUSES UPON THE PEOPLE *

"September 4, 1903.
" M. LE VICE GOUVERNEUR-GÉNÉRAL,

" I have the honour to draw your Excellency's attention to the fact that complaints have reached me from several members of the Congo Balolo Mission as to restrictions placed upon their freedom of direct dealing, chiefly for food supplies, with the Natives dwelling around those of their stations situated in the basins of the Lopori and Maringa Rivers.

" These restrictions are represented to me as the outcome of the system of control established by the Society termed the 'A.B.I.R.' (formerly known as the Anglo-Belgian India-Rubber Company), whereby the Natives of the territory leased or conceded to it by the Government of the Congo Independent State are compelled, by armed force, to work in the exclusive interest of that Society.

" In drawing my attention to the effect upon their labours which this system of forced dealing induces, the members of the Congo Balolo Mission affected by it did not suggest or seek my intervention with the local authorities. But despite the fact that they have maintained silence on this point, doubtless from an earnest wish to cause no umbrage to the Society whose guests they are said to be, I feel it to be my duty to draw your Excellency's attention to the situation of the English Mission stations established within the A.B.I.R. Concession, since it is clear to me that the situation thus created is not only prejudicial to the prior rights secured to missionary enterprise in the Congo State by the terms of the Berlin Act, but is in direct conflict with the common law of this country.

"In making this representation I would, therefore, desire to emphasise the fact that it emanates from His Britannic Majesty's Consulate alone, and is directed not against individuals, but against a system which is, in my opinion, in conflict with the principles of an international obligation it is one of my duties as Consul to seek to see maintained in its integrity.

* A copy of this letter Consul Casement deemed necessary to send to the representative of the Mission on whose behalf he wrote. I am indebted to the head of that Mission in Europe, Dr. Guinness, for this copy.

APPENDIX 391

"I take this step all the more readily, in that I have been given to understand that the personal relations of the English missionaries with the local agents of the A.B.I.R. Company are, and have been, invariably friendly, and that no one of my countrymen seeks to attribute the responsibility for the state of affairs which prevails to the failure or misconduct of an individual agent of that Society.

"On the contrary, the missionaries who have sought my advice have one and all expressed themselves in cordial terms of their neighbours, and I believe they are very sensible of the many acts of personal kindness and of the help so frequently extended to them by the local agents of this Company.

"For my own part I have observed, during my recent stay at Bongandanga, how unceasing were the efforts of M. Lejeune, the local representative of the A.B.I.R. Society, to furnish the mission station there with all necessary food supplies, and to see that the comfort and welfare of its members were, in so far as he could provide for them, in no wise diminished by reason of the compulsion he was forced to exercise upon the surrounding district.

"I had, moreover, to thank M. Lejeune for much kindness and hospitality shown to myself during my few days' stay at Bongandanga.

"It is, therefore, in no sense a personal complaint that I feel it my duty to address to your Excellency, but one directed against a system of pressure exercised on the Native inhabitants which very seriously affects the work, both moral and material, of the English Mission stations established in their midst.

"This system, as I have seen it at work, I have no hesitation in denouncing as entirely illegal.

"By being forced to owe their daily and weekly food supplies to it, the English missionaries dwelling within the A.B.I.R. Concession are made participators in a systematic breach of the laws of this country, as well as sharers in a method of dealing with the Natives, which is contrary to the dictates of humanity, and which must fatally compromise their teaching in the eyes of the community they seek to instruct and lift up.

"I am sure your Excellency would share my feelings of indignation had the unhappy spectacles I have witnessed of late come before your Excellency's own eyes.

"I cannot believe that the full extent of the illegality of the system of arbitrary impositions, followed by dire and illegal punishments, which is in force over so wide an area of the country I have recently visited, is known to or properly appreciated by your Excellency or the central administration of the Congo State Government.

"I have seen women and young children summarily arrested, taken away from their homes and families, to be kept in wholly illegal and painful detention, guarded often by armed sentries, because, as I was informed by their captors, their villages, or their male relatives, had failed to bring in antelope meat or some other commodity desired by the local European.

APPENDIX

"I have seen recently, but not within the limits of the A.B.I.R. Concession, a number of Native women—eleven in all—with five infants at the breast, and three of them big with child, who had been taken from their homes and were tied together by the neck or ankle, guarded by two armed sentries—one of whom had a cap-gun, and the other a double-barrelled shot-gun.

"When I asked the reason of this detention, I was informed by the principal of these two guards (the man with the shot-gun) that this was but the customary measure of precaution the chief of the neighbouring European factory adopted to insure that each week's or fortnight's supply of indiarubber 'due' by the husbands of these women should be quite up to the mark.

"On the 2nd September I encountered at Bongandanga fifteen women and girls, one with a baby at the breast, being led to the prison (termed, I find, the 'maison des otages'), and guarded by three sentries of the A.B.I.R. Company; and in answer to my inquiry as to whom these women were, and why they were being thus led away, I was told by the acting representative of that Company, a M. Peters, that they were arrested and would be kept in detention until their husbands or male relatives had redeemed them in antelope or other meat which was required from their village for the use of the white man's table.

"I was further informed that a part of the meat furnished by this process of extortion would be sent over to the English Mission station, whose guest I was at the time, and that a further part would be (very kindly) sent for my own use on board my steamer when leaving.

"This method of obtaining supplies, I am informed, is in frequent operation, and I saw during my brief stay at Bongandanga several other cases of arrest and detention by the local agent of the A.B.I.R., which were, I believe, equally illegal. The effect produced on my mind from a very limited inspection of the system, revealing itself in such painful incidents as these, was that that system, and not the agents who are forced to keep it at work, was wrong in the extreme.

"I gather, too, that Bongandanga is, perhaps, noteworthy among the stations of the A.B.I.R. Concession for the forbearance and discretion shown by its agent, M. Lejeune, in his manner of imposing these exactions upon the local inhabitants, but I must confess with pain and astonishment that instead of a trading or commercial establishment, I felt I was visiting a penal settlement.

"I have no right of representation to your Excellency, save where the persons or interests of British subjects dwelling in this country are affected, and I would desire, in making this communication, to confine myself strictly to that aspect of the system, to which I now draw attention, which unduly presses upon them.

"I have a right to request, and one that I would urge with most respectful insistence, that my fellow-countrymen residing in any part of the Congo State should not be forced, in order to have food for themselves and households, to share in measures which are repugnant to the most vulgar sentiments of civilized society.

"Were the people of the Bongandanga villages around the mission left at complete liberty to dispose freely of their foodstuffs, as they have a legal right to do, my fellow-countrymen living there would hail the change with joy, even if it meant diminished supplies and enhanced prices.

"But as things are to-day the Mission at Bongandanga, with the exception of a stray fowl or an occasional egg, which may be bought direct from a Native, is entirely dependent on the neighbouring A.B.I.R. factory for all the local necessaries of life, which are furnished it daily or weekly, as the case may be, against a signed receipt.

"This system, I find, came into force in July of last year.

"Previous to that date, by an understanding arrived at between the missionaries and the local representative of the A.B.I.R. Society, certain villages in the *secteur* of Bongandanga, namely, Lilangi, Mpami, Lipongi, Bokoti, and Limboya, were permitted to deal direct with the English Mission there.

"This liberty of direct dealing with the Natives my countrymen at Bongandanga no longer effectively possess, as I have had opportunity of observing during my stay in that neighbourhood, and I am informed that a similar state of affairs prevails at Baringa—another station of the C.B.M. situated within the A.B.I.R. Concession.

"This is a liberty that I most respectfully submit these missionaries and the Native subjects of the Congo Independent State, who would deal with them, are entitled to enjoy in the fullest degree; and I would, therefore, beg that your Excellency will be pleased to require that no restrictions of any kind may be placed upon the legitimate intercourse of the Mission of Bongandanga, or any other station of the C.B.M., situated within the basins of the Lopori and Maringa Rivers, with the Natives of the surrounding districts.

"I have, etc.,
(Signed)   "ROGER CASEMENT."

ANNEXES TO RABINEK CASE

I. Penal Clause of the Decree of 30th October, 1892.
II. Text of M. Lévêque's Power of Attorney.
III. Lévêque's published Declaration.
IV. Agreement between Rabinek and the Katanga Company.
V. Report of Commandant Hennebert to the Governor-General *re* Rabinek's Death.

I

Penal Clause of the Decree of 30th October, 1892.

Décret du 30th Octobre, 1892.

(Bulletin Officiel, 1892, p. 307.)

" Celui qui exploitera ou fera exploiter le caoutchouc dans les terres visées aux art. 2 et 3 ou dans les biens concédés, affermés, ou vendus à des tiers, ou sans se conformer aux dispositions du présent décret ou qui achètera du caouchouc n'ayant pas acquitté la redevance prévue à l'art. 7, sera passible d'une amende de 10 à 1,000 francs et d'une servitude pénale d'un jour à un mois, ou d'une de ces peines seulement, le tout sans préjudice de dommages-intérêts au profit des ayants droit. Le tribunal ordonnera en outre la restitution aux ayants droit du caoutchouc recueilli illégalement et pourra retirer aux auteurs de l'infraction, l'autorisation conférée par le présent décret."

II

Text of M. Lévêque's Power of Attorney.

" Le Conseil d'Administration de la Compagnie du Katanga dans sa séance du 11 Octobre, 1899, agissant en vertu des Articles 25 et 26 des Statuts, a délégué à Monsieur Gustave Lévêque les pouvoirs nécessaires à l'effet d'y réprésenter celle-ci, de prendre les mesures de gestion journalière qu'il jugera utiles, notamment de traiter les affaires courantes et transiger sur celles-ci, acheter, échanger ou vendre toutes marchandises, faire toutes opérations du

APPENDIX

ressort de l'activité habituelle de la Compagnie en Afrique; prendre toutes les mesures disciplinaires prévues par les contrats à l'egard des agents; recevoir toutes sommes ou tous loyers dus à la compagnie, donner décharge pour toutes valeurs et quittances, émettre des traités en terrains concédés à la Compagnie par l'État du Congo, en reclamer les titres de propriété provisoires ou définitifs, signer tous actes, documents et pièces quelconques à ces fins; se substituer une ou plusieurs personnes dans tout ou partie de ces présents pouvoirs; révoquer les dites substitutions, en faire de nouvelles, passer et signer tous actes, élire domicile et *généralement faire, relativement aux pouvoirs ci-dessus conférés tout ce que le mandataire jugera convenable quoique non prévu en ces présentes.*"*

"Bruxelles, le douze Octobre, 1899, nonante neuf
"L'Administrateur   L'Administrateur
"Le Directeur   Délegué
(Signé)   "CAMBIER.   (Signé)   THYS.

"Vu pour légalisation de la signature de M.M. Thys et Cambier, Bruxelles, le 12th Octobre, 1899. Au nom du Sécrétaire d'Etat de l'État Indépendant du Congo.
"Le Directeur
(Signé)   "ED. P.............(?).†"

"I hereby certify that this document is a true and correct copy of a document this day produced to me.
(Signed)   "MARSHALL, Magistrate.
"Abercorn, N.E. Rhodesia, Aug. 6, 1901."

III

THE PUBLISHED DECLARATION OF M. LÉVÊQUE, THE DIRECTOR OF THE KATANGA COMPANY.

"Abercorn, le 12 Août 1901.
"Je soussigné, Gustave Lévêque, Ingénieur Civil, ex-directeur en Afrique de la Compagnie du Katanga, certifie que les faits suivants sont l'expression de l'exacte vérité:

"Le 11 Septembre, 1900, étant à Pweto, j'ai vu pour la première fois Rabinek arrivant par le schooner. Devant les bruits qui couraient sur son compte au Congo, relativement à la fraude du caoutchouc et de l'ivoire dans les térritoires du Katanga, je l'ai prié de bien vouloir m'accompagner au boma de Pweto, pour lui demander des explications à ce sujet, devant le Chef du Poste, M. Haubroe.
"Là, M. Rabinek nous exhiba:
"1. une 'Licence pour le Commerce dans le Congo,' du 10 Septembre, 1899, signée Cerckell à Kilwa (10 f. à payer par an).
"2. le Permis No 18 du 4 Fevrier, 1900, signé Hennebert à

---

* Italics mine.   † Name illegible.

Albertville, pour la licence pendant 5 ans de la chasse à l'éléphant (500 f. payés), permis imprimé, sur lequel CINQ ANNEÉS a été ajouté au timbre gras.

" 3. Un permis de port d'armes pour 39 fusils (somme payée 1950 f.) du 4 Février, 1900, signé Hennebert à Albertville. M. Hennebert est le Capitaine-Commandant à Mtoa, Chef de Zone du Tanganika-Katanga en 1900.

" M. Rabinek prétendit qu'il achetait aux noirs du caoutchouc et de l'ivoire à Kazembe seulement, où il avoit son store, c'est-à-dire en territoire anglais, et non au Katanga; sa présence au Katanga s'expliquait par suite de son permis de chasse.

" Le Lieutenant Haubroe lui demanda des renseignements sur les révoltés du Lualaba, d'où revenait Rabinek; cette conversation me confirma ce que je savais, que cette partie du territoire, d'où provenait beaucoup de caoutchouc vendu par les noirs au delà du Congo était inabordable à tout ce qui était officiel dans le Congo : Rabinek et des métis portugais connaissant parfaitement la langue du pays, et vivant avec les noirs, pouvaient seuls y circuler.

" Le caoutchouc du poste de Pweto provenait surtout du Luvule, à 2 ou 3 jours de marche, où pouvaient encore aller avec précautions les Europééns non officiels; les environs du poste de Pweto, qui autrefois produisaient beaucoup de caoutchouc, n'en produisaient plus, par suite du manque de surveillance de l'État Indépendant sur la façon de récolter ce caoutchouc, manque de surveillance dû surtout à l'hostilité des noirs contre les Officiels de l'État Indépendant du Congo; ces mêmes Officiels n'avaient pas commencé, à la fin de 1900, de replanter 150 pieds de caoutchouc par tonne récoltée par an, ainsi que le prescivent les lois de l'État Indépendant.

" Devant l'importance des frais faits et à faire par la Cie. du Katanga, pour la construction des stations et des Steamers, devant le manque total du caoutchouc sur le Tanganika; devant les difficultés de récolter le caoutchouc sur le lac Moero (Mweru) en quantité suffisamment grande pour payer les dépenses, je me résolus à accepter la proposition de Rabinek, c'est-à-dire : de lui donner la licence pour la récolte du caoutchouc et de l'ivoire dans les térrains de la Cie. du Katanga, *situés dans la zone des révoltés*,* moyennant le paiement de £10 par an, et de un franc par Kilo de caoutchouc ou d'ivoire récoltés et remis entre nos mains avant de quitter le Congo, et l'obligation de planter 150 pieds de caoutchouc par tonne exportée : nons assurions ainsi la conservation du caoutchouc.

" Rabinek estimait pouvoir faire par an 100 tonnes de caoutchouc, ce qui aurait fait pour la Cie. du Katanga un bénéfice de 100,000 francs par an, sans aucun risque ni débours, d'autant plus que nous n'étions suffisamment armés et en force pour aller dans le térritoire des révoltés. *Après avoir fait de nouveau constater les pouvoirs que m'avait donnés* † la Cie. du Katanga, je signai au nom de la Cie. du Katanga une convention avec Rabinek le 23 Septembre, 1900; celui-ci envoya aussitôt son agent Presquier au delà du Luvule, et

---

* Italics mine. † Ibid.

APPENDIX

alla à Blantyre pour y chercher des marchandises, qui faisaient défaut sur place.

"J'ai su depuis que Rabinek avait eu beaucoup de crédit près des A. L. C. African Lakes Corporation, de M.M. T. de Mattos, Ludgwi Deuss, etc. Dès la fin d'Octobre, je reçus des plaintes des capitãos de Rabinek, *maltraités et volés par les askaris de l'État Indépendant*,* et le 6 Décembre, M. Bouvier (?) successeur de M. Haubroe au poste de Pweto m'écrivit "veuillez me faire savoir si ce fusil (à piston) a été remis au capitão noir par vous ou par Rabinek.

"Un fusil entre les mains d'un capitão de Rabinek ne me sembla pas anormal, étant donné que celui-ci avait un permis de port d'armes pour 39 fusils, et qu'il était inadmissible que ce fut pour lui seul ; 39 fusils, c'est trop pour un seul homme.

"Je ne connus la nouvelle de l'amalgamation de la Cie. du Katanga avec l'État Indépendant que par la lettre du 9 Août, 1900, de la Cie., *reçue le 7 Novembre seulement à Luanja*.†

"Le 20 Avril, 1901, le steamer de la Cie. du Katanga arriva à Mvoa avec le Major Weyns et M. Rabinek qui avait été au devant du Major ; je communiquai à Rabinek, devant le Major Weyns, une lettre de la Cie. du Katanga du 12 Janvier, 1901, relative à sa licence, lettre reçu le 11 Avril à Mvoa, dans laquelle la Cie. du Katanga refusait de reconnaitre cette licence, ce que celui-ci refusa d'admettre.

"*La Major Weyns envoya Rabinek, avec le steamer de la Cie. à Kasanga, pour y acheter des provisions pour ses officiers restés sans ressources à Sumbu* ; ‡ ces provisions ne sont pas encore actuellement, payées, quoiqu'elles aient été consommées à Sumbu ainsi qu'il est facile de la faire constater par les blancs résidant à cet endroit.

"Dès le retour du steamer de Sumbu, le Major Weyns partit le 23 Avril pour Mtoa, et revint le 4 Mai à Mvoa nous annonçant qu'un mandat d'arrêt demandé quelque temps avant à Boma par le Commandant Hennebert venait d'arriver ; le Major Weyns ajouta, et cela devant M.M. Ferrier agent de la Cie. du Katanga, de Smet (sécrétaire du Major), Madame Lévêque et moi que celui qu'ils allaient arrêter, ils lui feraient un si gentil petit voyage que celui-ci ne recommencerait pas et que les autres s'en souviendraient. Il parla ensuite de Rabinek, prétendant que celui-ci avait fourni des armes aux révoltés, en envoyant des capitãos armés pour la chasse à l'éléphant dans cette contrée.

"Le 17 Mai, le Major Weyns quitta Sumbu pour Pweto, et le 7 Juin, M. Richards revint à Sumbu ; j'appris par ce dernier qu'il avait vu Rabinek prisonnier libre à Pweto, et qu'il avait pu lui parler.

"Le 19 Juin, 1901, le steamer allemand *von Wissmann* arriva à Sumbu nous apportant le nouvelle que Rabinek, à Mtoa était condamné à 1 an de prison et 1000 francs d'amende, et qu'on lui faisait faire le voyage de Mtoa à Boma pour passer de nouveau en jugement, les accusations portées contre lui étant très graves, *introduction illégale d'armes et de munitions dans le Congo*.§

* Italics mine.   † Ibid.   ‡ Ibid.   § Ibid.

"Le 'si gentil petit voyage' dont parlait le Major Weyns était donc destiné à Rabinek ; il reste à espérer que celui-ci pourra le supporter, étant donnée le façon dont les blancs sont traités par les askaris, même quand il n'y a aucun mandat d'amener, comme pour M. Van den Bosch pour lequel des excuses officielles ont été faites. Celui-ci a été plusieurs fois mis en joue par les askaris de l'État Indépendant à Chiniama, puis maltraité par eux d'une façon honteuse, puis ceux-ci l'ont trainé jusqu'à Lukafu, le sergent noir lui enlevant son casque, sa machilla, une chèvre que celui-ci avait achetée pour manger, et ne lui donnant que de la viande pourrie, et cela après avoir volé M.M. Juber et Van den Bosch, et avoir pillé la station de Chiniama. M. Bosch en est revenu avec un coup de soleil et un état permanent de fièvre, qui ne l'avait pas quitté en juin dernier.

"Un voyage pareil de Mtoa à Boma est certainement la mort,* et le Major Weyns a été bien mal inspiré de dire que celui qui serait arrêté 'ne recommencerait pas.'

"Je ne connais rien des marchandises introduites dans l'État du Congo par Rabinek, *mais je sais qu'il en payait régulièrement les droits d'entrée d'après les quittances que j'ai vues au poste de Pweto.*†

"Je ne connais rien aussi des quantités de caoutchouc et d'ivoire qu'il y avait achetées depuis la licence donnée par la Cie. du Katanga. Je sais que les marchandises qu'il avait achetées à Blantyre ont passé par Fife, Kasama et peut être sont elles toutes à son store de Kazembe; M. Lucas, agent de Rabinek à Kazembe est arrivé á Sumbu le 14 Juin, me disant qu'il avait remis les clefs et les livres du store au Dr. Watson à Kalongwise (?) : Lucas est parti le 20 Juin pour Kasanga. Relativement aux événements-ci-dessus relaté, je ferai les reflexions suivantes :

"*Endroit où Rabinek a été arrêté.*—D'après ce que lui a appris Rabinek, M. Richards m'a dit que celui-ci avait été arrêté à bord du steamer anglais *Scotia*, dans la baie de Pweto ; le Capitaine Mils des A.L.C. étant descendu à terre, a appris à M. Bouvier que Rabinek était à son bord, et M. Bouvier est venu procéder à son arrestation.‡

"D'un autre côté, si on consulte l'Arrangement du 12 Mai, 1894, conclu entre l'Angleterre et l'État Indépendant du Congo, il est dit que : 'La frontière entre l'État Indépendant du Congo et la sphère d'influence britannique au Nord du Zambèze (Zambesi) suivra une ligne allant directement de l'extrémité du Cap Akalunga sur le Lac Tanganika, situé au point le plus septentrional de la Baie de Cameroun, par environ 8° 15′ latitude sud, à la rive droite de la rivière Luapula, au point où cette rivière sort du Lac Mweru. La ligne sera ensuite prolongée directement jusqu'à l'embouchure de cette rivière dans le lac ; toutefois, vers le sud du lac, elle déviera

---

* This declaration, of course, was written in ignorance of Rabinek's fate.

† Italics mine.

‡ Later details show that the officer who served the warrant upon Rabinek was Lieut. Saroléa.

de façon à laisser l'île de Kilwa à la Grande Bretagne. Dans ces conditions, si on examine la carte officielle de l'Etat du Congo, mise à jour par le Lieutenant Lemaire, le dessin ci-dessous provenant d'un calque qu'en a fait Van den Bosch à Lukafu, on constate que le steamer en rade de Pweto se trouve fatalement dans les eaux anglaises.

"D'un autre côté, les observations du Lieutenant Belge Lemaire ont donné comme latitudes pour Moliro 8° 14', pour Pweto 8° 29'; la ligne joignant le Cap Akalunga à la rive droite du Luapula, de l'est à l'ouest, est donc inclinée vers le sud; la méridienne tracée avec des briques et partant d'un socle en briques par le même Lieutenant Lemaire, faite (?) la boma de Pweto, fait un angle aigue avec la route y conduit du lac: on peut donc en conclure, avec toute certitude, que la plage même de Pweto est Anglaise et non Belge.

"Tout ceci permet de déclarer formellement qu'il y a eu double violation de frontière, sur les eaux du lac et sur le beach, aggravée par le fait que Rabinek a été arrêté sur un steamer Anglais.

"*Pénalité encourue.*—Rabinek ayant été condamné à un an de prison et à 1000 francs d'amende, ce ne peut être pour l'exploitation illégale du caoutchouc, car le décret du 30 Octobre, 1892, dit: 'Art. 10. Celui qui exploitera ou fera exploiter le caoutchouc dans les terres visées aux art. 2 et 3 (terres domaniales) ou dans des biens concédés, affermés ou vendus à des tiers, ou sans se conformer aux dispositions du présent décret, ou qui achetera du caoutchouc n'ayant pas acquitté la redevance prévu à l'article 7, sera passible d'une amende de 10 à 1000 francs, et d'une servitude pénale d'un jour à un mois, ou d'une de ces peines seulement, le tout sans préjudice de dommages et intérêts au profit des ayants droit. Le tribunal ordonnera en outre la restitution aux ayants droit du caoutchouc recueilli illégalement, et pourra retirer aux auteurs de l'infraction l'autorisation conférée par le present décret (autorisation d'exploiter le caoutchouc).'

"Relativement au trafic des armes, le Major Weyns a insinué devant moi que Rabinek avait vendu des armes aux révoltés; je n'ai jamais rien su de semblable, et ce ne peut être que pour les 39 fusils à piston qu'il était autorisé à avoir au Congo, pour sa licence relative à la chasse de l'éléphant: quelques fusils ont pu être perdus ou volés à ses capitaõs, l'un d'eux a été saisi par les askaris du poste de Pweto. C'est ce qui expliquerait sa condamnation, car le décret du 10 Mars, 1892, 'Armes & Munitions,' dit: 'Art. 9. Quinconque commettra ou laissera commettre par ses subordonnés des infractions au present décret, ainsi qu'aux arrêtés et règlements d'exécution, sera puni de 100 à 1000 francs d'ammende, on d'une servitude pénale n'excédant pas une année, ou de l'une de ces peines seulement. La peine de servitude pénale sera toujours prononcée, et elle pourra être portée à cinq ans lorsque le délinquant se sera livré au trafic des armes à feu ou de leurs munitions dans les régions où sévit la traite. Dans les cas prévus ci-dessus, les armes, la poudre, les balles et les cartouches seront confisquées.' Le Major Weyns a prétendu que la licence pour la chasse à l'éléphant était pour un an ; je déclare formellement avoir vu la licence avec *Cinq Années imprimées au timbre gras.*

"Quant aux permis de port d'armes, le décret du 10 Mars, 1892, dit : Art. 3. 'Les permis de port d'armes sont valuables *pour cinq années et peuvent être* renouvelés.'

(Signé) " G. LÉVÊQUE."

IV

AGREEMENT BETWEEN RABINEK AND THE KATANGA COMPANY.

Companie du Katanga Soc. anon. Siège Social Bruxelles.

" ENTRE les soussignés Gustave Maria Rabinek demeurant actuellement à Kasembe, North-Eastern Rhodesia, d'une part, et Gustave Lévêque, agissant au nom de la Cie. du Katanga dont il est le directeur en Afrique d'autre part, a été convenu ce qui suit :

"A. La Cie. du Katanga donne à M. Rabinek *la concession pendant cinq anneés /5 ans/ de l'exploitation du caoutchouc et de l'ivoire sur les territoires de la Cie.* du Katanga, *actuellement sous l'influence des révoltés,* c'est à dire compris entre :

" 1. une ligne partant du confluent des rivières Lufira et Lungweze jusqu'au sud du Lac Kebele ;

" 2. la rivière Lualaba jusqu'au nord du Lac Kalomba ;

" 3. le parallèle 7° 50′ sud depuis le Lac Kalomba jusqu'à la rivière Luvna ;

" 4. la rivière Luvna jusqu'à son confluent avec la rivière Luwule ;

" 5. la rivière Luwule jusqu'à 28 longitude est ;

" 6. le 28 longitude est jusqu'à la rivière Lungweze ;

" 7. la rivière Lungweze jusqu'à son confluent avec la rivière Lufira.

"Le plan annexé ci-joint, fait d'après les cartes de M. Wauters, publiées dans le journal le 'Mouvement Géographique' du 24 Juillet 1898 et 27 Novembre, 1898, complète la description ci-dessus.

"B. *La licence* annuelle à payer par M. Rabinek est fixée à dix £Str./£10/ par blanc, travaillant dans le territoire ci-dessus.

"C. *La redevance* que M. Rabinek devra payer à la Cie. du Katanga pour l'exploitation du caoutchouc et de l'ivoire est fixée à un franc/ fr. 1/ par kilogramme.

"D. M. Rabinek est tenu de faire apporter tout le caoutchouc et l'ivoire qu'il exploitera dans la région ci-dessus désignée, à la Station de la Cie. du Katanga près de Mubanga, où tous les trois mois, aux 1er Janvier, 1er Avril, 1er Juillet, 1er Octobre, et suivant les circonstances, il sera pesé contradictoirement devant lui pour pouvoir régler la Cie. du Katanga, règlement qui devra être fait avant la sortie du caoutchouc et de l'ivoire de la station de la Compagnie.

"E. M. Rabinek est tenu de faire faire *tous ses transports* par la

Cie. du Katanga sur les Lacs Moero et Tanganyika, dès que celle-ci sera en mesure de le faire, et celle-ci s'engage à ne pas dépasser les prix des Compagnies concurrentes.

"F. Si M. Rabinek cesse son contrat pour quelque cause que ce soit, la Compagnie du Katanga deviendra propriétaire de son caoutchouc et de son ivoire accumulé dane la station de Mubanga.

"G. M. Rabinek s'engage à se conformer aux lois de l'Etat Indépendant du Congo, c'est à dire : d'introduire ses marchandises par les postes de douane de Moliro, Pweto, Mulenga : à payer les droits d'entrée de ses marchandises, à signifier à la Cie. du Katanga et aux postes de l'Etat Indépendant du Congo l'emplacement de ses stations, dès qu'elles seront construites ; de tenir ses livres conformément à la loi ;—ses livres de comptabilité pourront être vérifiés par les agents de la Cie. du Katanga à Mubanga ; à payer les droits de sortie de son caoutchouc et de son ivoire ; à planter *cent cinquante pieds* /150 *pieds/ de caoutchouc par tonne de caoutchouc récoltée par an.*

"H. *La licence* sera retirée de plein droit par la Cie. du Katanga en cas de fraude ou de tentative de fraude, ou si M. Rabinek ne se conforme pas aux clauses ci-dessus.

"I. Toutes les contestations qui pourraient surgir entre la Cie. du Katanga et Monsieur Rabinek, seront jugées par les autorités de l'Etat Indépendant du Congo.

"Fait et signé *en triple* exemplaire à Mbango, *le vingt-trois Septembre mil neuf cents.*

"Signé le Directeur en
Afrique de la Cie. du Katanga,
G. LÉVÊQUE.
" Signé par les témoins
MAURICE GREEN,
E. R. LUCAS.

"I, C. P. Caudy, do hereby declare the above is a true copy of the original which was placed before me on the thirtieth of October, 1900.

(Signed) "C. P. CAUDY,
Acting Collector, Karonga,
North Nyassa.

Dated 30.10.1900."

V

COMMANDANT HENNEBERT'S REPORT TO THE GOVERNOR-GENERAL ON THE CIRCUMSTANCES UNDER WHICH RABINEK DIED. Copy of Extract.

"Boma, le 18 Septembre, 1901.

"MONSIEUR LE GOUVERNEUR-GÉNÉRAL,

. . . .

"Le 20 Août, je m'embarquais à Bumba sur la *Hainaut*. Ce bateau venant de Stanleyville, avait à bord plusièurs passagers, dont Rabinek. Je constatai que celui-ci avait accès sur le pont et à la salle à manger au même titre que les autres passagers. Je fis observer au Commissaire du Bord l'irrégularité de cette situation. Il me fut répondu que le substitut du Procureur d'Etat de Stanleyville, en faisant embarquer Rabinek, avait déclaré qu'il pouvait être traité comme un passager quelconque, parce qu'il désirait faire entendre sa cause par le tribunal d'appel. Je m'abstins de modifier ces instructions.

" Durant le voyage, Rabinek s'est montré insouciant d'humeur. La plupart des passagers frayaient avec lui et il se tenait généralement parmi les groupes parlant haut et gaiement.

"Je citerai parmi ses compagnons habituels, le capitaine du bateau Otto et le commissaire Pahaut, le sous-lieutenant Rosendael, l'agronome WenWaert, le premier officier Rovero, le poseur Carrey, etc.

"Rabinek s'alita le 27 ou le 28 Août. Il avait des accès de fièvre et des vomissements de bile. Le 29, le médecin attaché au camp d'Irébu examina le malade, lui reconnut une fièvre bilieuse, mais ne manifesta aucune crainte. La maladie suivit son cours jusqu'au 1er Septembre. Le malade était soigné par le commissaire du bord; plusieurs passagers et particulièrement M. Carrey le visitaient fréquemment.

"Le dimanche le Septembre vers 8 heures du soir l'état de Rabinek, qui n'avait jamais été inquiétant, empira, et je fus averti que la température du malade était très élevée. Je reconnus en effet l'urgence de lui administrer une hypodermique de quinine.

" Ce médicament n'eut pas l'éffet souhaité, la température du patient s'éleva encore, et une demiheure après il expira.

" J'ai entendu émettre l'avis général que Rabinek, par son long séjour aux tropiques et par la passion de la morphine qui le dominait, n'était pas en état de résister à un accès violent de fièvre.

" Tout ce qu'il laissait fut enfermé dans ses malles et la malle cabine qui les contenait mise sous scellés jusqu'à Léopoldville.

" Le lendemain matin Rabinek fus inhumé au poste de Black River, où le *Hainaut* avait séjourné la nuit.

" Le suivis le corps avec la presque totalité des passagers."

JUDGMENT OF THE APPEAL COURT OF BOMA IN THE CASE OF CAUDRON AND JONES

March, 1904.

(Translation.)

"*Judgment in Appeal respecting the Cases of M. Caudron and S. Jones.*

"The Court of Appeal at Boma, sitting for the consideration of Criminal Cases, has pronounced the following Judgment:—

"*Public hearing of March* 15, 1904.

"(No. on the list 395.)

"The Public Prosecutor *versus*—

"(1) Caudron, Phillip Charles François, born at Auderlecht, Belgium, Superintendent of the Melo Commercial Zone, in the service of the Société Anversoise du Commerce au Congo; and

"(2) Jones, Silvanus, a native of Lagos, clerk in the service of the said Company:

"The charges against the first-named were that, at the end of 1902, and at the beginning of 1903, when he was Superintendent of the Melo Commercial Zone, in the service of the Société Anversoise du Commerce au Congo:

1. He caused the village of Liboké to be attacked at night by the servants of the Society, armed with Albini rifles, thus directly bringing about the death of a certain number of Natives of the said village of Liboké;

2. That he went about the country with a force composed of sixty State soldiers and of twenty servants of the Société Anversoise du Commerce au Congo, armed with Albinis, and caused the Natives of the villages of Magugu, Teriba, Mandingia, Muibembetti, and Kakoré to be attacked by this force, divided into small detachments, thus directly bringing about the death of a great number of Natives of the said villages;

3. That he, at Muibembetti, deliberately wounded the woman Menniegbiré by discharging a shot-gun into her breast;

4. That he arbitrarily detained at Mimbo for nearly a month about twenty prisoners taken during his expeditions in the villages of Magugu, Teriba, Mandingia, Muibembetti, and Kakoré;

5. That at Mimbo he directly caused the death of a prisoner,

having previously given instructions to the armed sentries under his orders to kill any prisoner who might attempt to escape;

6. That at the station of Binga-Etat he gave an order to the sentries to kill a Mogwande Chief, an order which was executed by the soldier Kamassi;

7. That he established, or allowed to be established, at Bussu-Baya, and at Dengeseke, commercial factories where workmen were installed, armed with Albinis and cartridges, forming part of the armament of the factories of Mimbo and Binga, these arms and ammunition having been moved without authority, and having been used in committing the breaches of law, for which Silvanus Jones, chief of the factory of Bussu-Baya, and Bangi, his servant, are being prosecuted;

8. That, at the post of Mimbo, he handed over to his Headman ("Capita") Kassango 100 Albini cartridges belonging to the State, and, at the post of Binga, handed over 200 cartridges to Houart, head of that factory; which proceedings constituted a fraudulent abstraction of cartridges, the property of the State; and, in the second place, a breach of the Regulations in regard to fire-arms, offences covered by Articles 1, 2, 3, 4, 11, 18, 19 of the Penal Code, 101 *bis*, 101 (4) of the Penal Code, Decree of 27th March, 1900; 2 and 9 of the Decree of 10th March, 1892, and the Order of 30th August, 1901, respecting fire-arms.

The charges against the second were that, at the end of 1902, he sent workmen of the Société Anversoise du Commerce au Congo, armed with Albinis, into the neighbourhood of the factory of Bussu-Baya, with instructions to kill the Natives, and thus directly caused the death of a woman of Bassango, who was killed by a rifle-shot by his servant Bangi—offences covered by Articles 1 and 9 of the Decree of 10th March, 1892, and by the Order of 30th April, 1901, respecting fire-arms, and 1 and 2 of the Penal Code;

In view of the terms of the indictment against the above-named persons, and the verdict of the Court of First Instance of the Lower Congo, dated the 12th January, 1904, condemning the first-named to twenty years' penal servitude and to seven-eighths of the costs of the action, and the second to ten years' penal servitude and to one-eighth of the costs of the action;

Whereas appeals against the said verdict were made by the Public Prosecutor and by the accused Caudron, according to declarations received at the office of the Registrar of Court of Appeal on the 12th February, 1904;

Whereas the said appeals were notified to the Public Prosecutor and to the accused on the same day;

Whereas a summons was served on the accused on the 22nd February, 1904;

Whereas Judge Albert Sweerts has reported on the case;

Whereas the case has been heard before the Court of Appeal;

Whereas the Procureur d'État has addressed the Court for the prosecution;

APPENDIX 405

Whereas the statements and defence of the accused have been heard, being presented on behalf of Caudron by M. de Neutor, the defending Counsel accepted by the Court;

Whereas the Court of Appeal has received the appeal of the accused Caudron, and the appeal of the Public Prosecutor relating to the latter, and to the other accused, Silvanus Jones;

Whereas the appeal of the accused Caudron is inadmissible, the appellant not having deposited the costs in advance, in conformity with Article 78 of the Decree of the 27th April, 1889;

Whereas, nevertheless, the appeal of the Public Prosecutor reopens the whole case even in the interest of those served with the notice of appeal.

With regard to the accused Caudron;

On the first and second counts:

Whereas it is proved by the evidence of the witnesses and by the documents included in the "dossier": (1) that, on the night of the 15th to 16th October, 1902, at the station of Akula in the district of the Melo, the accused Caudron, District Superintendent of the Société Anversoise du Commerce au Congo, with a view to punish the inhabitants of the village of Liboké for not furnishing the forced labour required of them, gave orders to five of his workmen, armed with Albinis, to go to the said village and fire on the inhabitants, orders which the workmen executed, killing the Chief and several inhabitants of the village;

(2) That in the course of the months of January, February, and March, 1903, in order to force the Natives of the region of the Banga to furnish a greater supply of rubber, he conducted an expedition into the said region with twenty of his workmen, armed with Albinis, and accompanied by a non-commissioned officer and fifty soldiers of the State; that in the course of this expedition he despatched the workmen, armed with Albinis, and the soldiers, in small detachments, into the localities of Magugu, Teriba, Bongu, Muibembetti, and Kakoré, with instructions to fire upon any Natives they might meet—instructions which the workmen and soldiers carried out, thereby causing the death of a large number of Natives;

Whereas the accused acknowledges the general truth of these facts, but pleads in extenuation that he acted in accordance with the authorization, and even by the order, of the authorities, represented, in the case of the Liboké incident, by M. Nagant, and, in the case of the expedition against the Banga, by M. Jamart, both Heads of the police-station at Binga;

Whereas, in the case of the Liboké incident, all the witnesses questioned on this point before the Court of First Instance and before the Court of Appeal denied categorically that M. Nagant was at Akula when the attack against that village took place, and that consequently he could not have authorized by his presence the order given by the accused Caudron, as the latter maintains;

Whereas the "dossier" contains, however, certified copies of two letters addressed by M. Collet, Manager of the station of Akula, to M. Nagant, the first dated the 12th October, 1902, asking him to take action against the village of Liboké, and the second dated the 16th October—that is, the day after the attack—thanking him for his action, and informing him that the Natives had come in in the morning to the station and had undertaken to accomplish their allotted tasks with regularity; and the authenticity of these letters is denied by the prosecution, who maintain that they were forged subsequently in the interest of the accused;

Whereas, however, the three facts: that they have been included in the "dossier" by the Magistrate in charge of the case; that they were found in the office of the police-station, and that they were admitted by M. Collet in the course of the preliminary inquiry, do not allow of their being considered as forgeries and consequently rejected;

Whereas, since a doubt exists, the version most favourable to the accused must be accepted—that is to say, that the Chief of the police-station, Nagant, was at Akula when the attack on the village of Liboké took place, and that he was aware of, and authorized that attack;

Whereas, consequently, any supplementary examination relative to the said circumstances would be absolutely useless in the interest of the defence;

Whereas, in the case of the expedition against the Banga, the presence in that expedition of the Chief of Police, Jamart, with fifty soldiers of the State, is not denied, and it is, moreover, proved that the accused acted throughout on that occasion in perfect accord with the former; whereas it remains, therefore, to be determined whether the presence and the authorization of these representatives of authority may be taken as justifying the action of the accused;

Whereas it is a principle, expressly recognized by the codes on which our legislation is based, that, in order to exclude the idea of an offence, it is not enough that the action may have been ordered by the Executive authorities, but it is necessary also that it should be prescribed by the law;

Whereas there is no doubt in the present instance that it is a case of offences against common law, that is to say, of manslaughter committed for a private purpose with the object of forcing the Natives to supply labour or produce;

Whereas, although the restoring of order has been occasionally vaguely mentioned, it is clearly shown by the evidence of all the witnesses, and even by the reports addressed by the accused to the Director of the Company, and by his letters to the officers of the district, that, in committing these acts of hostility against the Natives, he only had in view the interest of his Company's trade, and more especially the increase in the amount of rubber collected;

Whereas, even if there could be any doubt as to the nature of the previous expedition against the Gwakas, no doubt can exist in this respect in connection with the facts which are the subject of the prosecution;

APPENDIX

Whereas, in any case, it is a well-established fact that at the time these acts took place order had in no way been disturbed, either at Liboké or among the Banga; that it does not appear that the victims of these actions had committed any other fault than that of failing to furnish the Company with the amount of labour required by it;

On the other hand, seeing that the sole fact of not having paid the taxes, even if they had been legally due (which they were not in this case, because no law had yet authorized their collection), could not justify such sanguinary measures;

In the present instance it is still less possible to speak of war-like acts, because to attack peaceable people and to fire upon single and inoffensive individuals is certainly not making war;

Whereas it is proved by the evidence of the witnesses, and by the statements of the accused himself, that on no occasion during these events did the Natives attack or commit any sort of hostile act;

Whereas there was not one killed or wounded among the soldiers or among the Company employés;

Whereas, therefore, it would be absurd to call it war; and killing under such circumstances constitutes a crime which no law or necessity authorizes, and which is punishable by the Penal Code, whether it be committed by a private person or by a representative of authority;

Whereas, on the other hand, the accused cannot plead in extenuation the principle of official subordination, in view of the fact that such a plea is only valid in the case of representatives of authority who carry out the orders of an official superior, and then only so far as the authority of that superior extends;

Whereas the accused was not a representative of authority and he did not owe official obedience to any one; it was in no way part of his duty as an agent of a Company to co-operate in measures of repression; he was, therefore, fully entitled to refuse to execute the orders which might be given him to this effect, and, if he executed them, it was at his own risk;

Whereas, moreover, it is a principle of law that even obedience to one's official superior does not constitute a valid plea when the illegality of the order is obvious;

Further, whereas there is no truth in the statement that the accused, as he affirms, only obeyed the orders of the Chiefs of the police-station;

Whereas the truth, on the contrary, is that the latter were, in point of fact, under his orders;

Whereas a mere non-commissioned officer like Nagant; a mere military assistant (corporal) like Jamart, could not have any authority over the accused, who occupied the high position of a District Superintendent of the Société Anversoise du Commerce au Congo, and had under his orders a large staff of white men and Natives;

Whereas all the witnesses were unanimous in stating that in

all the expeditions which he made with the Chiefs of the police-station, it was he who commanded, gave orders to, and punished, not only his own men, but even the soldiers of the State; whereas, especially in the case of the expedition against the Banga, it is evident that Corporal Jamart, quite young and but recently arrived in Africa, knowing neither the language nor the country, and, besides, so ill that he nearly always had to be carried, and remained several days' journey to the rear, was simply a lay figure made use of by the accused in the belief that by Jamart's presence he would be able to cover his own illegal actions and to involve the State in his own responsibility;

Whereas it is therefore useless for the accused to plead good faith in having acted in accord with the representatives of authority;

Whereas he knew that he ought not to kill, and that he was even less justified in so doing in the interests of trade;

He knew that it is not tolerated by the laws of the State;

He knew, also, that several of his predecessors and colleagues in the same region and belonging to the same Company had received very severe sentences from the Court for similar offences;

He thought he would be cleverer than the others in trying to cover his responsibility by making use of State employés;

But if this precaution turns out to be ineffectual—if he realizes too late that criminal responsibility cannot be so easily eluded—he has no right to describe himself as the victim of an error;

Whereas, if he was mistaken, it was not with regard to the morality of the actions which he committed, but with regard to the value of the ruse which he made use of to cover them;

Whereas, however, the accused insists upon the request which he had already made in First Instance—to wit, that the Tribunal should order a supplementary inquiry, in order to have incorporated in the "dossier" the political reports sent by the higher administrative authorities of the region to the local government—which would show that the said authorities had known and approved of the actions of which he is accused, and even of previous and subsequent expeditions which he had made with the troops of the State; whereas the local government, questioned by the examining Magistrate, declared that, as a matter of principle, it did not think it possible to produce these documents, and, moreover, the said documents contained nothing that could refer to the facts mentioned by the accused;

Whereas the defence contests these declarations in law and in fact;

Whereas the right of the judicial authority to demand, and even to search for in any public or private place, any document which might lead to a conviction or an acquittal, cannot be denied in principle;

Whereas this right, which is given to the judicial authority by law, can only be curtailed also by law; whereas neither the Congo legislation, nor the legislation on which it is founded, fixes any limitation in favour of the Public Departments;

APPENDIX 409

Whereas if an exception be made in the case of diplomatic representatives, that is on account of the fiction of the extra-territoriality of their residence; whereas there is no place of asylum;

Whereas, however, it is the duty of the judicial authority to proceed in such matters with the greatest circumspection, and only if the documents demanded are of obvious use to the prosecution or the defence;

Whereas, in the present instance, the defence thinks that it can deduce from these documents the approval, and, in any case, the toleration of the authorities in connection with these actions;

Whereas, as has been set forth above, even the definite order, and, therefore, still less the toleration of the authorities, could not be held to justify acts contrary to the law;

Whereas this principle has already, for a long time past, and on several occasions, been affirmed by the Tribunals of the State;

Whereas, consequently, in no case could the accused find in the documents, the production of which he demands, justification for the actions with which he is charged;

Whereas the utmost he could do would be to adduce the toleration of the authorities as an extenuating circumstance;

Whereas, in this connection, it may be fittingly observed that the documents of the "dossier" itself, and the evidence of witnesses, go to prove the existence of a certain toleration on the part of the authorities;

Whereas, indeed, the presence and the co-operation of the heads of the police-station of Binga, at the time of the Qiboke affair, and of the expedition against the Banga, have been admitted by the Tribunal. Whereas the evidence of the witnesses also goes to prove that the accused, accompanied by agents and soldiers of the State, had, previously and subsequently, conducted other punitive expeditions against the Natives;

Whereas this is sufficient ground at least for presuming the toleration of the higher authorities of the district, and for admitting this toleration as an extenuating circumstance in favour of the accused;

Whereas, consequently, all supplementary inquiry on this subject, even if it might serve to prove the responsibility of other persons, could be of no service to the accused;

On the third count:

Whereas it is proved by the evidence of witnesses, and admitted by the men accused, that at Muibembetti, in the course of an expedition against the Banga, the accused in question, having lost his temper owing to a delay on the part of the carriers, fired upon them with his shot-gun loaded with small shot; one of the two discharges wounded a native woman in the back; and the wound was slight and did not cause her to be incapacitated from work;

On the fourth count:

Whereas the accused admits having caused to be detained at the factory of Mimbo some twenty Natives who had been taken prisoners in the course of the expedition against the Banga, and that their detention had no other object than to force their villages to collect rubber; whereas he alleges in his defence that these people had been arrested with the authorization and assistance of Jamart, the Chief of the police-station; whereas they were awaiting at Mimbo the instructions of the Commander of the police forces; whereas he maintains that this act was perfectly legal because the Government had, since the month of April, 1901, authorized the Société Anversoise du Commerce au Congo to exact rubber as a tax from the people, and had decreed the penalty of detention in the case of refusal;

Whereas, in fact, the Public Prosecutor declared in the course of a trial before the Court of First Instance that he was authorized to state that a letter was in existence from the Governor-General to the Commissioner of the district of Nouvelle-Anvers, granting to the Société Anversoise du Commerce au Congo the right to exact rubber as a tax; whereas this letter adds that the Commander of the police force may, in case of refusal, put in force the penalty of detention; that he may delegate that right to an agent of the Société Anversoise du Commerce au Congo, but that it will always rest with him to decide if the detention is to be confirmed or not;

Whereas it is quite evident that taxes could not be established, or detention in case of non-payment decreed, by a mere letter;

And whereas the right of imposing taxes on the people, and of fixing penalties can only belong to the King Sovereign, or to those to whom he has legally delegated his authority for that purpose;

And whereas the Judicature would fail in its duty and its mission if it recognized in any other authority those powers which are reserved to the sovereign authority;

And whereas a law duly decreed and published would therefore have been necessary;

And whereas such a law has only appeared quite recently, a very long time after the acts which form the subject of the prosecution, and it requires, moreover, in order to render the penalty of detention applicable, conditions which do not exist in this case;

Whereas, consequently, the letter of the Governor-General being unable to run counter to the Penal Code could not justify the violation of individual liberty;

And whereas it is quite possible that the accused may have been mistaken on this point, but the fact of acting in good faith cannot be taken as a justification for a breach of the law;

Whereas it is just, however, to take this into consideration in order to give the accused, on this head, the benefit of extenuating circumstances to the greatest extent possible;

On the fifth count:

Whereas it is established and admitted by the men accused that

APPENDIX 411

one of the prisoners detained at Mimbo, having attempted to escape during the night, was killed with an Albini rifle by the sentry on guard;

And whereas the accused maintains that he had absolutely nothing to do with this act;

Whereas, although it is established by the evidence of the witnesses that the accused had always given his men orders to fire on prisoners who tried to escape, it is not, however, proved that the sentry who fired was one of the men placed directly under his orders;

Whereas, on the contrary the proceedings seem to show that the man in question was a workman of the post of Mimbo, and that he had been placed as a sentry by the Manager of that factory;

And whereas the murder, therefore, could not be imputed to the accused;

On the sixth count:

Whereas the accused admits that upon his return from the expedition against the Banga, a native Chief was killed in the prison of the police-station of Banga by the soldiers of that station;

Whereas he admits that on two occasions, when he was in the company of Jamart, the soldiers came to ask for instructions relating to this prisoner, who was making a disturbance; and he also admits that he was actually present in the prison when the prisoner was killed; whereas, however, he affirms that neither he, nor Jamart, gave any order to the soldiers, and that he went to the prison solely to induce the prisoner to remain quiet;

Whereas all the witnesses interrogated on this point in the course of the preliminary inquiry, and at the hearing of the case, did, in a manner the most precise, and consistent in the most minute details, affirm that the accused twice gave the order to kill; first to Sergeant Tangua, who had come for instructions; and on the second occasion to the same sergeant and to the soldier Rixassi when they returned to get the order confirmed; and that it was the accused himself, who, in the prison, after the sergeant had fired upon the prisoner and missed him, handed the gun to the soldier Rixassi, who killed him;

Whereas the latter detail was also given by the witness Houart, confined in the prison at Boma, when the other witnesses were still in the Upper Congo; and it is, therefore, impossible that it was invented;

Whereas these two circumstances, absolutely established by other evidence as well as that of native witnesses, that the accused was in the prison and that he handed the gun to the man who fired, confirm in the most positive manner the fact that it was he who gave the order to fire, an order which the soldiers who were returning from the expedition, on which they had always looked upon the accused as their Commandant, could not hesitate to execute;

Whereas it is, moreover, amply evident that they certainly would not have killed without instructions, even in the presence of the accused;

On the seventh count:

Whereas the facts cited in the prosecution are established, and admitted by the accused, and constitute breaches of the Regulations as to fire-arms;

On the eighth count:

Whereas, as the first Judge declared, it is merely a question in this case of a simple exchange of ammunition between the troops of the State and the Company's armed men; and whereas a simple exchange cannot constitute a fraudulent abstraction, or (when it is only a question of cartridges, and not of the weapon itself) a contravention of the Regulations as to fire-arms;

Whereas, for the reasons given above, the accused must be declared guilty of murders with premeditation, as the moral author, through abuse of authority, of the deeds he is charged with on the first, second, and sixth counts; of blows and wounds on the third count; of arbitrary detention on the fourth count; of contraventions of the Regulations as to fire-arms on the seventh count; and he should be acquitted on the remainder of the counts;

Whereas there are reasons for granting extenuating circumstances to the accused, not only on account of the considerations submitted on the first, second, and fourth counts, but also on account of his good previous character during his long stay in Africa, and the great difficulties under which he must have laboured, as he had to do his duty in the midst of a population entirely hostile to all idea of work, and which only respects the law of force, and knows no other argument than terror;

Whereas it must be recognized that it must be very difficult to act within the law in a country still absolutely barbarous and savage, more especially when the laws to be obeyed in that country are the same as those which govern the most civilized peoples;

Whereas, to conclude, it is just to bear in mind that, although the acts are in themselves very grave, they lose a part of their gravity when they are considered in connection with the surroundings, in which, according to immemorial custom, human life has no value, and pillage, murder, and cannibalism were, until the other day, of ordinary occurrence.

As regards the accused Silvanus Jones:

Whereas it is duly established by the consistent testimony of the witnesses, and even by the contradictory evidence of the accused himself, that, during the month of October, 1902, when he was Chief of the post of the Société Anversoise du Commerce au Congo at Bussa-Baya, he ordered the men placed under his orders to proceed to the neighbourhood of the factory, and to kill the Natives that they met, to punish them for not having furnished a sufficient quantity of rubber, an order which his servant Bongi executed by killing a woman;

Whereas the accused maintains, as a subsidiary plea, that in any case he acted, as in other circumstances, in accordance with the orders of his superiors, especially with those of the District Chief, M. Caudron;

Whereas—although these orders are not well established—the methods adopted by the District Chief Caudron to obtain rubber from the Natives, and the fact that the accused had been placed at Bussa-Baya secretly, and that that post had been armed with eight Albini rifles without permission, give colour to the supposition, in favour of the accused, that, in point of fact, he did but follow the instructions of his Chiefs;

And whereas, however, for the reasons already given, these orders could in no way justify or exculpate the accused;

And whereas he could not even be regarded as a passive and unconscious instrument in the hands of his Chiefs, because, although a black, he possesses some mental culture and belongs to a country already partly civilised;

And whereas he must have known perfectly well that to kill is a crime;

And whereas he, moreover, acted in his personal interest because he was paid in proportion to the rubber he collected;

Whereas, however, it is just to concede to him extenuating circumstances to the greatest possible extent, taking into account his surroundings and the example set by his Chief; and whereas it must be admitted that it would have been very difficult for a black man to withstand the influence of example;

And whereas, therefore, the Court of Appeal expresses the hope that the rigour of the penalty, which, according to law, it is compelled to confirm, may, in the case of this prisoner, be modified as soon as possible, by his conditional release;

For these reasons, and those cited by the First Judge, which do not conflict with them;

The Court of Appeal:

Taking into consideration Articles 78 of the Decree of the 27th April, 1889; 3, 4, 11, 98, 101 (*bis*), and 101 (4) of the Penal Code; 2 and 9 of the Decree of the 10th March, 1892, and the Order of the 30th April, 1901;

Declares the appeal of the accused Caudron to be inadmissible;

And, on the appeal of the Public Prosecutor—

Amends the Judgment appealed against with respect to the accused Caudron, in regard to the penalty pronounced, and condemns him on the count of murders with premeditation, of blows and wounds, of arbitrary detention, and contraventions of the Regulations as to fire-arms, with extenuating circumstances, to five years' penal servitude;

Confirms in other respects the Judgment which was the subject of appeal, also as regards the accused Silvanus Jones;

Ordains that the costs of the appeal shall be borne by the State.

Thus judged and pronounced in public sitting by the Tribunal, composed of M. Giacomo Nisco, President; MM. Albert Sweerts and Michel Cuciniello, Judges; M. Fernand Waleffe, Public Prosecutor; M. Paul Hodüm, Clerk.

                                      The President,
                          (Signed)   G. NISCO.

    The Judges,
 (Signed)   Sweerts.
            M. Cuciniello.
    The Clerk,
        P. Hodüm.

LETTERS* RECEIVED FROM THE CONGO THIS YEAR SINCE THE PRESENT VOLUME WAS COMPLETED

IN THE DOMAINE DE LA COURONNE. LETTER FROM THE REV. A. E. SCRIVENER.

MR. SCRIVENER'S appalling account of a three months' journey into the *Domaine de la Couronne*, in July, August, and September, 1903, is given in Chapter XV. In the Official Report (Africa, No. 1, 1904), Mr. Roger Casement describes the conversations he had with refugees from the district visited by Mr. Scrivener. Confirmation was thus complete. Mr. Scrivener has made another journey into a part of the country peopled by some wretched survivors of the rubber-hunting orgies in the Lake region. He sends me some of the stories he has gathered from the lips of these victims of moral and material regeneration.

"Bolobo Mission, May 27, 1904.

"MY DEAR MR. MOREL,
   "You may possibly have heard of my having been invited to Leopoldville to a conference with a *Substitut* (judicial officer) there, concerning the statements which have appeared in the *West African Mail*, and other papers, from my pen. I answered all the questions he put to me with the exception of those concerning the conversation I had with Dooms at Mbongo. I demanded that he should be allowed to make a statement himself to the proper authorities, and also that I myself desired to seek advice before saying to the *Substitut* what Dooms told me. On returning from Leopoldville I was asked by the *Substitut* to seek other witnesses who could bear out my statements (I happened to have four Basengele eye-witnesses with me of atrocities committed by some of the soldiers in charge of various posts), and this I have been able to do in a recent little journey while visiting our outposts.

"Without any seeking, other than to question the visitors to my camps, I have already succeeded in obtaining the testimony of eye-witnesses of some of the deeds credited to certain white men who have gained a notoriety in these parts. I have written the

---

* Some of these letters were written to the author personally, others to friends, who have communicated the same to the author.

Substitut asking him to name a date when he could visit these parts, so that I may arrange to have the witnesses ready.

"While several days in from the river, I heard a rumour (it was only once removed from the man who brought it from the Lake), that Dooms has been drowned while hunting hippopotamus somewhere on the Lake. It seems too circumstantial not to be true. If it is, then a valuable witness to much that I have brought forward has been removed. His management of his district was so mild compared to that of his predecessor, although he by no means excused them the amount of rubber he thought they should bring in, that he was much liked by the people generally, and many expressions of sorrow were heard when the news was announced.

"For some time I have been trying to enter a district, which shall be nameless, where I knew a great many refugees were living.

"So great was the dread of the people that my going might mean their further persecution, that I failed, until this last trip, to obtain any guides. I have just returned from a journey of a day and a half into that part. The country appears to have been uninhabited until the arrival of these folk. There are hardly any palms, and no signs of old cultivation. The people are scattered about in the forests in small villages of from six to thirty huts, and these are often heavily barricaded. Even now the huts are for the most part of a temporary character, and not like the neat structures they generally build. The majority of my carriers were boys of sixteen or eighteen, but the fact that they were wearing clothes was sufficient to empty the villages of all the women and children as soon as we approached. I hope before very long to go again and learn something more about them.

"Here are some specimens of the stories I have heard from some of the Basengele and Bakutu—

"—— went with others to the white man's station with their rubber. They were one basket short. For this basket the white man demanded that a man should be given him, and took from amongst them ——, made him stand at some little distance from the others, and then shot him with a gun he brought from his house. Another day he was at the same place, and saw —— shot in the same way by the white man. This was because the man had killed a goat (his own), but they were told that nothing they had was their own, but belonged to the State. Another day he was at the same place, and saw a party of people come in with their rubber. It was short of the proper amount. The white man received it and sent them home, and soon afterwards sent six soldiers with rifles to shoot them in their own village. Ten men and two women were killed.

"—— said he went to the same post mentioned above, with other people, taking rubber with them. One of their number was of very light complexion, for a Native. A soldier called the white man's attention to this, when he called out angrily that one like himself should not live on the station with him, and took his gun and shot the man as he stood a little apart from his friends.

APPENDIX

"—— was going with a soldier in the direction of the rubber forest. They met a man coming from the forest.

"'Why have you no rubber?' said the soldier. 'It is coming behind with my boy.' But the soldier shot and killed the man as he stood in the road. Another day he was with the same soldier, and went with him to the gardens. They saw a man working in the cassava. 'Why are you not away cutting rubber?' 'Look at my cassava, it is all being eaten by the buffaloes, and I want to save a little of it to eat.' Then the soldier shot him.

* * * * * * *

"—— went with forty men to the white man's post at —— with their rubber, each man carrying one little basket full.

"The white man was very furious and fired blank cartridges at them at almost blank range, in some cases searing them, and killing a fowl one man was holding. A soldier tried to pacify the white man, and he eventually sent them away with many threats if they did not bring more rubber next time.

* * * * * * *

"—— went with others to the post at ——, where the same white man mentioned was then living. He grumbled at the quantity of rubber they brought, and took a man named —— by the arm, led him a short distance away, and shot him. The others ran away, and heard afterwards that the soldiers had dragged the body into the grass, close to the post. At the same place he was engaged with other men thatching a roof. The white man called a soldier, told him to go into the village, and if he saw any men there to shoot them at once. He heard afterwards that a man named ——, who was working at something in his hut, was seen by the soldier, and shot, although he offered to go at once and assist in the thatching. Another day he was on the station, a man named —— came along with some cassava bread he had purchased close by. 'You've been stealing,' said the white man. 'No; I've just bought this over there.' But a soldier was called and told to kill the man. He led him away, tied him to a palm tree, and shot him, and dragged his body into the grass.

"The chief —— told me the following as one of the reasons why he ran away. He went with a lot of his people to the post of ——. They were short by several baskets. The white man took ——, gave him to a soldier to tie to a tree, and then himself shot him. The others (some twenty-nine) were standing shivering with fear, when the white man told the soldiers to fire on them. This they did, and killed twenty-seven, only two poor wretches managing to get away.

"They were made to work on the roads, and men were shot at the whim of the soldiers on the slightest excuse. A man resting, or tying up an ulcer, or trying to get a light for his pipe, was shot down without hardly a word of warning.

"——, a soldier, was placed in charge of ——. He had no gun, but tied up men and women, and threw them into a river close by to make the others bring more rubber.

"——, the chief of ——, one of the newest of refugees, supports this evidence, and says this same soldier on one occasion tied up four men and three women and sent them to the white man at ——. The women were put in prison, and the men were shot in front of the white man's house.

"I met some men from a district of which I had heard nothing. This is situated more to the south and is largely grass country. The usual demand was made for the rubber. The people asked that some other work should be assigned to them, as the rubber forest was far away. But no change was made, and the people had to buy what they could from their neighbours, but totally insufficient to meet the demands. Then began a series of massacres which would be incredible were it not for so much of a like character that, alas ! has been proved only too well. The district is now a waste.

"These are simply a few samples of the stories one hears in going in and out amongst these poor folk. I would listen to nothing but what could be vouched for by eye-witnesses. But they are practically all eye-witnesses. The suffering and starvation they underwent at the time of their flight, and during the first months after their arrival in this neighbourhood, is in itself evidence that what they fled from must have been something very terrible. If a proper inquiry is ever instituted, there will be no lack of evidence of a most convincing nature to all who are willing to accept the truth.

"There are rumours that all the rubber posts in the regions which I passed through have been abandoned. I shall not be surprised if this is found to be true, for the paucity of the population remaining must have made it very difficult to support the posts. Here, in our immediate neighbourhood, the soldiers have been taken away from the State post, and thirty miles away a State training camp has been practically abandoned, only a few soldiers and white men being left. The relief this is to the people of the vicinity of this camp is of course very great. But there is already talk of new demands to be made upon them. The talk of these new taxes and the preparatory taking of names has already resulted in a few going over to the French side.

"If you think the publication of the foregoing likely to do good, I am perfectly willing that any or all should be published. In every case where I have put dashes I have the names, and where white men are mentioned as such, I have the native names by which they were known. I refrain from supplying these at this time, because I do not wish to endanger any of these people who have given me information. If a competent and impartial inquiry is made, I shall be able to produce the necessary evidence to more than substantiate all I have written, saving that, of course, supplied by Dooms. His reported death may lead to difficulties.

"With very kind regards and all good wishes.

"I remain,
"Yours sincerely,
(Signed) "A. E. SCRIVENER."

APPENDIX 419

IN THE ABIR CONCESSION. LETTER FROM MR. JOHN H. HARRIS.

I have been favoured with a copy of the following letter, written by Mr. John H. Harris, of the Congo Balolo Mission, at Baringa, to a well-known British nobleman. The letter is dated May 1, 1904.

"MY LORD,
"We have heard with much pleasure from Mr. —— of the interest you take in the deplorable condition of the Congo Natives, and as lately we have had to deal with some gross outrages, I have thought it wise to acquaint you with the facts.

"You have, of course, already seen in the 'White Book,' published and presented to both Houses, many similar instances to those I have to relate.

"In the reply of the Congo Government to Lord Lansdowne it is stated that atrocities are 'exceptional,' 'long ago,' or that they are 'only asserted.' I sincerely wish these deeds were either 'long ago,' or 'exceptional;' this they certainly are not. Under the present system they are the inevitable outcome.

"The district of Baringa would not number less than 20,000 men, who for the most part spend their time at forced labour, gathering the rubber as taxes imposed *by* the Company *for* the Company's benefit, who seem to have bought the land, the people, and all their belongings. The people recognise that they are the slaves of the Company. Every village has an armed sentry or sentries of the Company, according to its size, and these men are little kings, who rule most despotically, helping themselves to the people's wives and goods to an incredible extent. Any one daring to oppose their slightest wish—from the Chief to the child—is dealt with summarily.

"*During the last two months* the following outrages, amongst others, have been committed in the immediate vicinity of this station:—

"At the village Bolumboloko the sentry shot Bokama.

"At the village Lotoko, the sentry Jangi shot the Chief Ilumbu and two others.

"At Ekolongo the sentry Bomolo shot Isekalasumba.

"At Ekolongo the sentry Ikombi shot Bosasa.

"At Bolima, Ilangala and others shot six men and two women.

"The cases have been investigated by the judge—the first I have ever seen on the Congo—and whose district is larger than France and Germany put together. All these cases were proved beyond doubt to have been mere acts of bullying. Even the required rubber was completed! Hardly was his investigation complete before I had to call attention to some more dark deeds close at hand.

"A month or six weeks ago, my boy, Bomolo, was allowed to

visit his friends on the opposite bank of the river. When he came back, he told me of the usual stealing and blackmailing by these armed bullies, but as these things are normal, I said nothing to the officials. Three days ago I sent him to buy some nets that I required, but the poor lad arrived at his friend's house only to find that his brother-in-law had been shot by Ilanga.

"Another sentry, Bofoja, had shot the woman Boali. Ekofa, another sentry, had shot the man Nsala. Another brute of a sentry named Ifutu had demanded fish of a woman named Bongwalanga. She gave him all she had got, but because it was not sufficient, he cut off her head and that of her daughter, a young girl named Lofinda.

"Besides other witnesses, I have the sworn testimony of Ifeko, who picked up the headless corpses of his relatives and helped to bury them.

"I need not tell you the state of the people, or the sorrow of the relatives.

(Signed)   "JOHN H. HARRIS."

IN THE DOMAINE PRIVÉ. LETTER FROM THE REV. J. H. WEEKS.

"Monsembe Station, Haut Congo,
"May 17, 1904.

"To E. D. Morel.

"DEAR SIR,

"I desire in this letter to lay before your readers some examples of Congo Free State justice (?) that have come to my notice during the past eight or ten months. However good laws may look on paper, however imposing in diction, and righteous in tone and aim; yet it is the application, or rather the harsh, wrong, and whimsical application of them that affects the people who, by force of circumstances, are compelled to live under them. In the following examples of the civilising methods of the State, I have confined myself to a bare statement of facts, and have not allowed my indignation to express itself.

"Libulula, on the south bank of the river, was formerly a large town, stretching for a considerable distance along the bank. The Chief, with his family, lived at the upper end of it. During the last eight or nine years the town has gradually decreased, until at last at the lower end of the town was a collection of nineteen miserable huts. At the other end Ngwa, the Chief, lived with his wives and family, and for hundreds of yards in between, where formerly people had lived, there was nothing but grass. Last year the *commissaire* of the district ordered Ngwa to remove his houses to the lower end and live with the people. Ngwa did not wish to leave the place where his fathers had lived before him; he paid his share of the taxes, and could not see any reason for the order to move lower down the river. As the *commissaire* insisted, Ngwa had to comply, but being undesirous to leave he was naturally slow to obey, so he was taken a prisoner, put in chains, and made to carry bricks. His treatment was such that before his time had expired he died on August 16, 1903.

"The crime: slowness to obey a whimsical and unreasonable order of the *commissaire*. Punishment: chains and treatment resulting in death. Ngwa's share of the taxes was divided among the rest of the people, so the State lost nothing by his death, but the burden of the people was increased. When I was visiting that part a few weeks ago, I asked an intelligent Native where all the people were. He said, 'Some have died of sleep-sickness, some have run away, but plenty have died from worry and grief of the heart because of oppression.'

"Mangumbe, a headman of Monsembe, was appointed a Chief by the State, and given a medal certificate to that effect. He received no remuneration, but was made responsible for the fortnightly tax due from this section of the district. Mangumbe was appointed a medal chief in the early part of 1902, and things went along fairly well until June and July of last year. Sometimes he went up with the tax, at other times he sent a responsible headman with it. During the above months the State officials began to worry him to go up with every fortnightly tax himself, a most unreasonable demand to make of a headman, who had affairs of his own to occasionally attend to; but then, of course, he should have no affairs of his own. It is two days' hard paddling to Bangala—one day to deliver the tax, and one day paddling down, leaving ten days to procure his own share of the next tax and gather the rest from the people.

"Last July Mangumbe sent the tax up by a headman, and he himself went twenty to twenty-five miles down river to buy a goat ready for the next tax. Down came a messenger calling him to Bangala (Nouvelle Anvers), but not finding him there, the messenger had to go down to Malele, where Mangumbe was bargaining for a goat. Mangumbe returned at once, collected the next tax, and went with it to Bangala. No fault was found with the tax, but because he did not take up the previous tax himself, he was sentenced by the commandant in charge (the *commissaire* was up the Mongala River) to eight days carrying bricks in the chains. Mangumbe said, 'I did not come with the tax because I went to buy a goat for the next tax.' That made no difference; soldiers were called, and he was taken away to the chains.

"Just before his eight days were up the *commissaire* (who in the mean time had received my letter of June 13) returned, and increased the sentence to twenty-two days. We cannot help putting the increase of sentence down to the *commissaire's* irritation at receiving our communication from the same town to which Mangumbe belonged. Did he suspect that Mangumbe had given me the information about Mabata's irregular fine of 57,000 rods, and to punish him for it increased his sentence to twenty-two days?

"Mangumbe was chained next to Ngwa, and between them they had to carry a heavy box of bricks. A soldier always accompanied them, and there are witnesses to prove that the butt end of the gun was used often on Mangumbe's back and side. Their treatment of him was such that he died within twenty-four hours of Ngwa, and his corpse was brought here on August 18. Mangumbe's share of the tax was divided among the people, so their burden became heavier, but the State lost nothing.

"The crime: not going up personally every fortnight with the tax. Punishment: chains and ill-treatment resulting in death.

"Bokunji is a small town on the north bank of the river, about fifteen miles above Bangala. The folk there have to take every fortnight to Bangala a bush pig as a part of their tax. Through constantly hunting them the pigs have become not only scarcer, but more wary, and consequently more difficult to trap and kill. I would challenge any State officer, with his weapons of precision, to kill, year in and year out, a wild bush pig every fortnight.

"In March last, Makake, the chief of Bokunji, failed to trap and send to Bangala one of the pigs due for that month. My colleague was itinerating in that part of the district last April, and happened to be staying in Bokunji on the very day that Makake returned from Bangala, where he had done a fortnight in the chains. Nor was that the only punishment: for when he was set free he was given forty-eight hours to paddle up to his town, collect 3000 brass rods, and take down to the *commissaire* as a fine.

"Crime: failing one fortnight to trap and kill a wild bush pig. Punishment: a fortnight in the chains, and a fine of 3000 rods, worth up here £9 15s. He receives for the pigs taken 100 rods each—equal to 6s. 6d.

"These, sir, are a few instances of justice (?) that have come under our notice without any seeking on our part. Is there any need for comment?

"On November 30 last I wrote to M. Mardelier, the then *commissaire* of this district, a letter bringing to his notice the killing of twenty-two men and women in the lower part of his district by soldiers alleged to have been under the orders of Commandant Mazy (native name Mabata). A copy of the same I sent to the Governor-General on December 12. Thinking it was on public service, I did not stamp the letter, so on its arrival at Boma it was opened by the postal authorities to ascertain the address of the writer, and was sent back to me because it had no stamp on it. It reached me on January 12, and on the 19th it was on its way down again, this time duly stamped.

"Early in February—7th or 8th—M. Mazy (Mabata) and his superior officer, M. Mardelier, the *Commissaire-Général*, left Bangala for Europe. Although my letter containing so grave a charge against the former arrived at Boma on January 30, some three weeks before him, yet he was allowed to proceed to Belgium, where I hear on very good authority that he cannot be arrested without much trouble and expense. It is all the more astonishing that he was allowed to proceed, as I have heard that both he and M. Mardelier were interrogated at Boma, and that their replies were unsatisfactory. Is there any need to point out the difference between the justice (?) meted out to Natives and that meted out to a white officer of the State?

"Early in April, four months after the charge is made, and several weeks after the accused is allowed to quit the country, the judge for this district called upon us on his way to officially investigate the charge against M. Mazy. He spent four or five days in the towns where the people had been killed. On his return he again called on us. He told us many people had been killed, and that others had died of starvation in the bush and on the islands, as they were afraid to return while the white man and the soldiers were in occupation of their towns.

The following conversation took place in the presence of my colleague—*

"Question by myself: 'Did you find the names I gave in my letter of November 30 tally with the names you got down there?'

"Answer by the judge: 'Yes, all except two; but I got one name that you had not written down in your list. A man named Mowandi was killed at Bokumela.'

"'Yes,' I said, 'I have the name and place in my notes. Here it is (showing him my notes), but I did not put it down because I did not receive the information from the Chief himself.'

"Judge: 'I can tell you another thing. When M. Mazy arrived at the town of Bomunga the soldiers rushed up the bank, and seeing a woman running away, they fired at her and killed her at about 100 metres from the beach.'

"Is it necessary to comment on the above facts? I think not; they speak for themselves.

"Believe me to be,
"Yours very sincerely,
(Signed) "JOHN H. WEEKS."

IN THE DOMAINE PRIVÉ. THE YANDJALI MASSACRE. LETTER FROM THE REV. W. B. FRAME.

"B.M.S. Wathen, Tumba, Congo Free State, S.W. Africa,
"March 10, 1904.
"E. D. Morel, Esq., Liverpool.

"DEAR SIR,

"In recent issues of your paper I have seen my name mentioned as an eye-witness of the shocking outrage at Yandjali, on

* I have before me a joint declaration signed by Mr. Weeks and Mr. Kirkland, giving the conversation between them and Judge Grenade in ample detail.

the Upper Congo. Allow me to state that the account given in the *West African Mail* is substantially correct, although I do not remember that any of the witnesses swore to the person shot in the canoe being a woman.* One need not repeat the details of the barbarous scene, but time can never wipe it from our memory.

"The mutilated dead, the mad rushing and firing of the soldiers let loose, and the hasty flight of the poor people hunted from their homes like wild beasts, made us sick at heart, and when we looked into the faces of our black crew we were ashamed; for were not these things done in the name of the State, and under the eyes of its white officers?

"I do not know the running of the Congo State Courts of Justice, but it is only fair to state that, in obedience to a summons from the Procurator Fiscal, I appeared before him at Matadi on February 5, and in answer to questions similar to those put to us by the *Commissaire* at Basoko on October 30, 1903, gave evidence on what I saw at Yandjali on October 29, 1903. I have been resident in this district † since 1896, and until my recent visit to the Upper Congo, made in the interests of health, my impression of the Congo State was very favourable. Coming just when the days of transport by road were ending, my experience had been that of seeing the State at its best, and did the order of things obtain elsewhere that obtains in the Tumba district, we should have heard no cry of oppressive taxation, slavery, and murder.

"*It does not obtain,*‡ and I am convinced that, with the exception of this very limited district, and perhaps that of Stanley Falls, the title of "Slave State" is very fitting to the *régime* that exists.

"For example, it fits it in the Stanley Pool district. As I traversed the old caravan route to the Pool, my eyes were opened. Crowds of people passed me every now and then, bearing heavy loads of *kwanga* (cassava puddings), and all were for the State.§

"Some were little girls of twelve years of age carrying eight and ten; some were women converted into sweating beasts of burden, for besides the twelve *kwanga* on the head, they often had a baby on the back; some were men, and some were little boys. No one will accuse me of exaggeration if I say each *kwanga* weighs 3½ to 4 lbs., so that the women often had loads varying from 42 to 50 lbs.

"It is quite true that the State does not fix the loads that the women should carry. What it does demand is, that such and such a town shall bring in, say, 250 *kwanga* every fourth, eighth, or twelfth day, according to distance; and if the people fail to do it, then punishment follows. What it means to the people is nothing to the State, and the cry of the poor women who have to grind from morning till night to provide, and often to carry, is not heard by the

---

* One of the accounts published mentioned the incident referred to.
† That is the Tumba district (Lower Congo).
‡ W. B. Frame's italics.
§ Part of the forced tax in food-stuffs. See specially Africa, No. 1, 1904 (White Book).

State officer. *The labour is forced.** If in reply it be said that the people are paid for it, let it be understood that the payment is very small compared with local rates, and, as a matter of fact, if a man pays another to carry his load of *kwanga*, he has to pay all he gets from the State, and something on top. Some have to carry three days' journey. These have to bring in every twelfth day. That means they spend five days on the road and seven in their towns, which have to be spent in planting and cooking for the State. They have time for nothing else. *They are slaves.*†

"All up the river it is the same thing, and on a single trip one sees enough and hears enough to convince him that the lot of the Natives in the town is that of the harassed and crushed slave. Messrs. Weeks, Bond, and others have told us the system in force in the Bangala and Coquilhatville districts, and its effects on the Natives. The sad state of things about Monsembe is becoming true of other places.

"At one place, where crowds of people ought to have been on the beach, we found the whole town had all fled. Young and old, male and female, were hiding in the bush because the fish-tax was not complete. By sad experience they had learned what it would mean. Under similar circumstances they had often had their women tied up, even to the number of fifty, and the chain and lash are well known in the camp. I was told by one who knows, that in order to make up the tax the men would have to begin work on Monday, and do nothing else all the week. Surely, *this is slavery?* ‡

"In a town some distance from the big State camp we saw it in another form. A hundred youths and boys were marched past us in one gang, carrying firewood to the State post. They were accompanied by a soldier. As there is no forced labour, I suppose he was simply there to keep them in step!

"Some exception has been taken to Mr. Scrivener's remarks, but it is only too true that the cruel rule of the whites in the interior has become unbearable to many, and the remnant seek for refuge in other parts.

"We visited a town near to Lisali, where the people had recently come from inland to escape the cruelties attached to rubber collecting.

"I have written thus because of the attempts made to discredit the story of oppression and wrong. Yandjali is fact. The slavery of the people on this side of Stanley Pool to the Nkissi river is fairly complete, WITH NO HOPE OF IMPROVEMENT. The whole truth about Congo will never be known, but enough is known to fill us with pity for those unfortunate Africans placed at the mercy of unscrupulous men.

"Yours sincerely,
"W. B. FRAME."

---

* W. B. Frame's italics.   † Ibid.   ‡ Ibid.

In the Lower Congo. Letter from an English Trader.

I have received the following letter from an English trader in Matadi, dated May, and it shows that the Congo Government, in its determined violation of every clause and principle of the Berlin Act, is now extending the worst features of its methods to the reaches of the lower river.

"The Consul's report has got the State's back up. They say they'll end this matter their way by getting rid of us all. From all I hear, things up country are worse than ever. In the Mayumbe country, behind Boma even, the State has begun collecting rubber by force from the Natives. We were supposed to have 'free trade' below Stanley Pool, but even that narrow belt is now to be invaded by the 'tax-collector.' What do we pay our trade-taxes, licences, and customs duties for, I wonder? The oil and kernel trade has almost died out at Boma as a consequence of these Mayumbe *prestations*. The State are founding a camp of 1000 soldiers, independent of the one already at Luki, seventeen miles inland of Boma, where Mrs. Meyer and the Sierra Leone men were arrested, and so many of them done to death. This new camp is at Boma-Sundi, or, rather, between that place and the Lukula river, about thirty-five or forty miles from Boma, in the heart of the Mayumbe country, where the people have brought oil and kernels from time immemorial to the Boma factories. This invasion of these ancient trading rights will damage considerably the old-established trade in the Chilango district, and the exports there, through the Portuguese province, will also fall over. Everything in the country is for the Government. We traders, who are not concession holders, but who made such trade as exists, are only to be taxed and thwarted, and the poor Natives are to pay the piper. Of course, as soon as this camp is established, the State will begin to force the people in the usual way to bring in food, etc., for the soldiers.

"I see no possible future for the country and the poor people unless something is done by the Powers. Nearly all the shops at Matadi have commenced to liquidate, or will do so in a month or less. They cannot continue at this rate long; they are all losing money. I don't know what will be the end of it."

In the "Equateur" District.*

I have received from a gentleman residing in this country a long letter, dated December 26, 1903, to hand from a relative, who is a missionary in the Upper Congo. This communication has been kindly placed at my disposal on the understanding that the name of

---

* The district is not further specified—at least the writer desires that it shall not be specified.

APPENDIX 427

the writer shall not be given, a request made by the writer himself on the grounds of apprehension of personal illtreatment, which I at first believed to be exaggerated, but no longer believe so. The writer dates his communication from a town in the Equateurville district. In the covering letter to his relative accompanying the communication, the writer says: "I am almost certain that unless England and other signatory Powers intervene, a great calamity must soon come upon the Congo. I should not be surprised at anything happening."

The writer describes as follows the "normal state of affairs" in the district in which he resides—

"How is the rubber obtained by the monopolists? It is not bought.... The Company has bought from the State the absolute right to tax the people, and this they do.... The agents of the Companies are too often drawn from the most ignorant and unscrupulous classes.... They are sent in twos and threes to districts, one being *Chef de Factorerie*. The aim of the *Chef* is to get more rubber from the district than the agent whom he has superseded, and he therefore sets to work to find out which villages in his district can bear a heavier imposition.... Each man must bring a basket of rubber *every fortnight* ($2\frac{1}{2}$ kilos), and armed sentries are placed in each village to see that the right amount is forthcoming *every fortnight*. These sentries are generally the worst characters, and stop at nothing. Of course, the Chief must supply them to the full with the very best of food, and such women as they may demand. No man's wife is safe from them. Beyond a shadow of doubt, large numbers of Natives are done to death by these abominable bullies. When the rubber is brought to the factory the Natives line up and present their baskets, and woe betide the boy who brings $2\frac{1}{4}$ kilos: It must be a 'measure pressed down and running over.' Generally, such an individual is *chicotted*, or put in prison. If the quantity is correct, four men's baskets are weighed together, *i.e.* 10 kilos. For this they are given a something—sometimes one yard of cheap cloth, but with my own eyes I have seen twenty spoonfuls of salt given, value 10d. (?) per kilo! Of course the payment is a mere farce. Now, supposing the rubber does not come up to the right quantity. The sentries will report that the people surpass in wickedness, and forthwith a number of other sentries are added, who proceed to the village, catch a number of men and women—the latter often big with child, or with babies at the breast—they are tied neck by neck in long files, and imprisoned at the factory until 'redeemed' by a large quantity of rubber. Then they are set at liberty to return to their ruined homes, for the sentries always leave their mark. Sometimes people say, 'Come and kill us; we cannot find more rubber.' This happens fairly often. A number of Natives are then killed and villages burnt, and the people are 'subdued and willing to bring in an increased toll of rubber.' ... Sometimes the Government troops are asked to co-operate. These perform the work much better (!!) and strike terror far and wide. No one can contradict these statements. Of course a few people round Boma and Matadi know nothing of these things except by hearsay. . . . The system is practically a traffic in human beings.

"You may wonder whether I have anything to say about atrocities. Yes, a great deal; but this is a difficult subject, because the State now refuses to accept native evidence. But the recent books by Fox Bourne and E. D. Morel are certainly most fair representations of the truth. They are by no means exaggerated. In fact, Mr. Morel, in several places, seems to me to have minimised several generally accepted facts."

The writer then goes on to give samples of conversations he has had with Natives.

Q. "Where is your father?"
A. "Shot by X."
Q. "Under what circumstances?"
A. "My brother was his servant, and, owing to cruelty, ran away. X. came with the sentry, and asked my father where my brother was. He said he did not know. 'Shoot him,' said X., which was immediately done."
Q. "Where's your mother?"
A. "Shot, with the baby at the breast; also my brother at the same time, because the rubber was incomplete."

The writer describes the following incident. The name of the town, the name of the chief, and the name of the Europeans responsible are given in full in the "Notes" accompanying the communication. I am precluded from quoting them, but as I understand that the communication is to be placed in the hands of a member of the House of Commons, it is to be hoped that they may transpire eventually—not, after all, that it is of much importance, such incidents being common, as witness, for example, the Yandjali massacre and cannibalistic orgie, which took place last autumn, actually on the main river, while the incident narrated above occurred in a much more remote district—and are the direct outcome of the entire system prevailing. . . .

"The town of C—— and surrounding villages had been for some time bringing short toll of rubber. A sentry was sent to 'arrest' the chief. The 'arrest' led to the killing of the Chief I—— Four of his wives were also killed, and the best portions of the bodies carried away to the sentry's town and eaten. Naturally the villages were enraged at this, and stopped bringing rubber at all. Thereupon they were reported as in open revolt. M. M—— and another white man collected a considerable force of the fiercest cannibals for a set-to fight. The white men accompanied the sentries and native warriors. About sixty men, women, and children were killed. These were cut up and eaten, and the houses of the defaulting chiefs decorated with the intestines of the killed. The chiefs who remained sent in to say that they would bring in the required amount of rubber, and are doing it to-day. The people employed in this cannibalistic raid still openly gloat over the grand feast of human flesh they enjoyed when the Chief I—— was fought against."

The above incident is somewhat similar to the confessions of an agent of the *Société Anversoise du Commerce au Congo* some years ago, as given in Chapter XI., which occurred, of course, in quite a different part of the Congo.

The writer summarises the condition of affairs prevailing in his district as follows—

"(1) White men fighting against native towns is a normal condition out here.

"(2) All concessions have their 'prisons.'*

"(3) The monopolist is the absolute administrator.

"(4) I have been nearly six years on the Congo, and have never seen a State 'judge.'

"(5) In the 'prisons' † can always be seen men and children, and women in all stages of pregnancy, all herded together.

"(6) Rubber is not bought. It is brought in as an 'imposition.'

"(7) Unless some steps are soon taken to alter the present state of affairs, the white man will be swept from the Upper Congo. A prominent white man here told me the other day he expected a revolution within two years.

"(8) The missionaries are at the mercy of those in authority here—the monopolists. This explains why missionaries are silent on so many atrocities; and why others, when they do say anything, require that their names should be kept strictly secret. In almost any State, missionaries keeping silence, as they do here, could be prosecuted for connivance. But here they *simply dare not speak out.* Reporting law-breakers is received here as a hostile act, and generally followed by further restrictions."

IN AND AROUND THE BARINGA DISTRICT OF THE "ABIR" CONCESSION DURING THE FIRST SIX MONTHS OF THE PRESENT YEAR.

In the three following accounts, (1) that by Mr. Herbert Frost, (2) Mr. J. H. Harris, (3) Mr. Edgar Stannard, we have a complete and consecutive picture of the inconceivable condition of affairs in a small part of the Abir concession from January to June, 1904. Wholesale murders, mutilations, and open cannibalism by the soldiers of this so-called "Company," in which the Congo Government holds 50 per cent. of the shares; their European masters, the only representatives of authority in the district, callous and brutalised by their task, which is to obtain rubber to enrich the "Company" and themselves, entirely indifferent to the means, and only anxious that their ill-deeds shall be concealed from the resident British missionaries, whom they hate, and are beginning to threaten;

---

* *Maisons des ôtages.*

† For similar instances of a common practice, see official White Book, Africa, No. 1, 1904.

the cannibal soldiers laughingly stating that they are merely carrying out instructions, and in effect masters of the country; a perambulating "judge," with no powers other than those of "investigation," who can only "report," who is bound to be the guest of the very people whose infamies he is supposed to denounce, and who is the one Government official in a country as large as a European State. The other side shows us the miserable inhabitants of the territory, "hunted animals," tortured, mutilated, killed, and food for their cannibal oppressors. No opium-haunted brain could conjure a more terrible picture of criminality *in excelsis*, of unbridled lust, of unchecked wickedness, or of human misery, degradation, and despair.

MR. HERBERT FROST'S DIARY.*

"February 13, 1904.

"Whilst at work in the carpenter's shed this morning, the town of Lotoko passed along the palm avenue close to me, accompanied by their armed soldiers. By the town of Lotoko I mean a company of boys from about eight years old to men, who have been seized to keep up the stock of hostages. They were heavily laden with baskets of rubber, soon to be deposited at the doors of the rubber-shed.

"This afternoon we learned that the soldiers had killed four men, they themselves making no secret of the matter, it being to them apparently quite an ordinary occurrence. I inquired somewhat into the details, and find that the soldiers—

"(Wunju) killed a man named Bokama, of Bolomboloko.

"(Basumbelo) killed a man named Eyamba, of Nsongo.

"(Likio) killed a man named Isekofo, of Lotoko.

"(Jange) killed a man named Elumbu, of Lotoko.

"February 14, 1904. Sunday.

"After service this morning Mr. X—— and I walked across to the Abir factory, and saw the second agent (the chief agent—*chef de poste*—being away up the river). When I referred to the above report, he said that he had heard something about some men being killed, but did not know the details; he would inquire.

"February 17, 1904.

"Happening to be in conversation with some of the Natives this evening, I was told that Mr. —— has given orders to his capita, Ilangala, to the effect that he and the sentries under him may kill, and there will be 'no palaver'—that is to say, no trouble will ensue from their outrages. Also, in reference to the matter of my walk in Baringa with my wife and child, when I photographed the rubber hostages at work, I am told that Iyema, the soldier guarding the

* Communicated to the author by Mr. Frost.

APPENDIX 431

hostages, was straightway charged by his master, the rubber agent, that if I appeared again with my camera, and he did not drive me away, he should be chicotted. The same threats, they say, are held out to the soldiers if they do not kill.

"The same men assure me that if I could go out to the towns where the men were shot last Friday, the people would certainly give me all particulars, and would even disinter the bodies, they are so angry. Though still weak from fever, I feel impelled to go. Will see my colleague about it to-morrow."

"February 18, 1904.

"After talking over recent matters with my wife and colleague, I have decided to go to Lotoko to-morrow morning, and return on Saturday."

"February 19, 1904. Friday.

"Left this morning at 7.15 for the town of Lotoko. My aim was to reach the home of Elumbu, the blacksmith (an elderly man, and much esteemed by his townsfolk), and then return. As we passed on through Baringa I inquired more carefully as to the distance, and the men asserted that it was not possible to reach his place and return the following day. I therefore sent back a messenger saying that I should not be able to return until Sunday evening, or even Monday morning. Passing through Baringa and Boeringa, we struck the forest, and after about an hour's walk, reached the town of Bolomboloko. Here I had the opportunity to inquire into the circumstances of the shooting of the man Bokama by the sentry Wunju on the previous Friday, the 12th instant. The Chief ——* showed me the place where he was threatened, how he ran away, was chased and caught, and, being brought back, was tied to a small tree; the rifle barrel being placed at the back of the neck, was discharged in an upward direction, blowing the head to pieces. I asked the reason why Bokama was shot, and, in dismay, the Chief held out his hands, saying, 'I do not know. The rubber was complete; we cannot understand.' We then proceeded to the place where he was buried, the people being prepared to disinter the body, so that I might see it. Three men dug away the soil with pointed sticks, and I took a snap of them as they worked; but when they had partly unearthed the body, I found it had so far decomposed that I told them to desist. The people were greatly distressed, and complained bitterly of the treatment received at the hands of the soldiers.

"In this same village, and about the same time, a most abominable and bestial outrage was committed by the same soldier upon a brother and sister. The soldiers use the most abusive language, heaping the greatest insults upon those who have natural authority among their fellows. They thrash the old men, abuse and rob the women, set fire to their houses, are intolerant and high-

* See footnote at end of diary.

handed in their demands for the best food. Upon the rumour of their approach, the inhabitants flee into the bush, or cower when they find themselves within range of the soldier's rifle.

"At twelve o'clock we were in the forest, I sitting on my bag of bedding, the men squatting around, the boy heating some soup for me, when suddenly an armed soldier made his appearance in our midst. I was not surprised, for although I had never before in all my journeys through the Abir Concessions been followed by a soldier, I rather expected it this time, for, in my judgment, the new agent (*chef de factorie*) is a man of extreme measures. He greeted me with the native salutation, and I then asked what his business was, and he said his white man had sent him to follow me. I knew this, and that he was also to warn the resident soldiers, and set them to intimidate the people, so that I might not gain the information I was seeking. He sat down, and journeyed with us.

"We reached Lokoto to-day at 1.15, and after a cup of tea, proceeded on our way. About two o'clock we passed the sentries' settlement, when one of the boys came up to me and said, 'Bondele, we have passed the place where Iyambu was shot.' I said, 'All right, we will go back,' and telling some of the men to sit down and wait, I and the other returned. Reaching the bush that divided the native compounds of Ilemba and Bolondo, the spot was pointed out to me where the soldier Basumbelo shot Iyamba, from whence they had dragged the body into the bush. Following up the track made by the soldiers as they dragged the body, we presently came upon the corpse. There was a terrible stench and swarms of flies, but the body seemed in fairly good preservation. With some difficulty I secured a photograph, my boys and the soldier standing behind me at some distance.

"At 3.45 I reached the compound of Isekalongoi. It was here that Isekefofo was shot by the sentry Lokio, the body being carried away by his relatives and buried in the forest. Being tired, and expecting to pass this way to-morrow, I did not go to see the grave. This afternoon a young man named ——, who had as a boy been taken down river, had worked at Bassankusu, Wangata, Irebo, and Leopoldville, told me that he had stood by when Isekefofo was shot. There was abundant testimony from his near male relatives, and the evidences of mourning bore silent proof. In this town, as in most others, the resident sentries have their own houses, an effort to imitate the white man in size and style, built by the Natives in whose town the soldier dwells. In the vicinity of the soldiers' houses the native huts are deserted, the owners being unable to bear their intolerance, preferring to spend their time in the bush or build houses elsewhere.

"In conversation this evening, I learned that Ilangala, otherwise Ilinhiofe, the head captain of the soldiers, gave them orders to the effect that if they did not kill the people, they themselves would be thrashed and imprisoned. Also that many have been killed in

Bolima.* Such distressing tales of bloodshed, torture, and robbery have I listened to this evening that I feel bound to continue my journey through the whole district.

"The power of an armed soldier amongst these enslaved people is absolutely paramount. By chief or child, every command, wish, or whim of the soldier must be obeyed or gratified. At his command, with rifle ready, a man will eat his own dung, outrage his own sister, give to his persecutor the wife he loves most of all—say or do anything, indeed, to save his life. The woes and sorrows of the race whom King Leopold has enslaved have not decreased, for his commissaires, officers, and agents have introduced and maintain a system of devilry hitherto undreamed of by his victims.

"Whilst they strive to satisfy the demands of the white man for rubber, he allows soldiers a free hand to worry and wear them out by perpetual robbery, torture, and violence. No wonder that the cry breaks from them, 'What shall we do?' No wonder if they sink their own petty differences to combine against a common foe! No wonder that the king's own emissaries anticipate rebellion!

"February 20, 1904.

"Six o'clock.—The owner of the hut in which I have slept, being threatened by the soldiers, is not to be found this morning.

"9.15.—In Elumbu's smithing-shed. Whilst having a cup of tea, I learned the following facts from eye-witnesses: That Elumbu was shot by the sentry Jange behind the houses at mid-day on Friday, the 19th. Binding his victim to a small tree, the sentry placed the rifle near the mouth, discharging it down Elumbu's throat, the shot passing out behind, between the shoulders. This was witnessed by his younger brother E E and his son L L, as also by Jange's boys. Afterwards I took a photograph of the spot where he was buried, his son C C, who buried him, standing in the foreground. (In each case, planned, deliberate, cold-blooded murders—not the results of fights or quarrels.)

"Left Lotoko at 10.15. For two hours we descended, until we reached a swamp. The soil was of a light brown colour, full of iron-stone pebbles. I also saw some very large boulders. Reached Ekolongo at 4.15. This appears to be a populous town, though much smaller in area than Lotoko.

"Soon after my arrival, whilst talking to the people who gathered around, the two soldiers Ikombe and Basunbulu came and saluted me. Ikombe and Bomolo are the two sentries resident in the town, and the presence of Basumbelo is accounted for by the fact that it is a common thing for the soldiers to go about in bands to other villages than those to which they are appointed, for the purpose of more effective pillaging.

"Each soldier has a following of from one to eight or ten boys

* See notes at end.

and men, their business being to aid him in all his plunderings or seizures, and to carry the stuff.

"I learned here this evening that two men were shot in this town in the same day, and about the same time as the previous cases, the soldier Bomolo shooting his man, named Bosasa, and Ikombe the other man, named Isekalasumba. Both these were shot at the same time and in the same place.

"I give here the names and number of soldiers appointed to and resident in each village, and also the number of baskets of rubber produced fortnightly in each village.

Village.	Resident sentries.	Baskets per fortnight.
Bolomnoloko	Wunju	... 30
Lotoko	Jange Lokomba Basumbelo Mboyo	... 127
Ekolongo	Bomolo Ikombe ...	... 40
Bolima	Boyo Ilangala Nsala Efanza Bosefe Iyele Likio	... 200

The required quantity for each basket is four kilos.*

"February 21, 1904. Sunday.

"Ekolongo.—Left my lodgings at eight o'clock for a walk through the town. Found the people very quiet and uncommunicative, having, no doubt, been threatened by the soldiers. After an hour's walk, I reached the soldiers' settlement, that of Bomolo. I had heard that Bomolo was ill, but, upon asking him, found it was merely a headache. Ikombe and Basumbelo were with him, and also some of their boys.

"I asked them and the people to gather in the large house, as I had something to say to them. This they did, the soldiers placing themselves in a conspicuous position, and a stool for me in the centre. The people, both men and women, came, and also my own carriers. Just as I was about to speak, I noticed a man named Bofundu, a big, stout fellow, whose acquaintance I had made, sitting under the eaves of another hut some distance away. He was one of the local capitas, and I had found him out to be both liar and coward. I therefore called him, twitted him as to his size and

* Thus these four villages alone would supply over 1½ tons of rubber every fortnight, or, say, 41 tons annually (41,288 kilos). The value of the labour of these people to their taskmasters would therefore be £11,150 per annum in rubber.

cowardice, and shamed him to come in with the others. My theme was the difference between beast and man, both in practical life and ultimate end—the annihilation of the one, and continued existence of the other. How that a man might kill his dog for food without fear of a palaver, but should he kill a man, the palaver was by no means finished. The people well understood the difference, and assented. I then turned to Bomolo and said, 'Did you kill Bosasa?' And before all the people he answered, 'Yes, I did.' And to Ikombe I said, 'Did you not kill Isekalasumba?' And before all he gave the same answer.

"As I was speaking, about fifteen men and women passed by, hostages released from the Baringa factory's prison (Abir) by the agent on the previous day—a silent, half-starved line, wending their weary way to their distant homes, a demonstration of the fact that these unfortunate people are not only subjected to all kinds of abuse in their own villages, but are always liable to be caught and carried away to the factory prison as so-called rubber hostages. They have done no wrong, and the rubber may be complete, but the agent must keep down the expenses of his factory, and must have this kind of unpaid labour. These men, women, and children are bound and borne off by these brutal soldiers, and committed to an indefinite term of imprisonment without knowing the reason why. Whilst there they are often ill-used, ill-fed, and hard-worked, which means disease and death, and the homes they have been forced to forsake run to ruin.

"After I had finished speaking, I took a snap of the large hut in which we had gathered. Returning to the hut where I had slept, I had a slight meal, and came on to Bolima town.

"Ilafa, the soldier who was sent to follow me, was not present whilst I was speaking to the people, he having remained in the house of Ikombe, some three miles' distance away.

"12.30.—Resting in the bush on our way to Bolima—indeed, the men say we are nearly there. Two parties have just passed us, one of three, and another of four, men and boys of the head capita Ilangalla, loaded with spears, shields, knives, food, dogs, and riches of every kind, the spoil of pillage. I hear that twenty persons at least were killed the last time the rubber was brought in, but can get no details.

"Arriving at the first house in Bolima, we found it occupied by about thirty boys with their rubber. Being small boys, I asked them why they were carrying rubber to the factory instead of those who collected it. 'Oh,' they replied, 'we collect it ourselves.' Upon further inquiry, I found that these little fellows of nine to fourteen years of age, actually did collect rubber.

"They told me the place where they went to gather it. They had to be at the Baringa factory the next day, and were then waiting for the contingents of workers now on their way from the more distant parts of Bolima town. Here I met the soldier Boyo, to whose settlement I presently went to await the later rubber contingents.

"2.45.—Whilst speaking to a large crowd just now in the soldiers' house, I noticed a bit of a stir amongst them, and heard the word 'bónyóló' (prisoners) mentioned. Picking up my camera and getting free from the crowd, I saw passing by about a dozen men and women tied together neck by neck. They were from the Ngombe town of Bongwonga, having been hunted and caught in the bush, and in charge of the two sentries Likio and Iela, with two guns. The soldiers hurried them along, and I took a snap of them from behind; but as the sun was shining right into the lens of my camera, the picture produced proved to be very dim.

"About fifteen minutes after the above went by, the soldier Bofasa appeared on the scene, and upon inquiry I learned from him that the renowned tyrant Ilangalla was close behind, bringing up the final contingent of rubber workers. Listening to the conversation, I heard Ilafa telling the other soldiers that I had come to find out about the men who had been killed. Bofasa's boy, Ngidima, carried his rifle, and slung by his side was a bundle of small arrows, the kind used for shooting at monkeys. His master carried the small stiff bow in his hand, and I needed no telling that he used these upon the naked bodies of his unfortunate fellows.

"After a few minutes, Ilangalla arrived, and I invited him and the other soldiers, with the people, to rest awhile, as I wished to speak to them. We then gathered in the house close by, and after much fuss, the great Ilangalla (Ilingiofe) was seated in his travelling chair, and we became quiet. My address was brief and pointed. Ilangalla sat close to me and listened in stolid silence, broken once only when he admitted boastfully that they had killed many people in Bolima. He wore a long black coat; his frightful features exhibited a character of exceptional and unrelenting brutality. Having finished, there was a quick exit. I also went out, and sat under the eaves of another hut. The sentries gathered in the open street, and some discussion followed, during which I took a picture of them.

"Then all went off, intending to sleep at Ekolongo that night, and get to the Abir factory next midday.

"My men were anxious to get on, so getting into my hammock, we went along at a trot for two hours, reaching the soldier Nsala's house about 5.30. I was very tired, but sat down outside and chatted to the people, it not requiring much exertion to interest them. I took my supper of bottled soup and bread in the centre of a thick ring of natives. They considered it a proof of great strength that I should eat my meal amid such a crowd of eyes. Having finished my supper, the children begged for a little salt and volunteered to sing one of their native songs. I assented, and they went through a most amusing performance, after which they received some salt to divide between them. I slept in a house close to Nsala's, but did not fall asleep until about eleven oclock. At midnight I was awakened by a heavy thunderstorm. The rain fell in torrents, and ran through the house under my bed. About two o'clock I fell asleep again.

"February 22, 1904.

" Packed up at 8.30. At midday we reached the settlement of Ilangalla. The two soldiers Efanza and Bosefe were here. A large house was being built, and a sleeping apartment had been erected on the top of an ant-hill, with wooden steps leading up to it.

" Whilst travelling through the town this morning, and before reaching the settlement of Ilangalla, I met parties of men and boys, amounting to quite a dozen, heavily laden with the spoils of robbery and extortion. I saw also many houses which had been destroyed, the walls and roofs being scattered about. I asked the reason, and was informed that the adult owners had been killed and their children driven away to find homes where they could. I also met not a few mourners covered with charcoal dust, but when these were interrogated they were afraid to tell me by what means their relatives had met their death. When any questions were put, or recent matters referred to, the frightened tell-tale glances, the peculiar denials that any one had been killed, were in themselves an evidence of something seriously wrong. Bolima has long been the happy hunting-ground of soldiers and their followers.

NOTES.

"(1) The names which are omitted in the above diary I have in my original notes.

"(2) It has subsequently come to light that Ilangalla—the capita of the soldiers—and others, killed six men and two women in Bolima on the same occasion.

"(3) It was not an insignificant fact to all who were acquainted with the affair, that the chief Agent of the Abir factory at Baringa passed through these villages the previous week, ending February 6, as the outrages were committed on the following Friday.

"(4) A reason for the occurrence was furnished us by one of the Abir Agents, viz. That when the director of the Company brought the Agent to the factory in December, 1903, he promised him the post only on the condition that he increased the quantity of rubber by half a ton per month, than the previous Agent.

"(5) On Sunday, April 18, the director of the Abir visited Baringa factory, accompanied by the judge. The matter was investigated, and the cases proved, but up to June 1, no arrests had been made, the judge having power only to make inquiries.

HERBERT FROST.

LETTER FROM MR. JOHN H. HARRIS.*

Baringa, May 30, 1904.

" This letter you may do as you like with. It is useless to expect anything better from the Congo Free State in the way of

* To a relative in England.

administration. From the *Times* issue of March 18, just received, we learn that the British Consul was the victim of a hoax, that his report is founded upon native evidence; and from another source we learn that these atrocities are the outcome of "morbid imagination of missionaries.' We also learn that Congo pigs have a rare fancy for human hands! Suppose it were admitted for a moment, for the sake of argument, that the British Consul is the ignorant fool the Congo State depicts him, and that a pig took Epondo's hand, what about all the other handless people on the Congo? What about the little lad I saw a few weeks ago, not more than four years old, with his hand off? Again, what about the chief I know who has only one hand, and another whose now useless arm, mutilated by 'sentries,' mutely appeals to-day for justice. Perhaps these things also are due to 'pigs'!

"We know a few things about the investigation of Epondo's case, but let this pass for the moment.

"So much for the 'morbid imagination of the missionaries.' Who is most likely to know the truth—the resident missionary, and the missionary of years' experience, or the occasionally passing State official, who does not know the native language, and does everything through an interpreter?

"Another question I should like to ask is, why, when an agent of a rubber 'company' enters a town, do all the women and children run helter-skelter into the forest to hide, carrying with them all their possessions?

"Another most interesting question is, why, if the Congo State is anxious to put down these atrocities, do they treat those who report gross breaches of the law as little better than enemies to the State? I think I can state, without fear of contradiction, that every time we have called attention to outrages our positions have been rendered more difficult. In fact, a late Commissaire of Equator District told two of our missionaries at Basankusu, that if I made any trouble at Baringa he would put a chain round my neck and put me in prison. The 'trouble' refers, of course, to speaking about atrocities.

"The state of affairs is the natural outcome of the system. The Congo officials want rubber. The State says that the collection of rubber is a collection of taxes; but how can this be, considering that so-called private 'companies' fix the quantity of rubber to be brought in, and the rubber brought to them is for these companies' benefit? Surely taxes ought not to be used to benefit private individuals, but for the development of the State.*

"Again, we are told that 'the taxes are fixed between the officials and the native chiefs.' This a wicked and barefaced untruth; the chiefs are never *consulted*,† they are *ordered* † to bring in so much rubber every fortnight, and sentries with their retinue are

* And for the benefit of the people who pay the taxes.
† Italics, Mr. Harris's.

quartered upon them and force the rubber out of the people. The relative position of the 'sentries' and the chiefs is that of master and slave. No respect whatever is shown to the chiefs. How often, for instance, have the chiefs of this district, at one time or another, suffered the greatest degradations. Have I not seen them again and again with chains round their necks, carrying soil and other rubbish with the commonest slaves, and left in this position for weeks, absolutely without trial? Again, a number of them have, to my certain knowledge, been publicly flogged. These chiefs may be inferior to the white man, but amongst their own people they are greatly respected.

"I see a great deal is being made in Europe about the new regulations—that Natives are only to work in future forty hours per month!* A great deal is also being made of this on the Congo—a great deal of ridicule—by State officials, rubber agents and missionaries! Every one realises that it is only a 'blind.' If it were carried out, not a single kilo of rubber could reach Europe. I have not yet heard a single person speak seriously of that law. It is like many other 'State' laws, only made to be broken.

"I want now to tell you how this rubber is collected. By some secret process, a company of magnates in Europe apparently buy a tract of country out here, including the people. (I understand what are called the 'Abir people' number about two millions.) These magnates choose a director and agents in Africa.† The Agents have districts assigned to them to rule, and to get in all the rubber they can.

"The agent is supplied with guns and ammunition; these he gives to a number of men whom he 'calls' for the purpose. These men are named 'sentries,' and are placed in the towns in the numbers of two to ten according to the size of the town.

"These sentries in their turn, quarter themselves upon the chiefs—in itself a considerable hardship when it is remembered that the sentries are little despots, and have a considerable retinue of 'boys' and wives, all living upon the chief. For the use of the sentries, women, food, and sundries must be supplied; the women must be of the finest type and the food of the best quality. Added to this there are constant acts of blackmailing. In fact, the sentries are simply 'terrors' to the poor people, who know that their refusal to supply them, or even one of their 'boys,' with what they ask, will probably mean death. A case in point is that of Bongwalanga and her daughter Lofinda, both of whose heads were cut off for refusing

* The writer has evidently heard of this for the first time. It is noteworthy to see what he says on the subject, in view of the fact that this utterly ridiculous statement about "forty hours' work" has figured for at least twelve months among the varied assortment of official plausibilities.

† This, of course, is how it appears to the man on the spot. We, in Europe, know that the principal "magnate" is the so-called "Government" of the Congo itself, which holds the fact part of the shares, and otherwise benefits by these "commercial" operations.

to give Ifuta all the fish he asked for.* Every fortnight these sentries collect the rubber and accompany a number of people to the nearest post, and carefully watch the people lest they tell tales to the white man, who, I may say from experience, is never very anxious to listen, and if he does so has to hear a palaver through an interpreter, who is probably 'in' with the sentries.

"Occasionally one comes across a more humane agent, but, generally speaking, they are the kind who get the Irishman's rise, because they do not increase the toll of rubber.

"It has been sometimes argued that the State official sanctions the quantity of rubber. He may do so in his half-yearly visits, which are of only a few hours' duration, but he knows nothing of the ability of the people to bring in the rubber beyond what the 'Company's' Agent likes to tell him, and, moreover, every agent, when sent to the 'post,' is ordered to increase the quantity. In a word, the poor people are absolutely under the control of the so-called 'trading' companies, who can do just as they like with them. Law is not operative here, and if we sometimes quote law to prove some action illegal, we are laughed at, as I was on April 23 last, and told, 'What is State law to me? I am sent to get plenty of rubber, not to carry out law.' Can you wonder that, under these circumstances, the wretched sentries take the cue from their masters, and rule the country according to their standard of right, which is to become despots, to enrich themselves by tyranny and blackmail, and at the same time to live in unparalleled luxury, whilst at their very names even the chief of a town trembles.

"In what does the Congo State 'Government' differ from slavery? Honestly, I confess I do not know.

"Think for a few minutes what a harrowing time the people have been through lately, and but for us I am confident worse would have been still the order of the day.

"Close to us are the towns of Balumboloko, Lotoko, Ekelongo, and Bolima. The last few months these brutes of sentries have cruelly murdered in these towns at least twelve people, including a chief and two women.

"The worst part appears to be that these were mere acts of brutality committed with the sole object of terrorising people. At Esanga, a district of small villages on the opposite bank, these 'sentries' murdered at least five people, including two women and one girl. It was necessary for me to go down to Jikau on business a few days ago, and whilst I was away a terrible affair was enacted close here at the Nsongo towns, which, for sickening brutality, surpasses all I have heard of lately. On Sunday morning, May 15, the man Noala brought the foot and hand of his child in to prove to the Agent that the sentry Lifumba and others had cut up this child and eaten her, also his wife Bogindangoa; also that they had

* This particular act occurred last March, and was reported by Mr. Harris.

APPENDIX

killed Esanga, a boy of about ten; Esekolumbo, a chief, was mortally wounded, and since dead; also Elisi, another chief, was wounded, but will probably recover.

" One girl child, killed and eaten.
" One woman, mother, killed and eaten.
" One boy, killed and eaten.
" One chief, killed, not eaten.
" One chief wounded.

"I arrived here Thursday, May 19, and on Friday afternoon three Nsongo men brought in the hands of Bolenga and Lingomo, who had been killed at their town, two days before, by the sentries Loteri, Bomolo, and others. Also they had killed, cooked, and eaten the woman Balengolo.

" Two men killed.
" One woman killed and eaten.
" On May 22, Bolima suffered once more.

" One of the sentry's retinue—a ' boy '—demanded more meat from the people, and on their refusal became abusive, and threatened them. The sentry loaded his gun and shot a man and a woman, killing the man and probably mortally wounding the woman; there seems very little hope of her recovery.

" One man killed.
" One woman wounded.

"Thus, you see, during the last few months twenty-five persons have lost their lives, and two badly wounded. Amongst these were several women and children; quite a number of these were cooked and eaten.

"The evidence is not disputed—in fact, up to the present the sentries admit it and blame the agent, saying that it was by his orders. Moreover, we have names and details beyond dispute, and yet—can you believe it?—such a state of things exists here, that the sentries are as free as you or I.

" If these things go on close to the Mission Station, what goes on further afield? If half the gruesome stories we hear are true (and I have good reason to believe most of them are), such a story could be written as would shock the civilised world.

" Some time ago a chief, 200 miles away, sent a message begging us to establish a Mission Station near him, ' or,' said he, ' we shall soon all be killed.' In the light of this, is it any wonder that the State refuses to grant us any new sites?

" Two months ago a chief near here was offered a native fortune if he could influence us to go to a certain district on a visit, because it was hoped that our visit might put an end to the devilry that was in progress; needless to say, we discountenanced such a proceeding.

"You may find some difficulty in getting people at home to believe this, but I can assure you every word is true to fact.

" May God rouse the hearts of the people in Europe to demand a new system for this poor country."

Letter from Mr. E. Stannard.*

"C.B.M., Baringa, Upper Congo,
"Congo Independent State,
"May 21, 1904.

"I regret to say that during the last few months, instead of there being any signs of improvement in this district, the condition of things is becoming infinitely worse, and we are forced to believe that, under present conditions, this will be increasingly so. The treatment to which these poor people are subjected is simply atrocious—no less strong word than that describes it.

"The State authorities appear to resent the word 'atrocities.' I wish they were equally concerned about the atrocities themselves. It is a marvel to us that the people can submit to such treatment. They are getting desperate, and one wonders what the end of it all will be. They seem so hopeless and helpless, and there is no remedy provided for them by the State—in fact, it is the State that is oppressing them.

"Quite recently Judge Bosco was here making inquires regarding the murders that were committed by sentries in the towns at the back of us just before Mr. Frost left for England, and which he personally investigated. The murders were proved up to the hilt—in fact, a larger number than we at first had known of definitely. Relatives of the murdered people, and witnesses from the towns, came and testified before the judge, and the sentries confessed to having killed the people. The judge said it was certain that the murders had taken place, and the only question in dispute was as to upon whom the responsibility rested. All the sentries, without exception, affirmed that they were instructed by M. Van Calcken, the agent, to kill people, and that those who did not were censured. The agent, on the other hand, denied that he had done so.

"The power and authority of the judge seemed to be very limited, and it appeared that he could do no more than make an investigation. He said that, as a white man was involved, all he could do was to report the facts to Boma, and he would probably have a reply on the subject in about three months' time. We pointed out that these sentries admitted having committed the murders, and that being so, asked him what he was going to do with them; but he confessed his inability to do more in the matter, as the responsibility was not established, and it was connected with rubber. So that, in the face of these confessed murders, nobody has been arrested or punished, and the same kind of things are being repeated. One would have thought that the very least that would have been done would have been to put the sentries under arrest. Do you wonder that the people say it is useless to report these things? They come

* To Dr. Guinness.

APPENDIX

and tell us of these things, often at great risk, but with no better result than the above, and often not as much. The judge did arrest Ilangala, the capita, or head sentry; but he explained to us that he did so solely because he had killed a woman, and he said it was illegal for a woman to be punished on account of rubber. These particular men have ceased to be sentries, but they are in their towns and quite free, and it is probable that if they are wanted in three months' time they may have disappeared, and then their charge against the agent will be unsubstantiated, and the whole thing will fall through and nothing more be heard of it.

"That is the usual way with these palavers in which people are murdered. The sentries invariably affirm that they are told to kill people, whilst when murders come to light the agents discredit them, and disclaim responsibility. It is significant, however, that scarcely ever, if ever, do they take action, except in cases we report to them. My own distinct impression is that they are acquainted with the actions of their sentries, and largely responsible for them. They are compelled to get their full demand of rubber, and good rubber, if it is possible to be got, and will use any means to that end. Of course, they prefer not to do the horrible work actually themselves, and the sentries are only too willing to use the gun. The agents should know the kind of men they arm and send out with guns and rifles, and should know what is done with the cartridges and powder that have been used. Is it right that it should be possible to shirk responsibility in the easy fashion these men seem to be able to do it?

"The way in which some of these men regard the seriousness of these charges is illustrated by the following. Whilst the judge was here, another series of murders came to light through one of our station lads visiting the Esanga District. One woman was decapitated by a sentry, and one of the murdered men was a relative of our lad. The judge, Mr. Harris, and I were sitting talking in Mr. Harris's house, when the two agents came across to get particulars about the affair. After the lad had enumerated the four people who were killed and the sentries implicated, Mr. ——* said, with half a laugh and affected surprise, 'Is that all? I thought there were a lot killed.' He then added, 'I can't be everywhere, and I am not a policeman.' And we are told by the State that these men have the entire surveillance of the district. We are put under their jurisdiction, and have to recognise them as the representatives of the State; in any kind of difficulty we are told we must apply to them. Mr. ——† says he has since made inquiries, and admits that the allegations are true, but says the murders were committed in the time of his predecessor, who went to Europe last January. He evidently does not mind admitting the facts, as long as he is cleared of the responsibility.

"The judge remarked to us that the work given to him to do

---

* The name is given in the letter. † Ibid.

is not serious, *i.e.* it is impossible. In this Equator District, as large as a great European State, he is the only judicial officer, and he can scarcely visit the whole of his district during his term of service. When he goes to investigate a charge it is possibly a year old, and it is impossible to get witnesses. Then whilst he is travelling he knows there is a tremendous lot of work accumulating for him at Coquilhatville, and that there is no proper administration of justice.

"Mr. Harris has already intimated to you in a letter of his that while he was down at Jikau, attending a committee meeting, a horrible case of murder and cannibalism on the part of rubber sentries occurred in this district. It was of a shocking nature, and has greatly distressed us. On Sunday morning, May 15, just after eight o'clock, I had gone across to Mr. Harris's house, and we were just going to commence morning worship when two boys rushed breathlessly in, and said that some sentries had killed a number of people, and that two men had gone by to tell the rubber white men, and that they also had some hands to show him, in case he did not believe them. It greatly upset us, and we told them to watch for the men as they came back, and to tell us, so that we could see them. Shortly afterwards the two men came along the path, and we heard the boys calling to them to come and show us; but they seemed afraid, and so we went out quickly and overtook them, and asked them where the hands were. Thereupon one of them opened a parcel of leaves, and showed us the hand and foot of a small child, who could not have been more than five years old. They were fresh and clean cut. It was an awful sight, and even now, as I write, I can feel the shudder and feeling of horror that came over me as we looked at them, and saw the agonised look of the poor fellow, who seemed dazed with grief, and said they were the hand and foot of his little girl. I can never forget the sight of that horror-stricken father. We asked them to come into the house and tell us about the affair, which they did, and the following is the story they told us—

"'The father of the little girl said his name was Nsala, and he was a native of Wala, which is a section of the Nsongo District and connected with Lifinda, the outpost of Baringa. On the previous day, although it was three days before they were due to take in the rubber, fifteen sentries came from Lifinda, all except two being armed with Albini rifles, and they were accompanied by followers. They began making prisoners and shooting, and killed Bongingangoa, his wife; Boali, his little daughter of about five years of age; and Esanga, a boy of about ten years. These they at once cut up, and afterwards cooked in pots, putting in salt which they had brought with them, and then ate them.

"'They also shot three other people who, although wounded, managed to run into the forest. They were :

"'Eikitunga, a woman who, although wounded, ran as far as a stream, named the Loali, where she fell in and was drowned.

"'Isekolumbo, a chief. Shot with an Albini, and the bullet

APPENDIX 445

passed through right arm, and then through his body and out at back. They say he will not live.

"'Elisi, a chief. Shot with an Albini in the thigh; he will probably live, as the bone was not broken.

"'The chiefs, they say, are not supposed to go out and get rubber, and, I might add, neither are the women and innocent children. The sentries took ten prisoners, of whom nine were women. The people, however, afterwards redeemed four women for a thousand rods, and later, another four for a large basketful of rods and a dog. The other two prisoners were taken to the rubber posts at Lifinda. They were Isekolanganga, a man, and Bòkombi, a woman, who was the wife of Elisi, the chief who was shot in the thigh. She had brass anklets on when taken, but these the sentries stole.

"'Nsala said that when the sentries were not looking, he snatched up the foot and hand of his little girl, to bring and show to the white man, in case he should disbelieve what he said. We asked him whether he had cut off the hand and foot, but he looked horrified, and protested that he had not done so. He added that when they came away the sentries were still hunting the people, and that they were then going to hide in the bush, as they were afraid to go back.'

"Mrs. Harris then took a photo of the sorrowing man and all that was left to him of his wife and little daughter. We were sickened as we looked, and thought of the innocent little child, and pictured her running about but a short time before. We tried to enter a little into the feelings of the unhappy father, and involuntarily there arose from our hearts a prayer that God himself would intervene on behalf of these people.

"They say the natives are 'adequately paid.' This is the price paid for rubber on the Congo!

"When Judge Bosco was here, he said it was absolutely illegal to imprison women on account of rubber. This is the way the law is observed on the Congo. Could things be much worse if there were no law?

"Later in the morning a note was sent to M. Van Calcken, the agent, informing him of what we had seen and been told, and saying we expected him to report the matter. He afterwards came across and said the men had been across to him in the morning, but that he had not seen the hand and foot. This is certainly strange, because we met them coming straight from the rubber factory, and asked them whether they had shown the white man, and what he said. They replied that they had done so, and that he said he would talk the palaver with the other white man, who was coming next day. If they did not show the hand and foot, it illustrates the fear with which people go and report any matter to the rubber agents.

"On the next morning (Monday) we heard the canoe of M. Y——*

* The name is given in the letter.

had arrived from Lifinda, and on Tuesday afternoon, about 3.30, two men came up to me whilst I was superintending some brick-making on the station, and said they wanted to tell me some more about how the sentries had been killing and eating their people. Poor fellows, they looked like hunted animals, and terror was stamped on their features. Their names were Bompenju and Lofiko. Bompenju said he was the elder brother of Lofiko and Nsala, who came to us on Sunday. They had just come from the forest, where they had been hiding. Their account was substantially the same as that given to us on Sunday, but somewhat amplified. Fourteen days, they said, were allowed to them in which to get their rubber, of which they spent ten days in the forest collecting it. On the previous Saturday, Bompenju was still in the jamba (swamp) gathering his, and Lofiko was in his house, as he had his rubber, and was sitting down for three days before they had to take it in. Although they were not due with their rubber for three days, fifteen sentries with their followers appeared, two of whom had cap-guns, whilst the rest were armed with Albini rifles, and commenced shooting. They also affirmed that previously they had sentries who were natives of the Nsongo district, but that the white man recalled them and took away their guns, because he said they did not kill their own people. He then sent them others from places where the people are known to be notorious cannibals, with the above result. Whilst we were interrogating the man, Mrs. Harris mentioned that M. Van Calcken said he had not seen the hand and foot on Sunday, whereupon Botondo, one of our workmen, exclaimed, 'That is falsehood itself, because I was returning from the river at the time, and saw Nsala show him the hand and foot.' Bokalo, a house boy, also spoke up and said, ' Yes, and when I saw them coming along the path, and told them to come and show the English, they said they were afraid, because the rubber white man had told them not to do so.'

"We were also informed that M. X——,* on his way down by canoe, put on shore at a landing near the Nsongo district five sentries, with instructions that they were to go and kill some more people. When, however, he got to Baringa, M. X——,† told him that the missionaries knew about the affair, and two sentries, named Lote and Lolenga, were sent overland to tell the other sentries not to kill any more, and they had returned to Baringa to-day, with a lot of women prisoners. At 6.45 that evening, Longombo, a workman of the Mission, came and told me that he had just been told by Ikala, a sentry, that the prisoners brought in from Nsongo that day numbered ten—eight women and two men, and that one woman and one man had been released, leaving seven women and one man in prison. Lianza, a station lad, told me later that Inumga, a boy who previously worked for Mr. Frost, but who now works at the factory, had told him that a number of women prisoners had been

---

* The name is given in the letter.   † Ibid.

brought in, but he had not counted them. I was further told next morning by Botondo, Basombo, and Ifomi, three station lads, that they had been over at the sentries' houses the previous night, and had seen the women prisoners, who are in charge of the sentries. Lomboto, the headman, is responsible for them, and they are not put in the prison itself. The reason given for this procedure is that M. X——* does not want the English to know that he has women prisoners. And all this has taken place immediately after the judge had emphasised, in our presence and his, that women must not be made prisoners by Abir agents on account of rubber.

"With the present strained relations we were in a very difficult position. If I had personally gone looking round his sentries' houses and asking questions, he would have got very angry; on the other hand, had I gone and asked him about it, he would have taken care that the women were kept out of the way.

"On Thursday, May 19, at midday, Mr. Harris returned from Jikau, and we hoped that these horrors were at an end, anyway for a time. Unfortunately such was not the case, for on Friday afternoon, about 4.30, whilst I was with Mr. Harris, three men came up to us with a small bundle, and opening it said, 'Look! this is the hand of Lingomo, and this is the hand of Bolengo. We couldn't bring the hand of Balengola, as they have eaten the whole of her body.' I recognised two of the men as Bompenju and Lofiko, who had come to us on the previous Tuesday. We said, 'What, have they killed some more?' 'Yes,' they replied; 'three more; one of whom they have eaten.' 'White men,' they went on, 'what *are* we to do? They are finishing us all off. Whilst we came here three days ago they killed a man, a boy, and a woman.' Mrs. Harris took a photo of the men with the hands, and Mr. Harris and I stood in the group, as we thought it would be additional testimony. Mr. Harris then went across with the men to the agent. I had had a very unpleasant interview with him some time ago in connection with some other murderous outrages. Just after, I noticed a number of people at the end of the station path, and found that they were people who had come from Wala with rubber, and were waiting for the other three men. Mrs. Harris and I walked along, and had a talk with them. They told us that the sentries had killed a man, woman, and lad, and had also eaten the woman. In answer to our question as to when it took place, they said it was three days ago, and that the sentries, who were armed with Albini rifles, had also taken five prisoners, of whom two were women with their children. We asked whether Isekolumbo and Elisi, the two wounded chiefs, were still alive, and they said they were.

"I am afraid Mr. Harris and I look rather angry in the photo, but I confess that I felt angry. It made my blood boil to think of these things—horror upon horror—which are being perpetrated upon these persecuted people."

* The name is given in the letter.

"Thursday, May 26, 1904.

"This afternoon I returned from a visit to Wala in the Nsongo district. I left here last Tuesday morning and reached there about 4 p.m. On passing through Boeringa we met two natives of Wala, who accompanied us. Just before reaching Wala they said to me, 'Come in here and we will show you where they killed the little girl Boali.' So I turned aside into a small side-path in the forest, and there, a short way in, I saw a large number of leaves covered with old blood-stains. They told me she had run into the forest and was overtaken, killed, and cut up. The parts were then carried into the town, cooked, and eaten.

"On reaching Wala itself, I met Mpombo the chief, a man of considerable influence amongst the natives, and widely known throughout the surrounding districts. I was informed that Isekolumbo, the man who had been seriously wounded, had died on the morning of that day. They said that his compound was some distance away, and that they might have buried him. However, as I said I should like to see his body, they sent off for it at once, and also sent a message on the 'lokoli' telling the people there not to bury it. It arrived just before dark. I examined the body, and the wounds showed clearly that he had been shot with a rifle. The bullet had passed through the right arm, and then through the side of the body and out at the back. The arm bone was also broken. The wound could only have been caused by a bullet. He was a big man and seems to have been of good standing and much respected in the district.

"The next morning, while I was having breakfast, they brought me in Elisi, the other man who had been wounded in the thigh. I examined him and found the bullet-wound through the fleshy part of the thigh. It was of such a nature that it could only have been caused by a bullet. I dressed the wound and he promised to come to the station to be treated. He said he was shot by an Albini rifle by Lifumba, the capita of the Lifinda sentries. When the sentries first arrived they commenced making a number of prisoners, and Elisi asked Lifumba why they were doing that, as the rubber was not due for three days, whereupon he lifted up his rifle and shot him, saying at the same time, 'take that.'

"I was told by Mpombo and a number of others that after Elisi had been shot, the sentries came through to Mpombo's part, and killed, cooked, and ate, Bongindangoa, Boali, and the boy Esanga.

> Bongindangoa was shot with an Albini by Mboyo.
> Boali " " " Likilo.
> Esanga " " " Lomboto.

Mpombo said that had he remained in his house they would have shot him. After their cannibal feast the sentries slept in the same house, and started back next morning for Lifinda. On their way through the town they met Isekolumbo, and he said to them, 'Why

APPENDIX 449

are you killing us?' The rubber is not due for three days.' The sentry, Bokumgu, then lifted up his rifle and shot him, also saying, 'take that.' He managed to run into the bush. The above refers to the first killing palaver.

"Three days later (on Monday) five sentries came to Mpombo's part from the river, armed with Albini rifles. They were Bompasu, Bopambo, Lomboto, Mboyo, and Isekombali. They did not kill or wound, but made a number of prisoners, some of whom were women. Later on two sentries, Loto and Lolenga, arrived from Baringa, and told them that they were not to kill any people. They slept there that night and left next morning with the prisoners.

"That same morning (Tuesday), Lifumba and some other sentries, including Lomboto, Loteri, Bokungu, Lokilo, and Efomo, came again from Lifunda to the other end of Wala, but did not reach Mpombo's part. On this occasion they killed three people, one of whom was a woman, whom they ate. The people killed were Lingongo, a man; Bolengo (also named Lofembe), a lad; and Balengola, a woman. The woman was speared by Lontulu, a 'boy' of one of the sentries, after which they cut her up and ate her.

"The house that I slept in was next to the open house in which the first cannibal feast of the sentries had taken place, and my food was actually cooked in the same house. I asked Mpombo if it would not be possible to find me some of the bones of the people who had been eaten, but he said it was then about ten days since the first took place, and that the sentries burnt most of the bones or else threw what remained right away. However, he said he would send a man at once to the place where the last woman had been eaten, at the other end of Wala (nearly a day's journey further on), to see if he could find any. Later in the day they brought me a piece of bone charred at one end, which they had found in the house where the feast had taken place, and which they said belonged to Boali. They thought it was part of one of the bones of the forearm.

"Just before I left, the man returned from the other place, bringing a piece of bone which he said belonged to the woman Balengola, and which he found outside the house where she was eaten. He said that was all he was able to find of her, and that had been lying outside, and the white ants had started eating one end. That was so, because even after my return to the station I found two white ants still on it. They thought it was a part of the leg bone. These I am sending on to you just as they were given to me, tied on to the ends of pieces of stick. For superstitious reasons the people would not handle the bones themselves, as they were parts of the remains of their relatives.

"I left them, saying I would do what I could for them, and hoped that those who had done such awful things to them would be severely punished. These things have been reported to the judge, and we are anxiously awaiting another visit from him.

"According to the present written law of the State, these people are only required to work forty hours a month, but so far as those for whom it is intended are concerned, it might as well never have been written. It is merely a blind, for I do not suppose it is acted upon anywhere in the State. The rubber agents here openly ridiculed it in the presence of the judge, and said it was only written for European consumption. They are constantly receiving circulars instructing them to increase the amount of rubber. The people's work is not reckoned by time, but by the amount of rubber they must bring in. They are practically always working for the State or rubber companies. The agents sometimes complain to us that a number of people have gone away from their towns, as though they had committed a great crime which demands severe measures. And yet can the people be blamed for running away from such treatment? They can hardly be expected to do less than that. Can they be expected to remain quietly and receive such treatment as the Nsongo people have lately had meted out to them? However, it is seldom that they get far, and usually only out of one rubber district into another. These rubber agents have but one thought and apparently but one interest, viz. rubber. And one would almost imagine that their hearts must be made of rubber, or something harder, else they could not but feel some pity for the unfortunate people who are at their mercy, and whom they seem to be willing to do to death with so little compunction.

"You will be able to understand our feelings of indignation and disgust when we read of the defenders of the State in Europe denying the charges that are made against it, and asserting that the people are happy and receive just treatment, whilst we are living in the midst of these horrors which are being perpetrated upon the people at the *present* time.

"Whilst Judge Bosco was here, he said that he had received instructions to investigate the British Consul's statement to the Governor-General that he had seen at Bongandanga fifteen women prisoners tied by the neck. I told him that I was at Bongandanga during the Consul's visit, and had seen those women being marched to the factory by sentries, and I also said that I had seen very many others besides. I added that whilst I was at Bongandanga, it was by no means exceptional for women to be put in prison, but on the other hand, that it was an ordinary everyday occurrence. I signed a statement to that effect. At that time he had not seen a copy of the Consul's report, and we showed him ours. If he is the Marquis Bosco referred to in the papers, as having investigated the charges made by the British Consul in his report, and proved them unfounded, it is a false statement. When he was here in April, he told us he had not yet seen a copy of the report, and what he saw here went to confirm the Consul's charges.

"We very much need the prayers of God's people to know always how to act for the best under most trying circumstances. The work is certainly beset with great difficulties and there is much that might discourage us, but, in spite of all, God is giving us signs of his blessing and evidences of His working. We take courage and press forward. One thing is certain, and never was the Gospel message of love, peace, and goodwill more needed that it is at the present time in this land of oppression and darkness."

"June 5, 1904.

"Yesterday afternoon Judge Bosco arrived by the Abir steamer. He came along to the Mission, and we spoke to him about these fresh acts of murder and cannibalism by rubber sentries. He seemed to think things were very bad, and said he would report the matter to Boma. That was all he could do, and if these things still continued afterwards it would not be his fault.

"This morning he came and interrogated Mr. Harris and myself. I gave him a full account of the whole affair, and signed a declaration embodying the main features of the case. The judge appears to be a very fair man, and desirous of doing what is just; but his hands seem to be tied, and all he can do is to investigate. He is virtually a judge only in name, for he seems to lack the authority and power attaching to that office. I sincerely wish we could feel some confidence in the desire of the State to mete out justice, not only to those who actually commit these crimes, but to those who are really responsible for them.

"It is difficult for people at home to understand how extremely hard it is for these natives to give any kind of evidence against the rubber agents. Try and put yourself in their position. For all practical purposes, the rubber company is supreme in this part of the country. It is the rubber agent with whom these people have to do and whom they fear. A judge may come along and ask them a few questions, but he then passes on, and they are left with the rubber agent. They know that if they have said anything against him they will have to suffer for it pretty severely afterwards. They have repeatedly expressed themselves to us in this way. They argue that if they say anything about the agent, nothing comes of it—no change for the better is made, and they are afterwards punished for saying it. Fear, therefore, closes their mouths. The men implicated know all this only too well.

"From Mr. Harris's letter you will be able to appreciate our position here now, which is not a very enviable one. We cannot say what developments may take place, but we shall keep you informed. The attitude of the rubber Company is openly and actively hostile. They have made it clear that the only way in which we can receive anything like proper treatment is by closing our eyes, ears, and mouths with reference to their atrocious doings. But that is impossible.

"Since last Christmas, in the districts surrounding Baringa, to our knowledge about twenty-five people, including men, women, and children, have been brutally murdered, some of whom have been cooked and eaten by rubber sentries. Can we, in the face of these things, remain silent? Is not our duty as Christian missionaries perfectly clear, regardless of consequences? We must speak or our conscience will condemn us!

"EDGAR STANNARD."

THIRTEEN YEARS OF CONGO STATE RULE IN KATANGA. EXTRACTS FROM A LETTER WRITTEN BY THE REV. DUGALD CAMPBELL.*

"The Mission, Johnstone Falls,
"N. E. Rhodesia, May 14, 1904.

"DEAR SIR,

"I have just returned from a three weeks' journey in the Congo State, having paid a visit to our Mission Station at Koni Hill, on the Lufire River, and to the Belgian post, Lufaku, as also to Msiri's Town, where I spent four days with chiefs and old friends. Old Msiri's son, Kitanika, and Kalama, one of the principal *capitas* † in Katanga, have been here on a week's visit, and have just left. The afore-mentioned *capita*, Kalama, has served the State faithfully since the appearance of the first yellow flag star, brought by Paul Le Marinel, whom he accompanied on his return journey to Luluaburg. With these two loyal Congolese I went over the principal events of State history in Katanga, since the advent of Congo Government, and particularly since my own arrival about eleven years ago. To be sure of being accurate, I thus refreshed my memory as to facts, names of places, people, etc., relating thereto, and much else, and I beg to send you the following observations and narrative of experiences in the hope that they may prove useful and help to put an end to the abuses prevailing in poor oppressed Congoland.

Ivory Régime.—" Shortly prior to my arrival at Lufoi (Katanga) from Bihe, on the West Coast, Lieutenant, afterwards Captain Legat, left, and was replaced by Lientenant, afterwards Captain X——,‡ who welcomed me to the country. The Mission Station was fifteen minutes' walk from the State post. Just a month or so before I arrived, Lieutenant X—— had set out with a large party to avenge a supposed insult to two of his messengers—Dioko, the State interpreter (a Loanda black left at Msiri's by the Portuguese travellers Capello and Ivens), and Magabe, a local native. He attacked the large village of Mutwila, a Sanga chief. There was great slaughter, including women and little children. Heads were brought back for a wardance. Gangs of slaves, men and women, were taken—some of whom are still in slavery. The village was burnt and everything destroyed. The women were given mostly to the soldiers. Lots of ivory was taken.

"Kafwimbi, a big chief with a large village on the Luapula

---

* To Mr. H. R. Fox-Bourne, Secretary of the Aborigines Protection Society.
† Chief of State Soldiers.
‡ The name is given in the letter.

River (he is now in British territory and visited me a few days ago), was also known to have much ivory, and consequently attacked. The chief escaped across the river under a hail of bullets, but M. Y——* told me many were shot and sunk while trying to reach the British side. Others were killed in the village, and all the women and children roped together. The women became soldiers' property, and some were, as they say here, "married" to the whites. The village was burnt and pillaged, and everything destroyed, including a parting kick at any undamaged pots—the usual thing even in time of quiet.

"A journey from Lufoi post to Mtoa (Tanganyika Zone) by Sub-Lieutenant P——,† was the occasion of further burning, pillaging, and killing. The officer in question was conducting a large gang of prisoners in chains, and on his return journey, he burnt out our local chief Chipungu, ten minutes' distance from whose village was our second Mission Station on Lake Mweru, also the villages of chiefs Nswioa and Kafungo. These burnings were accompanied with the usual plunder and devastation—carrying off stock and destroying food, much to our chagrin, as the missionaries were more or less dependent on them for fowls, eggs, and native produce. Leaving there, Sub-Lieutenant P—— crossed the Bukongolo Mountains, murdered old chief Mbogo and chief Lukona, with further burning, destroying, and fighting *en route* back—that is, if you call shooting down helpless natives by such a dignified appellation as fighting. To the west of Lufoi post, among the mountains which in parts are honeycombed with caves, live the Bena Mitumba, or people of the hills, a branch of the Va-Sanga tribe, who have been an incessant thorn in the State's side, as they have been almost inaccessible, and are splendid elephant-hunters, with, of course, heaps of ivory. Between this tribe—the aborigines of the country—and the Va-Yeke, Msiri's people, there has been a perpetual feud. Really a stranger from the north of Tanganyika, Msiri was considered an unwelcome intruder. To strengthen himself, therefore, he killed and oppressed the Va-Sanga, and cropped off the ears of one of their principal chiefs, Mulowanyama. This chief was afterwards burnt alive in a cave with about seventy or eighty of his people, including women and children, by a State force under Captain Z——.‡ The State took sides with Msiri's people against the Va-Sanga, whom they (Msiri's people) hated and persecuted under State flags and with State guns, caps, and powder. Result, the Va-Sanga resented and refused to bring in the ivory. (N.B.— Verbal guarantees had been given by Captain Stairs,§ on the Va-Sanga submitting to the State and taking the flag, that no Yeke chief would again dominate them. Hence the bitterness was due to

* The name is given in the letter.
† Ibid.
‡ Ibid.
§ Captain Stairs, an Englishman, was one of the earliest exploring pioneers in Katanga.

this violation of a promise solemnly given.) Kalela, one of the strongest of these chiefs, from a mountaineer's point of view, was next chosen for punishment. A war-party was got together, and, with Captain X———* set out to attack him. The people, being forewarned, rushed to their canoes, and in the attack killed two and wounded two of the State forces. The mouth of their cave was filled with firewood and straw, and an attempt made to burn them out; but they escaped, as we were told, by an exit some distance off. The usual destruction and pillage followed, *plus* the burning of another village on the way back. In the attack Captain X———† shot two of his own local natives for 'disobeying orders,' and one of these, by name Chonobaruti, brother of the State *capita* who left here yesterday, had two fingers shot off; the other, Mukolokolo, was shot in the leg. Both are still alive.

"One of the biggest and most bloody journeys was that undertaken by Captain X———‡ and Lieut. Y———§ to Lubaland, extending over a period of about two months. After about a ten days' journey from Lufoi post, through a semi-subjugated people, the very populous district of Chivanda was reached in Lubaland. The principal chief, Munongo, fled, but leaving a fat goat tied up in the middle of the village, and a big basket of native flour, as a propitiatory present to the white man. As he did not show himself, having learnt lessons by bitter previous experience, his town was forthwith pillaged and burnt, goats, fowls, pigeons, and all stock taken, and all else destroyed. No prisoners were taken, though the adjacent country was scoured; the people having got timely warning. The village of another big chief, Chikomo, was similarly treated, but as the news had spread of the State's approach, and the treatment meted out at Chivanda, the people got well away. Next Kaluira, a very large chief, hearing of the former burning and pillaging, fled. A number of women were caught in the fields and roped together, and the village was plundered and burnt to the ground. Kayombo was the next large Luban chief dealt with. Having taken refuge among reeds, *in a marsh, he was caught and hung up by the feet to a palm tree; then a fire was kindled underneath, over which he was slowly roasted to death. Several more women were added to the rope-gang, and the village was pillaged and burnt.*

"After that, Katoro, another very large chief, living near the apex of Western and Eastern Lualaba, was attacked. The crowds were fired into promiscuously, and fifteen were killed, including four women and a baby on its mother's breast. The heads were cut off and brought to the officer in charge, who then sent the men to cut off the hands also, and these were pierced, strung, and dried over the camp fire. The heads, with many others, I saw myself. The town, prosperous once, was burnt, and what they could not carry off was destroyed. Crowds of people were caught, mostly old women and

---

* The name is given in the letter.
† Ibid.   ‡ Ibid.   § Ibid.

young women, and three fresh rope-gangs were added. One died shortly after, from being driven by the butts of soldiers' guns. These poor 'prisoner' gangs were mere skeletons of skin and bone, and their bodies cut up frightfully with *la chicotte*, when I saw them. I have travelled with Bihean slave-caravans, and lived among them, and seen the Portuguese Angola slave-trade in full swing, but I think the Congo soldiery far more brutal than either the Bihean or the Arab. Of course the Arab and Bihean slavers are kind to their slaves from a commercial point of view.*

"Chiyombo's very large town, which Captain X——* told me it took him four days to devastate and burn, was next attacked. A lot of people were killed, and heads and hands cut off, and taken back to the officers.

"The wanton destruction of live stock was enormous.

"These towns were prosperous, and the centre of a healthy native trade in grass-cloths, iron, beads, and palm oil. This was their introduction to the yellow star flag and the State, and the same people suffered the bitter fruits of State misrule shortly afterwards, as the Batetla revolters,† pressed hard from the north, entrenched themselves hereby and razed the country to the ground. When they left for Lake Kisale the place was a howling wilderness, and the few remaining people had to eke out a precarious existence in the bush. Shortly after the State caravans, with flags flying and bugles blowing, entered the mission village at Luanza, on Lake Mweru, where I was then alone, and I shall not soon forget the sickening sight of deep baskets of human heads. These baskets of 'war trophies' were used by Msiri's people for a big 'kutomboka,' or war-dance, to which was added the State quota of powder and percussion caps to celebrate their 'victories.'

"Another journey was made to the Lamba country, as far south as Ntenke's and Katanga's, and still another to the Luapala, with the customary plunderings and devastation. I made a journey myself to the copper hills in the west, to the caves, to Ntenke's, Katanga's, Makaka's, and Katete's all in South Lamba, and found the sentries everywhere living like kings, plundering, killing and burning villages, in the name of the State. I append a list of the villages and Chiefs at 'sentry posts' known to me, and each manned by two black soldiers.

"Kazembe's: on the West Lualaba.

"Nguba: three days east of the West Lualaba.

"Kalungumi: principal Va-Sanga chief, a few hours from Kambone copper mines.

"Ntenke: a big Lamba Chief, South Lamba.

"Katanga: owner of some copper mines.

"Katete: a big Lamba Chief.

"Nwachia: Chief of Lufira salt pans.

* The name is given in the letter.
† Rebels. See Chapter XVIII.

"Molenga : Chief of other salt pans.
"Kipazila : near Luapula.
"Kiwele : near Chinama.
"Kashobwe : Yeke Chief, Luapula.
"Mukove : two days south-east of Lake Mweru.
"Kasongo : Luapula.
"Kalanombe : in the Chivanda direction.
"Muvanga : Lake Mweru Chief.
"Kalonga : Valomotwa Chief.
"Kipwayila : near Luapula.
"Muyofia : near Lake Mweru.
"Kiaka : on the mountain near Lake Mweru.
"Kayumba : Luaba Chief near Kisale.

"Each of the posts was manned, as stated, by two black soldiers—dare-devils they—to look after State interests, chiefs, and ivory.

"During the incipient stages of State administration, and under Captain Legat, the first resident official in Katanga after Msiri's downfall, quiet and peace reigned, and the initiatory *régime* augured well for future relations with the natives. Upon Captain Legat's replacement by Captain X—— * (then Lieutenant) the pacific *régime* changed with a vengeance, and there being no State demand then for rubber,† the collection of ivory on which I was told the officers received a large premium, to give impetus to their efforts, was pushed to murder point, and the death penalty was verbally threatened on all Katanga Chiefs who hid or smuggled ivory. No stone was left unturned and no means untried that might make the Natives disgorge ivory, and armed soldiers and Natives were let loose over the country, with results that are obvious to-day.

"Mukandu-Bantu, as Msiri II. was called, and whom Captain X—— ‡ termed his 'commander-in-chief' was sent off by him at the head of a large war-party of armed natives—armed at State expense—on an ivory and head-hunting expedition in the Chivanda direction. Mukandu-Bantu received strict secret instructions to punish old Kasangula, a Bona-Mitumba chief, who was known, or reputed to have ivory, on pretence of having insulted his soldiers with poor food, and the net result was twenty-one heads and the same number of tusks of ivory. I saw the heads and war-dance, and heard the story of the deceitful and bloody business. One of the male prisoners, I was told by eye-witnesses, was sacrificed at the grave of old Msiri unknown to the State.

"Perhaps you will say, 'Why did you not speak out and report all this?' My first experience in Katanga was Captain X——'s § threat to imprison my colleague for denouncing these doings. Every time I made representations, these were declared impossible, or the answer was, 'I will ask my *capita* to make inquiries'—his *capita*

---

* The name is given in the letter.
† Previous to the inauguration of the rubber *régime*.
‡ The name is given in the letter.
§ Ibid.

being one of the worst blackguards in the country. Nothing was ever proved. He would not believe his soldiers would be guilty of such misconduct or, 'Well, they must have *carte blanche*, or the Natives would not respect the State.' Sometimes, 'might is right,' would be the curt reply. What could one say? There were no judges or courts of appeal, and the officer, often at his wits' end, would say, 'What can I do? I MUST get ivory. I have no law or regulation book. I am the only law and only god in Katanga.'

"For several years, owing to the Batetla revolt, these officers received no European supplies *Absolutem rein*, and had to live entirely on the produce of the country. All labour, roads, buildings, cultivations, caravans, etc., were unpaid for or rewarded by plunder and slaves, and as a rule, the soldiers and employees were paid from the loot taken from Bihean slave caravans or raided villages, on the plea of having brought no ivory as tribute.

"Two fruitless trips to the Arab town of Chivala, on the Luapula, ended in loss of prestige, tents, papers, and almost the lives of the two officers. Shortly after this Captain Verdick arrived, with an artillery officer and a small cannon, and arrangements were made for a final fight and break-up of Chivala's town. He had lots of ivory, and traded with the Portuguese on the Zambesi, and had two small cannon. Of course, he did lots of raiding in Arab fashion, and was a small State within a State. Captain X——'s * term of service had fully expired, and he was quite elated at the thought of furlough. One evening he said to me, 'Monsieur Campbell, je vais retourner en Europe mais je voudrais bien prendre part dans une bataille sanglante avant de partir.' A few weeks later they set out for the Arabs' Chivala, and Captain X——,† who was so keen on his 'bloody battle' before leaving, was the first man to be shot, and died four days after. It was his successor who fired the cave near the Western Lualuba, where about eighty people perished.

"*Inauguration of rubber régime.*—Here, on the arrival of Captain Y——, the rubber *régime* was inaugurated, and a large, new-burnt, brick fort store, mess-room, officers' quarters, etc., were built at Lukafu by forced labour. That was one hour distant from Moena Mission Station, where I then lived.

"After Captain Y——,‡ during whose term I had a change home and returned, Captain O—— § assumed command. Through him I sent a report of a big slave caravan of about 3000 slaves, met in the Congo State near Lake Dilolo. These had been purchased principally from the Batetla revolters then entrenched at Lake Kisale. (I may say here that the revolters, computed at 1000 warriors, consisted of two camps—Batetla and Swahili, the former preponderating. The latter, though they joined issue when fighting against the State forces, hated the former for their cannibalism, being Moslem. These revolters took to themselves the name of 'Va

---

* The name is given in the letter.
† Ibid.   ‡ Ibid.   § Ibid.

Huni,' a term of the utmost reproach, which means 'the despisers of all Europeans,' and it will take the fair Luba country long years to recuperate from their killing, looting, and devastation.) This report on the slave caravan, though signed by myself and my wife, never received a reply, though it would have given them the key to the situation from an anti-slavery point of view, and enabled them, by means of a post on the Lutemlewe River, near Lake Dilolo, and others on the Kasia, to have for ever closed the State western door against Bihean and Portuguese slavers. I have crossed the continent between Benguela and Mozambique several times, and I do not hesitate to say that the only regular slave trade that goes on to a large extent is in the southern and south-western corners of the Congo State. From the West Lualaba to beyond Lake Dilolo there is not a single State post, and the slave trade through that door is brisker than ever. The revolters, who were supposed to have been defeated by Major Malfeyt, in March, 1901, are to-day, May, 1904, as lively and as busy as ever in the districts around the Lubidi River. Not only so, but they are well supplied with guns, rifles, and ammunition; and regularly supply the Bihe and Benguela slave markets through Bihean and Ovimbunda traders.

"Under Captain O——'s* *régime* the whole country, from the Lufira River to the Luapula River, was looted of almost all sheep, goats, fowls, and pigeons—friendly and disloyal Natives sharing alike. The disorder in the country and amongst the soldiers, brought about a small revolt, which was only nipped in the bud by timely concessions to the soldiers, who absolutely ruled the Katanga. I complained then, as before, about the abuses of the soldiers, but to no purpose, Congo State soldiers were immaculate, and could not be punished.

"A new officer replaced Captain O——; but did that bring a change of *régime* and better treatment to the Natives? During the whole of his term the brutal and inconsiderate treatment of the Natives all over his *secteur* was just a continuation of State policy. Close to the post at Lukafu, during the making of a wide road from there to the Kambone copper mines, which road passed by our mission at Koni Hill, on the Lufira, practically everything of market value was cleared, even up to our mission door. The Natives were kicked and abused (to put it mildly), and being afraid to appeal to the judge then come to Lukafu, for fear of being intercepted by soldiers and treated worse for daring to complain, the pillaging and flogging continued. Meanwhile, on the Luapula, similar abuses existed, and women were raped and made to serve both white and black, until many of the best and biggest villages crossed into British territory, where they live in peace and are to-day settled contentedly under the protection of the British flag.

"The following are a few of the villages hereabouts whose chiefs have crossed over: 1, Chipungu; 2, Muyofia; 3, Chiva; 4, Kaf-

---

* The name is given in the letter.

wimbi; 5, Chilongoshi; 6, Kashiva; 7, Makungu; 8, Kasongo; 9, Kasandala; 10, Munene; 11, Kanyemba; 12, Muyamunsenga; 13, Chalwe; 14, Chikungu; 15, Mutipula; 16, Chitungu; 17, Nkango; 18, Mboto; 19, Chisompola; 20, Chitwambi. Up to the south bend of the Luapula, the country on the Belgian side is empty, the people having literally rushed to this side for safety and protection, where they live to-day a law-abiding people, and give no trouble to the Government here. The wholesale exodus is due to Belgian raiding, the sentry system, and the maltreatment of the natives.

"Kasongo,* whom I put among the twenty villages, has just come out from hiding in the bush, and a few days ago got permission from the Civil Commissioner to build here. The ultimate reason of his fleeing was because the Belgian officer took his wives. He says he first gave him (M———†) his niece, a young girl, whom, after living with, the officer sent back, taking instead one of the Chief's own wives. Then, after living with her, he sent her back, and took by force the Chief's other wife, whereupon the chief, not daring to refuse, determined to flee. This is only one story out of thousands, for the women in these parts, like the men, have no redress.

"In conclusion, permit me to make the following observations:

"*Treatment of Natives.*—This is, and ever has been, shocking, and the cause of revolts, troubles, and, when possible, exodus into the territories of other Powers. The treatment of the down-trodden Congolese, since State occupation, has brought about a moral and material degeneration. Through the gross and wholesale immorality, and forcing of women and girls into lives of shame, African family life and its sanctities have been violated, and the seeds of disease, sown broadcast over the Congo State, are producing their harvest already. Formerly Native conditions put restrictions on the spread of disease, and localised it to small areas. But the 17,000 black Congo soldiers, moved hither and thither to districts removed from their wives and relations to suit Congo policy, must have women wherever they go, and these must be provided from the district Natives. . . . Native institutions, rights, and customs, which one would think ought to be the basis of permanent good government, are ignored. . . . Much of the evil in this respect is due to complete ignorance of the Native customs and Native language. There are very few *chefs de poste* who are not at the mercy of black interpreters, who are, as a rule, the greatest ruffians, and frequently the most wealthy and influential men in the land—or rather, become so after a few years in this office. For example, Mukevo, the State interpreter now at Lukafu, who was formerly a miserable slave, has now a large village, women, and slaves.

"*Forced Labour.*—There is no such thing as freedom in the

---

* The name of the chief as well as of his village; villages often take their name from their chiefs.

† Name not given in letter.

'Congo Free State,' that is freedom as we understand it. ALL labour is forced, and 'voluntary engagements' or 're-enlistments,' as suggested in the Congo Government's reply to the British Note, are a most rare occurrence, and only due to some special circumstance. The mode of getting police I once saw working. Captain O—— * sent to Msiri and other villages for workmen. A large crowd came reluctantly with their Chiefs. Then they were told they were now soldiers. A guard was put over them, and drill commenced. Great dissatisfaction was expressed, and threats were muttered all over. As the revolters were then but seven or eight days' distant, at Kisale, it only wanted a spark to ignite the whole, a leader to rally the people against the State, and every officer's throat would have been cut, and the scenes of revolt and bloodshed enacted elsewhere would have been reproduced in Katanga. Thanks to the influence of the missionaries the Chiefs remained loyal. Carriers were sent for in the same manner, and if the prescribed number were not forthcoming, the Chiefs and women were usually tied up, when men would offer themselves to ransom their Chiefs. Women, too, were impressed into service, and it was a common sight to see women working with babies pickaback. . . . Formerly we reckoned fully 3000 people in Msiri's town, and I should say a fifth of these were men. To-day, the Chief tells me, there are only thirty men left. Many of his people, he says, have been called up and despatched to other parts of the State for work, mainly road-making. These latter have been away over a year, and do not know when they may be permitted to return to their homes.

"*The Mayanga or Sentry System.*—This is the greatest curse which has befallen the once prosperous country of Katanga. Old Msiri was undoubtedly a tyrant, and ruled the Katanga or Garengonze kingdom with a rod of iron. But I do not think there was anything in his rule a thousandth part so execrable or so oppressive as the Congo State sentry system is. After all, with a Native despot, it was Native dealing with Native on Native lines and according to established African law. But what did the sentry system represent? It was inaugurated to serve one end, and that was to collect all the ivory in the country, and see that the Chiefs and the hunters sold none elsewhere. Ivory had to be brought, the alternative being villages burned and pillaged, and people taken to serve as State prisoners—that is, to build State buildings, plant State gardens, cut State roads, and all to the tune of the State *chicotte*.

"When two black soldiers were deputed to a sentry post, how did they proceed to fulfil their duty? The Chief's wives were paraded, and village women, and several of the best looking were picked out to become sentries' wives. The remainder, and the men, were then paraded and told off to build (*a*) a large house for the white men, and camp for the carriers in the event of their visiting;

* The name is given in the letter.

APPENDIX

(*b*) two large houses for the sentries. They had to plant gardens and do whatever other work was required. Beer also had to be brewed regularly and brought; goats, fowls, and other food had to be produced. These sentries sometimes lived eight or ten days from any European officer. I have known them tie up Chiefs for a week in ropes and keep them tied until a sufficient ransom was brought. Ordinary Natives, especially women, were being continually caught and held up to ransom, and the soldiers used to tell me it was the only means they had of obtaining calico to clothe their women. I have met them on the road on plundering expeditions, travelling in hammocks with from twenty to thirty carriers—these, of course, impressed into the work—besides other carriers who carried their pots, cloth, provisions, and guns wherever they went, and helped them in their raiding, sometimes sharing the spoils. I say emphatically and solemnly, from what I have seen, that these sentries exercise more power over the Natives than their masters, and lived like little kings. I have complained of this and told the *chef de poste*, who would say he would inquire or send the interpreter to inquire; consequently no charge was ever proved. . . These sentries had to appear with the chiefs before the white officers each new moon, and, if the tale of tribute fell short, they were always in terror of punishment. It was a common practice to remove the sentries who were unsuccessful in securing sufficient ivory, and to replace them by others more ruffianly disposed, whose ivory-extorting powers had been previously tested. Thus the State made the sentry system produce what should have been the outcome of honest trade.

"*Free Trade, so-called.*—In all Katanga there is not a single trader outside the *Comité Spécial du Katanga*,* whose monopoly is thereby ensured. The only man who did succeed in getting a trading licence from M. Lévêque, the then representative of the *Compagnie du Katanga*, was Herr Rabinek, whose licence, etc., were signed and sealed in the Mission premises of Luanza; and what befel him, his licence, goods, and rubber, is now well known. A Mr. Carson, and a German trader, Herr Frerk, living on the British side, tried to obtain trading licences, but their applications, which I forwarded, to ensure their reaching Mr. N———,† the present representative of the *Comité Spécial*, must have been ignored, for up till now they have received no reply. On speaking recently with Judge Jenniges at Lukafu, I mentioned these matters to him, and he said, 'Of course, legally and according to State laws they must, if they force matters, receive a licence for trade, but I don't think they will receive it. The State will not cede a licence where the monopoly of trade is in the hands of a big Company.‡ It is against all precedent.' There are many other traders here who would gladly pay all licence, costs, and import and export dues, could permission to

---

* The State under another name, as previously explained.
† Name given in letter.
‡ Not a " Company " at all, but the Government itself.

trade in Katanga be obtained. But the door of Katanga is unquestionably fast shut to all the legitimate trade, and will be until the State's hand is forced, and the State becomes free in more than name.

"You may form an idea of the condition of things in Katanga when I tell you that M. Binard, the officer in Kasenga post (one hour from here across the Luapula), sends his large quota of fowls, etc., to supply the officers' mess at Lukafu and Lukonzolwa, the two largest posts in Katanga. These are bought in British territory this side of the Luapula, by Natives sent by him, which the British official good-naturedly permits. . . .

"A great farce is the Sunday market, so-called, to which the Natives are compelled to bring food to supply the soldiers and their families and Europeans. Each Chief has to attend with his people, his flour, manioc, potatoes, fish, or whatever it be. An officer is supposed to be present to prevent stealing and cheating. The baskets are emptied out, a few beads are thrown into the empty basket, and the Natives have to smile and march back home contentedly. 'We do it to save our heads,' is the Native explanation.

"I hope that these details may help in the campaign against this legalised State iniquity. If I get home this year I shall be pleased to give what further information I can or reply to questions arising out of the subjects on which I have written."

KING LEOPOLD'S PROMISES. MANIFESTO OF THE INTERNATIONAL ASSOCIATION *

(WHICH AFTERWARDS BECAME THE "CONGO INDEPENDENT STATE")

THE Association have declared to the Government of the United States that the Congo States have resolved to levy no customs duties whatever upon goods imported into their territories, whether by land or water, *the sole object being to enable commerce to follow the Association's advance into inner equatorial Africa;* that a guarantee is given to foreigners settling in their territories of the right to purchase, sell, or lease lands and buildings situated therein, to establish houses, and trade upon the sole condition of obedience to the laws of the State. The Association pledge themselves also not to grant to the citizens of one nation any advantage without extending the same to the citizens of all other nations, and to *do all in their power to prevent the slave trade.*

The Secretary of State of the Government of the United States acknowledged the receipt of the foregoing notification, and declared that the Government of the United States announced its sympathy with, and approval of, the humane and benevolent purposes of the Association, administering, as it does, the interests of the *Free States there established,* and will order the officers of the United States both on land and sea to recognise the flag of the Association as the flag of a friendly Government.

From the date of these reciprocal declarations the Congo territory became *open to free commerce,* and the forces at the disposal of the Association *were able to ensure order and tranquillity in the country.*

The head-quarters of the Association are established in Brussels, because from thence flow the financial resources which have sustained the enterprise for the last six years. Liberia was upheld financially for thirty-nine years by the American Colonisation Society. When the new State shall have been recognised by Europe, the fountain-head will continue to furnish supplies which are a substitute for the customs dues which have been publicly

* Communicated by Stanley to the members of the Manchester Chamber of Commerce at the special meeting held at the Town Hall on October 21, 1884.

renounced.* It is reasonably hoped that *commerce will be attracted by the exceptional advantages to be found in the new State, and that a considerable impulse will be given to trade*, this enhancing the hitherto undeveloped natural resources of the country, and creating public wealth. The European traders on the Congo are unanimous in their desire that the present condition of things shall not be disturbed, by which all can *freely enter into commercial negotiations with the Natives*. Full satisfaction to this desire is given by the Association; *absolute freedom of trade is ensured*, with the advantage of a civilised Power to assist them in case of necessity. However it may be, the Association does not press England to recognise their sovereignty. They simply say, "Examine this work impartially, and judge of its merits, and until you are satisfied, make no engagements which shall close for ever the commercial liberty in the Congo valley for which we are striving."

With regard to the question how it is proposed to govern the Congo *States*,† the legislation of the Congo territory, subject to the supervision and control of the Association, shall be based upon the principles of law recognised by civilised nations, and upon the philanthropic principles set forth in the well-known plan of the Association, whose aim is to *civilise Africa by encouragement given to legitimate trade*. At first, account will be taken of the actual state of the Native population; administration and judicial organisation will march in a parallel line with the *progress of these populations*. Meanwhile the country will be governed as it is at present by an Administrator-General, who will have at his disposal the necessary means for the maintenance of public order. It may be asked, How do you propose to support the Government without customs duties? Far from constituting the only resources of a State, the customs duties only represent a part of its revenue, and the least important part of it. Eminent economists condemn customs from a fiscal point of view. They admit their usefulness only as a temporary means for the protection of some new-born trade with a future before it. In any other case they regard customs in the light of a tax that is more costly than productive, because by thwarting commercial liberty it burdens the production of wealth. This doctrine is also that of Richard Cobden and John Bright, and has been adopted by the Association. They consider, like these two illustrious representatives of the Manchester school, that when two nations freely exchange the produce of their countries they both increase respectively their capital and derive benefit from the transaction. The exchange of produce between two nations is generally followed by interchange of ideas, and it will then be seen how judicious was the decision taken by the Association not to

---

* Five years later leave was given for these to be imposed (Brussels Act), despite the protests of the Mercantile community.

† The fiction of Free "States" was dropped as soon as the end had been obtained. As Consul Pickersgill has subsequently remarked, "Nothing is free on the Congo State except fevers."

establish customs of their frontiers, and it will then be understood how deserving is the Association of the congratulations of those who take an interest in the *moral and material progress of the African races*. *By granting entire freedom to trade,* and by abolishing custom-house vexations, the Association wish to attract to their territories commerce and capital. The Congo region abounds in produce of various kinds now lost to the world, although industry might turn it to such marvellous account. Thanks to trade, all this produce will enter into circulation; the *counterpart of its value will return to Africa,* for which it will prove a source of prosperity. The Congo State will then be in the same circumstances as all civilised countries we know, and will then be able to bear the expenses of its public services by and through the wealth obtained by its natural resources.

The Association possess a capital at their disposal of which the interest has sufficed hitherto to cover the expenses of their work. As soon as the State shall have been recognised by the civilised nations, and its political existence assured, this capital will be employed to endow the new State which will then have been founded. The interest derived from this endowment fund will be equal to the revenue which might be obtained by a system of custom-house duties. It will suffice to defray all expenses of the new State until such time as the increase of public wealth, the natural increase in the white population, will allow of its fulfilling all its engagements, as has just been explained.

Thus the future of the new State has been secured, and the death of its founders would no more imperil its existence than that of King Leopold I. imperilled the existence of Belgium, or the death of George Peabody imperilled the endowment fund that bears his name.

When a large number of white men shall have permanently settled in the country, will they, it may also be asked, have any part in the government? The legislation given to the new State will decide after what manner the divers interests are to be represented in the government. It is impossible to give more precise information as to what will be the legislation of the future, just as it is impossible to predict the changes that will be introduced into the constitution of the different nations of the world. The first laws given will be nearly similar to those adopted for the colonies of the British Crown. The central power will reside in Belgium so long as the revenues emanate from the head-quarters of the Association. By that power shall be chosen the functionaries for the different posts in Europe or in Africa. The selection will be made without references to nationality, competency being the principal requirement.

When the new State is definitely established, the direction in Africa shall consist of a Governor-General, assisted by a legislative council and an executive committee. The judicial organisation is to comprise commercial courts of justice, inferior courts for civil causes, a superior court, and a court of appeal. The cases which may be referred to the central power are fully determined by law. The Natives are admitted on an equality with the Europeans before the law, provided they fulfil the obligations prescribed by law. Every sensible and practical man will understand that the authorities will have to show some consideration for the habits and ideas of the Natives in matters of administration and justice. Before laying down new laws and regulations applicable to them, a period of transition must be allowed to pass, during which they may continue to follow their own customs as long as these are not atrocious and inhuman.

The new State has formally declared that there shall be no customs duties established. The revenue derived from the endowment fund will be in lieu of the funds which the customs dues would have furnished. To obtain the complementary resources which will be necessary to ensure the regular working of the public services, the new State will have recourse to the same expedients, when necessary, as those employed by other civilised Governments, though for the present such considerations are altogether premature. The right to settle, purchase, or sell or lease lands and buildings, establish houses, and trade freely, has been formally granted in the declaration to the United States Government. Provisionally, differences between Natives will be settled according to existing local customs. Quarrels and disputes between Europeans and Natives are to belong to the jurisdiction of the law courts that will be established.

The despatch addressed on the 29th of September last by the French Ambassador, M. de Courcel, to Prince Bismarck, states that in case of any cession of territory to France by the Association, the French Government promises to maintain in that territory the absolute freedom of commerce established by the Association. The Association will never part with any of its possessions without stipulating that the buyer shall maintain the *absolute freedom of trade and the complete individual liberty which it has established*. So much for the principle, for, in practice, far from seeking to sell its possessions, the Association is engrossed by the wish to develop their prosperity.

THE END